FRANK WOOD'S

A-LEVEL ACCOUNTING
GCE Year 2

PEARSON
Education

We work with leading authors to develop the
strongest educational materials in business and finance,
bringing cutting-edge thinking and best learning
practice to a global market.

Under a range of well-known imprints, including
Financial Times Prentice Hall, we craft high quality print
and electronic publications which help readers to
understand and apply their content, whether studying
or at work.

To find out more about the complete range of our
publishing, please visit us on the World Wide Web at:
www.pearsoned.co.uk

A Companion Website support *Frank Wood's A-Level Accounting*, fourth edition by Alan Sangster

Visit the ***Business Accounting 1 and 2*** Companion Website at
www.booksites.net/wood to find valuable teaching and learning material
relevant to this text, including:

For Students:
● Study material designed to help you improve your results
● Multiple choice questions to test your learning
● Accounting standards updates
● A fully searchable glossary

For Lecturers:
● A secure, password-protected site with teaching material
● Complete, downloadable Instructor's Manual with information relevant to this text
● Powerpoint slides that can be downloaded and used as OHTs

Also: This site has a syllabus manager, search functions, and email results functions.

FRANK WOOD'S

A-LEVEL ACCOUNTING
GCE Year 2

FOURTH EDITION

Alan Sangster BA, MSc, Cert TESOL, CA

Prentice Hall
FINANCIAL TIMES

An imprint of **Pearson Education**
Harlow, England • London • New York • Boston • San Francisco • Toronto • Sydney • Singapore • Hong Kong
Tokyo • Seoul • Taipei • New Delhi • Cape Town • Madrid • Mexico City • Amsterdam • Munich • Paris • Milan

Pearson Education Limited
Edinburgh Gate
Harlow
Essex CM20 2JE
England

and Associated Companies throughout the world

Visit us on the World Wide Web at:
www.pearsoned.co.uk

First edition published in Great Britain under the
 Pitman Publishing imprint in 1994
Second edition published under the Financial Times Pitman Publishing imprint in 1998
Third edition published under the Financial Times Prentice Hall imprint in 2001
Fourth edition published 2004

© Longman Group UK Limited 1994
© Financial Times Professional Limited 1998
© Pearson Education Limited 2001, 2004

ISBN 0 273 68532 5

British Library Cataloguing-in-Publication Data
A catalogue record for this book is available from the British Library

10 9 8 7 6 5 4 3 2
08 07 06 05

Typeset in 10/12pt Garamond Book by 35
Printed in China
GCC/02

The publisher's policy is to use paper manufactured from sustainable forests.

Contents

Detailed contents   vii

Preface   xv

Introduction: The scope of this book   1

| Part 1 | FURTHER ASPECTS OF FINANCIAL ACCOUNTING |

1 Incomplete records   7
2 Non-profit-oriented organisations   26
3 Partnership accounts   40
4 Valuation of assets   93
5 Types of organisations and sources of finance   120

Part 2 PUBLISHED FINANCIAL STATEMENTS OF LIMITED COMPANIES AND ACCOUNTING STANDARDS

6 Published financial statements and requirements of user groups   131
7 Reserves, bonus issues and rights issues   189
8 Published financial statements and ratio analysis   205
9 Cash flow statements   251
10 Accounting standards   275
11 Limitations of published financial statements   295

Part 3 FURTHER ASPECTS OF ACCOUNTING FOR MANAGEMENT AND DECISION MAKING

12 Absorption costing, marginal costing and decision making   303
13 Standard costing and variance analysis   333
14 Capital investment appraisal   372
15 Other factors affecting decision making – social accounting   395

Contents

Part 4 MANAGEMENT ACCOUNTING PRINCIPLES AND BUDGETING

16	Elements of costing	407
17	Contract accounts	419
18	Job, batch and process costing	428
19	Budgeting and budgetary control	444
20	Cash budgets	451
21	Co-ordination of budgets	465

Part 5 SUPPLEMENTARY TOPICS

22	Break-even analysis	483
23	The accounting equation and the balance sheet	500
24	The double entry system	512
25	Accounting concepts	521
Appendix I	Examination techniques	530
Appendix II	Glossary	535
Appendix III	Answers to review questions	545
Index		596

Detailed contents

Preface   xv

Introduction: The scope of this book   1

Part 1   FURTHER ASPECTS OF FINANCIAL ACCOUNTING

1   Incomplete records   7
  1.1   Why double entry is not used   7
  1.2   Profit as an increase in capital   7
  1.3   Drawing up the financial statements   10
  1.4   Incomplete records and missing figures   13
  1.5   Where there are two missing pieces of information   14
  1.6   Cash sales and purchases for cash   15
  1.7   Goods stolen or lost by fire, etc.   15

2   Non-profit-oriented organisations   26
  2.1   Non-profit-oriented organisations   26
  2.2   Receipts and payments accounts   26
  2.3   Income and expenditure accounts   27
  2.4   Profit or loss for a special purpose   28
  2.5   Accumulated fund   28
  2.6   Drawing up income and expenditure accounts   28
  2.7   Outstanding subscriptions and the prudence concept   32
  2.8   Life membership   33
  2.9   Donations   33
  2.10 Entrance fees   33
  2.11 The differences in headings   33

3   Partnership accounts   40
  3.1   The need for partnerships   40
  3.2   The characteristics of a partnership   41
  3.3   Limited partners   41
  3.4   Partnership agreements   41
  3.5   An example of the distribution of profits   44
  3.6   The profit and loss appropriation account   45
  3.7   Capital accounts and current accounts   46
  3.8   The balance sheet   48
  3.9   Structural changes in the ownership of a partnership 49
  3.10 Goodwill   49
  3.11 Goodwill in the partnership accounts   51
  3.12 Asset revaluation   58

3.13   Partnership dissolution — 60
3.14   The rule in *Garner* v. *Murray* — 67
3.15   Piecemeal realisation of assets — 68

4 Valuation of assets — 93
Part I: Valuation of stock — 93
4.1   Different valuations of stock — 93
4.2   First in, first out method — 94
4.3   Last in, last out method — 95
4.4   Average cost method — 95
4.5   Stock valuation and the calculation of profits — 96
4.6   Reduction of stock valuation to net realisable value — 96
4.7   Stock groups and valuation — 97
4.8   Some other bases in use — 98
4.9   Periodic stock valuation — 99
4.10   Factors affecting the stock valuation decision — 99
4.11   SSAP 9, *Stocks and long-term contracts* — 100
4.12   The conflict of aims — 101
4.13   Work in progress — 101
4.14   Goods on sale or return — 102
4.15   Stocktaking and the balance sheet date — 102
4.16   Stock levels — 103
Part II: Revaluation of assets — 105
4.17   Fixed asset revaluation — 105
Part III: Measurement of income and asset values — 106
4.18   Measurement of income — 106
4.19   Asset valuation alternatives — 107
4.20   Capital maintenance — 111
4.21   A worked example — 112
4.22   Combinations of different values and capital maintenance concepts — 112
4.23   A worked example — 113
4.24   Operating capital maintenance concept — 113
4.25   Problems during a period of changing price levels — 114

5 Types of organisations and sources of finance — 120
5.1   Types of business ownership — 120
5.2   Companies — 121
5.3   Long-term sources of finance — 123
5.4   Other sources of finance — 126

Part 2   PUBLISHED FINANCIAL STATEMENTS OF LIMITED COMPANIES AND ACCOUNTING STANDARDS

6 Published financial statements and requirements of user groups — 131
6.1   The functions of accounting — 131
6.2   Company trading and profit and loss account differences — 133
6.3   Company balance sheet differences — 135
6.4   Users of published financial statements and their needs — 137
6.5   Aspects of company financial statements for external use — 140

6.6	Published financial statements	145
6.7	Published profit and loss account: Format 1	145
6.8	Published balance sheet: Format 1	153
6.9	Published balance sheets and GCE A-level examinations	156
6.10	Other statements and notes required in the annual report	157
6.11	Additional requirements introduced or amended by FRS 3	159
6.12	Small and medium-sized company reporting requirements	160
6.13	Summary financial statements	161
6.14	Other issues	161
6.15	Illustrative company financial statements: example 1	164
6.16	Illustrative company financial statements: example 2	168

7 Reserves, bonus issues and rights issues — 189
7.1	Shareholders' funds	189
7.2	The nature of reserves	189
7.3	Revenue reserves	190
7.4	General reserves	190
7.5	Capital reserves	190
7.6	Profits available for payments of dividends in cash	191
7.7	Allowable reductions of capital reserves	193
7.8	Bonus shares	193
7.9	Rights issues	196

8 Published financial statements and ratio analysis — 205
Part I: Accounting ratios — 206
8.1	Why use ratios?	206
8.2	How to use ratios	207
8.3	Users of ratios	207
8.4	Liquidity	208
8.5	Profitability	213
8.6	Efficiency ratios	217
8.7	Capital structure ratios	217
8.8	Shareholder ratios	221
8.9	Overtrading	222
Part II: The analysis and interpretation of accounting statements — 224
8.10	Interpretation of ratios – trends and comparability	224
8.11	Sector relevance	225
8.12	Trend analysis	225
8.13	Comparisons over time	227
8.14	Comparisons with other businesses	228
8.15	Pyramid of ratios	229
8.16	Return on capital employed: company policy	230
8.17	Fixed and variable expenses	231
8.18	Summary of ratios	233

9 Cash flow statements — 251
9.1	Need for cash flow statements	251
9.2	FRS 1, *Cash flow statements*	252
9.3	Businesses other than companies	252
9.4	Profit and liquidity not directly related	252

9.5	Where from: where to	252
9.6	Construction of a cash flow statement for a sole trader	253
9.7	Note on the use of brackets	255
9.8	Adjustments needed to net profit	255
9.9	Example of adjustments	256
9.10	A comprehensive example	257
9.11	UK companies and FRS 1	259
9.12	Cash flow	260
9.13	Operating activities and cash flows	261
9.14	Dividends from joint ventures and associates	262
9.15	Returns on investment and servicing of finance	262
9.16	Taxation	262
9.17	Capital expenditure and financial investment	263
9.18	Acquisitions and disposals	263
9.19	Equity dividends paid	263
9.20	Management of liquid resources	263
9.21	Financing	264
9.22	Material transactions not resulting in any cash flows	264
9.23	Exceptional and extraordinary items	264
9.24	Two further examples	264
9.25	Uses of cash flow statements	268

10 Accounting standards — 275

10.1	Why do we need financial statements?	275
10.2	The background	276
10.3	The Accounting Standards Board	276
10.4	International accounting standards	277
10.5	GCE A-levels and accounting standards	278
10.6	FRS 18, *Accounting policies* (issued 2000)	278
10.7	SSAP 9, *Stocks and long-term contracts* (revised 1988)	279
10.8	FRS 15, *Tangible fixed assets* (issued 1999)	280
10.9	FRS 10, *Goodwill and intangible assets* (*companies*)	282
10.10	FRS 11, *Impairment of fixed assets and goodwill*	282
10.11	SSAP 13, *Accounting for research and development*	283
10.12	Other standards that may be relevant to your syllabus	285
10.13	Further thoughts on concepts and conventions	288

11 Limitations of published financial statements — 295

11.1	The historical perspective of financial statements	295
11.2	Lack of disclosure	295
11.3	Changes to the sources of information	296
11.4	One set of financial statements for all purposes	296
11.5	Aggregation	297
11.6	Objectivity vs. subjectivity	298
11.7	Timing differences	299

Part 3	FURTHER ASPECTS OF ACCOUNTING FOR MANAGEMENT AND DECISION MAKING	

12	Absorption costing, marginal costing and decision making	303
12.1	Absorption and marginal costing	303
12.2	Allocation of indirect manufacturing costs	303
12.3	Absorption costing: effect upon future action	304
12.4	The lesson to be learnt	306
12.5	Fixed and variable costs	306
12.6	Cost behaviour	306
12.7	Marginal costing and absorption costing contrasted	307
12.8	Comparison of reported profits – constant sales and uneven production	310
12.9	Pricing policy	311
12.10	Full cost pricing	312
12.11	Example of full cost pricing	313
12.12	Contribution	315
12.13	Using marginal costs	315
12.14	Maximisation of total contribution	317
12.15	Activity-based costing (ABC)	319

13	Standard costing and variance analysis	333
	Part I: Standard costing and variance analysis	333
13.1	Comparison with actual costs	333
13.2	Setting standards	334
13.3	Variance analysis	335
13.4	Adverse and favourable variances	336
13.5	Computation of variances	336
	Part II: Materials and labour variances	337
13.6	Materials variances	337
13.7	Materials variances – analysis	342
13.8	Key questions of variances	342
13.9	Formulas for materials variances	343
13.10	Inventory records under standard costing	343
13.11	Disposition of variances	343
13.12	Costing for labour	343
13.13	Labour variances	344
13.14	Labour variances – analysis	347
13.15	Formulas for labour variances	347
	Part III: Overhead and sales variances	347
13.16	Management overheads	347
13.17	Predetermined rates	348
13.18	Variances in overhead recovery	348
13.19	Assessing variances	351
13.20	Formulas for overhead variances	352
13.21	A comprehensive example	353
13.22	Variances and management action	356
13.23	Sales variances	356

14 Capital investment appraisal
14.1	Introduction	372
14.2	Accounting rate of return	372
14.3	Payback method	373
14.4	The time value of money	374
14.5	Cost of capital	375
14.6	Present values	376
14.7	Net present value	376
14.8	Internal rate of return (IRR)	378
14.9	Relevant and irrelevant costs	379
14.10	Sunk costs	380
14.11	A comparison of the methods	380
14.12	Merits and demerits of the techniques	381
14.13	Surveys of practice	382
		383

15 Other factors affecting decision making – social accounting
15.1	Introduction	395
15.2	Costs and measurement	395
15.3	The pressure for social actions and social accounting	395
15.4	Corporate social reporting	396
15.5	Types of social accounting	397
15.6	National social income accounting	397
15.7	Social auditing	397
15.8	Financial social accounting in profit-oriented organisations	398
15.9	Managerial social accounting in profit-oriented organisations	399
15.10	Financial and/or managerial social accounting in non-profit organisations	399
15.11	Conflict between shareholders' interests and social considerations	400
15.12	Reports from companies	401
		402

Part 4 MANAGEMENT ACCOUNTING PRINCIPLES AND BUDGETING

16 Elements of costing
16.1	Costs for different purposes	407
16.2	Past costs in trading companies	407
16.3	Past costs in manufacturing companies	409
16.4	Product costs and period costs	409
16.5	Advantages of a costing system	412
16.6	The control of costs	412
16.7	Costing: manufacturing firms compared with retailing or wholesale firms	413
		414

17 Contract accounts
17.1	Accounts and the business cycle	419
17.2	Opening contract accounts	419
17.3	Certification of work done	419
17.4	Allocation of overheads	420
17.5	Example	420
17.6	Profit estimation	420
17.7	Anticipated losses	422
17.8	SSAP 9	422
		423

18   Job, batch and process costing   428
    18.1   Introduction   428
    18.2   The choice of job costing or process costing   428
    18.3   Job costing   430
    18.4   Cost centres – job costing and responsibility   433
    18.5   Process costing   434
    18.6   Normal and abnormal losses   435
    18.7   Under/overabsorption of overheads   436
    18.8   Other kinds of firms   437
    18.9   The problem of joint costs   437

19   Budgeting and budgetary control   444
    19.1   Financial budgets   444
    19.2   Budgets and people   444
    19.3   Budgets, planning and control   445
    19.4   Preparation of estimates   446
    19.5   The production budget   446
    19.6   Even production flow   447
    19.7   Uneven production levels   448

20   Cash budgets   451
    20.1   The need for cash budgets   451
    20.2   Timing of cash receipts and payments   452
    20.3   Advantages of cash budgets   454
    20.4   Profits and shortages of cash funds   455

21   Co-ordination of budgets   465
    21.1   Master budgets   465
    21.2   Capital budgeting   469
    21.3   The advantages of budgeting   469
    21.4   The use of computers in budgeting   471
    21.5   Flexible budgets   471

Part 5   SUPPLEMENTARY TOPICS

22   Break-even analysis   483
    22.1   Introduction   483
    22.2   The break-even chart   484
    22.3   Changes and break-even charts   487
    22.4   The limitations of break-even charts   490
    22.5   Contribution graph   492

23   The accounting equation and the balance sheet   500
    23.1   What is accounting?   500
    22.2   What is bookkeeping?   501
    22.3   Accounting is concerned with . . .   501
    23.4   Users of accounting information   501
    23.5   The accounting equation   502
    23.6   The balance sheet and the effects of business transactions   503

23.7 Equality of the accounting equation 506
23.8 More detailed presentation of the balance sheet 507

24 The double entry system 512
24.1 Nature of a transaction 512
24.2 The double entry system 512
24.3 The accounts for double entry 513
24.4 Worked examples 514
24.5 A further worked example 516
24.6 Abbreviation of 'limited' 518

25 Accounting concepts 521
25.1 Introduction 521
25.2 One set of financial statements for all purposes 521
25.3 Objectivity and subjectivity 522
25.4 Accounting standards and financial reporting standards 523
25.5 Accounting standards and the legal framework 523
25.6 Underlying accounting concepts 523
25.7 Fundamental accounting concepts 524
25.8 Materiality 528
25.9 The assumption of the stability of currency 528
25.10 FRS 18, *Accounting policies* 529

Appendix I Examination techniques 530
Appendix II Glossary 535
Appendix III Answers to review questions 545

Index 596

Preface

This book is for students in their second year of study for GCE A-level Accounting for the various examining bodies in the United Kingdom. The subjects covered meet the needs of the second year of both the OCR and AQA syllabuses.

The book assumes that the first year of the A-level course (the Advanced Subsidiary GCE) has been completed. Under the AQA syllabus, this first year comprises (i) the accounting information system *or* introduction to published accounts; (ii) financial accounting; and (iii) introduction to management accounting. Under OCR, the first year comprises (i) accounting principles; (ii) financial accounting; and (iii) final accounts. These topics are listed in greater detail in Section 5 of the Introduction to this book and they are covered in *Frank Wood's Business Accounting 1*.

The second year of the A-level is in three parts. For AQA, these are:

1 Further aspects of financial accounting
2 Published accounts of limited companies
3 Further aspects of management accounting

and for OCR, they are:

1 Management accounting – budgeting, control and capital expenditure
2 Management accounting – principles and systems
3 Company accounts and interpretation.

As you may imagine from these two short lists, the two bodies examine different topics at each of the two years of the A-level. Partnership accounts is the major difference between the two syllabuses, being a first-year topic under OCR and a second-year topic under AQA. In comparison, AQA spreads management accounting over both years of the syllabus, whereas OCR places it in the second year.

In addition to covering the second-year topics of both these bodies, this book includes some of the topics considered most fundamental to the study of accounting which are normally covered in the first year of the A-level course. These are given as supplementary chapters at the end of the book. This is in response to numerous requests from teachers and lecturers who have indicated that the topics covered in these supplementary chapters are those for which students have been found to need some reinforcement at this stage of their studies. In particular, Chapter 25, **Accounting concepts**, is relevant to the study of accounting at any level. It should be referred to as appropriate and read in its entirety at least once during this year of A-level study.

The depth in which each section is given is that most suitable for A-level examinations. A-level students should not only know how to tackle accounting problems, but should also understand the basic reasoning which underlies accounting and its methods.

A very welcome aspect of A-level examinations is that examiners want students to see that there are factors other than purely financial considerations which should affect decisions in the world of business and government. In terms of simply getting better marks in examinations, students would be well advised to bring environmental factors into their answers, but the fact that these examinations expect an approach which is not blinkered by accounting knowledge should make these examinations more challenging and interesting for both students and teachers.

The questions in this book are mainly either from GCE A-level examination papers or devised by ourselves. A few have been selected from examinations of the professional accounting bodies as they relate to topics that are covered in the A-level syllabus. The answers shown at the back of the book are the result of combined work and checking by ourselves, John Whiteside, Peter Beazeley, David Welch and Christina Mulligan. Should any error(s) remain, then we must accept full responsibility. The fact that approximately 50 per cent of the answers are shown in the book means that students can attempt a considerable number of questions and be able to check their own work. The remainder of the questions will be useful for other forms of supplementary work.

A time-saving *Solutions Manual*, including fully-displayed answers to all questions with the suffix 'X' in the text, is available free of charge to teachers who recommend this book on their courses.

As an additional feature, Appendix II contains a *Glossary* of all the important terms covered in this book.

We wish to acknowledge the permission to reproduce past examination papers granted by the following examining bodies and institutions: the Assessment and Qualifications Alliance (AQA) which includes former AEB, NEAB and SEG questions; the Association of Accounting Technicians (AAT); the Association of Chartered Certified Accountants (ACCA); the Chartered Institute of Management Accountants; London Qualifications Limited (formely Edexcel Foundation) which includes former University of London questions; the Oxford, Cambridge and RSA Examinations (OCR) which includes former MEG questions; the Scottish Qualifications Authority and the Welsh Joint Education Committee (WJEC).

We should also like to thank Noel Williams, Chief Examiner, University of Oxford Delegacy of Local Examinations, and G L Brownlee, Chief Examiner, University of Cambridge Local Examinations Syndicate, for their assistance in reviewing the content of the first edition of this book and Muhammad Hanif Ghanchi for his most helpful and illuminating advice concerning the content and focus of the book.

Frank Wood and Alan Sangster

Note on the review questions

With reference to the answers to questions set by the Assessment and Qualifications Alliance (AQA) the solutions given are the responsibility of the authors and may not necessarily constitute the only possible solutions.

London Qualifications Limited accepts no responsibility whatsoever for the accuracy or method of working in the answers given.

Oxford, Cambridge and RSA Examinations (OCR) bears no responsibility for the example answers to questions taken from past question papers which are contained in this publication.

The scope of this book

This book has been written specifically for the second year of study for those who are taking GCE A-level examinations in Accounting for the various UK examining bodies.

It is assumed that you have already covered the first year's work. You should check against the list of topics as shown in Section 5 of this Introduction to ensure that you have properly covered the work that you should have done in the first year.

1 The syllabuses

This book focuses upon the syllabuses for the second year of the *Assessment and Qualifications Alliance* (AQA) and the *Oxford, Cambridge and RSA Examinations* (OCR) Advanced GCE (A-level) in Accounting. As the coverage of the syllabuses of these two bodies encompasses virtually all the topics included in the syllabuses of the other A-level examining bodies, the contents of this book should be sufficient to give those with the necessary application and intelligence the ability to achieve marks at the highest grade, whichever UK A-level examining body's exam they are studying for.

For this edition, the sequence of material has been changed so it closely follows the AQA syllabus.

If you are using this book for the AQA examinations, you will find that Module 5 is covered in Part 1, Module 6 is covered in Part 2 and Module 7 is covered in Part 3.

If you are using this book for the OCR examinations, you will find that the topics not covered in Parts 1 to 3 are covered in Part 4. The coverage in the chapters of this book for each Paper is as follows:

Paper 4	Paper 5	Paper 6
19	16	6
20	12	8
21	4	9
13	17	7
14	18	10
15		

In response to requests from teachers and lecuers, material has been added to Chapter 12 on limiting factor (key factor) and the partnership, and on company accounting, and the standard costing chapters have been combined into three chapters so as to facilitate coverage of these topics. A chapter on the limitation of published financial statements (Chapter 11) has been added.

2 Supplementary chapters

The second year of the AQA and OCR Advanced GCE (A-level) syllabuses is covered in the first 21 chapters. Chapters 22 to 25 are provided as a supplement to that material. They contain material which it is anticipated that you will have covered in the first year of your A-level course. They are included here at the request of a number of teachers and lecturers who have indicated that these relate to topics for which students have been found to need some reinforcement at this stage of their studies.

3 Review questions

Many of the review questions at the end of each chapter are from the A-level examinations themselves. Sometimes there are questions devised by the authors to fill in gaps or to give a more straightforward approach to the topic.

Practice is essential for success in accounting examinations. Simply reading the text of this book, even though you may fully understand it when you are reading it, is not sufficient. Some of the questions in the examinations will be of the essay variety, but the other questions do demand that you have practical work to carry out. There is no doubt that the more practice you can manage to carry out, the greater will be the corresponding increase in the grades you can achieve in the examination.

4 Quality newspapers

It would certainly be beneficial for you to read a 'quality' newspaper regularly, such as *The Times*, the *Guardian*, the *Daily Telegraph*, the *Independent*, *The Scotsman* or the *Financial Times*. Many of the business issues of the day affect accounting in all sorts of ways. At first, some of the articles may seem to be very hard work indeed to assimilate but, as your studies progress, you should find the going easier. Such reading may also help you to give your answers a business background which you might otherwise be lacking.

5 The first year's coverage

During your first year of study you should have covered many of the following topics. Precisely which of them you should have covered will, of course, depend upon the syllabus of the examining body you followed.

● The accounting equation (this is included in supplementary Chapter 23)
● Double entry bookkeeping, including the books of original entry – cash book, day books and journal (double entry is included in supplementary Chapter 24)
● The trial balance
● Accounting concepts and conventions (included in supplementary Chapter 25)
● Capital and revenue expenditure
● Changing asset values, including depreciation
● Ledger entries and adjustments, including accruals and prepayments, bad debts and provision for doubtful debts
● Trading and profit and loss account and balance sheet for sole traders
● Cost behaviour and cost volume profit analysis (included in supplementary Chapter 22)
● Errors and suspense accounts
● Control accounts
● Stock valuation, including SSAP 9, just-in-time, and economic order quantity (this is covered in Chapter 4)

- Single entry and incomplete records (this is covered in Chapter 1)
- The use of computers in accounting
- Organisations and finance
- Accounting for partnerships, including appropriation accounts, changes in profit sharing ratios, goodwill, asset revaluation and partnership changes (this is covered in Chapter 3)
- Accounting for clubs and societies, including receipts and payments and income and expenditure accounts (this is covered in Chapter 2)
- Manufacturing accounts
- Departmental accounts
- Analysis and evaluation of accounting statements, including ratio analysis
- Social accounting (this is covered in Chapter 15)
- Recording VAT

All of these topics are fully covered in *Business Accounting 1* by Frank Wood and Alan Sangster, published by Pearson Education Limited. You will also find them in most other basic texts for first-year courses.

6 A note on figures

Generally, the values used in exhibits and exercises are relatively small amounts. This has been done deliberately to make the work of the user of this book that much easier. Constantly handling large figures does not add anything to the study of the principles of accounting; instead it simply wastes a lot of the student's time, and he/she will probably make far more errors if larger figures are used.

It could lead to the authors being accused of not being 'realistic' with the figures given, but we believe that it is far more important to make learning easier for the student.

Part 1

FURTHER ASPECTS OF
FINANCIAL ACCOUNTING

1 Incomplete records

2 Non-profit-making organisations

3 Partnership accounts

4 Valuation of assets

5 Types of organisations and sources of finance

CHAPTER 1

Incomplete records

Learning objectives

By the end of this chapter, you should be able to:

- deduce the figure of profits where only the increase in capital and details of drawings are known;
- draw up a trading and profit and loss account and balance sheet from records not kept on a double entry system;
- deduce the figure for cash drawings when all other cash receipts and cash payments are known;
- deduce the figures of sales and purchases from incomplete records.

1.1 Why double entry is not used

For every small shopkeeper, market stall or other small business to keep its books using a full double entry system would be ridiculous. First of all, a large number of the owners of such firms would not know how to write up double entry records, even if they wanted to.

It is more likely that they would enter details of transactions once only, using a single entry system. In many cases, they won't even do that, resulting in what is referred to as 'incomplete records'.

It is perhaps only fair to remember that accounting is supposed to be an aid to management. It is not something to be done as an end in itself. Therefore, many small firms, especially retail shops, can have all the information they want by merely keeping a cash book and having some form of record, not necessarily in double entry form, of their debtors and creditors.

Somehow, however, the profits will have to be calculated, if for no other reason than so as to enable the income tax payable by the owner to be calculated. How can profits be calculated if the bookkeeping records are inadequate or incomplete?

1.2 Profit as an increase in capital

Probably the best way to start is to recall that unless there has been an introduction of extra cash or resources into the firm, the only way that capital can be increased is by making profits. Therefore, profits can be found by comparing capital at the end of the last period with capital at the end of this period.

To do this, you do not need to know what net profit is in order to find the end of year capital figure. Instead, you rely on the accounting equation and simply subtract the total liabilities from the total assets. What is left must be the end of year capital figure.

Let's look at an example where capital at the end of 20X4 was £2,000. During 20X5 there have been no drawings, and no extra capital has been brought in by the owner. At the end of 20X5 the capital was £3,000.

$$\text{Net profit} = \underset{\text{capital}}{\underset{\text{This year's}}{£3,000}} - \underset{\text{capital}}{\underset{\text{Last year's}}{£2,000}} = £1,000$$

If drawings had been £700, the profits must have been £1,700, calculated thus:

$$\text{Last year's Capital} + \text{Profits} - \text{Drawings} = \text{This year's Capital}$$
$$£2,000 \quad + \quad ? \quad - \quad £700 \quad = \quad £3,000$$

We can see that £1,700 profits was the figure needed to complete the formula, filling in the missing figure:

$$£2,000 + £1,700 - £700 = £3,000$$

Exhibit 1.1 shows the calculation of profit where insufficient information is available to draft a trading and profit and loss account, only information concerning assets and liabilities being available.

EXHIBIT 1.1

H Taylor has not kept proper bookkeeping records, but he has kept notes in diary form of the transactions of his business. He is able to give you details of his assets and liabilities as at 31 December 20X5 and at 31 December 20X6 as follows:

At 31 December 20X5. *Assets:* Motor van £1,000; Fixtures £700; Stock £850; Debtors £950; Bank £1,100; Cash £100. *Liabilities:* Creditors £200; Loan from J Ogden £600.

At 31 December 20X6. *Assets:* Motor van (after depreciation) £800; Fixtures (after depreciation) £630; Stock £990; Debtors £1,240; Bank £1,700; Cash £200. *Liabilities:* Creditors £300; Loan from J Ogden £400; Drawings were £900.

First of all a **Statement of Affairs** is drawn up as at 31 December 20X5. This is the name given to what would have been called a balance sheet if it had been drawn up from a set of records. The capital is the difference between the assets and liabilities.

H Taylor
Statement of Affairs as at 31 December 20X5

	£	£
Fixed assets		
Van		1,000
Fixtures		700
		1,700
Current assets		
Stock	850	
Debtors	950	
Bank	1,100	
Cash	100	
	3,000	
Less Current liabilities		
Creditors	(200)	

	£	£
Net current assets		2,800
		4,500
Less Long-term liability: Loan from J Ogden		(600)
Net assets		3,900
Financed by:		
Capital		3,900

You now draw up a second statement of affairs, this time as at the end of 20X6. The formula of Opening Capital + Profit – Drawings = Closing Capital is then used to deduce the figure of profit.

H Taylor
Statement of Affairs as at 31 December 20X6

	£	£
Fixed assets		
Van		800
Fixtures		630
		1,430
Current assets		
Stock	990	
Debtors	1,240	
Bank	1,700	
Cash	200	
	4,130	
Less Current liabilities		
Creditors	(300)	
Net current assets		3,830
		5,260
Less Long-term liability: Loan from J Ogden		(400)
Net Assets		4,860
Financed by:		
Capital		
Balance at 1.1.20X6		3,900
Add Net profit	(C)	?
	(B)	?
Less Drawings		(900)
	(A)	

Deduction of net profit:
Opening Capital + Net Profit – Drawings = Closing Capital. Finding the missing figures (A), (B) and (C) by deduction:
(A) is the same as the total of the top half of the balance sheet, i.e. £4,860;
(B) is therefore £4,860 + £900 = £5,760;
(C) is therefore £5,760 – £3,900 = £1,860.

To check:
Capital

Balance at 1.1.20X6		3,900
Add Net profit	(C)	1,860
	(B)	5,760
Less Drawings		(900)
	(A)	4,860

Obviously, this method of calculating profit is very unsatisfactory as it is much more informative when a trading and profit and loss account can be drawn up. Therefore, whenever possible this 'comparisons of capital' method of ascertaining profit should be avoided and a full set of financial statements drawn up from the available records.

It is important to realise that a business would have exactly the same trading and profit and loss account and balance sheet whether they kept their books by single entry or double entry. However, as you will see, whereas the double entry system uses the trial balance in preparing the financial statements, the single entry system arrives at the same answer by different means.

1.3 Drawing up the financial statements

The following example shows the various stages of drawing up financial statements from a single entry set of records.

The accountant discerns the following details of transactions for J Frank's retail store for the year ended 31 December 20X5.

(a) The sales are mostly on a credit basis. No record of sales has been made, but £10,000 has been received, £9,500 by cheque and £500 by cash, from persons to whom goods have been sold.

(b) Amount paid by cheque to suppliers during the year = £7,200.

(c) Expenses paid during the year: by cheque, Rent £200, General Expenses £180; by cash, Rent £50.

(d) J Frank took £10 cash per week (for 52 weeks) as drawings.

(e) Other information is available:

	At 31.12.20X4 £	At 31.12.20X5 £
Debtors	1,100	1,320
Creditors for goods	400	650
Rent owing	–	50
Bank balance	1,130	3,050
Cash balance	80	10
Stock	1,590	1,700

(f) The only fixed asset consists of fixtures which were valued at 31 December 20X4 at £800. These are to be depreciated at 10 per cent per annum.

Stage 1: Draw up a Statement of Affairs on the closing day of the last accounting period. This is now shown:

J Frank
Statement of Affairs as at 31 December 20X4

	£	£
Fixed assets		
Fixtures		800
Current assets		
Stock	1,590	
Debtors	1,100	
Bank	1,130	
Cash	80	

	£	£
Less Current liabilities	3,900	
Creditors	(400)	
Working capital		3,500
		4,300
Financed by:		
Capital (difference)		4,300
		4,300

All of these opening figures are then taken into account when drawing up the financial statements for 20X5.

Stage 2: Next a cash and bank summary, showing the totals of each separate item, plus opening and closing balances, is drawn up.

	Cash	Bank		Cash	Bank
	£	£		£	£
Balances 31.12.20X4	80	1,130	Suppliers		7,200
Receipts from debtors	500	9,500	Rent	50	200
			General Expenses		180
			Drawings	520	
			Balances 31.12.20X5	10	3,050
	580	10,630		580	10,630

Stage 3: Calculate the figures for purchases and sales to be shown in the trading account. Remember that the figures needed are the same as those which would have been found if double entry records had been kept.

Purchases: In double entry, purchases means the goods that have been bought in the period irrespective of whether they have been paid for or not during the period. The figure of payments to suppliers must therefore be adjusted to find the figure for purchases.

	£
Paid during the year	7,200
Less Payments made, but which were for goods which were purchased in a previous year (creditors 31.12.20X4)	(400)
	6,800
Add Purchases made in this year, but for which payment has not yet been made (creditors 31.12.20X5)	650
Goods bought in this year, i.e. purchases	7,450

The same answer could have been obtained if the information had been shown in the form of a total creditors account, the figure for purchases being the amount required to make the account totals agree.

Total Creditors

	£		£
Cash paid to suppliers	7,200	Balances b/d	400
Balances c/d	650	Purchases (missing figure)	7,450
	7,850		7,850

Sales: The sales figure will only equal receipts where all the sales are for cash. Therefore, the receipts figures need adjusting to find sales. This can only be done by constructing a total debtors account, the sales figure being the one needed to make the totals agree.

Total Debtors

	£		£
Balances b/d	1,100	Receipts: Cash	500
		Cheque	9,500
Sales (missing figure)	10,220	Balances c/d	1,320
	11,320		11,320

Stage 4: Expenses. Where there are no accruals or prepayments either at the beginning or end of the accounting period, then expenses paid will equal expenses used up during the period. These figures will be charged to the trading and profit and loss account.

On the other hand, where such prepayments or accruals exist, then an expense account should be drawn up for that particular item. When all known items are entered, the missing figure will be the expenses to be charged for the accounting period. In this case only the rent account needs to be drawn up.

Rent Account

	£		£
Cheques	200	Rent (missing figure)	300
Cash	50		
Accrued c/d	50		
	300		300

Stage 5: Now draw up the financial statements.

J Frank
Trading and Profit and Loss Account for the year ended 31 December 20X5

	£	£
Sales (stage 3)		10,220
Less Cost of goods sold:		
Stock at 1.1.20X5	1,590	
Add Purchases (stage 3)	7,450	
	9,040	
Less Stock at 31.12.20X5	(1,700)	
		(7,340)
Gross profit		2,880
Less Expenses:		
Rent (stage 4)	300	
General expenses	180	
Depreciation: Fixtures	80	
		(560)
Net profit		2,320

Balance Sheet as at 31 December 20X5

	£	£	£
Fixed assets			
Fixtures at 1.1.20X5		800	
Less Depreciation		(80)	720
Current assets			
Stock		1,700	
Debtors		1,320	
Bank		3,050	
Cash		10	
		6,080	
Less Current liabilities			
Creditors	650		
Rent owing	50	(700)	
Working capital			5,380
			6,100
Financed by:			
Capital			
Balance 1.1.20X5 (per Opening Statement of Affairs)			4,300
Add Net profit			2,320
			6,620
Less Drawings			(520)
			6,100

<h2>1.4   Incomplete records and missing figures</h2>

In practice, part of the information relating to cash receipts or payments is often missing. If the missing information is in respect of one type of payment, then it is normal to assume that the missing figure is the amount required to make both totals agree in the cash column of the cash and bank summary. (This does not happen with bank items because another copy of the bank statement can always be obtained from the bank.) Exhibit 1.2 shows an example when the drawings figure is unknown; Exhibit 1.3 is an example where the receipts from debtors had not been recorded.

EXHIBIT 1.2

The following information on cash and bank receipts and payments is available:

	Cash	Bank
	£	£
Cash paid into the bank during the year	5,500	
Receipts from debtors	7,250	800
Paid to suppliers	320	4,930
Drawings during the year	?	–
Expenses paid	150	900
Balances at 1.1.20X5	35	1,200
Balances at 31.12.20X5	50	1,670

	Cash	Bank		Cash	Bank
	£	£		£	£
Balances 1.1.20X5	35	1,200	Bankings C	5,500	
Received from debtors	7,250	800	Suppliers		4,930
Bankings C		5,500	Expenses	320	900
			Drawings	150	
			Balances 31.12.20X5	?	
				50	1,670
	7,285	7,500		7,285	7,500

The amount needed to make the two sides of the cash columns agree is £1,265. Therefore, this is taken as the figure for drawings.

EXHIBIT 1.3

Information of cash and bank transactions is available as follows:

	Cash	Bank
	£	£
Receipts from debtors	?	6,080
Cash withdrawn from the bank for business use (this is the amount which is used besides cash receipts from debtors to pay drawings and expenses)		920
Paid to suppliers		5,800
Expenses paid	640	230
Drawings	1,180	315
Balances at 1.1.20X5	40	1,560
Balances at 31.12.20X5	70	375

	Cash	Bank		Cash	Bank
	£	£		£	£
Balances 1.1.20X5	40	1,560	Suppliers		5,800
Received from debtors	?	6,080	Expenses	640	230
Withdrawn from Bank C	920		Withdrawn from Bank C		920
			Drawings	1,180	315
			Balances 31.12.20X5	70	375
	1,890	7,640		1,890	7,640

Receipts from debtors is, therefore, the amount needed to make each side of the cash column agree, £930.

It must be emphasised that balancing figures are acceptable only when all the other figures have been verified. Should, for instance, a cash expense be omitted when cash received from customers is being calculated, then this would result in an understatement, not only of expenses but also, ultimately, of sales.

1.5 Where there are two missing pieces of information

If both cash drawings and cash receipts from customers were not known, it would not be possible to deduce both of these figures separately. The only course lying open would be to estimate whichever figure was more capable of being accurately assessed, use this as a known figure, then deduce the other figure. However, this is a most unsatisfactory position as both of the figures are no more than pure estimates, the accuracy of each one relying entirely upon the accuracy of the other.

1.6 Cash sales and purchases for cash

Where there are cash sales as well as sales on credit terms, then the cash sales must be added to sales on credit to give the total sales for the year. This total figure of sales will be the one shown in the trading account.

Similarly, purchases for cash will need to be added to the credit purchases to give the figure of total purchases for the trading account.

1.7 Goods stolen or lost by fire, etc.

When goods are stolen, destroyed by fire, or lost in some other way, then the value of them will have to be calculated. This could be needed to substantiate an insurance claim or to settle problems concerning taxation, etc.

If the stock had been properly valued immediately before the fire, burglary, etc., then the stock loss would obviously be known. Also if a full and detailed system of stock records were kept, then the value would also be known. However, as the occurrence of fires or burglaries cannot be foreseen, and not many businesses keep full and proper stock records, the stock loss will have to be calculated in some other way.

The methods described in this chapter and Chapter 25 are used instead. The only difference is that instead of computing closing stock at a year end, for example, the closing stock will be that as at immediately before the fire consumed it or it was stolen.

We will now look at Exhibits 1.4 and 1.5. The first exhibit will be a very simple case, where figures of purchases and sales are known and all goods are sold at a uniform profit ratio. The second exhibit is rather more complicated.

EXHIBIT 1.4

J Collins lost the whole of his stock by fire on 17 March 20X9. The last time that a stocktaking had been done was on 31 December 20X8, the last balance sheet date, when it was £1,950 at cost. Purchases from then to 17 March 20X9 amounted to £6,870 and Sales for the period were £9,600. All sales were made at a uniform gross profit margin of 20 per cent.

First, the trading account can be drawn up with the known figures included. Then the missing figures can be deduced afterwards.

J Collins
Trading Account for the period 1 January 20X9 to 17 March 20X9

		£	£
Sales			9,600
Less Cost of goods sold:			
Opening stock		1,950	
Add Purchases		6,870	
		8,820	
Less Closing stock	(C)	?	
	(B)		?
Gross profit	(A)		?

Now the missing figures can be deduced.

It is known that the gross profit margin is 20 per cent, therefore gross profit (A) is 20% of £9,600 = £1,920.

Now (B) + (A) £1,920 = £9,600, so that (B) is the difference, i.e. £7,680.

Now that (B) is known, (C) can be deduced: £8,820 − (C) = £7,680, so (C) is the difference, i.e. £1,140.

The figure for goods destroyed by fire, at cost, is therefore £1,140.

EXHIBIT 1.5

T Scott had the whole of his stock stolen from his warehouse on the night of 20 August 20X6. Also destroyed were his sales and purchases journals, but the sales and purchases ledgers were salvaged. The following facts are known:

(a) Stock was known at the last balance sheet date, 31 March 20X6, to be £12,480 at cost.
(b) Receipts from debtors during the period 1 April to 20 August 20X6 amounted to £31,745. Debtors were: at 31 March 20X6 £14,278, at 20 August 20X6 £12,333.
(c) Payments to creditors during the period 1 April to 20 August 20X6 amounted to £17,270. Creditors were: at 31 March 20X6 £7,633, at 20 August 20X6 £6,289.
(d) The gross profit margin on sales has been constant at 25 per cent.

Before we can start to construct a trading account for the period, we need to find out the figures of sales and of purchases. These can be found by drawing up total debtors and total creditors accounts, sales and purchases figures being the difference on the accounts.

Total Creditors

	£		£
Cash and bank	17,270	Balances b/d	7,633
Balances c/d	6,289	Purchases (difference)	15,926
	23,559		23,559

Total Debtors

	£		£
Balances b/d	14,278	Cash and bank	31,745
Sales (difference)	29,800	Balances c/d	12,333
	44,078		44,078

The trading account can now show the figures already known.

Trading Account for the period 1 April to 20 August 20X6

		£	£
Sales			29,800
Less Cost of goods sold:			
Opening stock		12,480	
Add Purchases		15,926	
		28,406	
Less Closing stock	(C)	?	
	(B)		?
Gross profit	(A)		?

Gross profit can be found, as the gross profit margin on sales is known to be 25%, therefore (A) = 25% of £29,800 = £7,450.

Cost of goods sold (B) + Gross profit £7,450 = £29,800, therefore (B) is £22,350. £28,406 − (C) = (B) £22,350, therefore (C) is £6,056.

The figure for cost of goods stolen is therefore £6,056.

Learning outcomes

You should now have learnt:

1 The difference between a single entry system and a double entry system.

2 How to calculate net profit for a small trader when you know the change in capital over a period and the amount of drawings during the period.

3 How to prepare a trading and profit and loss account and balance sheet from records not kept on a double entry system.

4 How to deduce the figures for purchases and sales from a total creditors account and a total debtors account.

REVIEW QUESTIONS

Note: In all the review questions in this book, questions with the letter X shown after the question number do not have answers shown at the back of the book. Answers to the others are shown in Appendix III.

The authors realise that students would like to have *all* the answers shown. However, teachers and lecturers would not then be able to test your knowledge with questions from this book, as you would already possess the answers. It is impossible to please everyone, and the compromise reached is that of putting a large number of review questions in the book.

This means that adequate use can be made by the student studying on his or her own, and by those studying under a lecturer or teacher.

1.1 B Arkwright started in business on 1 January 20X5 with £10,000 in a bank account. Unfortunately he did not keep proper books of account.

He is forced to submit a calculation of profit for the year ended 31 December 20X5 to the Inspector of Taxes. He ascertains that at 31 December 20X5 he had stock valued at cost £3,950, a motor van which had cost £2,800 during the year and which had depreciated by £550, debtors of £4,970, expenses prepaid of £170, bank balance £2,564, cash balance £55, trade creditors £1,030, and expenses owing £470.

His drawings were: cash £100 per week for 50 weeks, cheque payments £673.

Draw up statements to show the profit or loss for the year.

1.2X J Kirkwood is a dealer who has not kept proper books of account. At 31 August 20X6 his state of affairs was as follows:

	£
Cash	115
Bank balance	2,209
Fixtures	4,000
Stock	16,740
Debtors	11,890
Creditors	9,052
Motor van (at valuation)	3,000

During the year to 31 August 20X7, his drawings amounted to £7,560. Winnings from a football pool of £2,800 were put into the business. Extra fixtures were bought for £2,000.

At 31 August 20X7, his assets and liabilities were: Cash £84; Bank overdraft £165; Stock £21,491; Creditors for goods £6,002; Creditors for expenses £236; Fixtures to be depreciated £600; Motor van to be valued at £2,500; Debtors £15,821; Prepaid expenses £72.

Draw up a statement showing the profit and loss made by Kirkwood for the year ended 31 August 20X7.

1.3 Following is a summary of Kelly's bank account for the year ended 31 December 20X7:

	£		£
Balance 1.1.20X7	405	Payments to creditors for goods	29,487
Receipts from debtors	37,936	Rent	1,650
Balance 31.12.20X7	602	Rates	890
		Sundry expenses	375
		Drawings	6,541
	38,943		38,943

All of the business takings have been paid into the bank with the exception of £9,630. Out of this, Kelly has paid wages of £5,472, drawings of £1,164 and purchase of goods £2,994.

The following additional information is available:

	31.12.20X6	31.12.20X7
Stock	13,862	15,144
Creditors for goods	5,624	7,389
Debtors for goods	9,031	8,624
Rates prepaid	210	225
Rent owing	150	–
Fixtures at valuation	2,500	2,250

You are to draw up a set of financial statements for the year ended 31 December 20X7. Show all of your workings.

1.4X J Evans has kept records of his business transactions in a single entry form, but he did not realise that he had to record cash drawings. His bank account for the year 20X8 is as follows:

	£		£
Balance 1.1.20X8	1,890	Cash withdrawn from bank	5,400
Receipts from debtors	44,656	Trade creditors	31,695
Loan from T Hughes	2,000	Rent	2,750
		Rates	1,316
		Drawings	3,095
		Sundry expenses	1,642
		Balance 31.12.20X8	2,648
	48,546		48,546

Records of cash paid were: Sundry expenses £122; Trade creditors £642. Cash sales amounted to £698.

The following information is also available:

	31.12.20X7	31.12.20X8
	£	£
Cash in hand	48	93
Trade creditors	4,896	5,091
Debtors	6,013	7,132
Rent owing	–	250
Rates in advance	282	312
Motor van (at valuation)	2,800	2,400
Stock	11,163	13,021

You are to draw up a trading and profit and loss account for the year ended 31 December 20X8, and a balance sheet as at that date. Show all of your workings.

1.5 On 1 May 20X8 Jenny Barnes, who is a retailer, had the following balances in her books: Premises £70,000; Equipment £8,200; Vehicles £5,100; Stock £9,500; Trade debtors £150.

Jenny does not keep proper books of account, but bank statements covering the 12 months from 1 May 20X8 to 30 April 20X9 were obtained from the bank and summarised as follows:

	£
Money paid into bank:	
Extra capital	8,000
Shop takings	96,500
Received from debtors	1,400
Payments made by cheque:	
Paid for stock purchased	70,500
Purchase of delivery van	6,200
Vehicle running expenses	1,020
Lighting and heating	940
Sales assistants' wages	5,260
Miscellaneous expenses	962

It has been discovered that, in the year ending 30 April 20X9, the owner had paid into the bank all shop takings apart from cash used to pay (*i*) £408 miscellaneous expenses and (*ii*) £500 per month drawings.

At 30 April 20X9:

£7,600 was owing to suppliers for stock bought on credit.

The amount owed by trade debtors is to be treated as a bad debt. Assume that there had been no sales on credit during the year.

Stock was valued at £13,620.

Depreciation for the year was calculated at £720 (equipment) and £1,000 (vehicles).

You are asked to prepare trading and profit and loss accounts for the year ended 30 April 20X9. (Show all necessary workings separately.)

(London Qualifications Limited: GCE A-level)

1.6X Bill Smithson runs a second-hand furniture business from a shop which he rents. He does not keep complete accounting records, but is able to provide you with the following information about his financial position at 1 April 20X8: Stock of furniture £3,210; Trade debtors £2,643; Trade creditors £1,598; Motor vehicle £5,100; Shop fittings £4,200; Motor vehicle expenses owing £432.

He has also provided the following summary of his bank account for the year ended 31 March 20X9:

	£		£
Balance at 1 Apr 20X8	2,420	Payments of trade creditors	22,177
Cheques received from trade		Electricity	1,090
debtors	44,846	Telephone	360
Cash sales	3,921	Rent	2,000
		Advertising	1,430
		Shop fittings	2,550
		Insurance	946
		Motor vehicle expenses	2,116
		Drawings	16,743
		Balance at 31 Mar 20X9	1,775
	£51,187		£51,187

All cash and cheques received were paid into the bank account immediately.
You find that the following must also be taken into account:

● Depreciation is to be written off the motor vehicle at 20% and off the shop fittings at 10%, calculated on the book values at 1 April 20X8 plus additions during the year.
● At 31 March 20X9 motor vehicle expenses owing were £291 and insurance paid in advance was £177.
● Included in the amount paid for shop fittings were:
a table bought for £300, which Smithson resold during the year at cost;
some wooden shelving (cost £250), which Smithson used in building an extension to his house.

Other balances at 31 March 20X9 were:

	£
Trade debtors	4,012
Trade creditors	2,445
Stock of furniture	4,063

Required:

(a) For the year ended 31 March 20X9
  (i) calculate Smithson's sales and purchases;
  (ii) prepare his trading and profit and loss account.
(b) Prepare Smithson's balance sheet as at 31 March 20X9.

(OCR (MEG): GCE A-level)

1.7 Although Janet Lambert has run a small business for many years, she has never kept adequate accounting records. However, a need to obtain a bank loan for the expansion of the business has necessitated the preparation of 'final' accounts for the year ended 31 August 20X9. As a result, the following information has been obtained after much careful research:

1 Janet Lambert's business assets and liabilities are as follows:

As at	1 September 20X8	31 August 20X9
	£	£
Stock in trade	8,600	16,800
Debtors for sales	3,900	4,300
Creditors for purchases	7,400	8,900
Rent prepaid	300	420
Electricity accrued due	210	160
Balance at bank	2,300	1,650
Cash in hand	360	330

2 All takings have been banked after deducting the following payments:

Cash drawings – Janet Lambert has not kept a record of cash drawings, but suggests these will be in the region of	£8,000
Casual labour	£1,200
Purchase of goods for resale	£1,800

Note: Takings have been the source of all amounts banked.

3 Bank payments during the year ended 31 August 20X9 have been summarised as follows:

	£
Purchases	101,500
Rent	5,040
Electricity	1,390
Delivery costs (to customers)	3,000
Casual labour	6,620

4 It has been established that a gross profit of $33\frac{1}{3}\%$ on cost has been obtained on all goods sold.

5 Despite her apparent lack of precise accounting records, Janet Lambert is able to confirm that she has taken out of the business during the year under review goods for her own use costing £600.

Required:

(a) Prepare a computation of total purchases for the year ended 31 August 20X9.
(b) Prepare a trading and profit and loss account for the year ended 31 August 20X9 and a balance sheet as at that date, both in as much detail as possible.
(c) Explain why it is necessary to introduce accruals and prepayments into accounting.

(Association of Accounting Technicians)

1.8X Jean Smith, who retails wooden ornaments, has been so busy since she commenced business on 1 April 20X5 that she has neglected to keep adequate accounting records. Jean's opening capital consisted of her life savings of £15,000 which she used to open a business bank account. The transactions in this bank account during the year ended 31 March 20X6 have been summarised from the bank account as follows:

	£
Receipts:	
Loan from John Peacock, uncle	10,000
Takings	42,000
Payments:	
Purchases of goods for resale	26,400
Electricity for period to 31 December 20X5	760
Rent of premises for 15 months to 30 June 20X6	3,500
Rates of premises for the year ended 31 March 20X6	1,200
Wages of assistants	14,700
Purchase of van, 1 October 20X5	7,600
Purchase of holiday caravan for Jean Smith's private use	8,500
Van licence and insurance, payments covering a year	250

According to the bank account, the balance in hand on 31 March 20X6 was £4,090 in Jean Smith's favour.

While the intention was to bank all takings intact, it now transpires that, in addition to cash drawings, the following payments were made out of takings before bankings:

	£
Van running expenses	890
Postages, stationery and other sundry expenses	355

On 31 March 20X6, takings of £640 awaited banking; this was done on 1 April 20X6. It has been discovered that amounts paid into the bank of £340 on 29 March 20X6 were not credited to Jean's bank account until 2 April 20X6 and a cheque of £120, drawn on 28 March 20X6

for purchases, was not paid until 10 April 20X6. The normal rate of gross profit on the goods sold by Jean Smith is 50% on sales. However, during the year a purchase of ornamental goldfish costing £600 proved to be unpopular with customers and therefore the entire stock bought had to be sold at cost price.

Interest at the rate of 5% per annum is payable on each anniversary of the loan from John Peacock on 1 January 20X6.

Depreciation is to be provided on the van on the straight line basis; it is estimated that the van will be disposed of after five years' use for £100.

The stock of goods for resale at 31 March 20X6 has been valued at cost at £1,900.

Creditors for purchases at 31 March 20X6 amounted to £880 and electricity charges accrued due at that date were £180.

Trade debtors at 31 March 20X6 totalled £2,300.

Required:

Prepare a trading and profit and loss account for the year ended 31 March 20X6 and a balance sheet as at that date.

(Association of Accounting Technicians)

1.9 David Denton set up in business as a plumber a year ago, and he has asked you to act as his accountant. His instructions to you are in the form of the following letter.

Dear Henry,

I was pleased when you agreed to act as my accountant and look forward to your first visit to check my records. The proposed fee of £250 p.a. is acceptable. I regret that the paperwork for the work done during the year is incomplete. I started my business on 1 January last, and put £6,500 into a business bank account on that date. I brought my van into the firm at that time, and reckon that it was worth £3,600 then. I think it will last another three years after the end of the first year of business use.

I have drawn £90 per week from the business bank account during the year. In my trade it is difficult to take a holiday, but my wife managed to get away for a while. The travel agent's bill for £280 was paid out of the business account. I bought the lease of the yard and office for £6,500. The lease has ten years to run, and the rent is only £300 a year payable in advance on the anniversary of the date of purchase, which was 1 April. I borrowed £4,000 on that day from Aunt Jane to help pay for the lease. I have agreed to pay her 10% interest per annum, but have been too busy to do anything about this yet.

I was lucky enough to meet Miss Prism shortly before I set up on my own, and she has worked for me as an office organiser right from the start. She is paid a salary of £3,000 p.a. All the bills for the year have been carefully preserved in a tool box, and we analysed them last week. The materials I have bought cost me £9,600, but I reckon there was £580 worth left in the yard on 31 December. I have not yet paid for them all yet, I think we owed £714 to the suppliers on 31 December. I was surprised to see that I had spent £4,800 on plumbing equipment, but it should last me five years or so. Electricity bills received up to 30 September came to £1,122; but motor expenses were £912, and general expenses £1,349 for the year. The insurance premium for the year to 31 March next was £800. All these have been paid by cheque but Miss Prism has lost the council tax demand. I expect the Local Authority will send a reminder soon since I have not yet paid. I seem to remember that council tax was £180 for the year to 31 March next.

Miss Prism sent out bills to my customers for work done, but some of them are very slow to pay. Altogether the charges made were £29,863, but only £25,613 had been received by 31 December. Miss Prism thinks that 10% of the remaining bills are not likely to be paid. Other customers for jobs too small to bill have paid £3,418 in cash for work done, but I only managed to bank £2,600 of this money. I used £400 of the difference to pay the family's grocery bills, and Miss Prism used the rest for general expenses, except for £123 which was left over in a drawer in the office on 31 December.

Kind regards,

Yours sincerely,

David.

You are required to draw up a profit and loss account for the year ended 31 December, and a balance sheet as at that date.

(Association of Chartered Certified Accountants)

1.10 The following are summaries of the cash book and bank accounts of J Duncan who does not keep his books using the double entry system.

Bank Summary	£	£
Balance on 1 January 20X8		8,000
Receipts		
Debtors	26,000	
Cash banked	4,100	
		30,100
		38,100
Payments		
Trade creditors	18,500	
Rent	1,400	
Machinery	7,500	
Wages	6,100	
Insurance	1,450	
Debtors (dishonoured cheque)	250	
Loan Interest	300	
		35,500
Balance on 31 December 20X8		2,600

Cash Summary	£	£
Balance on 1 January 20X8		300
Receipts		
Cash sales	14,000	
Debtors	400	
		14,400
		14,700
Payments		
Drawings	9,500	
Repairs	300	
Electricity	750	
Cash Banked	4,100	
		14,650
Balance on 31 December 20X8		50

The following referred to 20X8:

	£
Bad debts written off	400
Discount received	350
Goods withdrawn by J Duncan for own use	300
Credit note issued	1,200

The following additional information is available.

	1 January 20X8	31 December 20X8
	£	£
Stocks	4,100	3,200
Machinery	12,600	15,900
Rent prepaid	200	
Rent owing		250
Debtors	6,300	5,000
Creditors	2,400	2,500
Loan from Bank at 8%	5,000	5,000
Loan interest owing		100

You are required to:

(*a*) Calculate the value of J Duncan's capital on 1 January 20X8.

(*b*) Prepare the Trading and Profit and Loss Accounts for the year ended 31 December 20X8.

(*Scottish Qualifications Authority*)

1.11 Using the information in Question 1.10, prepare J Duncan's Balance Sheet as at 31 December 20X8.

1.12X The following are summaries of the cash book and bank accounts of P Maclaran who does not keep her books using the double entry system.

Bank Summary	£	£
Balance on 1 January 20X8		6,000
Receipts		
Debtors	35,000	
Cash banked	2,200	
		37,200
		43,200
Payments		
Trade creditors	31,000	
Rent	1,100	
Machinery	3,400	
Wages	9,200	
Insurance	850	
Debtors (dishonoured cheque)	80	
Loan Interest	500	–
		(46,130)
Balance on 31 December 20X8		(2,930)

Cash Summary	£	£
Balance on 1 January 20X8		60
Receipts		
Cash sales	9,700	
Debtors	1,100	
		10,800
		10,860
Payments		
Drawings	6,600	
Repairs	1,400	
Electricity	570	
Cash Banked	2,200	
		(10,770)
Balance on 31 December 20X8		90

The following referred to 20X8:

	£
Bad debts written off	240
Discount received	600
Goods withdrawn by P Maclaran for own use	1,200
Credit note issued	640

The following additional information is available:

	1 January 20X8 £	31 December 20X8 £
Stocks	2,300	5,400
Machinery	9,800	10,400
Rent prepaid		100
Rent owing	150	
Debtors	8,100	9,200
Creditors	5,700	4,800
Loan from Bank at 10%	7,000	7,000
Loan interest owing		200

You are required to:

(*a*) Calculate the value of P Maclaran's capital on 1 January 20X8.

(*b*) Prepare the Trading and Profit and Loss Accounts for the year ended 31 December 20X8.

1.13X   Using the information in Question 1.12, prepare P Maclaran's Balance Sheet as at 31 December 20X8.

Non-profit-oriented organisations

2.1 Non-profit-oriented organisations

Clubs, associations and other non-profit-oriented organisations do not have trading and profit and loss accounts drawn up for them, as their main purpose is not trading or profit making. They are run so that their members can do things such as play football, bridge or chess.

The income and expenditure of many clubs and societies is often in cash, with credit transactions virtually unheard of. They often operate a system of incomplete records, frequently maintaining a cash book as the only written record of the transactions entered into. As a result, their financial statements are often based upon a mixture of cash book, bank statements and invoices and receipts.

The financial statements always prepared by these organisations are either a receipts and payments account (but only in the case of the very smallest non-accrual-oriented organisations) or an income and expenditure account. When an organisation has assets and liabilities, it will produce a balance sheet which some call a 'statement of affairs'.

2.2 Receipts and payments accounts

Receipts and payments accounts are a summary of the cash book for a period. Exhibit 2.1 is an example.

EXHIBIT 2.1

The Haven Running Club
Receipts and Payments Account for the year ended 31 December 20X5

Receipts	£	Payments	£
Bank balance at 1.1.20X5	236	Groundsman's wages	728
Subscriptions received in 20X5	1,148	Sports stadium expenses	296
Rent received	116	Committee expenses	58
		Printing and stationery	33
		Bank balance at 31.12.20X5	385
	1,500		1,500

Receipts and payments accounts of cash-based organisations that bank all their cash receipts are, in effect, another name for a cash account. They show *all* income for a period and all expenditure, irrespective of whether it is revenue expenditure or capital expenditure. They do *not* apply the accruals concept which you will have learnt about earlier in your accounting studies – that net profit is the difference between revenues and the expenses incurred in generating those revenues – the key to the application of which is that all income and charges relating to the financial period to which the financial statements relate should be taken into account without regard to the date of receipt or payment.

If there was no expenditure at all on fixed assets (i.e. capital expenditure) during the period and if there were no opening or closing accruals or prepayments, and no non-cash transactions or adjustments, such as depreciation, and no opening or closing stock, the difference between the opening and closing balance would represent the net profit, if it were a business or, the net surplus, if it were a non-profit-oriented organisation.

It may seem unlikely that this could be the case but, with very small non-profit-oriented organisations, it could be. However, a far better and more consistently applicable way to determine the net surplus (i.e. net profit) of a non-profit-oriented organisation is to prepare an income and expenditure account.

Income and expenditure accounts do apply the accruals concept, they do include non-cash transactions or adjustments, and they do produce a figure called 'net surplus', rather than leaving you to work it out, as is the case with the receipts and payments account. In other words, they are the non-profit-oriented organisation's equivalent of the trading and profit and loss account.

2.3 Income and expenditure accounts

When assets are owned, and there are liabilities, the receipts and payments account is not a good way of drawing up final accounts. Other than the cash received and paid out, it shows only the cash balances. The other assets and liabilities are not shown at all. What is required is:

(a) a balance sheet, and
(b) an account showing whether the association's capital has increased.

In a non-profit organisation, (a) is usually called a balance sheet, though some use the term, '**statement of affairs**' which, as you saw in Chapter 1, is more usually a summary statement of assets and liabilities before adjustment to create the balance sheet. In a profit-making organisation, (b) would be a trading and profit and loss account. In a non-profit organisation, (b) would be an income and expenditure account.

Thus, as mentioned above, an income and expenditure account follows the same rules as trading and profit and loss accounts. The only differences are the terms used. A comparison now follows:

Terms used

Profit-oriented organisation	Non-profit oriented organisation
1 Trading and Profit and Loss Account	1 Income and Expenditure Account
2 Net Profit	2 Surplus of Income over Expenditure
3 Net Loss	3 Deficit of Income over Expenditure

2.4 Profit or loss for a special purpose

Sometimes there are reasons why a non-profit-oriented organisation would want a profit and loss account.

This is where something is done to make a profit. The profit is not to be kept, but used to pay for the main purpose of the organisation.

For instance, a football club may hold dances which people pay to go to. Any profit from these helps to pay football expenses. For these dances, a trading and profit and loss account would be drawn up. Any profit (or loss) would be transferred to the income and expenditure account. Another obvious example would be a bar, as in the case of a rugby club, a bridge club or a snooker club.

2.5 Accumulated fund

Sole traders and partnerships have capital accounts. A non-profit-oriented organisation would, instead, have an **accumulated fund**. It is the same as a capital account, as it is the difference between assets and liabilities.

In a sole trader or partnership:

$$\text{Capital} = \text{Assets} - \text{Liabilities}$$

In a non-profit-making organisation:

$$\text{Accumulated Fund} = \text{Assets} - \text{Liabilities}$$

2.6 Drawing up income and expenditure accounts

We can now look at the preparation of an income and expenditure account and a balance sheet of a club in Exhibit 2.2. A separate trading account is to be prepared for a bar, where refreshments are sold to make a profit.

Probably the majority of clubs and associations keep their accounts using single entry methods. This example will therefore be from single entry records, using the principles described in the last chapter. We shall start with a receipts and payments account and adjust it so as to arrive at the figures necessary for the preparation of the income and expenditure account.

EXHIBIT 2.2

Long Lane Football Club
Receipts and Payments Account for the year ended 31 December 20X6

Receipts		£	Payments		£
Bank balance 1.1.20X6		524	Payment for bar supplies		3,962
Subscriptions received for			Wages:		
20X5 (arrears)		55	Groundsman and assistant		939
20X6		1,236	Barman		624
20X7 (in advance)		40	Bar expenses		234
Bar sales		5,628	Repairs to stands		119
Donations received		120	Ground upkeep		229
			Secretary's expenses		138
			Transport costs		305
			Bank balance 31.12.20X6		1,053
		7,603			7,603

The treasurer of the Long Lane Football Club has prepared a receipts and payments account, but members have complained about the inadequacy of such an account. He therefore asks an accountant to prepare a trading account for the bar, and an income and expenditure account and a balance sheet. The treasurer gives the accountant a copy of the receipts and payments account together with information on assets and liabilities at the beginning and end of the year:

Notes:	31.12.20X5	31.12.20X6
1	£	£
Stocks in the bar – at cost	496	558
Owing for bar supplies	294	340
Bar expenses owing	25	36
Transport costs	–	65

2 The land and football stands were valued at 31 December 20X5 at: land £4,000; football stands £2,000. The stands are to be depreciated by 10 per cent per annum.

3 The equipment at 31 December 20X5 was valued at £550, and is to be depreciated at 20 per cent per annum.

4 Subscriptions owing by members amounted to £55 on 31 December 20X5, and £66 on 31 December 20X6.

From this information, the accountant drew up the following accounts and statements.

Stage 1: Draw up a Statement of Affairs as at 31 December 20X5.

Statement of Affairs as at 31 December 20X5

	£	£	£
Fixed assets			
Land			4,000
Stands			2,000
Equipment			550
			6,550
Current assets			
Stock in bar		496	
Debtors for subscriptions		55	
Cash at bank		524	
		1,075	

	£	£	£
Less Current liabilities			
Creditors	294		
Bar expenses owing	25		
		(319)	
Working capital			756
			7,306
Financed by:			
Accumulated fund (difference)			7,306
			7,306

Stage 2: Draw up a Bar Trading Account.

Long Lane Football Club
Bar Trading Account for the year ended 31 December 20X6

	£	£
Sales		5,628
Less Cost of goods sold:		
Stock 1.1.20X6	496	
Add Purchases[Note 1]	4,008	
	4,504	
Less Stock 31.12.20X6	(558)	
		(3,946)
Gross profit		1,682
Less Bar expenses[Note 2]	245	
Barman's wages	624	(869)
Net profit to income and expenditure account		813

Notes:

1

Purchases Control

	£		£
Cash	3,962	Balances (creditors) b/d	294
Balances c/d	340	**Trading account (difference)**	**4,008**
	4,302		4,302

2

Bar Expenses

	£		£
Cash	234	Balance b/d	25
Balance c/d	36	**Trading account (difference)**	**245**
	270		270

Stage 3: Draw up the financial statements.

Long Lane Football Club
Income and Expenditure Account for the year ended 31 December 20X6

	£	£	£
Subscriptions for 20X6[Note 1]			1,302
Profit from the bar			813
Donations received			120
			2,235

	£	£	£
Less Expenditure			
Wages – Groundsman and assistant		939	
Repairs to stands		119	
Ground upkeep		229	
Secretary's expenses		138	
Transport costs[Note 2]		370	
Depreciation			
Stands	200		
Equipment	110		
		310	
			(2,105)
Surplus of income over expenditure			130

Notes:

1 Subscriptions Received

	£			£
Balance (debtors) b/d	55	Cash 20X5		55
Income and expenditure		20X6		1,236
account (difference)	**1,302**	20X7		40
Balance (in advance) c/d	40	Balance (owing) c/d		66
	1,397			1,397

2 Transport Costs

	£		£
Cash	305	**Income and expenditure**	
Accrued c/d	65	**account (difference)**	**370**
	370		370

It will be noted that subscriptions received in advance are carried down as a credit balance to the following period.

The Long Lane Football Club
Balance Sheet as at 31 December 20X6

	£	£	£
Fixed assets			
Land at valuation			4,000
Pavilion at valuation		2,000	
Less Depreciation		(200)	1,800
Equipment at valuation		550	
Less Depreciation		(110)	440
			6,240
Current assets			
Stock of bar supplies		558	
Debtors for subscriptions		66	
Cash at bank		1,053	
		1,677	
Less Current liabilities			
Creditors for bar supplies	340		
Bar expenses owing	36		

	£	£	£
Transport costs owing	65		
Subscriptions received in advance	40		
		(481)	
Working capital			1,196
			7,436
Financed by:			
Accumulated fund			
Balance as at 1.1.20X6			7,306
Add Surplus of income over expenditure			130
			7,436

2.7 Outstanding subscriptions and the prudence concept

So far we have treated subscriptions owing as being an asset. However, as any treasurer of a club would tell you, most subscriptions that have been owing for a long time are never paid. A lot of clubs do not therefore bring in unpaid subscriptions as an asset in the balance sheet. This is obviously keeping to the prudence concept which states that assets should not be over-valued. They are therefore ignored by these clubs for final accounts purposes.

However, **in an examination** a student should assume that subscriptions owing are to be brought into the final accounts unless instructions to the contrary are given.

Exhibit 2.3 shows an instance where subscriptions in arrears and in advance occur at the beginning and close of a period.

EXHIBIT 2.3

An amateur theatre organisation charges its members an annual subscription of £20 per member. It accrues for subscriptions owing at the end of each year and also adjusts for subscriptions received in advance.

(A) On 1 January 20X2, 18 members owed £360 for the year 20X1.
(B) In December 20X1, 4 members paid £80 for the year 20X2.
(C) During the year 20X2 we received cash for subscriptions £7,420.

For 20X1	£360	
For 20X2	£6,920	
For 20X3	£140	£7,420

(D) At close of 31 December 20X2, 11 members had not paid their 20X2 subscriptions.

Subscriptions

20X2			£	20X2			£
Jan 1 Owing b/d	(A)		360	Jan 1 Prepaid b/d	(B)		80
Dec 31 Income and expenditure			*7,220	Dec 31 Bank	(C)		7,420
Dec 31 Prepaid c/d	(C)		140	Dec 31 Owing c/d	(D)		220
			7,720				7,720
20X3				20X3			
Jan 1 Owing b/d	(D)		220	Jan 1 Prepaid b/d	(C)		140

* Difference between the two sides of the account.

2.8 Life membership

In some clubs and societies, members can make a payment for life membership. This means that by paying a fairly substantial amount now the member can enjoy the facilities of the club for the rest of his or her life.

Such a receipt should not be treated as income in the income and expenditure account solely in the year in which the member paid the money. It should be credited to a life membership account, and transfers should be made from that account to the credit of the income and expenditure account of an appropriate amount annually.

Exactly what is meant by an 'appropriate' amount is decided by the committee of the club or society. The usual basis is to establish, on average, how long members will continue to use the benefits of the club. To take an extreme case, if a club was in existence which could not be joined until one achieved the age of 70, then the expected number of years' use of the club on average per member would be relatively few. Another club, such as a golf club, where a fair proportion of the members joined when reasonably young, and where the game is capable of being played by members until and during old age, would expect a much higher average of years of use per member. The simple matter is that the club should decide for itself.

In an examination, candidates have to follow the instructions set for them by the examiner. The credit balance remaining on the account, after the transfer of the agreed amount has been made to the credit of the income and expenditure account, should be shown on the balance sheet as a liability. It is, after all, the liability of the club to provide amenities for members without any further payment by them.

2.9 Donations

Any donations received are usually shown as income in the year that they are received.

2.10 Entrance fees

New members often have to pay an entrance fee in the year that they join, in addition to the membership fee for that year. Entrance fees are normally included as income in the year that they are received. The club could, however, decide to treat them differently. It all depends on the circumstances.

2.11 The differences in headings

Students often get confused about the differences between the headings used in the financial statements of non-profit-oriented organisations and those used in a business context. When you look closely, you will see that there really are very few differences of this type:

● 'profits' are described as 'surpluses' and 'losses' are described as 'deficits';
● the 'trading and profit and loss account' is called an 'income and expenditure account';
● the 'capital account' is known as the 'accumulated fund'.

Make sure you know these, know how to account for subscriptions, life memberships and donations; learn how to deal with items for which a profit calculation is needed (such as a bar) and how to enter the profit into the income and expenditure account; and learn how to proceed from a receipts and payments account to an income and expenditure accounts and balance sheet. If you do, you will not find exam questions on this topic very difficult.

Learning outcomes

You should now have learnt:

1 That a receipts and payments account does not show the full financial position of an organisation, except for one where the only asset is cash and there are no liabilities.

2 That an income and expenditure account is drawn up to show either the surplus of income over expenditure or the excess of expenditure over income. These are the same as 'profit' or 'loss' in a profit-oriented organisation.

3 That the accumulated fund is basically the same as a capital account.

4 That although the main object of the organisation is non-profit oriented, certain activities may be run at a profit (or may lose money) in order to help finance the main objectives of the organisation.

5 That in an examination you should treat subscriptions owing at the end of a period in the same way as debtors, unless told otherwise.

6 That donations are usually treated as income in the period in which they are received.

7 That entrance fees are usually treated as income in the year in which they are received.

8 That the treatment of life membership fees is purely at the discretion of the organisation, but that they are usually amortised over an appropriate period.

REVIEW QUESTIONS

2.1 A summary of the Uppertown Football Club is shown below. From it, and the additional information, you are to construct an income and expenditure account for the year ended 31 December 20X4, and a balance sheet as at that date.

Cash Book Summary

	£		£
Balance 1.1.20X4	180	Purchase of equipment	125
Collections at matches	1,650	Rent for football pitch	300
Profit on sale of refreshments	315	Printing and stationery	65
		Secretary's expenses	144
		Repairs to equipment	46
		Groundsman's wages	520
		Miscellaneous expenses	66
		Balance 31.12.20X4	879
	2,145		2,145

Further information:

(*i*)   At 1.1.20X4 equipment was valued at £500.

(*ii*) Depreciate all equipment 20 per cent for the year 20X4.

(*iii*) At 31.12.20X4 rent paid in advance was £60.

(*iv*) At 31.12.20X4 there was £33 owing for printing.

2.2X   The following trial balance of Haven Golf Club was extracted from the books as on 31 December 20X8:

	Dr £	Cr £
Clubhouse	21,000	
Equipment	6,809	
Profits from raffles		4,980
Subscriptions received		18,760
Wages of bar staff	2,809	
Bar stocks 1 January 20X8	1,764	
Bar purchases and sales	11,658	17,973
Greenkeepers' wages	7,698	
Golf professional's salary	6,000	
General expenses	580	
Cash at bank	1,570	
Accumulated fund at 1 January 20X8		18,175
	59,888	59,888

Notes:

(*i*)   Bar purchases and sales were on a cash basis. Bar stocks at 31 December 20X8 were valued at £989.

(*ii*) Subscriptions paid in advance by members at 31 December 20X8 amounted to £180.

(*iii*) Provide for depreciation of equipment £760.

You are required to:

(*a*) Draw up the bar trading account for the year ended 31 December 20X8.

(*b*) Draw up the income and expenditure account for the year ended 31 December 20X8, and a balance sheet as at 31 December 20X8.

2.3   Read the following and answer the questions below.

On 1 January 20X8 The Happy Haddock Angling Club had the following assets:

	£
Cash at bank	200
Snack bar stocks	800
Club house buildings	12,500

During the year to 31 December 20X8 the Club received and paid the following amounts:

Receipts	£	*Payments*	£
Subscriptions 20X8	3,500	Rent and rates	1,500
Subscriptions 20X9	380	Extension to club house	8,000
Snack bar income	6,000	Snack bar purchases	3,750
Visitors' fees	650	Secretarial expenses	240
Loan from bank	5,500	Interest on loan	260
Competition fees	820	Snack bar expenses	600
		Games equipment	2,000

Notes:

The snack bar stock on 31 December 20X8 was £900.

The games equipment should be depreciated by 20%.

(*a*) Prepare an income and expenditure account for the year ended 31 December 20X8. Show, either in this account or separately, the snack bar profit or loss.

(*b*) Prepare a balance sheet as at 31 December 20X8.

(*OCR (MEG): GCE A-level*)

2.4X   The treasurer of the City Sports Club has produced the following receipts and payments account for the year ended 31 December 20X7:

Receipts	£	Payments	£
Balance at bank 1 January 20X7	1,298	Coffee supplies bought	1,456
Subscriptions received	3,790	Wages of attendants and cleaners	1,776
Profits and dances	186	Rent of rooms	887
Profit on exhibition	112	New equipment bought	565
Coffee bar takings	2,798	Travelling expenses of teams	673
Sale of equipment	66	Balance at bank 31 December 20X7	2,893
	8,250		8,250

Notes:

(*i*)   Coffee bar stocks were valued: 31 December 20X6 £59, 31 December 20X7 £103. There was nothing owing for coffee bar stocks on either of these dates.

(*ii*)   On 1 January 20X7 the club's equipment was valued at £2,788. Included in this figure, valued at £77, was the equipment sold during the year for £66.

(*iii*)   The amount to be charged for depreciation of equipment for the year is £279. This is in addition to the loss on equipment sold during the year.

(*iv*)   Subscriptions owing by members 31 December 20X6 nil, at 31 December 20X7 £29.

You are required to:

(*a*)   Draw up the coffee bar trading account for the year ended 31 December 20X7. For this purpose £650 of the wages is to be charged to this account; the remainder will be charged in the income and expenditure account.

(*b*)   Calculate the accumulated fund as at 1 January 20X7.

(*c*)   Draw up the income and expenditure account for the year ended 31 December 20X7, and a balance sheet as at 31 December 20X7.

2.5   The following is a summary of the receipts and payments of the Miniville Rotary Club during the year ended 31 July 20X9.

Miniville Rotary Club
Receipts and Payments Account for the year ended 31 July 20X9

	£		£
Cash and bank balances b/d	210	Secretarial expenses	163
Sales of competition tickets	437	Rent	1,402
Members' subscriptions	1,987	Visiting speakers' expenses	1,275
Donations	177	Donations to charities	35
Refund of rent	500	Prizes for competitions	270
Balance c/d	13	Stationery and printing	179
	£3,324		£3,324

The following valuations are also available:

as at 31 July	20X8	20X9
	£	£
Equipment (original cost £1,420)	975	780
Subscriptions in arrears	65	85
Subscriptions in advance	10	37
Owing to suppliers of competition prizes	58	68
Stocks of competition prizes	38	46

Required:

(a) Calculate the value of the accumulated fund of the Miniville Rotary Club as at 1 August 20X8.

(b) Reconstruct the following accounts for the year ended 31 July 20X9:
  (i) the subscriptions account,
  (ii) the competition prizes account.

(c) Prepare an income and expenditure account for the Miniville Rotary Club for the year ended 31 July 20X9 and a balance sheet as at that date.

(Association of Accounting Technicians)

2.6X The Milham Theatre Club has been in existence for a number of years. Members pay an annual subscription of £15 which entitles them to join trips to professional productions at a reduced rate.
On 1 February 20X7 the Club's assets and liabilities were as follows:

Cash in hand £80, Bank balance (overdrawn) £180, Subscriptions in arrears £150, Savings account with local building society £1,950, Amount owing for coach hire £60.

Required:

(a) A *detailed* calculation of the Milham Theatre Club's accumulated fund at 1 February 20X7.

The Club's treasurer was able to present the following information at 31 January 20X8:

Receipts and Payments Accounts for year ended 31 January 20X8

	£	£
Opening balances		
Cash in hand	80	
Cash at bank (overdrawn)*	(180)	
		(100)
Receipts		
Subscriptions		
for year ended 31 January 20X7	120	
for year ended 31 January 20X8	1,620	
for year ended 31 January 20X9	165	
Gift from member	1,000	
Interest on Building Society Account	140	
Theatre outings		
receipts from members for theatre tickets	2,720	
receipts from members for coach travel	1,240	
	7,005	
	6,905	

	£	£
Payments		
Transfer to Building Society Account	1,210	
Theatre trips		
tickets	3,120	
coach hire	1,540	
Secretarial and administrative expenses	55	
		(5,925)
		980
Closing balances		
cash in hand	35	
cash at bank	945	
		980

- On 31 January 20X8 the club committee decided to write off any arrears of subscriptions for the year ended 31 January 20X7; the membership secretary reported that £75 is due for subscriptions for the year ended 31 January 20X8.
- The treasurer has calculated that the full amount of interest receivable on the building society account for the year ended 31 January 20X8 is £155.
- The club committee has decided that the gift should be capitalised.

Required:

(*b*) An account showing the surplus or deficit made by the Milham Theatre Club on theatre trips.

(*c*) An income and expenditure account for the Milham Theatre Club for the year ended 31 January 20X8.

(*d*) An *extract* from the Milham Theatre Club's balance sheet as at 31 January 20X8, showing the accumulated fund and current liability sections only.

The club committee have been concerned by the fact that the club's income has been steadily declining over recent years.

Required:

(*e*) Advice for the committee on *four* ways in which they could improve the club's income.

(AQA (SEG): GCE A-level)

* *Note*: Figures in brackets represent minus amounts.

2.7 The accounting records of the Happy Tickers Sports and Social Club are in a mess. You manage to find the following information to help you prepare the accounts for the year to 31 December 20X8.

Summarised Balance Sheet 31 December 20X7

	£		£
Half-share in motorised roller	600	Insurance (3 months)	150
New sports equipment unsold	1,000	Subscriptions 20X8	120
Used sports equipment at valuation	700	Life subscriptions	1,400
Rent (2 months)	200		1,670
Subscriptions 20X7	60	Accumulated fund	2,900
Café stocks	800		
Cash and bank	1,210		
	4,570		4,570

		£
Receipts in the year to 31 December 20X8:		
Subscriptions – 20X7		40
– 20X8		1,100
– 20X9		80
– Life		200
From sales of new sports equipment		900
From sales of used sports equipment		14
Café takings		4,660
		6,994

		£
Payments in the year to 31 December 20X8:		
Rent (for 12 months)		1,200
Insurance (for 18 months)		900
To suppliers of sports equipment		1,000
To café suppliers		1,900
Wages of café manager		2,000
Total cost of repairing motorised roller		450
		7,450

Notes:

(*i*)   Ownership and all expenses of the motorised roller are agreed to be shared equally with the Carefree Conveyancers Sports and Social Club which occupies a nearby site. The roller cost a total of £2,000 on 1 January 20X6 and had an estimated life of 10 years.

(*ii*) Life subscriptions are brought into income equally over 10 years, in a scheme begun 5 years ago in 20X3. Since the scheme began the cost of £200 per person has been constant. Prior to 31 December 20X7 10 life subscriptions had been received.

(*iii*) Four more annual subscriptions of £20 each had been promised relating to 20X8, but not yet received. Annual subscriptions promised but unpaid are carried forward for a maximum of 12 months.

(*iv*) New sports equipment is sold to members at cost plus 50%. Used equipment is sold off to members at book valuation. Half the sports equipment bought in the year (all from a cash and carry supplier) has been used within the club, and half made available for sale, new, to members. The 'used equipment at valuation' figure in the 31 December 20X8 balance sheet is to remain at £700.

(*v*)   Closing café stocks are £850, and £80 is owed to suppliers at 31 December 20X8.

Required:

(*a*) Calculate the profit on café operations and the profit on sale of sports equipment.

(*b*) Prepare a statement of subscription income for 20X8.

(*c*) Prepare an income and expenditure statement for the year to 31 December 20X8, and balance sheet as at 31 December 20X8.

(*d*) Why do life subscriptions appear as a liability?

(*Association of Chartered Certified Accountants*)

CHAPTER 3

Partnership accounts

Learning objectives

By the end of this chapter, you should be able to:

- explain exactly what a partnership is;
- explain the difference between limited partners and the ones with unlimited liability;
- describe the main features of a partnership agreement;
- explain what will happen if no agreement has been made to share profits or losses;
- describe the main provisions of the Partnership Act 1890;
- draw up the final accounts of a partnership;
- explain why goodwill exists;
- explain why goodwill has a monetary value;
- calculate the amount of adjustments needed when there is some form of change in a partnership;
- make the adjustments for goodwill in the books of a partnership;
- explain why there may be the need for revaluation of assets in a partnership;
- make the necessary adjustments when assets are revalued;
- explain what happens upon dissolution of a partnership;
- record the entries relating to the dissolution of a partnership.

3.1 The need for partnerships

So far we have mainly considered businesses owned by only one person. As you have seen when you looked at company financial statements, businesses set up to make a profit can often have more than one owner. There are various reasons for multiple ownership:

1 The capital required is more than one person can provide.
2 The experience or ability required to manage the business cannot be found in one person alone.
3 Many people want to share management instead of doing everything on their own.
4 Very often the partners will be members of the same family.

There are two types of multiple ownership: **partnerships** and companies. This chapter deals only with partnerships.

3.2 The characteristics of a partnership

A partnership has the following characteristics:

1 It is formed to make profits.
2 It must obey the law as given in the Partnership Act 1890. If there is a limited partner, as described in section 3.3, there is also the Limited Partnership Act of 1907 to comply with as well.
3 Normally there can be a minimum of two partners and a maximum of 20 partners. Exceptions are banks, where there cannot be more than ten partners; also there is no maximum limit for firms of accountants, solicitors, stock exchange members or other professional bodies receiving the approval of the Board of Trade for this purpose.
4 Each partner (except for limited partners described below) must pay their share of any debts that the partnership could not pay. If necessary, they could be forced to sell all their private possessions to pay their share of the debts. This can be said to be unlimited liability.

3.3 Limited partners

Limited partners are not liable for the debts as in section 3.2(4) above. They have the following characteristics:

1 Their liability for the debts of the partnership is limited to the capital they have put in. They can lose that capital, but they cannot be asked for any more money to pay the debts.
2 They are not allowed to take part in the management of the partnership business.
3 All the partners cannot be limited partners, so that there must be at least one partner with unlimited liability.

3.4 Partnership agreements

Agreements in writing are not necessary. However, it is better if a proper written agreement is drawn up by a lawyer or accountant. Where there is a proper written agreement there will be fewer problems between partners. A written agreement means less confusion about what has been agreed.

Where no partnership agreement exists

Where no agreement exists, express or implied, section 24 of the Partnership Act 1890 governs the situation. The accounting content of this section states:

(*a*) Profits and losses are to be shared equally.
(*b*) There is to be no interest allowed on capital.
(*c*) No interest is to be charged on drawings.
(*d*) Salaries are not allowed.

(e) If a partner puts a sum of money into a firm in excess of the capital he has agreed to subscribe, he is entitled to interest at the rate of 5 per cent per annum on such an advance.

This section applies where there is no agreement. There may be an agreement not by a partnership deed but in a letter, or it may be implied by conduct, for instance when a partner signs a balance sheet which shows profits shared in some other ratio than equally. Where a dispute arises as to whether agreement exists or not, and this cannot be resolved by the partners, only the courts will be competent to decide.

Contents of partnership agreements

The written agreement can contain as much, or as little, as the partners want. The law does not say what it must contain. The usual accounting contents are:

1 The capital to be contributed by each partner.
2 The ratio in which profits (or losses) are to be shared.
3 The rate of interest, if any, to be paid on capital before the profits are shared.
4 The rate of interest, if any, to be charged on partners' drawings.
5 Salaries to be paid to partners.
6 Arrangements for the admission of new partners.
7 Procedures to be carried out when a partner retires or dies.

An appropriation account is used in order to make the adjustments relating to items 2 to 5 and allocate appropriate shares of profit between the partners.

1 Capital contributions

Partners need *not* contribute equal amounts of capital. What matters is how much capital each partner *agrees* to contribute.

2 Profit (or loss) sharing ratios

Partners can agree to share profits/losses in any ratio or any way that they may wish. However, it is often thought by students that profits should be shared in the same ratio as that in which capital is contributed. For example, suppose the capitals were Allen £2,000 and Beet £1,000, many people would share the profits in the ratio of two-thirds to one-third, even though the work to be done by each partner is similar. A look at the division of the first few years' profits on such a basis would be:

Years	1	2	3	4	5	Total
	£	£	£	£	£	£
Net profits	1,800	2,400	3,000	3,000	3,600	
Shared:						
Allen $^2/_3$	1,200	1,600	2,000	2,000	2,400	9,200
Beet $^1/_3$	600	800	1,000	1,000	1,200	4,600

It can now be seen that Allen would receive £9,200. That is, £4,600 more than Beet. To treat each partner fairly, the difference between the two shares of profit in this case, as the duties of the partners are the same, should be adequate to compensate Allen for putting extra capital into the firm. It is obvious that £4,600 extra profits is far more than adequate for this purpose, as Allen only put in an extra £1,000 as capital.

Consider too the position of capital ratio sharing of profits if one partner put in £99,000 and the other put in £1,000 as capital.

To overcome the difficulty of compensating for the investment of extra capital, the concept of interest on capital was devised.

3 Interest on capital

If the work to be done by each partner is of equal value but the capital contributed is unequal, it is reasonable to grant interest on each partner's capital. This interest is treated as a deduction prior to the calculation of and distribution of profits according to the profit-sharing ratio.

The rate of interest is a matter of agreement between the partners, but it should equal the return which they would have received if they had invested the capital elsewhere.

Taking Allen and Beet's firm again, but sharing the profits equally after charging 5 per cent per annum interest on capital, the division of profits would become:

Years	1	2	3	4	5	Total
	£	£	£	£	£	£
Net profit	1,800	2,400	3,000	3,000	3,600	
Interest on capitals						
Allen	100	100	100	100	100	= 500
Beet	50	50	50	50	50	= 250
Remainder shared:						
Allen $^{1}/_{2}$	825	1,125	1,425	1,425	1,725	= 6,525
Beet $^{1}/_{2}$	825	1,125	1,425	1,425	1,725	= 6,525

Summary	Allen	Beet
	£	£
Interest on capital	500	250
Balance of profits	6,525	6,525
	7,025	6,775

Allen has thus received £250 more than Beet, this being adequate return (in the partners' estimation) for having invested an extra £1,000 in the firm for five years.

4 Interest on drawings

It is obviously in the best interests of the firm if cash is withdrawn from the firm by the partners in accordance with the two basic principles of: (a) as little as possible, and (b) as late as possible. The more cash that is left in the firm the more expansion can be financed, the greater the economies of having ample cash to take advantage of bargains and of not missing cash discounts because cash is not available and so on.

To deter the partners from taking out cash unnecessarily the concept can be used of charging the partners interest on each withdrawal, calculated from the date of withdrawal to the end of the financial year. The amount charged to them helps to swell the profits divisible between the partners. The rate of interest should be sufficient to achieve this without being too harsh.

Suppose that Allen and Beet have decided to charge interest on drawings at 5 per cent per annum, and that their year end was 31 December. The following drawings are made:

Allen

Drawings			Interest		
					£
1 January	£100		£100 × 5% × 12 months	=	5
1 March	£240		£240 × 5% × 10 months	=	10
1 May	£120		£120 × 5% × 8 months	=	4
1 July	£240		£240 × 5% × 6 months	=	6
1 October	£ 80		£ 80 × 5% × 3 months	=	1
			Interest charged to Allen	=	26

Beet

Drawings			Interest		
					£
1 January	£ 60		£ 60 × 5% × 12 months	=	3
1 August	£480		£480 × 5% × 5 months	=	10
1 December	£240		£240 × 5% × 1 month	=	1
			Interest charged to Beet	=	14

5 Salaries to partners

One partner may have more responsibility or tasks than the others. As a reward for this, rather than change the profit and loss sharing ratio, he may have a salary which is deducted before sharing the balance of profits.

6 Performance-related payments to partners

Partners may agree that commission or performance-related bonuses be payable to some or all the partners linked to their individual performance. As with salaries, these would be deducted before sharing the balance of profits.

3.5 An example of the distribution of profits

Taylor and Clarke have been in partnership for one year sharing profits and losses in the ratio of Taylor ^{3}/5ths, Clarke ^{2}/5ths. They are entitled to 5 per cent per annum interest on capitals, Taylor having £2,000 capital and Clarke £6,000. Clarke is to have a salary of £500. They charge interest on drawings, Taylor being charged £50 and Clarke £100. The net profit, before any distributions to the partners, amounted to £5,000 for the year ended 31 December 20X7.

	£	£	£
Net profit			5,000
Add Charged for interest on drawings:			
Taylor		50	
Clarke		100	
			150
			5,150

	£	£	£
Less Salary: Clarke		500	
Interest on capital:			
Taylor	100		
Clarke	300		
	400		
		400	
			(900)
Balance of profits			4,250
Shared:			
Taylor ^{3}/5ths		2,550	
Clarke ^{2}/5ths		1,700	
			4,250

The £5,000 net profits have therefore been shared:

	Taylor	Clarke
	£	£
Balance of profits	2,550	1,700
Interest on capital	100	300
Salary	–	500
	2,650	2,500
Less Interest on drawings	50	100
	2,600	2,400

£5,000

3.6 The profit and loss appropriation account

If the sales, stock and expenses of partnership were exactly the same as that of a sole trader, then the trading and profit and loss account would be identical with that as prepared for the sole trader. However, a partnership would have an extra section shown under the profit and loss account. This section is called the **profit and loss appropriation account**, and it is in this account that the distribution of profits is shown. The heading to the trading and profit and loss account does not include the words 'appropriation account'. It is purely an accounting custom not to include it in the heading.

The trading and profit and loss account of Taylor and Clarke from the details given would appear:

Taylor and Clarke
Trading and Profit and Loss Account for the year ended 31 December 20X7

(Trading Account – same as for sole trader)

£

(Profit and Loss Account – same as for sole trader)

	£	£	£
Net profit			5,000
Interest on drawings:			
Taylor		50	
Clarke		100	
			150
			5,150

	£	£	£
Less:			
Interest on capitals			
Taylor	100		
Clarke	300		
		400	
Salary: Clarke		500	
			(900)
Balance of profits			4,250
Shared:			
Taylor ³/₅ths		2,550	
Clarke ²/₅ths		1,700	
			4,250

3.7 Capital accounts and current accounts

There is a choice of approach available as follows.

(a) Fixed capital accounts plus current accounts

The capital account for each partner remains year by year at the figure of capital put into the firm by the partners. The profits, interest on capital and the salaries to which the partner may be entitled are then credited to a separate current account for the partner, and the drawings and the interest on drawings are debited to it. The balance of the current account at the end of each financial year will then represent the amount of undrawn (or overdrawn) profits. A credit balance will be undrawn profits, while a debit balance will be drawings in excess of the profits to which the partner was entitled.

For Taylor and Clarke, capital and current accounts, assuming drawings of £2,000 each, will appear:

Taylor – *Capital*

		20X7		£
		Jan 1 Bank		2,000

Clarke – *Capital*

		20X7		£
		Jan 1 Bank		6,000

Taylor – *Current Account*

20X7		£	20X7		£
Dec 31 Cash: Drawings		2,000	Dec 31 Profit and loss		
,, 31 Profit and loss			appropriation account:		
appropriation account:			Interest on capital		100
Interest on drawings		50	Share of profits		2,550
,, 31 Balance c/d		600			
		2,650			2,650
			20X8		
			Jan 1 Balance b/d		600

Clarke – *Current Account*

20X7		£	20X7		£
Dec 31	Cash: Drawings	2,000	Dec 31	Profit and loss	
,, 31	Profit and loss			appropriation account:	
	appropriation account:			Interest on capital	300
	Interest on drawings	100		Share of profits	1,700
,, 31	Balance c/d	400		Salary	500
		2,500			2,500
			20X8		
			Jan 1	Balance b/d	400

Notice that the salary of Clarke was not paid to him, it was merely credited to his account. If in fact it was paid in addition to his drawings, the £500 cash paid would have been debited to the current account, changing the £400 credit balance into a £100 debit balance.

Examiners often ask for the capital accounts and current accounts to be shown in columnar form. For the previous accounts of Taylor and Clarke these would appear as follows:

Capital Accounts

	Taylor	Clarke			Taylor	Clarke
	£	£	20X7		£	£
			Jan 1	Bank	2,000	6,000

Current Accounts

		Taylor	Clarke			Taylor	Clarke
20X7		£	£	20X7		£	£
Dec 31	Cash: Drawings	2,000	2,000	Dec 31	Interest on capital	100	300
,, 31	Interest on drawings	50	100	,, 31	Share of profits	2,550	1,700
,, 31	Balances c/d	600	400	,, 31	Salary		500
		2,650	2,500			2,650	2,500
				20X8			
				Jan 1	Balances b/d	600	400

(b) Fluctuating capital accounts

The distribution of profits would be credited to the capital account, and the drawings and interest on drawings debited. Therefore the balance on the capital account will change each year, i.e. it will fluctuate.

If fluctuating capital accounts had been kept for Taylor and Clarke they would have appeared:

Taylor – *Capital*

20X7		£	20X7		£
Dec 31	Cash: Drawings	2,000	Jan 1	Bank	2,000
,, 31	Profit and loss		Dec 31	Profit and loss	
	appropriation account:			appropriation account:	
	Interest on drawings	50		Interest on capital	100
,, 31	Balance c/d	2,600		Share of profits	2,550
		4,650			4,650
			20X8		
			Jan 1	Balance b/d	2,600

Clarke – *Capital*

20X7	£	20X7	£
Dec 31 Cash: Drawings	2,000	Jan 1 Bank	6,000
„ 31 Profit and loss		Dec 31 Profit and loss	
appropriation account:		appropriation account:	
Interest on		Interest on capital	300
drawings	100	Salary	500
„ 31 Balance c/d	6,400	Share of profit	1,700
	8,500		8,500
		20X8	
		Jan 1 Balance b/d	6,400

Fixed capital accounts preferred

The keeping of fixed capital accounts plus current accounts is considered preferable to fluctuating capital accounts. When partners are taking out greater amounts than the share of the profits that they are entitled to, this is shown up by a debit balance on the current account and so acts as a warning.

3.8 The balance sheet

The capital part side of the balance sheet will appear:

Balance Sheet as at 31 December 20X7

			£	£
Capital accounts	Taylor		2,000	
	Clarke		6,000	
				8,000
Current accounts	*Taylor*	*Clarke*		
	£	£		
Interest on capital	100	300		
Share of profits	2,550	1,700		
Salary	–	500		
	2,650	2,500		
Less Drawings	(2,000)	(2,000)		
Interest on drawings	(50)	(100)		
	(2,050)	(2,100)		
	600	400		
				1,000

If one of the current accounts had finished in debit, for instance if the current account of Clarke had finished up as £400 debit, the figure of £400 would appear in brackets and the balances would appear net in the totals column:

	Taylor	*Clarke*	
	£	£	£
Closing balance	600	(400)	200

If the net figure turned out to be a debit figure then this would be deducted from the total of the capital accounts.

3.9 Structural changes in the ownership of a partnership

There are three main changes that can occur in the ownership of a partnership:

- A change in the profit-sharing ratios.
- Admission of a new partner.
- A partner leaves the partnership.

In each case, there is a need to revalue the business so as to enter the appropriate entries into the accounting records. The revaluation has two phases:

- Asset revaluations
- Goodwill.

We'll now consider these issues. First, let's consider goodwill, what it is, how it arises, and how it is treated in the partnership books of account. We will begin by looking at it in a context with which you are familiar, the sole trader.

3.10 Goodwill

Suppose you have been in a business for some years and you wanted to sell it. How much would you ask as the total sale price of the business? You decide to list how much you could get for each asset if sold separately. This list might be as follows:

	£
Buildings	225,000
Machinery	75,000
Debtors	60,000
Stock	40,000
	400,000

Instead. you sell the whole of the business as a going concern to Mr Lee for £450,000. He has therefore paid £50,000 more than the total for all the assets. This extra payment of £50,000 is called **goodwill**. He has paid this because he wanted to take over the business as a going concern. Thus:

Purchased Goodwill = Total amount paid *less* value of identifiable assets.

Reasons for payment of goodwill

In buying an existing business which has been established for some time there may be quite a few possible advantages. Some of them are listed here:

- A large number of regular customers will continue to deal with the new owner.
- The business has a good reputation.
- It has experienced, efficient and reliable employees.
- The business is situated in a good location.
- It has good contacts with suppliers.

None of these advantages is available to completely new businesses. For this reason, many people would decide to buy an existing business and pay an amount for goodwill.

Existence of goodwill

Goodwill does not necessarily exist in a business. If the business had a bad reputation, an inefficient labour force or other negative factors, the owner might be unlikely to be paid for goodwill on selling the business.

Methods of calculating goodwill

There is no single way of calculating goodwill to which everyone can agree. The seller will probably want more for the goodwill than the buyer will want to pay. All that is certain is that when an agreement is reached between buyer and seller, then that is the amount of goodwill. Various methods are used to help buyer and seller come to an agreed figure. The calculations give buyer and seller a figure with which to begin discussions of the value.

Very often each industry or occupation has its own customary way of calculating goodwill:

(a) In more than one type of retail business it has been the custom to value goodwill at the average weekly sales for the past year multiplied by a given figure. The given figure will, of course, differ between different types of businesses, and often changes gradually in the same types of business in the long term.

(b) With many professional firms, such as accountants in public practice, it is the custom to value goodwill as being the gross annual fees times a given number. For instance, what is termed a two years' purchase of a firm with gross fees of £6,000 means goodwill = 2 × £6,000 = £12,000.

(c) The average net annual profit for a specified past number of years multiplied by an agreed number. This is often said to be x years' purchase of the net profits.

(d) The super-profits method. It may be argued, as in the case of a sole trader for example, that the net profits are not 'true profits'. This is because the sole trader has not charged for the following expenses:

(i) Services of the proprietor. He has worked in the business, but he has not charged for such services. Any drawings he makes are charged to a capital account, not to the profit and loss account.

(ii) The use of the money he has invested in the business. If he had invested his money elsewhere he would have earned interest or dividends on such investments.

Super profits are what is left of the net profits after allowances have been made for (i) services of the proprietor and (ii) the use of the capital.

They are usually calculated as:

	£	£
Annual net profits		80,000
Less (i) Remuneration proprietor would have earned for similar work elsewhere	20,000	
(ii) Interest that would have been earned if capital had been invested elsewhere	10,000	
		(30,000)
Annual super profits		50,000

The annual super profits are then multiplied by a number agreed by the seller and the purchaser of the business.

3.11 Goodwill in the partnership accounts

Goodwill is not entered in a sole trader's accounts unless he has actually bought it. This will show that he did not start the business himself, but bought an existing business. For a partnership, sometimes it is necessary to enter goodwill in the partnership accounts even when it does not arise from initial purchase of the business by the partners.

Unless it has been agreed differently, a partner will own a share in the goodwill in the same ratio in which he shares profits. For instance, if A takes one-quarter of the profits he will be the owner of one-quarter of the goodwill. This is true even if there is no goodwill account.

This means that when something happens such as:

(*a*) existing partners decide to change profit- and loss-sharing ratios, or
(*b*) a new partner is introduced, or
(*c*) a partner retires or dies,

then the ownership of goodwill by partners changes in some way.

The change may involve cash passing from one partner to another, or an adjustment in the partnership accounts, so that the changes in ownership do not lead to a partner (or partners) giving away his or her share of ownership for nothing.

(a) Change in profit-sharing ratios of existing partners

Sometimes the profit- and loss-sharing ratios have to be changed. Typical reasons are:

- A partner may not work as much as he used to do, possibly because of old age or ill-health.
- His skills and ability may have changed.
- He may be doing much more for the business than he used to do.

If the partners decide to change their profit-sharing ratios, an adjustment will be needed.

To illustrate why this is so, let us look at the following example of a partnership in which goodwill is not already shown in a goodwill account at its correct value.

(*a*) A, B and C are in partnership, sharing profits and losses equally.
(*b*) On 31 December 20X5 they decide to change this to A one-half, B one-quarter and C one-quarter.
(*c*) On 31 December 20X5 the goodwill, which had never been shown in the books, was valued at £60,000. If, just before the profit-sharing change, the firm had been sold and £60,000 received for goodwill, then each partner would have received £20,000 as they shared profits equally.
(*d*) At any time after 31 December 20X5, once the profit sharing has changed, their ownership of goodwill is worth A £30,000, B £15,000 and C £15,000. If goodwill is sold for that amount then those figures will be received by the partners for goodwill.
(*e*) If, when (*b*) above happened there had been no change made to A by B and C, or no other form of adjustment, then B and C would each have given away a £5,000 share of the goodwill for nothing. This would not be sensible.

We can now look at how the adjustments can be made when a goodwill account with the correct valuation does not already exist.

EXHIBIT 3.1

E, F and G have been in business for ten years. They have always shared profits equally. No goodwill account has ever existed in the books. On 31 December 20X6 they agree that G will take only a one-fifth share of the profits as from 1 January 20X7, because he will be devoting less of his time to the business in the future. E and F will each take two-fifths of the profits. The summarised balance sheet of the business on 31 December 20X6 appears as follows:

Balance Sheet as at 31 December 20X6

	£
Net Assets	7,000
Capital: E	3,000
F	1,800
G	2,200
	7,000

The partners agree that the goodwill should be valued at £3,000. Answer (1) shows the solution when a goodwill account is opened. Answer (2) is the solution when a goodwill account is not opened.

1 **Goodwill account opened.** Open a goodwill account. Then make the following entries:
   Debit goodwill account: total value of goodwill.
   Credit partners' capital accounts: each one with his share of goodwill in old profit-sharing ratio.
   The goodwill account will appear as:

Goodwill

	£		£
Capitals: valuation shared		Balance c/d	3,000
E	1,000		
F	1,000		
G	1,000		
	3,000		3,000

The capital accounts may be shown in columnar fashion as:

Capital Accounts

	E £	F £	G £		E £	F £	G £
Balances c/d	4,000	2,800	3,200	Balances b/d	3,000	1,800	2,200
				Goodwill: old ratios	1,000	1,000	1,000
	4,000	2,800	3,200		4,000	2,800	3,200

The balance sheet items before and after the adjustments will appear as:

	Before £	After £		Before £	After £
Goodwill	–	3,000	Capitals: E	3,000	4,000
			F	1,800	2,800
Other assets	7,000	7,000	G	2,200	3,200
	7,000	10,000		7,000	10,000

2 **Goodwill account not opened.** The effect of the change of ownership of goodwill may be shown in the following form:

Before			After		Loss or Gain	Action Required
		£		£		
E	One-third	1,000	Two-fifths	1,200	Gain £200	Debit E's capital account £200
F	One-third	1,000	Two-fifths	1,200	Gain £200	Debit F's capital account £200
G	One-third	1,000	One-fifth	600	Loss £400	Credit G's capital account £400
		3,000		3,000		

The column headed 'Action Required' shows that a partner who has gained goodwill because of the change must be charged for it by having his capital account debited with the value of the gain. A partner who has lost goodwill must be compensated for it by having his capital account credited.

The capital accounts will appear as:

Capital Accounts

	E £	F £	G £		E £	F £	G £
Goodwill				Balances b/d	3,000	1,800	
adjustments	200	200		Goodwill			2,200
Balances c/d	2,800	1,600	2,600	adjustments			400
	3,000	1,800	2,600		3,000	1,800	2,600

As there is no goodwill account the balance sheet items before and after the adjustments will therefore appear as:

	Before	After			Before	After
	£	£			£	£
Net assets	7,000	7,000	Capitals: E		3,000	2,800
			F		1,800	1,600
			G		2,200	2,600
	7,000	7,000			7,000	7,000

Comparison of methods 1 and 2

Let us see how the methods compare. Assume that shortly afterwards the assets in answers 1 and 2 are sold for £7,000 and the goodwill for £3,000. The total of £10,000 would be distributed as follows, using each of the methods:

Method 1 The £10,000 is exactly the amount needed to pay the partners according to the balances on their capital accounts. The payments are therefore made of:

Capitals paid to	E	4,000
	F	2,800
	G	3,200
Total cash paid		£10,000

Method 2 First of all the balances on capital accounts, totalling £7,000, are to be paid. Then the £3,000 received for goodwill will be split between the partners in their profit and loss ratios. This will result in payments as follows:

	Capitals	Goodwill Shared	Total Paid
E	2,800	(2/5ths) 1,200	4,000
F	1,600	(2/5ths) 1,200	2,800
G	2,600	(1/5th) 600	3,200
	£7,000	£3,000	£10,000

You can see that the final amounts paid to the partners are the same whether a goodwill account is opened or not.

(b) Admission of new partners

New partners may be admitted, usually for one of two reasons:

1 As an extra partner, either because the firm has grown or someone is needed with different skills.
2 To replace partners who are leaving the firm. This might be because of retirement or death of a partner.

Goodwill on admission of new partners

The new partner will be entitled to a share in the profits. Normally, the new partner will also be entitled to the same share of the value of goodwill. It is correct to charge a new partner for her or his taking over that share of the goodwill.

Goodwill adjustments when new partners admitted

This calculation is done in three stages:

1 Show value of goodwill divided between old partners in old profit- and loss-sharing ratios.
2 Then show value of goodwill divided between partners (including new partner) in new profit- and loss-sharing ratio.
3 Goodwill gain shown: charge these partners for the gain.
4 Goodwill loss shown: give these partners an allowance for their losses.

This is illustrated in Exhibits 3.2 and 3.3.

EXHIBIT 3.2

	Stage 1		Stage 2		Stage 3	
Partners	Old profit shares	Share of goodwill £	New profit shares	Share of goodwill £	Gain or loss £	Adjustment needed
A	1/2	30,000	1/3	20,000	10,000 Loss	Cr A Capital
B	1/2	30,000	1/3	20,000	10,000 Loss	Cr B Capital
C		–	1/3	20,000	20,000 Gain	Dr C Capital
		60,000		60,000		

A and B are in partnership, sharing profits and losses equally. C is admitted as a new partner. The three partners will share profits and losses one-third each.

Total goodwill is valued at £60,000.

This means that A and B need to have their capitals increased by £10,000 each. C needs to have his capital reduced by £20,000.

Note that A and B have kept their profits in the same ratio to each other. While they used to have one-half each, now they have one-third each.

We will now see in Exhibit 3.3 that the method shown is the same even when existing partners take a different share of the profit to that before the change.

EXHIBIT 3.3

D and E are in partnership sharing profits one-half each. A new partner, F, is admitted. Profits will now be shared D one-fifth, and E and F two-fifths each. D and E have therefore not kept their shares equal to each other. Goodwill is valued at £60,000.

D needs his capital to be increased by £18,000. E's capital is to be increased by £6,000.

F needs his capital to be reduced by £24,000.

	Stage 1		Stage 2		Stage 3	
Partners	Old profit shares	Share of goodwill £	New profit shares	Share of goodwill £	Gain or loss £	Adjustment needed
D	1/2	30,000	1/5	12,000	18,000 Loss	Cr D Capital
E	1/2	30,000	2/5	24,000	6,000 Loss	Cr E Capital
F		–	2/5	24,000	24,000 Gain	Dr F Capital
		60,000		60,000		

Accounting entries for goodwill adjustments

These depend on how the partners wish to arrange the adjustment. Three methods are usually used:

1 Cash is paid by the new partner privately to the old partners for his share of the goodwill. No goodwill account is to be opened.

In Exhibit 3.3, F would therefore give £24,000 in cash, being £18,000 to D and £6,000 to E. They would bank these amounts in their private bank accounts. No entry is made for this in the accounts of the partnership.

2 Cash is paid by the new partner into the business bank account for his/her share of the goodwill. No goodwill account is to be opened. Assume that the capital balances before F was admitted were D £50,000, E £50,000, and F was to pay in £50,000 as capital plus £24,000 for goodwill.

The £24,000 payment is made in order to secure a share of the £60,000 existing goodwill. The £24,000 is shared between the two existing partners by increasing their capital accounts by the amounts shown in Stage 3 of Exhibit 3.3. The debit entry is to the bank account. The entries in the capital accounts are:

Capital Accounts

	D £	E £	F £		D £	E £	F £
Adjustments for goodwill			24,000	Balances b/d	50,000	50,000	
				Cash for capital			50,000
				Cash for goodwill			24,000
Balances c/d	68,000	56,000	50,000	Loss of goodwill	18,000	6,000	
	68,000	56,000	74,000		68,000	56,000	74,000

3 Goodwill account to be opened. No extra cash to be paid in by the new partner for goodwill.

In Exhibit 3.3, the opening capitals were D £50,000 and E £50,000. F paid in £50,000 as capital.

Here the situation is different from that under the second method. The new partner is not paying anything in order to secure a share of the £60,000 of existing goodwill. As a result, it is shared now between the two original partners in their original profit-sharing ratios (1/2 : 1/2) and the new partner's capital account is credited only with the £50,000 s/he is investing. This is done because the new partner is not entitled to any of the previously established goodwill and the only way to prevent that permanently is to recognise all the goodwill now and credit it to the existing partners' capital accounts. The action required is:

● Debit goodwill account with total value of goodwill.
● Credit capitals of old partners with their shares of goodwill in old profit-sharing ratios.

No adjustments for goodwill gains and losses are required as the capital accounts of D and E have been increased by the full value of the goodwill at the time of F's admission to partnership.

For Exhibit 3.3, the entries would appear as:

Goodwill

	£		£
Value divided:		Balance c/d	60,000
D Capital	30,000		
E Capital	30,000		
	60,000		60,000

Capital Accounts

	D £	E £	F £		D £	E £	F £
				Balances b/d	50,000	50,000	
				Cash for capital			50,000
Balances c/d	80,000	80,000	50,000	Goodwill	30,000	30,000	
	80,000	80,000	50,000		80,000	80,000	50,000

Were the partnership dissolved and realised the £210,000 it was valued at when F was admitted, it would first be used to repay the capital account balances. D and E would, therefore, be fully compensated for the value of the goodwill at the time of F's admission to partnership, and F would receive exactly the amount of her/his investment.

Where new partners pay for share of goodwill

Unless otherwise agreed, the assumption is that the total value of goodwill is directly proportionate to the amount paid by the new partner for the share taken by him/her. If a new partner pays £1,200 for a one-fifth share of the profits, then goodwill is taken to be £6,000. A sum of £800 for a one-quarter share of the profits would therefore be taken to imply a total value of £3,200 for goodwill.

(c) Goodwill on withdrawal or death of partners

This depends on whether or not a goodwill account exists.

If there was no goodwill account

If no goodwill account already existed the partnership goodwill should be valued because the outgoing partner is entitled to his or her share of its value. This value is entered in double entry accounts:

● Debit goodwill account with valuation.
● Credit each old partner's capital account in profit-sharing ratios.

EXHIBIT 3.4

H, I and J have been in partnership for many years sharing profit and losses equally. No goodwill account has ever existed.

   J is leaving the partnership. The other two partners are to take over his share of profits equally. Capitals entered before goodwill were £50,000 each. The goodwill is valued at £45,000.

Goodwill

	£		£
Valuation: Capital H	15,000	Balance c/d	45,000
Capital I	15,000		
Capital J	15,000		
	45,000		45,000
Balance b/d	45,000		

Capital Accounts

	H £	I £	J £		H £	I £	J £
Balances c/d	65,000	65,000	65,000	Balances b/d	50,000	50,000	50,000
				Goodwill shares	15,000	15,000	15,000
	65,000	65,000	65,000		65,000	65,000	65,000
				Balances b/d	65,000	65,000	65,000

When J leaves the partnership, his capital balance of £65,000 will be paid to him.

If a goodwill account exists

1 If a goodwill account exists with the correct valuation of goodwill entered in it, no further action is needed.
2 If the valuation in the goodwill account needs to be changed, the following will apply:

Goodwill undervalued: Debit increase needed to goodwill account.

Credit increase to old partners' capital accounts in their old profit-sharing ratios.

Goodwill overvalued: Debit reduction to old partners' capital accounts in their old profit-sharing ratios.

Credit reduction needed to goodwill account.

3.12 Asset revaluation

When:

- Existing partners decide to change profit- and loss-sharing ratios, or
- A new partner is introduced; or
- A partner retires or dies,

it is treated as if the business were being sold. Just as with the actual sale of a business, if the sale price of the assets exceeds their value, there will be a profit on the sale.

In the case of a change in the status of a partnership for one of the three reasons given above, this profit (or loss) will be shared between the partners in their profit- and loss-sharing ratios. In order to determine whether there is a profit or loss when one of these three events occurs, the assets have to be revalued to reflect their current value.

If this were not done a new partner admitted would benefit from increases in value before he joined the firm, without having to pay anything for it.

Similarly, if the value of assets had fallen before he had joined the firm, and no revaluation took place, he would share that loss of value without any adjustment being made for it.

Partners who leave or change their profit- and loss-sharing ratios would also be affected, if there were no payments or allowances for such gains or losses.

Profit or loss on revaluation

We have already seen that there should be a revaluation when there is a change in partners or a change in profit-sharing ratios.

If the revaluation shows no difference in asset values, no further action is needed. This will not happen very often, especially if assets include buildings. These are normally shown in the financial statements at cost less depreciation to date, but this is seldom the actual value after the buildings have been owned for a few years.

		£
If:	New total valuation of assets	90,000
Is more than:	Old total valuation of assets	(60,000)
The result is:	Profit on revaluation	30,000

		£
If:	Old total valuation of assets	50,000
Is more than:	New total valuation of assets	(40,000)
The result is:	Loss on revaluation	10,000

Accounting for revaluation

A revaluation account is opened:

1 For each asset showing a gain on revaluation:
    Debit asset account with gain.
      Credit revaluation account.

2 For each asset showing a loss on revaluation:
    Debit revaluation account.
      Credit asset account with loss.

3 If there is an increase in total valuation of assets:
    Debit profit to revaluation account.
      Credit old partners' capital accounts in old profit- and loss-sharing ratios.[Note]

4 If there is a fall in total valuation of assets:
    Debit old partners' capital accounts in old profit- and loss-sharing ratios.[Note]
      Credit loss to revaluation account.

Note: If partners' current accounts are kept, then the entries should be made in their current accounts.

EXHIBIT 3.5

Following is the balance sheet as at 31 December 20X5 of W and Y, who shared profit and losses in the ratios W two-thirds; Y one-third. From 1 January 20X6 the profit- and loss-sharing ratios are to be altered to W one-half; Y one-half.

Balance Sheet as at 31 December 20X5

	£	£
Premises at cost		6,500
Fixtures (at cost *less* depreciation)		1,500
		8,000
Stock	2,000	
Debtors	1,200	
Bank	800	
		4,000
		12,000
Capitals: W		7,000
Y		5,000
		12,000

The assets were revalued on 1 January 20X6 to be: Premises £9,000, Fixtures £1,100. Other assets remained at the same values.
    Accounts to show the assets at revalued amounts follow:

Revaluation

	£	£		£
Assets reduced in value:			Assets increased in value:	
Fixtures		400	Premises	2,500
Profit on revaluation carried to				
Capital accounts:				
W two-thirds	1,400			
Y one-third	700	2,100		
		2,500		2,500

Premises

	£		£
Balance b/d	6,500	Balance c/d	9,000
Revaluation: Increase	2,500		
	9,000		9,000
Balance b/d	9,000		

Fixtures

	£		£
Balance b/d	1,500	Revaluation: Reduction	400
		Balance c/d	1,100
	1,500		1,500
Balance b/d	1,100		

Capital: W

	£		£
Balance c/d	8,400	Balance b/d	7,000
		Revaluation: Share of profit	1,400
	8,400		8,400
		Balance b/d	8,400

Capital: Y

	£		£
Balance c/d	5,700	Balance b/d	5,000
		Revaluation: Share of profit	700
	5,700		5,700
		Balance b/d	5,700

3.13 Partnership dissolution

Reasons for dissolution include the following:

(a) The partnership is no longer profitable, and there is no longer any reason to carry on trading.

(b) The partners cannot agree between themselves how to operate the partnership. They therefore decide to finish the partnership.

(c) Factors such as ill-health or old age may bring about the close of the partnership.

What happens upon dissolution

Upon **dissolution** the partnership firm stops trading or operating. Then, in accordance with the Partnership Act 1890:

(a) the assets are disposed of;

(b) the liabilities of the firm are paid to everyone other than partners;

(c) the partners are repaid their advances and current balances – advances are the amounts they have put in above and beyond the capital;

(d) the partners are paid the final amounts due to them on their capital accounts.

Any profit or loss on dissolution would be shared by all the partners in their profit- and loss-sharing ratios. Profits would increase capitals repayable to partners. Losses would reduce the capitals repayable.

If a partner's final balance on his/her capital and current accounts is in deficit, he or she will have to pay that amount into the partnership bank account.

Disposal of assets

The assets do not have to be sold to external parties. Quite often one or more existing partners will take assets at values agreed by all the partners. In such a case the partner may not pay in cash for such assets; instead they will be charged to his or her capital account.

Accounting for partnership dissolution

The main account around which the dissolution entries are made is known as the realisation account. It is this account in which it is calculated whether the realisation of the assets is at a profit or at a loss.

A simple example

Exhibit 3.6 shows the simplest of partnership dissolutions. We will then look at a more difficult example in Exhibit 3.7.

EXHIBIT 3.6

The last balance sheet of A and B, who share profits A two-thirds : B one-third is shown below. On this date they are to dissolve the partnership.

Balance Sheet at 31 December 20X9

	£	£
Fixed assets		
Buildings		10,000
Motor vehicle		2,000
		12,000
Current assets		
Stock	3,000	
Debtors	4,000	
Bank	1,000	
	8,000	
Current liabilities		
Creditors	(2,000)	
		6,000
		18,000
Capitals: A		12,000
B		6,000
		18,000

The buildings were sold for £10,500 and the stock for £2,600. £3,500 was collected from debtors. The motor vehicle was taken over by A at an agreed value of £1,700, but he did not pay any cash for it. £2,000 was paid to creditors. The costs of the dissolution were paid which were £200.

The accounting entries needed are:

(A) Transfer book values of all assets to the realisation account:
   Debit realisation account
      Credit asset accounts
(B) Amounts received from disposal of assets:
   Debit bank
      Credit realisation account
(C) Values of assets taken over by partner without payment:
   Debit partner's capital account
      Credit realisation account
(D) Creditors paid:
   Debit creditors' accounts
      Credit bank
(E) Costs of dissolution:
   Debit realisation account
      Credit bank
(F) Profit or loss on realisation to be shared between partners in profit- and loss-sharing ratios:
   If a profit: Debit realisation account
                  Credit partners' capital accounts
   If a loss: Debit partners' capital accounts
                  Credit realisation account
(G) Pay to the partners their final balances on their capital accounts:
   Debit capital accounts
      Credit bank

The entries are now shown. The letters (A) to (G) as above are shown against each entry:

Buildings

	£			£
Balance b/d	10,000	Realisation	(A)	10,000

Motor Vehicle

	£			£
Balance b/d	2,000	Realisation	(A)	2,000

Stock

	£			£
Balance b/d	3,000	Realisation	(A)	3,000

Debtors

	£			£
Balance b/d	4,000	Realisation	(A)	4,000

Realisation

		£				£
Assets to be realised:			Bank: Assets sold			
Buildings	(A)	10,000	Buildings	(B)		10,500
Motor vehicle	(A)	2,000	Stock	(B)		2,600
Stock	(A)	3,000	Debtors	(B)		3,500
Debtors	(A)	4,000	Taken over by partner A:			
Bank:			Motor vehicle	(C)		1,700
Dissolution costs	(E)	200	Loss on realisation		£	
			A 2/3	(F)	600	
			B 1/3	(F)	300	900
		19,200				19,200

Bank

		£			£
Balance b/d		1,000	Creditors	(D)	2,000
Realisation: Assets sold			Realisation: Costs	(E)	200
Buildings	(B)	10,500	Capitals: to clear		
Stock	(B)	2,600	A	(G)	9,700
Debtors	(B)	3,500	B	(G)	5,700
		17,600			17,600

Creditors

		£		£
Bank	(D)	2,000	Balance b/d	2,000

A: Capital

		£		£
Realisation: Motor Vehicle	(C)	1,700	Balance b/d	12,000
Realisation: Share of loss	(F)	600		
Bank: to close	(G)	9,700		
		12,000		12,000

B: Capital

		£		£
Realisation: Share of loss	(F)	300	Balance b/d	6,000
Bank: to close	(G)	5,700		
		6,000		6,000

The final balances on the partners' capital accounts should always equal the amount in the bank account from which they are to be paid. For instance, in the above exhibit there was £15,400 in the bank from which to pay A £9,700 and B £5,700. If the final bank balance does not pay out the partners' capital accounts exactly, you will have made a mistake somewhere.

A more detailed example

Exhibit 3.6 did not show the more difficult accounting entries. A more difficult example appears in Exhibit 3.7.

The extra information is:

(*a*) Any provision such as bad debts or depreciation is to be transferred to the credit of the asset account: see entries (A) in Exhibit 3.7.

(*b*) Discounts on creditors – to balance the creditors' account, transfer the discounts on creditors to the credit of the realisation account: see entries (F) in the exhibit.

(*c*) Transfer the balances on the partners' current accounts to their capital accounts: see entries (I) of the exhibit.

(*d*) A partner who owes the firm money because his capital account is in deficit must now pay the money owing: see entries (J) of the exhibit.

EXHIBIT 3.7

On 31 December 20X8, P, Q and R decided to dissolve their partnership. They had always shared profits in the ratio of P 3 : Q 2 : R 1.

Their goodwill was sold for £3,000, the machinery for £1,800 and the stock for £1,900. There were three cars, all taken over by the partners at agreed values, P taking one for £800, Q one for £1,000 and R one for £500. The premises were taken over by R at an agreed value of £5,500. The amounts collected from debtors amounted to £2,700 after bad debts and discounts had been deducted. The creditors were discharged for £1,600, the difference being due to discounts received. The costs of dissolution amounted to £1,000.

Their last balance sheet is summarised as:

Balance Sheet as at 31 December 20X8

	£	£	£
Fixed assets			
Premises			5,000
Machinery			3,000
Motor vehicles			2,500
			10,500
Current assets			
Stock		1,800	
Debtors	3,000		
Less Provision for doubtful debts	(200)		
		2,800	
Bank		1,400	
		6,000	
Current liabilities			
Creditors		(1,700)	
			4,300
			14,800
Capital accounts: P			6,000
Q			5,000
R			3,000
			14,000
Current accounts: P		200	
Q		100	
R		500	
			800
			14,800

The accounts recording the dissolution are shown below. A description of each entry follows the accounts, the letters (A) to (K) against each entry indicating the relevant descriptions.

Premises

		£				£
Balance b/d		5,000	Realisation	(B)		5,000

Machinery

		£				£
Balance b/d		3,000	Realisation	(B)		3,000

Motor Vehicles

		£				£
Balance b/d		2,500	Realisation	(B)		2,500

Stock

		£				£
Balance b/d		1,800	Realisation	(B)		1,800

Debtors

		£				£
Balance b/d		3,000	Provisions for bad debts	(A)		200
			Realisation	(B)		2,800

Realisation

		£				£
Assets to be realised:			Bank: Assets sold			
Premises	(B)	5,000	Goodwill	(C)		3,000
Machinery	(B)	3,000	Machinery	(C)		1,800
Motor vehicles	(B)	2,500	Stock	(C)		1,900
Stock	(B)	1,800	Debtors	(C)		2,700
Debtors	(B)	2,800	Taken over by partners:			
Bank: Costs	(G)	1,000	P: Motor car	(D)		800
Profit on realisation:	(H)		Q: Motor car	(D)		1,000
		£	R: Motor car	(D)		500
P		600	R: Premises	(D)		5,500
Q		400	Creditors: Discounts	(F)		100
R		200	1,200				
		17,300				17,300

Creditors

		£			£
Bank	(E)	1,600	Balance b/d		1,700
Realisation (Discounts)	(F)	100			
		1,700			1,700

Bank

		£			£
Balance b/d		1,400	Creditors	(E)	1,600
Realisation: Assets sold			Realisation: Costs	(G)	1,000
Goodwill	(C)	3,000	P: Capital	(K)	6,000
Machinery	(C)	1,800	Q: Capital	(K)	4,500
Stock	(C)	1,900			
Debtors	(C)	2,700			
R: Capital	(J)	2,300			
		13,100			13,100

P: Capital

		£			£
Realisation: Motor car	(D)	800	Balance b/d		6,000
Bank	(K)	6,000	Current account transferred	(I)	200
			Realisation: Share of profit	(H)	600
		6,800			6,800

Provision for Bad Debts

		£			£
Debtors	(A)	200	Balance b/d		200

P: Current Account

		£			£
P: Capital	(I)	200	Balance b/d		200

Q: Current Account

		£			£
Q: Capital	(I)	100	Balance b/d		100

Q: Capital

		£			£
Realisation: Motor car	(D)	1,000	Balance b/d		5,000
Bank	(K)	4,500	Current account transferred	(I)	100
			Realisation: Share of profit	(H)	400
		5,500			5,500

R: Capital

		£			£
Realisation: Motor car	(D)	500	Balance b/d		3,000
Realisation: Premises	(D)	5,500	Current account transferred	(I)	500
			Realisation: Share of profit	(H)	200
			Bank	(J)	2,300
		6,000			6,000

R: Current Account

		£		£
R: Capital	(I)	<u>500</u>	Balance b/d	<u>500</u>

Description of transactions:

(A) The provision accounts are transferred to the relevant asset accounts so that the net balance on the asset accounts may be transferred to the realisation account. Debit provision accounts. Credit asset accounts.

(B) The net book values of the assets are transferred to the realisation account. Debit realisation account. Credit asset accounts.

(C) Assets sold. Debit bank account. Credit realisation account.

(D) Assets taken over by partners. Debit partners' capital accounts. Credit realisation account.

(E) Liabilities discharged. Credit bank account. Debit liability accounts.

(F) Discounts on creditors. Debit creditors' account. Credit realisation account.

(G) Costs of dissolution. Credit bank account. Debit realisation account.

(H) Profit or loss split in profit/loss-sharing ratio. Profit – debit realisation account. Credit partners' capital accounts. The opposite if a loss.

(I) Transfer the balances on the partners' current accounts to their capital accounts.

(J) Any partner with a capital account in deficit, i.e. debits exceeding credits, must now pay in the amount needed to cancel his or her indebtedness to the partnership firm. Debit bank account. Credit capital account.

(K) The credit balances on the partners' capital accounts can now be paid to them. Credit bank account. Debit partners' capital accounts.

The payments made under (K) should complete the payment of all the balances in the partnership books.

3.14 The rule in *Garner* v. *Murray*

It sometimes happens that a partner's capital account finishes up with a debit balance. Normally the partner will pay in an amount to clear his indebtedness to the firm. However, sometimes he will be unable to pay all, or part, of such a balance. In the case of *Garner* v. *Murray* in 1904 (a case in England) the court ruled that, subject to any agreement to the contrary, such a deficiency was to be shared by the other partners *not* in their profit- and loss-sharing ratios but in the ratio of their 'last agreed capitals'. By 'their last agreed capitals' is meant the credit balances on their capital accounts in the normal balance sheet drawn up at the end of their last accounting period.

It must be borne in mind that the balances on their capital accounts after the assets have been realised may be far different from those on the last balance sheet. Where a partnership deed is drawn up it is commonly found that agreement is made to use normal profit- and loss-sharing ratios instead, thus rendering the *Garner* v. *Murray* rule inoperative. **The *Garner* v. *Murray* rule does not apply to partnerships in Scotland.**

Before reading further you should check whether or not this topic is in the requirements for your examinations.

EXHIBIT 3.8

After completing the realisation of all the assets, in respect of which a loss of £4,200 was incurred, but before making the final payments to the partners, the balance sheet appears:

Balance Sheet

		£	£
Cash at bank			6,400
			6,400
Capitals: R		5,800	
S		1,400	
T		400	
		7,600	
Less Q (debit balance)		(1,200)	6,400
			6,400

According to the last balance sheet drawn up before the dissolution, the partners' capital account credit balances were: Q £600; R £7,000; S £2,000; T £1,000; while the profits and losses were shared Q 3 : R 2 : S 1 : T 1.

Q is unable to meet any part of his deficiency. Each of the other partners therefore suffers the deficiency as follows:

$$\frac{\text{Own capital per balance sheet before dissolution}}{\text{Total of all solvent partners' capitals per same balance sheet}} \times \text{Deficiency}$$

This can now be calculated.

$$R \quad \frac{£7,000}{£7,000 + £2,000 + £1,000} \times £1,200 = £840$$

$$S \quad \frac{£2,000}{£7,000 + £2,000 + £1,000} \times £1,200 = £240$$

$$T \quad \frac{£1,000}{£7,000 + £2,000 + £1,000} \times £1,200 = £120$$

$$\underline{£1,200}$$

When these amounts have been charged to the capital accounts, then the balances remaining on them will equal the amount of the bank balance. Payments may therefore be made to clear their capital accounts.

	Credit balance b/d £		Share of deficiency now debited £		Final credit balances £
R	5,800	–	840	=	4,960
S	1,400	–	240	=	1,160
T	400	–	120	=	280
Equals the bank balance					6,400

3.15 Piecemeal realisation of assets

Frequently the assets may take a long time to realise. The partners will naturally want payments made to them on account as cash is received. They will not want to wait for payments until the dissolution is completed just for the convenience of the accountant. There is, however, a danger that if too much is paid to a partner, and he is unable to repay it, then the person handling the dissolution could be placed in a very awkward position.

To counteract this, the concept of prudence is brought into play. This is done by:

(*a*) Treating each receipt of sale money as being the final receipt, even though more could be received.

(*b*) Any loss then calculated so far to be shared between partners in profit- and loss-sharing ratios.

(*c*) Should any partner's capital account after each receipt show a debit balance, then that partner is assumed to be unable to pay in the deficiency. This deficit will be shared (failing any other agreement) between the partners using the *Garner* v. *Murray* rule.

(*d*) After payments of liabilities and the costs of dissolution the remainder of the cash is then paid to the partners.

(*e*) In this manner, even if no further money were received, or should a partner become insolvent, the division of the available cash would be strictly in accordance with the legal requirements. Exhibit 3.9 shows such a series of calculations.

EXHIBIT 3.9

The following is the summarised balance sheet of H, I, J and K as at 31 December 20X8. The partners had shared profits in the ratios H 6 : I 4 : J 1 : K 1.

Balance Sheet as at 31 December 20X8

	£
Assets	8,400
	8,400
Capitals:	
H	600
I	3,000
J	2,000
K	1,000
Creditors	1,800
	8,400

On 1 March 20X9 some of the assets were sold for cash £5,000. Out of this the creditors' £1,800 and the cost of dissolution £200 are paid, leaving £3,000 distributable to the partners.

On 1 July 20X9 some more assets are sold for £2,100. As all of the liabilities and the costs of dissolution have already been paid, then the whole of the £2,100 is available for distribution between the partners.

On 1 October 20X9 the final sale of the assets realised £1,200.

First distribution: 1 March 20X9	H	I	J	K
	£	£	£	£
Capital balances before dissolution	600	3,000	2,000	1,000
Loss if no further assets realised:				
Assets £8,400 – Sales £5,000				
= £3,400 + Costs £200 = £3,600 loss				
Loss shared in profit/loss ratios	(1,800)	(1,200)	(300)	(300)
	1,200 Dr	1,800 Cr	1,700 Cr	700 Cr
H's deficiency shared in				
Garner v. *Murray* ratios		³/₆ (600)	²/₆ (400)	¹/₆ (200)
Cash paid to partners (£3,000)		1,200	1,300	500

Second distribution: 1 July 20X9	H £	I £	J £	K £
Capital balances before dissolution	600	3,000	2,000	1,000
Loss if no further assets realised:				
Assets £8,400 – Sales (£5,000 + £2,100)				
= £1,300 + Costs £200 = £1,500 loss				
Loss shared in profit/loss ratios	(750)	(500)	(125)	(125)
	150 Dr	2,500 Cr	1,875 Cr	875 Cr
H's deficiency shared in *Garner* v. *Murray* ratios		(75)	(50)	(25)
		2,425	1,825	850
Less First distribution already paid		(1,200)	(1,300)	(500)
Cash now paid to partners (£2,100)		1,225	525	350

Third and final distribution: 1 October 20X9	H £	I £	J £	K £
Capital balances before dissolution	600	3,000	2,000	1,000
Loss finally ascertained:				
Assets £8,400 – Sales (£5,000 + £2,100				
+ £1,200) = £100 + Costs £200 = £300 loss				
Loss shared in profit/loss ratios	(150)	(100)	(25)	(25)
	450 Cr	2,900 Cr	1,975 Cr	975 Cr
(No deficiency now exists on any capital account)				
Less First and second distributions	(–)	(2,425)	(1,825)	(850)
Cash now paid to partners (£1,200)	450	475	150	125

In any subsequent distribution following that in which all the partners have shared, i.e. no partner could then have had a deficiency left on his capital account, all receipts of cash are divided between the partners in their profit- and loss-sharing ratios. Following the above method would give the same answer for these subsequent distributions but obviously an immediate division in the profit- and loss-sharing ratios would be quicker. The reader is invited to try it to satisfy him/herself that it would work out at the same answer.

Learning outcomes

You should now have learnt:

1 That there is no limited liability in partnerships except for 'limited partners'.

2 That the contents of a partnership agreement can override anything written in this chapter. Partners can agree to anything they want to, in as much or as little detail as they wish.

3 If there is no partnership agreement, then the provisions of the Partnership Act (details shown in Section 3.4) will apply.

4 Partners can agree to show their capital accounts using either the fixed capital or fluctuating capital methods.

5 If more than 20 owners of an organisation are needed, then a partnership would not be suitable; instead, a limited company would be preferable.

6 That the true value of goodwill can be established only when the business is sold, but for various reasons of fairness between partners it is valued the best way possible when there is no imminent sale of a business.

7 If the old partners agree, a new partner can be admitted without paying anything in as capital.

8 Goodwill is usually owned by the partners in the ratio in which they share profits.

9 If there is a change in partnership without adjustments for goodwill, then some partners will make an unfair gain while others will quite unfairly lose money.

10 If a new partner pays a specific amount for his or her share of the goodwill, then that payment is said to be a 'premium'.

11 That when a new partner joins a firm, or a partner retires or dies, the partnership assets should be revalued.

12 Revaluation of assets should also occur when there is a change in the profit- and loss-sharing ratios of partners.

13 Profits on revaluation of assets are credited to the old partners' capital accounts in the old profit- and loss-sharing ratios.

14 Losses on revaluation of assets are debited to the old partners' capital accounts in the old profit- and loss-sharing ratios.

15 The asset accounts also show the revalued amounts. Losses will have been credited to them and profits debited.

16 Upon dissolution, a partnership firm stops trading or operating, any profit or loss on dissolution being shared by the partners in their profit-sharing ratio.

17 That the *Garner* v. *Murray* rule does not apply to partnerships in Scotland.

REVIEW QUESTIONS

3.1 Stephens, Owen and Jones are partners. They share profits and losses in the ratios of $^2/_5$, $^2/_5$ and $^1/_5$ respectively.

For the year ended 31 December 20X6, their capital accounts remained fixed at the following amounts:

	£
Stephens	6,000
Owen	4,000
Jones	2,000

They have agreed to give each other 10 per cent interest per annum on their capital accounts.

In addition to the above, partnership salaries of £3,000 for Owen and £1,000 for Jones are to be charged.

The net profit of the partnership, before taking any of the above into account, was £25,200.

You are required to draw up the appropriation account of the partnership for the year ended 31 December 20X6.

3.2   Read the following and answer the questions below.

Roach and Salmon own a grocery shop. Their first financial year ended on 31 December 20X9.

The following balances were taken from the books on that date:

Capital:	Roach – £60,000;	Salmon – £48,000.
Partnership salaries:	Roach – £9,000;	Salmon – £6,000.
Drawings:	Roach – £12,860;	Salmon – £13,400.

The firm's net profit for the year was £32,840.
Interest on capital is to be allowed at 10% per year.
Profits and losses are to be shared equally.

(*a*) From the information above prepare the firm's appropriation account and the partners' current accounts.

(*b*) If there is no partnership agreement, to which Act of Parliament do the partners then refer?

(*OCR (MEG): GCE A-level*)

3.3   Draw up a profit and loss appropriation account for the year ended 31 December 20X7 and balance sheet extracts at that date, from the following:

(*i*)   Net profits £30,350.
(*ii*)   Interest to be charged on capitals: Williams £2,000; Powell £1,500; Howe £900.
(*iii*)   Interest to be charged on drawings: Williams £240; Powell £180; Howe £130.
(*iv*)   Salaries to be credited: Powell £2,000; Howe £3,500.
(*v*)   Profits to be shared: Williams 50%; Powell 30%; Howe 20%.
(*vi*)   Current accounts: balances b/fwd Williams £1,860; Powell £946; Howe £717.
(*vii*)   Capital accounts: balances b/fwd Williams £40,000; Powell £30,000; Howe £18,000.
(*viii*) Drawings: Williams £9,200; Powell £7,100; Howe £6,900.

3.4X   Penrose and Wilcox are in partnership, sharing profits and losses in the ratio 3 : 2. The following information was taken from their books for the year ended 31 December 20X9, before the completion of their profit and loss appropriation account.

		£	
Current accounts (1 January 20X9)			
	Penrose	640	(*Dr*)
	Wilcox	330	(*Cr*)
Drawings	Penrose	3,000	
	Wilcox	2,000	
Net trading profit		6,810	
Interest on capital	Penrose	540	
	Wilcox	720	
Salary	Penrose	2,000	
Interest on drawings	Penrose	270	
	Wilcox	180	

(*a*) Prepare, for the year ended 31 December 20X9:
    (*i*) the profit and loss appropriation account of Penrose and Wilcox;
    (*ii*) the current accounts in the ledger for Penrose and Wilcox.
(*b*) Why in many partnerships are current accounts prepared as well as capital accounts?
(*c*) At 1 January 20X9 Penrose had a debit balance in his current account. What does this mean?

(d) In partnership accounts what is the purpose of preparing:
    (i) a profit and loss account?
    (ii) a profit and loss appropriation account?
(e) In partnership accounts why is:
    (i) interest allowed on capital?
    (ii) interest charged on drawings?

(*AQA (NEAB): GCE A-level*)

3.5   Bee, Cee and Dee have been holding preliminary discussions with a view to forming a partnership to buy and sell antiques.

The position has now been reached where the prospective partners have agreed the basic arrangements under which the partnership will operate.

Bee will contribute £40,000 as capital, and up to £10,000 as a long-term loan to the partnership, if needed. He has extensive other business interests and will not therefore be taking an active part in the running of the business.

Cee is unable to bring in more than £2,000 as capital initially, but, because he has an expert knowledge of the antique trade, will act as the manager of the business on a full-time basis.

Dee is willing to contribute £10,000 as capital. He will also assist in running the business as the need arises. In particular, he is prepared to attend auctions anywhere within the United Kingdom in order to acquire trading stock which he will transport back to the firm's premises in his van. On occasions he may also help Cee to restore the articles prior to sale to the public.

At the meeting, the three prospective partners intend to decide upon the financial arrangements for sharing out the profits (or losses) made by the firm, and have approached you for advice.

You are required to prepare a set of explanatory notes, under suitable headings, of the considerations which the prospective partners should take into account in arriving at their decisions at the next meeting.

(*Association of Chartered Certified Accountants*)

3.6   Mendez and Marshall are in partnership sharing profits and losses equally. The following is their trial balance as at 30 June 20X9.

	Dr £	Cr £
Buildings (cost £75,000)	50,000	
Fixtures at cost	11,000	
Provision for depreciation: Fixtures		3,300
Debtors	16,243	
Creditors		11,150
Cash at bank	677	
Stock at 30 June 20X8	41,979	
Sales		123,650
Purchases	85,416	
Carriage outwards	1,288	
Discounts allowed	115	
Loan interest: King	4,000	
Office expenses	2,416	
Salaries and wages	18,917	
Bad debts	503	
Provision for doubtful debts		400

	Dr £	Cr £
Loan from J King		40,000
Capitals: Mendez		35,000
Marshall		29,500
Current accounts: Mendez		1,306
Marshall		298
Drawings: Mendez	6,400	
Marshall	5,650	
	244,604	244,604

Required:

Prepare a trading and profit and loss appropriation account for the year ended 30 June 20X9, and a balance sheet as at that date.

(*a*) Stock, 30 June 20X9, £56,340.
(*b*) Expenses to be accrued: Office Expenses £96; Wages £200.
(*c*) Depreciate fixtures 10 per cent on reducing balance basis, buildings £1,000.
(*d*) Reduce provision for doubtful debts to £320.
(*e*) Partnership salary: £800 to Mendez. Not yet entered.
(*f*) Interest on drawings: Mendez £180; Marshall £120.
(*g*) Interest on capital account balances at 10 per cent.

3.7X Oscar and Felix are in partnership. They share profits in the ratio: Oscar 60 per cent; Felix 40 per cent. The following trial balance was extracted as at 31 March 20X9.

	Dr £	Cr £
Office equipment at cost	6,500	
Motor vehicles at cost	9,200	
Provision for depreciation at 31.3.20X8:		
Motor vehicles		3,680
Office equipment		1,950
Stock at 31 March 20X8	24,970	
Debtors and creditors	20,960	16,275
Cash at bank	615	
Cash in hand	140	
Sales		90,370
Purchases	71,630	
Salaries	8,417	
Office expenses	1,370	
Discounts allowed	563	
Current accounts at 31.3.20X8		
Oscar		1,379
Felix		1,211
Capital accounts: Oscar		27,000
Felix		12,000
Drawings: Oscar	5,500	
Felix	4,000	
	153,865	153,865

Required:

Draw up a set of final accounts for the year ended 31 March 20X9 for the partnership. The following notes are applicable at 31 March 20X9.

(*a*) Stock 31 March 20X9 £27,340.
(*b*) Office expenses owing £110.
(*c*) Provide for depreciation: motor 20 per cent of cost, office equipment 10 per cent of cost.
(*d*) Charge interest on capitals at 10 per cent.
(*e*) Charge interest on drawings: Oscar £180; Felix £210.

3.8   The following list of balances as at 30 September 20X9 has been extracted from the books of Brick and Stone, trading in partnership, sharing the balance of profits and losses in the proportions 3 : 2 respectively.

	£
Printing, stationery and postage	3,500
Sales	322,100
Stock in hand at 1 October 20X8	23,000
Purchases	208,200
Rent and rates	10,300
Heat and light	8,700
Staff salaries	36,100
Telephone charges	2,900
Motor vehicle running costs	5,620
Discounts allowable	950
Discounts receivable	370
Sales returns	2,100
Purchases returns	6,100
Carriage inwards	1,700
Carriage outwards	2,400
Fixtures and fittings: at cost	26,000
provision for depreciation	11,200
Motor vehicles: at cost	46,000
provision for depreciation	25,000
Provision for doubtful debts	300
Drawings: Brick	24,000
Stone	11,000
Current account balances at 1 October 20X8:	
Brick	3,600 credit
Stone	2,400 credit
Capital account balances at 1 October 20X8:	
Brick	33,000
Stone	17,000
Debtors	9,300
Creditors	8,400
Balance at bank	7,700

Additional information:

1 £10,000 is to be transferred from Brick's capital account to a newly opened Brick Loan Account on 1 July 20X9.
   Interest at 10 per cent per annum on the loan is to be credited to Brick.
2 Stone is to be credited with a salary at the rate of £12,000 per annum from 1 April 20X9.
3 Stock in hand at 30 September 20X9 has been valued at cost at £32,000.
4 Telephone charges accrued due at 30 September 20X9 amounted to £400 and rent of £600 prepaid at that date.
5 During the year ended 30 September 20X9 Stone has taken goods costing £1,000 for his own use.

6 Depreciation is to be provided at the following annual rates on the straight line basis:

Fixtures and fittings   10%
Motor vehicles   20%

Required:

(*a*) Prepare a trading and profit and loss account for the year ended 30 September 20X9.
(*b*) Prepare a balance sheet as at 30 September 20X9 which should include summaries of the partners' capital and current accounts for the year ended on that date.

Note: In both (*a*) and (*b*) vertical forms of presentation should be used.

(*Association of Accounting Technicians*)

3.9X   Menzies, Whitlam and Gough share profits and losses in the ratios 5 : 3 : 2 respectively. Their trial balance as at 30 September 20X9 was as follows:

	Dr £	Cr £
Sales		210,500
Returns inwards	6,800	
Purchases	137,190	
Carriage inwards	1,500	
Stock 30 September 20X8	42,850	
Discounts allowed	110	
Salaries and wages	18,296	
Bad debts	1,234	
Provision for doubtful debts 30.9.20X8		800
General expenses	945	
Rent and rates	2,565	
Postages	2,450	
Motor expenses	3,940	
Motor vans at cost	12,500	
Office equipment at cost	8,400	
Provisions for depreciation at 30.9.20X8:		
Motor vans		4,200
Office equipment		2,700
Creditors		24,356
Debtors	37,178	
Cash at bank	666	
Drawings: Menzies	12,610	
Whitlam	8,417	
Gough	6,216	
Current accounts: Menzies		1,390
Whitlam	153	
Gough		2,074
Capital accounts: Menzies		30,000
Whitlam		16,000
Gough		12,000
	304,020	304,020

Draw up a set of final accounts for the year ended 30 September 20X9. The following notes are relevant at 30 September 20X9:

(*i*)   Stock 30 September 20X9, £51,060.
(*ii*) Rates in advance £120; Stock of postage stamps £190.
(*iii*) Increase provision for doubtful debts to £870.
(*iv*) Salaries: Whitlam £1,200; Gough £700. Not yet recorded.
(*v*)   Interest on Drawings: Menzies £170; Whitlam £110; Gough £120.
(*vi*) Interest on Capitals at 10 per cent.
(*vii*) Depreciate Motor vans £2,500, Office equipment £1,680.

3.10 The partners have always shared their profits in the ratios of X 4 : Y 3 : Z 1. They are to alter their profit ratios to X 3 : Y 5 : Z 2. The last balance sheet before the change was:

Balance Sheet as at 31 December 20X7

	£
Net Assets (not including goodwill)	14,000
	14,000
Capitals:	
X	6,000
Y	4,800
Z	3,200
	14,000

The partners agree to bring in goodwill, being valued at £12,000 on the change.

Show the balance sheets on 1 January 20X8 after goodwill has been taken into account if:

(*a*) Goodwill account was opened.
(*b*) Goodwill account was not opened.

3.11X The partners are to change their profit ratios as shown:

	Old ratio	*New ratio*
A	2	3
B	3	4
C	4	3
D	1	2

They decide to bring in a goodwill amount of £18,000 on the change. The last balance sheet before any element of goodwill has been introduced was:

Balance Sheet as at 30 June 20X8

	£
Net assets (not including goodwill)	18,800
	18,800
Capitals:	
A	7,000
B	3,200
C	5,000
D	3,600
	18,800

Show the balance sheets on 1 July 20X8 after necessary adjustments have been made if:

(*a*) Goodwill account was opened.
(*b*) Goodwill account was not opened.

3.12 X and Y are in partnership, sharing profits and losses equally. They decide to admit Z. By agreement, goodwill valued at £6,000 is to be introduced into the business books. Z is required to provide capital equal to that of Y after he has been credited with his share of goodwill. The new profit-sharing ratio is to be 4 : 3 : 3 respectively for X, Y and Z.

The balance sheet before admission of Z showed:

	£
Fixed and current assets	15,000
Cash	2,000
	17,000
Capital X	8,000
Capital Y	4,000
Current liabilities	5,000
	17,000

Show:

(a) Journal entries for admission of Z.

(b) Opening balance sheet of new business.

(c) Journal entries for writing off the goodwill which the new partners decided to do soon after the start of the new business.

3.13X L, M and S are in partnership. They shared profits in the ratio 2 : 5 : 3. It is decided to admit R. It is agreed that goodwill was worth £10,000, but that this is not to be brought into the business records. R will bring £4,000 cash into the business for capital. The new profit-sharing ratio is to be L 3 : M 4 : S 2 : R 1.

The balance sheet before R was introduced was as follows:

	£
Assets (other than in cash)	11,000
Cash	2,500
	13,500
Capitals: L	3,000
M	5,000
S	4,000
Creditors	1,500
	13,500

Show:

(a) The entries in the capital accounts of L, M, S and R, the accounts to be in columnar form.

(b) The balance sheet after R has been introduced.

3.14 T, U and V are in partnership. They shared profits in the ratio 4 : 5 : 1. It is decided to admit W. It is agreed that goodwill was worth £30,000 and that it was to be brought into the business records. W will bring £20,000 cash into the business for capital. The new profit-sharing ratio is to be T 6 : U 7 : V 2 : W 5.

The balance sheet before W was introduced was as follows:

	£
Assets (other than in cash)	40,000
Cash	6,000
	46,000
Capitals: T	14,000
U	18,000
V	5,000
Liabilities	9,000
	46,000

Show:

(a) The entries in the capital accounts of T, U, V, and W, the accounts to be in columnar form.

(b) The balance sheet after W has been introduced.

3.15 A new partner has joined the business during the year and has paid in £10,000 for 'goodwill'. This £10,000 has been credited by the bookkeeper to the account of the new partner. The senior partner had objected to this, but the bookkeeper had replied: 'Why not credit the £10,000 to the account of the new partner? It is his money after all.'

Required:

Give your advice as to the proper treatment of this £10,000. Explain your reasons fully.

(Association of Chartered Certified Accountants)

3.16 Owing to staff illnesses, the draft final accounts for the year ended 31 March 20X9 of Messrs Stone, Pebble and Brick, trading in partnership as the Bigtime Building Supply Company, have been prepared by an inexperienced, but keen, clerk. The draft summarised balance sheet as at 31 March 20X9 is as follows:

	£	£
Tangible fixed assets: At cost *less* depreciation to date		45,400
Current assets	32,290	
Less: Trade creditors	6,390	25,900
		£71,300

Represented by:	Stone	Pebble	Brick	Total
	£	£	£	£
Capital accounts: at 1 April 20X8	26,000	18,000	16,000	60,000
Current accounts:				
Share of net profit for the year ended				
31 March 20X9	12,100	12,100	12,100	
Drawings year ended 31 March 20X9	(8,200)	(9,600)	(7,200)	
At 31 March 20X9	3,900	2,500	4,900	11,300
				£71,300

The partnership commenced on 1 April 20X8 when each of the partners introduced, as their partnership capital, the net tangible fixed and current assets of their previously separate businesses. However, it has now been discovered that, contrary to what was agreed, no adjustments were made in the partnership books for the goodwill of the partners' former businesses now incorporated in the partnership. The agreed valuations of goodwill at 1 April 20X8 are as follows:

	£
Stone's business	30,000
Pebble's business	20,000
Brick's business	16,000

It is agreed that a goodwill account should not be opened in the partnership's books.

It has now been discovered that effect has not been given in the accounts to the following provisions in the partnership agreement effective from 1 January 20X9:

1 Stone's capital to be reduced to £20,000, the balance being transferred to a loan account upon which interest at the rate of 11% per annum will be paid on 31 December each year.
2 Partners to be credited with interest on their capital account balances at the rate of 5% per annum.
3 Brick to be credited with a partner's salary at the rate of £8,500 per annum.
4 The balance of the net profit or loss to be shared between Stone, Pebble and Brick in the ratio 5 : 3 : 2 respectively.

Notes:
1 It can be assumed that the net profit indicated in the draft accounts accrued uniformly throughout the year.
2 It has been agreed between the partners that no adjustments should be made for any partnership goodwill as at 1 January 20X9.

Required:

(*a*) Prepare the profit and loss appropriation account for the year ended 31 March 20X9.
(*b*) Prepare a corrected statement of the partners' capital and current accounts for inclusion in the partnership balance sheet as at 31 March 20X9.

(*Association of Accounting Technicians*)

3.17

Hughes, Allen and Elliott
Balance Sheet as at 31 December 20X8

	£
Buildings at cost	8,000
Motor vehicles (at cost *less* depreciation)	3,550
Office fittings (at cost *less* depreciation)	1,310
Stock	2,040
Debtors	4,530
Bank	1,390
	20,820

Capitals:	£
Hughes	9,560
Allen	6,420
Elliott	4,840
	20,820

The above partners have always shared profits and losses in the ratio: Hughes 5, Allen 3, Elliott 2.

From 1 January the assets were to be revalued as the profit-sharing ratios are to be altered soon. The following assets are to be revalued to the figures shown: Buildings £17,500, Motor vehicles £2,600, Stock £1,890, Office fittings £1,090.

Required:

(a) You are required to show all the ledger accounts necessary to record the revaluation.

(b) Draw up a balance sheet as at 1 January 20X9.

3.18X Avon and Brown have been in partnership for many years sharing profits and losses in the ratio 3 : 2 respectively. The following was their balance sheet as at 31 December 20X6.

	£
Goodwill	2,000
Plant and machinery	1,800
Stock	1,960
Debtors	2,130
Cash at bank	90
	£7,980
Capital: Avon	4,000
Brown	3,000
	7,000
Sundry creditors	980
	£7,980

On 1 January 20X7, they decided to admit Charles as a partner on the condition that he contributed £2,000 as his capital but that the plant and machinery and stock should be revalued at £2,000 and £1,900 respectively, the other assets, excepting goodwill, remaining at their present book values. The goodwill was agreed to be valueless.

You are required to show:

(a) The ledger entries dealing with the above in the following accounts:
  (i) Goodwill account,
  (ii) Revaluation accounts,
  (iii) Capital accounts.
(b) The balance sheet of the partnership immediately after the admission of Charles.

3.19 Alan, Bob and Charles are in partnership sharing profits and losses in the ratio 3 : 2 : 1 respectively. The balance sheet for the partnership as at 30 June 20X6 is as follows:

	£	£
Fixed assets		
Premises		90,000
Plant		37,000
Vehicles		15,000
Fixtures		2,000
		144,000
Current assets		
Stock	62,379	
Debtors	34,980	
Cash	760	98,119
		£242,119
Capital		
Alan		85,000
Bob		65,000
Charles		35,000
		185,000

Current account	£	£
Alan	3,714	
Bob	(2,509)	
Charles	4,678	5,883
Loan – Charles		28,000
Current liabilities		
Creditors		19,036
Bank overdraft		4,200
		£242,119

Charles decides to retire from the business on 30 June 20X6, and Don is admitted as a partner on that date. The following matters are agreed:

(*a*) Certain assets were revalued:
- Premises £120,000
- Plant £35,000
- Stock £54,179

(*b*) Provision is to be made for doubtful debts in the sum of £3,000.

(*c*) Goodwill is to be recorded in the books on the day Charles retires in the sum of £42,000. The partners in the new firm do not wish to maintain a goodwill account so that amount is to be written back against the new partners' capital accounts.

(*d*) Alan and Bob are to share profits in the same ratio as before, and Don is to have the same share of profits as Bob.

(*e*) Charles is to take his car at its book value of £3,900 in part payment, and the balance of all he is owed by the firm in cash except £20,000 which he is willing to leave as a loan account.

(*f*) The partners in the new firm are to start on an equal footing so far as capital and current accounts are concerned. Don is to contribute cash to bring his capital and current accounts to the same amount as the original partner from the old firm who has the lower investment in the business.

The original partner in the old firm who has the higher investment will draw out cash so that his capital and current account balances equal those of his new partners.

Required:

(*a*) Account for the above transactions, including goodwill and retiring partners' accounts.

(*b*) Draft a balance sheet for the partnership of Alan, Bob and Don as at 30 June 20X6.

(*Association of Accounting Technicians*)

3.20 S, W and M are partners. They share profits and losses in the ratios of $^2/_5$, $^2/_5$ and $^1/_5$ respectively.

For the year ended 31 December 20X9 their capital accounts remained fixed at the following amounts:

	£
S	6,000
W	4,000
M	2,000

They have agreed to give each other 10 per cent interest per annum on their capital accounts.

In addition to the above, partnership salaries of £3,000 for W and £1,000 for M are to be charged.

The net profit of the partnership before taking any of the above into account was £25,200.

You are required to draw up the appropriation account of the partnership for the year ended 31 December 20X9.

3.21X Draw up a profit and loss appropriation account for Winn, Pool and Howe for the year ended 31 December 20X7, and balance sheet extracts at that date, from the following:

(*i*) Net profits £30,350.
(*ii*) Interest to be charged on capitals: Winn £2,000; Pool £1,500; Howe £900.
(*iii*) Interest to be charged on drawings: Winn £240; Pool £180; Howe £130.
(*iv*) Salaries to be credited: Pool £2,000; Howe £3,500.
(*v*) Profits to be shared: Winn 50%; Pool 30%; Howe 20%.
(*vi*) Current accounts: Winn £1,860; Pool £946; Howe £717.
(*vii*) Capital accounts: Winn £40,000; Pool £30,000; Howe £18,000.
(*viii*) Drawings: Winn £9,200; Pool £7,100; Howe £6,900.

3.22 Moore and Stephens, who share profits and losses equally, decide to dissolve their partnership as at 31 March 20X9. Their balance sheet on that date was as follows:

	£		£
Buildings	800	Capital account: Moore	2,000
Tools and fixtures	850	Stephens	1,500
Debtors	2,800		3,500
Cash	1,800	Sundry creditors	2,750
	6,250		6,250

The debtors realised £2,700, the buildings £400 and the tools and fixtures £950. The expenses of dissolution were £100 and discounts totalling £200 were received from creditors.

Required:

Prepare the accounts necessary to show the results of the realisation and of the disposal of the cash.

3.23 X, Y and Z have been in partnership for several years, sharing profits and losses in the ratio 3 : 2 : 1. Their last balance sheet which was prepared on 31 October 20X9 is as follows:

Balance Sheet of X, Y and Z
as at 31 October 20X9

		£		£	£
Fixed assets			Capital X		4,000
At cost	20,000		Y		4,000
Less Depreciation	6,000		Z		2,000
		14,000			10,000
Current assets			*Current liabilities*		
Stock	5,000		Bank	13,000	
Debtors	21,000		Creditors	17,000	
		26,000			30,000
		£40,000			£40,000

Despite making good profits during recent years they had become increasingly dependent on one credit customer, Smithson, and in order to retain his custom they had gradually increased his credit limit until he owed the partnership £18,000. It has now been discovered that Smithson is insolvent and that he is unlikely to repay any of the money owed by him to the partnership. Reluctantly X, Y and Z have agreed to dissolve the partnership on the following terms:

(*i*) The stock is to be sold to Nelson Ltd for £4,000.

(*ii*) The fixed assets will be sold for £8,000 except for certain items with a book value of £5,000 which will be taken over by X at an agreed valuation of £7,000.

(*iii*) The debtors, except for Smithson, are expected to pay their accounts in full.

(*iv*) The costs of dissolution will be £800 and discounts received from creditors will be £500. Z is unable to meet his liability to the partnership out of his personal funds.

Required:

(*a*) the realisation account;

(*b*) the capital accounts to the partners recording the dissolution of the partnership.

(*AQA (AEB): GCE A-level*)

3.24X   The following trial balance has been extracted from the books of Gain and Main as at 31 March 20X8; Gain and Main are in partnership sharing profits and losses in the ratio 3 to 2:

	£	£
Capital accounts:		
Gain		10,000
Main		5,000
Cash at bank	1,550	
Creditors		500
Current accounts:		
Gain		1,000
Main	2,000	
Debtors	2,000	
Depreciation: Fixtures and fittings		1,000
Motor vehicles		1,300
Fixtures and fittings	2,000	
Land and buildings	30,000	
Motor vehicles	4,500	
Net profit (for the year to 31 March 20X8)		26,250
Stock, at cost	3,000	
	£45,050	£45,050

In appropriating the net profit for the year, it has been agreed that Main should be entitled to a salary of £9,750. Each partner is also entitled to interest on his opening capital account balance at the rate of 10 per cent per annum.

Gain and Main have decided to convert the parnership into a limited company, Plain Limited, as from 1 April 20X8. The company is to take over all the assets and liabilities of the partnership, except that Gain is to retain for his personal use one of the motor vehicles at an agreed transfer price of £1,000.

The purchase consideration will consist of 40,000 ordinary shares of £1 each in Plain Limited, to be divided between the partners in profit-sharing ratio. Any balance on the partners' current accounts is to be settled in cash.

You are required to:

Prepare the main ledger accounts of the partnership in order to close off the books as at 31 March 20X8.

(*Association of Accounting Technicians*)

3.25X   A, B & C are partners sharing profits and losses in the ratio 2 : 2 : 1. The balance sheet of the partnership as at 30 September 20X7 was as follows:

	£			£	£
Freehold premises	18,000	Capital accounts			
Equipment and machinery	12,000	A		22,000	
Motor cars	3,000	B		18,000	
Inventory*	11,000	C		10,000	
Debtors	14,000				50,000
Bank	9,000	Loan account – A			7,000
		Creditors			10,000
	£67,000				£67,000

Author's note: Inventory is another word for stock.

The partners agreed to dispose of the business to CNO Limited with effect from 1 October 20X7 under the following conditions and terms:

(*i*) CNO Limited will acquire the goodwill, all fixed assets and the inventory for the purchase consideration of £58,000. This consideration will include a payment of £10,000 in cash and the issue of 12,000 10 per cent preference shares of £1 each at par, and the balance by the issue of £1 ordinary shares at £1.25 per share.

(*ii*) The partnership business will settle amounts owing to creditors.

(*iii*) CNO Limited will collect the debts on behalf of the vendors.

Purchase consideration payments and allotments of shares were made on 1 October 20X7.

The partnership creditors were paid off by 31 October 20X7 after the taking of cash discounts of £190.

CNO Limited collected and paid over all partnership debts by 30 November 20X7 except for bad debts amounting to £800. Discounts allowed to debtors amounted to £400.

Required:

(*a*) Journal entries (including those relating to cash) necessary to close the books of the partnership, and

(*b*) Set out the basis on which the shares in CNO Limited are allotted to partners.
Ignore interest.

(*Institute of Chartered Secretaries and Administrators*)

3.26 Amis, Lodge and Pym were in partnership sharing profits and losses in the ratio 5 : 3 : 2. The following trial balance has been extracted from their books of account as at 31 March 20X8:

	£	£
Bank interest received		750
Capital accounts (as at 1 April 20X7):		
Amis		80,000
Lodge		15,000
Pym		5,000
Carriage inwards	4,000	
Carriage outwards	12,000	
Cash at bank	4,900	
Current accounts:		
Amis	1,000	
Lodge	500	
Pym	400	
Discounts allowed	10,000	
Discounts received		4,530

	£	£
Drawings:		
Amis	25,000	
Lodge	22,000	
Pym	15,000	
Motor vehicles:		
at cost	80,000	
accumulated depreciation (at 1 April 20X7)		20,000
Office expenses	30,400	
Plant and machinery:		
at cost	100,000	
accumulated depreciation (at 1 April 20X7)		36,600
Provision for bad and doubtful debts (at 1 April 20X7)		420
Purchases	225,000	
Rent, rates, heat and light	8,800	
Sales		404,500
Stock (at 1 April 20X7)	30,000	
Trade creditors		16,500
Trade debtors	14,300	
	£583,300	£583,300

Additional information:

(*a*) Stock at 31 March 20X8 was valued at £35,000.

(*b*) Depreciation on the fixed assets is to be charged as follows:
      Motor vehicles – 25 per cent on the reduced balance.
      Plant and machinery – 20 per cent on the original cost.
    There were no purchases or sales of fixed assets during the year to 31 March 20X8.

(*c*) The provision for bad and doubtful debts is to be maintained at a level equivalent to 5 per cent of the total trade debtors as at 31 March 20X8.

(*d*) An office expense of £405 was owing at 31 March 20X8, and some rent amounting to £1,500 had been paid in advance as at that date. These items had not been included in the list of balances shown in the trial balance.

(*e*) Interest on drawings and on the debit balance on each partner's current account is to be charged as follows:

	£
Amis	1,000
Lodge	900
Pym	720

(*f*) According to the partnership agreement, Pym is allowed a salary of £13,000 per annum. This amount was owing to Pym for the year to 31 March 20X8, and needs to be accounted for.

(*g*) The partnership agreement also allows each partner interest on his capital account at a rate of 10 per cent per annum. There were no movements on the respective partners' capital accounts during the year to 31 March 20X8, and the interest had not been credited to them as at that date.

Note: The information given above is sufficient to answer part (*a*)(*i*) and (*ii*) of the question, and notes (*b*) and (*i*) below are pertinent to requirements (*b*)(*i*), (*ii*) and (*iii*) of the question.

(*b*) On 1 April 20X8, Fowles Limited agreed to purchase the business on the following terms:
    (*i*) Amis to purchase one of the partnership's motor vehicles at an agreed value of £5,000, the remaining vehicles being taken over by the company at an agreed value of £30,000;

(ii) the company agreed to purchase the plant and machinery at a value of £35,000 and the stock at a value of £38,500;

(iii) the partners to settle the trade creditors: the total amount agreed with the creditors being £16,000;

(iv) the trade debtors were not to be taken over by the company, the partners receiving cheques on 1 April 20X8 amounting to £12,985 in total from the trade debtors in settlement of the outstanding debts;

(v) the partners paid the outstanding office expense on 1 April 20X8, and the landlord returned the rent paid in advance by cheque on the same day;

(vi) as consideration for the sale of the partnership, the partners were to be paid £63,500 in cash by Fowles Limited, and to receive 75,000 in £1 ordinary shares in the company, the shares to be apportioned equally amongst the partners.

(i) Assume that all the matters relating to the dissolution of the partnership and its sales to the company took place on 1 April 20X8.

Required:

(a) Prepare:

(i) Amis', Lodge's and Pym's trading, profit and loss and profit and loss appropriation account for the year to 31 March 20X8;

(ii) Amis', Lodge's and Pym's current accounts (in columnar format) for the year to 31 March 20X8 (the final balance on each account is to be then transferred to each partner's respective capital account);

and

(b) Compile the following accounts:

(i) the partnership realisation account for the period up to and including 1 April 20X8;

(ii) the partners' bank account for the period up to and including 1 April 20X8; and

(iii) the partners' capital accounts (in columnar format) for the period up to and including 1 April 20X8.

Note: Detailed workings should be submitted with your answer.

(Association of Accounting Technicians)

3.27X   Proudie, Slope and Thorne were in partnership sharing profits and losses in the ratio 3 : 1 : 1. The draft balance sheet of the partnership as at 31 May 20X9 is shown below:

	£000 Cost	£000 Depreciation	£000 Net book value
Fixed assets			
Land and buildings	200	40	160
Furniture	30	18	12
Motor vehicles	60	40	20
	£290	£98	192
Current assets			
Stocks		23	
Trade debtors	42		
Less Provision for doubtful debts	(1)		
		41	
Prepayments		2	
Cash		10	
		76	

	£000 Cost	£000 Depreciation	£000 Net book value
Less Current liabilities			
Trade creditors	15		
Accruals	3		
		(18)	
			58
			£250
Financed by:			
Capital accounts			
Proudie		100	
Slope		60	
Thorne		40	
			200
Current accounts			
Proudie		24	
Slope		10	
Thorne		8	
			42
			242
Loan			
Proudie			8
			£250

Additional information:

1 Proudie decided to retire on 31 May 20X9. However, Slope and Thorne agreed to form a new partnership out of the old one, as from 1 June 20X9. They agreed to share profits and losses in the same ratio as in the old partnership.

2 Upon the dissolution of the old partnership, it was agreed that the following adjustments were to be made to the partnership balance sheet as at 31 May 20X9.
   (*a*) Land and buildings were to be revalued at £200,000.
   (*b*) Furniture was to be revalued at £5,000.
   (*c*) Proudie agreed to take over one of the motor vehicles at a value of £4,000, the remaining motor vehicles being revalued at £10,000.
   (*d*) Stocks were to be written down by £5,000.
   (*e*) A bad debt of £2,000 was to be written off, and the provision for doubtful debts was then to be adjusted so that it represented 5 per cent of the then outstanding trade debtors as at 31 May 20X9.
   (*f*) A further accrual of £3,000 for office expenses was to be made.
   (*g*) Professional charges relating to the dissolution were estimated to be £1,000.

3 It has not been the practice of the partners to carry goodwill in the books of the partnership, but on the retirement of a partner it had been agreed that goodwill should be taken into account. Goodwill was to be valued at an amount equal to the average annual profits of the three years expiring on the retirement. For the purpose of including goodwill in the dissolution arrangement when Proudie retired, the net profits for the last three years were as follows:

	£000
Year to 31 May 20X7	130
Year to 31 May 20X8	150
Year to 31 May 20X9	181

The net profit for the year to 31 May 20X9 had been calculated before any of the items listed in 2 above were taken into account. The net profit was only to be adjusted for items listed in 2(*d*), 2(*e*) and 2(*f*) above.

4 Goodwill is not to be carried in the books of the new partnership.

5 It was agreed that Proudie's old loan of £8,000 should be repaid to him on 31 May 20X9, but any further amount owing to him as a result of the dissolution of the partnership should be left as a long-term loan in the books of the new partnership.

6 The partners' current accounts were to be closed and any balances on them as at 31 May 20X9 were to be transferred to their respective capital accounts.

Required:

(*a*) Prepare the revaluation account as at 31 May 20X9.
(*b*) Prepare the partners' capital accounts as at the date of dissolution of the partnership, and bring down any balances on them in the books of the new partnership.
(*c*) Prepare Slope and Thorne's balance sheet as at 1 June 20X9.

(*Association of Accounting Technicians*)

3.28 Lock, Stock and Barrel have been in partnership as builders and contractors for many years. Owing to adverse trading conditions it has been decided to dissolve the partnership. Profits are shared Lock 40 per cent, Stock 30 per cent, Barrel 30 per cent. The partnership deed also provides that in the event of a partner being unable to pay off a debit balance the remaining partners will treat this as a trading loss.

The latest partnership balance sheet was as follows:

	Cost	Depreciation	
	£	£	£
Fixed tangible assets			
Freehold yard and buildings	20,000	3,000	17,000
Plant and equipment	150,000	82,000	68,000
Motor vehicles	36,000	23,000	13,000
	206,000	108,000	98,000
Current assets			
Stock of land for building		75,000	
Houses in course of construction		115,000	
Stocks of materials		23,000	
Debtors for completed houses		62,000	
		275,000	
Current liabilities			
Trade creditors	77,000		
Deposits and progress payments	82,000		
Bank overdraft	132,500		
		291,500	
Excess of current liabilities over current assets			(16,500)
			81,500
Partners' capital accounts			
Lock		52,000	
Stock		26,000	
Barrel		3,500	
			81,500

During the six months from the date of the latest balance sheet to the date of dissolution the following transactions have taken place:

	£
Purchase of materials	20,250
Materials used for houses in course of construction	35,750
Payments for wages and subcontractors on building sites	78,000
Payments to trade creditors for materials	45,000
Sales of completed houses	280,000
Cash received from customers for houses	225,000
Payments for various general expenses	12,500
Payments for administration salaries	17,250
Cash withdrawn by partners: Lock	6,000
Stock	5,000
Barrel	4,000

All deposits and progress payments have been used for completed transactions.

Depreciation is normally provided each year at £600 on the freehold yard and buildings, at 10 per cent on cost for plant and equipment and 25 per cent on cost for motor vehicles.

The partners decide to dissolve the partnership on 1 February 20X7 and wish to take out the maximum cash possible, as items are sold. At this date there are no houses in course of construction and one-third of the stock of land had been used for building.

It is agreed that Barrel is insolvent and cannot bring any money into the partnership. The partners take over the partnership cars at an agreed figure of £2,000 each. All other vehicles were sold on 28 February 20X7 for £6,200. At the same date stocks of materials were sold for £7,000, and the stock of the land realised £72,500. On 30 April 20X7 the debtors paid in full and all the plant and equipment was sold for £50,000.

The freehold yard and buildings realised £100,000 on 1 June 20X7, on which date all remaining cash was distributed.

There are no costs of realisation or distribution.

Required:

(a) Prepare a partnership profit and loss account for the six months to 1 February 20X7, partners' capital accounts for the same period and a balance sheet at 1 February 20X7.

(b) Show calculations of the amounts distributable to the partners.

(c) Prepare a realisation account and the capital accounts of the partners to the final distribution.

(*Association of Chartered Certified Accountants*)

3.29X Grant and Herd are in partnership sharing profits and losses in the ratio 3 to 2. The following information relates to the year to 31 December 20X8:

	Dr £000	Cr £000
Capital accounts (at 1 January 20X8):		
Grant		300
Herd		100
Cash at bank	5	
Creditors and accruals		25
Debtors and prepayments	18	
Drawings during the year: Grant (all at 30 June 20X8)	40	
Herd (all at 31 March 20X8)	40	
Fixed assets: at cost	300	
accumulated depreciation (at 31 December 20X8)		100
Herd – salary	10	
Net profit (for the year to 31 December 20X8)		60
Stocks at cost (at 31 December 20X8)	90	
Trade creditors		141
Trade debtors	223	
	£726	£726

Additional information:

1 The partnership agreement allows for Herd to be paid a salary of £20,000 per annum, and for interest of 5 per cent per annum to be paid on the partners' capital account balances as at 1 January in each year. Interest at a rate of 10 per cent per annum is charged on the partners' drawings.

2 The partners decide to dissolve the partnership as at 31 December 20X8, and the business was then sold to Valley Limited. The purchase consideration was to be 400,000 £1 ordinary shares in Valley at a premium of 25p per share. The shares were to be issued to the partners on 31 December 20X8, and they were to be shared between them in their profit-sharing ratio.

   The sale agreement allowed Grant to take over one of the business cars at an agreed valuation of £10,000. Apart from the car and the cash and bank balances, the company took over all the other partnership assets and liabilities at their book values as at 31 December 20X8.

3 Matters relating to the appropriation of profit for the year to 31 December 20X8 are to be dealt with in the partners' capital accounts, including any arrears of salary owing to Herd.

Required:

(*a*) Write up the following accounts for the year to 31 December 20X8:
   (*i*)   the profit and loss appropriation account;
   (*ii*) Grant and Herd's capital accounts; and
   (*iii*) the realisation account.
(*b*) Prepare Valley's balance sheet as at 1 January 20X9 immediately after the acquisition of the partnership and assuming that no further transactions have taken place in the meantime.

(*Association of Accounting Technicians*)

3.30 Dinho and Manueli are in partnership sharing profits and losses equally after interest of 10 per cent on each partner's capital account in excess of £100,000. At 31 December 20X8, the partnership trial balance was:

	Dr £	Cr £
Bank		56,700
Capital accounts: Dinho		194,000
Manueli		123,000
Creditors		85,800
Debtors	121,000	
Equipment, at cost	85,000	
Long-term loan		160,000
Freehold property	290,000	
Provision for depreciation on equipment		20,000
Stocks	143,500	
	639,500	639,500

On 31 December 20X8, the partnership was converted to a limited company, Bin Ltd. All the partnership assets and liabilities were taken over by the company in exchange for shares in Bin Ltd valued at £304,000. The share capital was allocated so as to preserve the rights previously enjoyed by the partners under their partnership agreement.

   The assets and liabilities and shares issued were all entered in the books of Bin Ltd at 31 December. In the company's books, the debtors were recorded at £116,000 and the freehold property was valued at £260,000.

On 1 January 20X9, Pa invested £120,000 in the company and was issued shares on the same basis as had been applied when deciding the share allocations to Dinho and Manueli – i.e. as if he had been an equal partner in the partnership.

Pa had previously been an employee of the partnership earning £40,000 per annum. The £120,000 he invested in the company had been earning interest of 6 per cent per annum from the bank. His salary will continue to be paid.

Assume that all profits will be paid as dividends. Ignore taxation.

Required:

(*a*) Prepare the partnership realisation account after the sale of the business to Bin Ltd had been completed and recorded in the partnership books.

(*b*) Prepare Bin Ltd's balance sheet as at 1 January 20X9 after the purchase of shares by Pa.

(*c*) Calculate the annual profit that Bin Ltd needs to make before it pays any dividends if Pa is to receive the same amount of income as he was receiving before buying shares in Bin Ltd.

CHAPTER 4

Valuation of assets

Learning objectives

After you have studied this chapter, you should be able to:

- calculate the value of stock using three different methods;
- explain why using the most appropriate method to value stock is important;
- explain what effect changing prices has on stock valuation under each of three different methods;
- explain why net realisable value is sometimes used instead of cost for stock valuation;
- adjust stock valuations, where necessary, by a reduction to net realisable value;
- explain how subjective factors influence the choice of stock valuation method;
- explain why goods purchased on 'sale or return' are not included in the buyer's stock;
- explain the rules relating to asset revaluation;
- describe some of the possible valuation alternatives to historical cost.

Part I   VALUATION OF STOCK

4.1   Different valuations of stock

Most people would think that there can be only one figure for the valuation of stock. This is not true. We will examine in this chapter how we can calculate different figures for stock.

Assume that a firm has just completed its first financial year and is about to value stock at cost price. It has dealt in only one type of goods. A record of the transactions is now shown in Exhibit 4.1.

EXHIBIT 4.1

Bought			Sold		
20X5		£	20X5		£
January	10 at £30 each	300	May	8 for £50 each	400
April	10 at £34 each	340	November	24 for £60 each	1,440
October	20 at £40 each	800			
	40	1,440		32	1,840

There are 8 units in stock at 31 December.

The total figure of purchases is £1,440 and that of sales is £1,840. The trading account for the first year of trading can now be completed if the closing stock is brought into the calculations.

But what value do we put on each of the 8 units left in stock at the end of the year? If all of the units bought during the year had cost £30 each, then the closing stock would be 8 × £30 = £240. However, we have bought goods at different prices. This means that the valuation depends on which goods are taken for this calculation, the units at £30 or at £34, or at £40.

Many firms do not know exactly whether they have sold all the oldest units before they sell the newer units. For instance, a firm selling spanners may not know if the oldest spanners had been sold before the newest spanners.

The stock valuation will therefore be based on an accounting custom, and not on the facts of exactly which units were still in stock at the year end. The three main methods of doing this are now shown.

4.2 First in, first out method

This is usually abbreviated to **FIFO**. This method says that the first goods to be received are the first to be issued. Using the figures in Exhibit 4.1 we can now calculate the closing figure of stock as follows:

	Received	Issued	Stock after each transaction		
20X5				£	£
January	10 at £30 each		10 at £30 each		300
April	10 at £34 each		10 at £30 each	300	
			10 at £34 each	340	640
May		8 at £30 each	2 at £30 each	60	
			10 at £34 each	340	400
October	20 at £40 each		2 at £30 each	60	
			10 at £34 each	340	
			20 at £40 each	800	1,200
November		2 at £30 each			
		10 at £34 each			
		12 at £40 each			
		24	8 at £40 each		320

The closing stock at 31 December 20X5 is therefore valued at £320.

4.3 Last in, first out method

This is usually abbreviated to **LIFO**. As each issue of goods is made, they are said to be from the last lot of goods received before that date. Where there is not enough left of the last lot of goods, then the balance of goods needed is said to come from the previous lot still unsold.

From the information shown in Exhibit 4.1 the calculation can now be shown.

	Received	Issued	Stock after each transaction		
				£	£
20X5 January	10 at £30 each		10 at £30 each		300
April	10 at £34 each		10 at £30 each	300	
			10 at £34 each	340	640
May		8 at £34 each	10 at £30 each	300	
			2 at £34 each	68	368
October	20 at £40 each		10 at £30 each	300	
			2 at £34 each	68	
			20 at £40 each	800	1,168
November		20 at £40 each			
		2 at £34 each			
		2 at £30 each			
		24	8 at £30 each		240

The closing stock at 31 December 20X5 is therefore valued at £240, i.e. £80 less than under FIFO.

4.4 Average cost method

This is usually abbreviated to **AVCO**. Under this method, with each receipt of goods the average cost for each item of stock is recalculated. Further issues of goods are then at that figure, until another receipt of goods means that another recalculation is needed. From the information in Exhibit 4.1 the calculation can be shown.

Received		Issued	Average cost per unit of stock held	Number of units in stock	Total value of stock
			£		£
January	10 at £30		30	10	300
April	10 at £34		32*	20	640
May		8 at £32	32	12	384
October	20 at £40		37*	32	1,184
November		24 at £37	37	8	296

* In April, this is calculated as follows: stock 10 × £30 = £300 + stock received (10 × £34 = £340) = total £640. 20 units in stock, so the average is £640 ÷ 20 = £32. In October this is calculated as

follows: stock 12 × £32 = £384 + stock received (20 × £40) £800 = £1,184. 32 units in stock, so the average is £1,184 ÷ 32 = £37.

The closing stock at 31 December 20X5 is therefore valued at £296, which is between the FIFO and LIFO valuations.

4.5 Stock valuation and the calculation of profits

Using the figures from Exhibit 4.1 with stock valuations shown by the three methods of FIFO, LIFO and AVCO, the trading accounts would be:

Trading Account for the year ended 31 December 20X5							
	FIFO £	LIFO £	AVCO £		FIFO £	LIFO £	AVCO £
Purchases	1,440	1,440	1,440	Sales	1,840	1,840	1,840
less Closing stock	320	240	296				
Cost of goods sold	1,120	1,200	1,144				
Gross profit	720	640	696				
	1,840	1,840	1,840		1,840	1,840	1,840

Not surprisingly (as the valuation of closing stock was different in each case) the different methods of stock valuation each result in a different profit figure being produced.

4.6 Reduction of stock valuation to net realisable value

The **net realisable value** of stock is calculated as follows:

**Saleable value – Expenses needed before completion of sale
= Net realisable value.**

The concept of prudence is used when stock is valued. Stock should not be overvalued, otherwise profits will be unrealistically high. If the net realisable value of stock is less than the cost of the stock, the figure to be taken for the final accounts is that of net realisable value.

A somewhat exaggerated example will show the necessity for this action. Assume that an art dealer has bought only two paintings during the financial year ended 31 December 20X8. He starts off the year without any stock, and then buys a genuine masterpiece for £6,000, which he sells later in the year for £11,500. The other painting is a fake, but he does not realise this when he buys it for £5,100. He only discovers this during the year. Its net realisable value is only £100. The fake remains unsold at the end of the year. The trading accounts, which are shown in Exhibit 4.2, would appear as (*a*) if stock is valued at cost, and (*b*) if stock is valued at net realisable value.

EXHIBIT 4.2

Trading Account for the year ended 31 December 20X8

Method		(a) £		(b) £
Sales		11,500		11,500
Purchases	11,100		11,100	
Closing stock	(5,100)	6,000	(100)	11,000
Gross profit		5,500		500

Method (a) ignores the fact that the dealer had a bad trading year owing to his skill being found wanting, when he bought an expensive fake. If this method was used, the loss on the fake would reveal itself in the following year's trading account. Method (b), however, realises that the loss really occurred at the date of purchase rather than at the date of sale. Following the concept of prudence, accountants would use method (b).

At one time the terminology was 'the lower of cost or market value'. Changing it to 'lower of cost or net realisable value' gives a more precise definition to the terms used.

4.7 Stock groups and valuation

If there is only one type of goods in stock, calculating the lower of cost or net realisable value is easy. If we have several or many types of goods in stock, we can use one of two ways of making the calculation.

From the information given in Exhibit 4.3, we will calculate the stock in two different ways.

EXHIBIT 4.3

Stock at 31 December 20X8			
Article	Different categories	Cost	Net realisable value
		£	£
1	A	100	80
2	A	120	150
3	A	300	400
4	B	180	170
5	B	150	130
6	B	260	210
7	C	410	540
8	C	360	410
9	C	420	310
		2,300	2,400

Articles 1, 2 and 3 are televisions. Articles 4, 5 and 6 are radios. Articles 7, 8 and 9 are videos.

The category method

The same sorts of items are put together in categories. Thus, articles 1, 2 and 3 are televisions and shown as category A. Articles 4, 5 and 6 are radios and shown as category B. Articles 7, 8 and 9 are videos and shown as category C.

A calculation showing a comparison of cost valuation and net realisable value for each category is now shown.

Category	Cost	Net realisable value
A	£100 + £120 + £300 = £520	£80 + £150 + £400 = £630
B	£180 + £150 + £260 = £590	£170 + £130 + £210 = £510
C	£410 + £360 + £420 = £1,190	£540 + £410 + £310 = £1,260

The lower of cost and net realisable value is, therefore:

	£
Category A: lower of £520 or £630 =	520
Category B: lower of £590 or £510 =	510
Category C: lower of £1,190 or £1,260 =	1,190
Stock is valued for final accounts at	2,220

Article method

By this method, the lower of cost or net realisable value for each article is compared and the lowest figure taken. From Exhibit 4.3 this gives us the following valuation:

Articles	Valuation
	£
1	80
2	120
3	300
4	170
5	130
6	210
7	410
8	360
9	310
	£2,090

The regulations governing how financial statements are produced mean that accountants must adopt the second approach – the article method.

4.8 Some other bases in use

Retail businesses often estimate the cost of stock by calculating it in the first place at selling price, and then deducting the normal margin of gross profit on such stock. Adjustment is made for items which are to be sold at other than normal selling prices.

Where standard costing is in use (*see* Chapter 13) the figure of standard cost is frequently used.

4.9   Periodic stock valuation

Some businesses do not keep detailed stock records like those shown in Exhibit 4.1. Instead, they wait until the end of a period before calculating the cost of their closing stock. In this case, AVCO is based upon the total cost of stock available for sale in the period divided by the number of units of stock available for sale in the period. You then multiply the closing stock by the overall average cost of the stock.

If you did this for the data in Exhibit 4.1 the closing stock value at cost would be £1,440 ÷ 40 = £36 × 8 = £288 (rather than £296, as calculated in Section 4.4). This method is also known as the 'weighted average cost method'.

If you used FIFO or LIFO in these circumstances, FIFO gives the same answer as under the method presented earlier. LIFO, on the other hand, would become the permanent opposite of FIFO, with all closing stock assumed to have come from the earliest batches of purchases.

You should assume that you are to calculate AVCO, FIFO and LIFO in the way they were presented earlier in this chapter *unless* an examiner asks you to calculate them on a periodic stock valuation basis.

4.10   Factors affecting the stock valuation decision

The regulations governing the preparation of financial statements (*see* Chapter 21) require that the overriding consideration applicable in all circumstances when valuing stock is the need to give a 'true and fair view' of the state of the affairs of the undertaking as on the balance sheet date and of the trend of the firm's trading results. There is, however, no precise definition of 'true and fair view'. It rests on the judgement of the persons concerned. In order to understand the factors that affect judgement, it is necessary to study the behavioural sciences. However, it should be possible to state that the judgement of any two persons will not always be the same in the differing circumstances of various firms.

In fact, the only certain thing about stock valuation is that the concept of consistency should be applied. That is, once adopted, the same basis should be used in the annual accounts until some good reason occurs to change it. If the amount involved is material, a reference should then be made in the final accounts concerning the effect of the change of basis on the reported profits.

It will, perhaps, be useful to look at some of the factors which cause a particular basis to be chosen. The list is intended to be indicative rather than comprehensive, and is merely intended as a first brief look at matters which will have to be studied in depth by those intending to make a career in accountancy.

1 Ignorance
The people involved may not appreciate the fact that there is more than one possible way of valuing stock.

2 Convenience
The basis chosen may not be the best for the purposes of profit calculation but it may be the easiest to calculate. It must always be borne in mind that the benefits which flow from possessing information should be greater than the costs of obtaining it. The only difficulty with this is actually establishing when the benefits do exceed the cost, but in some circumstances the decision not to adopt a given basis will be obvious.

3 Custom

It may be the particular method used in a certain trade or industry.

4 Taxation

The whole idea may be to defer the payment of tax for as long as possible. Because the stock figures affect the calculation of profits on which the tax is based the lowest possible stock figures may be taken to show the lowest profits up to the balance sheet date.

5 The capacity to borrow money or to sell the business at the highest possible price

The higher the stock value shown, then the higher will be the profits calculated to date, and therefore at first sight the business looks more attractive to a buyer or lender. Either of these considerations may be more important to the proprietors than anything else. It may be thought that those in business are not so gullible, but all business people are not necessarily well acquainted with accounting customs. In fact, many small businesses are bought, or money is lent to them, without the expert advice of someone well versed in accounting.

6 Remuneration purposes

Where someone managing a business is paid in whole or in part by reference to the profits earned, then one basis may suit them better than others. They may therefore strive to have that basis used to suit their own ends. The owner, however, may try to follow another course to minimise the remuneration that he/she will have to pay out.

7 Lack of information

If proper stock records have not been kept, then such bases as the average cost method or the LIFO method may not be calculable.

8 Advice of the auditors

Many firms use a particular basis because the auditors advised its use in the first instance. A different auditor may well advise that a different basis be used.

9 Accounting Standards

SSAP 9 contains the rules relating to how stock should be valued in financial accounting statements.

4.11 SSAP 9, *Stocks and long-term contracts*

Due to the many varying kinds of businesses and conditions in companies, there simply cannot be one system of valuation for stocks and work in progress. All that the standard can do is to narrow down the different methods that could be used.

Stocks should be stated at the total of the lower of cost and net realisable value of the separate items of stock or of groups of similar (which really means 'identical') items. Profit should not, except in the case of long-term contracts, be recognised in advance, but immediate account should be made for anticipated losses.

In the balance sheet (or in the notes), stocks should be sub-classified so as to indicate the amounts held in each of the main categories in the standard balance sheet formats (as adapted where appropriate) of the Companies Act 1985. (These categories are *raw materials and consumables, work in progress, finished goods and goods for resale* and *payments on account.*)

Net realisable value is the expected selling price less any expenses necessary to sell the product. This may be below cost because of obsolescence, deterioration and similar factors. SSAP 9 also defines 'cost' and certainly in the case of a manufacturing business it will also include overhead expenses, so that prime cost could not be used. **Cost** is defined in SSAP 9 in relation to the different categories of stocks and work in progress as being:

> *that expenditure which has been incurred in the normal course of business in bringing the product or service to its present location and condition. This expenditure should include, in addition to cost of purchase* [as defined later] *such costs of conversion* [as defined later] *as are appropriate to that location and condition.*

Cost of purchase comprises purchase price including import duties, transport and handling costs and any other directly attributable costs, less trade discounts, rebates and subsidies.

Cost of conversion comprises:

(a) costs which are specifically attributable to units of production, i.e. direct labour, direct expenses and subcontracted work;

(b) production overheads (as defined later);

(c) other overheads, if any, attributable in the particular circumstances of the business to bringing the product or service to its present location and condition.

Production overheads based on the normal level of activity and including fixed production overheads, taking one year with another, should all be included. Obviously, neither selling nor general administration costs should be included in cost.

Notice that abnormal costs should not be included, as they would not have the effect of increasing stock valuation.

The LIFO and base stock methods should not be used, as they do not provide an up-to-date valuation. Although LIFO is not accepted by the SSAP, the Companies Act 1985 accepts its use. However, where appropriate in order to maintain a true and fair view, LIFO may be used. This would be the case, for example, where you were valuing the stock of a coal distributor.

The Standard does accept that replacement cost may, in certain circumstances, be acceptable. As a result, the lower of replacement cost or net realisable value may be used. Again, this is in accord with the Companies Act 1985.

4.12   The conflict of aims

The list of some of the factors which affect decisions is certainly not exhaustive, but it does illustrate the fact that stock valuation is usually a compromise. There is not usually only one figure which is true and fair, there must be a variety of possibilities. Therefore the desire to borrow money, and in so doing to paint a good picture by being reasonably optimistic in valuing stock, will be tempered by the fact that this may increase the tax bill. Stock valuation is therefore a compromise between the various ends for which it is to be used.

4.13   Work in progress

The valuation of work in progress is subject to all the various criteria and methods used in valuing stock. Probably the cost element is more strongly pronounced than in stock valuation, as it is very often impossible or irrelevant to say what net realisable value or replacement price would be applicable to partly finished goods. Firms in industries such as those which have contracts covering several years have evolved their own methods.

4.14 Goods on sale or return

Goods received on sale or return

Sometimes we may receive goods from one of our suppliers on a **sale or return** basis. What this means is that we do not have to pay for the goods until we sell them. If we do not sell them we have to return them to our supplier.

This means that the goods do not belong to us. If we have some goods on sale or return at the stocktaking date, they should not be included in our stock valuation.

Goods sent to our customers on sale or return

We may send goods on a sale or return basis to our customers. The stock will belong to us until it is sold. At our stocktaking date any goods held by our customers on sale or return should be included in our stock valuation.

4.15 Stocktaking and the balance sheet date

Students often think that all the counting and valuing of stock is done on the last day of the accounting period. This might be true in a small business, but it is often impossible in larger businesses. There may be too many items of stock to do it so quickly.

This means that stocktaking may take place over a period of days. To get the figure of the stock valuation as on the last day of the accounting period, we will have to make adjustments. Exhibit 4.4 gives an example of such calculations.

EXHIBIT 4.4

Lee Ltd has a financial year which ends on 31 December 20X7. The stocktaking is not in fact done until 8 January 20X8. When the items in stock on that date are priced out, it is found that the stock value amounted to £28,850. The following information is available about transactions between 31 December 20X7 and 8 January 20X8:

1 Purchases since 31 December 20X7 amounted to £2,370 at cost.
2 Returns inwards since 31 December 20X7 were £350 at selling price.
3 Sales since 31 December 20X7 amounted to £3,800 at selling price.
4 The selling price is always cost price + 25 per cent.

Lee Ltd
Computation of stock as on 31 December 20X7

		£
Stock (at cost)		28,850
Add Items which were in stock on 31 December 20X7 (at cost)		
	£	
Sales	3,800	
Less Profit content (20 per cent of selling price)*	760	
		3,040
		31,890

Less Items which were not in stock on 31 December 20X7 (at cost)

	£		
Returns inwards	350		
Less Profit content (20 per cent of selling price)*	(70)		
	280		
Purchases (at cost)	2,370		
		(2,650)	
Stock in hand as on 31 December 20X7		29,240	

* Stock at cost (or net realisable value), and not at selling price. As this calculation has a sales figure in it which includes profit, we must deduct the profit part to get to the cost price. This is true also for returns inwards.

At one time it was very rare for the auditors to attend at stocktaking time as observers. The professional accounting bodies now encourage the auditors to be present if at all possible.

4.16 Stock levels

One of the most common faults found in the running of a business is that too high a level of stock is maintained.

A considerable number of firms that have problems with a shortage of finance will find that they can help matters by having a sensible look at the amounts of stock they hold. It would be a very rare firm indeed which, if they had not investigated the matter previously, could not manage to let parts of their stock run down. As this would save spending cash on items not really necessary, this cash could be better utilised elsewhere.

Let us look at how excessive stocks can have a detrimental effect upon the financial results of a firm:

1 Money tied up in unnecessarily large stocks is not earning anything. If, therefore, an extra £1 million is tied up in stocks which do not have to be so large, then the money which we could have earned from utilising that extra £1 million somewhere else has been lost. If we could have earned 10 per cent return on that money, then the unnecessary stocks have cost us £100,000 a year without any alternative benefit.

2 Too much stock needs extra storage space. Therefore the rent for the extra space, heating, lighting, insurance, wages of extra storekeepers, etc. is all money being spent for no benefit.

One thing that anyone should look for when examining the affairs of a business is to see if stocks are larger than they need be. For someone controlling the business there are three methods of cutting down on unnecessarily high stocks which have become much more popular in recent times. These are:

(*a*) **Economic Order Quantity** (**EOQ**). This is a mathematical method of deciding what is the lowest amount of stock that should be ordered at a time so that the costs of financing and keeping stock are kept down to the minimum.

The formula for this is:

$$\text{EOQ} = \sqrt{\frac{2CO}{S}}$$

where:

C = consumption (usage) per annum in units

O = cost of placing one order

S = cost of storage and holding of one unit per year

S will include the costs of operating the stores, transport and insurance, and also the costs concerned with interest on capital which has been invested in stock. We then take the square root of the above as the answer.

Exhibit 4.5 shows the calculation of the minimum order to be made.

EXHIBIT 4.5

Annual consumption = 800 units

Cost of reordering = £4

Storage and holding costs per unit = £1

$$\text{EOQ} = \sqrt{\frac{2 \times 800 \times £4}{£1}} = \sqrt{\frac{6{,}400}{1}} = 80 \text{ units (10 orders per year)}$$

(b) **Just-in-time** approach (JIT). This has been seen as one of the major factors which have resulted in the past success of Japanese manufacturers. It is an approach which is concerned not just with stock levels, but that is part of it.

The JIT approach requires that delivery of materials should occur immediately before their use. If arrangements are made with suppliers for more frequent deliveries then stocks can be cut to a minimum. Getting suppliers to inspect the materials before they deliver them, and getting them to guarantee their quality, also cuts down on costs, including the need to keep larger stocks in case there are deficiencies.

This sort of service is obtained by giving more business to fewer suppliers, and also placing longer-term orders. This enables the supplier to plan ahead more effectively to give a better service.

(c) The last few years have also seen a new approach to the management of production called **optimised production technology** (OPT). The object is to distinguish between 'bottleneck' and 'non-bottleneck' resources. To give an example, the 'bottleneck' resource might be a machine which has a limited capacity. As a result, everything else can only be operated at that same level. Rather than other parts of the business producing more than the 'bottleneck' machine can absorb, a lower overall level of activity takes place. This needs less stocks.

Of course if a 'bottleneck' can be eliminated it will be. The above applies when a bottleneck, for whatever reason, cannot be eliminated.

It is better to have a smooth-running business, operating within its 'bottleneck' capacities, than to have one which operates very irregularly. One run irregularly would have to have parts of the business shut down at times. One running smoothly, besides all the other economies, needs fewer stocks.

Part II REVALUATION OF ASSETS

4.17 Fixed asset revaluation

Fixed asset revaluation is permitted and governed by the rules of FRS 15, *Tangible fixed assets*. If a policy of revaluation is adopted, the valuations should be kept up to date. If one asset is revalued, all the assets of that class (i.e. those with a similar nature, function or use) must also be revalued.

Revaluation losses caused by use of the asset should be recognised in the profit and loss account. Other revaluation losses should be recognised in the statement of total recognised gains and losses until the carrying amount of the asset is less than the amount the asset would be carried at had depreciated historical cost been adopted rather than asset revaluation.

For example, imagine an asset is revalued from a carrying amount of £20,000 down to £6,000 because the asset had become obsolete. Had it never been revalued, its carrying amount would have been £11,000. The carrying amount of the asset (£6,000) is, therefore, below £11,000 and so the loss on revaluation of £14,000 would be split with £9,000 being recognised in the statement of total recognised gains and losses and £5,000 being recognised in profit and loss.

Revaluation gains should be recognised in the statement of total recognised gains and losses unless they relate to an asset that had previously had revaluation losses charged to the profit and loss acount. Where that is the case, the revaluation gain should also be charged to profit and loss, after adjusting for depreciation since the revaluation loss was recognised.

Depreciation should be charged irrespective of when the asset was revalued. An increased value arising from a revaluation does not mean that depreciation should not be charged. The new value is the one on which future depreciation should be based. Depreciation charged before revaluation should not be credited back to profit and loss.

According to paragraph 21 of FRS 3, *Reporting financial performance*, the profit or loss on the disposal of an asset should be accounted for in the profit and loss account of the period in which the disposal occurs as the difference between the net sale proceeds and the net carrying amount, whether carried at historical cost (less any provisions made) or at a valuation.

Land and buildings

Freehold land

As this normally lasts forever there is no need to depreciate, unless subject to depletion or loss of value for reasons which may be applicable in certain circumstances, such as desirability of location, land erosion, extraction of minerals, dumping of toxic waste, etc. It is rare to encounter circumstances under which freehold land should be subject to depreciation. The problem that most often occurs is the distinction between the cost/value of freehold land and the cost/value of the buildings upon it. FRS 15 states that the distinction should be made as only the buildings have a limited useful economic life and should be depreciated. Land has an unlimited life and should not be depreciated. Failure to separate the two elements of the cost/value will result in non-compliance with the standard.

Buildings

These have finite lives and should be depreciated.

Notes to accounts

The FRS requires that the following should be disclosed:

1 Methods of depreciation used.
2 Useful economic lives or the depreciation rates in use.
3 Total depreciation charged for the period.
4 Where material, the financial effect of a change in either useful economic lives or estimates of residual values.
5 The cost or revalued amount at both the start and end of the accounting period.
6 The cumulative amount of provisions for depreciation or impairment at the beginning and end of the financial period.
7 A reconciliation of the movements, separately disclosing additions, disposals, revaluations, transfers, depreciation, impairment losses and reversals of past impairment losses written back in the period.
8 The net carrying amount at the beginning and end of the financial period.

Part III MEASUREMENT OF INCOME AND ASSET VALUES

4.18 Measurement of income

'Income' and the words 'net profit' mean exactly the same thing. In this book the calculation of net profit is done within fairly strict guidelines. In Chapter 25, you will learn about the overall concepts ruling such calculations. However, just because the business world and the accounting profession use this basic approach does not mean it is the only one available. We will now consider possible alternatives to the basic method.

Let us start by looking at the simplest possible example of the calculation of profit, where everyone would agree with the way it is calculated. John is starting in business, his only asset being cash £1,000. He rents a stall in the market for the day, costing him £40. He then buys fruit for cash £90, and sells it all during the day for cash £160. At the end of the day John's only asset is still cash: £1,000 − £40 − £90 + 160 = £1,030. Everyone would agree that his profit for that day was £30, i.e. £160 sales − £90 purchases − £40 expenses = £30. In this case his profit equals the increase in his cash.

Suppose that John now changes his style of trading. He buys the market stall, and he also starts selling nuts and dried fruit, of which he can keep a stock from one day to another. If we now want to calculate profit we cannot do it simply in terms of cash, we will also have to place a value both on the stock of fruit and nuts and on his stall, both at the beginning and end of each day.

The argument just put forward assumes that we can all agree that profit represents an increase in wealth or 'well-offness'. It assumes that John will make a profit for a period if either:

(*a*) he is better off at the end of it than he was at the beginning; or
(*b*) he would have been better off at the end than the beginning had he not consumed some of the profits by taking drawings.

Sir John Hicks, the economist, expressed this view by saying that the profit was the maximum value which a person could consume during a period and still be as well off at the end of the period as at the beginning.

In terms of a limited company, the Sandilands Committee, which will be mentioned in greater detail later, said that a company's profit for the year is the maximum value which the company can distribute as dividends during the year, and still be as well off at the end of the year as it was at the beginning. There are some important questions which need answering. They are:

(a) How can we measure wealth at the beginning and end of a period?
(b) How do we measure the change in wealth over a period?
(c) When we have measured wealth over a period, how much can be available for consumption and how much should not be consumed?

There are basically two approaches to the measurement of wealth of a business:

(a) Measuring the wealth by finding the values of the individual assets of a business.
(b) Measuring the expectation of future benefits.

In Chapter 14, you will learn about the technique of discounting which can be used here to calculate the present value of the expected future net flow of cash into the firm.

We will look first at the different methods of valuation on an individual asset basis.

4.19 Asset valuation alternatives

1 Historical cost

This method is the one you have used so far in the financial accounting in this book. Even in that case there is not always one single figure to represent it. Let us look at a few examples.

(a) **Depreciation.** How do we 'precisely' charge the cost of using an asset to a particular period? As you have already seen, there is no one 'true' answer; the choice of method, expected length of use of the asset, etc., is quite arbitrary.
(b) Stocks to be used during the period can be charged out at FIFO, LIFO, AVCO and so on. There is no one 'true' figure.
(c) Suppose we buy a block of assets, e.g. we take over the net assets of another organisation. How do we allocate the cost exactly? There is no precise way, we simply use a 'fair value' for each asset. Any excess of cost over the total of fair values we call goodwill.

2 Adjusted historical cost

Because of the changes in the value or purchasing power of money, the normal historical cost approach can be very unsatisfactory. Take the case of a buildings account; in it we find that two items have been debited. One was a warehouse bought in 1970 for £100,000 and the other an almost identical warehouse bought in 2000 for £400,000. These two figures are added together to show cost of warehouses £500,000, quite clearly a value which has little significance.

To remedy this defect, the original historical cost of an asset is adjusted for the changes in the value or purchasing power of money over the period from acquisition to the present balance sheet date. The calculations are effected by using a price index.

This method does not mean that the asset itself is revalued. What is revalued is the money for which the asset was originally bought. This method forms the basis of what is known as **current purchasing power** accounting, abbreviated as CPP.

It does not remove the original problems of historical accounting which we have already described (*see* above). All this does is to take the original historical cost as accurate and then adjust it.

To illustrate this method, let us take an instance which works out precisely, just as the proponents of CPP would wish.

A machine which will last for five years, depreciated using the straight line method, was bought on 1 January 20X4 for £5,000. On 1 January 20X6 exactly the same kind of machine (there have been no technological improvements) is bought for £6,000. The price index was 100 at 1 January 20X4, 120 at 1 January 20X6 and 130 at 31 December 20X6. The machines would appear in the balance sheet at 31 December 20X6 as follows, the workings being shown in the box alongside.

	Historical cost £	Conversion factor £		Balance sheet CPP at 31 Dec 20X6 £
Machine 1	5,000	130/100	6,500	
Machine 2	6,000	130/120	6,500	13,000
Less Depreciation				
Machine 1	3,000	130/100	3,900	
Machine 2	1,200	130/120	1,300	(5,200)
				7,800

You can see that the CPP balance sheet shows two exactly similar machines at the same cost, and each has been depreciated £1,300 for each year of use. In this particular case CPP has achieved exactly what it sets out to do, namely put similar things on a similar basis.

Underlying this method are the problems inherent in the price index used to adjust the historical cost figures. Any drawbacks in the index will result in a distortion of the adjusted historical cost figures.

3 Replacement cost

Replacement cost, abbreviated as RC, is the estimated amount that would have to be paid to replace the asset at the date of valuation. You will often see it referred to as an 'entry value' as it is the cost of an asset entering the business.

How do we 'estimate' the replacement cost? As we are not in fact replacing the asset we will have to look at the state of the market at the date of valuation. If the asset is exactly the same as those currently being traded, perhaps we can look at suppliers' price lists.

Even with exactly the same item, there are still problems. Until you have actually negotiated a purchase it is impossible to say how much discount you could get – you might guess but you could not be certain. Also, if the asset consists of, say, ten drilling machines, how much discount could you get for buying ten machines instead of one only?

If we have those difficulties looking at identical assets, what happens when we are trying to find out these figures for assets which cannot still be matched on the market? Technological change has greatly speeded up in recent years. If there is a second-hand market, it may be quite possible to get a valuation. However, in second-hand markets the price is often even more subject to negotiation. It becomes even more complicated when the original asset was specially made and there is no exactly comparable item, new or second-hand.

The difficulties outlined above mean that solutions to valuation can be sought under three headings:

(*a*) **Market prices.** As already mentioned, there will often be a market, new or second-hand, for the assets. For instance, this is particularly true for motor vehicles. If our asset differs in some way an adjustment may be necessary, thus cutting into the desirable degree of objectivity.

(*b*) **Units of service.** Where a market price is unobtainable, this being especially so with obsolete assets, a value is placed on the units of service which the asset can provide, rather than trying to value the asset itself.

For instance, assume that a machine has an estimated future production capacity of 1,000 units. A new machine producing the same type of product might have a total future capacity of 5,000 units. If the running costs of the machines are the same, the value of the old machine can be said to be one-fifth of the cost of the new one, as that is the proportion its future capacity bears to the new one. If the running costs were different an adjustment would be made.

(*c*) **Cost of inputs.** If the asset was made or constructed by the owner, it may be possible to calculate the cost of replacing it at the balance sheet date. Present rates of labour and materials costs could be worked out to give the replacement cost.

4 Net realisable value

Net realisable value means the estimated amount that would be received from the sale of the asset less the estimated costs on its disposal. The term '**exit value**' is often used as it is the amount receivable when an asset leaves the business.

A very important factor affecting such a valuation is the conditions under which the assets are to be sold. To realise in a hurry would often mean accepting a very low price. Look at the sale prices received from stock from bankruptcies – usually very low figures. The standard way of approaching this problem is to value as though the realisation were 'in the normal course of business'. This is not capable of an absolutely precise meaning, as economic conditions change and the firm might never sell such an asset 'in the normal course of business'.

The difficulties of establishing an asset's net realisable value are similar to those of the replacement value method when similar assets are not being bought and sold in the market-place. However, the problems are more severe as the units of service approach cannot be used, since that takes the seller's rather than buyer's viewpoint.

5 Economic value (present value)

As any economist would be delighted to tell you, they would value an asset as the sum of the future expected net cash flows associated with the asset, discounted to its present value. The technicalities of discounting are discussed in Chapter 14.

Certainly, if you really did know (not guess) the future net cash flows associated with the asset and you had the correct discount rate, your valuation would be absolutely correct. The trouble is that it is impossible to forecast future net cash flows with certainty, neither will we necessarily have chosen the correct discount rate. It is also very difficult to relate cash flows to a particular asset, since a business's assets combine together to generate revenue.

6 Deprival value

The final concept of value is based on ideas propounded in the USA by Professor Bonbright in the 1930s, and later developed in the UK for profit measurement by Professor W T Baxter.

Deprival value is based on the concept of the value of an asset being the amount of money the owner would have to receive to compensate them exactly for being deprived of it. We had better point out immediately that the owner does not have to be deprived of the asset to ascertain this value, it is a hypothetical exercise. This leads to a number of consequences.

(*a*) Deprival value cannot exceed replacement cost, since if the owner were deprived of the asset they could replace it for a lesser amount. Here we will ignore any costs concerned with a delay in replacement.

(*b*) If the owner feels that the asset is not worth replacing, its replacement cost would be more than its deprival value. They simply would not pay the replacement cost, so the value to the owner is less than that figure.

(*c*) If the asset's deprival value is to be taken as its net realisable value, that value must be less than its replacement cost. It would otherwise make sense for someone to sell the asset at the net realisable value and buy a replacement at a lower cost. Again, delays in replacement are ignored.

(*d*) Take the case where an owner would not replace the asset, but neither would they sell it. It is possible to envisage a fixed asset which has become obsolete but might possibly be used, for example, when other machines break down. It is not worth buying a new machine, as the replacement cost is more than the value of the machine to the business. Such a machine may well have a very low net realisable value.

The benefit to the business of keeping such a machine can be said to be its 'value in use'. This value must be less than its replacement cost, as pointed out above, but more than its net realisable value for otherwise the owner would sell it.

It is probably easier to summarise how to find 'deprival value' by means of the diagram in Exhibit 4.6.

EXHIBIT 4.6 Deprival value

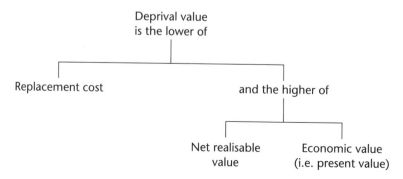

This can be illustrated by a few examples, using assets A, B and C.

	Asset A	Asset B	Asset C
	£	£	£
Replacement cost (RC)	1,000	800	600
Net realisable value (NRV)	900	500	400
Economic value (EV)	2,000	700	300

The deprival values can be explained as follows. Check them against Exhibit 4.6.

(a) **Asset A.** If the firm were deprived of asset A, what would it do? As economic value is greater than replacement cost it would buy another asset A. The deprival value to the business is therefore £1,000, i.e. replacement cost.

(b) **Asset B.** If deprived of asset B, what would the firm do? It would not replace it, as replacement cost £800 is greater than its value to the business – its economic value £700. If deprived, the firm would therefore lose the present value of future cash flows, i.e. economic value £700. This then is the deprival value for asset B.

(c) **Asset C.** With this asset there would be no point in keeping it, as its economic value to the firm is less than the firm could sell it for. Selling it is the logical way, so the deprival value is net realisable value £400.

4.20 Capital maintenance

Let us go back to Sir John Hicks's definition of income (profit): 'A man's income is the maximum value which he can consume during a week, and still expect to be as well off at the end of the week as he was at the beginning.'

We have looked at the different ways we could value assets as a preliminary to totalling them to find the wealth or 'well-offness' at a particular date. Before going any further we must examine the problems of measuring the maintenance of wealth (or 'well-offness') over a period. We could call this **capital maintenance**.

The basic method used in accounting, and described earlier, is that of **money capital maintenance**. Using this approach, we see that if a firm has £1,000 in capital or net assets on 1 January 20X1 it must have £1,000 in capital or net assets at 31 December 20X1 to be as well off at the end of the period. This means that, provided no new share capital has been issued and no dividends have been paid or share capital withdrawn, a company starting with capital of £1,000 on 1 January 20X2 and finishing with capital of £1,600 on 31 December 20X2 must have made a profit of £600, using this approach to capital maintenance.

Such a method would be acceptable to everyone in a period when there is no change in prices. However, most people would agree that the approach is not satisfactory when either prices in general, or specific prices affecting the firm, are changing. In these two cases, to state that £600 profit has been made for 20X2 completely ignores the fact that the £1,000 at 1 January 20X2 and the £1,000 at 31 December 20X2 do not have the same value. From this we can see the possibilities of three different concepts.

1 **Money capital maintenance.** The traditional system of accounting as already described.

2 **Real capital maintenance.** This concept is concerned with maintaining the general purchasing power of the equity shareholders. This takes into account changes in the purchasing power of money as measured by the retail price index.

3 **Maintenance of specific purchasing power of the capital of the equity.** This uses a price index which is related to the specific price changes of the goods in which the firm deals.

From these we can look at the following example, which illustrates three different figures of profit being thrown up for a firm.

4.21 A worked example

A company has only equity share capital. Its net assets on 1 January 20X5 are £1,000, and on 31 December 20X5 £1,400. There have been no issues or withdrawal of share capital during the year. The general rate of inflation, as measured by the retail price index, is 10 per cent, whereas the specific rate of price increase for the type of goods in which the company deals is 15 per cent. The profits for the three measures are as follows:

	(a) Money maintenance of capital	(b) Real capital maintenance	(c) Maintenance of specific purchasing power
	£	£	£
Net assets 31 Dec 20X5	1,400	1,400	1,400
Less What net assets would have to be at 31 Dec 20X5 to be as well off on 1 Jan 20X5			
(a) Money maintenance	(1,000)		
(b) Real capital £1,000 + 10%		(1,100)	
(c) Specific purchasing power maintenance £1,000 + 15%			(1,150)
Profit	400	300	250

Note that under the three methods:

(*a*) here the normal accounting method gives £400 profit;

(*b*) this case recognises that there has been a fall in the purchasing power of money;

(*c*) this takes into account that it would cost £1,150 for goods whose value at the start of the year was £1,000.

4.22 Combinations of different values and capital maintenance concepts

We have just looked at three ways of calculating profits based on historical cost allied with three capital maintenance concepts. This can be extended by using replacement cost or net realisable value instead. Each of these, when adjusted by each capital maintenance concept, will give three separate figures for profit. Together the three different means of valuation, multiplied by three different concepts of capital maintenance, will give us nine different profit figures.

At this stage in your studies it will be difficult to understand how such different profit measures could be useful for different purposes. We can leave this until your studies progress to more advanced examinations. However, we can use one simple example to illustrate how using only the traditional way of calculating profits can have dire consequences. The next example shows how this can happen.

4.23 A worked example

A company has net assets on 1 January 20X7 of £100,000 financed purely by equity share capital. During 20X7 there has been no injection or withdrawal of capital. At 31 December 20X7 net assets have risen to £115,000. Both the retail price index and the specific price index for the goods dealt in have risen by 25 per cent. Taxation, based on traditional historical cost calculations (maintenance of money capital), is at the rate of 40 per cent. The profit may be calculated as follows.

	Maintenance of money capital	Maintenance of real capital and of specific purchasing power
	£	£
Net assets on 31 Dec 20X7	115,000	115,000
Less Net assets needed to be as well off at 31 Dec 20X7 as with £100,000 on 1 Jan 20X7		
(a) Money capital	(100,000)	
(b) Both real capital and specific purchasing power £100,000 + 25%		(125,000)
Profit/loss	15,000	(10,000)

Tax payable is £15,000 × 40% = £6,000. Yet the real capital or that of specific purchasing power has fallen by £10,000. When tax is paid that would leave us with net assets of £115,000 − £6,000 = £109,000. Because of price changes £109,000 could not finance the amount of activity financed by £100,000 one year before. The operating capacity of the company would therefore be reduced.

Obviously it is not equitable for a company to have to pay tax on what is in fact a loss. It is only the traditional way of measuring profits that has thrown up a profit figure.

4.24 Operating capital maintenance concept

This approach looks at the output which could be generated by the initial holding of assets. A profit will only be made if the assets held at the end of the period are able to maintain the same level of output.

A very simple example of this is that of a trader who sells only one product, a particular kind of watch. The only costs the trader incurs are those of buying the watches. They have no assets apart from watches. In this case the operating capital consists solely of watches.

Using the historical cost concept the trader will recognise a profit if the revenue from the sale of a watch exceeded the historic cost of it. However, using the operating capital maintenance concept they will recognise a profit only if the revenue from the sale is greater than the cost of buying another watch to replace the watch sold.

4.25   Problems during a period of changing price levels

Obviously, the greater the rate of change in price levels, the greater will be the problems. They include:

1 **Fixing selling prices.** If you can change your prices very quickly, an extreme case being a market trader, this problem hardly exists. For a company setting prices which it is expected to maintain for a reasonably long period, the problems are severe. It dare not price too highly, as early demand may be reduced by an excessive price; on the other hand, the company has to guess how prices are going to change over a period so that sufficient profit is made.

2 **Financial planning.** As it is so difficult to guess how prices are going to change over a period, planning the firm's finances becomes particularly trying. Obviously, it would be better if the plans were revised frequently as conditions changed.

3 **Paying taxation and replacing assets.** We have seen earlier how, during a period of inflation, traditional historic accounting will tend to overstate profits. Such artificial 'profits' are then taxed. Unless various supplementary tax allowances are given, the taxation paid is both excessive and more than true profits, adjusted for inflation, can bear easily. This tends to lead to companies being short of cash, too much having been taken in tax. Therefore, when assets which have risen in price have to be replaced, adequate finance may not be available.

4 **Monetary assets.** If stocks of goods are held, they will tend to rise in money terms during a period of inflation. On the other hand, holding monetary assets, e.g. cash, bank and debtors, will be counter-productive. A bank balance of £1,000 held for six months, during which the purchasing power of money has fallen 10 per cent, will in real terms be worth only 90 per cent of its value six months before. Similarly, in real terms debt of £5,000 owed continually over that same period will have seen its real value fall by 10 per cent.

5 **Dividend distribution.** Just as it is difficult to calculate profits, so is it equally difficult to decide how much to pay as dividends without impairing the efficiency and operating capability of the company. At the same time the shareholders will be looking to payment of adequate dividends.

Learning outcomes

You should now have learnt:

1 That methods of valuing stocks, such as FIFO, LIFO and AVCO, are only that – methods of *valuing* stocks. It does not mean that goods are *physically* sold on a FIFO or LIFO basis.

2 That because different methods of valuing stock result in different closing stock valuations, the amount of profit reported for a particular accounting period is affected by the method of stock valuation adopted.

3 That using net realisable when this is lower than cost, so that profits are not overstated, is an example of the prudence concept in accounting.

4 That many subjective factors may affect the choice of stock valuation method adopted.

5 That without stock records of quantities of items, it would be very difficult to track down theft or losses or to detect wastage of goods.

6 That without proper stock records, it is unlikely that AVCO and LIFO can be applied in the way described at the start of this chapter.

7 That goods sold on sale or return should be included in the stock of the seller until the buyer has sold them.

8 That stocktaking is usually done over a period of time around the end of the accounting period.

9 That the stock levels identified at a stocktake need to be adjusted to the level they would have been at had the stocktake taken place on the balance sheet date.

10 The rules relating to the revaluation of fixed assets.

11 That changing price levels distort historic cost values and that various approaches have been suggested to deal with this issue.

12 Some of the possible valuation alternatives to historical cost.

REVIEW QUESTIONS

4.1 From the following figures calculate the closing stock-in-trade that would be shown using (*i*) FIFO, (*ii*) LIFO, (*iii*) AVCO methods.

Bought		Sold	
January	10 at £30 each	April	8 for £46 each
March	10 at £34 each	December	12 for £56 each
September	20 at £40 each		

4.2 For question 4.1 draw up the trading account for the year showing the gross profits that would have been reported using (*i*) FIFO, (*ii*) LIFO, (*iii*) AVCO methods.

4.3X From the following figures calculate the closing stock-in-trade that would be shown using (*i*) FIFO, (*ii*) LIFO, (*iii*) AVCO methods on a perpetual inventory basis.

Bought		Sold	
January	24 at £10 each	June	30 at £16 each
April	16 at £12.50 each	November	34 at £18 each
October	30 at £13 each		

4.4X Draw up trading accounts using each of the three methods from the details in question 4.3X.

4.5 The sixth formers at the Broadway School run a tuck shop business. They began trading on 1 December 20X9 and sell two types of chocolate bar, 'Break' and 'Brunch'.

Their starting capital was a £200 loan from the School Fund.

Transactions are for cash only.

Each Break costs the sixth form 16p and each Brunch costs 12p.

25% is added to the cost to determine the selling price.

Transactions during December are summarised as follows:

December 6	Bought 5 boxes, each containing 48 bars, of Break; and 3 boxes, each containing 36 bars, of Brunch.
December 20	The month's sales amounted to 200 Breaks and 90 Brunches.

(a) Record the above transactions in the cash, purchases and sales accounts. All calculations must be shown.

(b) On 20 December (the final day of term) a physical stocktaking showed 34 Break and 15 Brunch in stock. Using these figures calculate the value of the closing stock, and enter the amount in the stock account.

(c) Prepare a trading account for the tuck shop, calculating the gross profit/loss for the month of December 20X9.

(d) Calculate the number of each item that should have been in stock. Explain why this information should be a cause for concern.

(*London Qualifications Limited: GCE A-level*)

4.6 Thomas Brown and Partners, a firm of practising accountants, have several clients who are retail distributors of the Allgush Paint Spray guns.

The current price list of Gushing Sprayers Limited, manufacturers, quotes the following wholesale prices for the Allgush Paint Spray guns:

Grade A distributors	£500 each
Grade B distributors	£560 each
Grade C distributors	£600 each

The current normal retail price of the Allgush Paint Spray gun is £750.

Thomas Brown and Partners are currently advising some of their clients concerning the valuation of stock in trade of Allgush Paint Spray guns.

1 Charles Gray – Grade B distributor

On 30 April 20X9, 15 Allgush Paint Spray guns were in stock, including 1 gun which was slightly damaged and expected to sell at half the normal retail price. Charles Gray considers that this gun should remain in stock at cost price until it is sold.

K. Peacock, a customer of Charles Gray, was expected to purchase a spray gun on 30 April 20X9, but no agreement was reached owing to the customer being involved in a road accident and expected to remain in hospital until late May 20X9.

Charles Gray argues that he is entitled to regard this as a sale during the year ended 30 April 20X9.

2 Jean Kim – Grade C distributor

On 31 May 20X9, 22 Allgush Paint Spray guns were in stock. Unfortunately Jean Kim's business is suffering a serious cash flow crisis. It is very doubtful that the business will survive and therefore a public auction of the stock in trade is likely. Reliable sources suggest that the spray guns may be auctioned for £510 each; auction fees and expenses are expected to total £300.

Jean Kim has requested advice as to the basis upon which her stock should be valued at 31 May 20X9.

3 Peter Fox – Grade A distributor

Peter Fox now considers that stock valuations should be related to selling prices because of the growing uncertainties of the market for spray guns.

Alternatively, Peter Fox has suggested that he uses the cost prices applicable to Grade C distributors as the basis for stock valuations – 'after all this will establish consistency with Grade C distributors'.

Required:

A brief report to each of Charles Gray, Jean Kim and Peter Fox concerning the valuation of their stocks in trade.

Note: Answers should include references to appropriate accounting concepts.

(*Association of Accounting Technicians*)

4.7X Mary Smith commenced trading on 1 September 20X9 as a distributor of the Straight Cut garden lawn mower, a relatively new product which is now becoming increasingly popular.

Upon commencing trading, Mary Smith transferred £7,000 from her personal savings to open a business bank account.

Mary Smith's purchases and sales of the Straight Cut garden lawn mower during the three months ended 30 November 20X9 are as follows:

20X9	Bought	Sold
September	12 machines at £384 each	–
October	8 machines at £450 each	4 machines at £560 each
November	16 machines at £489 each	20 machines at £680 each

Assume all purchases are made in the first half of the month and all sales are in the second half of the month.

At the end of October 20X9, Mary Smith decided to take one Straight Cut garden lawn mower out of stock for cutting the lawn outside her showroom. It is estimated that this lawn mower will be used in Mary Smith's business for 8 years and have a nil estimated residual value. Mary Smith wishes to use the straight line basis of depreciation.

Additional information:
1 Overhead expenses paid during the three months ended 30 November 20X9 amounted to £1,520.
2 There were no amounts prepaid on 30 November 20X9, but sales commissions payable of $2\frac{1}{2}\%$ of the gross profit on sales were accrued due on 30 November 20X9.
3 Upon commencing trading, Mary Smith resigned a business appointment with a salary of £15,000 per annum.
4 Mary Smith is able to obtain interest of 10% per annum on her personal savings.
5 One of the lawn mowers not sold on 30 November 20X9 has been damaged in the show-room and is to be repaired in December 20X9 at a cost of £50 before being sold for an expected £400.

Note: Ignore taxation.

Required:
(a) Prepare, in as much detail as possible, Mary Smith's trading and profit and loss account for the quarter ended 30 November 20X9 using:
  (i) the first in first out basis of stock valuation, and
  (ii) the last in first out basis of stock valuation.
(b) Using the results in (a) (i) above, prepare a statement comparing Mary Smith's income for the quarter ended 30 November 20X9 with that for the quarter ended 31 August 20X9.
(c) Give one advantage and one disadvantage of each of the bases of stock valuations used in (a) above.

(Association of Accounting Technicians)

4.8 'The idea that stock should be included in accounts at the lower of historical cost and net realisable value follows the prudence convention but not the consistency convention.'

Required:
(a) Do you agree with the quotation?
(b) Explain, with reasons, whether you think this idea (that stocks should be included in accounts at the lower of historical cost and net realisable value) is a useful one. Refer to at least two classes of user of financial accounting reports in your answer.

(Association of Chartered Certified Accountants)

4.9X After stocktaking for the year ended 31 May 20X9 had taken place, the closing stock of Cobden Ltd was aggregated to a figure of £87,612.

During the course of the audit which followed, the undernoted facts were discovered:

(a) Some goods stored outside had been included at their normal cost price of £570. They had, however, deteriorated and would require an estimated £120 to be spent to restore them to their original condition, after which they could be sold for £800.

(b) Some goods had been damaged and were now unsaleable. They could, however, be sold for £110 as spares after repairs estimated at £40 had been carried out. They had originally cost £200.

(c) One stock sheet had been over-added by £126 and another under-added by £72.

(d) Cobden Ltd had received goods costing £2,010 during the last week of May 20X9 but, because the invoices did not arrive until June 20X9, they have not been included in stock.

(e) A stock sheet total of £1,234 had been transferred to the summary sheet as £1,243.

(f) Invoices totalling £638 arrived during the last week of May 20X9 (and were included in purchases and in creditors) but, because of transport delays, the goods did not arrive until late June 20X9 and were not included in closing stock.

(g) Portable generators on hire from another company at a charge of £347 were included, at this figure, in stock.

(h) Free samples sent to Cobden Ltd by various suppliers had been included in stock at the catalogue price of £63.

(i) Goods costing £418 sent to customers on a sale or return basis had been included in stock by Cobden Ltd at their selling price, £602.

(j) Goods sent on a sale or return basis to Cobden Ltd had been included in stock at the amount payable (£267) if retained. No decision to retain had been made.

Required:

Using such of the above information as is relevant, prepare a schedule amending the stock figure as at 31 May 20X9. State your reason for each amendment or for not making an amendment.

(*Association of Chartered Certified Accountants*)

4.10 The following information relates to the actual sales of Griffton Ltd during the last four months of its financial year.

	March	*April*	*May*	*June*
Quantity (units)	900	900	900	1,000
Price each	£55	£55	£55	£55

The budgeted information below relates to the next financial year commencing 1 July 20X2:

(i) The company forecasts that sales quantity will decrease in July by 10 per cent of the level in June. The reduced quantity will remain for August and September, but will then increase by 10 per cent in October, and remain fixed for the next three months.

The sales price will remain at £55 each until 1 September when it will be increased to £60 per unit, this price will be effective for a minimum of six months.

50 per cent of sales are on a cash basis and attract a 2 per cent cash discount, the remaining 50 per cent of sales are paid two months in arrears.

The company arranges its purchases of raw materials such that the closing stock at the end of each month exactly meets the requirement for the following month's sales. Each unit sold requires 2 kg of material at £15 per kg; this price is fixed until December 20X3.

(ii) As a separate exercise, the managing director asks for stock levels to be reviewed, and asks you about the use of Economic Order Quantities at some time in 20X3. The following budgeted data would apply to this exercise:

Material	2,000 kg per month
Price	£15 per kg
Stockholding costs	20% p.a. on average stock value
Ordering costs	£10 per order

Required:

From the budgeted information given in note (ii) calculate the Economic Order Quantity for the company. Briefly outline the limitations of this ordering method. *(4 marks)*

(OCR – University of Oxford Delegacy of Local Examinations: GCE A-level)

4.11 Nyree Chan owns a manufacturing business which produces light switches. She transfers the production cost of completed light switches to the business trading account at cost plus 20%.

Nyree provides you with the following information for the year ended 31 August 20X1.

	as at 1 September 20X0	as at 31 August 20X1
Stocks of finished goods at cost plus 20%	£32,400	£34,200

Provision for unrealised profit at 1 September 20X0 was £5,400.

Required:

(*a*) Calculate the adjustment to the provision for unrealised profit to be shown in the profit and loss account for the year ended 31 August 20X1. *(5 marks)*

(*b*) Prepare a balance sheet extract as at 31 August 20X1 showing how the provision for unrealised profit calculated in (*a*) should be treated. *(4 marks)*

(*c*) Explain why Nyree Chan makes a provision for unrealised profit in her final accounts.
(3 markrs)

(AQA: GCE A-level, Paper ACC3, Q2, 16/1/2002)

CHAPTER 5

Types of organisations and sources of finance

Learning objectives

By the end of this chapter, you should be able to:

- explain how limited companies differ from other forms of organisation;
- calculate how distributable profits available for dividends are divided between the different classes of shares;
- explain the differences between shares and debentures;
- describe a range of source of finance for companies, partnerships and sole traders;
- explain the advantages and disadvantages of each of a range of sources of finance for companies, partnerships and sole traders;
- prepare company profit and loss accounts for internal purposes;
- prepare company balance sheets for internal purposes.

5.1   Types of business ownership

We are going to focus on the three most common forms of business ownership:

1   **Sole traders.** You covered this type of ownership at length in your previous accounting studies. It is the type of ownership typified by the local independent newsagent and the local independent grocer shop. Other examples include jewellers and gift shops, as well as sole practitioner professionals, such as lawyers, accountants and dentists. Nowadays, there are far fewer businesses of this type than twenty or thirty years ago, partly because of the increase in large competitors and partly because of the financial risks in being a sole trader. However, they still represent a major form of business.

2   **Partnerships.** You covered this form of business in Chapter 3.

3   **Limited liability companies.** (More comonly, these are simply referred to as 'companies'.) You may have been introduced to this type of business and to its characteristics in your previous studies of accounting. If so, the next few pages will serve as a useful reminder before you look in detail at the financial statements they produce when you proceed to Chapter 6.

We shall return to sole traders and partnerships later in this chapter, when we review the alternative sources of finance available to each of these three types of business. Before doing so, let's look at the third type of business, companies, in some detail.

5.2 Companies

Limited companies came into existence originally because of the growth in the size of businesses, and the need to have a lot of people investing in the business who would not be able to take part in its management. Partnerships were not suitable for such businesses because:

● Normally they cannot have more than 20 partners, not counting limited partners.
● If a partnership business fails, partners could lose part, or all, of their private assets to pay the debts of the business.

The form of organisation which does not have these limitations is the limited liability company, normally known as the limited company. The law governing the preparation and publication of the final accounts of limited companies in the United Kingdom is contained in two Acts of Parliament. These are the Companies Acts of 1985 and 1989. Both Acts are in force for this purpose, the 1989 Act adding to and amending the 1985 Act.

Limited liability

The capital of a limited company is divided into **shares**. These can be shares of £1 each, £5 each, £10 each or any other amount per share. To become a member of a limited company, or a shareholder, a person must buy one or more of the shares.

If shareholders have paid in full for their shares, their liability is limited to what they have already paid for those shares. If a company loses all its assets, all those shareholders can lose is their shares. They cannot be forced to pay anything more in respect of the company's losses.

Shareholders who have only partly paid for their shares, can be forced to pay the balance owing on the shares, but nothing else.

This is known as limited liability and the company is known as a limited company. You can see that these limited companies meet the need for limited liability for their owners, and make it possible to have a large amount of capital invested in the company.

There are, in fact, a few companies which have unlimited liability, but these are outside the scope of this book.

Public and private companies

There are two classes of company, the public company and the private company. In the UK, private companies far outnumber public companies. In the Companies Acts, a public company is defined as one which fulfils the following conditions:

● Its memorandum states that it is a public company, and has registered as such.
● It has an authorised share capital of at least £50,000.
● Minimum membership is two. There is no maximum.
● Its name must end with the words 'public limited company' or the abbreviation 'plc'. It can have the Welsh equivalent if registered in Wales.

A private company is usually, but not always, a smaller business, and may be formed by one or more persons. It is defined by the Companies Act as a company which is not a public company. The main differences between a private company and a public company are that a private company:

- can have an authorised capital of less than £50,000;
- cannot offer its shares for subscription to the public at large, whereas public companies can;
- cannot use the term 'public limited company' or 'plc' in its name. Instead, it uses the single word 'Limited', often abbreviated to 'Ltd'.

This means that if you were to walk into a bank, or similar public place, and see a prospectus offering anyone the chance to take up shares in a company, then that company would be a public company.

The shares that are dealt in on the Stock Exchange are all of public limited companies. This does not mean that all public companies' shares are traded on the Stock Exchange, as, for various reasons, some public companies have either chosen not to, or not been allowed to, have their shares traded there. The ones whose shares are traded are known as 'quoted companies' meaning that their shares have prices quoted on the Stock Exchange. They have to comply with Stock Exchange requirements in addition to those laid down by the Companies Acts and accounting standards.

Directors of the company

The day-to-day business of a company is not carried out by the shareholders. The possession of a share normally confers voting rights on the holder, who is then able to attend general meetings of the company. At one of these, the shareholders will meet and will vote for **directors**, these being the people who will be entrusted with the running of the business. They are shareholders of the company and usually receive a salary. At each **Annual General Meeting** the directors will have to report on their stewardship, and this directors' report is accompanied by a set of financial statements for the year – the 'annual report'. (The directors' report is discussed in the next chapter.)

Auditors

Auditors perform the role of overseeing the quality of the financial statements. In contrast to directors, they are neither shareholders nor employees of the companies they audit. They report to the Annual General Meeting and their duties lie to the shareholders, not to the directors. (The audit report is discussed in the next chapter.)

Contrary to what most of the public think, auditors do not guarantee to discover any fraud that may have occurred. That is not what the audit is for. As a result of financial scandals including Enron, WorldCom, the Maxwell affair, the BCCI bank, Polly Peck and Barlow Clowes there has been continuous and continually growing pressure exerted upon the accounting profession to reconsider its position regarding the discovery of fraud when auditing the financial statements of a company.

Legal status of a limited company

A limited company is said to possess a 'separate legal identity' from that of its shareholders. Put simply, this means that a company is not seen as being exactly the same as its shareholders. For instance, a company can sue one or more of its shareholders, and similarly, a shareholder can sue the company. This would not be the case if the company and its shareholders were exactly the same thing, as one cannot sue oneself.

5.3	Long-term sources of finance

There are three major long-term sources of capital:

1 Share capital
2 Debentures
3 **Other loans, including bank loans and mortgages**

Companies have access to all three but, partnerships and sole traders have no share capital and they cannot issue debentures.

1 Share capital

Share capital comprises shares in the company. Holders of share capital own a part of the company. When companies are performing poorly, with few exceptions, they need pay nothing to the holders of share capital. As such, this source of finance represents a low level of risk to companies when they are not performing well – they cannot be forced out of business for failing to pay a dividend. In addition, a shareholder cannot force a company to buy back its shares.

Shares can normally only be sold on the stock market. As a result, companies do not need to worry about having to repay investors. Because of the risk being accepted by any shareholder (that the company may not perform well and may not pay any dividends), companies need to pay a dividend that compensates for that risk whenever they are doing reasonably well. Otherwise, no one would buy the company's shares.

When we talk about share capital, we tend to mean the amount of shares issued by a company and held by its shareholders. However, the term 'share capital' can have any of the following meanings:

1 **Authorised share capital.** Sometimes known as registered capital or nominal capital. This is the total of the share capital which the company is allowed to issue to shareholders.
2 **Issued share capital.** This is the total of the share capital actually issued to shareholders.

If all of the authorised share capital has been issued, then 1 and 2 above would be the same amount.

3 **Called-up capital.** Where only part of the amounts payable on each share has been asked for, the total amount asked for on all the shares is known as the called-up capital.
4 **Uncalled capital.** This is the total amount which is to be received in future, but which has not yet been asked for.
5 **Calls in arrears.** The total amount for which payment has been asked (i.e. called for), but has not yet been paid by shareholders.
6 **Paid-up capital.** This is the total of the amount of share capital which has been paid for by shareholders.

Exhibit 5.1 illustrates these different meanings.

EXHIBIT 5.1

1 Better Enterprises Ltd was formed with the legal right to be able to issue 100,000 shares of £1 each.
2 The company has actually issued 75,000 shares.

3 None of the shares has yet been fully paid up. So far the company has made calls of 80p (£0.80) per share.

4 All the calls have been paid by shareholders except for £200 owing from one shareholder.

    (a) Authorised or nominal share capital is: 1 £100,000.
    (b) Issued share capital is: 2 £75,000.
    (c) Called-up capital is: 3 $75,000 \times £0.80 = £60,000$.
    (d) Calls in arrear amounted to: 4 £200.
    (e) Paid-up capital is: (c) £60,000 *less* (d) £200 = £59,800.

Forms of share capital

There are two principal forms of share capital – **ordinary shares** and **preference shares**. Both are issued in the same way and both reward their holders through a share of the profits, known as a **dividend**. However, the manner in which the amount of dividend received by each of the two groups of shareholders is determined differs. Preference shareholders get a fixed percentage rate of dividend. That is all they can receive, no matter how well the company is performing. They get paid their dividend before the ordinary shareholders receive anything. The rest of the amount available for dividend then passes to the ordinary shareholders.

The amount to be paid out in dividends is determined by the directors. Anything not paid out in this way is retained in the business. Such matters as government directives to reduce dividends, the effect of taxation, the availability of bank balances to pay the dividends and the possibility of takeover bids will all be taken into account in coming to this decision.

The dividend is usually expressed as a percentage. Ignoring income tax, a dividend of 10 per cent in Firm A on 500,000 Ordinary Shares of £1 each will amount to £50,000, or a dividend of 6 per cent in Firm B on 200,000 Ordinary Shares of £2 each will amount to £24,000. A shareholder having 100 shares in each firm would receive £10 from Firm A and £12 from Firm B.

For example, if a company had 10,000 5 per cent preference shares of £1 each and 20,000 ordinary shares of £1 each, then the dividends would be payable as in Exhibit 5.2.

EXHIBIT 5.2

Year	1	2	3	4	5
	£	£	£	£	£
Profits appropriated for dividends	900	1,300	1,600	3,100	2,000
Preference dividends (5%)	500	500	500	500	500
Ordinary dividends	(2%) 400	(4%) 800	(5½%) 1,100	(13%) 2,600	(7½%) 1,500

The two main types of preference shares are:

1 Non-cumulative preference shares

These can receive a dividend up to an agreed percentage each year. If the amount paid is less than the maximum agreed amount, the shortfall is lost by the shareholder. The shortfall cannot be carried forward and paid in a future year.

2 Cumulative preference shares

These also have an agreed maximum percentage dividend. However, any shortfall of dividend paid in a year can be carried forward. These arrears of preference dividends will have to be paid before the ordinary shareholders receive anything.

EXHIBIT 5.3

A company has 5,000 £1 ordinary shares and 2,000 5 per cent non-cumulative preference shares of £1 each. The profits available for dividends are: year 1 £150, year 2 £80, year 3 £250, year 4 £60, year 5 £500.

Year	1	2	3	4	5
	£	£	£	£	£
Profits	150	80	250	60	500
Preference dividend (non-cumulative)					
(limited in years 2 and 4)	100	80	100	60	100
Dividends on ordinary shares	50	–	150	–	400

EXHIBIT 5.4

Assume that the preference shares in Exhibit 5.3 had been cumulative. The dividends would have been:

Year	1	2	3	4	5
	£	£	£	£	£
Profits	150	80	250	60	500
Preference dividend	100	80	120*	60	140*
Dividends on ordinary shares	50	–	130	–	360

* including arrears.

2 Debentures

The term debenture is used when a limited company receives money on loan and, in return, issues certificates called 'debentures' to the lender. Interest will be paid to the holder, the rate of interest being shown on the certificate. Instead of always being called debentures they are often known as 'loan stock' or 'loan capital'.

Debenture interest has to be paid whether profits are made or not. They are, therefore, different from shares, where dividends depend on profits being made. This makes debentures a higher risk source of finance than share capital, especially when a company is performing badly – companies can be forced out of business for failing to pay interest on their debentures. However, when a company is performing well, debentures can be a far cheaper source of finance than share capital (as the amount paid to debenture holders is the same no matter how much profit a company is making).

A debenture may be either:

● Redeemable, i.e. repayable at or by a particular date, or
● Irredeemable, normally repayable only when the company is officially terminated, known as liquidation.

If a date is shown behind a debenture, e.g. 2001/2008, it means that the company can redeem it during the period shown, e.g. during any of the years 2001 to 2008 inclusive.

People lending money to companies in the form of debentures will be interested in how safe their investment will be. Some debentures are given the legal right that on certain happenings the debenture holders will be able to take control of specific assets, or of the whole of the assets. They can then sell the assets and recoup the amount due under their debentures, or deal with the assets in ways specified in the deed under which the debentures were issued. Such debentures are known as being '**secured**' against the assets, the term 'mortgage' debenture often being used. Other debentures have no prior right to control the assets under any circumstances. These are known as **simple** or **naked** debentures.

3 Other loans

Any business, whether it be a company, a partnership or a sole trader, may have other sources of long-term finance in the form of loans from banks and other financial institutions. These would normally be secured on the assets of the business and may require that the lender has some say in the running of the business. For companies, this form of finance is often of higher risk than debentures, as the penalties that can form part of the loan agreement are liable to be far more severe than those that can be set in motion by aggrieved debenture holders.

For sole traders and partnerships this is the cheapest source of capital other than reinvestment of profits and low interest bearing loans from the owner or a partner. However, as with companies, it carries a significant risk if the business fails to perform well and the lender chooses to exercise whatever rights are written into the loan concerning failure to make payments of interest when due.

Some companies have another source of long-term loans. When a company is part of a group, long-term loans may be granted by other companies within the group. This probably carries the lowest level of risk to the company of all the alternative sources of long-term finance. However, this form of long-term finance may arise as a result of a takeover of the company and could, therefore, indicate that the company has already surrendered a significant element of, if not all of its independence.

5.4 Other sources of finance

Among other sources of finance are:

- **Government aid** – typically in the form of grants relating to the form of expenditure, such as the purchase of fixed assets; or relating to the nature of the activities of or size of the business.
- **Hire purchase** – enables use of a fixed asset during the period it is being paid for. In exchange for use of the asset (e.g. a vehicle or a machine), the business pays the supplier the price of the asset plus interest. Over the term of the hire purchase agreement, the buyer may pay twice or more times the amount in interest that would have been paid had a bank loan been obtained instead. At the end of the hire purchase period, the buyer has an option to take over the ownership of the asset, normally for a nominal sum. This is a relatively expensive way to fund asset purchase, but it has the benefit of enabling businesses to use an asset at times when banks and other lenders may be unwilling to lend the funds required to buy it.
- **Leasing** – enables use of an asset without any of the problems of ownership. The apparent cost may not be very different from that relating to hire purchase, but all the costs can be charged to profit and loss rather than, in the case of hire purchase, having to be included in the total asset value in the balance sheet. This may have considerable tax advantages for the buyer. Very rigid rules are applied through accounting standards to determine whether a lease agreement is actually a hire purchase agreement in disguise.

- **Sale and lease back** – an arrangement whereby a business sells a fixed asset, such as a building or some equipment, to another entity and immediately leases it back for a long period of time. This has the advantage that a significant amount of funds may be received immediately. It has two disadvantages. First, the lease rental must be paid when due and, secondly, when the lease expires, the holder of the asset may decline to renew it, resulting in the original holder of the asset having to fund the acquisition of a replacement.
- **Mortgages** – a source of finance for sole traders and partnerships whereby the home of the owner or a partner is mortgaged and the funds received are invested in the business. It has a similar advantage to sale and lease back, a significant amount of funds may be received immediately. It also has the advantage that, provided all payments are made to the lender, the house will revert to the ownership of the mortgagee at the end of the mortgage term. However, not only do interest payments have to be made, but the capital lent must also be repaid and, if the business runs into serious financial difficulties, the mortgagee may not only lose the business but the home as well.

Learning outcomes

You should now have learnt:

1 What is meant by the term 'limited liability'.

2 The difference between public and private companies.

3 The difference between ordinary shares and preference shares.

4 How dividends are calculated.

5 The difference between shares and debentures.

6 How to prepare company profit and loss accounts for internal purposes.

7 How to prepare company balance sheets for internal purposes.

REVIEW QUESTIONS

5.1 The chairman of a public limited company has written his annual report to the shareholders, extracts of which are quoted below.

Extract 1

'In May 20X6, in order to provide a basis for more efficient operations, we acquired PAG Warehousing and Transport Ltd. The agreed valuation of the net tangible assets acquired was £1.4 million. The purchase consideration, £1.7 million, was satisfied by an issue of 6.4 million equity shares, of £0.25 per share, to PAG's shareholders. These shares do not rank for dividend until 20X7.'

Extract 2

'As a measure of confidence in our ability to expand operations in 20X7 and 20X8, and to provide the necessary financial base, we issued £0.5 million 8% Redeemable Debenture Stock, 2000/2007, 20 million 6% £1 Redeemable Preference Shares and 4 million £1 equity shares. The opportunity was also taken to redeem the whole of the 5 million 11% £1 Redeemable Preference Shares.'

Required:

Answer the following questions on the above extracts.

Extract 1

(*a*) What does the difference of £0.3 million between the purchase consideration (£1.7m) and the net tangible assets value (£1.4m) represent?

(*b*) What does the difference of £0.1 million between the purchase consideration (£1.7m) and the nominal value of the equity shares (£1.6m) represent?

(*c*) What is the meaning of the term 'equity shares'?

(*d*) What is the meaning of the phrase 'do not rank for dividend'?

Extract 2

(*e*) In the description of the debenture stock issue, what is the significance of
  (*i*) 8%?
  (*ii*) 2000/2007?

(*f*) In the description of the preference share issue, what is the significance of
  (*i*) 6%?
  (*ii*) Redeemable?

(*g*) What is the most likely explanation for the company to have redeemed existing preference shares but at the same time to have issued others?

(*h*) What effect will these structural changes have had on the gearing of the company?*

(*j*) Contrast the accounting treatment, in the company's profit and loss accounts, of the interest due on the debentures with dividends proposed on the equity shares.

(*k*) Explain the reasons for the different treatments you have outlined in your answer to (*j*) above.

(*Association of Chartered Certified Accountants*)

* This part of the question is covered in the text in Chapter 8.

5.2   Explain what you understand by the accounting term 'debentures' and indicate the circumstances under which a debenture issue would or would not be an appropriate form of financing.

(*Scottish Qualifications Authority*)

Part 2

PUBLISHED FINANCIAL STATEMENTS OF LIMITED COMPANIES AND ACCOUNTING STANDARDS

6 Published financial statements and requirements of user groups

7 Reserves, bonus issues and rights issues

8 Published financial statements and ratio analysis

9 Cash flow statements

10 Accounting standards

11 Limitations of published financial statements

Published financial statements and requirements of user groups

Learning objectives

By the end of this chapter, you should be able to:

- describe and distinguish between the two functions of acccounting – the management function and the stewardship function;
- explain the differences in content between the financial statements of sole traders, partnerships, and companies;
- prepare the trading and profit and loss accounts for a company for internal purposes;
- prepare the balance sheet for a company for internal purposes;
- demonstrate a knowledge of the corporate report requirements of different user groups;
- explain the need for notes to the accounts concerning accounting policies, fixed assets, capital structure, directors' remunerations, employees' remuneration, debtors and creditors;
- identify the main elements of annual reports;
- explain why limited companies are required to publish their financial statements;
- describe and explain the contents of the published financial statements of a limited company;
- describe the content of the directors' report;
- describe the content of the auditor's report;
- distinguish between the duties of the auditors and the directors.

6.1 The functions of accounting

Accounting information is used to assist two main functions, management and stewardship. You will be looking at the major forms of accounting information that fulfil a management function in Part 3, *Further aspects of accounting for management and decision making*. However, the accounting information you will be learning about in that section of this book forms the major part of the branch of accounting known as 'management accounting'.

So far as the management and stewardship functions of accounting are concerned, management accounting provides most of the accounting information to assist management – i.e. the accounting information used in decision making by managers within an organisation.

Financial accounting, on the other hand, while it does provide some accounting information to assist management, provides much of the accounting information used to assist in stewardship – i.e. the overall running of an organisation by its senior management who, in the case of a company, are the directors of that company. It is the duty of the directors to steward or guide the company so that the returns achieved from its resources are at a level that is acceptable to its shareholders.

To that end, the contents of the financial statements are viewed as being very clear indicators of the success or otherwise of the directors in their fulfilment of their stewardship responsibilities. The profits shown, the financial position and the generation and use of cash as reported in the financial statements are fundamental examples of how accounting performs its stewardship function.

By producing those statements, accounting enables the owners of the company to assess the effectiveness of the stewardship of the company during the period they report upon. As they are of such importance, companies are required to produce their financial statements annually and submit them to the Registrar of Companies. They must also present them to their shareholders at a general meeting (the 'annual general meeting'). They must do both within seven months of the end of the company's financial year, unless it is a private company, in which case they must do so within 10 months rather than seven.

Nevertheless, although financial accounting produces information principally for stewardship, some of that information is also relevant and of use for the management of the organisation. The published profit and loss account and balance sheet are examples of accounting information produced to assist in an assessment of stewardship that can be rewritten so as to be of direct use for management.

Prior to the UK Companies Act 1981, a company could, provided it disclosed the necessary information, draw up its balance sheet and profit and loss account for publication in any way that it wished. As a result, many companies simply provided the same profit and loss account and balance sheet for external use as they prepared for management. The 1981 Act, however, stopped such freedom of display, and laid down the precise details to be shown. These were repeated in the Companies Acts of 1985 and 1989.

As a result, some companies produce two forms of profit and loss and balance sheet: the published versions and the versions for internal use. There are two major differences between these two versions.

First, the internal profit and loss accounts and balance sheets may be far more detailed than the summary versions required when they are prepared for publication.

Secondly, there are no rules concerning how the internal versions are presented, nor any concerning how any of the figures are calculated – accounting standards (which must be observed when preparing financial statements for publication) do not apply to internal reports. Nevertheless, it would be very unusual for companies to use different bases for the preparation of internal profit and loss accounts and balance sheets from those they adopt when preparing the external versions of these statements.

These *internal* profit and loss accounts and balance sheets are very similar to those produced for sole traders and partnerships. From them, managers are able to see such things as the amount spent on individual expense items, such as wages, energy and fuel and, in the balance sheet, such things as how much depreciation has been charged against each class of fixed asset and the book value of the company. However, they typically contain some additional items that do not appear in the financial statements of sole traders and partnerships. The next two sections describes these additional items.

6.2 Company trading and profit and loss account differences

The trading and profit and loss accounts for both private and public companies are drawn up in exactly the same way.

The trading account of a limited company is no different from that of a sole trader or a partnership. However, some differences may be found in the profit and loss account. Interest on drawings and interest on capital do not appear in company profit and loss accounts. The two main expenses that would be found only in company accounts are directors' remuneration and debenture interest.

1 **Directors' remuneration.** As directors exist only in companies, this type of expense is found only in company accounts.

   Directors are legally employees of the company, appointed by the shareholders. Their remuneration is charged to the profit and loss account.

2 **Debenture interest.** The interest payable for the use of the funds raised from issuing debentures is an expense of the company, and is payable whether profits are made or not. This means that debenture interest is charged as an expense in the profit and loss account itself. Contrast this with dividends which are dependent on profits having been made.

Another item that appears in company profit and loss accounts but not in sole trader accounts, and not in the same form in partnership accounts, is an appropriation account.

The appropriation account

Below the profit and loss account is a section called the profit and loss appropriation account. As with partnerships, the appropriation account of companies shows how the net profits are to be appropriated, i.e. how the profits are to be used.

You may find any of the following in the appropriation account:

Items that increase the balance

1 **Net profit for the year.** This is the net profit brought down from the main profit and loss account.

2 **Balance brought forward from last year.** As you will see, some of the profits may not be appropriated during a period. If so, they are described as retained profits. The total of retained profits at the start of a period is shown in the appropriation account as the balance brought forward from the previous year.

Items that reduce the balance

3 **Transfers to reserves.** The directors may decide that some of the profits should not be included in the calculation of how much should be paid out as dividends. These profits are transferred to **reserve accounts**.

   There may be a specific reason for the transfer such as a need to replace fixed assets. In this case an amount would be transferred to a fixed assets replacement reserve.

   Or the reason may not be specific. In this case an amount would be transferred to a general reserve account.

4 **Amounts written off as goodwill.** Goodwill may require to be amortised (which is the intangible fixed asset equivalent of depreciation). When this is done, the amount written off should be shown in the appropriation account, **not** in the main profit and loss account.

5 **Preliminary expenses.** When a company is formed, there are many kinds of expenses concerned with its formation. These include, for example, legal expenses and various government taxes. They cannot be shown as an asset in the balance sheet, but can be charged to the appropriation account.

6 **Taxation payable on profits.** At this point in your studies you do not need to know very much about taxation. However, it does affect the preparation of accounts, and so we will tell you here as much as you need to know now. Sole traders and partnerships pay income tax based on their profits. Such income tax, when paid out of the business bank account, is simply charged as drawings – it is not an expense.

   In the case of companies, the taxation levied upon them is called **corporation tax**. It is also based on the amount of profits made. At this point in your accounting studies, you will be told how much it is, or be given a simple arithmetical way of ascertaining the amount.

   Corporation tax is *not* an expense, it is an appropriation of profits. This was established by two legal cases many years ago. However, for the sake of presentation and to make the accounts more understandable to the general reader, it is not shown with the other appropriations. Instead, as in Exhibit 6.1, it is shown as a deduction from profit for the year before taxation (i.e. this is the net profit figure) to show the net result, i.e. profit for the year after taxation.

7 **Dividends.** Out of the remainder of the profits the directors propose what dividends should be paid.

8 **Balance carried forward to next year.** After the dividends have been proposed there will probably be some profits that have not been appropriated. These retained profits will be carried forward within the profit and loss account (which is one of the reserve accounts in the ledger and is not to be confused with the profit and loss account financial statement) to the following year.

Exhibit 6.1 shows the profit and loss appropriation account of a new business for its first three years of trading.

EXHIBIT 6.1

IDC Ltd has an ordinary share capital of 40,000 ordinary shares of £1 each and 20,000 5 per cent preference shares of £1 each.

● The net profits for the first three years of business ended 31 December are: 20X4, £10,967; 20X5, £14,864; and 20X6, £15,822.
● Transfers to reserves are made as follows: 20X4, nil; 20X5, general reserve, £1,000; and 20X6, fixed assets replacement reserve, £2,250.
● Dividends were proposed for each year on the preference shares at 5 per cent and on the ordinary shares at: 20X4, 10 per cent; 20X5, 12.5 per cent; 20X6, 15 per cent.
● Corporation tax, based on the net profits of each year, is 20X4 £4,100; 20X5 £5,250; 20X6 £6,300.

IDC Ltd
Profit and Loss Appropriation Accounts
(1) For the year ended 31 December 20X4

	£	£
Profit for the year before taxation		10,967
Less Corporation tax		(4,100)
Profit for the year after taxation		6,867
Less Proposed dividends:		
Preference dividend of 5%	1,000	
Ordinary dividend of 10%	4,000	
		(5,000)
Retained profits carried forward to next year		1,867

(2) For the year ended 31 December 20X5

	£	£	£
Profit for the year before taxation			14,864
Less Corporation tax			(5,250)
Profit for the year after taxation			9,614
Add Retained profits from last year			1,867
			11,481
Less Transfer to general reserve		1,000	
Proposed dividends:			
Preference dividend of 5%	1,000		
Ordinary dividend of 12$\frac{1}{2}$%	5,000		
		6,000	(7,000)
Retained profits carried forward to next year			4,481

(3) For the year ended 31 December 20X6

	£	£	£
Profit for the year before taxation			15,822
Less Corporation tax			(6,300)
Profit for the year after taxation			9,522
Add Retained profits from last year			4,481
			14,003
Less Transfer to fixed assets replacement reserve		2,250	
Proposed dividends:			
Preference dividend of 5%	1,000		
Ordinary dividend of 15%	6,000		
		7,000	
			(9,250)
Retained profits carried forward to next year			4,753

In the balance sheet, corporation tax owing can normally be found as a current liability.

6.3 Company balance sheet differences

Corporation tax will often appear as a separate item in company balance sheets, virtually always as a creditor, as will dividends payable to shareholders. In addition, a new section replaces the capital section of the balance sheet. This section contains details of the issued share capital and the reserves. For obvious reasons, (partners') current accounts do not appear in company balance sheets. Company balances sheets also contain notes explaining some of the figures. These are a set of statements, some compulsory under the Companies Act and some voluntary or only required when it is appropriate to do so, that, when combined with the relevant figure(s) presented in the financial statements, provide an improved true and fair view. The notes required by the Companies Act are covered later in this chapter.

Notes to the accounts

Among those items for which notes may be needed are:

(*i*) **Accounting policies**

The accounting policies adopted when the financial statements were prepared must be described in notes, either notes relating to the item in question, such as stock, or in a separate note concerning accounting policies. This is so that any user of the information contained in the financial statements is in a position to understand the bases underlying the figures being presented, thereby making realistic analysis and comparison possible.

(*ii*) **Fixed assets**

Details of the opening cost and depreciation amounts for each class of asset, along with details of acquisitions and disposals, and the depreciation charged during the period may all be included in a note. Also, if any fixed assets are revalued during the period, details of the basis of valuation or the qualification of the person who conducted the valuation will be given in a note. If any of the fixed assets are secured by creditors (against the possibility of the company failing to honour its debts) this may be disclosed in a note. Any information about fixed assets disclosed in a note is provided in order to enable the user of the information to better assess the worth of the fixed assets.

(*iii*) **Capital structure**

The authorised share capital, where it is different from the issued share capital, is shown as a note. This reveals how much additional capital the company is currently authorised to raise.

(*i*) **Creditors**

Where a detailed breakdown is omitted from the balance sheet, a note will be included breaking down the creditors figures shown in current liabilities into the Companies Act categories, such as trade creditors, accruals and overdrafts. When the true and fair view is enhanced by doing so, these categories may be further broken down in the note. For example, the 'other creditors including taxation and social security' category may be broken down into dividends proposed and corporation tax.

(*ii*) **Debtors**

Where a detailed breakdown is omitted from the balance sheet, a note will be included breaking down the debtors figure into the Companies Act categories, such as trade debtors and prepayments. Similarly to creditors, these categories may be further broken down if it enhances the true and fair view.

(*iii*) **Stock**

Where a detailed breakdown is omitted from the balance sheet, a note will be included showing the breakdown of the balance sheet stock figure between the various categories – raw materials and consumables, work in progress, finished goods and goods for resale and payments on account.

6.4 Users of published financial statements and their needs

When accounting information is used to produce financial statements, it is important to remember why they are being prepared and why the information is being presented in the format adopted. At the end of the day, the reason is that it is done in order to meet the needs of the users of the accounting information. You have already heard of how one version of the financial statements may be prepared for internal use and another for external use. Let's consider who these external users are, and what their interests are in the financial statements.

Users of financial statements

The main users of published financial statements are:

1 **Shareholders of the company,** both existing and potential. As you've already learnt, they want to know how effectively the directors are performing their steward-ship function. They will use the financial statements as a base for decisions to dispose of some or all of their shares, or to buy some.

2 **The loan stockholder group.** This consists of existing and potential debenture and loan stock holders, and providers of short-term secured funds. They will want to ensure that interest payments will be made promptly and capital repayments will be made as agreed. Debenture and loan stock holders, whether redeemable or irre-deemable, will also want to be able to assess how easily they may dispose of their debentures or loan stocks, should they so wish.

3 **Employee groups,** including existing, potential and past employees. These can include trade unions whose members are employees. Past employees will be mainly concerned with ensuring that any pensions, etc., paid by the company are main-tained. Present employees will be interested in ensuring that the company is able to keep on operating, so maintaining their jobs and paying them acceptable wages, and that any pension contributions are maintained. In addition, they may want to ensure that the company is being fair to them, so that they get a reasonable share of the profits accruing to the firm from their efforts. Trade unions will be upholding the interests of their members, and will possibly use the financial statements in wage and pension negotiations. Potential employees will be interested in assessing whether or not it would be worth seeking employment with the company.

4 **Bankers.** Where the bank has not given a loan or granted an overdraft, there will be no great need to see the financial statements. Where money is owed to the banks, they will want to ensure that payments of interest will be made when due, and that the company will be able to repay the loan or overdraft at the correct time.

5 **The business contact group.** This includes trade creditors and suppliers, who will want to know whether or not they will continue to be paid, and the prospects for a profitable future association. Customers are included, since they will want to know whether or not the company is a secure source of supply. Business rivals in this group will be trying to assess their own position compared with the reporting com-pany. Potential takeover bidders, or those interested in a merger, will want to assess the desirability of any such move.

6 **The analyst/adviser group.** These will need information for their clients or their readers. Financial journalists need information for their readers. Stockbrokers need it

to advise investors. Credit agencies want it to be able to advise present and potential suppliers of goods and services to the company as to its creditworthiness.

7 **The Inland Revenue** will need the financial statements to assess the tax payable by the company.

8 **Other official agencies.** Various organisations concerned with the supervision of industry and commerce may want the financial statements for their purposes.

9 **Management.** As you have already learnt, in addition to the internally produced management accounts, the management is also vitally concerned with any published financial statements. It has to consider the effect of such published financial statements on the world at large.

10 **The public.** This consists of groups such as taxpayers, political parties, pressure groups and consumers. The needs of these parties will vary accordingly. They could include such things as information concerning the ethical practices of the company and its position regarding the maintenance of the environment.

Apart from containing the information a particular user group seeks, whether the information presented in the financial statements is helpful to any of these user groups depends upon the information actually being 'useful'.

Characteristics of useful information

From various reports which have appeared since 1975, the following characteristics of useful information have been noted. Published financial statements that fail to exhibit one or more of these characteristics will be of limited use to the various user groups.

1 **Relevance.** This is regarded as one of the two main qualities. The information supplied should be that which will satisfy the needs of its users.

2 **Reliability.** This is regarded as the other main quality. Obviously, if such information is also subject to an independent check, such as that of the auditor, this will considerably enhance the reliance people can place on the information.

3 **Objectivity.** Information which is free from bias will increase the reliance people place on it. It is, therefore, essential that the information is prepared as objectively as possible. Management may often tend to give a better picture of its own performance than is warranted, and is therefore subjective. It is the auditor's task to counter this view, and to ensure objectivity in the financial statements.

4 **Ability to be understood.** Information is not much use to a recipient if it is presented in such a manner that no one can understand it. This is not necessarily the same as simplicity.

5 **Comparability.** Recipients of financial statements will want to compare them both with previous financial statements of that company and with the results of other companies; without comparability the financial statements would be of little use.

6 **Realism.** This can be largely covered by the fact that financial statements should show a 'true and fair' view. It has also been contended that financial statements should not give a sense of absolute precision when such precision cannot exist.

7 **Consistency.** This is one of the basic concepts, but it is not to be followed slavishly if new and improved accounting techniques indicate a change in methods.

8 **Timeliness.** Up-to-date information is of more use to recipients than outdated news.

9 **Economy of presentation.** Too much detail can obscure the important factors in financial statements and cause difficulties in understanding them.

10 **Completeness.** A rounded picture of the company's activities is needed.

Problems of information production in accounting

All the user groups have differing needs and priorities relating to the information that they seek to obtain from the published financial statements. We have already considered the differing needs of the management versus the needs of the outside world. In an ideal world, specific financial reports would be produced, not just for the company management, but for each group of users, tailored to their special needs.

However, we have not arrived at a level of sophistication in our reporting capabilities that is sufficient to support such a range of report production. There are occassions when companies do produce special reports for certain groups of users. A bank, for instance, will almost certainly want to see a forecast of future cash flows before granting a loan or overdraft. The Inland Revenue will often require various analyses in order to agree the tax position. Some companies produce special reports for the use of their employees. However, such extra reports are a very small sub-set of the reports which could be issued and would be produced were a report to be produced for every user group.

Of course, producing reports is not costless. Even if we could produce a complete range of customised reports, exactly tailored to every possible group of users, it would be an extremely costly and time-consuming process. It is hardly likely that any company at present would wish to do so. There is, however, no doubt that this is the way things are moving and will continue to move.

As a result, most companies produce one set of financial statements for all the possible external users. Not surprisingly, they are multi-purpose documents very much geared to the needs of the primary stakeholder – the shareholder – while, at the same time, designed and regulated so as to provide as much of the information as possible that is sought by the remaining wide range of user groups. Obviously such a multi-purpose document cannot satisfy all the users. In fact, it will almost certainly not fully satisfy the needs of any one user group – save that it must satisfy the legal requirements of the Companies Act and comply with accounting standards.

Published financial statements are, therefore, a compromise between the requirements of users and the maintenance of accounting concepts, subject to the overriding scrutiny of the auditor. Judgement has a major impact on the information presented. It can be said that if two large companies operating in the same industry and in the same location had identical share capitals, liabilities, numbers of employees, assets, turnover, costs, transactions and so on, the published financial statements of the two companies would not be identical. Differences would arise for a number of reasons. For example, depreciation methods and policies may vary, as may stock valuation assessments, doubtful debt provisions, figures for revaluation of properties, etc. There will also probably be rather more subtle distinctions, many of which you will come across in the later stages of your studies.

Let's now consider some features of published financial statements that are intended to widen as far as possible the range of user groups who will find them useful.

6.5 Aspects of company financial statements for external use

True and fair view

When the financial statements of a company are published for external use, no one, neither the directors nor the auditors, ever states that 'the financial statements are correct'. This is because, in the preparation of company financial statements, many subjective estimates and judgements affect the figures. The valuation of stock, or the estimates of depreciation, cannot be said to be 'correct', just as it is impossible to say that the provision for doubtful debts is 'correct'. Only time will tell whether these estimates and judgements will turn out to have been 'correct'.

The expression that is used is that, in the opinion of the auditors, the financial statements give a *'true and fair view'* of the state of affairs and financial performance of the company.

Notes to the accounts

For internal use, companies would normally include notes showing details of items of key interest to management, such as fixed assets, stock, debtors and creditors.

When publishing financial statements for external use, companies may include as many notes as they wish to accompany them, including those mentioned above. They must include a statement concerning the accounting policies they have adopted and there are some notes that the Companies Acts require to be included:

1 Particulars of turnover

An analysis of turnover into:

(*a*) each class of business; and by
(*b*) geographical markets;

and, in addition, the amount of profit or loss before taxation, in the opinion of the directors, attributable to each class of business.

Such disclosure does not have to be made if it would be prejudicial to the business of the company. The fact of non-disclosure would have to be stated. An example of such a note might be as in Exhibit 6.2.

EXHIBIT 6.2

Analysis of turnover

	Turnover £	Profit £
Motors	26,550,000	2,310,000
Aircraft	58,915,000	4,116,000
	85,465,000	6,426,000

The geographical division of turnover is:

	£
UK	31,150,000
The Americas	43,025,000
Rest of the World	10,290,000
	84,465,000

It should be noted that these requirements were extended by SSAP 25, *Segmental reporting*, but only for:

- plcs or parent undertakings that have one or more plcs as a subsidiary;
- banking and insurance companies or groups;
- private companies and other entities that exceed the criteria, multiplied in each case by ten, for defining a medium-sized company under section 247 of the Companies Act 1985. (**Currently, a 'small' company is one for which two of the following are true for the financial year in question and the year that preceded it: turnover does not exceed £2.8 million; the balance sheet total does not exceed £1.4 million; the average number of employees does not exceed 50. For 'medium-sized' companies, the equivalent limits are £11.2 million, £5.6 million and 250 employees.**)

It requires that for each segment, turnover (analysed between sales to external customers and sales between segments), results and net assets should be disclosed. Geographical segmental analysis should, in the first instance, be on the basis of source (i.e. the geographical location of the supplying segment). In addition, turnover to third parties should be segmentally reported on the basis of destination (i.e. the geographical location of the receiving segment).

Where associated undertakings (companies in which the reporting company has a controlling interest) account for at least 20 per cent of the total results or net assets of the reporting entity, additional disclosure should be made in aggregate for all associated undertakings. This comprises segmental disclosure of the reporting entity's share of the aggregate profits or losses before tax, minority interests and extraordinary items of the associated undertakings, and the reporting entity's share of the net assets of the associated undertakings (including goodwill to the extent that it has not been written off) after attributing, where possible, fair values to the net assets at the date of acquisition of the interest in each associated undertaking.

2 Particulars of staff

(*a*) Average number employed by the company (or by the group in consolidated accounts), divided between categories of workers, e.g. between manufacturing and administration.

(*b*) (*i*) Wages and salaries paid to staff.
   (*ii*) Social security costs of staff.
   (*iii*) Other pension costs for employees.

(*c*) Number of employees (excluding those working wholly or mainly overseas) earning over £30,000. This is analysed under successive multiples of £5,000. Pension contributions are excluded.

Exhibit 6.3 is an example of a note concerning higher-paid employees.

EXHIBIT 6.3

The number of employees earning over £30,000 was 28, analysed as follows:

Gross salaries	Number of employees
£30,001–35,000	16
£35,001–40,000	8
£40,001–45,000	4
	28

3 Directors' emoluments

(*a*) Aggregate amounts of:
  - (*i*) emoluments, including pension contributions and benefits in kind. Distinction to be made between those emoluments as fees and those for executive duties;
  - (*ii*) pensions for past directors;
  - (*iii*) compensation for loss of office.
(*b*) The chairman's emoluments and those of the highest paid director, if paid more than the chairman. In both cases pension contributions are to be excluded.
(*c*) Number of directors whose emoluments, excluding pension contributions, fall within each bracket of £5,000.
(*d*) Total amounts waived by directors and numbers concerned.

The disclosures under (*b*) and (*c*) above are not needed for a company being neither a parent nor subsidiary undertaking where its directors' emoluments under (*a*) do not exceed £60,000. The disclosures under (*b*) and (*c*) are also not necessary for directors working wholly or mainly overseas.

An illustration is now given in Exhibit 6.4.

EXHIBIT 6.4

Name	Fee (as directors)	Remuneration (as executives)	Pension contributions
A (Chairman)	£5,000	£85,000	£20,000
B	£2,500	£95,000	£30,000
C	£2,500	£55,000	£15,000
D	£1,500	£54,000	£12,500
E	£1,500	£30,000	£10,000

Note to accounts:
Directors' remuneration: the amounts paid to directors were as follows:

Fees as directors	£13,000
Other emoluments, including pension contributions	£406,500

Emoluments of the Chairman – excluding pension contributions – amounted to £90,000, and those of the highest paid director to £97,500. Other directors' emoluments were in the following ranges:

£30,001 to £35,000	1
£55,001 to £60,000	2

4 Various charges to be shown as notes

(*a*) Auditors' remuneration, including expenses.
(*b*) Hire of plant and machinery.
(*c*) Interest payable on (*i*) bank loans, overdrafts and other loans repayable by instalments or otherwise within five years; (*ii*) loans of any other kind.
(*d*) Depreciation:
  - (*i*) amounts of provisions for both tangible and intangible assets;
  - (*ii*) effect on depreciation of change of depreciation method;
  - (*iii*) effect on depreciation of revaluation of assets.

5 Income from listed investments

6 Rents receivable from land, after deducting outgoings

7 Taxation

(*a*) Tax charges split between:
  (*i*)   UK corporation tax, and basis of computation;
  (*ii*) UK income tax, and basis of computation;
  (*iii*) irrecoverable VAT;
  (*iv*) tax attributable to franked investment income.
(*b*) If relevant, split between tax on ordinary and tax on extraordinary activities.
(*c*) Show, as component part, charge for deferred tax.
(*d*) Any other special circumstances affecting tax liability.

8 Extraordinary and exceptional items and prior period adjustments

See FRS 3, *Reporting financial performance*, which is dealt with in Section 6.7.

9 Redemption of shares and loans

Show amounts set aside for these purposes.

10 Earnings per share (listed companies only)

See FRS 14, *Earnings per share*, which is dealt with in Section 10.12.

11 Statement showing movements on reserves

The directors' report

When financial statements are published for external use, as well as a balance sheet and profit and loss account, the shareholders must also receive a directors' report. The contents of the report are given in the Companies Acts, but no formal layout is given. Such a report is additional to the notes, which have to be attached to the financial statements; the directors' report does not replace such notes. The report should include:

(*a*) A fair review of the development of the business of the company (and its subsidiaries) during the financial year and of the position at the end of the year. The dividends proposed and transfers to reserves should be given.
(*b*) Principal activities of the company and any changes therein.
(*c*) Post-balance sheet events, i.e. details of important events affecting the company (and its subsidiaries) since the end of the year.
(*d*) Likely future developments in the business.
(*e*) An indication of research and development carried on.
(*f*) Significant changes in fixed assets. In the case of land, the difference between book and market values, if significant.
(*g*) Political and charitable contributions; if, taken together, these exceed £200 there must be shown:
  (*i*) separate totals for each classification;
  (*ii*) where political contributions exceeding £200 have been made, the names of recipients and amounts.
(*h*) Details of own shares purchased.

(*i*) Employees:
  (*i*) statement concerning health, safety and welfare at work of company's employees;
  (*ii*) for companies with average workforce exceeding 250, details of employment of disabled people.

(*j*) Directors:
  (*i*) names of all persons who had been directors during any part of the financial year;
  (*ii*) their interests in contracts;
  (*iii*) for each director, the name; also:
    ● the number of shares held at the start of the year;
    ● the number of shares held at the end of the year;
    ● for each director elected in the year there shall also be shown shares held when elected;
    ● all the above to show nil amounts where appropriate.

Note: Under the Companies Acts, the directors' report is considered during the external audit. If the external auditors' judgement is that the directors' report is inconsistent with the audited company accounts, then this must be stated in the auditors' report.

The audit report

The Companies Act requires that all but the smallest companies be audited every year. The auditors are appointed each year by the shareholders at the company annual general meeting (AGM). The auditors complete the report after examining the books and accounts and, in the report, they must say whether or not they agree that the financial statements give a *true and fair view*. The report is presented to the shareholders at the same time as the financial statements are presented to them at the AGM.

In preparing the audit report, the auditor must consider whether:

● the accounts have been prepared in accordance with the Companies Act;
● the balance sheet shows a true and fair view of the state of the company's affairs at the end of the period and the profit and loss account shows a true and fair view of the results for the period;
● proper accounting records have been kept and proper returns received from parts of the company not visited by the auditor;
● the accounts are in agreement with the accounting records;
● the directors' report is consistent with the accounts.

Smaller companies (those with turnover below £1 million) are exempt from the requirement to have their financial statements audited. However, they may still do so, if they wish.

Organisations that are not required to have their financial statements audited, such as sole traders, partnerships, clubs and societies, can still have their accounts audited. In this case, the audit is described as a *non-statutory audit*.

A qualified audit report inducates that the auditor is not satisfied that the financial statements present a true and fair view. When a company receives a qualified audit report, it acts as a signal to all stakeholders that something may be amiss. As such, it is a vitally important safeguard of the interests of the shareholders.

6.6　Published financial statements

The Companies Acts give companies the choice of two alternative formats (layouts) for balance sheets, and four alternative formats for profit and loss accounts. The Acts leave the choice of a particular format for the balance sheet and the profit and loss account to the directors. Once adopted, the choice must be adhered to in subsequent years except in the case that there are special reasons for the change. If a change is made, then full reasons for the change must be stated in the notes attached to the financial statements.

As you will most probably be studying this topic for the first time, it would be inappropriate (and unnecessary) to give you all the details of all the formats. The format we will use in this book for the published profit and loss account is called Format 1, as is the one we shall use for the published balance sheet.

In this section, you will be shown a profit and loss account produced for use within the company (an 'internal' profit and loss account) which can easily be adapted to cover publication requirements under the Acts, along with a balance sheet.

All companies, even the very smallest, have to produce financial statements for shareholders that adhere to the requirements of the Companies Acts. 'Small' and 'medium-sized' companies can, however, file summarised financial statements with the Registrar of Companies, but they must still prepare full financial statements for their shareholders. In addition, listed companies may send their shareholders summary financial statements in place of the full version, unless a shareholder specifically requests a full version. We will consider these points later.

6.7　Published profit and loss account: Format 1

The Companies Acts show Format 1 as in Exhibit 6.5.

EXHIBIT 6.5

Profit and loss account
Format 1

1　Turnover
2　Cost of sales
3　Gross profit or loss
4　Distribution costs
5　Administrative expenses
6　Other operating income
7　Income from shares in group undertakings
8　Income from participating interests
9　Income from other fixed asset investments
10　Other interest receivable and similar income
11　Amounts written off investments
12　Interest payable and similar charges
13　Tax on profit or loss on ordinary activities
14　Profit or loss on ordinary activities after taxation
15　Extraordinary income
16　Extraordinary charges
17　Extraordinary profit or loss
18　Tax on extraordinary profit or loss
19　Other taxes not shown under the above items
20　Profit or loss for the financial year

This is simply a list and it does not show where subtotals should be placed. The important point is that the items 1 to 20 have to be displayed in that order. If some items do not exist for the company in a given year, then those headings are omitted from the published profit and loss account. Thus, if the company has no investments, items 7, 8, 9, 10 and 11 will not exist, and item 6 will be followed by item 12 in that company's published profit and loss account. The category reference numbers on the left-hand side of items do not have to be shown in the published accounts.

Before going any further, let's show you another trading and profit and loss account drawn up for internal use.

Trading and profit and loss account for internal use

Exhibit 6.6 shows a trading and profit and loss account drawn up for internal use by a company. As mentioned earlier, there are no statutory rules concerning how financial statements are drawn up for internal use. However, if the internal financial statements were drawn up in a completely different fashion to those needed for publication, then there would be quite a lot of work needed in order to reassemble the figures into a profit and loss account for publication. Unsurprisingly, many companies use the same format but expand some of the detail for the internal version.

In Exhibit 6.6, the internal accounts have been drawn up in a style which makes it easy to get the figures for the published profit and loss account.

EXHIBIT 6.6 (for internal use)

Block plc
Trading and Profit and Loss Account for the year ended 31 December 20X6

	£000	£000	£000
Turnover			800
Less Cost of sales:			
Stock 1 January 20X6		100	
Add Purchases		525	
		625	
Less Stock 31 December 20X6		(125)	
			(500)
Gross profit			300
Distribution costs:			
Salaries and wages	30		
Motor vehicle costs: Distribution	20		
General distribution expenses	5		
Depreciation: Motors	3		
Machinery	2		
		60	
Administrative expenses			
Salaries and wages	25		
Motor vehicle costs: Administration	2		
General administration expenses	7		
Auditors' remuneration	2		
Depreciation: Motors	3		
Machinery	1		
		40	
			(100)
			200

	£000	£000	£000
Other operating income			30
			230
Income from shares in group undertakings		20	
Income from participating interests		10	
Income from shares from non-related companies		5	
Other interest receivable		15	
			50
Amounts written off investments			280
		4	
Interest payable:			
Loans repayable within five years	10		
Loans repayable in ten years' time	6		
		16	
			(20)
Profit on ordinary activities before taxation			260
Tax on profit on ordinary activities			(95)
Profit on ordinary activities after taxation			165
Retained profits brought forward from last year			60
			225
Transfer to general reserve		40	
Proposed ordinary dividend		100	
			(140)
Retained profits carried forward to next year			85

Now, let's look at the same information, this time prepared for publication using Format 1. Look carefully at it and compare it with the one for internal use.

Published profit and loss accounts

Note that there are no items in Exhibit 6.6 that would appear under items 15 to 19 in Companies Act Format 1. Exhibit 6.7 redrafts Exhibit 6.6 into a form suitable for publication according to Format 1. However, as before, the category reference numbers to the left-hand side of Exhibit 6.7 are for your benefit, they do not have to be included.

EXHIBIT 6.7 (for publication presented according to Format 1)

Block plc
Profit and Loss Account for the year ending 31 December 20X6

	£000	£000
1 Turnover		800
2 Cost of sales		(500)
3 Gross profit		300
4 Distribution costs	60	
5 Administrative expenses	40	
		(100)
		200
6 Other operating income		30
		230
7 Income from shares in group undertakings	20	
8 Income from participating interests	10	

	£000	£000
9 Income from other fixed asset investments	5	
10 Other interest receivable and similar income	15	
		50
		280
11 Amounts written off investments	4	
12 Interest payable and similar charges	16	
		(20)
Profit or loss on ordinary activities before taxation		260
13 Tax on profit or loss or loss on ordinary activities		(95)
14 Profit or loss on ordinary activities after taxation		165
Transfer to reserves	40	
Dividends paid and proposed	100	
		(140)
Retained profits for the period		25

Note that the retained profits from the previous year is not shown. This category would normally appear in a note to the financial statements concerning movements on the reserves.

The Companies Act does not force companies to publish fully detailed financial statements, but neither does it prohibit such disclosure. It simply states the minimum information which must be disclosed. Companies can publish detailed financial statements if they wish. Thus, it would be legally possible for the internal profit and loss account, as shown in Exhibit 6.6, to be published in that form, because all the items are shown in the correct order. This would not have been possible if they had been shown in a different order.

Definition of items in Format 1

Format Item 1

Turnover is defined as the amounts derived from the provision of goods and services falling within the company's ordinary activities, net after deduction of VAT and trade discounts.

Format Items 2, 4 and 5

The figures for cost of sales, distribution costs and administrative expenses must include any depreciation charges connected with these functions. In the case of Block plc, because of the type of business, there are depreciation charges as part of distribution costs and administration expenses, but not cost of sales.

Format Item 6

This is operating income which does not fall under Item 1. Such items as rents receivable or royalties receivable might be found under this heading.

Format Item 7

Accounting for groups lies outside the A-level syllabus. However, in brief, parent undertakings control subsidiary undertakings. A parent is able to exert a dominant influence (i.e. control) over the activities of the subsidiary usually, but not necessarily, as a result of its owning a majority of the voting rights in the subsidiary. The parent and all its subsidiaries are a 'group'. Any dividends received by a company from its investments in shares in any member of the 'group' have to be shown separately.

Format Item 8

The term 'participating interest' means one where the parent company has a long-term holding of shares or their equivalent in an undertaking for the purpose of securing a contribution to the investor's own activities by the exercise of control or influence arising from or related to that interest. Where the equity stake exceeds 20 per cent, there is a presumption of such influence unless the contrary is shown.

Format Item 12

This includes bank interest on loans and overdrafts, debenture interest, etc.

The profit and loss account produced in Exhibit 6.7 is not precisely as presented in Exhibit 6.5. As can be seen in Exhibit 6.7, it contains no items in categories 15, 16, 17, 18, 19 or 20. In addition, after item 14, there are several more lines, those of transfer to reserves, and proposed dividends. Although in Exhibit 6.7 the format omits them, when they have a value, they are required according to the detailed rules accompanying the format. This also applies to line 20 'Profit or loss for the financial year' shown in Exhibit 6.5, when that line is included.

It would also have been possible to amalgamate items, for instance 4 and 5 could have been shown together as 'Net operating expenses £100,000'. In this case, included in the notes appended to the financial statements would be an item showing the composition of the figure of £100,000.

In the notes attached to the profit and loss account, the Companies Acts require that the following be shown separately:

(*a*) interest on bank loans, overdrafts and other loans:
  (*i*) repayable within 5 years from the end of the accounting period;
  (*ii*) finally repayable after 5 years from the end of the accounting period;
(*b*) amounts set aside for redemption of share capital and for redemption of loans;
(*c*) rents from land, if material;
(*d*) costs of hire of plant and machinery;
(*e*) auditors' remuneration, including expenses.

Where a company carries on business of two or more classes differing substantially from each other, a note is required of the amount of turnover for each class of business, and the division of the profit and loss before taxation between each class. Information also has to be given of the turnover between geographical markets.

Notes are also required concerning numbers of employees, wages and salaries, social security costs and pension costs.

Three further disclosure requirements of the Companies Act were expanded by FRS 3:

● the effect must be stated of any amount relating to any preceding financial year included in any item in the profit and loss account;
● particulars must be given of any extraordinary income or charges arising in the financial year; and
● the effect of any transaction of exceptional size or incidence that falls within the ordinary activities of the company must be stated.

Layout of the published profit and loss account

If Block plc had items relevant to the other Format 1 categories, i.e. 15–19, the profit and loss account would have been presented as shown in Exhibit 6.8. Note that the lines added have been included simply to show what the statement would look like. Where a category has no value, it would normally be omitted from the statement, as was the case in Exhibit 6.7. In addition, Exhibit 6.8 shows the extra lines that must be included, but were not shown in Format 1 in the Companies Act. It is also worthwhile noting that the four lines in Format 1 that relate to *extraordinary items* are virtually eliminated as a result of the definition of the term that was introduced in FRS 3, *Reporting financial performance*. As a result of its issuing FRS 3, the Accounting Standards Board does not expect any company to identify an item as 'extraordinary' in their financial statements and so items 15–18 are unlikely to be seen in any future published profit and loss accounts.

EXHIBIT 6.8

Block plc
Profit and Loss Account for the year ending 31 December 20X6

		£000	£000
1	Turnover		800
2	Cost of sales		(500)
3	Gross profit		300
4	Distribution costs	60	
5	Administrative expenses	40	
			(100)
			200
6	Other operating income		30
			230
7	Income from shares in group undertakings	20	
8	Income from participating interests	10	
9	Income from fixed asset investments	5	
10	Other interest receivable and similar income	15	
			50
			280
11	Amounts written off investments	4	
12	Interest payable and similar charges	16	
			(20)
	Profit or loss on ordinary activities before taxation		260
13	Tax on profit or loss on ordinary activities		(95)
14	Profit or loss on ordinary activities after taxation		165
15	Extraordinary income	0	
16	Extraordinary charges	0	
17	Extraordinary profit or loss	0	
18	Tax on extraordinary profit or loss	0	
			0
			165
19	Other taxes not shown under the above items		0
20	Profit or loss for the year		165
	Transfer to reserves	40	
	Dividends paid and proposed	100	
			(140)
	Retained profits for the year		25

Allocation of expenses

It will be obvious under which heading most expenses will be shown, whether they are:

(*a*) cost of sales; or
(*b*) distribution costs; or
(*c*) administrative expenses.

However, as the Companies Acts do not define these terms, some items are not so easy to allocate with certainty. Some companies may choose one heading for a particular item, while another company will choose another. These items can now be examined.

1 **Discounts received.** These are for prompt payment of amounts owing by the company. Where they are for payments to suppliers of goods they could be regarded as either being a reduction in the cost of goods or, alternatively, as being a financial recompense – i.e. the reward for paying money on time. If regarded in the first way they would be deducted from cost of sales, whereas the alternative approach would be to deduct them from administrative expenses. However, these discounts are also deducted when paying bills in respect of distribution costs or administrative expenses, and it would also be necessary to deduct from these headings if the cost of sales deduction approach is used. As this raises complications in the original recording of discounts received, this book takes the approach that all cash discounts received are deducted in arriving at the figure of administrative expenses.

2 **Discounts allowed.** To be consistent in dealing with discounts, this should be included in administrative expenses.

3 **Bad debts.** These could be regarded as an expense connected with sales: after all, they are sales which are not paid for. The other point of view is that for a debt to become bad, at least part of the blame must be because the proper administrative procedures in checking on customers' creditworthiness has not been thorough enough. In this book all bad debts will be taken as being part of administrative expenses.

FRS 3, *Reporting financial performance*

Accounting is not a static subject. Changes occur over the years as they are seen to be necessary, and also as there is general agreement on their usefulness. Since the advent of accounting standards, the number of changes that practitioners and students have had to learn has increased at a very fast rate. A prime example of this is the introduction of FRS 3, which necessitated changes to the formats of profit and loss accounts when certain events have occurred.

This standard superseded SSAP 6, *Extraordinary items and prior year adjustments*, temporarily amended SSAP 3, *Earnings per share* (FRS 14, *Earnings per share*, was issued five years after FRS 3), and also made changes as a consequence to various other accounting standards.

Suppose that you are considering the affairs of a business over the years. The business has not changed significantly, there have been no acquisitions, no discontinued operations, no fundamental reorganisation or restructuring of the business, nor have there been any extraordinary items affecting the financial statements. In these circumstances, when comparing the financial statements over the years, you are comparing like with like, subject to the problem of the effect of inflation or deflation.

On the other hand, suppose that some of the things mentioned have occurred. When trying to see what the future might hold for the company, if you simply base your opinions on what has happened in the past the result can be very confusing.

To help you to distinguish the past and the future, and to give you some idea of what changes have occurred, FRS 3 requires that the following are highlighted in the profit and loss account if they are material in amount:

(*a*) *What the results of continuing operations are, including the results of acquisitions.* Obviously acquisitions affect future results, and are therefore included in continuing operations.

(*b*) *What the results of discontinued operations have been.* This should help distinguish the past from the future.

(*c*) *The profits or losses on the sale or termination of an operation, the costs of fundamental reorganisation or restructuring* and *the profits and losses on the disposal of fixed assets.* The profits and losses concerning these matters are not going to happen again, and so this also helps us distinguish the past from the future.

We can see how FRS 3 requires (*a*), (*b*) and (*c*) to be shown on the face of the profit and loss account in Exhibit 6.9. Not only is the turnover split to show the figures relevant to continuing operations, acquisitions and discontinued operations, the operating profit is split in a similar fashion. In addition any profit or loss on the disposal of the discontinued operations would also be shown. Exhibit 6.9 is restricted to the first six categories of Format 1 as this is the part of the statement affected by these FRS 3 requirements. Once again, it uses Block plc for the example.

EXHIBIT 6.9

Block plc
Profit and Loss Account for the year ending 31 December 20X6 (extract)

	£000	£000
1 Turnover		
Continuing operations	520	
Acquisitions	110	
	630	
Discontinued operations	170	
		800
2 Cost of sales		(500)
3 Gross profit		300
4 Distribution costs	60	
5 Administrative expenses	40	
		(100)
		200
Operating profit		
Continuing operations	160	
Acquisitions	60	
	220	
Discontinued operations (loss)	(20)	
		200
Profit on disposal of discontinued operations (*i*)		10
		210
6 Other operating income		20
Profit or loss on ordinary activities before interest		230

The item marked (*i*) can be described as an exceptional item. It is material in amount, falls within the ordinary activities of the firm and needs to be shown so that the financial statements will give a 'true and fair view'.

It is exceptional in that it is not the ordinary daily occurrence, but remember that it falls within the ordinary activities of the company. FRS 3 requires that three categories of exceptional items be shown separately on the face of the profit and loss account after operating profit and before interest, and included under the appropriate heading of continued or discontinued operations:

- profits or losses on the sale or termination of an operation;
- costs of a fundamental reorganisation or restructuring having a material effect on the nature and focus of the reporting entity's operations;
- profits or losses on the disposal of fixed assets.

Other exceptional items should be credited or charged in arriving at the profit or loss on ordinary activities by inclusion under the heading to which they relate. The amount of each exceptional item should be disclosed in a note, or on the face of the profit and loss account, if necessary in order to give a true and fair view.

6.8 Published balance sheet: Format 1

Format 1 is shown as Exhibit 6.10. Monetary figures have been included to illustrate it more clearly.

EXHIBIT 6.10

<table>
<tr><th colspan="5" style="text-align:center">Balance Sheet – Format 1</th></tr>
<tr><td></td><td></td><td></td><td>£000s</td><td></td></tr>
<tr><td></td><td></td><td>£</td><td>£</td><td>£</td></tr>
<tr><td>A CALLED-UP SHARE CAPITAL NOT PAID*</td><td></td><td></td><td></td><td>10</td></tr>
<tr><td>B FIXED ASSETS</td><td></td><td></td><td></td><td></td></tr>
<tr><td>I Intangible assets</td><td></td><td></td><td></td><td></td></tr>
<tr><td> 1 Development costs</td><td></td><td>20</td><td></td><td></td></tr>
<tr><td> 2 Concessions, patents, licences, trade marks
     and similar rights and assets</td><td></td><td>30</td><td></td><td></td></tr>
<tr><td> 3 Goodwill</td><td></td><td>80</td><td></td><td></td></tr>
<tr><td> 4 Payments on account</td><td></td><td>5</td><td></td><td></td></tr>
<tr><td></td><td></td><td></td><td>135</td><td></td></tr>
<tr><td>II Tangible assets</td><td></td><td></td><td></td><td></td></tr>
<tr><td> 1 Land and buildings</td><td></td><td>300</td><td></td><td></td></tr>
<tr><td> 2 Plant and machinery</td><td></td><td>500</td><td></td><td></td></tr>
<tr><td> 3 Fixtures, fittings, tools and equipment</td><td></td><td>60</td><td></td><td></td></tr>
<tr><td> 4 Payments on account and assets in course of construction</td><td></td><td>20</td><td></td><td></td></tr>
<tr><td></td><td></td><td></td><td>880</td><td></td></tr>
<tr><td>III Investments</td><td></td><td></td><td></td><td></td></tr>
<tr><td> 1 Shares in group undertakings</td><td></td><td>15</td><td></td><td></td></tr>
<tr><td> 2 Loans to group undertakings</td><td></td><td>10</td><td></td><td></td></tr>
<tr><td> 3 Participating interests</td><td></td><td>20</td><td></td><td></td></tr>
<tr><td> 4 Loans to undertakings in which the company has a
     participating interest</td><td></td><td>5</td><td></td><td></td></tr>
<tr><td> 5 Other investments other than loans</td><td></td><td>30</td><td></td><td></td></tr>
<tr><td> 6 Other loans</td><td></td><td>16</td><td></td><td></td></tr>
<tr><td> 7 Own shares</td><td></td><td>4</td><td></td><td></td></tr>
<tr><td></td><td></td><td></td><td>100</td><td></td></tr>
<tr><td></td><td></td><td></td><td></td><td>1,115</td></tr>
</table>

C	CURRENT ASSETS			
I	Stock			
	1 Raw materials and consumables	60		
	2 Work in progress	15		
	3 Finished goods and goods for resale	120		
	4 Payments on account	5		
			200	
II	Debtors			
	1 Trade debtors	200		
	2 Amounts owed by group undertakings	20		
	3 Amounts owed by undertakings in which the company has a participating interest	10		
	4 Other debtors	4		
	5 Called-up share capital not paid*	–		
	6 Prepayments and accrued income**	–		
			234	
III	Investments			
	1 Shares in group undertakings	40		
	2 Own shares	5		
	3 Other investments	30		
			75	
IV	Cash at bank and in hand		26	
			535	
D	PREPAYMENTS AND ACCRUED INCOME**		15	
			550	
E	CREDITORS: AMOUNTS FALLING DUE WITHIN ONE YEAR			
	1 Debenture loans	5		
	2 Bank loans and overdrafts	10		
	3 Payments received on account	20		
	4 Trade creditors	50		
	5 Bills of exchange payable	2		
	6 Amounts owed to group undertakings	15		
	7 Amounts owed to undertakings in which the company has a participating interest	6		
	8 Other creditors including taxation and social security	54		
	9 Accruals and deferred income***	–		
			(162)	
F	NET CURRENT ASSETS (LIABILITIES)			388
G	TOTAL ASSETS *LESS* CURRENT LIABILITIES			1,513
H	CREDITORS: AMOUNTS FALLING DUE AFTER MORE THAN ONE YEAR			
	1 Debenture loans	20		
	2 Bank loans and overdrafts	15		
	3 Payments received on account	5		
	4 Trade creditors	25		
	5 Bills of exchange payable	4		
	6 Amounts owed to group undertakings	10		
	7 Amounts owed to undertakings in which the company has a participating interest	5		
	8 Other creditors including taxation and social security	32		
	9 Accruals and deferred income***	–		
			116	

I	PROVISIONS FOR LIABILITIES AND CHARGES				
	1 Pensions and similar obligations		20		
	2 Taxation, including deferred taxation		40		
	3 Other provisions		4		
				64	
J	ACCRUALS AND DEFERRED INCOME***			20	
					(200)
					1,313
K	CAPITAL AND RESERVES				
I	Called-up share capital				1,000
II	Share premium account				100
III	Revaluation reserve				20
IV	Other reserves:				
	1 Capital redemption reserve		40		
	2 Reserve for own shares		10		
	3 Reserves provided for by the articles of association		20		
	4 Other reserves		13		
					83
V	Profit and loss account				110
					1,313

(*)(**)(***) These items may be shown in any of the positions indicated.

It should be noted that various items can be shown in alternative places, i.e.:

- **called-up share capital not paid**, either in position A or position CII 5;
- **prepayments and accrued income**, either CII 6 or as D;
- **accruals and deferred income**, either E9 or H9, or in total as J.

Items preceded by letters or roman numerals must be disclosed on the face of the balance sheet, e.g. B Fixed assets, KII Share premium account, whereas those shown with arabic numerals (you may call them ordinary numbers, 1, 2, 3, 4, etc.) may be combined where they are not material or the combination facilitates assessment of the company's affairs. Where they are combined, the details of each item should be shown in the notes accompanying the financial statements. The actual letters, roman numerals or arabic numbers do *not* have to be shown on the face of the published balance sheets.

Further details for Format 1

The following also apply to the balance sheet in Format 1.

- BI Intangible assets are assets not having a 'physical' existence compared with tangible assets which do have a physical existence. For instance, you can see and touch the tangible assets of land and buildings, plant and machinery, etc., whereas goodwill does not exist in a physical sense.

- For each of the items under fixed assets, whether they are intangible assets, tangible assets or investments, full details must be given in the notes accompanying the financial statements of (*a*) cost, at beginning and end of financial year, (*b*) effect on that item of acquisitions, disposals, revaluations, etc. during the year, and (*c*) full details of depreciation, i.e. accumulated depreciation at start of year, depreciation for year, effect of disposals on depreciation in the year and any other adjustments.

- All fixed assets, including property and goodwill, must be depreciated over the period of the useful economic life of each asset. Prior to this many companies had not depreciated property because of rising money values of the asset. Costs of research must not be treated as an asset, and development costs may be capitalised only in special cases. Any hire purchase owing must not be deducted from the assets concerned. Only goodwill which has been purchased can be shown as an asset; internally generated goodwill must not be capitalised.

- Where an asset is revalued, normally this will be fixed assets being shown at market value instead of cost. Any difference on revaluation must be debited or credited to a revaluation reserve – *see* KIII in the Format.

- Investments shown as CIII will be in respect of those not held for the long term.

- Two items which could previously be shown as assets, (*a*) preliminary expenses (these are the legal expenses, etc. in forming the company), and (*b*) expenses of and commission on any issue of shares or debentures, must not now be shown as assets. They can be written off against any share premium account balance; alternatively they should be written off to the profit and loss account.

- Full details of each class of share capital, and of authorised capital, will be shown in notes accompanying the balance sheet.

Notes to the financial statements: two illustrative questions on published company financial statements including notes required by law are shown at the end of this chapter.

6.9 Published balance sheets and GCE A-level examinations

You will not be expected to remember the full detail for such a balance sheet. This is simply outside the demands of your syllabus. If you can remember the main structure then that will be sufficient.

What you should remember are the main headings and these can be shown as follows:

Balance Sheet – Format 1

	£	£	£
FIXED ASSETS			
Intangible assets		xxx	
Tangible assets		xxx	
Investments (long term)		xxx	
			xxxx
CURRENT ASSETS			
Stock	xxx		
Debtors	xxx		
Investments (short term)	xxx		
		xxxx	
Cash at bank and in hand		xxx	
		xxxx	
CREDITORS: AMOUNTS FALLING DUE WITHIN ONE YEAR		(xxx)	
NET CURRENT ASSETS			xxxx
TOTAL ASSETS *LESS* CURRENT LIABILITIES			xxxx
CREDITORS: AMOUNTS FALLING DUE AFTER MORE THAN ONE YEAR			(xxx)
			xxxx

	£	£	£
CAPITAL AND RESERVES			
Called-up share capital			xxxx
Share premium account			xxx
Revaluation reserve			xxx
Other reserves			xxx
Profit and loss account			xxx
			xxxx

If you can remember these headings, you can then place the individual items under them.

6.10 Other statements and notes required in the annual report

FRS 3 requires three additional items to be published in the annual report along with the profit and loss account, balance sheet and cash flow statement.

1 Statement of total recognised gains and losses

The *statement of total recognised gains and losses* is one of two new primary statements introduced by FRS 3. It shows the extent to which shareholders' funds have increased or decreased from all the various gains and losses recognised in the period, and enables users to consider all recognised gains and losses of a reporting entity in assessing its overall performance; an example of what would be included in the statement would be unrealised gains on fixed asset revaluations. Exhibit 6.11 presents an example of the statement using the data from Block plc.

Note: only the profit figure can be found in the profit and loss account. The others have been inserted to demonstrate what the statement looks like. Also, as with all these statements, including the profit and loss account, comparative figures would also be shown.

EXHIBIT 6.11

Block plc
Statement of Total Recognised Gains and Losses

	20X6 £000
Profit for the financial year	165
Unrealised surplus on revaluation of properties	12
Unrealised (loss)/gain on trade investment	(8)
	169
Currency translation differences on foreign currency investments	(5)
Total recognised gains and losses relating to the year	164
Prior period adjustment	(19)
Total gains and losses recognised since last annual report	145

2 Note of historical cost profits and losses

Where assets have been revalued, which obviously affects depreciation, it may have a material effect upon the results shown in the financial statements using the revalued figures. If this is the case, FRS 3 requires that there should also be shown as a note what the profit and loss account would have been if the account had been shown using historical (i.e. not revalued) figures. The note should also show how the reported profit on ordinary activities (using accounts with revalued assets) can be reconciled with that calculated using historical figures, and should also show the retained profit figure for the financial year reported on the historical cost basis. The note should be presented immediately following the profit and loss account or the statement of total recognised gains and losses. An example of the note is presented in Exhibit 6.12.

Note: as with the statement of total recognised gains and losses, only the profit figure can be identified in the profit and loss account. Also, comparative figures should be shown.

EXHIBIT 6.12

Block plc
Note of Historical Cost Profits and Losses

	20X6
	£000
Reported profit on ordinary activities before taxation	260
Realisation of property revaluation gains of previous years	12
Difference between a historical cost depreciation charge and the actual depreciation charge of the year calculated on the revalued amount	1
Historical cost profit on ordinary activities before taxation	273
Historical cost profit for the year retained after taxation, minority interests, extraordinary items and dividends (273 – 95 – 100)	78

3 Reconciliation of movements in shareholders' funds

The profit and loss account and the statement of total recognised gains and losses reflect the performance of a reporting entity in a period, but there are other changes that can occur in shareholders' funds that these two statements do not disclose, and which can be important in understanding the change in the financial position of the entity – for example, a new share issue or goodwill written off. For this reason, FRS 3 also gave the *reconciliation of movements in shareholders' funds* the status of a primary statement, its purpose being to highlight these other changes in the financial position. When shown as a primary statement (there is an option to show it as a note), the reconciliation should be shown separately from the statement of total recognised gains and losses. Exhibit 6.13 presents an example of the statement. (*Note*: the figures can be found in the other statements except for the new share capital, the goodwill written off and the opening shareholders' funds amounts. As before, comparative figures should also be presented.)

EXHIBIT 6.13

Block plc
Reconciliation of Movements in Shareholders' Funds

	20X6
	£000
Profit for the financial year	165
Dividends	(100)
	65

	20X6 £000
Other recognised gains and losses relating to the year (net)	(1)
New share capital subscribed	20
Goodwill written off	(25)
Net addition to shareholders' funds	59
Opening shareholders' funds (originally £321,000 before deducting prior period adjustment of £19,000)	302
Closing shareholders' funds	361

6.11 Additional requirements introduced or amended by FRS 3

FRS 3 and extraordinary items

You have just seen that in FRS 3 some of the exceptional items have to be highlighted on the face of the profit and loss account, while others can be put under appropriate headings with notes giving details being attached to the financial statements.

In Exhibit 6.7 all of these exceptional items will have been dealt with by the time that item 14, profit for the year on ordinary activities after taxation, has been reached. Extraordinary items, as per Format 1, would be shown after that as items 15, 16, 17 and 18.

Before FRS 3, the distinction between what was an exceptional item and what was an extraordinary item was not as well defined as it could have been. This led to directors of companies sometimes manipulating the figures for their own ends while keeping within the necessary legal boundaries.

They did this because the profit per item 14 was a very well-used figure for assessing how well, or otherwise, a company was being managed. It was a vital part of calculating the earnings per share (EPS) which is a main indicator to many people of the company's performance. If a favourable item could be called an 'exceptional item' it would increase the size of the profit item per 14. On the other hand, should an item be unfavourable, and therefore lower the figure of profit per item 14, then perhaps it could be (and it often was) called an 'extraordinary item' instead. In this way, the profit per item 14 could be shown at a higher figure than was really justified. Such actions could affect the stock exchange values of the company's shares.

FRS 3 is more strict about what is, or is not, an extraordinary item, and thus to be shown after item 14 in the profit and loss account. Extraordinary items should be:

(a) material items possessing a high degree of abnormality which arise from events or transactions that fall outside the ordinary activities of the business, and

(b) are not expected to recur, and

(c) do not include exceptional items, and

(d) do not include items relating to a prior period merely because they relate to a prior period.

Extraordinary items fall *outside* the 'ordinary' activities of a company, whereas exceptional items fall *within* them. 'Ordinary activities' are any activities undertaken by a reporting entity as part of its business and such related activities in which the reporting entity engages in furtherance of, incidental to or arising from these activities. Ordinary activities include the effects on the reporting entity of any event in the various environments in which it operates. It is little wonder that the ASB did not believe that anything could ever be described as an extraordinary item after the introduction of FRS 3.

FRS 3 and prior period adjustments

A prior period adjustment is a material adjustment applicable to prior periods arising from changes in accounting policies or from the correction of fundamental errors. They do not include normal recurring adjustments or corrections of accounting estimates made in prior periods.

They are accounted for by restating the comparative figures for the preceding period in the primary statements and notes and adjusting the opening balance of reserves for the cumulative effect. The cumulative effect of the adjustments should also be noted at the foot of the statement of total recognised gains and losses of the current period (*see* Exhibit 6.11). The effect of prior period adjustments on the results for the preceding period should be disclosed where practicable.

FRS 3 and comparative figures

Comparative figures should be shown for all items in the primary statements and the notes to the statements required by FRS 3. The comparative figures in respect of the profit and loss account should include in the continuing category only the results of those operations included in the current period's continuing operations.

6.12 Small and medium-sized company reporting requirements

Small and medium-sized companies do not have to file a full set of financial statements with the Registrar of Companies. They could, if they wished, send a full set of financial statements, but what they *have* to file is a minimum of 'modified financial statements'. They would still have to send a full set to their own shareholders – the 'modified financial statements' refer only to those filed with the Registrar.

The definition of 'small' and 'medium-sized' companies is if, for the financial year in question and the previous year, the company comes within the limits of at least two of the following three criteria:

	Small	*Medium-sized*
Turnover not more than	£2.8 million	£11.2 million
Balance sheet total not more than	£1.4 million	£5.6 million
Employees not more than	50	250

In addition, there is no longer an audit requirement for small companies with a turnover of not more than £1 million and a balance sheet total of not more than £1.4 million, unless 10 per cent or more of shareholders sign a formal notice requesting an audit and lodge this at the registered office.

Modified financial statements of small companies

(*a*) Neither a profit and loss account nor a directors' report has to be filed with the Registrar.

(*b*) A modified balance sheet showing only those items to which a letter or roman numeral are attached (*see* Format 1, Exhibit 6.10) has to be shown. For example, the total for CI Stock has to be shown but not the figures for each of the individual items comprising this total.

Modified financial statements of medium-sized companies

(*a*) The profit and loss account per Format 1 does not have to show item 1 (Turnover), or item 2 (Cost of sales) or item 6 (Other operating income). It will therefore begin with the figure of gross profit or loss.

(*b*) The analyses of turnover and profit normally required as notes to the financial statements need not be given.

(*c*) The balance sheet, however, must be given in full.

6.13 Summary financial statements

A plc may send a summary financial statement to members in place of the full statements, but any member who requests the full statements must be sent them. The summary statement must:

(*a*) state that it is only a summary of information in the company's financial statements and the directors' report;

(*b*) contain a statement by the company's auditors of their opinion as to whether the summary financial statement is consistent with those financial statements and that report and complies with the requirements of the section 251 in the Companies Act 1985 (CA 85) that permits the distribution of this summary financial statement and the regulations made under it;

(*c*) state whether the auditors' report on the financial statements was unqualified or qualified, and if it was qualified set out the report in full together with any further material needed to understand the qualification;

(*d*) state whether the auditors' report on the annual accounts contained a statement under either:
- CA 85, section 237(2) – accounting records or returns inadequate or financial statements not agreeing with records or returns; or
- CA 85, section 237(3) – failure to obtain necessary information and explanations and, if so, set out the statement in full.

6.14 Other issues

Fundamental accounting principles

The Companies Acts set out the accounting principles (or 'valuation rules' as they are called in the Fourth Directive of the EC) to be followed when preparing company financial statements.

The following principles are stated in the Acts. (They are covered in fuller detail in supplementary Chapter 25.)

(*a*) A company is presumed to be a going concern.

(*b*) Accounting policies must be applied consistently from year to year.

(*c*) The prudence concept must be followed.

(*d*) The accruals concept must be observed.

(*e*) Each component item of assets and liabilities must be valued separately. As an instance of this, if a company has five different types of stock, each type must be valued separately at the lower of cost and net realisable value, rather than be valued on an aggregate basis.

(*f*) Amounts in respect of items representing assets or income may *not* be set off against items representing liabilities or expenditure. Thus an amount owing on a hire-purchase contract cannot now be deducted from the value of the asset in the balance sheet, although this was often done before 1981.

Bills of exchange

A detailed knowledge of this topic is not needed by A-level students. You do need to know the basic ideas underlying bills of exchange, and so it is introduced here as they are part of the format of published company balance sheets.

When goods are supplied to someone on credit, or services are performed for a person, then that person becomes a **debtor**. The creditor firm would normally wait for payment by the debtor. Until payment is made the money owing is of no use to the creditor firm as it is not being used in any way. This can be remedied by factoring the debtors, which involves passing the debts over to a finance firm. They will pay an agreed amount for the legal rights to the debts.

Another possibility is that of obtaining a bank overdraft, with the debtors accepted as part of the security on which the overdraft has been granted.

Yet another way that can give the creditor effective use of the money owed by a debtor is for the creditor to draw a bill of exchange on the debtor. This means that a document is drawn up requiring the debtor to pay the amount owing to the creditor, or to anyone nominated by the creditor at any time, on or by a particular date. The creditor sends this document to the debtor who, if it is acceptable, is said to 'accept' it by writing on the document that he or she will comply with it and appends his or her signature. The debtor then returns the bill of exchange to the creditor. This document is then legal proof of the debt. The debtor is not then able to contest the validity of the debt but only for any irregularity in the bill of exchange itself.

The creditor can now act in one of three ways:

1 The creditor can negotiate the bill to another person in payment of a debt. That person may also renegotiate it to someone else. The person who possesses the bill at maturity, i.e. the date for payment of the bill, will present it to the debtor for payment.

2 The creditor may 'discount' it with a bank. 'Discount' here means that the bank will take the bill of exchange and treat it in the same manner as money deposited in the bank account. The bank will then hold the bill until maturity when it will present it to the debtor for payment. The bank will make a charge to the creditor for this service known as a discounting charge.

3 The third way open to the creditor is to hold the bill until maturity when the creditor will present it to the debtor for payment. In this case, apart from having a document which is legal proof of the debt and could therefore save legal costs if a dispute arose, no benefit has been gained from having a bill of exchange. However, action 1 or 2 could have been taken if the need had arisen.

Bills receivable as contingent liabilities

The fact that bills had been discounted, but had not reached maturity by the balance sheet date, could give an entirely false impression of the financial position of the business unless a note to this effect is made on the balance sheet. That such a note is necessary can be illustrated by reference to the following balance sheets.

Balance Sheet as at 31 December 20X7

	(a) £	(a) £	(b) £	(b) £
Fixed assets		3,500		3,500
Current assets:				
Stock	1,000		1,000	
Debtors	1,200		1,200	
Bills receivable	1,800		–	
Bank	500		2,300	
	4,500		4,500	
Less Current liabilities	(3,000)		(3,000)	
Working capital		1,500		1,500
		5,000		5,000
Financed by:		£		£
Capital		5,000		5,000

Balance Sheet (*a*) shows the position if £1,800 of bills receivable were still in hand. Balance Sheet (*b*) shows the position if the bills had been discounted, ignoring discounting charges. To an outsider, Balance Sheet (*b*) seems to show a much stronger liquid position with £2,300 in the bank. However, should the bills be dishonoured on maturity the bank balance would slump to £500. The appearance of Balance Sheet (*b*) is therefore deceptive unless a note is added, e.g. *Note:* There is a contingent liability of £1,800 on bills discounted at the balance sheet date. This note enables the outsider to view the bank balance in its proper perspective of depending on the non-dishonour of the bills discounted.

Bills of exchange and the balance sheet

Besides bills of exchange to be received there are also bills of exchange in which we have agreed to pay a creditor at a future date. To distinguish between them:

● **Bills receivable:** These are bills for debts owing to us which people are going to pay us in the future.
● **Bills payable:** These are bills for debts which are owed to other people, and which we are going to have to pay in the future.

Bills receivable are assets, as they are money owing to us, and will therefore be shown as debit balances in the books and trial balance. They will be shown under current assets in the balance sheet.

Bills payable, being money owing by us, are liabilities, and are credit balances. Whether they will be shown under item E5 (*see* Exhibit 6.10) or under H5 will depend on whether we have agreed to pay the amount within the next 12 months, or at a later date.

FRS 4, *Capital instruments*

If a company can make short-term debt (i.e. payable within the next 12 months) look as though it does not have to be paid off within that period but, instead, it looks as though the company has several years in which to pay it, then the balance sheet shows what appears to be a much healthier liquidity position. Investors may then be fooled into investing in a company which appears to have no short-term problems of shortage of cash funds, only to see the company quickly fall into such problems.

FRS 4 is aimed at preventing devices which could mislead an investor or shareholder. A-level students do not need to know all the technical details, which include such methods as certain types of debentures, convertible debt and auction market preferred stock. The main provisions of FRS 4 are as follows:

- Liabilities should *not* be shown as being amounts which fall due after one year if in fact a strict interpretation of their contractual maturity means that they are amounts falling due within one year.
- Shareholders' funds must be analysed between equity and non-equity interests.

6.15 Illustrative company financial statements: example 1

F Clarke Ltd are specialist wholesalers. This is their trial balance at 31 December 20X4.

	Dr £	Cr £
Ordinary share capital: £1 shares		1,000,000
Share premium		120,000
General reserve		48,000
Profit and loss account as at 31.12.20X3		139,750
Stock: 31.12.20X3	336,720	
Sales		4,715,370
Purchases	2,475,910	
Returns outwards		121,220
Returns inwards	136,200	
Carriage inwards	6,340	
Carriage outwards	43,790	
Warehouse wages (average number of workers 59)	410,240	
Salesmen's salaries (average number of workers 21)	305,110	
Administrative wages and salaries	277,190	
Plant and machinery	610,000	
Motor vehicle hire	84,770	
Provisions for depreciation: plant and machinery		216,290
General distribution expenses	27,130	
General administrative expenses	47,990	
Directors' remuneration	195,140	
Rents receivable		37,150
Trade debtors	1,623,570	
Cash at bank and in hand	179,250	
Trade creditors (payable before 31.3.20X5)		304,570
Bills of exchange payable (payable 28.2.20X5)		57,000
	6,759,350	6,759,350

Notes:

(*a*) Stock at 31.12.20X4: £412,780, consists of goods for resale.

(*b*) Plant and machinery is apportioned: distributive 60 per cent; administrative 40 per cent.

(*c*) Accrue auditors' remuneration: £71,000.

(*d*) Depreciate plant and machinery: 20 per cent on cost.

(*e*) Of the motor hire, £55,000 is for distributive purposes.

(*f*) Corporation tax on profits, at a rate of 35 per cent, is estimated at £238,500, and is payable on 1.10.20X5.

(*g*) There is a proposed ordinary dividend of 37$\frac{1}{2}$ per cent for the year.

(*h*) All of the sales are of one type of goods. Net sales of £3,620,000 have been made in the UK with the remainder in Europe, and are shown net of VAT.

(*i*) Pension contributions for staff amounted to £42,550 and social security contributions to £80,120. These figures are included in wages and salaries in the trial balance. No employee earned over £30,000.

(*j*) Plant of £75,000 had been bought during the year.

(*k*) Directors' remuneration has been as follows:

	£
Chairman	46,640
Managing Director	51,500
Finance Director	46,000
Marketing Director	43,000
	187,140

In addition each of them drew £2,000 as directors' fees. Pensions are the personal responsibility of directors.

Required:

Subject to the limits of the information given you, draw up a profit and loss account for the year ended 31 December 20X4, and a balance sheet as at that date. They should be in published form and accompanied by the necessary notes prescribed by statute.

Specimen answer 1

Workings to accompany the answer

	£		£	£
Turnover: Sales	4,715,370	Cost of sales:		
Less Returns in	(136,200)	Opening stock		336,720
	4,579,170	*Add* Purchases	2,475,910	
		Less Returns out	(121,220)	
			2,354,690	
		Add Carriage in	6,340	2,361,030
				2,697,750
		Less Closing stock		(412,780)
				2,284,970
Distribution costs:		Administrative expenses:		
Warehouse wages	410,240	Wages and salaries		277,190
Salesmen's salaries	305,110	Motor hire		29,770
Carriage out	43,790	General expenses		47,990
General expenses	27,130	Directors' remuneration		150,140
Motor hire	55,000	Auditor's remuneration		71,000
Depreciation: plant	73,200	Depreciation: plant		48,800
Marketing Director's	45,000			624,890
remuneration	959,470			

F Clarke Ltd
Profit and Loss Account for the year ended 31 December 20X4

	£	£
Turnover		4,579,170
Cost of sales		(2,284,970)
Gross profit		2,294,200
Distribution costs	959,470	
Administrative expenses	624,890	
		(1,584,360)
		709,840
Other operating income		37,150
Profit on ordinary activities before taxation		746,990
Tax on profit on ordinary activities		(238,500)
Profit on ordinary activities after taxation		508,490
Proposed ordinary dividend		(375,000)
Retained profits for the year		133,490

F Clarke Ltd
Balance Sheet as at 31 December 20X4

Fixed assets	£	£	£
Tangible assets: Plant and machinery			271,710
Current assets			
Stock: Finished goods and goods for resale		412,780	
Debtors: Trade debtors		1,623,570	
Cash at bank and in hand		179,250	
		2,215,600	
Creditors: amounts falling due within one year			
Trade creditors	304,570		
Bills of exchange payable	57,000		
Other creditors including taxation and social security	684,500		
		(1,046,070)	
Net current assets			(1,169,530)
Total assets less current liabilities			1,441,240
Capital and reserves			£
Called-up share capital			1,000,000
Share premium account			120,000
Other reserves:			
General reserve			48,000
Profit and loss account			273,240
			1,441,240

Notes to the accounts

1 Turnover

This is the value, net of VAT, of goods of a single class of business. Turnover may be analysed as follows:

	£
United Kingdom	3,680,000
Europe	899,170
	4,579,170

2 Employees

Average number of workers was:

Warehousing	59
Sales	21
	80

Remuneration of employees was:

	£
Wages and salaries	869,870
Social security costs	80,120
Pension contributions	42,550
	992,540

3 Directors' remuneration

The amounts paid to directors were as follows:

	£
Fees as directors	8,000
Other emoluments	187,140

Emoluments of the Chairman amounted to £46,640, and those of the highest-paid director £51,500. Other directors' emoluments were in the following ranges:

£40,001–45,000	1
£45,001–50,000	1

4 Operating profit is shown after charging

	£
Auditor's remuneration	71,000
Hire of motors	84,770

5 Fixed assets

	£	£
Plant and machinery		
Cost at 1.1.20X4	535,000	
Additions	75,000	
		610,000
Depreciation to 31.12.20X3	216,290	
Charge for the year	122,000	
		(338,290)
		271,710

6 Other creditors including taxation

	£	£
Proposed dividend	375,000	
Auditor's remuneration	71,000	
Corporation tax	238,500	
		684,500

6.16 Illustrative company financial statements: example 2

The trial balance of Quartz plc on 31 December 20X3 was as follows:

	Dr £000	Cr £000
Preference share capital: £1 shares		200
Ordinary share capital: £1 shares		1,000
Exchange reserve		75
General reserve		150
Profit and loss account 31.12.20X2		215
Sales		4,575
Purchases	2,196	
Carriage inwards	38	
Stock 31.12.20X2	902	
Wages (adding value to goods)	35	
Wages: warehousing	380	
Wages and salaries: administrative	120	
Wages and salaries: sales	197	
Motor expenses	164	
Bad debts	31	
Debenture interest	40	
Bank overdraft interest	19	
General distribution expenses	81	
General administrative expenses	73	
Directors' remuneration	210	
Investments in undertakings in which the company has a participating interest	340	
Income from shares in undertakings in which the company has a participating interest		36
Discounts allowed and received	55	39
Buildings: at cost	1,200	
Plant and machinery: at cost	330	
Motor vehicles: at cost	480	
Provisions for depreciation:		
Land and buildings		375
Plant and machinery		195
Motors		160
Goodwill	40	
Patents, licences and trade marks	38	
Trade debtors and creditors	864	392
Bank overdraft (repayable any time)		21
Debentures 10 per cent		400
	7,833	7,833

Notes:

(a) Stock at 31.12.20X3: £1,103,000 at cost.

(b) Motor expenses and depreciation on motors to be apportioned: Distribution 75 per cent; Administrative 25 per cent.

(c) Depreciation on buildings and plant and machinery to be apportioned: Distribution 50 per cent; Administrative 50 per cent.

(*d*) Depreciate on cost: Motor vehicles 25 per cent; Plant and machinery 20 per cent.

(*e*) Accrue corporation tax on profits of the year £266,000. This is payable 1 October 20X4.

(*f*) A preference dividend of 10 per cent is to be paid and an ordinary dividend of 50 per cent is to be proposed.

(*g*) During the year new vehicles were purchased at a cost of £60,000.

(*h*) During June 20X3 one of the buildings, which had originally cost £130,000, and which had a written-down value at the date of the sale of £80,000, was sold for £180,000. Depreciation on buildings to be charged against the year's profits is £60,000. The buildings are revalued by B & Co., Chartered Surveyors, at £1,500,000 at 31.12.20X3 (and this figure is to be included in the financial statements).

(*i*) Directors' remuneration was as follows:

	£
Marketing	42,000
Chairman	37,000
Managing	61,000
Finance	50,000
	190,000

In addition each director drew £5,000 fees.

(*j*) Of the goodwill, 50 per cent is to be written off during this year, and 50 per cent in the following year.

(*k*) The debentures are to be redeemed in five equal annual instalments, starting in the following year 20X4.

(*l*) The investments are in listed companies with a market value at 31 December 20X3 of £438,000.

(*m*) Auditor's remuneration, including expenses, was £7,000.

You are required to prepare a balance sheet as at 31 December 20X3. It should:

(*a*) conform to the requirements of the Companies Act 1985;

(*b*) conform to the relevant accounting standards;

(*c*) give the notes necessary to the accounts.

Specimen answer 2

Workings to accompany the answer

	£000		Dist. £000	Admin. £000
Cost of sales:		Wages	577	120
Opening stock	902	Motor expenses	123	41
Add Purchases	2,196	General	81	73
Add Carriage in	38	Depreciation: plant	33	33
	3,136	motors	90	30
Less Closing stock	(1,103)	buildings	30	30
	2,033	Directors	47	163
Wages (added value)	35	Discounts (net) 55 – 39		16
	2,068	Bad debts		31
			981	537

Quartz plc
Profit and Loss Account for the year ended 31 December 20X4

	£000	£000
Turnover		4,575
Cost of sales		(2,068)
Gross profit		2,507
Distribution costs	981	
Administrative expenses	537	
		(1,518)
		989
Income from shares in undertakings in which the company has a participating interest		36
		1,025
Interest payable and similar charges		(59)
Profit on ordinary activities before taxation		966
Tax on profit on ordinary activities		(266)
Profit for the year on ordinary activities after taxation		700
Goodwill written off	20	
Dividends paid and proposed	520	
		(540)
Retained profits for the year		160

Quartz plc
Balance Sheet as at 31 December 20X3

	£000	£000	£000
Fixed assets			
Intangible assets			
Patents, licences and trade marks		38	
Goodwill		20	
		58	
Tangible assets			
Buildings	1,500		
Plant and machinery	69		
Vehicles	200		
		1,769	
Investments			
Shares in undertakings in which the company has a participating interest		340	
			2,167
Current assets			
Stock	1,103		
Trade debtors	864		
		1,967	
Creditors: amounts falling due within one year			
Debenture loans	80		
Bank overdraft	21		
Trade creditors	392		
Other creditors	786		
		(1,279)	
Net current assets			688
			2,855

Creditors: amounts falling due after more than one year	£000	£000	£000
Debenture loans			(320)
			2,535
Capital and reserves			
Called-up share capital			1,200
Revaluation reserve			735
Profit and loss account			375
Other reserves			225
			2,535

Notes to the accounts

1 Share capital called up

	£
200,000 10 per cent preference shares of £1 each	200,000
1,000,000 ordinary shares of £1 each	1,000,000
	1,200,000

2 Accounting policies

Goodwill has been written off £20,000 against this year. The directors intend to write off the remaining £20,000 against next year's profits.

3 Tangible assets

	Buildings £000	Plant £000	Vehicles £000
Cost at 1.1.20X4	1,330	330	480
Disposals (at cost)	(130)	–	–
Adjustment for revaluation	735		
	1,935	330	480
Depreciation at 1.1.20X4	425	195	160
Provided in year	60	66	120
Disposals	(50)	–	–
	435	261	280
Net book values	1,500	69	200

4 Investments

The market value of investments at 31 December 20X3 was £438,000.

5 Ten per cent debenture loans

These are redeemable in five equal annual instalments, starting next year. Interest of £40,000 is charged in this year's accounts.

6 Other creditors including taxation

	£
Preference dividend proposed	20,000
Ordinary dividend proposed 50 per cent	500,000
Corporation tax based on year's profits	266,000
	786,000

7 Other reserves

	£
Exchange reserve	75,000
General reserve	150,000
	225,000

8 Directors' remuneration

The amounts paid to directors were as follows:

	£	£
Fees as directors	20,000	
Other emoluments	190,000	210,000

Emoluments of the chairman amounted to £42,000 and those of the highest-paid director £66,000. Other directors' emoluments were in the following ranges:

£45,001 to £50,000	1
£50,001 to £55,000	1

9 Operating profit is shown after charging

	£
Auditor's remuneration	7,000
Bank overdraft interest	19,000

Learning outcomes

You should now have learnt:

1 The Companies Acts require that additional notes be prepared and included with the published financial statements.

2 In some cases, the contents of these notes have been extended through the issuing of an accounting standard. For example, SSAP 25, *Segmental reporting*, extended the disclosure required of many entities concerning segmental performance.

3 Along with the notes to the financial statements, a directors' report must be presented that summarises the activities and performance of the entity, along with specific details on a number of matters, including directors' shareholdings and information concerning significant changes in fixed assets.

4 The notes to the accounts and the Directors' Report are both audited and covered by the Auditors' Report that is attached to companies' published annual reports.

5 There are set formats for the preparation of published financial statements.

6 Financial statements for internal use need not comply with these set formats.

7 Accounting standards have statutory recognition and must, therefore, be complied with when preparing financial statements intended to present a true and fair view.

8 How the Companies Act defines company size.

9 There are set formats for the preparation of published financial statements.

10 Accounts for internal use need not comply with these set formats.

11 FRS 3, *Reporting financial performance*, has altered the set format for the profit and loss account by requiring further details to be disclosed concerning:
 (a) continuing and discontinued operations;
 (b) restructuring; and
 (c) disposal of fixed assets.

12 In addition, by defining extraordinary items out of existence, FRS 3 effectively made obsolete a number of the categories contained in the set format profit and loss accounts relating to extraordinary items.

13 FRS 3 introduced two additional primary financial statements:
 (a) the statement of total recognised gains and losses; and
 (b) the reconciliation of movements in shareholders' funds (may be shown as a note).

14 FRS 3 introduced a new note – the note of historical cost profits and losses.

15 Some 'small' companies are exempted from having their financial statements audited.

16 'Small' and 'medium-sized' companies may file modified financial statements with the Registrar if they wish.

17 Plcs may send a summary financial statement to members in place of the full statements, but any member who requests the full statements must be sent them.

18 How bills of exchange are treated in the balance sheet.

19 The main proivisions of FRS 4, *Capital Instruments*.

REVIEW QUESTIONS

Advice: You are not expected to know all the very detailed requirements concerning the format of published profit and loss accounts and balance sheets. Your examination board may not even require you to be able to prepare profit and loss accounts and balance sheets in a form suitable for publication. However, you will be expected to understand the contents of published financial statements.

You should remember that both the published profit and loss account and balance sheet of a company must show certain items in a given order. And, it goes without saying that, if you can remember the basic outline of a published company profit and loss account and balance sheet, it will make commenting on one or more of the items that may appear in them far easier than if you cannot.

The contents of FRS 3 are likely to attract quite a lot of questions in future. In particular the definition of extraordinary items per FRS 3 will undoubtedly see quite a crop of questions. Some will come in the form of the directors of a company wanting to class something as extraordinary, and therefore shown after item 14, *Profit or loss on ordinary activities after taxation*, rather than before it. That could make their stewardship performance look better than it may actually have been.

6.1 GWR Ltd started in business on 1 January 20X6. Its issued share capital was 100,000 ordinary shares of £1 each and 50,000 10 per cent preference shares of £1 each.

Its net profits for the first two years of business were: 20X6 £42,005; 20X7 £34,831.

Preference dividends were paid for each of these years, while ordinary dividends were proposed as 20X6 12 per cent and 20X7 9 per cent.

Corporation tax, based on the profits of these two years, was: 20X6 £13,480; 20X7 £11,114.

Transfers to general reserve took place as: 20X6 £6,000; 20X7 £4,000.

Draw up profit and loss appropriation accounts for each of the years ended 31 December 20X6 and 20X7.

6.2   LMS Ltd has an authorised capital of £200,000, consisting of 160,000 ordinary shares of £1 each and 40,000 8 per cent preference shares of £1 each. Of these 120,000 ordinary shares had been issued and all the preference shares when the business first started trading.

The business has a financial year end of 31 December. The first three years of business resulted in net profit as follows: 20X7 £27,929; 20X8 £32,440; 20X9 £36,891.

Dividends were paid each year on the preference shares. Dividends on the ordinary shares were proposed as follows: 20X7 8 per cent; 20X8 10 per cent; 20X9 11 per cent.

Corporation tax, based on the profits of each year, was: 20X7 £8,331; 20X8 £10,446; 20X9 £12,001.

Transfers to reserves were made as: General reserve 20X7 £3,000, 20X8 £4,000, and Foreign exchange reserve 20X9 £2,000.

You are to show the profit and loss appropriation accounts for each of the years 20X7, 20X8 and 20X9.

6.3   A balance sheet is to be drawn up from the following as at 30 June 20X6:

	£
Issued share capital: ordinary shares £1 each	100,000
Authorised share capital: ordinary shares of £1 each	200,000
10 per cent debentures (repayable 30 June 20X9)	40,000
Buildings at cost	105,000
Motor vehicles at cost	62,500
Fixtures at cost	11,500
Profit and loss account	5,163
Fixed assets replacement reserve	8,000
Stock	16,210
Debtors	14,175
General reserve	6,000
Creditors	9,120
Proposed dividend	5,000
Depreciation to date: Motor vehicles	15,350
Premises	22,000
Fixtures	3,750
Bank (balancing figure for you to ascertain)	?

6.4X   From the information given below you are required to prepare for Streamline plc:

(*a*) a profit and loss appropriation account for the year ended 31 December 20X9;
(*b*) a balance sheet as at 31 December 20X9.

Streamline plc has an authorised share capital of £520,000, divided into 500,000 £1 ordinary shares and 20,000 5% preference shares of £1 each. Of these shares, 300,000 ordinary shares and all of the 5% preference shares have been issued and are fully paid.

In addition to the above information, the following balances remained in the accounts after the profit and loss account had been prepared for the year ended 31 December 20X9.

	Dr	Cr
	£	£
Plant and machinery, at cost	140,000	
Provision for depreciation on plant and machinery		50,000
Premises at cost	250,000	
Profit and loss account balance (1 January 20X9)		34,000
Net trading profit for year ended 31 December 20X9		15,000
Wages owing		3,900
Bank balance	15,280	
Stock (31 December 20X9)	16,540	
Trade debtors and creditors	12,080	3,000
Advertising prepaid	2,000	
General reserve		10,000

The directors have proposed the payment of the preference share dividend, and an ordinary share dividend of 6%. They also recommend a transfer of £20,000 to the general reserve.

(AQA (NEAB): GCSE)

6.5 The trial balance extracted from the books of Chang Ltd at 31 December 20X8 was as follows:

	£	£
Share capital		100,000
Profit and loss account 31 December 20X7		34,280
Freehold premises at cost	65,000	
Machinery at cost	55,000	
Provision for depreciation on machinery account as at 31 December 20X7		15,800
Purchases	201,698	
Sales		316,810
General expenses	32,168	
Wages and salaries	54,207	
Rent	4,300	
Lighting expenses	1,549	
Bad debts	748	
Provision for doubtful debts at 31 December 20X7		861
Debtors	21,784	
Creditors		17,493
Stock in trade 31 December 20X7	25,689	
Bank balance	23,101	
	485,244	485,244

You are given the following additional information:
(*i*)   The authorised and issued share capital is divided into 100,000 shares of £1 each.
(*ii*) Stock in trade at 31 December 20X8, £29,142.
(*iii*) Wages and salaries due at 31 December 20X8 amounted to £581.
(*iv*) Rent paid in advance at 31 December 20X8 amounted to £300.
(*v*)   A dividend of £10,000 is proposed for 20X8.
(*vi*) The provision for doubtful debts is to be increased to £938.
(*vii*) A depreciation charge is to be made on machinery at the rate of 10 per cent per annum on cost.

Required:

A trading and profit and loss account for 20X8 and a balance sheet as at 31 December 20X8.

6.6X The following is the trial balance of BCC Ltd as on 31 December 20X7:

	Dr £	Cr £
Share capital issued: ordinary shares £1		75,000
Debtors and creditors	28,560	22,472
Stock 31 December 20X6	41,415	
Bank	16,255	
Machinery at cost	45,000	
Motor vehicles at cost	28,000	
Depreciation provisions at 31.12.20X6:		
Machinery		18,000
Motor vehicles		12,600
Sales		97,500
Purchases	51,380	
Motor expenses	8,144	
Repairs to machinery	2,308	
Sundry expenses	1,076	
Wages and salaries	11,372	
Directors' remuneration	6,200	
Profit and loss account as at 31.12.20X6		6,138
General reserve		8,000
	239,710	239,710

Given the following information, you are to draw up a trading and profit and loss account for the year ended 31 December 20X7, and a balance sheet as at that date:

(*i*) Authorised share capital: £100,000 in ordinary shares of £1.
(*ii*) Stock at 31 December 20X7 £54,300.
(*iii*) Motor expenses owing £445.
(*iv*) Ordinary dividend proposed of 20 per cent.
(*v*) Transfer £2,000 to general reserve.
(*vi*) Provide for depreciation of all fixed assets at 20 per cent reducing balance method.

Required:

A trading and profit and loss account for 20X7 and a balance sheet as at 31 December 20X7.

6.7 You are to draw up a trading and profit and loss account for the year ended 31 December 20X8, and a balance sheet as at that date from the following trial balance and details of T Howe Ltd:

	Dr £	Cr £
Bank	6,723	
Debtors	18,910	
Creditors		12,304
Stock at 31 December 20X7	40,360	
Buildings at cost	100,000	
Equipment at cost	45,000	
Profit and loss account as at 31.12.20X7		15,286
General reserve		8,000
Foreign exchange reserve		4,200
Authorised and issued share capital		100,000
Purchases	72,360	

	Dr	Cr
	£	£
Sales		135,486
Carriage inwards	1,570	
Carriage outwards	1,390	
Salaries	18,310	
Rates and occupancy expenses	4,235	
Office expenses	3,022	
Sundry expenses	1,896	
Provisions for depreciation at 31.12.20X7:		
Buildings		32,000
Equipment		16,000
Directors' remuneration	9,500	
	323,276	323,276

Notes at 31 December 20X8:

(*i*)   Stock at 31 December 20X8 £52,360.

(*ii*)   Rates owing £280; Office expenses owing £190.

(*iii*) Dividend of 10 per cent proposed.

(*iv*) Transfers to reserves: General £1,000; Foreign exchange £800.

(*v*)   Depreciation on cost: Buildings 5 per cent; Equipment 20 per cent.

6.8X   Here is the trial balance of RF Ltd as at 30 June 20X8:

	Dr	Cr
	£	£
Share capital: authorised and issued		50,000
Stock as at 30 June 20X7	38,295	
Debtors	26,890	
Creditors		12,310
10% debentures		20,000
Fixed assets replacement reserve		10,000
General reserve		6,000
Profit and loss account as at 30 June 20X7		3,964
Debenture interest	1,000	
Equipment at cost	35,000	
Motor vehicles at cost	28,500	
Bank	3,643	
Cash	180	
Sales		99,500
Purchases	66,350	
Returns inwards	1,150	
Carriage inwards	240	
Wages and salaries	10,360	
Rent, rates and insurance	5,170	
Discounts allowed	1,246	
Directors' remuneration	2,500	
Provision for depreciation at 30 June 20X7:		
Equipment		8,400
Motors		10,350
	220,524	220,524

Given the following information as at 30 June 20X8, draw up a set of final accounts for the year to that date:

(*i*)   Stock 30 June 20X8: £49,371.

(*ii*) The share capital consisted of 25,000 ordinary shares of £1 each and 25,000 10 per cent preference shares of £1 each. The dividend on the preference shares was proposed to be paid as well as a dividend of 20 per cent on the ordinary shares.

(*iii*) Accrued rent: £700; Directors' remuneration: £2,500.

(*iv*) Debenture interest: ½ year's interest owing.

(*v*)   Depreciation on cost: Equipment 10 per cent; Motors 20 per cent.

(*vi*) Transfers to reserves: General reserve £2,000; Fixed assets replacement reserve £1,000.

6.9   Burden plc has an authorised capital of 500,000 ordinary shares of £0.50 each.

(*a*) At the end of its financial year, 31 May 20X9, the following balances appeared in the company's books:

	£
Issued capital: 400,000 shares fully paid	200,000
Freehold land and buildings at cost	320,000
Stock in trade	17,800
10% debentures	30,000
Trade debtors	6,840
Trade creditors	8,500
Expenses prepaid	760
Share premium	25,000
General reserve	20,000
Expenses outstanding	430
Profit and loss account balance (1 June 20X8)	36,200
Bank overdrawn	3,700
Fixtures, fittings and equipment	
at cost	54,000
provision for depreciation	17,500

The company's trading and profit and loss accounts had been prepared and revealed a net profit of £58,070. However, this figure and certain balances shown above needed adjustment in view of the following details which had not been recorded in the company's books.

(*i*)   It appeared that a trade debtor who owed £300 would not be able to pay. It was decided to write his account off as a bad debt.

(*ii*) An examination of the company's stock on 31 May 20X9 revealed that some items shown in the accounts at a cost of £1,800 had deteriorated and had a resale value of only £1,100.

(*iii*) At the end of the financial year some equipment which had cost £3,600 and which had a net book value of £800 had been sold for £1,300. A cheque for this amount had been received on 31 May 20X9.

Required:

1 A statement which shows the changes which should be made to the net profit of £58,070 in view of these unrecorded details.

(*b*) The directors proposed to pay a final dividend of 10% and to transfer £50,000 to general reserve on 31 May 20X9.

Required:

For Burden plc (taking account of *all* the available information)

2 The profit and loss appropriation account for the year ended 31 May 20X9.
3 Two *extracts* from the company's balance sheet as at 31 May 20X9, showing in detail:
   (*i*) the current assets, current liabilities and working capital
   (*ii*) the items which make up the shareholders' funds.

(*c*) The directors are concerned about the company's liquidity position.

Required:

4 **THREE** transactions which will increase the company's working capital. State which balance sheet items will change as a result of each transaction and whether the item will increase or decrease in value.

(AQA (SEG): GCSE)

6.10X The accountant of Fiddles plc has begun preparing final accounts but the work is not yet complete. At this stage the items included in the trial balance are as follows:

	£000
Land	100
Buildings	120
Plant and machinery	170
Depreciation provision	120
Share capital	100
Profit and loss balance brought forward	200
Debtors	200
Creditors	110
Stock	190
Operating profit	80
Debentures (16%)	180
Provision for doubtful debts	3
Bank balance (asset)	12
Suspense	1

Notes (*i*) to (*vii*) below are to be taken into account:

(*i*) The debtors control account figure, which is used in the trial balance, does not agree with the total of the debtors ledger. A contra of £5,000 has been entered correctly in the individual ledger accounts but has been entered on the wrong side of both control accounts.

  A batch total of sales of £12,345 had been entered in the double entry system as £13,345, although individual ledger account entries for these sales were correct. The balance of £4,000 on sales returns account has inadvertently been omitted from the trial balance, though correctly entered in the ledger records.

(*ii*) A standing order received from a regular customer for £2,000, and bank charges of £1,000, have been completely omitted from the records.

(*iii*) A debtor for £1,000 is to be written off. The provision for doubtful debts balance is to be adjusted to 1% of debtors.

(*iv*) The opening stock figure had been overstated by £1,000 and the closing stock figure had been understated by £2,000.

(*v*) Any remaining balance on suspense account should be treated as purchases if a debit balance and as sales if a credit balance.

(*vi*) The debentures were issued three months before the year end. No entries have been made as regards interest.

(*vii*) A dividend of 10% of share capital is to be proposed.

Required:

(*a*) Prepare journal entries to cover items in notes (*i*) to (*v*) above. You are NOT to open any new accounts and may use only those accounts included in the trial balance as given.

(*b*) Prepare final accounts for internal use in good order within the limits of the available information. For presentation purposes all the items arising from notes (*i*) to (*vii*) above should be regarded as material.

(*Association of Chartered Certified Accountants*)

6.11 The directors of the company by which you are employed as an accountant have received the forecast profit and loss account for 20X9 which disclosed a net profit for the year of £36,000.

This is considered to be an unacceptably low figure and a working party has been set up to investigate ways and means of improving the forecast profit.

The following suggestions have been put forward by various members of the working party:

(*a*) 'Every six months we deduct income tax of £10,000 from the debenture interest and pay it over to the Inland Revenue. If we withhold these payments, the company's profit will be increased considerably.'

(*b*) 'I see that in the three months August to October 20X9 we have forecast a total amount of £40,000 for repainting the exterior of the company's premises. If, instead, we charge this amount as capital expenditure, the company's profit will be increased by £40,000.'

(*c*) 'In November 20X9, the replacement of a machine is forecast. The proceeds from the sale of the old machinery should be credited to profit and loss account.'

(*d*) 'There is a credit balance of £86,000 on general reserve account. We can transfer some of this to profit and loss account to increase the 20X9 profit.'

(*e*) 'The company's £1 ordinary shares, which were originally issued at £1 per share, currently have a market value of £1.60 per share and this price is likely to be maintained. We can credit the surplus £0.60 per share to the 20X9 profit and loss account.'

(*f*) 'The company's premises were bought many years ago for £68,000, but following the rise in property values, they are now worth at least £300,000. This enhancement in value can be utilised to increase the 20X9 profit.'

You are required, as the accounting member of the working party, to comment on the feasibility of each of the above suggestions for increasing the 20X9 forecast profit.

(*Association of Chartered Certified Accountants*)

6.12 From the following selected balances of Rogers plc as at 31 December 20X2 draw up (*i*) a trading and profit and loss account for internal use, and (*ii*) a profit and loss account for publication.

	£
Profit and loss account as at 31 December 20X1	15,300
Stock 1 January 20X2	57,500
Purchases	164,000
Sales	288,000
Returns inwards	11,500
Returns outwards	2,000
Carriage inwards	1,300
Wages and salaries (see note (*b*))	8,400

	£
Rent and rates (see note (*c*))	6,250
General distribution expenses	4,860
General administrative expenses	3,320
Discounts allowed	3,940
Bad debts	570
Debenture interest	2,400
Motor expenses (see note (*d*))	7,200
Interest received on bank deposit	770
Income from shares in related companies (gross)	660
Motor vehicles at cost: Administrative	14,000
Distribution	26,000
Equipment at cost: Administrative	5,500
Distribution	3,500
Royalties receivable	1,800

Notes:

(*a*) Stock at 31 December 20X2 £64,000.

(*b*) Wages and salaries are to be apportioned: Distribution costs one-third, Administrative expenses two-thirds.

(*c*) Rent and rates are to be apportioned: Distribution costs 60 per cent, Administrative expenses 40 per cent.

(*d*) Apportion Motor expenses equally between Distribution costs and Administrative expenses.

(*e*) Depreciate Motor vehicles 25 per cent and Equipment 20 per cent on cost.

(*f*) Accrue auditors' remuneration of £500.

(*g*) Accrue corporation tax for the year on ordinary activity profits £30,700.

(*h*) A sum of £8,000 is to be transferred to general reserve.

(*i*) An ordinary dividend of £30,000 is to be proposed.

6.13 You are given the following selected balances of Federal plc as at 31 December 20X4. From them draw up (*i*) a trading and profit and loss account for the year ended 31 December 20X4 for internal use and (*ii*) a profit and loss account for publication.

	£
Stock 1 January 20X4	64,500
Sales	849,000
Purchases	510,600
Carriage inwards	4,900
Returns inwards	5,800
Returns outwards	3,300
Discounts allowed	5,780
Discounts received	6,800
Wages (putting goods into saleable condition)	11,350
Salaries and wages: Sales and distribution staff	29,110
Salaries and wages: Administrative staff	20,920
Motor expenses (see note (*c*))	15,600
Rent and rates (see note (*d*))	25,000
Investments in related companies (market value £66,000)	80,000
Income from shares in related companies	3,500
General distribution expenses	8,220
General administrative expenses	2,190
Bad debts	840
Interest from government securities	1,600

	£
Haulage costs: Distribution	2,070
Debenture interest payable	3,800
Profit and loss account: 31 December 20X3	37,470
Motor vehicles at cost: Distribution and sales	75,000
Administrative	35,000
Plant and machinery at cost: Distribution and sales	80,000
Administrative	50,000
Production	15,000
Directors' remuneration	5,000

Notes:

(*a*) The production department puts goods bought into a saleable condition.

(*b*) Stock at 31 December 20X4 £82,800.

(*c*) Apportion Motor expenses: Distribution two-thirds, Administrative one-third.

(*d*) Apportion Rent and rates: Distribution 80 per cent, Administrative 20 per cent.

(*e*) Write £14,000 off the value of investments in related companies.

(*f*) Depreciate Motor vehicles 20 per cent on cost, Plant and machinery 10 per cent on cost.

(*g*) Accrue auditors' remuneration £2,000.

(*h*) Accrue corporation tax on ordinary activity profits £74,000.

(*i*) A sum of £20,000 is to be transferred to debenture redemption reserve.

(*j*) An ordinary dividend of £50,000 is to be proposed.

6.14X The following selected balances are from the books of Falconer plc as on 31 August 20X4. From them draw up (*i*) a trading and profit and loss account, for internal use, for the year ended 31 August 20X4, also (*ii*) a profit and loss account for publication for the year.

	£
Purchases	540,500
Sales	815,920
Returns inwards	15,380
Returns outwards	24,620
Carriage inwards	5,100
Wages – productive	6,370
Discounts allowed	5,890
Discounts received	7,940
Stock 31 August 20X3	128,750
Wages and salaries: Sales and distribution	19,480
Wages and salaries: Administrative	24,800
Motor expenses: Sales and distribution	8,970
Motor expenses: Administrative	16,220
General distribution expenses	4,780
General administrative expenses	5,110
Rent and rates (see note (*c*))	9,600
Directors' remuneration	12,400
Profit and loss account: 31 August 20X3	18,270
Advertising costs	8,380
Bad debts	1,020
Hire of plant and machinery (see note (*b*))	8,920
Motor vehicles at cost: Sales and distribution	28,000
Administrative	36,000
Plant and machinery: Distribution	17,500
Debenture interest payable	4,800

	£
Income from shares in group companies	12,800
Income from shares in related companies	10,500
Preference dividend paid	15,000
Profit on disposal of investments	6,600
Tax on profit on disposal of investments	1,920

Notes:

(*a*) Stock at 31 August 20X4 £144,510.

(*b*) The hire of plant and machinery is to be apportioned: Productive £5,200, Administrative £3,720.

(*c*) Rent and rates to be apportioned: Distribution two-thirds, Administrative one-third.

(*d*) Motors are to be depreciated at 25 per cent on cost, Plant and machinery to be depreciated at 20 per cent on cost.

(*e*) Auditors' remuneration of £1,700 to be accrued.

(*f*) Corporation tax on profit from ordinary activities for the year is estimated at £59,300.

(*g*) Transfer £25,000 to general reserve.

(*h*) Ordinary dividend of £60,000 is proposed.

6.15X From the following balance of Danielle plc you are to draw up (*i*) a trading and profit and loss account for the year ended 31 December 20X6, for internal use, and (*ii*) a profit and loss account for publication:

	£
Plant and machinery, at cost (see note (*c*))	275,000
Bank interest receivable	1,850
Discounts allowed	5,040
Discounts received	3,890
Hire of motor vehicles: Sales and distribution	9,470
Hire of motor vehicles: Administrative	5,710
Licence fees receivable	5,100
General distribution expenses	11,300
General administrative expenses	15,800
Wages and salaries: Sales and distribution	134,690
Administrative	89,720
Directors' remuneration	42,000
Motor expenses (see note (*e*))	18,600
Stock 31 December 20X5	220,500
Sales	880,000
Purchases	405,600
Returns outwards	15,800
Returns inwards	19,550
Profit and loss account as at 31 December 20X5	29,370

Notes:

(*a*) Stock at 31 December 20X6 £210,840.

(*b*) Accrue auditor's remuneration £3,000.

(*c*) Of the Plant and machinery, £150,000 is distributive in nature, whilst £125,000 is for administration.

(*d*) Depreciate plant and machinery 20 per cent on cost.

(*e*) Of the Motor expenses two-thirds is for Sales and distribution and one-third for Administration.

(*f*) Corporation tax on ordinary profits is estimated at £28,350.

(g) Proposed ordinary dividend is £50,000.

(h) A sum of £15,000 is to be transferred to general reserve.

6.16   The draft accounts of Wilkinson Ltd for the year ended 31 December 20X0 showed a gross profit of £97,000, and a net profit on ordinary activities after taxation of £25,000. Certain errors, listed below, had been made in arriving at these figures.

1 Taxation of £20,000 had been deducted, but no adjustment had been made for the fact that the previous year's provision of £18,000 had proved to be an overestimate when compared to the actual tax liability in that year of £16,000.

2 A building, which was bought on 1 January 20X8 on a fifty year lease at a cost of £80,000, had been revalued on 1 January 20X0 at £100,800. Amortisation in the draft accounts had been calculated at £1,600 for the year.

3 Goods returned to suppliers, totalling £4,025 (including Value Added Tax at 15%), had been added to the sales figure instead of being deducted from the purchases.

4 Value Added Tax (VAT) had been included in the sales figure as shown in the draft trading account. VAT is charged at 15% on all sales, and the amount of sales shown in the draft trading account, including the returns noted in paragraph 3 above, was £199,525.

There was a difference on the draft balance sheet, which was shown in a suspense account.

Required:

(a) A detailed summary of the effect of items 1 to 4 above on the draft gross profit and draft net profit on ordinary activities before taxation.   (16 marks)

(b) A reconstruction of the suspense account showing any entries which may have been made in the account as a result of items 1 to 4.   (4 marks)

(London Qualifications Limited (University of London): GCE A-level)

6.17X   The accountants of Jarndyce plc, a shoe manufacturer, are considering how they should treat the following items in the profit and loss account of the company for the year ended 31 May 20X1.

(i)   A loss of £200,000 caused by the seizure of company assets during a revolution in Gondwanaland.

(ii)   £150,000 redundancy money paid to the former employees of a subsidiary which is continuing to trade.

(iii) £100,000 written off as a bad debt. The average total of debtors during the year was £140,000.

(iv) £50,000 error relating to an undervaluation of the opening stock.

(v)   £70,000 loss on the closure of the company's printing division.

Revenue reserves at 1 June 20X0 total £620,000 and profit for the year ended 31 May 20X1 was £465,000 before any adjustments which might be required by (i)–(v) above.

   The accountants have some knowledge of extraordinary items, exceptional items and prior year adjustments, but are unsure if these terms are relevant to any of the above items.

Prepare:

(a) the amended profit and loss account for the year ended 31 May 20X1, in as much detail as is possible from the information given.   (12 marks)

(b) a statement of the changes in the company's revenue reserves during the year. (3 marks)

(London Qualifications Limited (University of London): GCE A-level)

6.18 The following balances remained in the books of Owen Ltd on 31 December 20X1, *after* the profit and loss account and appropriation account had been drawn up. You are to draft the balance sheet as at 31 December 20X1 in accordance with the Companies Act.

	Dr £	Cr £
Ordinary share capital: £1 shares		50,000
Preference share capital: 50p shares		25,000
Calls account (ordinary shares)	150	
Development costs	3,070	
Goodwill	21,000	
Land and buildings – at cost	48,000	
Plant and machinery – at cost	12,500	
Provision for depreciation: Buildings		16,000
Provision for depreciation: Plant and machinery		5,400
Shares in undertakings in which the company has a participating interest	35,750	
Stock: Raw materials	3,470	
Stock: Finished goods	18,590	
Debtors: Trade	17,400	
Amounts owed by undertakings in which company has participating interest	3,000	
Prepayments	1,250	
Debentures (*see* note 1)		10,000
Bank overdraft (repayable within 6 months)		4,370
Creditors: Trade (payable within 1 year)		12,410
Bills payable (*see* note 2)		3,600
Share premium		20,000
Capital redemption reserve		5,000
General reserve		4,000
Profit and loss account		8,400
	164,180	164,180

Notes:
1. Of the debentures £6,000 is repayable in 3 months' time, while the other £4,000 is repayable in 5 years' time.
2. Of the bills payable, £1,600 is in respect of a bill to be paid in 4 months' time and £2,000 for a bill payable in 18 months' time.
3. The depreciation charged for the year was: Buildings £4,000, Plant and machinery £1,800.

6.19 After the profit and loss appropriation account has been prepared for the year ended 30 September 20X4, the following balances remain in the books of Belle Works plc. You are to draw up a balance sheet in accordance with the Companies Act.

	£	£
Ordinary share capital		70,000
Share premium		5,000
Revaluation reserve		10,500
General reserve		6,000
Foreign exchange reserve		3,500
Profit and loss account		6,297
Patents, trade marks and licences	1,500	
Goodwill	17,500	

	£	£
Land and buildings at cost	90,000	
Provision for depreciation: Land and buildings		17,500
Plant and machinery at cost	38,600	
Provision for depreciation: Plant and machinery		19,200
Stock of raw materials: 30 September 20X4	14,320	
Work in progress: 30 September 20X4	5,640	
Finished goods: 30 September 20X4	13,290	
Debtors: Trade	11,260	
Debtors: Other	1,050	
Prepayments and accrued income	505	
Debentures (redeemable in 6 months' time)		6,000
Debentures (redeemable in 4½ years' time)		12,000
Bank overdraft (repayable in 3 months)		3,893
Trade creditors (payable in next 12 months)		11,340
Trade creditors (payable after 12 months)		1,260
Bills of exchange (payable within 12 months)		4,000
Corporation tax (payable in 9 months' time)		14,370
National insurance (payable in next month)		305
Pensions contribution owing		1,860
Deferred taxation		640
	193,665	193,665

6.20X The trial balance of Payne Peerbrook plc as on 31 December 20X6 is as follows:

	Dr	Cr
	£	£
Preference share capital: £1 shares		50,000
Ordinary share capital: 50p shares		60,000
General reserve		45,000
Foreign exchange reserve		13,600
Profit and loss account as on 31 December 20X5		19,343
Stock 31 December 20X5	107,143	
Sales		449,110
Returns inwards	11,380	
Purchases	218,940	
Carriage inwards	2,475	
Wages (putting goods into a saleable condition)	3,096	
Wages: Warehouse staff	39,722	
Wages and salaries: Sales staff	28,161	
Wages and salaries: Administrative staff	34,778	
Motor expenses (see note 2)	16,400	
General distribution expenses	8,061	
General administrative expenses	7,914	
Debenture interest	10,000	
Royalties receivable		4,179
Directors' remuneration	18,450	
Bad debts	3,050	
Discounts allowed	5,164	
Discounts received		4,092
Plant and machinery at cost (see note 3)	175,000	
Provision for depreciation: Plant and machinery		58,400

	Dr	Cr
	£	£
Motor vehicles at cost (see note 2)	32,000	
Provision for depreciation: Motor vehicles		14,500
Goodwill	29,500	
Development costs	16,320	
Trade debtors	78,105	
Trade creditors		37,106
Bank overdraft (repayable any time)		4,279
Bills of exchange payable (all due within 1 year)		6,050
Debentures (redeemable in 5 years' time)		80,000
	845,659	845,659

Notes:

1 Stock of finished goods on 31 December 20X6 £144,081.
2 Motor expenses and depreciation on motors to be apportioned: Distribution $^3/_4$ths, Administrative $^1/_4$th.
3 Plant and machinery depreciation to be apportioned. Cost of sales $^1/_5$th: Distribution $^3/_5$ths: Administrative $^1/_5$th.
4 Depreciate the following fixed assets on cost: Motor vehicles 25 per cent, Plant and machinery 20 per cent.
5 Accrue corporation tax on profits of the year £14,150. This is payable 1 October 20X7.
6 A preference dividend of £5,000 is to be paid and an ordinary dividend of £10,000 is to be proposed.

You are to draw up:

(*a*) A trading and profit and loss account for the year ended 31 December 20X6 for internal use, and

(*b*) A profit and loss account for publication, also a balance sheet as at 31 December 20X6.

6.21X The following financial information is available for Oakcroft plc, a retailing organisation, as at 31 March 20X2.

	£000
Aggregate depreciation on furniture and fittings at 1 April 20X1	31
Trade debtors	104
Trade creditors	86
Share premium account	50
Purchases	880
Sales	1,534
Issued share capital	370
Furniture and fittings at cost	395
Debenture interest	11
Cash at bank and cash in hand	328
Auditors' remuneration	30
Administration expenses	170
11% Debenture loan stock (20X8)	100
Distribution costs	110
Fixed assets: investments at cost	190
Hire charges: distribution equipment and vehicles	200
Interim dividend: paid 1 October 20X1	8
Profit and loss account: 1 April 20X1	320 Cr
Dividends received: 1 January 20X2	45
Stock in trade: 1 April 20X1	110

Additional information:

1 The authorised share capital is 450,000 ordinary shares of £1 each.
2 The directors have proposed that a final ordinary share dividend of 7 per cent be paid for the year ended 31 March 20X2.
3 Stock in trade was valued at £135,000 as at 31 March 20X2.
4 The market value of the investments at 31 March 20X2 was £208,000.
5 Depreciation of £28,000 is to be charged on furniture and fittings for the year to 31 March 20X2. One quarter of this depreciation is a distribution expense. There were no purchases or sales of furniture during the year.
6 Expenses in arrears as at 31 March 20X2:

	£000
Administration	12
Distribution	16

Required:

(*a*) A trading and profit and loss account for the year ended 31 March 20X2. *(9 marks)*

(*b*) A profit and loss appropriation account for the year ended 31 March 20X2. *(3 marks)*

(*c*) A balance sheet as at 31 March 20X2. *(8 marks)*

(*d*) From the final accounts of Oakcroft plc give the minimum information required to be shown by the Companies Acts (including the relevant figures) for each of the following:
  (*i*) The trading account.
  (*ii*) The revenue expenditure of the profit and loss account. *(5 marks)*

Note: Ignore all exemptions permitted for small and medium size companies.

(AQA (AEB): GCE A-level)

6.22 The Chairman's statement in the accounts of Great Traders plc contained the following:

'I am pleased to report that the total operating profit for the year to 30 November 20X1 was £143 million. These good results were achieved despite higher costs. After interest of £19.5 million the profit before tax of £123.5 million was 12 per cent up on the same period in 20X0. Future investment will be concentrated on those areas offering the highest returns and the greatest growth prospects.'

This reported profit would have pleased the following interested groups but for different reasons.

Required

Give reasons why the following groups would be pleased to hear of the increase in the profits of Great Traders plc.

(*a*) Shareholders *(3 marks)*
(*b*) Debenture holders *(3 marks)*
(*c*) Employees *(3 marks)*

(AQA: GCE A-level, Paper ACC2, Q7, 16/1/2002)

CHAPTER 7

Reserves, bonus issues and rights issues

Learning objectives

By the end of this chapter, you should be able to:

- explain the difference between revenue reserves and capital reserves;
- describe how capital reserves may be used;
- explain the difference between bonus issues and rights issues;
- make the entries in the accounts for bonus issues and rights issues.

7.1 Shareholders' funds

Shareholders' funds comprise the issued share capital and reserves. There are occasions when it is desirable for companies to alter the make-up of shareholders' funds, perhaps through the issue of new shares or by the conversion of reserves into share capital.

7.2 The nature of reserves

In the next three sections we will look at how revenue reserves and capital reserves are created. Before doing so, we must get rid of a misconception, common among students and some businessmen alike, that reserves mean that somewhere there is an investment held in cash, or shares or similar, which could be used to pay for whatever was needed by the company. With students, this misconception is most commonly found in relation to depreciation, which is a reserve created to reflect the reduction in worth of a fixed asset. It is not created in order to establish a fund to replace the asset, and it does not and cannot do so.

The creation of a reserve has come about by a debit entry and a credit entry in the books. No transaction has taken place. It is purely an adjustment of the entries in the books. A general reserve, for instance, is created by debiting the appropriation account and crediting a general reserve account. It does not involve, at the same time, putting some money into a special bank account.

A company can, therefore, have quite large amounts of reserves and yet have a very large bank overdraft. Obviously if (say) £200,000 had been appropriated as a general reserve then that amount could not, in that year, have been paid out as a dividend.

Labelling that amount as transferred to a general reserve account is a way of saying that we do not want to pay that amount out as dividends in that year. Therefore, the bank overdraft will be £200,000 less than it would have been if the reserve had not been made, and it had instead been paid out as a dividend.

Let's now look at the three classes of reserves.

7.3   Revenue reserves

A **revenue reserve** is where an amount has been voluntarily transferred from the profit and loss appropriation account by debiting it, thus reducing the amount of profits left available for cash dividend purposes, and crediting a named **reserve account**. The reserve may be for some particular purpose, such as a **foreign exchange reserve account** created just in case the firm should ever meet a situation where it would suffer loss because of devaluation of a foreign currency, or it could be a **general reserve account**.

Such transfers are, in fact, an indication to the shareholders that it would be unwise at that particular time to pay out all the available profits as dividends. The resources represented by part of the profits should more wisely and profitably be kept in the firm, at least for the time being. Revenue reserves can be called upon in future years to help swell the profits shown in the profit and loss appropriation account as being available for dividend purposes. This is effected quite simply by debiting the particular reserve account and crediting the profit and loss appropriation account in that future year.

7.4   General reserves

A **general reserve** may be needed because of the effect of inflation. If in the year 20X3 a firm needs a working capital of £4,000, the volume of trade remains the same for the next three years but the price level increases by 25 per cent, then the working capital requirements will now be £5,000. If all the profits are distributed, the firm will still only have £4,000 working capital which cannot possibly finance the same volume of trade as it did in 20X3. Transferring annual amounts of profits to a general reserve instead of paying them out as dividends is one way to help overcome this problem. On the other hand it may just be the convention of conservatism asserting itself, with a philosophy of 'it's better to be safe than sorry', in this case to restrict dividends because the funds they would withdraw from the business may be needed in a moment of crisis. This is sometimes overdone, with the result that the firm has excessive amounts of liquid funds being inefficiently used, whereas if they were paid out to the shareholders, who after all are the owners, then the shareholders could put the funds to better use themselves.

Under normal circumstances the remaining balance carried forward on the profit and loss account is treated as a revenue reserve.

7.5   Capital reserves

A **capital reserve** is normally quite different from a revenue reserve. It is a reserve which is *not* available for transfer to the profit and loss appropriation account to swell the profits shown as available for cash dividend purposes. Most capital reserves can never be utilised for cash dividend purposes.

Note the use of the word 'cash'. As you will see later in this chapter, bonus shares may be issued as a 'non-cash' dividend.

The ways that capital reserves are created must, therefore, be looked at.

Capital reserves created in accordance with the Companies Acts

The Companies Acts state that the following are capital reserves and can never be utilised for the declaration of dividends payable in cash:

(*a*) Capital redemption reserve – the Companies Act 1985 includes a regulation which states that, other than when financed by a new issue of shares, when shares are redeemed an amount equal to the nominal value of shares redeemed is to be transferred from distributable profits to a capital redemption reserve.

(*b*) Share premium account.

(*c*) Revaluation reserve – where an asset has been revalued then an increase is shown by a debit in the requisite asset account and a credit in the Revaluation Account. The recording of a reduction in value is shown by a credit in the asset account and a debit in the Revaluation Account.

Capital reserves created by case law

There have been quite a few legal cases to establish exactly whether an item would be a distributable profit or not and therefore available for cash dividend purposes. The difference determines whether an item should be transferred to a capital reserve account as not being distributable, or else to a revenue reserve account if it is distributable. These cases will have to be studied at the more advanced stages of accounting, and so will not be dealt with here.

7.6 Profits available for payments of dividends in cash

Only the 'realised profits' and 'realised losses' come into the calculations of how much can be paid (distributed) as cash dividends, the word 'cash' including payments by cheque. The Companies Acts define realised profits and losses as 'those profits and losses which are treated as realised in the accounts, in accordance with principles generally accepted with respect to the determination of realised profits and losses for accounting purposes at the time when those accounts are prepared'.

This means that what the accounting profession, at the time the accounts are prepared, accepts as 'realised profits and losses' is exactly what the law will also accept as correct. In accounting, the realisation concept recognises profit or loss at the point when a contract is made in the market to buy or sell assets. The realisation concept should have been part of your earlier studies.

You have already been told that the law says that capital reserves can never be utilised in the calculation of the amount out of which dividends can be paid in cash. However, reserves which are not capital reserves can be brought into the calculations.

The reserves which are revenue reserves (i.e. they are not capital reserves) have been voluntarily transferred to reserve accounts named for each specific reserve, or else they are in the balance on the profit and loss account after appropriations. They have not been so appropriated because of the need to do it by law. Should the company at any future time, in its wisdom, decide to transfer any or all of them back to the credit of the profit and loss account, and then pay cash dividends out of the then total amount in the profit and loss account, there is nothing in law that says that this cannot be done.

Whether it would be wise from a financial point of view is another matter, and we cannot be too specific about it; it all depends on the circumstances. Let us also be aware that a reserve does not equal cash available for dividend purposes. Let us look at two companies, which, for whatever reason, wish to pay as large a dividend as possible. Their reserves and cash and bank balances are as follows:

	Company A £	Company B £
General reserve	50,000	20,000
Foreign exchange reserve	–	10,000
Asset replacement reserve	70,000	–
Inflation protection reserve	–	5,000
Balance on profit and loss account	30,000	25,000
Cash and bank balances	60,000	90,000

You can see that Company A has a total of £50,000 + £70,000 + £30,000 = £150,000, which would be the total of profits available for dividend purposes. In theory it could pay out a dividend of £150,000 in cash. Would it do so?

Immediately you can see that Company A only has £60,000 cash and bank balances. It would need another £90,000 from somewhere to be able to pay a dividend of £150,000. It is more than doubtful whether the bank, or anyone else, under normal circumstances would lend the company £90,000 for this reason. It is possible that there are extreme circumstances, which demand extreme answers.

For A-level examinations you are often called upon to use your imagination and some knowledge of what happens in the real business world, in order to come up with answers which are rational enough but cannot be found within the pages of a textbook. Try to visualise when Company A may in fact decide to pay a dividend of £150,000 given the above facts about the reserves and the cash and bank balances.

Here are some possibilities:

● An unwelcome takeover bidder has appeared. The company is advised that if it pays the maximum dividend possible, the takeover bid will be averted.
● A new system of taxation will mean that dividends will suffer tax at the rate of 98 per cent (a number of wealthy taxpayers did pay at this rate in the 1970s). Payment of dividends before the new tax year will only suffer tax at 40 per cent. Most of the shareholders are wealthy people. The answer – pay out as big a dividend as possible now.

The £90,000 needed might possibly be raised by the issue of shares or debentures, or by selling off some unwanted fixed assets.

Under normal circumstances, it is likely that a much smaller dividend would be paid. If it was desired to pay a dividend of £50,000, then £20,000 could be transferred to the credit of the profit and loss account which, added to the existing balance of £30,000, would give profits available of £50,000. The company would decide how much to transfer from the other revenue reserves to make up this amount.

Company B has a total of £20,000 + £10,000 + £5,000 + £25,000 = £60,000 available for distribution as dividends. It has £90,000 cash and bank balances and, under normal circumstances, it could pay such a dividend. Whether it would do so would depend on the circumstances and needs of the company.

We must remember that the cash and bank balances are needed, not just for dividend purposes, but for all sorts of other necessary expenditures. We have to look at the company as a whole, and to understand all of its needs, before we can say whether or not it would make sense to pay a particular rate of dividend.

7.7 Allowable reductions of capital reserves

We have already seen that capital reserves cannot be used for the purpose of increasing profits available for *cash* dividend purposes. Within the confines of the GCE A-level syllabuses, what they can be used for now follows. Beware, there are other uses, but these include topics which are not covered in your examinations and are, therefore, beyond the scope of this textbook.

Capital redemption reserve

To be applied in paying up unissued shares of the company as fully-paid shares. These are commonly called 'bonus shares', and will be covered later in this chapter.

Share premium account

(*a*) The same provision referring to bonus shares as exists with the capital redemption reserve.
(*b*) Writing off preliminary expenses.
(*c*) Writing off expenses and commission paid on the issue of shares or debentures.
(*d*) In writing off discounts on shares or debentures issued.
(*e*) Providing any premium payable on redemption or purchases of shares or debentures.

Revaluation reserve

Where the directors are of the opinion that any amount standing to the credit of the revaluation reserve is no longer necessary then the reserve must be reduced accordingly. An instance of this would be where an increase in the value of an asset had been credited to the revaluation account, and there had subsequently been a fall in the value of that asset.

Reserves created by case law

These can be used in the issue of bonus shares or in the paying up of partly paid shares.

Let's now look at shares issued 'free' to existing shareholders – bonus shares – and then at shares issued for money to existing shareholders through what is known as a rights issue.

7.8 Bonus shares

Bonus shares are shares issued to existing shareholders free of charge. An alternative name is **scrip issue**.

If the articles give the power, and the requisite legal formalities are observed, the following may be applied in the issuing of bonus shares:

1 the balance of the profit and loss appropriation account;
2 any other revenue reserve;
3 any capital reserve, e.g. share premium.

This thus comprises all of the reserves.

The reason why this should ever be needed can be illustrated by taking the somewhat exaggerated example shown in Exhibit 7.1.

EXHIBIT 7.1

Better Price Ltd, was founded 50 years ago with 1,000 ordinary shares of £1 each and £1,000 in the bank. The company has constantly had to retain a proportion of its profits to finance its operations, thus diverting them from being used for cash dividend purposes. By electing to hold the amounts retained in cash rather than invest them in fixed assets, the company has built up its working capital to a point where it now finds it has no operational need for some of the funds retained.

Its balance sheet as at 31 December 20X7 is:

Better Price Ltd
Balance Sheet as at 31 December 20X7
(before bonus shares are issued)

	£
Fixed assets	5,000
Current assets *less* current liabilities	5,000
	10,000
Share capital	1,000
Reserves (including profit and loss appropriation balance)	9,000
	10,000

If an annual profit of £1,500 was now being made, this being 15 per cent on capital employed, and £1,000 could be paid annually as cash dividends, then the dividend declared each year would be 100 per cent, i.e. a dividend of £1,000 on shares of £1,000 nominal value.

It is obvious that the dividends and the share capital have got out of step with one another. Owing to their lack of accounting knowledge, there is a risk that employees and trade unions may well become concerned that the firm was making unduly excessive profits. Customers, especially if they are members of the general public, may also be deluded into thinking that they are being charged excessive prices, or, even though this could be demonstrated not to be true because of the prices charged by competitors, they may well still have the feeling that they are somehow being duped.

In point of fact, an efficient firm in this particular industry or trade may well be only reasonably rewarded for the risks it has taken by making a profit of 15 per cent on capital employed. The figure of 100 per cent for the dividend is due to the very misleading convention in accounting in the UK of calculating dividends in relationship to the nominal amount of the share capital rather than their market price.

If it is considered that net assets should never fall below £8,000 this would mean that only £2,000 needs to be kept in reserves. The remaining £8,000 could be share capital, so ensuring that net assets do not fall below £8,000 even were all the reserves paid out as dividends.

In order to have £8,000 in share capital, £7,000 must be transfered from the reserves into share capital. This is done through issuing bonus shares to the existing shareholders in proportion to their existing shareholdings. In this case, they would receive 7 bonus share for every share they hold.

The balance sheet after issuing the bonus shares would be:

Better Price Ltd
Balance Sheet as at 31 December 20X7
(after bonus shares are issued)

	£
Fixed assets	5,000
Current assets *less* current liabilities	5,000
	10,000
Share capital (£1,000 + £7,000)	8,000
Reserves (£9,000 − £7,000)	2,000
	10,000

When the dividends of £1,000 per annum are declared in the future, they will amount to:

$$\frac{£1,000}{£8,000} \times \frac{100}{1} = 12.5 \text{ per cent}$$

This will cause less disturbance in the minds of employees, trade unions and customers.

Of course the issue of bonus shares may be seen by any of the interested parties to be some form of diabolical liberty. To give seven shares of £1 each free for one previously owned may be seen as a travesty of social justice. In point of fact the shareholders have not gained at all. Before the bonus issue there were 1,000 shareholders who owned between them £10,000 of net assets. Therefore, assuming just for this purpose that the book 'value' is the same as any other 'value', each share was worth £10. After the bonus issue, each previous holder now has eight shares for every one share he held before. If he had owned one share only, he now owns eight shares. He is therefore the owner of $^8/_{8,000}$ part of the firm, i.e. a one-thousandth part. The 'value' of the net assets is £10,000, so that he owns £10 of them, so his shares are worth £10. This is exactly the same 'value' as that applying before the bonus issue was made.

It would be useful, in addition, to refer to other matters for comparison. Anyone who had owned a £1 share 50 years ago, then worth £1, would now have (if he was still living after such a long time) eight shares worth £8. A new house of a certain type 50 years ago might have cost £x; it may now cost £$8x$. The cost of a bottle of beer may now be y times greater than it was 50 years ago, a packet of cigarettes may be z times more and so on. Of course, the firm has brought a lot of trouble on itself by waiting so many years to capitalise reserves. It should have been done by several stages over the years.

This is all a very simplified, and in many ways an exaggerated version. There is, however, no doubt that misunderstanding of accounting and financial matters has caused a great deal of unnecessary friction in the past and will probably still do so in the future. Yet another very common misunderstanding is that the assumption the reader was asked to accept, namely that the balance sheet values equalled 'real values', is often one taken by the reader of a balance sheet. Thus a profit of £10,000 when the net assets' book values are £20,000 may appear to be excessive, yet in fact a more realistic value of the assets may be saleable value – in this case the value may be £100,000.

The accounting entries necessary are to debit the reserve accounts utilised, and to credit a bonus account. The shares are then issued and the entry required to record this is to credit the share capital account and to debit the bonus account. The journal entries would be:

The Journal

	Dr £	Cr £
Reserve account(s) (show each account separately)	7,000	
Bonus account		7,000
Transfer of an amount equal to the bonus payable in fully paid shares		
Bonus account	7,000	
Share capital account		7,000
Allotment and issue of 7,000 shares of £1 each, in satisfaction of the bonus declared		

Clearly, issuing bonus shares affects the capital structure of a company. Another type of share issue that results in an increase in share capital and also, obviously, affects the capital structure of a company is a rights issue.

7.9 Rights issues

A company can also increase its share capital by making a **rights issue**. This is the issue of shares to existing shareholders at a price lower than the ruling market price of the shares.

The price at which the shares of a very profitable company are quoted on the Stock Exchange is usually higher than the nominal value of the shares. For instance, the market price of the shares of a company might be quoted at £2.50 while the nominal value per share is only £1.00. If the company has 8,000 shares of £1 each and declares a rights issue of one for every eight held at a price of £1.50 per share, it is obvious that it will be cheaper for the existing shareholders to buy the rights issue at this price instead of buying the same shares in the open market for £2.50 per share. Assume that all the rights issue were taken up, then the number of shares taken up will be 1,000 (i.e. 8,000 ÷ 8), and the amount paid for them will be £1,500. The journal entries will be:

The Journal

	Dr £	Cr £
Cash	1,500	
Share capital		1,000
Share premium		500
Being the rights issue of 1 for every 8 shares held at a price of £1.50 nominal value being £1.00		

It is to be noted that because the nominal value of each share is £1.00 while £1.50 was paid, the extra 50p constitutes a share premium to the company.

Notice also that the market value of the shares will be reduced or 'diluted' by the rights issue, as was the case for bonus shares. Before the rights issue there were 8,000 shares at a price of £2.50, giving a market capitalisation of £20,000. After the issue there are 9,000 shares and the assets have increased by £1,500. The market value may therefore reduce to £2.39 [(20,000 + 1,500)/9,000)], although the precise market price at the end of the issue will have been influenced by the information given surrounding the sale about the future prospects of the company and may not be exactly the amount calculated.

You should now have learnt:

1 That there are two main categories of reserves:
   (*a*) revenue reserves (can be freely distributed); and
   (*b*) capital reserves (subject to restrictions on their distribution).

2 That there is often no need to transfer amounts from profit and loss into a revenue reserve. However, doing so does signal the likelihood of some future event and so could improve the true and fair view of the financial statements.

3 Some of the uses that can be made of capital reserves.

4 The difference between bonus issues and rights issues.

5 How to make the entries in the accounts for bonus issues and rights issues.

6 The effect upon the balance sheet of bonus issues and rights issues.

REVIEW QUESTIONS

Advice: You can expect quite a lot of questions which have some bearing on this chapter. These are mainly:

(i)   to what uses you can put the reserves
(ii) the differences between capital and revenue reserves
(iii) an issue of bonus shares and the use of reserves thereby
(iv) to calculate exactly what dividends can be paid by cash from the balances of reserves and the profit and loss account
(v)   the use of the revaluation reserve

   Which kinds of reserves can be brought into the calculation of the maximum amount that could be paid out as *cash* dividends? This asks you to distinguish between *revenue* reserves which can be used for cash dividend purposes, whilst *capital* reserves cannot. On the other hand, capital reserves can be used in the calculations of how many (free) bonus shares can be issued to shareholders.

Examples:

(i) A question which asks you to transfer a capital reserve back to the credit side of the profit and loss appropriation account. This cannot be allowed as it means in effect that it would swell the amount of profits available for distribution as cash dividends.

(ii) A question which asks you to revalue the property and to show the increase in the value on the credit side of the profit and loss appropriation account. This should be credited to a capital reserve account instead.

Remember that a 'rights issue' is entered exactly the same as an ordinary issue of shares. The only difference is that the rights issue is pitched at a somewhat lower price than would be asked from people who were to become shareholders for the first time. Also, remember that a bonus issue of shares means changing equivalent amounts from being reserves into being share capital.

7.1 The following constitutes the share capital and reserves of Seeds Ltd and Plant Ltd:

	Seeds Ltd	Plant Ltd
	£	£
Share capital: £1 ordinary	200,000	300,000
£1 Preference 10%	50,000	80,000
Share premium account	35,000	24,000
Asset revaluation reserve	10,000	–
General reserve	40,000	70,000
Foreign exchange reserve	5,000	–
Fixed assets replacement reserve	–	20,000
Profit and loss account before dividends	45,000	63,000

The companies have the following dividend policies:

Seeds Ltd: to retain a balance of £25,000 on the profit and loss account and to pay a preference dividend and the highest possible dividend on ordinary shares. All the relevant reserves can be called on for this purpose.

Plant Ltd: the same policy as Seeds Ltd, except that £40,000 is to be left in the general reserve account.

Required:

Showing your workings, calculate the percentage dividends which can be paid on ordinary shares for each company in keeping with the policies laid down.

7.2X The directors of Dennis plc are to meet shortly to consider the amount of dividend which they should pay to the shareholders of the company. The draft audited balance sheet shows the following reserves:

	£
Share premium account	60,000
Capital redemption reserve	100,000
Asset revaluation reserve	200,000
General reserve	50,000
Profit and loss account	100,000

The asset revaluation reserve arose during the year when a building was revalued from £300,000 to £500,000.

(*a*) State, with reasons, the extent to which each of the five reserves can be used for the payment of dividends.
(*5 marks*)

(*b*) Calculate the maximum *percentage* dividend which could be paid, assuming that the issued share capital at the balance sheet date consisted of 2 million ordinary shares of 25p each.
(*5 marks*)

(*c*) The company intends to replace its buildings in four years' time, at an anticipated cost of £1,500,000. It proposes to create an asset replacement reserve to ensure that sufficient cash is available to purchase the new buildings at the appropriate time. Comment on this proposal.
(*5 marks*)

(London Qualifications Limited (University of London): GCE A-level)

7.3 Grimble Limited's trial balance at 31 December 20X0 includes the following credit balances.

	£
Net profit for the year (before taxation and dividends)	265,500
Retained profits brought forward	188,300
9% Preference share capital (fully paid)	56,000
Ordinary share capital (fully paid)	280,000
Capital redemption reserve	147,000
7% Debentures	95,000

The directors make the following decisions which affect the draft accounts.

1 Taxation of £60,000 is to be provided for on the profits.
2 Capital redemption reserves are to be used for an issue of bonus shares in the ratio of one bonus share for every two shares held.
3 Whilst the first half-year's debenture interest and interim preference dividend had been paid and included within the draft accounts, the remaining amounts are still to be provided for.
4 Fixed assets are to be revalued upwards by £20,000.
5 No interim dividend on the ordinary shares has been paid, but a final dividend of 20p per share is proposed. No final dividend is to be paid on the bonus shares issued.

Required:

(a) The profit and loss appropriation account for the year ended 31 December 20X0.

(8 marks)

(b) A revised extract from the company's trial balance after the five decisions have been incorporated within the accounts, showing all outstanding balances which can be calculated from the information available.

(7 marks)

(London Qualifications Limited (University of London): GCE A-level)

7.4X After the trading and profit and loss accounts had been drawn up for Lemon Limited for the year ended 31 May 20X9, the following balances remained in the accounts:

	Dr £	Cr £
Ordinary share capital (£1 shares)		170,000
10% redeemable £1 preference shares		50,000
Debtors and creditors	96,800	65,302
Goodwill	20,000	
Fixed assets	187,600	
Stock	34,080	
Bank balance	94,200	
Profit and loss account		117,378
Share premium account		30,000
	432,680	432,680

After the trial balance was extracted, the directors decided to:

1 convert the existing £1 ordinary shares into shares with a nominal value of 50p;
2 redeem the 10% redeemable £1 preference shares at a premium of 5% (the shares had been issued originally at a premium of 10%);
3 issue bonus shares by utilising the value remaining in the share premium account after allowing for the premium payable on the redemption of the preference shares;

4 write off the goodwill;

5 propose a dividend of 10p per share on all ordinary shares of 50p each, including those issued by way of bonus.

Required:

(a) Show the ordinary share capital account, the share premium account and the ordinary dividend account as they would appear after the above decisions were implemented.

(9 marks)

(b) Prepare the (unpublished) balance sheet as at 31 May 20X9, after the implementation of all the directors' decisions and assuming no other transactions. *(10 marks)*

(c) Give two reasons why a company might wish to issue *bonus* shares to its existing shareholders.

(6 marks)

(London Qualifications Limited (University of London): GCE A-level)

7.5 Expansion plc is to issue shares to the public at the same time as a rights issue is made to its existing members. Bonus shares will also be issued.

The company's most recent balance sheet provides the following information:

	£
Paid up share capital	
100,000 preference shares at £1	100,000
500,000 ordinary shares at 50p	250,000
Reserves	
Share premium account	100,000
Capital redemption reserve	75,000
Revaluation reserve	100,000
General reserve	200,000
Asset replacement reserve	50,000
Profit and loss account	75,000
	£950,000

Authority to increase the company's capital has been obtained.

An extraordinary meeting of members has resolved the following:

(i)   One bonus share is to be issued for each five ordinary shares held.

(ii) Both preference and ordinary shareholders will be allowed to subscribe for ten ordinary shares for every ten shares (excluding bonus shares) of either class held: 10p per share is payable on application and 80p on allotment.

(iii) Additional shares may be applied for both by existing shareholders and by the public. Applications from existing shareholders are to be accepted in full before any allotments are made to the public: 25p per share is payable on application and £1.50 on allotment.

When the application lists closed it was found that:

(i)   The rights issue was entirely taken up and no shareholder at the time held less than 10 shares. No shareholders held any fraction of 5 shares.

(ii) Existing shareholders applied for and were allotted 50,000 shares.

(iii) Members of the public sent in application monies for a further 75,000 shares, of which only 50,000 were allotted. The directors allotted two shares for every three applied for. No fractional adjustments were required.

Required:

(a) An extract from the company's balance sheet showing the shares and reserves after the allotments have taken place but before amounts due on allotment have been paid.

(10 marks)

(b) A statement of the entries to be included in the bank account.

(4 marks)

(c) An explanation of why shares are sometimes issued at a premium.

(4 marks)

(Welsh Joint Education Committee: GCE A-level)

7.6 The summarised draft balance sheet as at 30 April 20X0 of T. Torrents Limited is as follows:

	Cost	Aggregate depreciation	
	£	£	£
Fixed assets			
Freehold land and buildings	60,000	4,000	56,000
Plant and machinery	47,000	14,100	32,900
Motor vehicles	16,000	9,600	6,400
	123,000	27,700	95,300
Current assets			
Stock		29,000	
Trade debtors and amounts prepaid		14,000	
Balance at bank		7,000	
		50,000	
Amounts falling due within one year			
Trade creditors and accrued charges		(9,800)	
			40,200
			135,500
Amounts falling due after more than one year			
8% Debenture stock			(40,000)
			£ 95,500
Represented by capital and reserves			
Ordinary shares of £1 each fully paid			60,000
Share premium account			10,000
Retained earnings			25,500
			£ 95,500

It has now been discovered that effect has not yet been given in the company's accounts for the year ended 30 April 20X0 to the following matters:

(i) On 1 May 20X9, the company sold machine KM623 for £5,000; this machine had been bought on 1 May 20X6 for £12,000. The company received goods valued at £5,000 in settlement for the machine. It is company policy for all plant and machinery to be depreciated at 12½ per cent per annum on cost.

(ii) On 30 April 20X0, the company purchased £6,000 of its 8 per cent Debenture stock for £5,200. The relevant cheque was not presented for payment until 4 May 20X0 and has been omitted from the company's cash book.

(iii) A provision for doubtful debts of 2½ per cent of debts outstanding at 30 April 20X0 is to be created; amounts prepaid at 30 April 20X0 amounted to £400.

(iv) The freehold land and buildings has been revalued at 30 April 20X0 at £70,000; it is proposed to give effect to this revaluation in the accounts.

(*v*) It has been discovered that a piece of equipment belonging to a customer and held by the company for repair was inadvertently added to the company's stock valuation at 30 April 20X0; the item was valued at £2,000.

(*vi*) The company made a bonus (scrip) issue of one ordinary share of £1 each for every twelve held on 31 December 20X9.

(*vii*) A final dividend for the year ended 30 April 20X0 on the ordinary share capital of 10p per share is being proposed.

Required:

(*a*) A corrected balance sheet as at 30 April 20X0 of T. Torrents Limited. (*22 marks*)

(*b*) Explain the reason for the creation of a share premium account. (*3 marks*)

(*OCR: from the University of Cambridge Local Examinations Syndicate*)

7.7 The balance sheet of De Vere Carter plc included the following information at 31 May 20X2:

	£
Issued share capital:	
Ordinary shares of £1 each, fully paid	240,000
10% Preference shares of £1 each, fully paid	90,000
Reserves:	
Share premium account	65,000
Capital redemption reserve	40,000
Revaluation reserve	120,000
Profit and loss account	56,000

On 1 June 20X2, the company is planning to increase its ordinary share capital in the following ways:

(*i*) An issue of bonus shares to existing members, with one bonus share being issued for every three ordinary shares held. The directors wished to retain the maximum flexibility regarding future dividend payments, so an appropriate choice of reserves was to be made for the purpose of the bonus issue.

(*ii*) A rights issue, whereby existing shareholders (both of ordinary and preference shares) may subscribe for five ordinary shares at £1.90 each for every three shares of either class held (excluding bonus shares). £1 is payable on application (by 30 June 20X2), and 90p on allotment (by 31 July 20X2).

(*iii*) A public issue of 100,000 ordinary shares to be made at £2.50 each, with £1.10 payable on application (by 30 June 20X2) and the balance on allotment (by July 20X2). Existing shareholders are to be given priority, as their applications will be accepted before those of the general public.

Applications were received as follows:

1 90% of the rights issue was taken up, and paid for by the due dates.

2 Existing shareholders applied for, and were allotted, 60,000 of the share issue. Other applications totalled 90,000 shares, and these were scaled down on a pro-rata basis, with excess application money being refunded on 10 July 20X2. All application and allotment monies were paid by the due date, with the exception of £3,000 allotment money due from existing shareholders.

(*a*) Show the company's application and allotment account, and ordinary share capital account for the period 1 June 20X2 to 31 July 20X2. (*12 marks*)

(b) Calculate the final number of shares held by a shareholder with an initial holding of 900 ordinary shares, who applied for the rights issue and 500 shares in the new share issue. *(3 marks)*

(c) Explain two advantages and two disadvantages to a company of raising funds by a share issue, and suggest three alternative ways of raising funds that the company could have considered. *(10 marks)*

(London Qualifications Limited (University of London): GCE A-level)

7.8X Aggressive Marketing plc, whose entire equity is made up of 100,000 25 pence shares, is in need of finance for planned expansion. It has therefore duly registered the required prospectus and attracted applications for 250,000 shares at a premium of 10 pence. Applicants have paid 20 pence on application, the balance (which includes the premium) being due on notification of allotment. The existing shareholders have only approved a further issue of 200,000 shares so the directors have resolved to allot the new issue to applicants as follows:

(i) Applicants for 5,000 shares are to be refused as their individual applications are for insufficient shares to justify the administration costs involved. Their application monies are to be returned to them.

(ii) Applicants for 15,000 shares are to be allotted shares in accordance with their applications.

(iii) Other applicants will be allotted the remaining shares in proportion to their individual applications but, rather than refunding application monies, these are to be retained by the company on account of the balance due on allotment.

It has also been resolved that existing shareholders should have the advantage of a rights issue of 50,000 shares at nominal value. The terms of the issue are that 25 pence is to be paid on application. No shareholder has an odd number of shares. After formal notification to those qualified, application monies for 40,000 shares have been received. The only asset the company has is cash.

Required:

(i) Application and allotment, share capital and share premium accounts to reflect the above transactions. *(16 marks)*

(ii) A calculation of the worth of one share owned by an investor who has subscribed for his rights and paid the monies due from him. *(7 marks)*

(iii) The company's balance sheet at the completion of the above transactions. *(5 marks)*

(Welsh Joint Education Committee: GCE A-level)

7.9 The directors of Shapers plc are considering an expansion of the company's operations which it is estimated will require a further £5,000,000 to be invested in the company.

The following information has been extracted from the latest published balance sheet of the company:

	£
Ordinary shares of 25p each, fully paid	2,600,000
8% Preference shares of £1.00 each, fully paid	1,400,000
Share premium account	200,000
Revaluation reserve	400,000
General reserve	500,000
Retained earnings	800,000
6% Loan stock 20X4/X5	1,000,000

The current price of the company's ordinary shares is 60p whilst that of the preference shares is par.

The directors are now considering how to raise the additional capital and have asked the company's financial adviser to report on the advantages and disadvantages of each of the following in meeting the company's projected capital needs:

A rights issue of ordinary shares at par
A rights issue of ordinary shares at a premium of 20p per share
A bonus issue of ordinary shares
An issue of 8% preference shares of £1.00 each at par
An issue of 6% loan stock at par.

Required:

As the company's financial adviser, prepare a report to the directors on their proposals.

(25 marks)

(OCR: from the University of Cambridge Local Examinations Syndicate)

CHAPTER 8

Published financial statements and ratio analysis

Learning objectives

By the end of this chapter, you should be able to:

- describe various groups of accounting ratios, where they would be used, why they would be of interest, and to whom;
- calculate a number of commonly used accounting ratios and interpret the results;
- calculate capital gearing and interpret the results;
- comment on company performance, as revealed by ratio analysis, from the viewpoint of investors;
- describe some of the difficulties that may arise in the calculation and interpretation of accounting ratios;
- explain the dangers in overtrading and how ratio analysis can be used to identify it;
- explain the importance of comparing the results of an organisation with other similar organisations;
- explain the importance of looking at the trend over time when assessing the financial position and performance of an organisation;
- explain the pyramid of ratios that can be used in order to enhance the view obtained from ratio analysis;
- explain how sensitivity to changes in the level of performance is linked to whether costs are fixed or variable;
- explain that different groups of users of financial statements have access to different sources of information that may help in developing an understanding of and explanation for the results of ratio analysis.

Part I ACCOUNTING RATIOS

8.1 Why use ratios?

You learnt about accounting ratios in the first year of your A-level course. This chapter takes that material forward, re-examining it for reinforcement and developing greater depth of knowledge and understanding.

Information is data organised for a purpose. Information contained in financial statements is organised so as to enable users of the financial statements to draw conclusions concerning the financial well-being and performance of the reporting entity. In the case of the financial statements of companies, independent auditors review the manner in which the data have been presented and provide a filter mechanism attesting to the reliability of the information presented. For partnerships and sole traders, there is generally no such independent review. However, as the financial statements are generally subject to review by the tax authorities, there is some justification in assuming that they are a reasonable reflection of reality.

Yet, being 'reasonably assured' of their reliability is not generally sufficient for tax authorities and they will review the financial statements of partnerships and sole traders to determine whether there may be cause to doubt their reliability. One of the key instruments at their disposal is ratios, and they use ratio analysis to compare those found in the entity under review with those typically existing in that sector of the economy. Hence, through ratio analysis, factors can be identified that would not otherwise be apparent.

Ratio analysis can also be used to review trends and compare entities with each other. A number of commercial organisations specialise in this service, providing detailed ratio analysis of the financial statements of plcs to subscribers and enabling analysts to see, at a glance, how one entity is performing, or how its financial structure compares to that of others of a similar nature.

Without ratios, financial statements would be largely uninformative to all but the very skilled. With ratios, financial statements can be interpreted and usefully applied to satisfy the needs of the reader.

For example, let's take the performance of four companies, all dealing in the same type of goods:

	Gross profit £	Sales £
Company A	10,000	84,800
Company B	15,000	125,200
Company C	25,000	192,750
Company D	17,500	146,840

Suppose you want to know which company gets the best profit margins. Simply inspecting these figures and trying to decide which performance was the best, and which was the worst, is virtually impossible. To bring the same basis of comparison to each company we need some form of common measure. The common measure used would be a ratio – the amount of gross profit on sales as a percentage. The comparison now becomes:

	%
Company A	11.79
Company B	11.98
Company C	12.97
Company D	11.91

Company *C*, with 12.97% gross profit on sales (i.e. £12.97 gross profit per £100 sales) has performed better than the other companies.

8.2	How to use ratios

You can only sensibly compare like with like. There is not much point in comparing the gross profit percentage of a wholesale chemists with that of a restaurant, for example.

Similarly, figures are only comparable if they have been built up on a similar basis. The sales figures of Company *X* which treats items as sales only when cash is received cannot be properly compared with Company *Z* which treats items as sales as soon as they are invoiced.

Another instance of this could be that of stock turnover, if Company *K* is compared with Company *L*. They are both toy shops so would seem to be comparable. However, although both companies have sales of £100,000 the average stock of *K* is £40,000 whilst that of *L* is £10,000. Cost of sales is £50,000, so **stock turnover** ratios are:

$$\begin{array}{ccc} & K & L \\[4pt] \dfrac{\textbf{Cost of sales}}{\textbf{Average stock}} & \dfrac{50{,}000}{40{,}000}=1.25 & \dfrac{50{,}000}{10{,}000}=5 \end{array}$$

It looks as though *L* has managed to turn its stock over five times during the year compared with *K*, 1.25 times. Is it true? Well, it depends. Let's imagine that *K* had a financial year end of 30 November, just before Christmas, so toy stocks would be extremely high; that *L* had a year end of 31 January when, following the Christmas sales, its stock had dropped to the year's lowest level; and that at 30 November, *L* also had stock valued at £40,000. Can you see how the difference in the timing of the year end can affect this ratio significantly?

Ratios therefore need very careful handling. They are extremely useful if used properly, but can be very misleading otherwise.

8.3	Users of ratios

There are vast number of parties interested in analysing financial statements – shareholders, lenders, customers, suppliers, employees, government agencies and competitors are just some of the groups who may all be interested in the financial statements of an entity. Yet, in many respects they will be interested in different things, and so there is no definitive, all-encompassing list of points for analysis that would be useful to all the groups. Nevertheless, it is possible to construct a series of ratios that together will provide all these groups with something that they will find relevant, and from which they can choose to investigate further, if necessary. Ratio analysis is a first step in assessing an entity. It removes some of the mystique surrounding the financial statements and makes it easier to pinpoint items which it would be interesting to investigate further.

Exhibit 8.1 shows some of categories of ratios and indicates some of the groups that would be interested in them.

EXHIBIT 8.1

Ratio category	Examples of interested groups
Liquidity	Shareholders, suppliers, creditors, competitors
Profitability	Shareholders, management, employees, creditors, competitors, potential investors
Efficiency	Shareholders, potential purchasers, competitors
Capital structure	Shareholders, lenders, creditors, potential investors
Shareholder	Shareholders, potential investors

Note: At the end of this chapter, in Section 8.17, you will find a list of all the main ratios. You may find it useful to refer to it while reading through the next few sections.

8.4 Liquidity

The return on profit on capital employed, as you will see, gives an overall picture of profitability. It cannot always be assumed, however, that profitability is everything that is desirable. It must be stressed that accounting is needed, not just to calculate profitability, but also to know whether or not the business will be able to pay its creditors, expenses, loans falling due, etc. at the correct times. Failure to ensure that these payments are covered effectively could mean that the business would have to be closed down. Being able to pay one's debts as they fall due is known as being 'liquid'.

It is essential that a business is aware if a customer or borrower is at risk of not repaying the amount due. New customers are usually vetted prior to being allowed to trade on credit rather than by cash. For private individuals, there are credit rating agencies with extensive records of the credit histories of many individuals. For a small fee, a company can receive a report indicating whether a new customer might be a credit risk. Similarly, information can be purchased concerning companies that indicates their solvency, i.e. whether they are liable to be bad credit risks.

The difference between these two sources of information is that, while the information on private individuals is based on their previous credit record, that of the companies is generally based on a ratio analysis of their financial statements. The ratio analysis will focus upon the liquidity (or solvency) ratios. Of these the best known are the current ratio and the acid test ratio.

Current ratio

This compares assets which will become liquid within approximately 12 months (i.e. total current assets) with liabilities which will be due for payment in the same period (i.e. total current liabilities) and is intended to indicate whether there are sufficient short-term assets to meet the short-term liabilities:

$$\text{Current ratio} = \frac{\text{Current assets}}{\text{Current liabilities}}$$

Traditionally, in order to provide some general guide, a value is given that may generally be taken to be the 'norm'. This has become increasingly less meaningful and is really more misleading (as it instils undue confidence) than helpful – the ratio is so sector dependent as to be incapable of being defined as 'generally best if around x'. Consequently, no such guidance will be given here. Rather, a set of factors will be suggested that ought to be considered:

- What is the norm in this industrial sector?
- Is this company significantly above or below that norm?
- If so, can this be justified after an analysis of the nature of these assets and liabilities, and of the reasons for the amounts of each held?

The ratio when calculated may be expressed as either a ratio to 1, with current liabilities being set to 1, or as a 'number of times', representing the relative size of the amount of total current assets compared with total current liabilities.

Example

If total current assets are £40,000 and total current liabilities are £20,000, the current ratio could be expressed as either:

$$£40,000 : £20,000 \quad = 2 : 1$$

or as:
$$\frac{£40,000}{£20,000} \quad = 2 \text{ times}$$

Acid test ratio

This shows that provided creditors and debtors are paid at approximately the same time, a view might be made as to whether the business has sufficient liquid resources to meet its current liabilities.

$$\text{Acid test ratio} = \frac{\text{Current assets} - \text{Stock}}{\text{Current liabilities}}$$

As with the current ratio, there is little benefit in suggesting a norm for the value to expect. The only difference in the items involved between the two ratios is that the acid test (or 'quick') ratio does not include stock. Otherwise, it is identical to the current ratio, comparing current assets, excluding stock, to current liabilities. Stock is omitted as it is considered to be relatively illiquid, because it depends upon prevailing and future market forces and may be impossible to convert to cash in a relatively short time.

Exhibit 8.2 shows how two businesses may have similar profitability, yet their liquidity positions may be quite different.

EXHIBIT 8.2

	E		F	
	£	£	£	£
Fixed assets		40,000		70,000
Current assets				
Stock	30,000		50,000	
Debtors	45,000		9,000	
Bank	15,000		1,000	
	90,000		60,000	
Less Current liabilities: creditors	(30,000)		(30,000)	
		60,000		30,000
		100,000		100,000
Capital				
Opening capital		80,000		80,000
Add Net profit		36,000		36,000
		116,000		116,000
Less Drawings		(16,000)		(16,000)
		100,000		100,000

Sales for both E and F amounted to £144,000. Gross profits for E and F were identical at £48,000.

Profitability is the same for both businesses. However, there is a vast difference in the liquidity of the two businesses.

$$\text{Current ratios } E = \frac{90{,}000}{30{,}000} = 3{:}1 \quad F = \frac{60{,}000}{30{,}000} = 2{:}1$$

This looks adequate on the face of it, but the acid test ratio reveals that F is in distress, as it will probably find it difficult to pay its current liabilities on time.

$$\text{Acid test ratio } E = \frac{60{,}000}{30{,}000} = 2{:}1 \quad F = \frac{10{,}000}{30{,}000} = 0.33{:}1$$

It is not enough for a business to be profitable. It should also be adequately liquid.

However, although a business should be adequately liquid, it is possible for it to have too high a current ratio or acid test ratio. While too much was being kept as current assets, which would raise the values of the two ratios, those assets may not be being used profitably. For instance, a high stock figure would increase the current ratio, but we may have more money tied up in stock than is necessary, meaning that we are not using our money to best effect. Too high a balance in the bank account could also mean that the money is just lying there, not being used properly.

There are some other ratios that will usually also be considered when assessing liquidity: stock turnover, debtor/sales and creditor/purchases. These are often classified as *efficiency* ratios, as they indicate how efficient the management of the items they consider has been. In order to understand their relationship to the current ratio and asset test ratios, we'll consider them now rather than in the section that deals with efficiency ratios.

Stock turnover

A reduction in stock turnover can mean that the business is slowing down. Stocks may be piling up and not being sold. This could lead to a liquidity crisis, as money may be being taken out of the bank simply to increase stocks which are not then sold quickly enough. It is hardly surprising, therefore, that this ratio is included in virtually every case where accounting ratios are being calculated. It measures the number of times (approximately) that stock is replenished in an accounting period.

For Exhibit 8.2 the cost of sales for each company was £144,000 − £48,000 = £96,000. If opening stocks had been E £34,000 and F £46,000 stockturns would have been:

	E	F
$\dfrac{\textbf{Cost of sales}}{\textbf{Average stock}}$	$\dfrac{96{,}000}{(34{,}000 + 30{,}000) \div 2}$	$\dfrac{96{,}000}{(46{,}000 + 50{,}000) \div 2}$
	$= \dfrac{96{,}000}{32{,}000} = 3 \text{ times}$	$= \dfrac{96{,}000}{48{,}000} = 2 \text{ times}$

It appears that F's stock is starting to pile up, perhaps because it is having difficulty selling it compared with E. The ratio can also be expressed as a number of days – the number of days stock held. In the case of E, 365 would be divided by 3 producing a result of 121.7 days. For F, it would be 182.5 days.

There are two major difficulties in computing this ratio: if cost of sales is not available, it is tempting to use sales instead. This should not be done other than as a last resort, and the results should be appropriately described, analysed and interpreted. Sales are expressed at selling prices; stock is expressed at cost price. Use of sales instead of cost of sales in the equation will not be comparing like with like.

In addition, there are at least three possible stock values that could be used – opening, closing and the average of these figures. The average figure would be the more commonly used, but use of any of the three can be justified.

Whichever stock value is used, the result will, at best, be a crude estimate. Due to seasonality of the business, stock, as shown in the balance sheet for example, may not be representative of the 'normal' level of stock. However, it is still useful for comparing trends over time and should be used mainly for that purpose. The result it produces needs careful consideration. A rising stock turnover may indicate greater efficiency, or it may be an indicator that stocks are being run down and that there may be problems in meeting demand in future. A falling stock turnover may indicate lower efficiency, perhaps with a build-up of obsolete stocks, or it could indicate higher stock volumes are being held because stock purchasing has become more efficient and the higher stock levels are financially beneficial for the company. In addition, it is important not to overlook that any change in the ratio may have nothing to do with the stock, but may be due to changes in factors relating to the sales for the period.

Debtor/sales ratio (or debtor days ratio)

This indicates how efficient the company is at controlling its debtors. The resources tied up in debtors is an important ratio subject. Funds tied up unnecessarily in debtors is unproductive. In the example in Exhibit 8.2, this can be calculated for the two companies as:

$$E \qquad\qquad F$$

$$\frac{\textbf{Debtor}}{\textbf{Sales}} \qquad \frac{45{,}000}{144{,}000} = 1:3.2 \qquad \frac{9{,}000}{144{,}000} = 1:16$$

This relationship is often translated into the length of time a debtor takes to pay. This turns out to be:

$$E \qquad\qquad F$$

$$365 \times \frac{1}{3.2} = 114 \text{ days} \qquad 365 \times \frac{1}{16} = 22.8 \text{ days}$$

Why Company E should have allowed so much time for its debtors to pay is a matter for investigation. Possibly the company was finding it harder to sell goods, and to sell at all it was forced to sell to customers on long credit terms. It could well be that E has no proper credit control system, whereas F has an extremely efficient one.

Strictly speaking, the debtors and sales figures are not comparable when companies charge VAT on their sales. Debtors include the VAT on sales; the figure for sales excludes VAT. However, the adjustment is not difficult to make if required for clarity.

As with stock, the amount shown in the balance sheet for debtors may not be representative of the 'normal' level. Nevertheless, this is generally a very useful ratio to calculate and comparison with those of other companies in the same industrial sector may be very interesting. However, as with stock turnover, its strength lies in trend analysis between periods.

Creditor/purchases ratio (or creditor days ratio)

This ratio indicates how the company uses short-term financing to fund its activities and further investigation will reveal whether or not the result is due to efficiency.

Assuming that purchases for E amounted to £92,000 and were £100,000 for F, the ratios are:

$$
\begin{array}{ccc}
 & E & F \\
\dfrac{\textbf{Creditor}}{\textbf{Purchases}} & \dfrac{30,000}{92,000} = 1:3.07 & \dfrac{30,000}{100,000} = 1:3.3
\end{array}
$$

This also is often translated into the length of time we take to pay our creditors. This turns out to be:

$$
\begin{array}{cc}
E & F \\
365 \times \dfrac{1}{3.07} = 118.9 \text{ days} & 365 \times \dfrac{1}{3.3} = 110.6 \text{ days}
\end{array}
$$

The purchases figure is not usually available in published financial statements, and the cost of sales amount would be used in its place. As with stock turnover and debtor days, its strength lies in trend analysis between periods.

Let's consider another example which shows why you need to consider all these ratios when looking at liquidity.

Example

Many companies operate with acid test ratios below 1 : 1. That is, they have insufficient liquid assets to meet their short-term liabilities. The great majority of companies in this situation have no problem paying their creditors when due.

If total current assets, including stock of £22,000, are £40,000 and total current liabilities stand at £20,000, the acid test ratio will be £18,000 : £20,000 = 0.9 : 1 (or 0.9 times). This means that if all current liabilities had been due for payment at the balance sheet date, it would not have been possible to do so without converting into cash some assets (e.g. stock, or fixed assets) that were likely to be convertible into cash only at a discount on their true value – that is, the company would have had to pay a premium in order to meet its obligations, and would not be able to continue to do so indefinitely.

However, the reality is generally that the current liabilities are due for payment at varying times over the coming financial period and some, for example a bank overdraft, may not, in reality, ever be likely to be subject to a demand for repayment. Trade creditors usually allow flexibility concerning the date when payment must be made, so the date of payment can be aligned with when there are funds available to make it. (However, taking too much time to pay suppliers can result in their refusing to supply more goods, so care must be taken not to abuse the flexibility in payment date that theoretically exists.)

The current assets, on the other hand, are within the control of the company and can be adjusted in their timing to match the due dates for payment to creditors. They can be renewed many times before one or other of the current liabilities is due for payment. For example, debtors may be on a ten-day cycle while trade creditors are paid after 90 days' credit has expired. Clearly, in this case, receipts from nine times the balance sheet debtors' figure could be received and available to meet the trade creditor figure shown in the balance sheet. A similar position may hold for stock.

As with the current ratio, the acid test ratio should be compared to the norms for the industrial sector, and the underlying assets and liabilities should be considered to determine whether there is any cause for concern in the result obtained. Again, they also should be compared to the norms for the industrial sector.

8.5 Profitability

These measures indicate whether the company is performing satisfactorily. They are used, among other things, to measure the performance of management, to identify whether a company may be a worthwhile investment opportunity, and to determine a company's performance relative to its competitors.

There are a large number of these ratios. Some of the most commonly used are:

Gross profit : Sales

The formula is
$$\frac{\text{Gross profit}}{\text{Sales}} \times 100$$

If gross profit is £120,000 and sales are £480,000, the ratio would be 25 per cent. (This should not be confused with the gross margin : cost of sales ratio which compares the gross profit to the cost of sales which, in this case, would have a value of 33.33 per cent.)

Net profit : Sales

The formula is
$$\frac{\text{Net profit}}{\text{Sales}} \times 100$$

If net profit is £38,400 and sales are £480,000, the ratio would be 8 per cent. It indicates how much safety there is in the price, i.e. current prices could be reduced by up to 8 per cent without causing the company to make a loss. Of course, it is much more complex than this. As any student of economics knows only too well, if a commodity's price falls, demand for it tends to rise. This could result in costs increasing (if unexpected demand has to be met in a hurry) or falling (as bulk purchasing discounts become available that were not previously obtainable due to the lower level of demand). Nevertheless, as a general guide, it is a sensible indicator of safety, as well as an indicator of success.

While a high value for this ratio may suggest successful performance, it is not always the case. It is possible for selling prices to be so high that demand is reduced causing overall profitability to be significantly lower than it could be were a lower price being used. In this circumstance, the ratio would produce a high percentage, but performance would certainly not be as good as it ought to have been.

Return on capital employed

This is one of the more awkward ratios to deal with, but it is also one of the most important of all the profitability ratios, as it encompasses all the other ratios, and the hope of an adequate rate of return is why investors put their money into the business in the first place. Unlike most other ratios, for example, there is no widely agreed definition of return on capital employed (ROCE). Hence, care must be taken when comparing this ratio as calculated for one company and as reported by another. Use of financial analysis bureaux that use the same formula to calculate the ratios of all the companies they consider is one way around this difficulty. Another is to ensure that you know the formula used by the companies you are comparing and, where necessary, the result is revised to bring it into line with the internally calculated ratio.

The ratio compares the profit earned (usually before interest and tax) to the funds used to generate that return (often the total of shareholders' funds at the beginning of the accounting period plus long-term creditors – most simply defined as total assets minus current liabilities). Were the profit before interest and tax £40,000 and the opening capital employed shown in the balance sheet £800,000, the return on capital employed would be 5 per cent. In theory, the higher the ratio, the more profitably the resources of the company have been used.

There is no one accepted definition of the term 'capital employed'. In this chapter, the average of the capital account will be used, i.e. (opening balance + closing balance) ÷ 2.

To consider this ratio appropriately, you first need to look separately at it in the context of sole traders and then in the context of limited companies.

In sole trader businesses C and D in Exhibit 8.3, the same amount of net profits has been made, but their respective capital employed figures are different.

EXHIBIT 8.3

Balance Sheets

	C £	D £
Fixed + Current assets – Current liabilities	10,000	16,000
Capital accounts		
Opening balance	8,000	14,000
Add Net profit	3,600	3,600
	11,600	17,600
Less Drawings	1,600	1,600
	10,000	16,000

Return on capital employed is:

$$\frac{\text{Net profit}}{\text{Capital employed}} \times 100$$

$$C \quad \frac{3,600}{(8,000 + 10,000) \div 2} \times \frac{100}{1} = 40\%$$

$$D \quad \frac{3,600}{(14,000 + 16,000) \div 2} \times \frac{100}{1} = 24\%$$

Return on share capital

Another form of words is frequently used instead of 'return on capital employed' when dealing with companies:

$$\frac{\text{Profit before tax}}{\text{Share capital} + \text{Reserves}} \times 100$$

Despite the different wording, this is the same ratio as the return on capital employed ratio. Now it is known as the '*Return on Share Capital*'. The ratio illustrates that what is important is not simply how much profit has been made but how well the capital has been employed. Business C has made far better use of its capital, achieving a return of

£40 net profit for every £100 invested, whereas *D* has received only a net profit of £24 per £100.

Profit on ordinary activities before tax is compared with share capital and reserves. In theory, the higher the ratio, the more profitably the shareholders' investment in the company has been used, and it is often used to compare performance between accounting periods, rather than to draw comparison with the ROSC of other companies.

Due to their often more complex financial structures, different meanings are attached to **capital employed** when discussing companies as opposed to sole traders. The main differences concern:

(*a*) return on capital employed by ordinary shareholders;
(*b*) return on capital employed by all long-term suppliers of capital.

To distinguish between these two meanings, as you've just seen, in a limited company (*a*) is usually known as 'Return on Share Capital' (ROSC). [It is also sometimes referred to as 'Return on Owners' Equity' (ROOE). These are just different names for the same ratio.]

In this case, the word 'Return' represents the net profit for the period. The words 'Owners' Equity' mean the book value of all things owned by the owners of the ordinary share capital. This is calculated: Ordinary Share Capital + all Reserves including Profit and Loss Account.

In the case of (*b*), this is often known simply as 'Return on Capital Employed' (ROCE). The word 'Return' in this case means net profit + any preference share dividends + debenture and long-term loan interest. The word 'Capital' means Ordinary Share Capital + Reserves including Profit and Loss Account + Preference Shares + Debentures and other Long-term Loans. (Another way of calculating this is: Total Assets − Current Liabilities.)

Given the following balance sheets of two companies, *P* Ltd and *Q* Ltd, the calculations of (*a*) and (*b*) can be attempted:

Balance Sheets as at 31 December

	P Ltd		*Q Ltd*	
	£	£	£	£
	20X8	*20X9*	*20X8*	*20X9*
Fixed assets	5,200	5,600	8,400	9,300
Net current assets	2,800	3,400	1,600	2,700
	8,000	9,000	10,000	12,000
Less: 10% debentures			(1,200)	(1,200)
	8,000	9,000	8,800	10,800
Share capital (ordinary)	3,000	3,000	5,000	5,000
Reserves	5,000	6,000	3,800	5,800
	8,000	9,000	8,800	10,800

Profit and Loss Accounts for years to 31 December 20X9

	P Ltd	*Q Ltd*
	£	£
Net profit	2,200	3,800
Dividends	(1,200)	(1,800)
	1,000	2,000

Note: In this example, we are going to use the average of the denominator values as we are provided with the opening and closing balance sheets. Often, you may only be given one balance sheet, in which case you use the figures within it. Unless you are told otherwise, if you are given both opening and closing balance sheets, you should assume that you should use the average of both sets of balance sheet values.

Return on Owners' Equity (ROOE)

P Ltd	Q Ltd

$$\frac{2,200}{(8,000 + 9,000) \div 2} \times \frac{100}{1} = 25.9\% \qquad \frac{3,800}{(8,800 + 10,800) \div 2} \times \frac{100}{1} = 38.8\%$$

The return on capital employed by all long-term suppliers of capital is not relevant in the case of *P Ltd*, as there are only ordinary shareholders in *P Ltd*. For *Q Ltd*, ROCE is:

$$\text{ROCE: } Q \text{ Ltd} = \frac{3,800 + 120^*}{(10,000 + 12,000) \div 2} \times \frac{100}{1} = 35.6\%$$

* The debenture interest 10% of £1,200 = £120 must be added back here, as it was an expense in calculating the £3,800 net profit.

Net profit after tax : Total assets

Net profit after tax is compared to the total of all assets other than current assets, plus working capital (i.e. current assets less current liabilities). If working capital is £20,000 and all non-current assets total £820,000, total assets are £840,000. If net profit after tax is £30,000, the ratio is £30,000/£840,000, i.e. 3.57 per cent.

There are problems with the integrity of this ratio – some items of expenditure that are relevant, e.g. interest on debentures, will have been charged against the profit in arriving at the figure for profit after tax. Strictly speaking, these other payments to investors and creditors ought to be reviewed and included in the profit figure used in the ratio, otherwise the profit may be significantly understated, giving a less healthy view than would be appropriate to present.

Intangible assets, e.g. goodwill, are included in the value of total assets used in the ratio. However, many would argue that this is inappropriate as there is not an agreed view on how such assets should be valued, thus inter-company comparisons may be difficult.

Net operating profit : Operating assets

This is an alternative to *Net profit after tax : Total assets*. It takes the net profit before interest, taxes and dividends, and before inclusion of any investment income. This is then compared with the assets other than intangibles and investments outside the company. Working capital would be included, but bank overdrafts would be excluded from the current liabilities on the basis that they are not generally short term in nature. If net operating profit before interest, tax and dividends is £36,000, tangible fixed assets excluding investments made outside the company are £600,000, working capital is £20,000, and there is a bank overdraft of £5,000, the ratio is:

$$\frac{£36,000}{£625,000} = 5.76\%$$

8.6　Efficiency ratios

Profitability is affected by the way that the assets of a business are used. If plant and machinery are only used for a few hours a day, the business is failing to utilise these assets efficiently. This may be because there is limited demand for the product produced. It could be due to the business restricting supply in order to maximise profitability per unit produced. On the other hand, it could be that there is a shortage of skilled labour and that there is no one to operate the plant and machinery the rest of the time. Alternatively, it could be that the plant and machinery is unreliable, breaking down a lot, and that the limited level of use is a precautionary measure designed to ensure that production targets are met.

In common with all accounting ratios, it is important that the results of efficiency ratio computations are not treated as definitively good or bad. They must be investigated further through consideration both of the underlying variables in the ratios, and of the broader context of the business and its relation to the industrial sector in which it operates.

We have already considered three of these ratios when we looked at the *liquidity ratios* – stock turnover, debtor/sales, and creditor/purchases. The other key one is asset turnover.

Asset turnover

This is a measure of how effectively the assets are being used to generate sales. It is one of the ratios that would be considered when interpreting the results of profitability ratio analyses like ROCE, but is of sufficient importance to be calculated and analysed irrespective of that fact. The calculation involves dividing sales by total assets less current liabilities.

As a general guide, where a company's asset turnover is significantly lower than those of its competitors, it suggests there may be over-investment in assets which could, in turn, make it vulnerable to takeover from a company interested in selling off any surplus assets while otherwise retaining the business in its current form. However, considerable care must be taken when interpreting this ratio: the assets may be much newer than those of other companies; the company may use a lower rate of depreciation than its competitors; or the company may purchase its plant and machinery, whereas the industry norm is to lease them. On the other side of the ratio, the result may be high because selling prices are being suppressed in order to maximise volume.

8.7　Capital structure ratios

There are a number of ratios that can be used to assess the way in which a company finances its activities. One, creditor days, was referred to earlier in this chapter. The ratios discussed within this section differ in that they are longer term in nature, being more concerned with the strategic rather than the operational level of corporate decision making. The formulae for these ratios are at the end of the chapter in Section 8.18.

Some of the more commonly analysed ratios of this type are:

Net worth : Total assets

This ratio indicates the proportion of fixed and current assets that are financed by net worth (the total of shareholders' funds, i.e. share capital plus reserves). If fixed assets are shown at a value of £500,000, current assets £100,000 and net worth is £300,000, 50 per cent of total assets are financed by shareholders' funds.

As with many accounting ratios, it is the trend in this ratio between periods that is important. Large falls in this ratio will tend to indicate a difficulty with long-term solvency.

Fixed assets : Net worth

This ratio focuses on the longer-term aspects of the net worth : total assets ratio. By matching long-term investment with long-term finance it is possible to determine whether borrowing has been used to finance some long-term investment in assets. Where this has occurred, there may be a problem when the borrowing is to be repaid (as the fixed assets it was used to acquire cannot be readily converted into cash). Again, this ratio is of most use when the trend over time is analysed.

Fixed assets : Net worth + Long-term liabilities

This ratio focuses on whether sufficient long-term finance has been obtained to meet the investment in fixed assets.

Debt ratio

This ratio compares the total debts to total assets and is concerned with whether the company has sufficient assets to meet all its liabilities when due. For example, if total liabilities are £150,000 and total assets are £600,000, the debts represent 25 per cent of total assets. Whether this is good or bad will, as with all accounting ratios, depend upon the norm for the industrial sector in which the company operates and on the underlying items within the figures included in the ratio.

Capital gearing ratio

This ratio provides the proportion of a company's total capital that has a prior claim to profits over those of ordinary shareholders. Prior claim (or prior charge) capital includes debentures, other long-term loans and preference share capital and is any capital carrying a right to a fixed return. Total capital includes ordinary share capital and reserves, preference shares and long-term liabilities.

There is more than one way of calculating this ratio. The most widely used method is:

$$\frac{\text{Long-term loans} + \text{Preference shares}}{\text{Ordinary share capital} + \text{Reserves} + \text{Preference shares} + \text{Long-term liabilities}} \times 100$$

This formula is sometimes abbreviated to

$$\frac{\text{Prior charge capital}}{\text{Total capital}} \times 100$$

which is exactly the same.

Long-term loans include debentures. Total shareholders' funds include preference shares and ordinary shares and all the reserves.

Let us look at the calculations of the gearing of two companies, *A Ltd* and *B Ltd* in Exhibit 8.4. Both have already been trading for five years.

EXHIBIT 8.4

Year 5: items per balance sheet	A Ltd £	B Ltd £
10% debentures	10,000	100,000
10% preference shares	20,000	50,000
Ordinary shares	100,000	20,000
Reserves	70,000	30,000
	200,000	200,000

Gearing ratios:

$$\text{A Ltd: } \frac{10,000 + 20,000}{10,000 + 20,000 + 100,000 + 70,000} \times \frac{100}{1} = 15\% \text{ (low gearing)}$$

$$\text{B Ltd: } \frac{100,000 + 50,000}{100,000 + 50,000 + 20,000 + 30,000} \times \frac{100}{1} = 75\% \text{ (high gearing)}$$

Now let us look at how dividends are affected, given the same level of profits made before payment of debenture interest and preference dividends. All the profits made in these years are to be distributed.

A Ltd: Low gearing		Year 6 £	Year 7 £	Year 8 £	Year 9 £
Profits before deducting the following:		20,000	15,000	30,000	40,000
Debenture interest	1,000				
Preference dividend	2,000	(3,000)	(3,000)	(3,000)	(3,000)
Profits left for ordinary dividend		17,000	12,000	27,000	37,000
Rate of ordinary dividend		17%	12%	27%	37%

B Ltd: High gearing		Year 6 £	Year 7 £	Year 8 £	Year 9 £
Profits before deducting the following:		20,000	15,000	30,000	40,000
Debenture interest	10,000				
Preference dividend	5,000	(15,000)	(15,000)	(15,000)	(15,000)
Profits left for ordinary dividend		5,000	–	15,000	25,000
Rate of ordinary dividend		25%	–	75%	125%

A company with a high percentage gearing ratio is said to be *high geared*, whereas one with a low percentage gearing is said to be *low geared*. As you can see from the above example, the proportionate effect gearing has upon ordinary shareholders is far greater in a high geared company, ranging from 0 to 125 per cent dividend for *B Ltd*, whilst the range of ordinary dividends for *A Ltd* varied far less and lay between 17 and 37 per cent.

A high rate of debt (i.e. long-term loans and preference shares) means that in bad times very little might be left over for ordinary shareholders after payment of interest on the debt items and preference dividends. In good times, however, the ordinary shareholders will enjoy a far higher return than in a low geared company.

This means that people investing in ordinary shares in a high geared company are taking a far greater risk with their money than if they had invested instead in a low geared company. It would have only required a drop of profits of £5,000 in Year 6 for *B Ltd* to find that there would be no ordinary dividends at all for both Years 6 and 7. Such a drop in Year 6 for *A Ltd* would still have allowed a dividend of 12 per cent for both of Years 6 and 7.

The choice of an investor will always be related to the amount of acceptable risk. We can list the possible investments under the headings of risk.

Lowest risk:

Debenture holders have their interest paid to them whether or not profits are made. This contrasts with shares, both preference and ordinary, where there have to be profits available for distribution as dividends.

In addition, should there be insufficient cash funds available to pay debenture dividends, many debentures give their holders the right to sell off some or all of the assets of the company, and to recoup the amount of their debentures before anyone else has a claim. Such an investment does not have as much security as, say, government stocks, but it certainly ranks above the shares of that same company.

Medium risk:

Preference shares have their dividends paid after the debenture interest has been paid, but before the ordinary shareholders. They still are dependent upon profits being available for distribution. If they are of the cumulative variety then any shortfall can be carried forward to future years and paid before any ordinary dividends are taken.

Highest risk:

Ordinary shares. Holders must give way to both debenture holders and preference shares for interest and dividends. However, should the remaining profits for distribution be very high then they may get a very high return on their money.

Investors, therefore, who are prepared to risk their money in the hope of large dividends would have chosen *B Ltd*. Those who wanted to cut down on their risk and be more certain about receiving dividends would choose *A Ltd*.

The management might decide that for various reasons it would like to change the gearing of the company. It can do this as follows:

To reduce gearing	*To increase gearing*
1 By issuing new ordinary shares	1 By issuing debentures
2 By redeeming debentures	2 By buying back ordinary shares in issue
3 By retaining profits	3 By issuing new preference shares

Such changes will be influenced by what kinds of investors the company wishes to attract. A highly geared company will attract risk-taking buyers of ordinary shares, whilst a low geared company will be more attractive to potential ordinary shareholders who wish to minimise risk.

Debt : Equity ratio

This is the ratio of prior charge capital to ordinary share capital and reserves.

Borrowing : Net worth

This ratio indicates the proportion that borrowing represents of a company's net worth. If long-term liabilities are £100,000 and current liabilities are £50,000, total borrowing is £150,000. If net worth is £300,000, the ratio is 1 : 2, or 50 per cent.

This and the *debt : equity ratio* indicate the degree of risk to investors in ordinary shares in a company. The higher these ratios are, the greater the possibility of risk to ordinary shareholders – both in respect of expectations of future dividends (especially in times of depressed performance where much of the profits may be paid to the holders of prior charge capital), and from the threat of liquidation should there be a slump in perform-ance that leads to a failure to meet payments to holders of prior charge capital. Whether these risks may be relevant can be investigated by reference to the next ratio, interest cover.

Interest cover

This ratio shows whether enough profits are being earned to meet interest payments when due. It is calculated by dividing profit before interest and tax by the interest charges. Thus, the interest cover is 20 times if profit before interest and tax is £400,000 and the total interest charges are £20,000. In this case, there would be little cause for immediate concern that there was any risk of the company failing to meet its interest charges when due. However, just because a company is making profits does not guar-antee that there will be sufficient cash available to make the interest charge payments when due.

Operating profit : Loan interest

This is another way of looking at interest payments and profit and gearing. It indicates how much of the profits are taken up by paying loan interest. Too great a proportion would mean that the company was borrowing more than was sensible, as a small fall in profits could mean the company operating at a loss with the consequent effect upon long-term solvency.

8.8 Shareholder ratios

Investors want to see ratios suitable for their purposes. These will not only be used on a single company comparison, but also with the average of the same type of ratios for other companies in the same industry. These ratios are those most commonly used by anyone interested in an investment in a company. They indicate how well a company is perform-ing in relation to the price of its shares and other related items including dividends and number of shares in issue. The ratios usually calculated are described below.

Dividend yield

This measures the real rate of return by comparing the dividend paid to the market price of a share. It is calculated as:

$$\frac{\textbf{Gross dividend per share}}{\textbf{Market price per share}}$$

Earnings per share (EPS)

This is the most frequently used of all the accounting ratios and is generally felt to give the best view of performance. It indicates how much of a company's profit can be attributed to each ordinary share in the company. FRS 14 (*Earnings per share*) provides the formula:

$$\frac{\textbf{Net profit or loss attributable to ordinary shareholders}}{\textbf{The weighted average number of ordinary shares outstanding during the period}}$$

This gives the shareholder (or prospective shareholder) a chance to compare one year's earnings with another in terms easily understood. (*Note*: 'outstanding' = 'issued'.)

Dividend cover

This compares the amount of profit earned per ordinary share with the amount of dividend paid, thereby giving the shareholder some idea as to the proportion that the ordinary dividends bear to the amount available for distribution to ordinary shareholders. It differs from EPS only in having a different denominator. The formula is:

$$\frac{\textbf{Net profit or loss attributable to ordinary shareholders}}{\textbf{Net dividend on ordinary shares}}$$

Usually, the dividend is described as being so many times covered by profits made. For example, if the dividend is said to be *three times covered*, it means that one-third of the available profits is being distributed as dividends.

Price earnings (P/E) ratio

This relates the earnings per share to the market price of the shares. It puts the price into context as a multiple of the earnings. The greater the P/E ratio, the greater the demand for the shares. A low P/E means there is little demand for shares. It is calculated by:

$$\frac{\textbf{Market price}}{\textbf{Earnings per share}}$$

and is a useful indicator of how the stock market assesses the company. It is also very useful when a company proposes an issue of new shares, in that it enables potential investors to better assess whether the expected future earnings make the share a worthwhile investment.

8.9 Overtrading

A very high proportion of new businesses fail within the first two years of trading. This can occur because there was insufficient demand for the goods or service provided, because of poor management, or for a number of other reasons of which possibly the most common to arise would be **overtrading** – basically, it runs out of cash. However, unlike the other common causes of business failure, overtrading often arises when a business, whether it be 'new' or 'old', is performing profitably.

'Profit' does not equal 'cash'

Just because a firm is making good profits it does not mean that it will not be short of cash funds. Let us look at how some firms may have good profits and yet still be short of cash funds, possibly having bank overdrafts or loans which are getting steadily bigger.

1 **Firm A has increased its sales by 50 per cent, is making the same percentage gross profit and its expenses have hardly increased, yet its overdraft has got bigger. The reason is that it increased its sales by giving all of its customers four months to pay instead of the usual one month. This has attracted a lot of new customers.**

This means that the debtors are increasing by very large amounts, as they can wait another three months in which to pay their bills. Thus the equivalent of three months' cash receipts have not come into the bank. Meanwhile the firm is making extra purchases for goods for the new customers, with a consequent outflow of more cash than usual, especially if it has not got longer credit terms from its suppliers. So hardly any cash is coming in in the short term, whilst more cash than usual is going out.

The answer to this is: large increase in profits and fewer cash funds probably resulting in higher bank overdrafts or loans.

2 **Firm B has the same sales, purchases and expenses as usual. However, the proprietor, for whatever reason, is now taking much higher drawings than before. In fact his drawings are exceeding the profits he is making.**

Such a situation cannot go on for ever. He will start to find his cash funds in the business are decreasing, possibly meaning higher loans or overdrafts being needed.

3 **Firm C has just spent a lot of money on fixed assets. It will be several years before the firm recoups the money it has paid out. In the meantime only the depreciation provisions are charged against profits. However, the cash funds have seen the disappearance of the whole amount paid for fixed assets. The net result is that profits may be recorded but the firm is hard-up for cash funds.**

4 **Firm D is going through a bad patch in that sales are very difficult to make, but it does not want to get rid of any of its workforce. Production is kept going at normal rates, and the products not sold are simply kept in stock. Thus the stock is increasing at an alarming rate.**

If stock is not being sold then cash obviously is not being received in respect of such production. Meanwhile all the expenses and wages are still being paid for. This can result in a severe shortage of funds if carried on for long if no further finance is received.

5 **A long-term loan has been paid off but no extra finance from anywhere else has been received. This could equally apply to a partner retiring and the balance due to him being paid out of the firm's funds, without a new partner being introduced. Similarly a company buying back its shares without a new issue of shares could face the same situation.**

In the long term, there is a connection between profits and cash funds available, even though it may not be very marked. In the short term you can see that there may be no relationship at all. This simple fact is one that surprises most people. It is because the calculation of profits follows one set of concepts (the accruals concept), whereas the calculation of cash funds follows a completely different set of rules.

Overtrading

Overtrading occurs when there is insufficient control over working capital resulting in there being insufficient liquid funds to meet the demands of creditors. As the cash dries up, so do the sources of supply of raw materials and other essential inputs – they will not continue to supply a business that fails to settle its bills when due. Overtrading is generally the result of sales growth being at too fast a rate in relation to the level of trade debtors, trade creditors and stock.

Take an example where, over a 12-month period, profits increased by 20 per cent, sales doubled from £1 million to £2 million, trade debtors doubled from £80,000 to £160,000, trade creditors quadrupled from £60,000 to £240,000, stock quadrupled from £50,000 to £200,000 and the bank balance moved from positive £20,000 to an overdraft of £80,000. No changes occurred during the period to the long-term financing of the business, though £100,000 was spent on some new equipment needed as a result of the expansion.

Working capital was 2.5 : 1; now it is 1.125 : 1 and the acid test ratio is now 0.5 : 1 from 1.67 : 1. Liquidity appears to have deteriorated significantly (but may have been high previously compared to other businesses in the same sector). Debtor days are unchanged (as the ratio of sales to debtors is unaltered). However, creditor days have probably doubled (subject to a slight reduction due to some cheaper purchasing costs as a result of the higher volumes involved). If the bank overdraft is currently at its limit, the business would be unable to meet any requests from creditors for immediate payment, never mind pay wages and other regular expenses.

This situation can be addressed by raising long-term finance, or by cutting back on the expansion – clearly, the first option is likely to be the more attractive one to the business.

Signals suggesting overtrading include:

- significant increases in the volume of sales;
- lower profit margins;
- deteriorating debtor, creditor and stock turnover ratios;
- increasing reliance on short-term finance.

Once identified, overtrading must be swiftly and appropriately dealt with, otherwise it may not be very long before the entire business comes to a halt.

Part II THE ANALYSIS AND INTERPRETATION OF ACCOUNTING STATEMENTS

8.10 Interpretation of ratios – trends and comparability

When shareholders receive the annual financial statements of a business, many simply look to see whether it has made a profit, and then put the document away. They are aware of only one thing – that the company made a profit of £x. They do not know if it was a 'good' profit. Nor do they know whether it was any different from the profit earned in previous years. (Even if they had noticed the previous period's profit figure in the comparative column, they would be unaware of the equivalent figures for the periods that preceded it.) In addition, they would have no perception of how the performance compared to those of other companies operating in the same sector.

In order that performance within a period can be assessed, ratio analysis may be undertaken. However, such analysis is relatively useless unless a similar task is undertaken on the financial figures for previous periods. Trend analysis is very important in the interpretation of financial statements, for it is only by means of this that the relative position can be identified, i.e. whether things are improving, etc.

If financial statements are to be usefully interpreted, of similar importance is comparison of the position shown with that of other companies operating in the same sector.

8.11 Sector relevance

The importance of ensuring that any comparison of analysis between companies is between companies in the same sector can best be illustrated through an extreme example – that of the contrast between service companies and manufacturing companies.

Stating the obvious, a firm of consultants that advise their clients on marketing strategies will have far fewer tangible assets than a company with the same turnover which manufactures forklift trucks. The service industry will need premises, but these could easily be rented and, in addition, would need very little in the way of machinery. Some computer equipment and office equipment as well as motor cars would be all that would be needed.

Compared with the service industry firm, a manufacturing company, such as that making forklift trucks, would need a great deal of machinery as well as motor lorries and various types of buildings, and so on. The manufacturing firm would also have stocks of materials and unsold trucks. The service firm would have very little in the way of stocks of tangible assets.

Especially with the service industries, it is also likely that the number of people working for the firm, but who do most, sometimes all, of their work in their homes will grow apace. The need for people to turn up at offices at given times every day is falling dramatically with the wider use of computers and various communication and link-up devices.

All of this has an effect on the ratios of performance calculated from the accounts of manufacturers and service industry firms. The figure of return on capital employed for a service firm, simply because of the few tangible assets needed, may appear to be quite high. For a manufacturing firm the opposite may well be the case.

If this distinction between these completely different types of organisation is understood, then the interpreter of the accounts will judge them accordingly. Failure to understand the distinction will bring forth some very strange conclusions.

8.12 Trend analysis

In examinations, a student is often given just one year's accounting figures and asked to comment on them. Obviously, lack of space on an examination paper may preclude several years' figures being given, also the student lacks the time to prepare a comprehensive survey of several years' accounts.

In real life, if more information was available, it would be extremely stupid for anyone to base decisions on just one year's accounts. What is important for a business is not just what, say, accounting ratios are for one year, but what the trend has been.

Given two similar types of businesses G and H, both having existed for five years, if both of them had *exactly* the same ratios in year 5, are they both equally desirable as investments? Given one year's accounts it may appear so, but if you had all five years' figures they might not give the same picture, as Exhibit 8.5 illustrates – note that the year 5 figures for G and H are identical.

From these figures, G appears to be the worse investment for the future, as the trend appears to be downwards. If the trend for G is continued it could be in a very dangerous financial situation in a year or two. Business H, on the other hand, is strengthening its position all the time.

Of course, it would be ridiculous to assert that H will continue on an upward trend. One would have to know more about the business to be able to judge whether or not that could be true.

EXHIBIT 8.5

Period:	X1	X2	X3	X4	X5 (now)
Gross profit as % of sales	G 40	38	36	35	34
	H 30	32	33	33	34
Net profit as % of sales	G 15	13	12	12	11
	H 10	10	10	11	11
Net profit as % of capital employed	G 13	12	11	11	10
	H 8	8	9	9	10
Current ratio	G 3.0	2.8	2.6	2.3	2.0
	H 1.5	1.7	1.9	1.9	2.0

However, given all other desirable information, trend figures would be an extra important indicator. Let's look more closely at the five-year ratios for G.

EXHIBIT 8.6

Period:	X1	X2	X3	X4	X5 (now)
Gross profit as % of sales	40	38	36	35	34
Net profit as % of sales	15	13	12	12	11
Net profit as % of capital employed	13	12	11	11	10
Current ratio	3.0	2.8	2.6	2.3	2.0

If the trends in these four ratios are considered, it is clear that they are all deteriorating, but there is no indication whether there should be cause for concern as a result. For example, the industry may be becoming more competitive, causing margins to shrink, and the falling current ratio may be due to an increase in efficiency over the control of working capital.

A company with this trend of figures could state that these were the reasons for the decline in margins and for the reduction in liquidity. A reader of the financial statements could then accept the explanation and put the calculations away. However, there is no guarantee that an explanation of this kind actually indicates a beneficial situation, whether or not it is accurate. In order to gain a fuller view of the company, comparison with other comparable companies in the same sector is needed, as shown above in Exhibit 8.5.

Another way in which these results may be compared is through graphs. Exhibit 8.7 compares the trend in gross profit as a percentage of sales of the two companies. (Note that the vertical axis does not show the percentage below 30 as there is no percentage below that amount. Omitting the lower figures on the graph allows for a more informative display of the information.)

The companies have identical ratios for the current period – does that make them equally desirable as investments? Given one year's accounts it appears so, but the five-year trend analysis reveals a different picture.

The graph reinforces what we saw in Exhibit 8.5 – G appears to be the worse investment for the future, as the trend for it appears to be downwards, while that of H is upwards. It suggests that the explanation made earlier for the falling margins may not be valid. If the trend for G is continued it could be in a very dangerous financial situation in a year or two. H, on the other hand, is strengthening its position all the time.

While it would be ridiculous to assert that H will continue on an upward trend, or that G will continue downwards, a consistent trend of this type does suggest that the

Chapter 8 • Published financial statements and ratio analysis

EXHIBIT 8.7 The trend of gross profit as a percentage of sales

situation may well continue into the foreseeable future. It is certainly cause for further investigation.

8.13 Comparisons over time

As shown in the previous section, one of the best ways of using ratios is to compare them with the ratios for the same organisation in respect of previous years. Take another example, the net profit percentage of a company for the past six years, including the current year 20X8:

Period:	20X3	20X4	20X5	20X6	20X7	20X8 (now)
Net profit %	5.4	5.2	4.7	4.8	4.8	4.5

This could be presented as a graph as in Exhibit 8.8.

EXHIBIT 8.8 The trend of net profit percentage over time

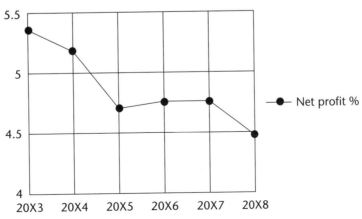

It is obvious that there is a long-term decline in net profit percentage. This prompts us to examine why this should be so. Without measuring against past years, our understanding of the direction in which the business seems to be heading would be much diminished.

We would not only look at the long-term changes in net profit percentages, but also compare similar long-term figures in relation to other aspects of the business.

When we consider trends, problems may arise from the use of the historical cost accounting concept when there have been significant price increases because of inflation.

8.14 Comparisons with other businesses

No one can say in isolation that a firm is 'very profitable'. It could be the case that it has made £6 million a year, which to most people may seem profitable. On the other hand, if firms of a similar size in the same type of industry are making £20 million a year, then the firm making £6 million cannot be said to be 'very profitable'.

Ideally, we would like to be able to compare the results of one firm with those of other similar firms in the same sort of industry. Then, and only then, would we really be able to judge how well, or how badly, it was doing.

The size of firm can have an important effect upon ratios. Just as we would not try to compare a chemist's shop with a building firm, it would also be wrong to judge a small supermarket against Sainsbury's, which owns hundreds of supermarkets.

Inter-firm comparisons are also sometimes misleading because of the different accounting treatment of various items, and the location and ages of assets. Some industries have, however, set up inter-firm comparisons with guidelines to the companies to ensure that the figures have been constructed using the same bases so that the information is properly comparable. The information does not disclose data which can be traced to any one firm, ensuring that full confidentiality is observed.

The information available may take the form shown in Exhibit 8.9.

EXHIBIT 8.9 Published ratios for the widget industry (extract)

| | Liquidity | | Efficiency | | | |
	Current	Acid test	Asset T/O	Stock T/O	Debtor days	Creditor days
20X6	2.4	0.7	5.4	8.2	56.4	80.4
20X7	2.2	0.8	5.7	9.3	52.6	66.8

The equivalent figures for the company being assessed can then be tabulated alongside the industry figures to enable comparisons to be made, as in Exhibit 8.10.

EXHIBIT 8.10

| | Company ratios | | Industry ratios | |
	20X6	20X7	20X6	20X7
Current ratio	2.9	2.8	2.4	2.2
Acid test ratio	0.5	0.6	0.7	0.8
Asset turnover	5.2	5.3	5.4	5.7
Stock turnover	4.4	4.7	8.2	9.3
Debtor days	65.9	65.2	56.4	52.6
Creditor days	58.3	56.8	80.4	66.8

The financial status of the company is now much clearer. What appeared to be a situation of improving liquidity and efficiency is now clearly shown to be an increasingly poorer liquidity and efficiency position compared to the industry as a whole.

However, it should be borne in mind that the industry figures probably include many companies that are either much larger or much smaller than the company being assessed. To obtain a more complete picture, information is needed concerning companies of a similar size, such as in the comparison between *G* and *H* earlier in this chapter (Section 8.12). This information may be available from the source of the inter-firm comparison. If not, other sources would need to be used, for example the published financial statements of appropriate companies.

The other information missing from the above comparison is data from previous periods. While not so relevant to the current position, such data can be useful in explaining why a situation has developed, and in determining whether the current position is likely to persist into the future.

8.15 Pyramid of ratios

Once ratios have been analysed and compared, explanations must be sought for the results obtained. Sometimes, it will be obvious why a certain result was obtained – for example, if a company has moved from traditional stock-keeping to a 'just-in-time' system during the period, its stock turnover will bear no resemblance to that which it had in the previous period.

For those inside the company – its directors and management – the management accounting records are available to assist in finding explanations, as are the company's staff. Outsiders – shareholders, analysts, lenders, suppliers, customers, etc. – do not have access to all this internal information (though some of these user groups will have access to more internal information than others – banks, for example, can usually obtain copies of a company's management accounts upon request). They must fall back upon other sources of information – newspaper reports and industry publications, for example. One source of additional information available to everyone is the **pyramid of ratios**. Most ratios can be further subdivided into secondary ratios, which themselves can also be subdivided. By following through the pyramid of a given ratio, the source of the original ratio can often be isolated, enabling a far more focused investigation than would otherwise be possible.

For example, one of the most important ratios is the return on the capital employed (ROCE). ROCE comes about as a result of all the other ratios which have underpinned it. It is the final summation of all that has happened in the pyramid of ratios as shown in Exhibit 8.11.

By itself the pyramid of ratios may not tell you much. It comes into full effect when compared with similar figures of the ratios for previous years, or with pyramids in respect of other firms. If ROCE has been falling over the past year then a study of the pyramids for the two years may enable you to pinpoint exactly where the changes have been made to bring about the worsening position. Investigation of these matters may then give you some answers for action to be taken.

EXHIBIT 8.11 Pyramid of ratios

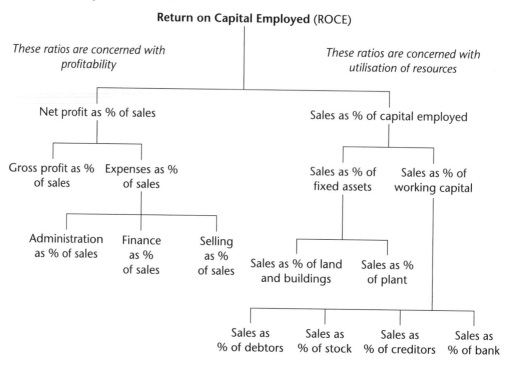

8.16 Return on capital employed: company policy

The pyramid of ratios in Exhibit 8.11 illustrates the interdependence of the ratios. This can be examined in greater detail by investigating the policies of two companies to achieve their desired return on capital employed.

The first part of the pyramid tells us that the ROCE is dependent on *both* net profit as a percentage of sales *and* also sales as a percentage of capital employed. This means that:

$$\text{ROCE} = \frac{\textbf{Net profit}}{\textbf{Capital employed}}$$

which by splitting the equation between profitability ratios and resource utilisation ratios means also that:

$$\text{ROCE} = \frac{\textbf{Net profit}}{\textbf{Sales}} \times \frac{\textbf{Sales}}{\textbf{Capital employed}}$$

This interrelationship of the subsidiary ratios can be illustrated through an example. At the same time, it can be seen that the result of computing a primary ratio is dependent upon the items comprising it; and that there is no guarantee that a value of x will be 'good', and y 'bad'. Whether the result obtained is 'good' or 'bad' depends on the underlying factors that give rise to the result obtained – what, for example, is the company's policy on depreciation and replacement of assets? This can significantly affect the ROCE. Also relevant are the sector in which the business operates and its relative size. Without knowledge of these items, comparison of the ratio analysis of two companies is likely to be misleading at best.

Two companies, both in the grocery business, may decide to aim for the same ROCE of 10 per cent. This can be achieved in completely different ways by the two companies.

A Ltd is a large company operating a supermarket. It seeks to attract customers by offering low prices and makes a net profit of only 1.25 per cent on sales. Its sales for the year are £8 million on which its net profit is £100,000. Its capital employed is £1 million. The ROCE is, therefore, 10 per cent (i.e. £100,000 net profit on capital employed of £1 million). This can also be expressed as:

$$\text{ROCE} = \frac{\text{Net profit}}{\text{Sales}} \times \frac{\text{Sales}}{\text{Capital employed}}$$

$$= \frac{£100,000}{£8,000,000} \times \frac{£8,000,000}{£1,000,000} = 10\%$$

B Ltd, by comparison, is a small local retailer. It seeks a higher margin per £100 sales, but because of higher prices it will achieve a lower volume of business. It makes a net profit of 5 per cent on sales. Its sales for the year amount to £200,000 on which it makes net profit of £10,000. The capital employed is £100,000. The ROCE is therefore 10 per cent (i.e. £10,000 on capital employed of £100,000). This can also be expressed as:

$$\text{ROCE} = \frac{\text{Net profit}}{\text{Sales}} \times \frac{\text{Sales}}{\text{Capital employed}}$$

$$= \frac{£10,000}{£200,000} \times \frac{£200,000}{£100,000} = 10\%$$

We can therefore see that two firms, *A Ltd* and *B Ltd*, with different sizes of business, and operating different pricing policies, can finish up with the same ROCE, even though one has a net profit on sales of 1.25 per cent and the other, 5 per cent.

8.17 Fixed and variable expenses

In any given time period, within any range of activity, some costs do not change. These are known as 'fixed costs'. Other costs do change as the level of activity changes – you need more material if you increase production, for example. These are known as variable costs. When comparing performance between organisations, or comparing the performance of the same organisation over time, it should be remembered that fixed expenses, such as rent, will remain constant whether activity increases or falls, at least within a given range of change of activity. This is especially relevant when managers are looking at their own organisations over time. They have access to far more detailed information than is available in the financial statements and can, therefore, account for the distinction between fixed and variable costs in their analysis of changes in the various ratios they examine.

Thus, for example, irrespective of whether sales rose or fell, the amount to be paid in rent would remain unchanged. The same would remain true of other fixed costs, such as rates, fire insurance and motor insurance.

Wages of shop assistants could also remain constant in such a case. If, for instance, the shop employed two assistants, then it would probably keep the same two assistants, on the same wages, whether sales increased or fell by 10 per cent.

Of course, such fixed expenses can only be viewed as fixed in the short term. If sales doubled, then the business might well need a larger shop or more assistants. A larger shop would also certainly mean higher rates, higher fire insurance and so on, and with more assistants the total wage bill would be larger.

On the other hand, variable expenses will change with swings in activity. Suppose that wrapping materials are used in the shop. It could well be that an increase in sales of 10 per cent may see 10 per cent more wrapping materials used. Similarly, if all sales are despatched by post, an increase of 10 per cent of sales could well see delivery charges increase by 10 per cent.

Some expenses may be part fixed and part variable. Suppose that because of an increase in sales of 10 per cent, telephone calls made increased by 10 per cent. With telephone bills the cost is in two parts, one for the rent of the phone and the second part corresponding to the actual cost of calls made. The rent does not change in such a situation and, therefore, this part of telephone expense is 'fixed'. The calls part of the expense is variable and could increase by 10 per cent if sales had risen by that amount.

This means that the effect of a percentage change in activity could have a greater or lesser percentage effect on net profit, because the fixed expenses (within that range of activity) may not alter.

Exhibit 8.12 compares the change in net profit in Business A (which has a low proportion of its expenses as 'fixed') with the change in net profit in Business B (which has 'fixed' expenses that represent a relatively high proportion of its expenses).

EXHIBIT 8.12

Business A

			(a) If sales fell 10%		(b) If sales rose 10%	
	£	£	£	£	£	£
Sales		50,000		45,000		55,000
Less Cost of goods sold		30,000		27,000		33,000
Gross profit		20,000		18,000		22,000
Less Expenses:						
Fixed	3,000		3,000		3,000	
Variable	13,000		11,700		14,300	
		(16,000)		(14,700)		(17,300)
Net profit		4,000		3,300		4,700

Business B

			(a) If sales fell 10%		(b) If sales rose 10%	
	£	£	£	£	£	£
Sales		50,000		45,000		55,000
Less Cost of goods sold		30,000		27,000		33,000
Gross profit		20,000		18,000		22,000
Less Expenses:						
Fixed	12,000		12,000		12,000	
Variable	4,000		3,600		4,400	
		(16,000)		(15,600)		(16,400)
Net profit		4,000		2,400		5,600

The comparison of percentage changes in net profit therefore works out as follows:

Decrease of 10% in sales   A   B

$$\frac{\text{Reduction in profit}}{\text{Original profit}} \times \frac{100}{1} \qquad \frac{700}{4,000} \times \frac{100}{1} = 17.5\% \qquad \frac{1,600}{4,000} \times \frac{100}{1} = 40\%$$

Increase of 10% in sales

$$\text{Increase in profit} \over \text{Original profit}} \times \frac{100}{1}$$

	A	B
	$\dfrac{700}{4,000} \times \dfrac{100}{1} = 17.5\%$	$\dfrac{1,600}{4,000} \times \dfrac{100}{1} = 40\%$

It can be seen that a change in activity in Business B, which has a higher fixed expense content, results in greater percentage changes in profit: 40% compared with 17.5% in *A*.

8.18 Summary of ratios

Ratio category	*Formula*
Liquidity	
Current ratio	$\dfrac{\text{Current assets}}{\text{Current liabilities}}$
Acid test ratio	$\dfrac{\text{Current assets} - \text{Stock}}{\text{Current liabilities}}$
Profitability	
Gross profit : Sales	$\dfrac{\text{Gross profit}}{\text{Sales}}$
Net profit : Sales	$\dfrac{\text{Net profit}}{\text{Sales}}$
Return on capital employed (sole trader)	$\dfrac{\text{Net profit}}{\text{Capital employed}}$
Return on capital employed (company)	$\dfrac{\text{Profit before interest and tax}}{\text{Total assets} - \text{Current liabilities}}$
Return on share capital	$\dfrac{\text{Profit before tax}}{\text{Share capital} + \text{Reserves}}$
Net profit after tax : Total assets	$\dfrac{\text{Net profit after tax}}{\text{Fixed and other non-current assets} + \text{Working capital}}$
Net operating profit : Operating assets	$\dfrac{\text{Net profit before interest, tax, dividends and investment income}}{\text{Tangible fixed assets} - \text{Outside investments} + \text{Working capital} + \text{Bank overdraft}}$
Efficiency	
Asset turnover	$\dfrac{\text{Sales}}{\text{Total assets} - \text{Current liabilities}}$
Stock turnover	$\dfrac{\text{Cost of sales}}{\text{Average stock}}$
Debtor days	$\dfrac{\text{Debtors}}{\text{Sales}} \times 365$
Creditor days	$\dfrac{\text{Creditors}}{\text{Purchases}} \times 365$
Capital structure	
Net worth : Total assets	$\dfrac{\text{Shareholders' funds}}{\text{Total assets}}$

Fixed assets : Net worth	$\dfrac{\text{Fixed assets}}{\text{Shareholders' funds}}$
Fixed assets : Net worth + Long-term liabilities	$\dfrac{\text{Fixed assets}}{\text{Shareholders' funds + Long-term liabilities}}$
Debt ratio	$\dfrac{\text{Total liabilities}}{\text{Total assets}}$
Capital gearing ratio	$\dfrac{\text{Prior charge capital}}{\text{Total capital}}$
Debt : Equity ratio	$\dfrac{\text{Prior charge capital}}{\text{Ordinary share capital and reserves}}$
Borrowing : Net worth	$\dfrac{\text{Total borrowing}}{\text{Shareholders' funds}}$
Interest cover	$\dfrac{\text{Profit before interest and tax}}{\text{Interest charges}}$
Operating profit : Loan interest	$\dfrac{\text{Loan interest}}{\text{Profit before interest and tax}}$

Shareholder ratios

Dividend yield	$\dfrac{\text{Gross dividend per share}}{\text{Market price per share}}$
Earnings per share	$\dfrac{\text{Net profit or loss attributable to ordinary shareholders}}{\text{Weighted average number of ordinary shares outstanding during the period}}$
Dividend cover	$\dfrac{\text{Net profit or loss attributable to ordinary shareholders}}{\text{Net dividend on ordinary shares}}$
Price/earnings ratio	$\dfrac{\text{Market price}}{\text{Earnings per share}}$

Learning outcomes

You should now have learnt:

1 There are many different categories of accounting ratios and many different ratios within each category.

2 Ratios that are of interest to one group of readers of financial statements may not be of interest to another.

3 Ratios may be used in order to review reliability of financial statements.

4 Ratios may be used to review trends between periods for the same company.

5 Ratios may be used to compare a company to others in the same industrial sector.

6 Some ratios in wide use but there is no agreed 'correct' formula for calculating them. This makes comparison between analysis reported elsewhere of limited value unless the formula used can be identified.

7 The ratios derived can be misleading if taken at face value. It is essential that they are placed in context and that interpretation goes beyond a superficial comparison to general norms.

8   Used casually, accounting ratios can mislead and result in poor quality decision making.

9   Used carefully, accounting ratios can provide pointers towards areas of interest in an entity, and provide a far more complete picture of an entity than that given by the financial statements.

10 Overtrading can be financially disastrous for a business and ratios can be used to help detect it.

11 Ratios on their own are frequently misleading – they should not be considered in isolation from similar computations:
    (*a*) in previous periods; and/or
    (*b*) on similar sized firms in the same sector.

12 The items in the financial statements are affected by company policy – for example, the rate of depreciation to use, and the policy of asset replacement – and the policies adopted, therefore, directly affect the ratio analysis.

13 Companies of very different size and in very different sectors can have the same ratio results despite their being different in every respect.

14 The importance and impact of size, sector and company policies upon ratios mean that there is no such thing as a 'good' or 'bad' value that can be treated as a yardstick for any ratio.

15 All ratios are part of one or more pyramids of ratios.

16 When the results of ratio analysis are being investigated further, the relevant pyramid of ratios can be analysed in order to pinpoint the element giving rise to the situation being investigated.

REVIEW QUESTIONS

Advice: Examiners at this level certainly do like to include a lot of questions concerned with the analysis and interpretation of accounting statements. This is almost certainly due to the fact that in no other topic can an examinee's *understanding* of accounts, as compared to his/her ability to *prepare* the accounts, be scrutinised so thoroughly.

There is no one set pattern to the questions, which depend upon the examiner's ingenuity and background experience. The usual shortcomings in the answers handed in by candidates can be listed as follows (you should avoid each of these – you'll only lose marks if you don't):

1   Not following the instructions as laid down. If the question says 'list the' then the examiner expects a list as an answer, 'Discuss the' means exactly that, 'Write a report' needs a report as the answer, and so on. You will lose a lot of marks for not giving the examiner exactly what has been asked for.

2   Very often all the ratios, etc. are calculated, but then the candidate does not offer any comments even though they have been asked for. Make certain you cover this part of the question.

3   Even where students have written something about the ratios, they often repeat what the calculations are and offer nothing else, e.g. 'you can see that the gross profit ratio has increased from 18 to 20 per cent' and the answer has finished there. The examiner can already see from your calculations that the gross profit percentage has increased, and wants you to write about why it might have increased, what conclusions, if any, can be arrived at, or what further information may be needed to proceed with why it has changed.

4 Remember that when the examiner asks you 'what other information you would like to have' about a firm when trying to interpret the accounts so as to give advice to someone then, ideally, you would like to know more about the plans for the future of the business, how it compares with others in the same industry, whether or not there are going to be changes in the management and so on. We should not limit ourselves to information about the past, we really need to know as much about the future as we possibly can.

5 Do not restrict your examination answers to what you have read in a textbook. Keep your eyes and ears open as you go shopping, visit factories, do part-time work in the supermarket, buy petrol at the filling station, go to the theatre and so on. Also reading a 'quality' newspaper helps, as there are quite a lot of items about business. Bring all of this sort of knowledge and experience into your answers. You will impress the examiners. They are bored to death reading regurgitations of textbook learning with nothing else added.

6 Quite a few questions will concern a type of business of which you will have first hand experience and you can introduce your own personal knowledge into your answer. A typical instance would be comparing two grocery businesses. One would be a large supermarket and the other would be a small corner shop. The policies of the two firms would be quite different. The supermarket would have decided on a policy of attracting new customers by lowering sales margins and yet boosting ROCE. The corner shop might have a policy of high margins, but remain open on Sundays and late at nights, and thus be a 'convenience shop', i.e. customers might well go there when other shops are closed or are too far away to be worth the extra cost in petrol, etc. when compared with the extra cost of shopping at the corner shop.

7 Last, but not least, not showing your workings.

8.1 Five categories of accounting ratios are described in this chapter. What are they?

8.2X Why should different groups of people be interested in different categories of accounting ratios?

8.3 Describe two ratios from each of the five groups of ratios, including how to calculate them.

8.4X What is the purpose in using each of the following ratios:

(a) current ratio;
(b) net profit after tax : sales;
(c) asset turnover;
(d) interest cover;
(e) dividend cover?

8.5 If you wished to assess the efficiency of a company, which of these ratios would you use:

(a) stock turnover;
(b) interest cover;
(c) return on capital employed;
(d) acid test ratio;
(e) dividend yield?

8.6X A company has capital of 1 million ordinary shares of £1 each. It pays a dividend of 6 per cent out of its profits after tax of £480,000 on sales of £4 million. The market price of the shares is £2.40. What is the:

(a) net profit after tax : sales;
(b) dividend yield;

(c) earnings per share;

(d) price/earnings ratio?

8.7 In respect of each of the following events, select all the effects resulting from that event that are shown in the list of effects:

(i) a bad debt written off;

(ii) an increase in the bank overdraft;

(iii) a purchase of six months' stock;

(iv) payment of all amounts due to trade creditors that had been outstanding for longer than 90 days;

(v) an offer of 5 per cent discount to all customers who settle their accounts within two weeks.

List of effects

(a) increased current ratio

(b) reduced current ratio

(c) increased acid test ratio

(d) reduced acid test ratio

8.8X Using the following balance sheet and profit and loss accounts, calculate and comment on ten accounting ratios (ignore taxation):

Balance Sheet as at 31 December 20X1 (£000s)

Fixed assets			
Equipment at cost			6,000
Less Depreciation to date			(2,000)
			4,000
Current assets			
Stock		600	
Debtors		60	
Bank		–	
		660	
Less Current liabilities			
Creditors	90		
Dividends payable	80		
Bank overdraft	450		
		(620)	
			40
			4,040
Long-term liabilities			
10% debentures			(500)
			3,540
Financed by			
Share capital – £1 ordinary shares			2,000
Reserves			
General reserve			800
Profit and loss account			740
			3,540

Profit and Loss Account for period ending 31 December 20X1 (£000s)

Sales		8,000
Less Cost of sales		
Opening stock	500	
Add Purchases	1,300	
	1,800	
Less Closing stock	(600)	
		(1,200)
Gross profit		6,800
Less Depreciation	800	
Other expenses	5,500	
		(6,300)
Net operating profit		500
Less Debenture interest		(50)
Net profit		450
Add Balance b/f		490
		940
Less Appropriations		
General reserve	120	
Dividend	80	
		(200)
		740

8.9 You are to study the following financial statements for two similar types of retail store and then answer the questions which follow.

Summary of Financial Statements

Trading and Profit and Loss Account	A		B	
	£	£	£	£
Sales		80,000		120,000
Less Cost of goods sold				
Opening stock	25,000		22,500	
Add Purchases	50,000		91,000	
	75,000		113,500	
Less Closing stock	(15,000)		(17,500)	
		(60,000)		(96,000)
Gross profit		20,000		24,000
Less Depreciation	1,000		3,000	
Other expenses	9,000		6,000	
		(10,000)		(9,000)
Net profit		10,000		15,000

Balance sheets	A		B	
Fixed assets				
Equipment at cost	10,000		20,000	
Less Depreciation to date	(8,000)		(6,000)	
		2,000		14,000
Current assets				
Stock	15,000		17,500	
Debtors	25,000		20,000	
Bank	5,000		2,500	
	45,000		40,000	

	A		B	
	£	£	£	£
Less Current liabilities				
Creditors	(5,000)		(10,000)	
Creditors		40,000		30,000
		42,000		44,000
Financed by:				
Capitals				
Balance at start of year		38,000		36,000
Add Net profit		10,000		15,000
		48,000		51,000
Less Drawings		(6,000)		(7,000)
		42,000		44,000

Required:

(*a*) Calculate the following ratios:

  (*i*)   gross profit as percentage of sales;   (*vi*)   current ratio;
  (*ii*) net profit as percentage of sales;   (*vii*) acid test ratio;
  (*iii*) expenses as percentage of sales;   (*viii*) debtor : sales ratio;
  (*iv*) stockturn;   (*ix*)   creditor : purchases ratio.
  (*v*)   rate of return of net profit on capital
        employed (use the average of the
        capital account for this purpose);

(*b*) Drawing upon all your knowledge of accounting, comment upon the differences and similarities of the accounting ratios for *A* and *B*. Which business seems to be the more efficient? Give possible reasons.

8.10X Study the following accounts of two companies and then answer the questions which follow. Both companies are stores selling textile goods.

Trading and Profit and Loss Accounts

	R Ltd		T Ltd	
	£	£	£	£
Sales		250,000		160,000
Less Cost of goods sold				
Opening stock	90,000		30,000	
Add Purchases	210,000		120,000	
	300,000		150,000	
Less Closing stock	(110,000)		(50,000)	
		(190,000)		(100,000)
Gross profit		60,000		60,000
Less Expenses				
Wages and salaries	14,000		10,000	
Directors' remuneration	10,000		10,000	
Other expenses	11,000		8,000	
		(35,000)		(28,000)
Net profit		25,000		32,000
Add Balance from last year		15,000		8,000
		40,000		40,000
Less Appropriations				
General reserve	2,000		2,000	
Dividend	25,000		20,000	
		(27,000)		(22,000)
Balance carried to next year		13,000		18,000

Balance Sheets

Fixed assets	R Ltd		T Ltd	
Equipment at cost	20,000		5,000	
Less Depreciation to date	(8,000)		(2,000)	
		12,000		3,000
Motor lorries	30,000		20,000	
Less Depreciation to date	(12,000)		(7,000)	
		18,000		13,000
		30,000		16,000
Current assets				
Stock	110,000		50,000	
Debtors	62,500		20,000	
Bank	7,500		10,000	
	180,000		80,000	
Less Current liabilities				
Creditors	(90,000)		(16,000)	
		90,000		64,000
		120,000		80,000
Financed by				
Issued share capital		100,000		50,000
Reserves				
General reserve	7,000		12,000	
Profit and loss	13,000		18,000	
		20,000		30,000
		120,000		80,000

Required:

(*a*) Calculate the following ratios for each of R Ltd and T Ltd:
  (*i*) gross profit as percentage of sales;
  (*ii*) net profit as percentage of sales;
  (*iii*) expenses as percentage of sales;
  (*iv*) stockturn;
  (*v*) rate of return of net profit on capital employed (for the purpose of this question only, take capital as being total of share capitals + reserves at the balance sheet date);
  (*vi*) current ratio;
  (*vii*) acid test ratio;
  (*viii*) debtor : sales ratio;
  (*ix*) creditor : purchases ratio.

(*b*) Comment briefly on the comparison of each ratio as between the two companies. State which company appears to be the most efficient, giving what you consider to be possible reasons.

8.11 The directors of L Ltd appointed a new sales manager towards the end of 20X2. This manager devised a plan to increase sales and profit by means of a reduction in selling price and extended credit terms to customers. This involved considerable investment in new machinery early in 20X3 in order to meet the demand which the change in sales policy had created.

The financial statements for the years ended 31 December 20X2 and 20X3 are shown below. The sales manager has argued that the new policy has been a resounding success because sales and, more importantly, profits have increased dramatically.

Profit and loss accounts	20X2	20X3
	£000	£000
Sales	900	2,800
Cost of sales	(360)	(1,680)
Gross profit	540	1,120
Selling expenses	(150)	(270)
Bad debts	(18)	(140)
Depreciation	(58)	(208)
Interest	(12)	(192)
Net profit	302	310
Balance b/fwd	327	629
	629	939

Balance sheets	20X2		20X3	
	£000	£000	£000	£000
Fixed assets:				
Factory		450		441
Machinery		490		1,791
		940		2,232
Current assets:				
Stock	30		238	
Debtors	83		583	
Bank	12		—	
	125		821	
Current liabilities:				
Creditors	(36)		(175)	
Bank	—		(11)	
	(36)		(186)	
Current assets *less* Current liabilities		89		635
		1,029		2,867
Borrowings		(100)		(1,600)
		929		1,267
Share capital		300		328
Profit and loss		629		939
		929		1,267

(*a*) **You are required to** explain whether you believe that the performance for the year ended 31 December 20X3 and the financial position at that date have improved as a result of the new policies adopted by the company. You should support your answer with appropriate ratios.

(*b*) All of L Ltd's sales are on credit. The finance director has asked you to calculate the immediate financial impact of reducing the credit period offered to customers. Calculate the amount of cash which would be released if the company could impose a collection period of 45 days.

(*Chartered Institute of Management Accountants*)

8.12X The financial information below was extracted from the balance sheets of two companies as at 30 June 20X0.

	Postgate plc £000	Coalux plc £000
Authorised share capital		
£1 Ordinary shares	500	400
11% £1 Preference shares	250	–
Called up share capital		
£1 Ordinary shares, fully paid	350	400
11% £1 Preference shares, fully paid	250	–
Reserves		
Share premium	150	200
Other capital reserves	250	100
Retained earnings	350	300
Loan capital		
9% Debenture stock (2008)	200	–
10% Debenture stock (2006)	–	50
Current liabilities	140	190

Additional information:

1 Both companies revalued their freehold land and buildings with effect from 1 July 20X0. The revaluations were as follows:

	Balance Sheet Value as at 30 June 20X0 £000	Balance Sheet Revaluation £000
Postgate plc	300	500
Coalux plc	150	200

2 The board of directors of Postgate plc had already approved a bonus issue of shares earlier in the year. The bonus issue is to be effected on 1 July 20X0 on the following terms:

One bonus share for every ordinary share currently held.

The issue is to be funded, one half from the capital reserves and one half from the retained earnings.

3 Coalux had approved a rights issue on the following terms:

One new ordinary share for every two ordinary shares currently held.

The issue price was fixed at £1.50 per share. The issue was fully subscribed and the funds received on 1 July 20X0.

Required:

(*a*) For each of the companies explain the significance of the items 1 to 3 above on the financing of the company subsequent to 1 July 20X0. *(8 marks)*

(*b*) When a limited company is considering the raising of further capital, briefly identify the relative merits of:
   (*i*) Ordinary shares
   (*ii*) Debenture stock
   as sources of capital. *(8 marks)*

(*c*) Explain what is meant by 'gearing', a term frequently used in the analysis of limited companies' balance sheets. *(4 marks)*

(*d*) Calculate a gearing factor for each of the companies, Postgate plc and Coalux plc, as at 2 July 20X0. *(5 marks)*

(AQA (AEB): GCE A-level)

8.13 The following information had been prepared for the board of directors of Positive plc who were considering the financial position of another company Minus plc, in which they held ordinary shares as an investment.

Financial Information as at 31 December 20X0

	Positive plc £000	Minus plc £000
Issued share capital		
£1 ordinary shares fully paid	1,500	
25p ordinary shares fully paid		500
12% Preference shares fully paid £1 each		100
Share premium account	750	350
General reserve	350	50
Retained earnings	600	20
Investment in Minus plc:		
500,000 Ordinary shares	240	–
Current assets	1,360	320
Fixed assets	2,100	1,000
Current liabilities	300	300
11% Debentures 20X2–X6	200	–

Note: The net trading profits reported by Minus plc for the last five years were:

20X6	20X7	20X8	20X9	20Y0
£125,000	£100,000	£75,000	£70,000	£10,000

Positive plc were considering the acquisition of further shares in Minus plc. The current ordinary share price was 30p. Positive plc wished to acquire sufficient shares to give them a 51 per cent stake in Minus plc.

Further investigation of the financial affairs of Minus plc by Positive plc revealed the following:

1 No dividends had been declared or paid for the year ended 31 December 20X0.
2 Raw material stocks held at 31 December 20X0 were valued at cost £160,000. Of these stocks £70,000 were redundant and of no value.
3 Cash and bank balances as at 31 December 20X0 amounted to £50,000.
4 Freehold land and buildings of £200,000 were included in the fixed assets. They had not been revalued for 11 years and the estimated market value was £2 million.

Required:

(*a*) A report on the financial position of Minus plc for the board of Positive plc. Your report should contain appropriate numerical analysis including an assessment of Minus plc's profitability and liquidity. *(9 marks)*

(*b*) A reasoned recommendation indicating whether or not Positive plc should increase its shareholding in Minus plc. *(6 marks)*

(*c*) If the board of Positive plc decided to acquire extra ordinary shares in Minus plc, explain the different ways in which Positive plc could, if need be, finance the acquisition of extra ordinary shares in Minus plc. *(5 marks)*

(*d*) Prepare a balance sheet for Positive plc as at 1 January 20X1, on the assumption that Positive plc purchased sufficient shares in Minus plc, for cash, at 30p per share on 1 January 20X1 to give them a 51 per cent stake. *(5 marks)*

(AQA (AEB): GCE A-level)

8.14 Janet James is considering the investment of £50,000 which she recently inherited from her late father's estate. After much thought, Janet has decided that her legacy will be invested in one of the following propositions:

A Placed on deposit with a building society; the interest rate being 10 per cent per annum.

B The outright purchase of the business of Thomas Smith for £50,000. Thomas Smith has been involved full time in the management of the business; the business's accounts have shown a net profit of £20,000 for each of the last three financial years.

C Purchase the entire ordinary share capital of Greater Deals Limited for £50,000. The share capital, reserves and loan capital of the company as shown in the company's last balance sheet are as follows:

	£	£
Ordinary share capital – ordinary shares of 50p each, fully paid up		30,000
10% Preference share capital – preference shares of £1.00 each, fully paid up		10,000
Reserves – Share premium	5,000	
General	10,000	
Retained earnings	8,000	
		23,000
10% Loan Stock		16,000

Note: The company's net profit, after taxation, for each of the last three years has been in the region of £7,000.

D Purchase 20 per cent of the ordinary share capital of Central Traders Limited for £50,000. The company's issued capital is entirely in ordinary shares. The company's net profit, after taxation, for each of the last three years has been in the region of £32,000.

Required:

As her financial adviser, address a report to Janet James setting out the disadvantages and advantages of each of the four propositions so far as her proposed investment is concerned. Reports should indicate whether any further information is required before a final decision is made.

(25 marks)

(OCR: from the University of Cambridge Local Examinations Syndicate)

8.15X The following financial information was available on Tecopac plc.

Balance Sheets as at 31 December

20X8 £m		20X9 £m
8.0	Fixed assets	11.0
5.4	Current assets	7.0
13.4		18.0
3.4	*Less* Current liabilities	4.5
10.0		13.5
6.0	Called-up capital – £1 Ordinary shares fully paid	6.0
2.0	Share premium	2.0
2.0	Retained earnings 1 January 20X9	2.0
	Net profit for year ended 31 December 20X9	3.5
10.0		13.5

In respect of the financial year ended 31 December 20X9 the directors recommended the payment of a final ordinary dividend of 10p per share and the transfer of £3.0m to a general reserve. No interim dividend had been paid.

Hartington, an ordinary shareholder, purchased 30,000 shares at £1.50 per share on 1 January 20X9 (market value at 31 December 20X9 £1.80 per share). On receiving the company's annual statement he was disappointed to learn that he would only receive a final dividend of 10p a share, and he regarded the profit of £3.5m for 20X9 as unsatisfactory since the company employed a substantial amount of capital.

Hartington decided to write to the company's Chief Accountant with a number of suggestions which he hoped would increase the return to shareholders and improve the profitability of Tecopac plc. The suggestions were as follows:

1 The company should make a bonus issue of shares to keep the shareholders happy.
2 Use the share premium account to pay an increase in the dividend. This will also conserve cash resources.
3 Invest £3m of the company's retained earnings in 8 per cent per annum fixed interest government securities.

Required:

(a) A profit and loss appropriation account for Tecopac plc for the year ended 31 December 20X9. *(4 marks)*

(b) (i) Calculate **two** suitable accounting ratios to show Tecopac's level of profitability. Comment on the results.
   (ii) Calculate Hartington's 20X9 return on his investment distinguishing between the income return and the capital return. *(12 marks)*

(c) As Chief Accountant of Tecopac write a reply to Hartington commenting on each of the suggestions **1** to **3** above. *(9 marks)*

(AQA (AEB): GCE A-level)

8.16X A small limited company is hoping to expand its activities. It has approached a potential investor, Mr Abdul, regarding the possibility of his buying 90,000 ordinary shares in the company, at a premium of 50p each. Mr Abdul has been shown only the latest balance sheet of the company, together with that at the end of the previous financial year. They are as follows:

		20X1 £		20X2 £
Fixed assets:				
Land and buildings		506,000		405,000
Machinery		75,000		85,000
Computers		15,000		18,000
Motor vehicles		18,000		26,000
		614,000		534,000
Current assets:				
Stock	67,000		105,000	
Debtors	50,000		80,000	
Bank	–		–	
	117,000		185,000	
Less: Current liabilities:				
Creditors	70,000		60,000	
Bank	8,000		50,000	
	78,000		110,000	
Net current assets		39,000		75,000
Total net assets		653,000		609,000

	20X1	20X2
	£	£
Share capital (£1)	100,000	100,000
Revenue reserves	363,000	319,000
	463,000	419,000
15% Debentures 20X7/20X9	190,000	190,000
	653,000	609,000

Annual net profit before debenture interest payments and dividends was £50,000 in 20X1 and £30,000 in 20X2.

You have been asked by Mr Abdul to comment on whether he should purchase shares in the company.

Write a report to Mr Abdul suggesting five areas of investigation prior to an investment decision being made.

(London Qualifications Limited (University of London): GCE A-level)

8.17 Adrian Frampton was considering the purchase of one of two businesses. However Frampton had only been provided with limited information about the businesses, as follows:

Summarised financial information for the year ended 31 December 20X9

	Business X	Business Y
Cost of goods sold	£400,000	£600,000
Administrative expenses	£50,000	£60,000
Average stock at cost	£40,000	£50,000
Working capital as at 31 December 20X9	£90,000	£250,000
Selling and distribution expenses	£15,000	£35,000
Proprietor's capital at 1 January 20X9	£200,000	£350,000
Gross profit percentage mark-up on cost	20	25

Additional information

1　Average stock had been calculated by using the year's opening and closing stocks. Subsequently it was discovered that Business *Y* had overvalued its stock on 31 December 20X9 by £10,000.

2　Business *X*'s administrative expenses included a payment for rent of £15,000 which covered a three-year period to 31 December 20X1.

3　A sum of £2,500 was included in the administrative expenses of Business *Y* in respect of a holiday taken by the owner and his family.

4　Cash drawings for the year ended 31 December 20X9 were:

	£
Business *X*	20,000
Business *Y*	25,000

5　The owners of the businesses had stipulated the following prices for their businesses:

	£
Business *X*	190,000
Business *Y*	400,000

Required:

(*a*) Based on the information available prepare comparative trading and profit and loss accounts for the year ended 31 December 20X9.　　　　　　　*(8 marks)*

(*b*) Using the information provided and the accounting statements prepared in (*a*), calculate relevant accounting ratios in order to give Frampton a basis for assessing the performances of the two businesses. Comment on the results.　　*(11 marks)*

(c) What additional information is needed in order to assess more accurately:
  (i) the liquidity of the businesses;
  (ii) the future prospects of the businesses?   (6 marks)

(AQA (AEB): GCE A-level)

8.18X The following information has been extracted from the final accounts of Dynamic Traders Limited:

Years ended 30 September	20X0	20X1	20X2
	£000	£000	£000
Sales	1,200	1,600	2,000
Cost of sales	800	1,000	1,200
Profit after tax	100	120	120
Dividends	60	60	–

As at 30 September	20X0	20X1	20X2
Fixed assets – Tangible	600	640	700
Current assets			
Stocks	60	90	260
Debtors	70	100	150
Bank	90	70	–
Current liabilities			
Bank overdraft	–	–	100
Creditors	16	36	26
Shareholders' funds			
Ordinary share capital	600	600	600
Retained earnings	204	264	384

John Thomas, a small shareholder in Dynamic Traders Limited, has asked Andrew Sharp, a financial adviser, to prepare a report on the financial position and profitability of the company.

Required:

In the name of Andrew Sharp prepare a report for John Thomas.   (25 marks)

Note: Make and state any necessary assumptions.

(OCR: from the University of Cambridge Local Examinations Syndicate)

8.19 The balance sheet of Trotwood Limited at 31 December 20X0 was as follows:

	£	£	£
Fixed assets (at book value)			
Freehold land and buildings			367,000
Machinery			35,000
Motor vehicles			120,000
Computer equipment			35,000
			557,000
Current assets			
Stock		34,000	
Debtors		7,000	
Bank		11,000	
		52,000	

	£	£	£
Current liabilities			
Creditors	16,000		
Taxation	24,000		
Dividend	8,000		
		48,000	
			4,000
			561,000
Share capital			
Authorised and issued capital:			
1,600,000 Ordinary Shares of 25p			400,000
Reserves			
Retained earnings (P & L a/c)			61,000
			461,000
Long-term liabilities:			
20% Debentures (repayable in the next two years)			100,000
			561,000

The earnings per share figures were 0.9p in 20X7, 0.7p in 20X8 and 20X9 and 0.6p in 20X0. Dividends per share in those years were 0.2p, 0.3p, 0.4p and 0.5p respectively.

You have been asked by a shareholder to prepare a report on the financial state of the company from the above information. The report should contain the following information.

(*a*) A comment on the company's working capital, liquidity and gearing position as shown on the balance sheet at 31 December 20X0. *(8 marks)*

(*b*) The significance of the earnings per share and dividends per share figures. *(8 marks)*

(*c*) Three questions which the shareholder could ask the company chairman at the Annual General Meeting in order to gain a fuller picture of the company's financial future.

(9 marks)

(London Qualifications Limited (University of London): GCE A-level)

8.19X 'Service companies such as advertising agencies have few tangible assets. Their main assets are the copywriters and other creative people who win business from admiring clients, but who never appear in the balance sheet. Accounting was developed to serve companies which traded or made physical goods, not businesses which make advertisements or provide similar services.'

From *The Guardian*

(*a*) Is it possible for a 'service company' to show a realistic statement of its assets on its balance sheet? Discuss. *(12 marks)*

(*b*) A major advertising company showed the following position at its balance sheet date:

	£m
Tangible assets	215
Associate companies and investments	22
Net current liabilities	(130)
Total net assets	107
Less Net borrowings	186
Shareholder value (negative)	(79)
(Stock market value £136m)	

Give two reasons why the stock market value of the company is so much higher than the (negative) shareholder value. *(8 marks)*

(London Qualifications Limited (University of London): GCE A-level)

8.21X The following are the summarised financial statements of Ball and Gregson Ltd, a trading company.

Trading and profit and loss account for the years ended 31 October

	20X4	20X5
	£000	£000
Sales	2,100	3,000
Less cost of sales		
Opening stock	350	420
Purchases	1,470	2,190
	1,820	2,610
Closing stock	420	510
	1,400	2,100
Gross Profit	700	900
Expenses	353	447
Net profit before tax	347	453
Taxation	87	113
	260	340
Dividends	90	120
Retained profit for the year	170	220

Balance sheets as at 31 October

	20X4		20X5	
	£000	£000	£000	£000
Fixed assets at net book value		1,700		2,100
Current assets				
Stock	420		510	
Debtors	400		450	
Bank and cash	100		120	
		920		1,080
Creditors less than one year				
Trade creditors	280		310	
Dividends	60		70	
Accruals	60		130	
Taxation	87		113	
		(487)		(623)
Creditors more than one year				
12% debentures 20X5		(400)		–
		1,733		2,557
£1 ordinary shares, fully paid		1,250		1,500
Share premium		250		604
Retained earnings		233		453
		1,733		2,557

Additional information

1 90% of all sales are on credit.

2 All purchases were made on credit.

3 Debtors and creditors figures at balance sheet dates may be taken as representative averages for each of the years in question.

Required:

(a) State and calculate **two** ratios relating to the profitability of Ball and Gregson Ltd for **each** of the years under review.

(6 marks)

(*b*) State and calculate **two** ratios relating to the liquidity of Ball and Gregson Ltd for **each** of the years under review. *(6 marks)*

(*c*) Write a report using the ratios calculated in (*a*) and (*b*) to analyse the profitability and liquidity of Ball and Gregson Ltd over the two year period. The report should include an outline of major difficulties encountered in making inter-year comparisons. *(16 marks)*

(*d*) State **two** ways in which a business could increase its working capital. *(6 marks)*

(*e*) What are the disadvantages to a business of having:
- (*i*) excessive working capital *(6 marks)*
- (*ii*) limited working capital. *(6 marks)*

(*f*) Explain briefly how a business could be profitable yet encounter a liquidity problem.
(4 marks)

(AQA (AEB): GCE A-level)

Cash flow statements

After you have studied this chapter, you should be able to:

- draw up a cash flow statement for any type of organisation;
- explain how cash flow statements can give a different view of a business to that simply concerned with profits;
- explain the purpose of cash flow information;
- explain the difference between cash flow and profit;
- prepare a cash flow statement for a company following the format given in FRS 1;
- explain some of the uses which can be made of cash flow statements.

9.1 Need for cash flow statements

For any business it is important to ensure that:

- Sufficient profits are made to finance the business.
- Sufficient cash funds are available as and when needed.

We ascertain the amount of profits in a profit and loss account. We also show what the assets, capital and liabilities are at a given date by drawing up a balance sheet. Although the balance sheet shows the cash balance (see definition later) at a given date, it does not show us how we have used our cash funds during the accounting year.

What we really need, to help throw some light on to the cash situation, is some form of statement which shows us exactly where the cash has come from during the year, and exactly what we have done with it. The statement that fulfils these needs is called a **cash flow statement**. Cash flow statements are not to be confused with 'cash budgets', which you will probably have learnt of earlier in your accounting studies. If you haven't, you will be able to learn about them in Chapter 20.

We take the word 'cash' to mean cash balances, plus bank balances plus 'cash equivalents'. These cash equivalents consist of the temporary investments of cash not required at present by the business. Such investments must be readily convertible into cash, or would mature within three months if left as investments.

9.2 FRS 1, *Cash flow statements*

In 1991, the Accounting Standards Board issued the first Financial Reporting Standard (FRS 1). It was revised and reissued in 1996. The standard, as its title suggests, supports the use of cash flow statements.

This had not always been the case. An earlier Accounting Standard had favoured the use of 'source and application of funds statements'. These funds were concerned with working capital and not cash. FRS 1 changed all of this, with cash as the central item.

The Accounting Standards Board requires only certain companies to include cash flow statements with their published final accounts and other matter. It does, however, encourage all other companies to use them.

9.3 Businesses other than companies

Although small companies, partnerships and sole traders do not have to prepare them, cash flow statements can be of considerable use to them.

FRS 1 prescribes a format for cash flow statements. An example is shown later in Exhibit 9.6. This is suitable for a company but, obviously, there are factors concerning partnerships and sole traders which do not occur in companies. It will be of help to students if the cash flow statements for sole traders and partnerships are fashioned to be as like those for companies as is possible. Such layouts will be followed in this book.

9.4 Profit and liquidity not directly related

Many people think that if we are making profits then there should be no shortage of cash. As you have learnt in Chapter 8, this is not necessarily so. Let us look at a few instances where, although reasonable profits are being made by each of the following firms, they could find themselves short of cash; if not now then they may do so in future.

● A sole trader is making £40,000 a year profits. However, his drawings have been over £60,000 a year for some time.
● A company has been over-generous with credit terms to debtors, and last year extended the time in which debtors could pay from one month to three months. In addition it has taken on quite a few extra customers who are not creditworthy and such sales may result in bad debts in the future.
● A partnership whose products will not be on the market for quite a long time has invested in some very expensive machinery. A lot of money has been spent now, but no income will result in the near future.

In all of these cases, each of the firms could easily run out of cash. In fact many businesses fail and are wound up because of cash shortages, despite adequate profits being made. Cash flow statements can help to show up such problems.

9.5 Where from: where to

Basically a cash flow statement shows where the cash funds came from, and where they have gone to. Exhibit 9.1 shows details of such cash flows.

EXHIBIT 9.1 Sources and applications of cash

Cash comes from (sources)	Cash funds		Cash goes to (applications)
	In	Out	

Cash comes from (sources)

1 Profits
2 Sales of Fixed Assets
3 Decrease in Stock
4 Decrease in Debtors
5 Capital Introduced
6 Loans Received
7 Increase in Creditors

Cash goes to (applications)

1 Losses
2 Purchases of Fixed Assets
3 Increase in Stock
4 Increase in Debtors
5 Drawings/Dividends
6 Loans Repaid
7 Decrease in Creditors

These can be explained as:

1 Profits bring a flow of cash into the firm. Losses take cash out of it.
2 The cash received from sales of fixed assets comes into the firm. A purchase of fixed assets takes it out.
3 Reducing stock in the normal course of business means turning it into cash. An increase in stock ties up cash funds.
4 A reduction in debtors means that the extra amount paid comes into the firm as cash. Letting debtors increase stops that extra amount of cash coming in.
5 An increase in a sole proprietor's capital, or issues of shares in a company, brings cash in. Drawings or dividends take it out.
6 Loans received bring in cash, while their repayment reduces cash.
7 An increase in creditors keeps the extra cash in the firm. A decrease in creditors means that the extra payments take cash out.

If we take the cash (and bank) balances at the start of a financial period, and adjust for cash flows in and out during the financial period, then we would arrive at the cash (and bank) balances at the end of the period. This can be shown as:

Cash per balance sheet (figures at the end of the previous period) + Changes – which must be because of cash flows during the intervening period = Cash per balance sheet (figures at the end of the following period)

9.6 Construction of a cash flow statement for a sole trader

We will first of all look at a cash flow statement drawn up for a sole trader's business, as this will be easier than looking at the more complicated example of a limited company.

We will start from Exhibit 9.2 and construct Exhibit 9.3, a cash flow statement.

EXHIBIT 9.2

The following are the balance sheets of T Holmes as at 31 December 20X6 and 31 December 20X7:

	20X6		20X7	
	£	£	£	£
Fixed assets				
Premises at cost		25,000		28,800
Current assets				
Stock	12,500		12,850	
Debtors	21,650		23,140	
Cash and bank balances	4,300		5,620	
	38,450		41,610	
Less Current liabilities				
Creditors	(11,350)		(11,120)	
Working capital		27,100		30,490
		52,100		59,290
Financed by:				
Capital				
Opening balances b/d		52,660		52,100
Add Net profit for year		16,550		25,440
		69,210		77,540
Less Drawings		17,110		18,250
		52,100		59,290

Note: For simpllicity, no depreciation has been charged in the accounts.

EXHIBIT 9.3

T Holmes
Cash Flow Statement for the year ended 31 December 20X7

	£
Net cash flow from operating activities (see Note 1)	23,370
Capital expenditure and financial investment	
Payment to acquire extra premises	(3,800)
Financing	
Drawings	(18,250)
Increase in cash	1,320

Notes:

1 Reconciliation of net profit to net cash inflow:

	£	£
Net profit		25,440
Less cash used for:		
Increase in stock	350	
Increase in debtors	1,490	
Decrease in creditors	230	
		(2,070)
Net cash flow from operating activities		23,370

2 Analysis of changes in cash during the year:

	£
Balance at 1 January 20X7	4,300
Net cash inflow	1,320
Balance at 31 December 20X7	5,620

9.7 Note on the use of brackets

As you know, in accounting it is customary to show a figure in brackets if it is a minus figure. This would be deducted from the other figures to arrive at the total of the column. These are seen very frequently in cash flow statements. For example, instead of bringing out a sub-total of the deductions, Note 1 accompanying Exhibit 9.3 would normally be shown as:

	£
Net profit	25,440
Increase in stock	(350)
Increase in debtors	(1,490)
Decrease in creditors	(230)
Net cash flow from operating activities	23,370

9.8 Adjustments needed to net profit

When net profit is included as a source of cash funds, we usually have to adjust the net profit figure to take account of items included which do not involve a movement of cash *in the period covered by the cash flow statement*. The most common examples are depreciation, provisions for doubtful debts, and book profits and losses on the sale or disposal of fixed assets.

Depreciation

For instance, suppose we bought equipment costing £3,000 in the year ended 31 December 20X6. It is depreciated at £1,000 per annum for three years and then scrapped, disposal value being nil. This would result in the following:

	Years to 31 December		
	20X6	20X7	20X8
	£	£	£
(*i*) Item involving flow of cash: Cost of equipment (as this is purchase of an asset this is not part of the net profit calculation)	3,000		
(*ii*) Net profit before depreciation	12,000	13,000	15,000
(*iii*) Items not involving flow of cash: Depreciation	(1,000)	(1,000)	(1,000)
(*iv*) Net profit after depreciation	11,000	12,000	14,000

Now the question arises as to which of figures (*i*) to (*iv*) are the ones to be used in cash flow statements. Let us examine items (*i*) to (*iv*) accordingly.

(*i*)   A payment of £3,000 is made to buy equipment. This *does* involve a flow of cash and should therefore be included in the cash flow statement for 20X6.

(*ii*)   Net profit before depreciation. This brings cash flowing into the firm and therefore *should* be shown in cash flow statements.

(*iii*) Depreciation is represented by a bookkeeping entry:
    Debit profit and loss:
        Credit provision for depreciation.

This does not involve any outflow of cash and *should not* be shown in a cash flow statement.

(*iv*) Net profit after depreciation. Depreciation does not involve cash flow, and therefore (*ii*) is the net profit we need.

In most examination questions (*iii*) will not be shown. As we will show you, the figure for net profit before depreciation will be calculated in the cash flow statement itself.

Doubtful debts provisions

If a debt is written off as bad, it represents an expense that does not involve a flow of cash during the period. A debt would have become cash when paid, and only does so at the time payment is received. Now you are saying that this will not happen and have written it off to the profit and loss account. You need to adjust both the profit (by adding it back) and the change in the debtor balance. Overall, they cancel each other out, so you need do nothing when preparing the cash flow statement.

On the other hand, a provision for doubtful debts is similar to a provision for depreciation. The cash flow occurs *when* a debt *is* paid, not when provisions are made in case there may be bad debts in the future. As a result, when preparing the cash flow statement, you need to add back to profit any increase in doubtful debt provision or deduct from profit any decrease in the doubtful provision.

If an examination question gives you the net profits *after* doubtful debts provision, then the provision has to be added back to exclude it from the profit calculations.

Book profit/loss on sales of fixed assets

If a fixed asset with a net book value (after depreciation) of £5,000 is sold for £6,400 cash, then the flow of cash is £6,400. The fact that there has been a book profit of £1,400 does not provide any more cash above the figure of £6,400. Similarly, the sale of an asset with a net book value of £3,000 for £2,200 cash produces a flow of cash of £2,200. Similarly to depreciation, the £800 book loss does not involve a flow of cash during the period.

9.9 Example of adjustments

As the net profit figure in accounts is:

(*i*)   *after* adjustments for depreciation
(*ii*)   *after* adjustment to provisions for doubtful debts
(*iii*) *after* book profits/losses on sales of fixed assets

profits need to be adjusted in cash flow statements. However, the adjustments are only for depreciation in *that period*, and for fixed asset book profits/losses for *that period*. No adjustments are needed with reference to previous periods. Exhibit 9.4 shows examples of three firms.

EXHIBIT 9.4

	Firm A	Firm B	Firm C
	£	£	£
Depreciation for year	2,690	4,120	6,640
Increases in doubtful debt provision	540	360	
Decrease in doubtful debt provision			200
Book loss on sale of fixed assets	1,200		490
Book profit on sale of fixed assets		750	
Net profit after the above items included	16,270	21,390	32,410

Reconciliation of net profit to net cash inflow

	£	£	£
Net profit	16,270	21,390	32,410
Adjustment for items not involving the movement of funds:			
Depreciation	2,690	4,120	6,640
Book profit on sale of fixed assets		(750)	
Book loss on sale of fixed assets	1,200		490
Increase in doubtful debt provision	540	360	
Decrease in doubtful debt provision			(200)
Net cash flow from operating activities	20,700	25,120	39,340

You will notice that the items in brackets, i.e. (750) and (200), had been credits in the profit and loss accounts and need deducting, while the other items were debits and need adding back.

9.10 A comprehensive example

EXHIBIT 9.5

The balance sheets of R Lester are as follows:

	31.12.20X7			31.12.20X8		
	£	£	£	£	£	£
Fixed assets						
Equipment at cost		28,500			26,100	
Less Depreciation to date		(11,450)			(13,010)	
			17,050			13,090
Current assets						
Stock		18,570			16,250	
Debtors	8,470			14,190		
Less Bad debts provision	(420)			(800)		
		8,050			13,390	
Cash and bank balances		4,060			3,700	
		30,680			33,340	
Less Current liabilities						
Creditors		(4,140)			(5,730)	
Working capital			26,540			27,610
			43,590			40,700
Less Loan from J Gorsey			(10,000)			(4,000)
			33,590			36,700

	31.12.20X7			31.12.20X8	
	£	£	£	£	£	£

Financed by:
Capital

Opening balances b/d	35,760	33,590
Add Net profit	10,240	11,070
Add Cash introduced	–	600
	46,000	45,260
Less Drawings	(12,410)	(8,560)
	33,590	36,700

Notes: Equipment with a book value of £1,350 was sold for £900. Depreciation written off equipment during the year was £2,610.

The sole trader's cash flow statement will be as follows:

R Lester
Cash Flow Statement for the year ended 31 December 20X8

	£	£
Net cash flow from operating activities (*see* Note 1)		12,700
Capital expenditure and financial investment		
Receipts from sale of fixed assets		900
Financing		
Capital introduced	600	
Loan repaid to J Gorsey	(6,000)	
Drawings	(8,560)	
		(13,960)
Decrease in cash		(360)

Notes:

1 Reconciliation of net profit to net cash inflow:

	£	£
Net profit		11,070
Depreciation	2,610	
Loss on sale of fixed assets	450	
Increase in bad debts provision	380	
Decrease in stock	2,320	
Increase in creditors	1,590	
Increase in debtors	(5,720)	
		1,630
Net cash flow from operating activities		12,700

2 Analysis of changes in cash during the year:

	£
Balance at 1 January 20X8	4,060
Net cash inflow	(360)
Balance at 31 December 20X8	3,700

Cash flow statements of this type work well for a sole trader or a partnership. However, companies have far more complex funding and flows of cash. As a result, they must produce a cash flow statement according to the rules and layout contained in FRS 1, *Cash flow statements*.

9.11 UK companies and FRS 1

UK companies, except those defined as small under the Companies Act (*see* Chapter 6, Section 6.12), have to publish a cash flow statement for each accounting period. There are two approaches available under the standard: the 'direct' method, which shows the operating cash receipts and payments summing to the net cash flow from operating activities – in effect, it summarises the cash book; and the 'indirect' method, which identifies the net cash flow via a reconciliation to operating profit. As the reconciliation has also to be shown when the direct method is used, it is hardly surprising that the indirect method is the more commonly adopted one. It is also the method that the ASB recommends (because the cost of producing the data required for the direct method is felt likely to be greater than the benefit of doing so, in most cases).

It is the indirect method that you are required to know under the AQA and OCR syllabuses. The basic layout is shown in Exhibit 9.6.

EXHIBIT 9.6

X LIMITED
Cash Flow Statement for the year ended 31 December 20X7

	£000	£000
1 Net cash inflow/(outflow) from operating activities (*see* Note 1)		XXX
2 *Dividends from joint ventures and associates*		(XXX)
3 *Returns on investments and servicing of finance*		
Interest received	XXX	
Interest paid	(XXX)	
Preference dividends paid	(XXX)	
Net cash inflow/(outflow) from returns on investments and servicing of finance		XXX
4 *Taxation*		(XXX)
5 *Capital expenditure and financial investment*		
Payments to acquire intangible fixed assets	(XXX)	
Payments to acquire tangible fixed assets	(XXX)	
Receipts from sales of tangible fixed assets	XXX	
Net cash inflow/(outflow) from capital expenditure and financial investment		XXX
6 *Acquisitions and disposals*		
Purchase of subsidiary undertaking	(XXX)	
Sale of business	XXX	
Net cash inflow/(outflow) from acquisitions and disposals		XXX
7 *Equity dividends paid*		(XXX)
8 *Management of liquid resources*		
Cash withdrawn from 7-day deposit	XXX	
Purchase of government securities	(XXX)	
Sale of corporate bonds	XXX	
Net cash inflow/(outflow) from management of liquid resources		XXX
9 *Financing*		
Issue of ordinary share capital	XXX	
Repurchase of debenture loan	(XXX)	
Expenses paid in connection with share issues	(XXX)	
		XXX
Increase/(decrease) in cash in the period		XXX

Reconciliation of net cash flow to movement in net debt/funds	£000	£000
Increase/(decrease) in cash in the period	XXX	
Cash inflow/(outflow) from increase/decrease in debt and lease financing	XXX	
Cash inflow/(outflow) from decrease/increase in liquid resources	XXX	
Change in net debt resulting from cash flows		XXX
Loans and finance leases acquired with subsidiary		(XXX)
New finance leases		(XXX)
Exchange rate translation differences		XXX
Movement in net debt in the period		XXX
Net debt at 1 January 20X7		XXX
Net debt at 31 December 20X7		XXX

Note to the cash flow statement

1 *Reconciliation of operating profit to net cash inflow/(outflow) from operating activities*

	£000
Operating profit	XXX
Depreciation charges	XXX
(Profit)/Loss on sale of tangible fixed assets	XXX
(Increase)/Decrease in stocks	XXX
(Increase)/Decrease in debtors	XXX
Increase/(Decrease) in creditors	XXX
Net cash inflow/(outflow) from operating activities	XXX

Each of the nine headings of the cash flow statement can be shown as one line in the statement and the detail in a note. (The numbers have been shown in Exhibit 9.6 in order to make it clear what the nine headings are. These line numbers would not normally be included in the cash flow statement.)

The first seven headings should be in the sequence shown. The eighth and ninth can be combined under one heading, so long as their cash flows are shown separately and separate subtotals are given for each of them within it.

The reconciliation to net debt does not form part of the statement, nor does the reconciliation of operating profit to net cash flow from operating activities. Either can be shown in a separate note (as the reconciliation of operating profit to net cash flow from operating activities is shown above) or adjoining the statement (as in the case of the reconciliation of the movement of cash to net debt above).

Now, let's consider each of the elements of the cash flow statement in turn.

9.12 Cash flow

The cash flow statement reports cash flow. Cash flow is defined in paragraph 2 of FRS 1 as 'an increase or decrease in an amount of cash'. Anything that falls outside this definition is not a cash flow and should not appear in the statement (though it could appear in the notes).

Cash is defined as 'cash in hand and deposits repayable on demand with any qualifying financial institution, less overdrafts from any qualifying financial institution repayable on demand'.

'Deposits repayable on demand' are deposits that can be withdrawn at any time without notice and without penalty or if a maturity or period of notice of not more than 24 hours or one working day has been agreed.

Cash includes cash in hand and deposits denominated in foreign currencies.

9.13 Operating activities and cash flows

Operating activities are generally the cash effects of transactions and other events relating to operating or trading activities. The net cash flow from operating activities represents the net increase or decrease in cash resulting from the operations shown in the profit and loss account in arriving at operating profit.

The reconciliation between operating profit and net cash flow from operating activities for the period should disclose separately the movements in stocks, debtors and creditors related to operating activities, and other differences between cash flows and profits. It should also show separately the difference between dividends received and results taken into account for equity accounted entities.

In the cash flow statement, **operating cash flows** may be shown using either the **indirect** method or the **direct** method. Using the **indirect** method, it would be laid out in a manner similar to that shown in Exhibit 9.7.

EXHIBIT 9.7

	£
Operating profit	12,000
Depreciation charges	500
Loss on sale of tangible fixed assets	10
Increase in stocks	(200)
Increase in debtors	(100)
Increase in creditors	300
Net cash inflow from operating activities	12,510

FRS 1 requires that a reconciliation be shown between the net cash flow from operating activities and the operating profit as shown in the profit and loss account, which is precisely what is produced if the *indirect* method is adopted. Consequently, by adopting the *indirect* method, as the detailed information is to be included in a reconciliation, the main part of the statement may only include a single line 'net cash flow from operating activities'. Thus, instead of being included in the body of the cash flow statement, the details shown in Exhibit 9.7 would be included in the notes to the statement. When the *indirect* method is adopted, no details of the equivalent *direct* method analysis is required.

On the other hand, when the **direct** method is adopted for preparation of the statement, the reconciliation (i.e. the *indirect* method analysis) must also be prepared and included as a note to the statement. The **direct** method would produce an analysis in the cash flow statement similar to that shown in Exhibit 9.8.

EXHIBIT 9.8

	£
Operating activities	
Cash received from customers	120,000
Cash payments to suppliers	(40,000)
Cash paid to and on behalf of employees	(60,000)
Other cash payments	(7,490)
Net cash inflow from operating activities	12,510

It is generally easier for an entity to adopt the *indirect* method – the figures are readily available from the profit and loss account and balance sheet data. The *direct* method, on the other hand, requires that the cash book is analysed. Despite there being much more work involved in preparing it, in Appendix III to FRS 1, the ASB encourages the use of the *direct* method when the potential benefits to users outweigh the costs of doing so – it does help provide a far clearer view of cash flow than the bookkeeping adjustments to profit that are undertaken under the *indirect* method.

In an examination, if sufficient information on cash flows is provided for you to adopt the *direct* method, you should assume that is the approach to take – however, you would still require to adopt the *indirect* method when completing the reconciliation if that was also required by the question set.

9.14 Dividends from joint ventures and associates

This category was added following the issue of FRS 9, *Associates and Joint Ventures* in 1997. It was felt appropriate to show these dividends as a separate item as they were not part of operating income and they have a different nature to that of dividends from a company's returns on investment.

9.15 Returns on investment and servicing of finance

This section concerns receipts resulting from the ownership of an investment and payments to providers of finance, non-equity shareholders and minority interests.

Generally, the standard endeavours to classify all cash flows according to the substance of the transaction that gave rise to them. As a result, this section of the statement excludes any item that may be classified under one of the other headings. For example, payments to *non-equity* shareholders (e.g. holders of preference shares in the entity) are included in this section, but payments to *equity* shareholders appear in the 'equity dividends paid' section.

Among the cash inflows included in this section are interest and dividends received (other than dividends from equity accounted entities whose results are included as part of operating profit). Cash outflows in this section include interest paid; finance costs, as defined under FRS 4 (*Capital instruments*); the interest element of finance lease rental payments, as defined under SSAP 21 (*Accounting for leases and hire purchase contracts*); and dividends paid to minority interests and to non-equity shareholders of the entity.

9.16 Taxation

This section includes cash flows to and from taxation authorities in respect of the reporting entity's revenue and capital profits. Other tax cash flows should be included under the same heading as the cash flow which gave rise to them – property taxes, such as rates, and VAT, for example, are seen as relating to 'operating activities'. Thus, the net amount of VAT paid to or received from the tax authorities is included under that section. The exception to this arises when VAT is irrecoverable, in which case it is added to the originating transaction value and not distinguished from it within the cash flow statement.

9.17   Capital expenditure and financial investment

Capital expenditure means *buying and selling fixed assets*. **Financial investment** means *buying and selling shares held as investments*. Included in this section are cash flows relating to the acquisition or disposal of any fixed asset other than those required to be classified under the 'acquisitions and disposals' section of the statement, and those relating to any current asset investment not included in the 'management of liquid resources' section.

The heading can be reduced to 'capital expenditure' if there are no cash flows relating to financial investment.

The cash *inflows* include:

● receipts from the sale or disposal of property, plant or equipment, and
● receipts from the repayment of the reporting entity's loans to other entities and sales of debt instruments of other entities (other than receipts forming part of an acquisition or disposal or a movement in liquid resources and classified as falling within either of those two sections of the statement).

The cash *outflows* include:

● payments to acquire property, plant or equipment, and
● loans made by the reporting entity and payments to acquire debt instruments of other entities (other than payments forming part of an acquisition or disposal or a movement in liquid resources and classified as falling within either of those two sections of the statement).

9.18   Acquisitions and disposals

It is quite normal for businesses to buy and sell other businesses or interests in other businesses. This category of cash flow records the cash-related results of these activities. Included in this section are therefore those cash flows relating to the acquisition or disposal of any trade or business, or of an investment in an entity that is or, as a result of the transaction, becomes or ceases to be an associate, a joint venture or a subsidiary undertaking.

9.19   Equity dividends paid

This section includes the dividends paid on the reporting entity's or, in a group, the parent's equity shares.

9.20   Management of liquid resources

The FRS defines liquid resources as 'current asset investments held as readily disposable stores of value'. A 'readily disposable investment' is one that is disposable without curtailing or disrupting the entity's business and is either readily convertible into known amounts of cash or traded in an active market. In other words, this heading is concerned with short-term investments.

Cash inflows in this section include withdrawals from short-term deposits not qualifying as cash and inflows from the disposal or redemption of any other investments held as liquid resources.

Cash outflows in this section include payments into short-term deposits not qualifying as cash and outflows to acquire any other investment held as a liquid resource.

Each entity must explain what it includes in liquid resources and declare any change in its policy.

9.21 Financing

This category reports the cash flow effects of changes to share capital and long-term borrowings. Receipts and repayments of the principal amounts (i.e. the advance, not the interest) from or to external providers of finance are entered in this section. Examples include receipts from issuing and payments towards the redemption of shares and other equity instruments, debentures, loans, notes, bonds, and from long-term and short-term borrowings (other than overdrafts); the capital element of finance lease rental payment; and payments of expenses or commission on any issue of equity shares.

The amount of any financing cash flows received from or paid to an equity-accounted entity should be disclosed separately.

9.22 Material transactions not resulting in any cash flows

FRS 1 also requires that details of material transactions that do not result in any cash flows should be included in a note if it is necessary for an understanding of the underlying transactions. A possible example would be an operating lease. It would involve the acquisition of an asset, but the reporting entity is paying rent, not purchasing the asset.

9.23 Exceptional and extraordinary items

Cash flows relating to items classed as exceptional or extraordinary in the profit and loss account should be shown under the appropriate standard headings, according to their nature. They should be identified in the cash flow statement or a note to it and the relationship between the cash flows and the originating exceptional or extraordinary item should be explained.

Where the cash flows themselves are exceptional because of their size or incidence but the underlying event that gave rise to them is not, sufficient disclosure should be given to explain their cause and effect.

Now, let's look at two examples of cash flow statements, one using the indirect method and the other using the direct method.

9.24 Two further examples

Exhibits 9.9 and 9.10 further illustrate how a cash flow statement is prepared, this time using numbers to add clarity. Some key points to remember include:

● It is amounts paid rather than charged or accrued that are included. Thus for both tax and dividends, it is the actual payments and receipts that occurred during the period that are included in the statement, not the amounts provided for that will be paid or received in a future period.

- Profit on sale of fixed assets is already included in the sale amount and should not be included a second time.
- Care should be taken to identify and eliminate non-cash adjustments to the original profit before tax figure, for example depreciation and bad debt provisions.
- If the layout presented in Exhibits 9.9 and 9.10 is followed, the entries in the 'Financing' section will have the opposite signs to the others, i.e. income will be shown with negative values, rather than positive as is the case in the other sections of the statement.
- Exhibit 9.9 shows the indirect method.
- Exhibit 9.10 shows the direct method.

EXHIBIT 9.9

From the following profit and loss and balance sheet information, prepare a cash flow statement as required by FRS 1 *using the indirect method.*

Profit and Loss Account for the year ending 31 December 20X4

	£000	£000
Sales		10,000
Cost of goods sold		(6,000)
		4,000
Expenses		
Depreciation	600	
Interest	150	
Other expenses	2,100	
		(2,850)
Profit for the year before tax		1,150
Tax		(200)
Profit for the year after tax		950
Proposed dividend		(150)
Retained profit		800

Balance Sheet as at 31 December

	20X4		20X3	
	£000	£000	£000	£000
Fixed assets at cost		6,000		6,000
Less accumulated depreciation		(3,000)		(2,400)
Net book value		3,000		3,600
Current assets				
Stock	650		700	
Trade debtors	200		250	
Cash	1,610		150	
		2,460		1,100
Less current liabilities				
Trade creditors	310		300	
Taxation	200		150	
Proposed dividends	150		250	
		(660)		(700)
		4,800		4,000
Financed by				
Ordinary share capital		2,000		2,000
Revenue reserves		2,800		2,000
		4,800		4,000

Outline solution

**Cash Flow Statement (using the indirect method) for the year
ended 31 December 20X4**

	£000
Net cash inflow from operating activities	2,010
Dividends from joint ventures and associates	–
Returns on investments and servicing of finance	
Interest paid	(150)
Taxation	(150)
Capital expenditure and financial investment	–
Acquisitions and disposals	–
Equity dividends paid	(250)
Management of liquid resources	–
Financing	–
Increase in cash in the period	1,460

Notes to the cash flow statement

1 Reconciliation of operating profit to net cash inflow from operating activities:

Operating profit	1,300
Depreciation charges	600
Decrease in stocks	50
Decrease in debtors	50
Increase in creditors	10
Net cash inflow from operating activities	2,010

Working:

Operating profit = Retained profit (800) + Interest (150) + Dividend (150) + Tax (200)
= 1,300

EXHIBIT 9.10

From the summarised cash account and the fixed asset schedule of Thistle Ltd for 20X2, pre-pare a cash flow statement as required by FRS 1 *using the direct method*.

Summarised Cash Account

	£000		£000
Opening balance	500	Wages	1,350
Cash from cash sales	3,500	Other expenses	600
Cash from credit sales	5,750	Cash paid to suppliers	4,320
Cash from issue of shares	1,200	Tax paid	100
Cash from sale of building	970	Cash paid on finance lease	700
		Final dividend for 20X1	100
		Interim dividend 20X2	50
		Closing balance	4,700
	11,920		11,920

Fixed Asset Schedule

	Plant	Buildings	Total
	£000	£000	£000
Cost at 1.1.20X2	10,000	15,000	25,000
Acquisitions	4,730	–	4,730
Disposals	–	(5,000)	(5,000)
Cost at 31.12.20X2	14,730	10,000	24,730
Accumulated depreciation at 1.1.20X2	3,500	6,000	9,500
Charge for year	650	1,500	2,150
Disposals	–	(4,500)	(4,500)
Accumulated depreciation at 31.12.20X2	4,150	3,000	7,150

Other information

(a) The tax charge for the year was £400,000. The opening balance on the tax liability was £100,000.

(b) The proposed final dividend for 20X2 was £120,000.

(c) Other expenses include insurance, which is paid a year in advance, on 30 June. In 20X1, insurance of £300,000 was paid. The amount paid in 20X2 was £400,000.

(d) Accrued wages were £75,000 at 1.1.20X2, and £95,000 at 31.12.20X2.

(e) Stocks were £1,500,000 at 1.1.20X2, and £1,700,000 at 31.12.20X2.

(f) All £700,000 paid on the finance lease in 20X2 represented capital. This was the first year of the lease and interest was not paid until the second payment, which was made in 20X3. Interest of £403,000 was included in the 20X3 payment and was accrued in the 20X2 financial statements.

(g) Opening and closing trade debtors and trade creditors were:

	1.1.20X2	31.12.20X2
Trade debtors	300,000	450,000
Trade creditors	500,000	475,000

(h) 600,000 £1 ordinary shares were issued at a premium on 1.3.20X2.

(i) Retained profits for the year to 31.12.20X2 were £732,000.

Outline solution

Cash Flow Statement (using the direct method) for Thistle Ltd for the year ended 31 December 20X2

	£000	£000
Operating activities		
Cash received from customers	9,250	
Cash paid to suppliers	(4,320)	
Cash paid to employees	(1,350)	
Other cash payments	(600)	
Net cash inflow from operating activities		2,980
Dividends from joint ventures and associates		–
Returns on investment and servicing of finance		–
Taxation		(100)
Capital expenditure and financial investment		
Sale of buildings		970
Acquisitions and disposals		–
Equity dividend paid		(150)
Management of liquid resources		–

	£000	£000
Financing		
Issue of share capital	1,200	
Capital element of finance lease rental payments	(700)	
Net cash inflow from financing		500
Increase in cash in the period		4,200

Note to the cash flow statement:

1 Reconciliation of operating profit to net cash inflow from operating activities:

	£000
Operating profit	1,705
Depreciation charges	2,150
Profit on sale of building	(470)
Increase in stocks	(200)
Increase in debtors	(150)
Increase in prepayments	(50)
Decrease in creditors	(25)
Increase in accruals	20
Net cash inflow from operating activities	2,980

Workings

1 Dividends paid in 20X2 are the proposed dividends from the previous year, plus the interim dividend paid during 20X2. The dividend charge in the profit and loss account will be the interim dividend and the proposed dividend for 20X2.

2 Assume tax paid during 20X2 is the amount outstanding at the opening balance sheet date. The tax charge for 20X2 in the profit and loss account is £400,000.

3

	£
Retained profit	732,000
Add Dividends	170,000
Add Tax	400,000
Add Interest	403,000
Operating profit	1,705,000

9.25 Uses of cash flow statements

Cash flow statements have many uses other than meeting the legal requirement for some companies to prepare them.

Let us first of all list a few cases where a business might find them useful in helping to answer their queries:

(a) One small businessman wants to know why he now has an overdraft. He started off the year with money in the bank, he has made profits and yet he now has a bank overdraft.

(b) Another businessman wants to know why the bank balance has risen even though the firm is losing money.

(c) The partners in a business have put in additional capital this last year. Even so, the bank balance fell dramatically during the year. They want an explanation as to how this has happened.

A study of the cash flow statement in each case would reveal to them the answers to their questions. A study of the final accounts themselves would not give them the information that they needed.

Besides the answers to such specific queries, cash flow statements should also help businesses to assess the following:

- the cash flows which the business may be able to generate in the future;
- how far the business will be able to meet future commitments, e.g. tax due, loan repayments, interest payments, contracts that could possibly lose quite a lot of money;
- how far future share issues may be needed, or additional capital in the case of sole traders or partnerships;
- a valuation of the business.

Learning outcomes

You should now have learnt:

1 Why cash flow statements provide useful information for decision making.

2 A range of sources and applications of cash.

3 How to adjust net profit for non-cash items to find the net cash flow from operating activities.

4 How to prepare a cash flow statement as defined by FRS 1.

5 How to present the net cash flow from operating activities using the indirect method.

6 That the objective of FRS 1 is to require entities to report their cash generation and absorption for a period on a standard basis.

7 Cash flow statements aid comparison between entities.

8 The statement must show the flows of cash for the period under the nine headings:
- operating activities;
- dividends from joint ventures and associates;
- returns on investments and servicing of finance;
- taxation;
- capital expenditure and financial investment;
- acquisitions and disposals;
- equity dividends paid;
- management of liquid resources; and
- financing.

9 That the headings should be in that order and the statement should include a total for each heading.

10 That cash flow is an increase or decrease in cash resulting from a transaction.

11 That operating activities are generally the cash effects of transactions and other events relating to operating and trading activities.

12 That operating cash flows can be shown using either the *indirect* method or the *direct* method.

13 That reconciliations are presented between operating profit and net cash flow from operating activities for the period, and between the movement in cash in the period and the movement in net debt.

14 That the ASB recommends that the *direct* method be used *if the benefits of doing so outweigh the costs.*

15 Some of the uses that can be made of cash flow statements.

REVIEW QUESTIONS

9.1 The balance sheets of M Daly, a sole trader, for two successive years are shown below. You are required to draw up a cash flow statement for the year ended 31 December 20X4.

Balance Sheets as at 31 December

	20X3	20X4		20X3	20X4
	£	£		£	£
Land and premises			Capital account:		
(cost £3,000)	2,600	2,340	1 January	4,200	4,700
Plant and machinery			*Add* Net profit for		
(cost £2,000)	1,500	–	the year	1,800	2,200
(cost £3,000)	–	2,300		6,000	6,900
Stocks	660	630			
Trade debtors	1,780	1,260	Deduct drawings	(1,300)	(1,500)
Bank	–	710		4,700	5,400
			Trade creditors	1,200	840
			Bank overdraft	640	–
			Loan (repayable		
			December 20X9)	–	1,000
	6,540	7,240		6,540	7,240

9.2X

John Flynn
Balance Sheets as at 31 December

	20X8	20X9		20X8	20X9
	£	£		£	£
Buildings	5,000	5,000	Capital at 1 January	15,500	16,100
Fixtures *Less* Depreciation	1,800	2,000	*Add* Cash introduced	–	2,500
			,, Net profit for year	6,800	7,900
Motor van				22,300	26,500
Less Depreciation	2,890	5,470	*Less* Drawings	(6,200)	(7,800)
Stock	3,000	8,410		16,100	18,700
Debtors	4,860	5,970	Creditors	2,900	2,040
Bank	3,100	–	Bank overdraft	–	1,260
Cash	350	150	Loan (repayable in		
			10 years' time)	2,000	5,000
	21,000	27,000		21,000	27,000

Draw up a cash flow statement for John Flynn for the year ended 31 December 20X9. You are told that fixtures bought in 20X9 cost £400, while a motor van was bought for £4,000.

9.3 Malcolm Phillips is a sole trader who prepares his accounts annually to 30 April. His summarised balance sheets for the last two years are shown below.

Balance Sheets as at 30 April

	20X8	20X9		20X8	20X9
	£	£		£	£
Capital at 1 May	20,000	20,500	Fixed assets, at cost	15,500	18,500
Add			*Less* Provision for		
Profit for year	7,000	8,500	depreciation	1,500	1,700
Additional capital introduced	–	2,000		14,000	16,800
	27,000	31,000			
Less Drawings	6,500	8,000			
	20,500	23,000	Stock	3,100	5,900
Trade creditors	2,000	2,200	Debtors	3,900	3,400
Bank overdraft	–	900	Bank	1,500	–
	22,500	26,100		22,500	26,100

Malcolm is surprised to see that he now has an overdraft, in spite of making a profit and bringing in additional capital during the year.

Questions:

(*a*) Draw up a suitable financial statement which will explain to Malcolm how his overdraft has arisen.

(*b*) The following further information relates to the year ended 30 April 20X9.

	£
Sales (all on credit)	30,000
Cost of sales	22,500

Calculate Malcolm's
(*i*) gross profit margin
(*ii*) rate of stock turnover.

(*OCR (MEG): GCSE*)

9.4 From the following details you are to draft a cash flow statement for C Willis for the year ended 31 December 20X8.

C Willis
Profit and Loss Account for the year ended 31 December 20X8

	£	£
Gross profit		29,328
Add Discounts received	298	
„ Profit on sale of motor van	570	868
		30,196
Less Expenses		
Motor expenses	1,590	
Wages	8,790	
General expenses	2,144	
Bad debts	340	
Increase in bad debt provision	120	
Depreciation: Motor van	1,090	14,074
		16,122

Balance Sheets at 31 December

	20X7		20X8	
	£	£	£	£
Fixed assets				
Motor vans at cost	11,200		7,200	
Less Depreciation to date	(4,160)	7,040	(2,980)	4,220
Current assets				
Stock	10,295		17,150	
Debtors *less* provision*	5,190		3,380	
Bank	1,568		2,115	
	17,053		22,645	
Less Current liabilities				
Creditors	(2,770)	14,283	(2,920)	19,725
		21,323		23,945
Less Long-term liability				
Loan from P Bond		(6,000)		(5,000)
		15,323		18,945
Capital				
Opening balance b/d		12,243		15,323
Add Net profit		14,080		16,122
		26,323		31,445
Less Drawings		(11,000)		(12,500)
		15,323		18,945

* Debtors 20X7 £5,490 – provision £300.
  Debtors 20X8 £3,800 – provision £420.

Note: The motor van was sold for £2,300 during 20X8.

9.5X

You are required to draw up a cash flow statement for S Markham for the year ended 30 June 20X8 from the following information.

S Markham
Profit and Loss Account for the year ended 30 June 20X8

	£	£
Gross profit		139,940
Add Reduction in bad debt provision		170
		140,110
Less Expenses:		
Wages and salaries	49,220	
General trading expenses	14,125	
Equipment running costs	16,040	
Motor vehicle expenses	8,110	
Depreciation: Motor vehicles	3,090	
Equipment	2,195	
Loss on sale of equipment	560	(93,340)
Net profit		46,770

Balance Sheets at 30 June

Fixed assets	20X7 £	20X7 £	20X8 £	20X8 £
Equipment at cost	31,150		20,100	
Less Depreciation to date	(18,395)	12,755	(14,600)	5,500
Motor vehicles at cost	22,510		22,510	
Less Depreciation to date	(7,080)	15,430	(10,170)	12,340
		28,185		17,840
Current assets				
Stock	28,970		32,005	
Debtors less provision*	16,320		15,050	
Bank	9,050		28,225	
	54,340		75,280	
Less Current liabilities				
Creditors	(11,350)	42,990	(14,360)	60,920
		71,175		78,760
Less Long-term liability				
Loan from A White		(21,185)		(10,000)
		49,990		68,760
Capital				
Opening balance		38,340		49,990
Add Net profit		36,150		46,770
		74,490		96,760
Less Drawings		(24,500)		(28,000)
		49,990		68,760

* Debtors 20X7 £17,000 – provision £680.
 Debtors 20X8 £15,560 – provision £510.

Note: The equipment was sold for £4,500.

9.6 The Balance Sheets as at 31 December of Sharma plc are shown below.

	20X0 £	20X0 £	20X1 £	20X1 £
Fixed assets (net)		420,000		530,000
Current assets				
Stock	42,000		46,000	
Debtors	28,000		20,000	
Cash at bank	10,000		3,000	
	80,000		69,000	
Creditors for less than 1 year				
Creditors	16,000		25,000	
Corporation tax	40,000		42,000	
Dividends	20,000		30,000	
	76,000		97,000	
Net current assets		4,000		(28,000)
		424,000		502,000
Capital and reserves				
£1 ordinary shares		300,000		350,000
General reserve		44,000		77,000
Profit and loss		80,000		75,000
		424,000		502,000

Additional information:

1 Tangible fixed assets costing £180,000 were purchased during the year ended 31 December 20X1. There were no disposals of fixed assets.

2 Sharma plc paid an interim dividend of £18,000 during the year ended 31 December 20X1.

Required:

(*a*) Prepare a Cash Flow Statement, in accordance with good accounting practice, for the year ended 31 December 20X1.

(22 marks)

(*b*) Evaluate the usefulness of a cash flow statement for Sharma plc.

(8 marks)

(*c*) Assess the liquidity position of Sharma plc.

(10 marks)

(OCR: GCE A-level, Paper 2505, Q2, 20/6/2002)

Accounting standards

You may find it useful to read supplementary Chapter 25, Accounting concepts, before you read this chapter.

10.1 Why do we need accounting standards?

Accounting is used in every kind of business and organisation from large multinational organisations to your local shop, from sole traders to companies. It can cover activities as different as breweries, charities, churches, dentists, doctors, lawyers, mines, oil wells, betting shops, banks, cinemas, circuses, funeral undertakers, farms, waste disposal, deep-sea diving, airlines, estate agents and so on.

Let's assume that you have received a copy of the published financial statements of a company. You want to be sure that you can rely on the methods it selected to calculate its revenues, expenditures and balance sheet values. Without this assurance you would not be able to have any faith at all in the figures, and could not sensibly take any decision concerning your relationship with the company.

It is the same for all investors. People invest in organisations of all types and they would all like to have faith and trust in the figures reported in the financial statements of those organsisations. But this diversity of type of business, and also of size, means that, while general principles can be laid down, detailed regulations that would make sense in one company, it would be absolutely stupid to apply in another company. It is, quite simply, impossible to provide 100 per cent assurance of the validity of the financial statements of every conceivable organisation through the creation of a single set of rules and procedures. There has to be some flexibility within the rules laid down.

If it isn't feasible to produce a set of all-encompassing regulations, why bother with rules at all? To understand why there was a move to regulation, we need to look back to what happened in the 1960s.

10.2 The background

In the late 1960s there was a general outcry that the methods used by different businesses were showing vastly different profits on similar data. In the UK, a controversy had arisen following the takeover of AEI Ltd by GEC Ltd. In fighting the takeover bid made by GEC, the AEI directors had produced a forecast, in the tenth month of their financial year, that the profit before tax for the year would be £10 million. After the takeover, the financial statements of AEI for that same year showed a loss of £4.5 million. The difference was attributed to there being £5 million of 'matters substantially of fact' and £9.5 million of 'adjustments which remain matters substantially of judgement'.

The financial pages of the national press started demanding action, calling for the accounting profession to lay down consistent principles for businesses to follow.

In December 1969, the Institute of Chartered Accountants in England and Wales issued a *Statement of Intent on Accounting Standards in the 1970s*. The Institute set up the Accounting Standards Steering Committee in 1970. Over the following six years, it was joined by the five other UK and Irish accountancy bodies and, in 1976, the committee became the Accounting Standards Committee (ASC). The six accountancy bodies formed the Consultative Committee of Accountancy Bodies (CCAB).

Prior to the issue of any accounting standard by the ASC, a great deal of preparatory work was done culminating in the publication of an exposure draft (ED). Copies of the exposure draft were then sent to those with a special interest in the topic. The journals of the CCAB also gave full details of the exposure drafts. After full and proper consultation, when it was seen to be desirable, an accounting standard on the topic was issued. The Standards issued by the ASC were called Statements of Standard Accounting Practice (SSAPs).

10.3 The Accounting Standards Board

Because the ASC had to obtain approval from its six professional accountancy body members, it did not appear to be as decisive and independent as was desired. To overcome this, in 1990 a new body, the Accounting Standards Board (ASB), took over the functions of the ASC. The ASB is more independent of the accounting bodies and can issue its recommendations, known as Financial Reporting Standards (FRSs), without approval from any other body. The ASB endorsed the remaining SSAPs (25 had been issued by the ASC), each of which remains in force until it is replaced by an FRS. As with the ASC, the ASB issues exposure drafts – Financial Reporting Exposure Drafts (FREDs) – developed in a similar fashion to before.

In 1997, the ASB issued a third category of standard – the Financial Reporting Standard for Smaller Entities (FRSSE). SSAPs and FRSs had generally been developed with the larger company in mind. The FRSSE was the ASB's response to the view that smaller companies should not have to apply all the cumbersome rules contained in the SSAPs and FRSs. It is, in effect, a collection of some of the rules from virtually all the other accounting standards. Small companies can choose whether to apply it or, as seems unlikely, apply all the other accounting standards.

In addition to the FRSs and the FRSSE, the ASB also issues Urgent Issue Task Force Abstracts (UITFs). These are issued in response to an urgent need to regulate something pending the issue of a new or amended FRS. They have the same status as an FRS.

While there is no general law compelling observation of the standards, accounting standards have had statutory recognition since the Companies Act 1989 was issued. As a result, apart from entities exempted from certain standards or sections within standards – SSAPs 13 (*Research and development*) and 25 (*Segmental reporting*) and FRS 1 (*Cash flow statements*), for example, all contain exemption clauses based on company size – accounting standards must be complied with when preparing financial statements intended to present a true and fair view. The Companies Acts state that failure to comply with the requirements of an accounting standard must be explained in the financial statements.

The main method of ensuring compliance with the standards has always been through the professional bodies' own disciplinary procedures on their members. The ASB, however, set up a Review Panel that has power to prosecute companies under civil law where their financial statements contain a major breach of the standards.

10.4 International accounting standards

The Accounting Standards Board deals with the United Kingdom. Besides this there is an international organisation concerned with accounting standards. The International Accounting Standards Committee (IASC) was established in 1973 and changed its name to the International Accounting Standards Board (IASB) in 2000.

The need for an IASB has been said to be mainly due to:

(*a*) The considerable growth in international investment. This means that it is desirable to have similar methods the world over so that investment decisions are more compatible.

(*b*) The growth in multinational firms. These firms have to produce accounts covering a large number of countries. Standardisation between countries makes the accounting work that much easier, and reduces costs.

(*c*) As quite a few countries now have their own standard-setting bodies, it is desirable that their efforts should be harmonised.

(*d*) The need for accounting standards in countries that cannot afford a standard-setting body of their own.

The work of the IASB is overseen by 19 trustees, six from Europe, six from the USA, and four from Asia/Pacific. The remaining three can be from anywhere so long as geographical balance is retained. The IASB has 12 full-time members and two part-time members. Of the 14, at least five must have been auditors, three financial statement preparers, three users of financial statements and one academic.

The IASB issues International Accounting Standards (IASs). When the IASC was founded, it had no formal authority and the IASs were entirely voluntary and initially intended for use in countries that did not have their own accounting standards or which had considerable logistical difficulty in establishing and maintaining the infrastructure necessary to sustain a national accounting standards board.

Up until 2005, SSAPs and FRSs had and have precedence over IASs in the UK. However, the ASB has been at pains to ensure that most of the provisions of the relevant IASs are incorporated in existing SSAPs or FRSs and each FRS indicates the level of compliance with the relevant IAS.

This has all changed. In 2005, it will be mandatory for all listed companies within the European Union preparing consolidated financial statements (i.e. the financial statements of a group of companies of which they are the overall parent company) to publish them in accordance with IASs.

10.5 GCE A-levels and accounting standards

The examination syllabuses, and the questions set, do not require you to have anything like a full knowledge of all the accounting standards. Nor do they require you to have any knowledge of international accounting standards, but this is something that is likely to change and knowledge of the preceding section should enable you to answer any question referring to the topic, should one appear in your examination paper. Nevertheless, although some of the A-level syllabuses may appear to have very little interest in accounting standards, they are included in the syllabuses and questions about them do appear in the A-level examinations.

In this book we will deal with the accounting standards that appear in at least one A-level syllabus. In fact, so important are accounting standards that, even though it is not specifically mentioned each time, the financial statements shown to you in this book do conform with the accounting standards.

AQA requires you to know about SSAPs 2 and 9 and FRSs 1, 10 and 15. OCR requires that you know about four specific standards, SSAPs 2, 9, 12 (now replaced by FRS 15) and 13, in addition to those specifically mentioned elsewhere in the OCR syllabus. SSAP 2 was replaced by FRS 18 in 2000.

10.6 FRS 18 *Accounting policies* (issued 2000)

Users of financial statements issued by organisations want to analyse and evaluate the figures contained within them. They cannot do this effectively unless they know which accounting policies have been used when preparing such statements. This FRS was issued to help continue the improvement in the quality of financial reporting that had been started in 1971 by the accounting standard it replaced, SSAP 2.

The FRS focuses upon '**accounting policies**' and considers the '**estimation techniques**' used in implementing them. It also looks in details at the various accounting concepts that you will cover later in Chapter 25.

Accounting policies

These are defined in FRS 18 as:

those principles, bases, conventions, rules and practices applied by an entity that specify how the effects of transactions and other events are to be reflected in its financial statements through:

(i) *recognising,*
(ii) *selecting measurement basis for, and*
(iii) *presenting*

assets, liabilities, gains, losses and changes to shareholders' funds.

In other words, accounting policies define the processes whereby transactions and other events are reflected in the financial statements. The accounting policies selected should enable the financial statements to give a true and fair view and should be consistent with accounting standards, UITFs and company legislation.

When an accounting policy is selected, its appropriateness should be considered in the context of four 'objectives':

● *Relevance* –
does it produce information that is useful for assessing stewardship and for making economic decisions?

● *Reliability* –
does it reflect the substance of the transaction and other events that have occurred? Is it free of bias, i.e. neutral? Is it free of material error? If produced under uncertainty, has prudence been exercised?

● *Comparability* –
can it be compared with similar information about the entity for some other period or point in time?

● *Understandability* –
is it capable of being understood by users who have a reasonable knowledge of business and economic activities and accounting?

Estimation techniques

These are the methods adopted in order to arrive at estimated monetary amounts for items that appear in the financial statements.

Examples of accounting policies

● The treatment of gains and losses on disposals of fixed assets – they could be applied to adjust the depreciation charge for the period, or they may appear as separate items in the financial statements.

● The classification of overheads in the financial statements – for example, some indirect costs may be included in the trading account, or they may be included in administration costs in the profit and loss account.

● The treatment of interest costs incurred in connection with the construction of fixed assets – these could be charged to profit and loss as a finance cost, or they could be capitalised and added to the other costs of creating the fixed assets (this is allowed by FRS 15, *Tangible fixed assets*).

10.7 SSAP 9, *Stocks and long-term contracts* (revised 1988)

Stock

This is covered in detail in Chapter 4.

Long-term contract work

It is not proposed to discuss this subject here. It is excluded from A-level syllabuses. However, you will find some discussion of this topic in Chapter 16.

10.8 FRS 15, *Tangible fixed assets* (issued 1999)

This FRS replaced SSAP 12. It applies to all tangible fixed assets, except investment properties, which are dealt with in SSAP 19.

First of all, some definitions:

- **Depreciation:** the measure of the cost or revalued amount of the economic benefits of the tangible fixed asset that have been consumed during the period. Consumption includes the wearing out, using up or other reduction in the useful economic life of a tangible fixed asset whether arising from use, effluxion of time or obsolescence through either technology or demand for the goods and services produced by the asset.
- **Useful economic life:** the period over which the entity expects to derive economic benefit from that asset.
- **Residual value:** the net realisable value of an asset at the end of its economic life. Residual values are based on prices prevailing at the date of the acquisition (or revaluation) of the asset and do not take account of expected future price changes.
- **Recoverable amount:** the higher of net realisable value and the amount recoverable from its further use.

Depreciation should be provided in respect of all tangible fixed assets which have a finite useful economic life. It should be provided by allocating the cost (or revalued amount) less net realisable value over the periods expected to benefit from the use of the asset being depreciated. No depreciation method is prescribed, but the method selected should be that which produces the most appropriate allocation of depreciation to each period in relation to the benefit being received in that period through use of the asset. The depreciation should be calculated on the value as shown on the balance sheet and not on any other figure. It *must* be charged against the profit and loss account, and *not* against reserves.

When the useful economic life of an asset is longer than fifty years, impairment reviews must be perfomed so as to ensure that the carrying amount of the asset is not overstated.

Useful economic lives should be reviewed at the end of every reporting period. If it is revised, the carrying amount at the date of the revision should be depreciated over the revised remaining useful economic life of the asset.

The depreciation method may only be changed when to do so will give a fairer presentation of the results and of the financial position. A change in depreciation method does not constitute a change in accounting policy. When the method is changed, the carrying amount should be depreciated over the remaining useful economic life of the asset, commencing with the period when the change occurred. Where a change of method occurs, the effect, if material, should be shown as a note attached to the financial statements.

Urgent Issues Task Force (UITF) Abstract 5, issued in July 1992, introduced rules relating to situations where current assets are included in the balance sheet at the lower of cost and net realisable value. Specifically, it addressed the question of an appropriate transfer value when a current asset becomes a fixed asset through its being retained for use on a continuing basis. (This could arise, for example, when a motor dealer removes a second-hand car from sale and provides it as a company car to the company secretary.) To avoid entities being able to effect transfers from current assets to fixed assets at above net realisable value and subsequently write down the value through a debit to a revaluation reserve, UITF 5 requires that all such transfers are done at the lower of cost and net realisable value, with any diminution in value at that point being charged in the profit and loss account.

Asset revaluation

Asset revaluation is permitted and, if a policy of revaluation is adopted, the valuations should be kept up to date. If one asset is revalued, all the assets of that class (i.e. those with a similar nature, function or use) must also be revalued.

Revaluation losses caused by use of the asset should be recognised in the profit and loss account. Other revaluation losses should be recognised in the statement of total recognised gains and losses until the carrying amount of the asset is less than the amount the asset would be carried at had depreciated historical cost been adopted rather than asset revaluation.

For example, imagine an asset is revalued from a carrying amount of £20,000 down to £6,000 because the asset had become obsolete. Had it never been revalued, its carrying amount would have been £11,000. The carrying amount of the asset (£6,000) is, therefore, below £11,000 and so the loss on revaluation of £14,000 would be split with £9,000 being recognised in the statement of total recognised gains and losses and £5,000 being recognised in profit and loss.

Revaluation gains should be recognised in the statement of total recognised gains and losses unless they relate to an asset that had previously had revaluation losses charged to the profit and loss acount. Where that is the case, the revaluation gain should also be charged to profit and loss, after adjusting for depreciation since the revaluation loss was recognised.

Depreciation should be charged irrespective of when the asset was revalued. An increased value arising from a revaluation does not mean that depreciation should not be charged. The new value is the one on which future depreciation should be based. Depreciation charged before revaluation should not be credited back to profit and loss.

According to paragraph 21 of FRS 3, *Reporting financial performance*, the profit or loss on the disposal of an asset should be accounted for in the profit and loss account of the period in which the disposal occurs as the difference between the net sale proceeds and the net carrying amount, whether carried at historical cost (less any provisions made) or at a valuation.

Land and buildings

Freehold land

As this normally lasts forever there is no need to depreciate, unless subject to depletion or loss of value for reasons which may be applicable in certain circumstances, such as desirability of location, land erosion, extraction of minerals, dumping of toxic waste, etc. It is rare to encounter circumstances under which freehold land should be subject to depreciation. The problem that most often occurs is the distinction between the cost/value of freehold land and the cost/value of the buildings upon it. FRS 15 states that the distinction should be made as only the buildings have a limited useful economic life and should be depreciated. Land has an unlimited life and should not be depreciated. Failure to separate the two elements of the cost/value will result in non-compliance with the standard.

Buildings

These have finite lives and should be depreciated.

Notes to accounts

The FRS requires that the following should be disclosed:

1 Methods of depreciation used.
2 Useful economic lives or the depreciation rates in use.
3 Total depreciation charged for the period.
4 Where material, the financial effect of a change in either useful economic lives or estimates of residual values.
5 The cost or revalued amount at both the start and end of the accounting period.
6 The cumulative amount of provisions for depreciation or impairment at the beginning and end of the financial period.
7 A reconciliation of the movements, separately dislosing additions, disposals, revaluations, transfers, depreciation, impairment losses and reversals of past impairment losses written back in the period.
8 The net carrying amount at the beginning and end of the financial period.

10.9 FRS 10, *Goodwill and intangible assets (companies)*

This standard was issued in December 1997, replacing SSAP 22. It applies to companies, not to partnerships or sole traders:

1 Purchased goodwill and purchased intangible assets (e.g. patents, trade marks, etc.) should be capitalised as assets.
2 If goodwill has not been purchased then there should not be any entry of it in the company's books. (This is different from the situation applicable to partnerships.)
3 Internally developed intangible assets should be capitalised (i.e. entered in the company's books as an asset) only when they have a readily ascertainable market value.
4 The calculation of goodwill should be the excess of the value of the consideration given (the price paid) over the total of the fair values of the net assets acquired.
5 Goodwill and intangible assets should be amortised (i.e. depreciated) over their useful economic life. However, when goodwill or intangible assets are regarded as having indefinite useful economic lives, they should not be amortised.
5 The useful economic lives of goodwill and intangible assets should be reviewed at the end of each reporting period and revised if necessary.
6 The straight line method of amortisation should be adopted, unless another method can be demonstrated to better reflect the expected pattern of depletion of the goodwill or intangible asset.

10.10 FRS 11, *Impairment of fixed assets and goodwill*

This FRS was issued in July 1998. It applies to all fixed assets and purchased goodwill that is recognised in the balance sheet except:

● fixed assets within the scope of any FRS addressing disclosures of derivatives and other financial instruments. (This is covered by FRS 13, *Derivatives and other financial investments: disclosures*);
● investment properties as defined by SSAP 19, *Accounting for investment properties*;
● an entity's own shares held by an employee share ownership plan (ESOP) and shown as a fixed asset in the balance sheet under UITF 13 (*Accounting for ESOP trusts*); and

- costs capitalised while a field is being appraised under the Oil Industry Accounting Committee's Statement of Recommended Practice (SORP), *Accounting for oil and gas exploration and development activities.*

Investments in subsidiary undertakings, associates and joint ventures *do* fall within the scope of FRS 11. However, smaller entities applying the FRSSE are exempt from the FRS. A brief summary of the FRS is as follows:

1 An impairment review should be carried out if events or changes in circumstances indicate that the carrying amount of a fixed asset or of goodwill may not be recoverable.
2 Impairment is measured by comparing the carrying value of an asset with its recoverable amount (the higher of its net realisable value and its value in use).
3 Impairment losses are recognised in the profit and loss account except that impairment losses on revalued fixed assets are shown in the *Statement of total recognised gains and losses*. Impairments on both unrevalued and revalued assets below the depreciated historical cost are recognised in the profit and loss account.
4 If the recoverable amount of a previously impaired asset or investment increases because of a change in economic conditions or in the expected use of the asset, the resulting reversal of the impairment loss should be recognised in the current period to the extent that it increases the carrying amount up to the amount that it would have been had the original impairment not occurred. The reversal should be recognised in the profit and loss account unless it arises on a previously revalued fixed asset, in which case it should be recognised in the profit and loss account to the extent that the previous impairment loss (adjusted for subsequent depreciation) was recognised in the profit and loss account, any remaining impairment reversal balance being recognised in the *Statement of total recognised gains and losses.*

10.11   SSAP 13, *Accounting for research and development*

SSAP 13 divides research and development expenditure under three headings, except for the location or exploitation of oil, gas or mineral deposits, or where all expenditure will be reimbursed by a third party. The three headings are:

(a) **pure (or basic) research:** experimental or theoretical work undertaken primarily to acquire new scientific or technical knowledge for its own sake rather than directed towards any specific aim or application;
(b) **applied research:** original or critical investigation undertaken in order to gain new scientific or technical knowledge and directed towards a specific practical aim or objective;
(c) **development:** use of scientific or technical knowledge in order to produce new or substantially improved materials, devices, products or services, to install new processes or systems prior to the commencement of commercial production or commercial applications, or to improve substantially those already produced or installed.

Expenditure incurred on pure and applied research can be regarded as part of a continuing operation required to maintain a company's business and its competitive position. In general, one particular period rather than another will not be expected to benefit and therefore it is appropriate that these costs should be written off as they are incurred.

The development of new and improved products is, however, distinguishable from pure and applied research. Expenditure on such development is normally undertaken with a reasonable expectation of specific commercial success and of future benefits arising from the work, either from increased revenue and related profits or from reduced costs. However, development expenditure should be written off in the year of expenditure, except in the following circumstances when it may be deferred to future periods:

1 there is a clearly defined project; and
2 the related expenditure is separately identifiable; and
3 the outcome of such a project has been assessed with reasonable certainty as to:
   (*a*) its technical feasibility; and
   (*b*) its ultimate commercial viability considered in the light of factors such as:
      (*i*)   likely market conditions (including competing products);
      (*ii*) public opinion;
      (*iii*) consumer and environmental legislation;
4 furthermore, a project will be of value only if:
   (*a*) the aggregate of the deferred development cost and any further development costs to be incurred on the same project together with related production, selling and administration costs is reasonably expected to be exceeded by related future revenues; and
   (*b*) adequate resources exist, or are reasonably expected to be available, to enable the project to be completed and to provide any consequential increases in working capital.

The elements of uncertainty inherent in the considerations set out in points 1 to 4 are considerable. There will be a need for different persons having differing levels of judgement to be involved in assessing the technical, commercial and financial viability of the project. Combinations of the possible different assessments which they might validly make can produce widely differing assessments of the existence and amounts of future benefits.

If these uncertainties are viewed in the context of the concept of prudence, the future benefits of most development projects would be too uncertain to justify carrying the expenditure forward. Nevertheless, in certain industries it is considered that there are numbers of major development projects that satisfy the stringent criteria set out above.

The Standard says that if the criteria are satisfied then expenditure may be deferred to the extent that its recovery can reasonably be regarded as assured. It is also required that where this policy is adopted, all projects meeting the criteria should be included.

If development costs are deferred, they should be amortised over the period of sale or use of the product.

At each accounting date the unamortised balance of development expenditure should be examined project by project to ensure that it still fulfils the criteria. Where any doubt exists as to the continuation of those circumstances the balance should be written off.

Fixed assets may be acquired or constructed in order to provide facilities for research and/or development activities. The use of such fixed assets will usually extend over a number of accounting periods and accordingly they should be capitalised and written off over their usual life.

The Standard requires that accounting policy on research and development expenditure should be stated and explained. The total amount of research and development expenditure charged in the profit and loss account should be disclosed, analysed between the current year's expenditure and amounts amortised from deferred expenditure. Movement on deferred expenditure and the amount carried forward at the beginning and end of the period should be disclosed. Deferred development expenditure should be disclosed under intangible fixed assets in the balance sheet.

10.12 Other standards that may be relevant to your syllabus

FRSSE, *Financial Reporting Standard for Smaller Entities*

The FRSSE was first issued in 1997 and has been updated regularly since then. It contains a simplified, but lengthy set of requirements derived from those included in all the other standards and UITFs. It may be applied to all financial statements intended to give a true and fair view of the financial position and profit or loss (or income and expenditure) of all entities that are small companies or groups or entities (other than building societies) that would be classified as such were they incorporated under companies legislation.

Small companies are defined in the FRSSE according to the definition contained in sections 247 and 247A of the Companies Act 1985 (*see* Chapter 6 Section 6.12).

Application of the FRSSE is voluntary – reporting entities may chose, instead, to apply all the other accounting standards and UITFs. Those that do apply it are exempt from complying with the other accounting standards and UITFs.

SSAP 4, *Accounting for government grants* (revised 1990)

Many different types of grant are, or have been, obtainable from government departments. Where these relate to revenue expenditure, e.g. subsidies on wages, they should be credited to revenue in the period when the revenue expenditure is incurred. The principle is that the grants should be recognised in the profit and loss account so as to match with the expenditure to which they are intended to contribute.

Where there are grants relating to capital expenditure, SSAP 4 states that they should be credited to revenue *over the expected useful economic life of the asset*. This may be achieved by treating the amount of the grant as a deferred income, a portion of which is credited to the profit and loss account annually, over the life of the asset, on a basis consistent with depreciation. The amount of the deferred credit should, if material, be shown separately. It should not be shown as part of shareholders' funds.

The same effect as treating the grant as deferred income would be achieved by crediting the grant to the fixed asset account and depreciating only the net balance of the cost of the asset over its lifetime (depreciation is thus reduced by the grant). However, although this method is acceptable in principle, it is considered to be illegal under the Companies Act 1985, which requires the balance sheet value of a fixed asset to be its purchase price or production cost.

SSAP 17, *Accounting for post balance sheet events* (issued 1980)

Quite often there will be events occurring after a balance sheet date which will provide evidence of the value of assets, or of the amounts of liabilities, as at the balance sheet date. Obviously any event up to the balance sheet date will have affected the balance sheet. Once the board of directors has formally approved the financial statements it is very difficult to alter them. However, there is the period between these dates during which events may throw some light upon the valuation of assets or amounts of liabilities. SSAP 17 directs its attention to such events during this period.

SSAP 17 introduced two new terms – 'adjusting events' and 'non-adjusting events'.

Adjusting events

These are events which provide additional evidence relating to conditions existing at the balance sheet date. They require changes in amounts to be included in financial statements. Examples of adjusting events are:

(a) **Fixed assets.** The subsequent determination of the purchase price or of the proceeds of sale of assets purchased or sold before the year end.

(b) **Property.** A valuation which provides evidence of a permanent diminution in value.

(c) **Investments.** The receipt of a copy of the financial statements or other information in respect of an unlisted company which provides evidence of a permanent diminution in the value of a long-term investment.

(d) **Stocks and work in progress**
   (i) The receipt of proceeds of sales after the balance sheet date or other evidence concerning the net realisable value of stocks.
   (ii) The receipt of evidence that the previous estimate of accrued profit on a long-term contract was materially inaccurate.

(e) **Debtors.** The renegotiation of amounts owing by debtors, or the insolvency of a debtor.

(f) **Dividends receivable.** The declaration of dividends by subsidiaries and associated companies relating to periods prior to the balance sheet date of the holding company.

(g) **Taxation.** The receipt of information regarding rates of taxation.

(h) **Claims.** Amounts received or receivable in respect of insurance claims which were in the course of negotiation at the balance sheet date.

(i) **Discoveries.** The discovery of errors or frauds which show that the financial statements were incorrect.

Non-adjusting events

These are events which arise after the balance sheet date and concern conditions which did not exist at that time. Consequently they do not result in changes in amounts in financial statements. They may, however, be of such materiality that their disclosure is required by way of notes to ensure that financial statements are not misleading. Examples of non-adjusting events which may require disclosure are:

(a) **Mergers** and acquisitions.

(b) **Reconstructions** and proposed reconstructions.

(c) **Issues** of shares and debentures.

(d) **Purchases and sales of fixed assets** and investments.

(e) **Loss of fixed assets** or stocks as a result of a catastrophe such as fire or flood.

(f) **Opening new trading activities** or extending existing trading activities.

(g) **Closing a significant part of the trading activities** if this was not anticipated at the year end.

(h) **Decline in the value** of property and investments held as fixed assets, if it can be demonstrated that the decline occurred after the year end.

(i) **Changes in rates of foreign exchange.**

(j) **Government action**, such as nationalisation.

(k) **Strikes** and other labour disputes.

(l) **Augmentation of pension benefits.**

FRS 12, Provisions, contingent liabilities and contingent assets (issued 1998)

This FRS repealed SSAP 18. FRS 12 defines a provision as:

a liability that is of uncertain timing or amount, to be settled by the transfer of economic benefits.

A provision should only be recognised when it is probable that a transfer of economic benefits will have to occur and a reasonable estimate can be made of the amount involved.

It defines a contingent liability as:

either a possible obligation arising from past events whose existence will be confirmed only by the occurrence of one or more uncertain future events not wholly within the entity's control; or a present obligation that arises from past events but is not recognised because it is not probable that a transfer of economic benefits will be required to settle the obligation or because the amount of the obligation cannot be measured with sufficient reliability.

It defines a contingent asset as:

a possible asset arising from past events whose existence will be confirmed only by the occurrence of one or more uncertain events not wholly within the entity's control.

Neither contingent liabilities nor contingent assets should be recognised.

Smaller entities applying the FRSSE (*Financial Reporting Standard for Smaller Entities*) are exempt from FRS 12.

FRS 14, *Earnings per share*

This FRS was issued in October 1998, replacing SSAP 3. The figure for earnings per share is calculated by dividing the net profit or loss attributable to ordinary shareholders by the weighted average number of ordinary shares outstanding during the period.

The FRS prescribes how to adjust the average number of shares when events occur to change the number of ordinary shares, such as bonus issues, share splits and share consolidations. Students taking examinations which cover FRS 14 in detail should read the actual standard. It contains many examples concerning how the adjustment to the denominator should be made.

Earnings per share (EPS) is a widely used stock market measure. The FRS tries to bring about a more consistent method to aid comparability and reduce misunderstandings.

Basically, EPS is the profit per ordinary share calculated as follows:

	£	£
Profit on ordinary activities after taxation		XXXX
Extraordinary activities (less tax)		XXXX
		XXXX
Less Minority interest*	XXXX	
Preference dividends	XXXX	
		(XXXX)
Profit available to equity shareholders		XXXX

$$\text{EPS} = \frac{\text{Profit available to equity shareholders}}{\text{Number of ordinary shares}} = \text{EPS in pence}$$

* This only applies to group accounts, which are outside the scope of your syllabus. Minority interest only exists where the company controls another undertaking, and outsiders own part of that undertaking.

10.13 Further thoughts on concepts and conventions

In recent years there has been a considerable change in the style of examinations in accounting at all levels. At one time nearly every examination question was simply of a computational nature, requiring you to prepare final accounts, draft journal entries, extract a trial balance and so on. Now, *in addition* to all that (which is still important) there are quite a lot of questions asking such things as:

● Why do we do it?
● What does it mean?
● How does it relate to the concepts and conventions?

Such questions depend very much on the interests and ingenuity of examiners. They like to set questions worded to find out those who can understand and interpret financial information, and eliminate those who cannot and simply try to repeat information learned by rote.

The examiners will often draw on knowledge from any part of the syllabus. It is therefore impossible for a student (or an author) to guess exactly how an examiner will select a question and how it will be worded.

An example of this is where the examiner could ask you to show how different concepts contradict one another. Someone who has just read about the concepts, and memorised them, could not answer this unless they had thought further about it. Think about whether or not you could have answered that question before you read further.

One instance is the use of the concept of consistency. Basically it says that one should keep to the same method of entering an item each year. Yet if the net realisable value of stock is less than cost, then the normal method of showing it at cost should be abandoned and the net realisable value used instead. Thus, at the end of one period, stock may be shown at cost and at the end of the next period it will be shown at net realisable value. In this case the concept of prudence has overridden the concept of consistency.

Another instance of this is that of calculating profit based on sales whether they have been paid for or not. If the prudence concept were taken to extremes, then profit would only be calculated on a sale when the sale had been paid for. Instead the realisation concept has overridden the prudence concept.

Learning outcomes

You should now have learnt:

1 About the role of the Accounting Standards Board.

2 The status of the principal documents produced by the Accounting Standards Board.

3 About the role of the International Accounting Standards Board.

4 The status of International Accounting Standards.

5 The rules relating to many of the more fundamental accounting standards, including SSAPs 4, 13 and 17; FRSs 10, 11, 12, 14, 15 (which replaced SSAP 12) and 18 (which replaced SSAP 2); and the FRSSE.

REVIEW QUESTIONS

Advice: You are not supposed to know everything about the Accounting Standards and the Financial Reporting Standards. This chapter has covered the essential ones for your examinations.

Questions are mainly set in such a way as to see whether or not you can observe the standards. For example, a distinction has to be made as to what can be charged in the profit and loss account, or credited to it, when calculating net profit for the period. This brings out the point that some things have to be shown in the profit and loss appropriation account which is drawn up *after* the net profit for the period has been calculated, and under no circumstances can they be shown in the main profit and loss account itself.

If the rules were not adhered to then you could not in any way compare this year's net profit with that of last year or any other previous period. Most shareholders and would-be investors place a very high reliance on the net profit figure; therefore it must contain only those things that can properly be charged or credited.

Examples:

(*i*) A question which suggests that depreciation should be charged to the appropriation account instead of to the main profit and loss account. This would affect net profit calculations and cannot be allowed.

(*ii*) It might be suggested that depreciation should not be charged at all for the year on a fixed asset or group of fixed assets. This normally conflicts with FRS 15 and cannot be allowed.

(*iii*) Another suggestion may be to carry forward the closing stock at a higher figure than the lower of cost or net realisable value. Normally this cannot be allowed. You are not asked to have knowledge of the extreme cases where this could be otherwise.

10.1 Queries plc directors have asked you for your advice on items concerning their published accounts. Give your replies in brief form.

(*a*) Toxic waste has been dumped on some of the freehold land we own. We believe that land should not be depreciated; therefore we cannot charge anything against profits for depreciation.

(*b*) A fire occurred in the warehouse three days after the financial year end and destroyed £100,000 of goods.

(*c*) At the year end a law case concerning one of our products is in court. It looks likely that we will have damages estimated almost certainly at £10 million awarded against us.

(*d*) Another business has been taken over. Assets worth £100 million have been bought for £80 million. We wish to credit £20 million profit to profit and loss.

(*e*) Some stock of rare metals has shown a large appreciation because of world shortages. We would like to show that stock at its market price in the accounts.

(*f*) In the directors' opinion it is pointless showing the figure for earnings per share (EPS) as no shareholder has been known to ask for it.

(*g*) Shareholders prefer the old-type funds flow statement (working capital) rather than the cash flow statement. The directors want to publish the working capital type of statement.

10.2X Ponders Ltd has had a directors' board meeting to which you were invited. During the course of it you were asked the following questions:

(*a*) Some of our stock is valued at a very low figure as it is currently unusable, and is of no value to anyone else. However, we think there is a possibility of a world shortage of this material in ten years' time. Can we therefore show it at a higher value to reflect this?

(*b*) We have depreciated land at the same rate as buildings. Need we have done this?

(*c*) We want to revalue buildings upwards to show the current values. However, we would like to keep depreciation based on the old cost figures, as otherwise our profits will be depressed. Can we do this and keep within the law?

(*d*) We spend 10 per cent of expenditure on research and development. This amounted to £5 million in the last year. £1 million of this was for land and buildings for use and £4 million for pure and applied research. We can never forecast whether our products will be successful, ours is an industry of chance and luck. Do we have to charge all of the £5 million as expenses against profits? What is your advice to the directors?

10.3 Henry Tompkins who has a little accounting knowledge has just completed the draft final accounts of his company for the year ended 31 May 20X2. The profit, before taxation, of £40,000 is in line with forecast, a matter of much satisfaction for Henry Tompkins particularly during a period of recession.

However, in preparing the accounts it appears that Henry Tompkins made the following decisions:

(*i*)   Depreciation on all fixed assets, other than freehold property, has been provided at half the normal annual rate to allow for the reduced level of activity in the business, the relevant charge in the accounts being £4,000.

(*ii*)   No depreciation has been provided on the freehold property since a recent surveyor's report commented favourably on the standard of maintenance and indicated that overall the property had increased in value.

Note: In the previous year depreciation of freehold property amounted to £8,000.

(*iii*) A transfer of £18,000 was made from the share premium account to the profit and loss account. This transfer has resulted in the net profit being increased.

(*iv*) Loan stock interest paid of £15,000 (gross of tax) was included with dividends on the company's ordinary shares as an appropriation of profits. In the opinion of Henry Tompkins, loan stock and ordinary shares are both part of the long-term capital of the company.

Required:

A reasoned comment on the justification for each of Henry Tompkins' decisions.

Note: If any adjustments to the profit, before taxation, of £40,000 are considered necessary, answers should include a detailed statement of the corrected profit, before taxation, for the year ended 31 May 20X2.

(*25 marks*)

(*OCR: from the University of Cambridge Local Examinations Syndicate*)

10.4X The managing director of Ahlan plc was rather concerned that the provisional final accounts for the company's year ended 31 May 20X0 showed only a very small profit of £50,000.

Recently he had read an article on 'Creative Accounting' and as a consequence of the contents of this document he made the following proposals to the company accountant in order to improve the reported profit:

1 Transfer from general reserve a sum of £800,000 and add it to this year's profit. The managing director reasoned that reserves were there to be drawn upon when times were bad.

2 Revalue the company's freehold land and buildings (current valuation £10m; valued on 1 January 20X0) in anticipation of future rising inflation. The managing director anticipated that the land and buildings would be worth £15m in 5 years' time. The increase in the valuation could be credited to the profit and loss account since the anticipation of this profit could help to smooth out the profit trend.

3 A large stock of raw material (cost £250,000) was redundant. The market value was only £20,000. The loss on stock had already been written off the current year's profit. The managing director argued that it would not be inconvenient to carry the stock for a further year and retain its value at cost. This would show a higher profit.

4 Of the overheads entered in the profit and loss account £150,000 had not yet been paid. If they were temporarily removed from the profit and loss account, the net profit would be higher and the managing director was sure that the creditors would not mind waiting two or three months.

Required:

As the company accountant prepare a report to the managing director of Ahlan plc. Your report should carefully consider **each** of the proposals bearing in mind generally accepted accounting concepts and principles.   *(23 marks)*

(AQA (AEB): GCE A-level)

10.5 A trainee accounting clerk was presented with the following information for three different firms.

1

BDK Ltd

Balance Sheet Extract as at 1 January 20X1

	At cost £	Aggregate depreciation £	Net £
Fixed assets	150,000	(51,000)	99,000

Depreciation has been charged on a straight line basis at 10 per cent per annum on cost. The company charges a full year's depreciation on all fixed assets owned at the end of the accounting year.

During the year ended 31 December 20X1 additional fixed assets were bought for £110,000 on 1 May 20X1. There were no other purchases or sales of fixed assets.

After drawing up the final accounts for 20X1 the company accountant decided to change the basis of calculating depreciation on fixed assets to the reducing balance method. The rate is to be 20% per annum.

2 Paula Rowe Ltd, a retailer, reported the following information for the accounting year ended 31 March 20X1:

	£
Gross profit	50,000
Less Expenses	40,000
Net profit	10,000

The company had agreed and paid for an advertising campaign on 1 April 20X0 at a total cost of £15,000. The campaign commenced on that date and is to continue at a uniform rate until 31 March 20X2.

3 Rendell Stott Ltd, a wholesaler, provided the following information for the accounting year ended 30 April 20X2.

	£		£
Gross profit	80,000	Carriage onwards	3,400
Rent and rates	2,000	Other selling expenses	2,500
Heating and lighting	1,050	Depreciation of fixed assets	8,000
Wages and salaries	19,000	Discounts allowed	1,700
Bad debts written off	20,000	Bank interest	2,500
Advertising	1,500	Insurance	1,400
Motor vehicle expenses	4,600	Postage and stationery	900

Note: Over the last five years bad debts written off had averaged £3,000 per annum.

Required:

(a) Explain what is meant by the:
  (i)   going concern concept;
  (ii) consistency concept;
  (iii) accruals concept;
  (iv) materiality concept.

(10 marks)

(b) In each of the following identify which of the above accounting concepts should be applied and why:
  (i)   BDK Ltd's treatment of depreciation.
  (ii) Paula Rowe Ltd's treatment of advertising.
  (iii) Rendell Stott Ltd's treatment of bad debts.

(8 marks)

(c) (i)   Calculate the effect on profit for the year ended 31 December 20X1 caused by a change in depreciation in BDK Ltd.
  (ii) Calculate a revised profit for Paula Rowe Ltd for the year ended 31 March 20X1.
  (iii) Draft an appropriately **summarised** profit and loss account for Rendell Stott Ltd for the year ended 30 April 20X2.

(7 marks)

(AQA (AEB): GCE A-level)

10.6X Patrick and Bernard own, in equal shares, the capital of Pompadour Limited, a private manufacturing company formed just over one year ago. The first draft accounts have been prepared as follows:

Balance Sheet – 30 April 20X1

	£000s	£000s		£000s
Plant, equipment at cost	950		Ordinary share capital –	
Less Depreciation	285	665	£1 shares	500
Stock of finished units		240		
Debtors		230	Trade Creditors	535
Profit and loss account		165	Bank overdraft	265
		1,300		1,300

Profit and loss account – year ended 30 April 20X1

	£000s	£000s
Sales (50,000 units at £20 each)		1,000
Less Direct materials	290	
Direct labour	550	
Cost of 70,000 units	840	
Less Stock of 20,000 units	240	
	600	
Depreciation of plant and equipment	285	
Factory overheads	90	
Administration and selling expenses	140	
Research and development expenses	30	
Advertising	20	1,165
Loss for the year		165

You ascertain that:

1 Research and development expenditure is mainly salaries and the cost of materials used in technical experiments and then thrown away.

2 Advertising (£20,000 above) represents a non-returnable deposit to an advertising agency for a campaign to begin later in 20X1.

3 Depreciation has been provided using the reducing balance method (at a rate of 30 per cent) so as to substantially reduce the book value of plant and equipment. The plant and equipment has an estimated useful life of five years with no scrap value.

4 The company has no stocks of raw materials or work in progress.

Patrick and Bernard are surprised at the poor results shown in the above draft accounts. They tell you that sales in the first year were higher than expected and that production at 70,000 units is in line with productive capacity and expected future demand.

To improve the financial figures they propose that the following policies be adopted:

1 Depreciation is to be provided using the straight-line method.

2 A suitable proportion of depreciation and factory overheads is to be included in valuing the stock of finished goods.

3 Advertising and research and development expenditure is to be carried forward and charged next year when the benefit of the expenditure is expected to be seen.

4 The expected profits from an order for 5,000 units at £25 each received on 2 May 20X1 should be included in the accounts because the hard work to obtain the order was done in April 20X1.

5 Self-created goodwill of £25,000 should be included in the accounts at 30 April 20X1.

6 Cheques totalling £40,000 and received from debtors in May 20X1 and relating to sales made before 30 April 20X1 should be deducted from the bank overdraft and debtors at 30 April 20X1 so as to improve the current ratio.

Required:

(*a*) Calculate the effect of the various suggestions made on the accounts by redrafting the profit and loss account and balance sheet in accordance with the proposals made above.

(15 marks)

(*b*) Discuss the principles involved in each suggestion saying whether or not each should be adopted.

(10 marks)

(*OCR: from the University of Cambridge Local Examinations Syndicate*)

10.7X The practice of accounting is firmly based upon the application of the following concepts:

1 going concern
2 accruals
3 consistency
4 prudence
5 materiality

Required:

State clearly your understanding of **each** of these concepts and illustrate the manner in which **each** concept influences the accounts of a business.

(5 × 6 marks)

(*AQA (AEB): GCE A-level*)

10.8X 'Bad accounting drives out good, and that was what was happening from the mid-1980s on.'

Professor Sir David Tweedie, Chairman of the Accounting Standards Board

With reference to any four areas covered by Statements of Standard Accounting Practice (SSAPs) or Financial Reporting Standards (FRSs), explain why you think that the standards help or hinder 'good accounting'.

(20 marks)

(*London Qualifications Limited (University of London): GCE A-level*)

10.9X The directors of Noggs Limited have valued their stocks at £450,000 at 31 December 20X5. Some of the stock items have been drawn to the attention of the company's auditors:

(*i*) Two categories of stocks, Nimms and Quibs, have been valued at £23,000. The auditors ascertain that the valuation was based on what the directors considered was the lower of cost and net realisable value, calculated as follows:

	Cost of raw materials	Attributable production overheads incurred	Attributable distribution overheads to be incurred	Expected selling price
	£	£	£	£
Nimms	16,000	2,000	2,400	17,000
Quibs	4,000	1,000	2,000	8,000
	20,000	3,000	4,400	25,000
Cost		23,000		
Net Realisable Value				29,400

(*ii*) A raw material, Opprobrium, was bought at several different prices during the year, and the closing stock was valued on a Last In First Out (LIFO) basis. The stock has previously been valued on a First In First Out (FIFO) basis. Stock is valued on a periodic basis. Details of the stock are:

20X5	Received (tonnes)	Cost per tonne £	Issued (tonnes)
Jan	500	35	200
Mar	300	45	500
Jun	600	65	400
Nov	800	90	100

There were no stocks of Opprobrium on 1 January 20X5.

(*a*) Recalculate the value of Noggs Limited's closing stock at 31 December on the basis of generally accepted accounting principles. *(10 marks)*

(*b*) Explain the accounting concept which underlies the requirement to value stock at the lower of cost and net realisable value. *(5 marks)*

(London Qualifications Limited (University of London): GCE A-level)

CHAPTER 11

Limitations of published financial statements

11.1 The historical perspective of financial statements

You should by now be becoming aware of some of the limitations of financial statements. They show, in financial terms, what has happened *in the past*. Accounting standards have made the content of the financial statements more reliable than in the past, but they haven't changed their focus. While this historical information is better than having no information at all, more information is neeeded if you are to sensibly assess the performance or capital structure of an organisation. Nor, as you learnt in Chapter 8, can you sensibly compare two businesses which are completely unlike one another if all you have to rely upon is historical accounting information.

11.2 Lack of disclosure

In addition, there are a great many factors that these historically based accounts do not disclose. The desire to keep to the money measurement concept, and the desire to be objective, both dealt with in supplementary Chapter 25, exclude a great deal of desirable information. Some typical desirable information can be listed but, beware, the list is indicative rather than exhaustive:

(*a*) What are the future plans of the business? Without this, any investment in a business would be based upon guesswork.

(*b*) Has the firm got good quality staff?

(c) Is the business situated in a location desirable for such a business? A shipbuilding business situated a long way up a river which was becoming unnavigable, to use an extreme example, could soon be in trouble.

(d) What is its position as compared with its competitors? A business manufacturing a single product, which has a foreign competitor that has just invented a much improved product which will capture the whole market, is obviously in for a bad time.

(e) Will future government regulations affect it? Suppose that a business which is an importer of goods from Country X, which is outside the EU, finds that the EU is to ban all imports from Country X?

(f) Is its plant and machinery obsolete? If so, does the business have sufficient funds to be able to replace it?

(g) Is the business of a high-risk type or in a relatively stable industry?

(h) Has the business got good customers? A business selling largely to Country Y, which is getting into trouble because of a shortage of foreign exchange, could soon lose most of its trade. Also if one customer was responsible for, say, 60 per cent of sales, then the loss of that one customer would be calamitous.

(i) Has the business got reliable suppliers? A business in wholesaling could, for example, be forced to close down if manufacturers decided to sell direct to the general public.

(j) Problems concerned with the effects of distortion of accounting figures caused by inflation (or deflation).

You can see that the list would have to be an extremely long one if it was intended to cover all possibilities. Yet, to properly assess the position of an organisation, questions of this type must be asked, otherwise all you have to go on is what happened in the past, and the past is not always a good indicator of what will happen in the future.

11.3 Changes to the sources of information

One thing that can be done with the information presented in the financial statements is to at least ensure that it is objective, neutral, valid and reliable. However, that does not remove the fundamental limitation that financial statements report historical information. However, when the financial statements are published, they form part of the Annual Report. Included in that document is a Chairman's Report and the Directors' Report. In both cases, there is an opportunity for some forward-looking information to be included, and doing so is becoming more commonplace. However, the Chairman's Report is not audited and so less reliance can be placed on any information it contains.

Another, this time very recent, development is the impact the *World Wide Web* is having upon financial reporting. Many organisations are using their company website to provide information of a forward-looking type concerning their activities. Again, this information is not generally audited, and is often presented more as a selling promotion on the part of the company than an attempt to provide richer information for stakeholders than is provided through the more traditional means of the annual report.

11.4 One set of financial statements for all purposes

Another limitation of financial statements is that they are incapable of providing all the information any single stakeholder group may be seeking. If it had always been the custom to draft different kinds of financial statements for different purposes, so that one type was given to a banker, another type to someone wishing to buy the business, etc., then accounting would be very different from what it is today. However, this has not occurred and identical copies of the financial statements are given to all the different stakeholders, irrespective of why they wish to look at them.

This means that the banker, the prospective buyer of the business, the owner and the other people all see the same trading and profit and loss account and balance sheet.

This is not an ideal situation as the interests of each party are different and each party seeks different kinds of information from that wanted by the others. For instance, the bank manager would really like to know how much the assets would sell for if the business ceased trading. She could then see what the possibility would be of the bank obtaining repayment of its loan or the overdraft. Other people would also like to see the information in the way that is most useful to them.

Although this is hardly ideal, at least everyone receives the same basic financial information concerning an organisation and, because all financial statements are prepared in the same way, comparison between them is reasonably straightforward. Also, some of the users of these financial statements have other sources of information, financial and otherwise, about a business – the banker, for example, will also have access to the management accounts produced for use by the managers of the business.

Management accounts are far more than simple profit and loss accounts and balance sheets produced for internal purposes. They are considerably more detailed than this, giving details of each activity, rather than to the organisation as a whole.

Most bankers insist upon access to them when large sums of money are involved. The banker will also have information about other businesses in the same industry and about the state of the market in which the business operates, and will thus be able to compare the performance of the business against those of its competitors.

Thus, once again, there are ways of overcoming another of the limitations of financial statements, their lack of suitability to each of the stakeholder groups. However, the stakeholder groups who can benefit from this extra information are those who have the most to lose without it. For most stakeholder groups, including the shareholders, this option is not available.

11.5 Aggregation

Aggregation is a major limitation of financial statements – every figure in the financial statements is a summary of an entire stream of transactions. They contain only partial information. Some are broken down slightly in the notes to the financial statements but, nevertheless, all any reader of the financial statements receives is a view of what has happened after all the pluses and minuses surrounding each figure have been eliminated. This aggregation effect is bad enough with respect to financial statements prepared for internal purposes, but that is nothing compared to the loss of detail in the published version, prepared according to the Companies Act formats.

So, for example, it is unlikely that the amount deducted from trade debtors as bad debts will be visible anywhere in published financial statements, or even in the notes to those statements and, if it is, you can be sure there will be no indication of what proportions of the bad debts were material of themselves. All that the reader of the financial statements will see is the level of trade debt at the start and end of the period. Clearly, this makes it hard to assess the efficiency of the company in managing its debtors with respect to their creditworthiness. (They will, of course, be able to calculate the ratio of debtors to sales and the ratio of days sales in debtors.)

No information will be available concerning maintenance costs of fixed assets, equipment and vehicles, purchase and sales returns. Nor will any detail be available concerning how the figure for advertising and promotion (if shown in a note) was actually distributed across the company's product range.

While information concerning movements, costs, revaluations, depreciation and sales will be available concerning classes of assets, no information will be available concerning individual fixed assets. A figure in the notes showing a gain on sale of buildings of £500,000 may have been due to the sale of one building or due to any number of combination of building sales, such as three buildings being sold at a combined loss of £1 million while a fourth was sold at a profit of £1.5 million. This is the sort of detail those overseeing the stewardship of the company would like to see, as would the investors and lenders.

The notes concerning earnings by employees do not reveal the seniority of the people within the organisation, nor their role. Employees would like to know how much individual senior managers earn as it makes it easier to compare workloads with individuals rather than with 'someone' in the organisation. It could be, for example, that the highest earning employee is a sales manager operating single-handed in a life-threatening part of the world. His salary may be twice that of anyone else and the reasons for it relatively easy to justify, but other employees would simply see that someone was earning a huge salary and, not unnaturally, probably draw the wrong conclusions.

It has been suggested that the way to overcome this limitation is to make the underlying data available to anyone who wishes it. Yet, that has serious competitive advantage implications and is unlikely ever to be a serious possibility. What is possible is that more detail will be provided of items that are easy to break down and which are not commercially sensitive. In many ways, it is that sort of information that is becoming available as companies start increasing the amount of information they post on their websites. However, the regulators are a long way from making any regulatory adjustments that will overcome the aggregation limitation in published financial statements.

11.6   Objectivity vs. subjectivity

Perhaps this section should be entitled 'lack of objectivity'. Most non-accountants assume that the amounts shown in financial statements are based on clearly defined and unambiguous evidence, such as sales receipts, purchase invoices and bank statements.

What they do not realise is that while many of the underlying transaction data are clearly and unambiguously evidenced, by the time some of them reach the financial statements, they have been adjusted to such an extent (for accruals and prepayments, depreciation, loss of stock value, provisions, and revaluations) that it is unlikely that any two accountants working from the same raw transaction data would ever produce an identical set of financial statements.

Financial statements are simply not objective. They are full of subjectivity and anyone using a set of financial statements needs to understand and appreciate the extent to which subjectivity may have influenced the values they present. For this reason, the notes to the financial statements are of crucial importance and no user of financial statements should ever draw any conclusion concerning the results and position they portray without first reading all the notes. For most stakeholder groups, including the shareholders, this option is not available.

11.7 Timing differences

One further limitation of financial statements relates to their ignoring movements in the value of money over time. Inflation is a permanent feature of the modern world. As a result, a fixed asset purchased 20 years ago would have cost considerably less than the same fixed asset purchased today.

Yet, in the balance sheet, fixed assets are shown at cost irrespective of when they were acquired and all the various cost amounts are added together as if they were all purchased at the same time. You may as well take 20 US dollars, 20 UK pounds and 20 Euros, add them all up and announce that you had 60 UK pounds.

Of course, depreciation removes some of the misinformation and revaluation, when undertaken (it is voluntary), can do much to remove it. Nevertheless, the vast majority of balance sheets fail to truly reflect the 'real' cost of the fixed assets they contain. Consequently, anyone using financial statements to ascertain the financial position of an organisation needs to try to find the true nature of the fixed asset values it contains. Once again, there may be some useful information in the notes but, realistically, this is one limitation that is unlikely to be overcome through reliance on the information contained in the published financial statements and their accompanying notes.

Learning outcomes

You should now have learnt:

1 About the implications of the historical nature of published financial statements.

2 About some of the issues that are not addressed as a result of information not being included in published financial statements.

3 That the World Wide Web is improving the range of information relating to company performance available to all stakeholder groups.

4 About the lack of suitability of published financial statements to all user groups.

5 That some stakeholder groups are able to obtain additional information that is unavailable to others.

6 About the issues of aggregation, subjectivity and timing differences, and their implications for the users of financial statements.

Part 3

FURTHER ASPECTS OF ACCOUNTING FOR MANAGEMENT AND DECISION MAKING

12 Absorption costing, marginal costing and decision making

13 Standard costing and variance analysis

14 Capital investment appraisal

15 Other factors affecting decision making – social accounting

CHAPTER 12

Absorption costing, marginal costing and decision making

Learning objectives

After you have studied this chapter, you should be able to:

- explain why different costs are often relevant for decision making rather than those used for the calculation of net profit;
- explain the difference between fixed, variable, semi-variable and step-variable costs;
- explain the difference between absorption and marginal costing;
- discuss various factors underlying the pricing policy adopted by an organisation;
- explain why marginal costing, not absorption costing, should be used when deciding how to utilise spare capacity through additional production;
- explain what is meant by 'full cost pricing';
- explain the importance of contribution to pricing, production and selling decisions;
- explain the relevance of the 'limiting factor' to decision making;
- explain what is meant by activity-based costing (ABC);
- discuss the advantages and limitations of ABC.

12.1 Absorption and marginal costing

We're now going to have a look at the nature of different types of costs, including fixed, variable and semi-variable costs. Costs must be attributed to goods and services in order to arrive at a cost per unit that can then be used in order to set an appropriate selling price for the good or service. There are two main contrasting approaches – absorption (or, full) costing and marginal costing. First, let's look at how indirect manufacturing costs may be allocated to production.

12.2 Allocation of indirect manufacturing costs

The most commonly accepted cost accounting theory used for purposes of the determination of profit is where all the indirect manufacturing costs are allocated to the products manufactured. The indirect manufacturing costs are seen as adding to the value of work in progress and thence to finished goods stock. The production cost of any article is thus comprised of direct materials, direct labour, any direct expenses and a share of factory indirect expense.

After the end of the financial period, it is possible to look back and calculate exactly what the indirect manufacturing costs were. This means that this figure is used when calculating the valuation of the closing stock. Consider a firm which had produced 1,000 units, of which 200 units have not yet been sold, and a total production cost of £100,000. The closing stock valuation becomes:

$$\frac{\text{Unsold units}}{\text{Total units produced}} \times \text{Production cost of goods completed} = \frac{200}{1,000} \times £100,000$$

$$= £20,000 \text{ closing stock valuation}$$

Cost data is, however, used for purposes other than that of valuing stock. The question is, therefore, whether or not this method is suitable for all costing purposes. The method we have just used above, of allocating all indirect manufacturing costs to products, is known as **absorption costing**, sometimes called full costing.

12.3 Absorption costing: effect upon future action

We can now look at a decision we might have to come to about a future action. Exhibit 12.1 shows a firm which has to make a decision about whether or not to take on an extra order.

EXHIBIT 12.1

Donald Ltd's factory has been making 1,000 units annually of a particular product for the past few years. Last year costs were:

	£
Direct labour	2,000
Direct materials	3,000
Indirect manufacturing costs	4,000
Production cost	9,000
Administration and other expenses	1,500
	10,500

The 1,000 units had been sold for £12 each = £12,000.

The production cost per unit can be seen to be $\frac{£9,000}{1,000} = £9$.

The current year is following exactly the same pattern of production and costs. Suddenly, part-way through the year, a foreign buyer says he will take 200 units if the price for him can be cut from £12 each to £8 each. A meeting is held and the managing director says, 'What a pity. This could have been our first export order, something we have been waiting to happen for several years. The selling price overseas has no bearing on our selling price at home. But it costs us £9 a unit in production costs alone. We just cannot afford to lose money so as to export. Our shareholders would not tolerate the profits of the company falling to less than £1,500.'

'I think that you are wrong,' says John the accountant. 'Let's look at this year's results (*a*) if we do not accept the order and (*b*) if the order is accepted.' He then drafts the following:

	(a) Order not taken		(b) Order taken	
	£	£	£	£
Sales 1,000 × £12		12,000		
1,000 × £12 + 200 × £8				13,600
Less Expenses:				
Direct labour	2,000		2,400	
Direct materials	3,000		3,600	
Indirect manufacturing costs	4,000		4,200	
Other expenses	1,500		1,500	
		(10,500)		(11,700)
Net profit		1,500		1,900

'More profit. This means that we take the order,' says the sales director enthusiastically.

'Surely you've got your figures wrong, John' says the managing director. 'Check your arithmetic.'

'There's nothing wrong with my arithmetic,' says John, 'but perhaps it will be a little more enlightening if I draft (*b*), Order taken, more fully.'

	(a) Order not taken		(b) Order taken	
	£	£	£	£
Sales		12,000		13,600
Less Costs which vary with production:				
Direct labour. The workers are on piece work – i.e. they are paid according to how much they produce. In this case, this means 20 per cent more production brings 20 per cent more wages (i.e. £2,000 for 1,000 units, £2,400 for 1,200 units).	2,000		2,400	
Direct materials. 20 per cent greater production gives 20 per cent more materials (£3,000 + £600).	3,000		3,600	
Indirect manufacturing costs. Some would not change at all, e.g. factory rent, factory rates. Some would alter, e.g. cost of electric power because machines are used more. Of the indirect manufacturing costs one-quarter are variable. For this variable part, £1,000 costs for 1,000 units becomes £1,200 costs for 1,200 units.	1,000		1,200	
Marginal cost				
Sales *less* Variable costs		(6,000)		(7,200)
Costs: i.e. costs which will not alter at all if 200 more units are produced:		6,000		6,400
Indirect manufacturing costs: fixed part				
Administration and other expenses	3,000		3,000	
	1,500		1,500	
Net profit		(4,500)		(4,500)
		1,500		1,900

'We can do all this without borrowing any money,' says the managing director, 'so I'll phone now to tell them we will start production immediately. By the way, John, come to my office this afternoon and tell me more about variable and fixed costs.'

12.4   The lesson to be learnt

We must not get lost in the technicalities of accounting. It is easy to think that calculations which look complicated must give the right answer. Logic must be brought to bear on such problems. This last case shows that **different costs will often be needed when making decisions about the future than the costs which were used for calculating profit earned in the past**. £9 per unit had been taken for stock valuation, but this case proves that a firm could still manufacture units and sell at less than £9 each and still increase profits. The reason for this state of affairs is the very essence of the differences between fixed and variable costs which we will now consider.

12.5   Fixed and variable costs

The division of costs into those that are fixed and those that are variable is not an easy matter. Even factory rent is not always a fixed cost, for if production had to be increased to a certain figure the firm might have to rent further premises. Such a change would not usually happen in the short term, it would take a while to rent and set up a new factory or extra premises before production could start. **When fixed costs are mentioned it is normally assumed that this means costs which are fixed in the *short* term.**

In the firm Donald Ltd, Exhibit 12.1 assumed that variable costs were 100 per cent variable, by this meaning that if production rose by 20 per cent then the cost would rise by 20 per cent, if the production rose by 47 per cent then the cost would also rise by 47 per cent. This is not necessarily true. The cost of power may rise by 20 per cent if production rose by 20 per cent, but the cost of repairing and maintaining the machines may rise by only 10 per cent if production rose by 20 per cent. In this case, the machine maintenance would be a semi-variable cost, this being the term for a cost which varies with production but not at a proportionate rate.

12.6   Cost behaviour

Appropriate cost planning and control is dependent on the knowledge of how costs behave under certain conditions. What is important is how costs behave in a particular firm. There is no substitute for experience in this respect.

Raw materials are examples of variable costs which normally vary in strict proportion to the units manufactured. Labour costs, on the other hand, usually move in steps, thus the name 'step-variable' costs. For instance, a job may be done by two people, and then a slight increase in activity means that the two people, cannot manage it so that a third person is added. In fact it may represent only $2\frac{1}{3}$ people's work, but the acquisition of workers come in indivisible chunks. There can still be a further increase in activity without any more workers, but then the time will come when a fourth person is needed.

This is shown on the two graphs in Exhibit 12.2.

EXHIBIT 12.2 Variable cost behaviour

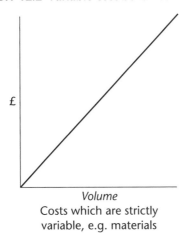

£

Volume
Costs which are strictly
variable, e.g. materials

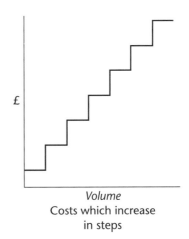

£

Volume
Costs which increase
in steps

12.7 Marginal costing and absorption costing contrasted

Where costing is used which takes account of the variable cost of products rather than the full production cost, then this is said to be **marginal costing**. We have seen that a marginal costing approach to the decision as to whether or not to accept the foreign order by Donald Ltd gave us the answer which increased the firm's profitability, whereas to use absorption costing of £9 a unit in a blind fashion would have meant our rejecting the order and therefore passing up the chance to increase profits and break into the foreign market. Let us look at the resulting stock valuation and gross profit amounts if we used either marginal costing or absorption costing in the calculation of profits for a whole firm, i.e. income determination.

EXHIBIT 12.3

The financial statements of a firm, Burke Ltd, are now shown drafted as if (A) marginal costing had been used, and (B) absorption costing had been used. The following information is available:

1 All fixed manufacturing costs amounted to £4,000 per annum.
2 Variable overheads amounted to £2 per unit.
3 Direct labour and direct materials total £3 per unit.
4 Sales remain constant at 1,000 units per annum at £12 per unit.
5 Production in year 1 is 1,200 units, year 2 is 1,500 units and year 3 is 900 units.

Year 1	(A) Marginal costing		(B) Absorption costing	
	£	£	£	£
Sales		12,000		12,000
Less Variable costs:				
Direct labour and material, 1,200 × £3	3,600		3,600	
Variable overheads, 1,200 × £2	2,400		2,400	
Total variable cost	6,000		6,000	
Less in (A) Valuation of closing stock				
$\dfrac{200}{1,200} \times £6,000$	(1,000)^Note			
Marginal cost of goods sold	5,000			
Fixed manufacturing cost	4,000		4,000	
		(9,000)		
Total production costs			10,000	
Less in (B) Valuation of closing stock				
$\dfrac{200}{1,200} \times £10,000$			(1,666)^Note	
				(8,334)
Gross profit		3,000		3,666

Year 2	(A) Marginal costing		(B) Absorption costing	
	£	£	£	£
Sales		12,000		12,000
Less Variable costs:				
Direct labour and material, 1,500 × £3	4,500		4,500	
Variable overheads, 1,500 × £2	3,000		3,000	
Total variable cost	7,500		7,500	
Add in (A) Opening stock b/d	1,000			
	8,500			
Less in (A) Closing stock				
$\dfrac{700}{1,500} \times £7,500$	(3,500)^Note			
Marginal cost of goods sold	5,000			
Fixed manufacturing cost	4,000		4,000	
		(9,000)		
Total production costs			11,500	
Add opening stock in (B) b/d			1,666	
			13,166	
Less Closing stock in (B)				
$\dfrac{700}{1,500} \times £11,500$			(5,366)^Note	
				(7,800)
Gross profit		3,000		4,200

	(A) *Marginal costing*		(B) *Absorption costing*	
Year 3	£	£	£	£
Sales		12,000		12,000
Less Variable costs:				
Direct labour and material, 900 × £3	2,700		2,700	
Variable overheads, 900 × £2	1,800		1,800	
Total variable cost	4,500		4,500	
Add in (A) Opening stock b/d	3,500			
	8,000			
Less in (A) Closing stock $\frac{600}{900}$ × £4,500	(3,000)^Note			
Marginal cost of goods sold	5,000			
Fixed manufacturing costs	4,000		4,000	
		(9,000)		
			8,500	
Add in (B) Opening stock b/d			5,366	
			13,866	
Less in (B) Closing stock $\frac{600}{900}$ × £8,500			5,666^Note	
				(8,200)
Gross profit		3,000		3,800

Note: The closing stock each year for (A) is made up of:

$$\frac{\text{Unsold units}}{\text{No. of units produced in year}} \times \text{Total } \textit{variable} \text{ cost of that year}$$

Units produced year 1   1,200 – 1,000 = Closing stock 200 units

Units produced year 2   1,500 + 200 opening stock – sales 1,000 = Closing stock 700 units

Units produced year 3   900 + 700 opening stock – sales 1,000 = Closing stock 600 units

So in year 1 unsold units are 200 units; units produced 1,200; total variable cost is £6,000, therefore stock valuation is:

$$\frac{200}{1,200} \times £6,000 = £1,000$$

The closing stock each year for (B) is made up of:

$$\frac{\text{Unsold units}}{\text{No. of units produced in year}} \times \text{Total } \textit{production} \text{ cost of that year.}$$

So in year 1 stock valuation becomes $\frac{200}{1,200} \times £10,000 = £1,666$.

Exhibit 12.4 shows in diagrammatic form the reported profits shown in Exhibit 12.3.

EXHIBIT 12.4 Gross profit calculated using marginal costs and absorption costs

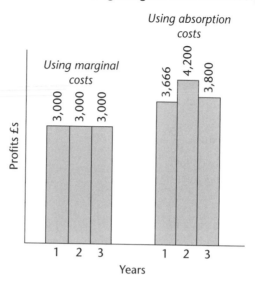

12.8 Comparison of reported profits – constant sales and uneven production

Exhibits 12.3 and 12.4 have illustrated that Burke Ltd, a firm which has had the same amount of sales each year at the same prices, and the same variable costs per unit, shows quite different gross profit figures using a marginal costing approach compared with absorption costing. As these were the gross profits that were calculated let us assume that the selling, distribution, administration and finance expenses were £1,000 for each of these years. The net profits would therefore be as follows:

	(A) *Marginal costing*	(B) *Absorption costing*
	£	£
Year 1	2,000	2,666
Year 2	2,000	3,200
Year 3	2,000	2,800

Because of the absorption costing approach, Year 2 shows the biggest net profit. As sales, etc. are the same, only production levels being different, this means that the year which has the greatest closing stock has shown the greatest profit. Because of greater production, the amount of fixed factory overhead per unit is less:

$$\frac{£4,000}{1,200} = £3.33 \text{ per unit, year 2 } \frac{£4,000}{1,500} = £2.67 \text{ per unit, year 3 } \frac{£4,000}{900} = £4.44 \text{ per unit}$$

Calculating the value of closing stock to include the fixed factory overhead means that less gets charged per unit for fixed factory overhead when production is greatest, and thus a greater gross profit is shown.

Of course the situation gets more complicated because the closing stock of one year is the opening stock of the next year and, under absorption costing, the values of units of stock will vary. Look at Year 3: the opening stock of 700 units is shown as £5,366 = £7.67; the closing stock of 600 units is shown as £5,666 = £9.44 per unit. Yet these are exactly the same kinds of things, and because we have made costs the same each year we have been ignoring inflation. To show a higher profit in a year when the closing stock is higher than usual may often give a false sense of security. The stock may be rising because we cannot sell the goods, we are really getting into trouble, yet the accounts sublimely show a higher profit!

Many experts have argued for or against the marginal and the absorption approach in the context of profit calculation. The marginal approach assumes that fixed factory overhead is a function of time and should not be carried forward to the next period by including it in stock valuations. The absorption approach assumes that such overhead is concerned with production and, therefore, that the goods produced in that year but not yet sold should include it in the calculation of their value carried forward to the next period.

Do such costs 'attach' to the product or to time? They attach to time. It does seem that the marginal approach is more appropriate for closing stock valuation.

Of course, **during the life of a business, the recorded profits of a firm will be the same in total whichever method is in use**. If A Ltd exists for 20 years before it closes down, the profits as calculated for each year using the different methods will result in different recorded profits year by year (except by coincidence). The total profit during the complete life of the business of (say) £20 million will be the same. However, the intermediate reporting of profits may induce decisions which may change the pattern of activities and, therefore, affect the future profitability of the business. Use of an inappropriate basis for calculating profits could lead to inappropriate decisions being made.

12.9 Pricing policy

One thing is clear – **in the long term the revenues of a firm must exceed its costs or else the firm will go out of business**. If it was a company, it would have to be liquidated. If it was a firm run by a sole trader, he might conceivably become bankrupt. On the other hand, firms may find that, in the short term, costs sometimes exceed revenues. In other words, the firm makes a net loss. Many firms do make losses from time to time without being forced out of business.

This being so, the way in which the prices of the goods sold by the firm are determined is of paramount importance. You may well expect that there are some definite rules which will be observed by a firm when it fixes its prices, and that these rules are followed by all businesses. Your expectations would, however, be quite wrong.

With pricing, each firm has certain features which may not apply to other firms, and this will affect its pricing policy. For instance, taking a simple illustration, let us look at the price of sugar sold by three different businesses dealing in groceries. The first business (A) is a grocer's shop in a village, it is the only grocer's shop, and the next shop at which the villagers can buy sugar is thirty miles away. The second shop (B) is also a grocer's shop in a town where there are plenty of other shops selling sugar. The last business (C) is a very large supermarket in a city, in a street where there are other large supermarkets. For a bag of sugar you might have to pay, at (A) 90p, (B) 80p, (C) 60p. The sugar may well be of exactly the same quality and be manufactured by the same company. Firm (A) buys in small quantities; consequently it pays a higher price than (B) or

(C) for its sugar, but it knows that none of its customers want to go thirty miles for sugar. The owner does not want to lose self-respect by overcharging anyway, so he settles for 90p. He always reflects that if he charged more, his customers might well buy sugar in large quantities when they went to the market town to shop. Firm (B) makes hardly any profit at all out of its sugar sales; it fears that if its regular customers were to go elsewhere for their sugar they might well decide to buy other things as well, so that (B) would lose not only its sugar sales but also a great many of its other sales. Supermarket (C) sells sugar at a loss – it does this quite deliberately to tempt in customers who come to buy cheap sugar, and then buy other items on which the supermarket makes reasonable profits.

If there can be such differences in the selling price of a bag of sugar when sold by three firms, none of which had, in fact, produced the sugar, then how much more complex is the position where firms manufacture goods and then have to fix prices. This is where a study of economics helps to get this in better perspective. Along with other economic factors, the elasticity of demand must be considered as well as whether or not the firm has a monopoly. Economics will give you a framework for your thinking but it is not the purpose of this book to be an economics text. Still, you can see that the thinking behind pricing relies on economic analysis. We will content ourselves with accepting that this is so, and will merely look at how accounting portrays it.

12.10 Full cost pricing

Although there may be no clearly defined rules on pricing, it can at least be said that views of pricing can be traced to one of two attitudes. These are:

1 Ascertain the cost of the product and then add something to that for profit, the sum being the selling price. This is usually known as **full cost pricing**.
2 Ascertain the price at which similar products are selling, and then attempt to keep costs below that level so as to make a profit.

Many of the problems connected with full cost pricing are those concerned with absorption costing and marginal costing. In absorption costing, the whole of the fixed costs are allocated to products whereas, in marginal costing, the 'contribution' identified was what fixed costs would have to come out of, leaving the profit as the difference.

Nevertheless, a considerable number of firms use the full cost basis, very probably because it is easy to apply. This is of itself not meant as a criticism – after all, the accounting that is used should be the simplest method of achieving the desired ends. There is certainly no virtue at all in using complicated methods when simple ones would suffice.

Complicated methods mean that the accounting system costs more to operate and, if the benefits are no greater than those derived from the simple system, the accounting system should be scrapped and replaced by the simple system. Using methods just because they are simple can, however, be harmful if they give the wrong data.

The information shown in Exhibit 12.5 has been drawn up on a full cost basis, using the following philosophy. The simple system of full cost pricing is to find the cost of direct materials and direct labour and then add relevant amounts to represent overheads and profit. The selling price is calculated in a manner similar to the following:

	£
Cost of direct materials and direct labour	10
Add Variable manufacturing overhead	5
Add Share of fixed manufacturing overhead	1
Absorption cost	16
Add Percentage (say 50 per cent in this case) for selling, administration and finance costs	8
Full cost	24
Add Percentage for profit (in this case, say, 25 per cent)	6
Selling price	30

The 50 per cent for selling, administration and finance costs is probably based on the figures for the previous year, when, as a total for the year, they would have approximated to 50 per cent of the total of direct materials + direct labour + variable manufacturing overhead + fixed manufacturing overhead (i.e. in this case they would have amounted to £16 for one unit). Therefore, taking 50 per cent of that figure (£8) as an addition is really saying that the basic situation is similar to the previous year.

Remember that this was an example. Full cost pricing is not always done in exactly the same manner, but the example just shown is a typical one. As you will see, when the selling price is based upon figures produced as a direct consequence of such arbitrary allocation, the result may not be all that the organisation wished.

12.11 Example of full cost pricing

We can now look at Exhibit 12.5. Three firms are making identical products. For the purpose of illustration, we will assume that the variable and fixed costs for each firm are the same. Different accountants use different methods of allocating fixed overhead between products even though, in each case, the allocation may seem to be quite rational. **There is usually no one 'right' way of allocating fixed overhead.** Instead, there are 'possible' ways. In this exhibit, each of the three firms manufactures two products and, because of the different ways in which they have allocated fixed overhead, they have come up with different selling prices for their products.

EXHIBIT 12.5

	Blue Ltd Products		Green Ltd Products		Red Ltd Products	
	A	B	A	B	A	B
	£	£	£	£	£	£
Direct labour and materials	10	12	10	12	10	12
Variable overhead	16	10	16	10	16	10
Marginal cost	26	22	26	22	26	22
Fixed overhead	6	26	22	10	14	18
Full cost	32	48	48	32	40	40
Add Profit: 12.5 per cent of full cost	4	6	6	4	5	5
	36	54	54	36	45	45

In real life, once the selling prices have been calculated the market prices of similar goods are looked at, and the price fixed on the basis of competition, etc. In this case, the price might well be adjusted to £45 for both products A and B. By a coincidence – the allocation of fixed overhead has been done on an arbitrary basis – Red Ltd has managed to get its selling prices calculated to exactly the average market price.

Suppose the firms had really placed their faith in their selling price calculations but now realised they would have to fix selling prices at £45. Blue might think that as the full cost of product B was £48 then it would lose £3 for every unit sold of product B. Green Ltd might, on the other hand, think that as the full cost of product A is £48 it would lose £3 on every unit sold of product A. Blue Ltd might decide to cease production of B, and Green Ltd decide to cease production of A.

If the plans had been for each firm to sell 100 of each of products A and B, then the plans have now altered to: Blue Ltd to produce and sell 100 of A only, Green Ltd to sell 100 of B only and Red Ltd to sell both 100 of A and 100 of B. The summarised profit and loss accounts will now be as shown in Exhibit 12.6.

EXHIBIT 12.6

	Blue Ltd £	Green Ltd £	Red Ltd £
Sales: 100 of A @ £45	4,500		4,500
100 of B @ £45		4,500	4,500
Total Revenue	4,500	4,500	9,000
Less Costs: Direct labour and materials			
Product A 100 × £10	1,000		1,000
Product B 100 × £12		1,200	1,200
Variable overhead:			
Product A 100 × £16	1,600		1,600
Product B 100 × £10		1,000	1,000
Fixed overhead: does not change			
Because of cessation of production in			
Blue Ltd and Green Ltd (see text)	3,200	3,200	3,200
Total costs	(5,800)	(5,400)	(8,000)
Net profit			1,000
Net loss	(1,300)	(900)	

Exhibit 12.6 shows that Blue Ltd and Green Ltd would incur losses if they ceased production of Product B and Product A respectively. Yet, if they had not ceased production they would both have made profits of £1,000 as Red Ltd has done. After all, they are *similar* firms with *exactly* the same costs – the only difference was the way they allocated fixed costs. The fixed costs in each firm totalled £3,200. Blue allocated this between products as A £6; B £26. Green allocated it as A £22; B £2. Red allocated it as A £14; B £18. With 100 units of each product this amounted to an allocation of £3,200 for each firm. **Fixed overhead does not change just because of ceasing production of one type of product.** The factory rent and rates will remain the same, so will the secretaries' salaries and other fixed costs.

12.12 Contribution

The question arises therefore as to which approach, absorption or marginal costing, is relevant in deciding whether to continue the manufacture of a certain product or to cease production. The answer to this is that the *marginal cost* figure is the one that is relevant. If the marginal cost is less than the selling price, then the difference will make a **contribution** towards fixed overheads, thus reducing the burden of the fixed overhead on the other products.

This can be seen in the following example concerning which of the two products we introduced in Section 12.11, A and B, to make when there is some spare production capacity:

	Product A	Product B
	£	£
Selling price	45	45
Marginal cost	(26)	(22)
Contribution towards fixed overhead and profit	19	23

Either product could be usefully considered, both making a positive contribution towards fixed costs. However, all other things being equal, Product B would appear the better option. Thus, if there is spare capacity, and an opportunity arises to use some of it, marginal costing would be used in order to determine whether the projected income exceeds the marginal cost. If it does, it would be appropriate to consider taking on the work. As absorption costing includes an element of fixed cost, it is not appropriate to use it when considering decisions of this type.

This is based on an important rule:

Contribution = Selling Price − Variable Cost

Contribution is also the basis of another important rule for decision making:

$$\textbf{Break-even point} = \frac{\textbf{Fixed costs}}{\textbf{Selling price per unit − Variable costs per unit}}$$

The break-even point is the volume of sales required in order to make neither a profit nor a loss. You'll learn more about these rules when you look at break-even analysis (also called cost volume profit analysis) in supplementary Chapter 22.

12.13 Using marginal costs

Let's test this out using a firm that produces five products and has the following cost and selling information. The firm would sell 100 of each product it manufactured. Total fixed overhead is £4,800 – allocated A £5 (100), B £7 (100), C £11 (100), D £15 (100), E £10 (100), i.e. £4,800 total. Exhibit 12.7 presents this in tabular form:

EXHIBIT 12.7

	Products				
	A	B	C	D	E
Cost: (per unit)	£	£	£	£	£
Direct labour and materials	8	9	16	25	11
Variable overhead	7	8	10	13	14
Marginal cost	15	17	26	38	25
Fixed overhead	5	7	11	15	10
Full cost	20	24	37	53	35
Selling price per unit	30	21	31	80	20

On the full-cost basis only A and D would seem to be profitable. Should production of B, C and E be discontinued? According to what has been said production should cease only when the selling price is less than marginal cost. In Exhibit 12.8 we will see if following our own advice brings about the greatest profit. We will also see at the same time what would have happened if production was not cut at all.

EXHIBIT 12.8

	(1) Following full-cost pricing, cease producing B, C and E		(2) Using marginal costing, cease producing E only		(3) Ignore costing altogether and produce all items	
		£		£		£
Sales: A 100 × £30		3,000		3,000		3,000
B 100 × £21				2,100		2,100
C 100 × £31				3,100		3,100
D 100 × £80		8,000		8,000		8,000
E 100 × £20						2,000
Total revenue		11,000		16,200		18,200
Less Costs:						
Direct labour and materials:						
100 × cost per product	(£33)	3,300	(£58)	5,800	(£69)	6,900
Variable cost: 100 × cost per product	(£20)	2,000	(£38)	3,800	(£52)	5,200
Fixed overhead (does not change)		4,800		4,800		4,800
Total costs		(10,100)		(14,400)		(16,900)
Net profit		900		1,800		1,300

The £s figures in brackets show the cost of each product, e.g. in (1) the Direct labour and materials are A £8 + D £25 = £33.

As you can see, in Exhibit 12.8 it would be just as well if we followed our own advice. This would give a profit of £1,800 compared with £900 using the full-cost method or £1,300 if we disregarded costing altogether. Sometimes the full-cost method will give far better results than ignoring costing altogether, but this case shows that in fact the wrong kind of costing can be even worse than having no costing at all! The marginal costing approach will, however, give the better answer in this sort of situation.

There is, however, a danger in thinking that if the marginal cost of each product is less than the selling price then activities will be profitable. This is certainly not so, and full consideration must be given to the fact that the total contributions from all the products should exceed the fixed costs, otherwise the firm will incur an overall loss. Different volumes of activity will affect this. Let us look at this in Exhibit 12.9 with a two-product firm making products A and B given different volumes of activity. Product A has a marginal cost of £10 and a selling price of £14. Product B has a marginal cost of £6 and a selling price of £8. Fixed costs are £1,400.

EXHIBIT 12.9

				Profit, or loss, at different volumes of activity				
	A	B	A	B	A	B	A	B
Units sold	100	100	200	200	300	300	400	400
	£	£	£	£	£	£	£	£
Contribution (Selling price less Marginal cost) A £4 per unit, B £2 per unit	400	200	800	400	1,200	600	1,600	800
Total contributions		600		1,200		1,800		2,400
Fixed overhead		(1,400)		(1,400)		(1,400)		(1,400)
Net loss		(800)		(200)				
Net profit						400		1,000

Here the selling price always exceeds marginal cost, but if activity is low the firm will incur a loss. This is shown where activity is only 100 or 200 units of each product.

The main lessons to be learnt about selling prices are that:

(a) a product should make a positive contribution (unless there is some overriding matter which makes the product a kind of loss-leader). That is, selling prices should exceed marginal costs; and

(b) the volume of sales should be sufficient so that in the long term (it may be different in the short term) the fixed overheads are more than covered by the total of all the contributions.

12.14 Maximisation of total contribution

It should be stressed that **it is the maximisation of the total contribution from a product that is important**. For this reason, the volumes of activity cannot be disregarded. Suppose a firm could only manufacture two products in future whereas, to date, it had manufactured three. The contribution per unit is A £10, B £8 and C £6. If a decision was made purely on the basis of contribution *per unit*, C would be discontinued. However, if the volumes were A 20, B 15 and C 30, then the total contributions *per product* would be A 20 × £10 = £200; B 15 × £8 = £120; C 30 × £6 = £180. As B has the lowest *total* contribution, it should be B that is discontinued, not C.

Where there is a limit of one of the items used in production of the product, the contribution *per product* for each unit of that limiting factor (or key factor) should be used as the basis for the decision taken.

For example, assume there are 200 spare hours of machine capacity available (this means that machine hours is the limiting factor) and a choice has to be made between increasing current production levels of a range of products. The contribution per machine hour of each product is: A £2; B £3; C £5; D £1. Product C should be produced. It will generate the greatest amount of contribution. If there is any spare capacity remaining after all Product C has been produced (for example, if there is only enough material available to make a few of product C) then Product B should be produced, etc.

Let's look at an example.

EXAMPLE 12.1

A firm produces two products, A and B. The firm can sell as many units of the products as it can make. Neither product is dependent for its market on the other. However, both products require skilled labour in their production and the firm has only 400 skilled labour hours available.

The cost and skilled labour hour details of both products are as follows:

	A	B
Unit selling price	£40	£20
Unit variable cost	(36)	(18)
Contribution per unit	4	2
Skilled labour hours per unit	4	1

At first glance, A appears to be more attractive. It has a contribution per unit of £4 compared to B's £2 per unit. However, A requires 4 hours of the limiting factor (skilled labour hours) compared to B's 1 hour.

The contribution per skilled labour hour for A is, therefore, £1 (i.e. £4 divided by 4 hours) while, for B, it is £2 (i.e. £2 divided by 1 hour).

Thus, B is the better choice. It earns more in terms of total contribution per hour of the limiting factor than A. This can be confirmed as follows:

If all the available units of the limiting factor (i.e. 400 skilled labour hours) are used to produce A, the total contribution earned will be £400. That is, 400 skilled labour hours divided by 4 (the number of hours of skilled labour required to make 1 unit of A) equals 100, which means that 100 units of A will be produced. These can then be sold, generating £4 of contribution per unit, i.e. £400.

On the other hand, if all the available units of the limiting factor are used to produce B, the total contribution earned will be £800. That is, 400 skilled labour hours divided by 1 (the number of hours of skilled labour required to make 1 unit of B) equals 400, which means that 400 units of B will be produced. These can then be sold, generating £2 of contribution per unit, i.e. £800.

Two or more scarce resources

Where a firm has two or more scarce resources (i.e. it has more than one limiting factor), it is likely that different products will be selected for production depending upon which of the scarce resources is viewed as being more important. It may be impossble to form a view on how many of each or any product to produce in this case if the only basis for the decision is the overall contribution by each product per unit of the limiting factor. In order to address situations of this type, another technique, known as linear programming, is used. It is not covered at this point in your accounting studies but is one you will encounter should you take your studies further in future.

12.15   Activity-based costing (ABC)

A single measure of volume is used for each production/service cost centre when traditional overhead absorption is in use. For example:

● machine hours
● direct labour hours
● direct materials cost
● direct labour cost

These bases are often unjustifiable when the nature of the activity at the cost centre and, more particularly, the nature of the item that is absorbing the cost is considered. In reality, the amount of overhead incurred may depend on any of a range of factors. An appropriate basis for cost absorption ought to adopt a basis that as truly as possible reflects the changes in overhead arising from the activities undertaken.

Cost drivers

Cost drivers are activities that generate cost. They are the factors that cause overhead to be incurred. A cost driver may be related to a short-term variable overhead (e.g. machine running costs) – where the cost is driven by production volume and the cost driver will be volume based, e.g. machine hours. Alternatively, it could be related to a long-term variable overhead (e.g. quality inspection costs) – where the cost is driven by the number of occasions the relevant activity occurs and where the cost driver will be transaction based, e.g. the number of quality inspections.

Activity-based costing is the process of using cost drivers as the basis for overhead absorption. Costs are attributed to cost units on the basis of benefit received from indirect activities, e.g. ordering, setting up, assuring quality.

While this sounds more appropriate than absorption costing, the information required to apply ABC is not generally available from the traditional accounting records and organisations that embrace ABC often require to develop a new information system to provide that information.

Cost pools

A cost pool is a collection of individual costs within a single heading, and in traditional overhead absorption, cost pools are production cost centres. Under ABC, a cost pool is created for each activity area. Then, in order to attribute costs held in a cost pool to an item, the cost pool is divided by the appropriate quantity of the related cost driver. This process of cost attribution is very similar to that used in traditional absorption costing – it is the terminology, the manner in which costs are built up and the type of basis used for cost attribution that differ.

ABC vs. absorption costing

It is claimed that traditional overhead absorption underallocates overheads to lower-volume products and overallocates overheads to higher-volume products – that is, it produces potentially misleading information at the two extremes. ABC directs attention to matters of interest that traditional overhead absorption is insufficiently sensitive to identify. It should, therefore, be capable of producing more useful information for decision making than traditional overhead absorption.

Because administration, selling and distribution overheads are excluded from financial accounting inventory and cost of sales calculations, traditional overhead absorption stops at the edge of the factory floor. A full analysis of product profitability requires consideration of these non-production overheads, which is one reason why some organisations have chosen to adopt ABC, which does include these overheads. When companies that use ABC to evaluate stock and cost of sales have to produce their financial statements, it should be straightforward to remove these non-production overheads from the calculated figures.

Limitations of ABC

While it is usually possible to implement an ABC system, in many cases it is not worthwhile:

- The costs of implementing and operating such a system often outweigh the benefits for smaller organisations.
- It can often be the case that the additional precision and accuracy that ABC brings is immaterial in the context of managerial decision making.
- For single product or single service organisations, ABC is of little benefit.
- Because of the need to exclude administration, selling and distribution overheads from stock and cost of sales in financial statements, many organisations that implement ABC operate an absorption costing accounting system in parallel with it. This simply adds to the complexity of the accounting system and is liable to confuse non-accounting-aware managers when they have two different 'cost' figures for the same product or item of stock.

However, where organisations have multiple products or services, ABC can prove to be a worthwhile and cost-effective way of increasing the reliability of managerial decision making.

Learning outcomes

You should now have learnt:

1 Why different costs are often relevant for decision making rather than those used for the calculation of net profit.

2 Different costs will often be needed when making decisions about the future than were used when calculating profit in the past.

3 The difference between fixed, variable, semi-variable and step-variable costs.

4 The difference between absorption and marginal costing.

5 How various factors underlie the pricing policy adopted by an organisation.

6 Why marginal cost, not full (or absorption) cost is the relevant cost when considering a change in what and/or how much is produced.

7 What is meant by 'full cost pricing'.

8 The importance of contribution to pricing, production and selling decisions.

9 The relevance of the 'limiting factor' to decision making.

10 That selling prices should exceed marginal costs. (Almost the only exception to this would be where a product was being promoted as a 'loss leader'.)

11 That, in the long term, the total contributions at given volumes must exceed the fixed costs of the firm.

13 What is meant by activity-based costing (ABC).

14 The advantages and limitations of ABC.

REVIEW QUESTIONS

Advice: The use of marginal costs in taking decisions is one which figures in quite a lot of A-level examinations. The idea of the 'contribution' which a project might make towards covering overheads and potential profits is one which has many applications in accounting.

12.1   Drake Ltd's cost and revenues for the current year are expected to be:

		£
Direct labour		6,000
Direct materials		7,000
Indirect manufacturing costs:		
Variable	4,500	
Fixed	500	
		5,000
Administration expenses		1,200
Selling and distribution expenses		600
Finance expenses		200
		£20,000

It was expected that 2,000 units would be manufactured and sold, the selling price being £11 each.

Suddenly during the year two enquiries were made at the same time which would result in extra production being necessary. They were:

(A) An existing customer said that he would take an extra 100 units, but the price would have to be reduced to £9 per unit on this extra 100 units. The only extra costs that would be involved would be in respect of variable costs.

(B) A new customer would take 150 units annually. This would mean extra variable costs and also an extra machine would have to be bought costing £1,500 which would last for 5 years before being scrapped. It would have no scrap value. Extra running costs of this machine would be £600 per annum. The units are needed for an underdeveloped country and owing to currency difficulties the highest price that could be paid for the units was £10 per unit.

On this information, and assuming that there are no alternatives open to Drake Ltd, should the company accept or reject these orders? **Draft the memo** that you would give to the managing director of Drake Ltd.

12.2X   Hawkins Ltd expects its cost per unit, assuming a production level of 100,000 per annum, to be:

	£
Direct materials	2.8
Direct labour	2.4
Indirect manufacturing costs: Variable	0.8
Fixed	0.4
Selling and distribution expenses	0.2
Administration expenses	0.3
Finance	0.1
	7.0

Selling price is £7.5 per unit.

The following propositions are put to the managing director. Each proposition is to be considered on its own without reference to the other propositions.

(a) If the selling price is reduced to £7.4 per unit, sales could be raised to 120,000 units per annum instead of the current 100,000 units. Apart from direct materials, direct labour and factory variable expenses there would be no change in costs.

(b) If the selling price is put up to £7.7 per unit, sales would be 80,000 per annum instead of 100,000. Apart from variable costs there would also be a saving of £2,000 per annum in finance costs.

(c) To satisfy a special order, which would not be repeated, 5,000 extra units could be sold at £6.3 each. This would have no effect on fixed expenses.

(d) To satisfy a special order, which would not be repeated, 3,000 extra units could be sold for £5.9 each. This would have no effect on fixed expenses.

Draft a memo stating what you would advise the managing director to do giving your reasons and workings.

12.3 Assume that by coincidence two firms have exactly the same costs and revenue, but that Magellan Ltd uses a marginal costing approach to the valuation of stock in trade in its final accounts, while Frobisher Ltd has an absorption cost approach. **Calculate** the gross profits for each company for each of their first three years of operating from the following:

(a) Fixed manufacturing cost is £9,000 per annum.
(b) Direct labour costs over each of the three years – £3 per unit.
(c) Direct material costs over each of the three years – £5 per unit.
(d) Variable overheads which vary in direct ratio to production were £2 per unit.
(e) Sales are: Year 1 900 units: Year 2 1,200 units: Year 3 1,100 units.
   The selling price remained constant at £29 per unit.
(f) Production is at the rate of: Year 1 1,200 units: Year 2 1,300 units: Year 3 1,250 units.

12.4X Your firm has been trading for three years. It has used a marginal costing approach to the valuation of stock in trade in its final accounts. Your directors are interested to know what the recorded profits would have been if the absorption cost approach had been used instead. **Draw up the three years' accounts using both methods.**

(a) Fixed manufacturing cost is £16,000 per annum.
(b) Direct labour costs per unit over each of the three years £4 per unit.
(c) Direct material costs over each of the three years £3 per unit.
(d) Variable overheads which vary in direct ratio to production were £5 per unit.
(e) Sales are: Year 1 9,000 units; Year 2 10,000 units; Year 3 15,000 units. All at £16 per unit.
(f) Production is at the rate of: Year 1 10,000 units; Year 2 12,000 units; Year 3 16,000 units.

12.5 Greatsound Ltd manufactures and sells compact disc players, the cost of which is made up as follows:

	£
Direct material	74.80
Direct labour	18.70
Variable overhead	7.50
Fixed overhead	30.00
Total cost	131.00

The current selling price is £187.

Greatsound Ltd works a day shift only, at present producing 120,000 compact disc players per annum, and has no spare capacity.

Market research has shown that there is a demand for an additional 60,000 compact disc players in the forthcoming year. However, these additional sales would have a selling price of

£150 each. One way of achieving the extra production required is to work a night shift. However, this would increase fixed costs by £2,500,000 and the labour force would have to be paid an extra 20 per cent over the day shift rate.

The company supplying the materials to Greatsound Ltd has indicated that it will offer a special discount of 10 per cent on total purchases if the annual purchases of materials increase by 50 per cent.

The selling price and all other costs will remain the same.

Assuming that the additional purchases will only be made if the night shift runs, **you are required to**:

(a) advise Greatsound Ltd whether it should proceed with the proposal to commence the night shift, based on financial considerations.
(b) calculate the minimum increase in sales and production required to justify the night shift.
(c) give **four** other matters which should be taken into consideration when making a decision of this nature.

(*AQA (NEAB): GCE A-level*)

12.6X (a) What is meant by the terms *contribution* and *marginal cost*?

(b) Barton & Co Ltd make and sell 2,000 units per month of a product 'Barco'. The selling price is £65 per unit, and unit costs are: direct labour £8; direct materials £17; variable overheads £11. Fixed costs per month are £29,400.

The company receives two export orders for completion in September 20X2. Order A requests 600 items at a special total price of £20,000; order B requires 750 items at a total price of £34,000. Order A will require no special treatment, but order B will demand extra processing at a cost of £6 per item. The company has sufficient capacity to undertake *either* A *or* B in addition to its current production, but only by paying its direct labour force an overtime premium of 25 per cent.

Calculate the company's contribution and the profits for the month if:
(*i*) normal production only takes place;
(*ii*) order A is accepted in addition to normal production;
(*iii*) order B is accepted in addition to normal production.

(c) Use your answer to (b) to demonstrate that a company will normally accept an order which produces a *contribution* towards overheads.

(*London Qualifications Limited: GCE A-level*)

12.7 Arncliffe Limited manufactures two types of product marketed under the brand names of 'Crowns' and 'Kings'. All the company's production is sold to a large firm of wholesalers.

Arncliffe is in something of a crisis because the chief accountant has been taken ill just as the company was about to begin negotiating the terms of future contracts with its customer. You have been called in to help and are given the following information relating to each product for the last year. This information has been prepared by a junior assistant.

Report on revenues/costs for the year just ended:

	Crowns	Kings
	£	£
Sales	60,000	25,000
Floor space costs (rent and rates)	10,000	5,000
Raw materials	8,000	2,000
Direct labour	20,000	10,000
Insurances	400	200
Machine running costs	12,000	3,000
Net profit	9,600	4,800

The junior assistant says in his report. 'As you can see, Crowns make twice as much profit as Kings and we should therefore stop manufacturing Kings if we wish to maximise our profits. I have allocated floor space costs and insurances on the basis of the labour costs for each product. All other costs/revenues can be directly related to the individual product.'

Further investigation reveals the following information:

(*i*) The wholesaler bought all the 20,000 Crowns and 10,000 Kings produced last year, selling them to their customers at £4 and £3 each respectively. The wholesaler is experiencing an increasing demand for Crowns and intends to raise his price next year to £4.50 each.

(*ii*) Crowns took 8,000 hours to process on the one machine the company owns, whereas Kings took 2,000 hours. The machine has a maximum capacity of 10,000 hours per year.

(*iii*) Because all production is immediately sold to the wholesaler no stocks are kept.

Required:

(*a*) Prepare the revenue/cost statement for the year just ended on a marginal cost basis, and calculate the rate of contribution to sales for each product.

(*b*) You are told that in the coming year the maximum market demand for the two products will be 40,000 Crowns and 36,000 Kings and that the wholesaler wishes to sell a minimum of 6,000 units of each product. Calculate the best product mix and resulting profit for Arncliffe Limited.

(*c*) Calculate the best product mix and resulting profit for Arncliffe Limited if another machine with identical running costs and capacity can be hired for £20,000 per annum. Floor space and insurance costs would not change and the maximum and minimum conditions set out in (*b*) above continue to apply.

(*d*) What points does Arncliffe Limited need to bear in mind when negotiating next year's contract with the wholesaler?

(*OCR: from the University of Cambridge Local Examinations Syndicate*)

12.8X Reed Ltd manufactures three products A, B and C. Budgeted costs and selling prices for the three months ending 30 September 20X2 are as follows:

	A	B	C
Sales (units per month)	6,000	8,000	5,000
	£	£	£
Selling price per unit	45	44	37
Unit costs			
Direct labour	6	9	6
Direct materials[Note]	20	24	16
Variable overhead	4	3	2
Fixed overhead	5	5	6

Labour costs are £3 per hour, and material costs are £4 per kilo for all products. The total fixed costs are of a general factory nature, and are unavoidable.

The company has been advised by its supplier that due to a material shortage, its material requirement for the month of September will be reduced by 15 per cent. No other changes are anticipated.

Required:

(*a*) A statement to show the maximum net profit for the three months ending 30 September 20X2, taking into account the material shortage for the month of September.

(b) Explain how the fixed cost element is dealt with in marginal costing and in absorption costing. Briefly explain how this affects any closing stock valuation.

(OCR – University of Oxford Delegacy of Local Examinations: GCE A-level)

Authors' note: assume that the materials used in each product are of the same kind.

12.9 Paul Wagtail started a small manufacturing business on 1 May 20X8. He has kept his records on the double entry system, and has drawn up a trial balance at 30 April 20X9 before attempting to prepare his first final accounts.

Extract from the trial balance of Paul Wagtail at 30 April 20X9

	£	£
Purchases of raw materials	125,000	
Sales		464,360
Selling expenses	23,800	
Insurance	4,800	
Factory repairs and maintenance	19,360	
Carriage on raw materials	1,500	
Heating and lighting	3,600	
Direct factory power	12,430	
Distribution expenses	25,400	
Production wages	105,270	
Factory supervisor's wages	29,600	
Administration expenses	46,700	
Plant and machinery at cost	88,000	
Delivery vehicles at cost	88,000	
Raw materials returned to supplier	2,100	

At 30 April 20X9, he has closing stocks of raw materials costing £8,900. He has manufactured 9,500 completed units of his product, and sold 8,900. He has a further 625 units that are 80 per cent complete for raw materials and production labour, and also 80 per cent complete for factory indirect costs.

He has decided to divide his insurance costs and his heating and lighting costs 40 per cent for the factory and 60 per cent for the office/showroom.

He wishes to depreciate his plant and machinery at 20 per cent p.a. on cost, and his delivery vehicles using the reducing balance method at 40 per cent p.a.

He has not yet made up his mind how to value his stocks of work in progress and finished goods. He has heard that he could use either marginal or absorption costing to do this, and has received different advice from a friend running a similar business and from an accountant.

Required:

(a) Prepare Paul Wagtail's manufacturing, trading and profit and loss accounts for the year ended 30 April 20X9 using *both* marginal and absorption costing methods, preferably in columnar format.

(b) Advise Paul Wagtail of the advantages and disadvantages of using each method.

(OCR – University of Oxford Delegacy of Local Examinations: GCE A-level)

12.10X The figures given below are all that could be salvaged from the records after a recent fire in the offices of Firelighters Limited. The company manufactures a single product, has no raw materials or work in progress and values its stocks at marginal cost (i.e. at variable manufacturing cost) using the FIFO basis. It is known that the unit closing stock valuation in 20X0 was the same as in 20X9.

	20X0	20X1
Selling price per unit	£10.00	£10.00
Variable manufacturing cost (per unit produced)	£4.00	£4.00
Variable selling cost (per unit sold)	£1.25	?
Quantity sold (units)	100,000	?
Quantity manufactured (units)	105,000	130,000
Contribution	?	£585,000
Fixed manufacturing costs	£105,000	£117,000
Other fixed costs	£155,000	?
Operating profit before interest charges	?	£292,000
Interest charges	£70,000	?
Opening finished stock (units)	?	?
Closing finished stock (units)	20,000	20,000
Net profit for the year	?	£210,000

Required:

Prepare a revenue statement for management showing contribution, operating profit and net profit for each year in as much detail as the information given above permits.

(OCR: from the University of Cambridge Local Examinations Syndicate)

12.11X Gainford Ltd is a manufacturing company which produces three specialist products – **A**, **B** and **C**. For costing purposes the company's financial year is divided into thirteen periods of four weeks. There is always sufficient raw material in stock to meet any planned level of production but there is a maximum number of labour hours available to the company. The production of each product requires a different physical layout of the factory equipment although the labour tasks are broadly similar. For this reason the company only produces one type of product at any time, and the decision as to which product to manufacture is taken before each four week period commences.

A forty hour working week is in operation and the following factory staff are employed:

Grade 1   28 staff paid at a rate of £8 per hour
Grade 2   12 staff paid at a rate of £6 per hour

In addition, a limited number of qualified part-time staff can be employed when required. Both full-time and part-time staff are paid at the same rate. The next four week period is number 7 and the following maximum part-time hours are available for that period:

Grade 1   2,240 hours
Grade 2   1,104 hours

The production costs and selling costs per unit for each product are:

	A £	B £	C £
Direct raw material	147	87	185
Direct labour: Grade 1	64	56	60
Grade 2	24	27	21
Variable overheads	15	10	15
Fixed overheads	12	12	12
Selling price of each product	400	350	450

There is a strong demand for all three products and every unit produced is sold.

Required:

(*a*) Explain the terms:
  (*i*) 'contribution'
  (*ii*) 'key factor'

(*b*) Calculate the contribution and profit obtained when **each** product is sold.

(*c*) Prepare a statement from the available information, for period number 7 which will assist management to decide which product to produce in order to maximise contribution. This statement should include details of the:
  (*i*) total production labour hours available
  (*ii*) number of hours required to produce one unit of **each** type of product
  (*iii*) maximum production (in units) possible of **each** type of product
  (*iv*) product which will give the greatest contribution in period number 7

(*d*) Outline the main steps in the manufacturing decision-making process which ought to be adopted by a business.

(AQA (AEB): GCE A-level)

12.12X Vale Manufacturing started in business on 1 April 20X3, and incurred the following costs during its first three years.

Year ending 31 March	20X4	20X5	20X6
	£	£	£
Direct materials	60,000	49,900	52,200
Direct labour	48,000	44,000	45,000
Variable overheads	24,000	30,000	40,000
Fixed costs	40,000	40,600	41,300

Sales during the first three years were all at £20 per unit.

	20X4	20X5	20X6
Production each year (units)	16,000	14,000	14,000
Sales each year (units)	14,000	14,000	15,000

Required:

(*a*) Prepare a statement showing the gross profit for each of the three years if the company used:
  (*i*) the marginal costing approach to valuing stock;
  (*ii*) the absorption costing approach to valuing stock.

(*b*) Advise the company of the advantages and disadvantages of using each method.

(OCR – University of Oxford Delegacy of Local Examinations: GCE A-level)

12.13 Glasses Ltd make four different products, Q, R, S and T. They have ascertained the cost of direct materials and direct labour and the variable overhead for each unit of product. An attempt is made to allocate the other costs in a logical manner. When this is done 10 per cent is added for profit. The cost of direct labour and materials per unit is Q £14; R £28; S £60; T £32. Variable overheads per unit are Q £4; R £8; S £13; T £12. Fixed overhead of £1,900 is allocated per unit as Q £2; R £4; S £7; T £6.

You are required to:

(*a*) Calculate the prices at which the units would be sold by Glasses Ltd if the full-cost system of pricing was adhered to.

(*b*) What would you advise the company to do if, because of market competition, prices had to be fixed at Q £33; R £39; S £70; T £49?

(c) Assuming production of 100 units of each item per accounting period, what would be the net profit (i) if your advice given in your answer to (b) was followed, (ii) if the firm continued to produce all of the items?

(d) What would you advise the company to do if, because of market competition, prices had to be fixed at Q £17; R £48; S £140; T £39?

(e) Assuming production of 100 units of each item per accounting period, what would be the net profit (i) if your advice given in your answer to (d) was followed, (ii) if the firm continued to produce all of the items?

12.14X Bottles Ltd makes six different products, F, G, H, I, J and K. An analysis of costs ascertains the following:

Per unit	F	G	H	I	J	K
	£	£	£	£	£	£
Direct labour and direct materials	15	17	38	49	62	114
Variable cost	6	11	10	21	22	23

Fixed costs of £11,400 are allocated per unit as F £4; G £7; H £7; I £10; J £16 and K £13. Using full-cost pricing 20 per cent is to be added per unit for profit.

You are required to:

(a) Calculate the prices that would be charged by Bottles Ltd if the full-cost pricing system was adhered to.

(b) What advice would you give the company if a survey of the market showed that the prices charged could be F £26; G £26; H £66; I £75; J £80; K £220?

(c) Assuming production of 200 units per period of each unit manufactured what would be the profit of the firm, (i) if your advice in (b) was followed, (ii) if the firm continued to produce all of the items?

(d) Suppose that in fact the market survey had revealed instead that the prices charged could be F £30; G £33; H £75; I £66; J £145 and K £130, then what would your advice have been to the company?

(e) Assuming that production of each item manufactured was 200 units per month, then what would have been the profit (i) if your advice in (d) had been followed, (ii) if the company chose to continue manufacturing all items?

12.15 Jason Ltd manufactures a product called Dufton. The normal annual output of this product is 200,000 units.

The following is a cost statement relating to the production of a Dufton:

	£	£
Materials		5.00
Wages		7.00
Factory overheads:		
Fixed	4.50	
Variable	1.00	5.50
Administration overheads:		
Fixed		2.00
Selling overheads:		
Fixed	3.50	
Variable	3.00	6.50
		26.00

The selling price of a Dufton is £36.

During the year the company received enquiries about two possible special orders each involving the production of 2,000 units. One enquiry related to the production of a Super Dufton (Ref. No. 610) and the other to a Premier Dufton (Ref. No. 620). Due to normal production commitments only one of these possible orders could be handled in the factory.

The conditions of order (Ref. No. 610) are that the variable costs will increase by 25 per cent but the selling price cannot exceed £25.00 per unit. The conditions relating to order (Ref. No. 620) are that variable costs will decrease by 25 per cent but the selling price will be £19.00 per unit.

Required:

(*a*) A computation of the break-even point of normal trading in terms of:

    (*i*)   sales revenue;

    (*ii*) units produced;

    (*iii*) percentage of normal capacity (assume all units sold).   *(11 marks)*

(*b*) What profit would be earned in normal trading if:

    (*i*)   the selling price was increased to £40 per unit and output restricted to 160,000 units;

    (*ii*) the selling price was reduced to £28 per unit and output increased to 260,000 units?

    (8 marks)

(*c*) Advise the board as to which of the two special orders should be accepted. Computations must be shown and a reason given for the choice made.   *(6 marks)*

(AQA (AEB): GCE A-level)

12.16X (*a*) What are the differences between marginal cost pricing and full cost pricing?

    (*b*) How far is it true to state that marginal cost pricing is a short-term strategy?

    (*c*) A.S. Teriod Ltd makes five different products – Ceres, Eros, Hermes, Icarus and Vesta. The various costs per unit of the products are respectively: direct labour, £14, £8, £22, £18 and £26; direct materials, £8, £10, £13, £12 and £17; variable overheads, £11, £9, £16, £15 and £19.

The fixed expenses for the month of February 20X1 are estimated at £8,200, and this has been allocated to the units produced as Ceres £17, Eros £13, Hermes £19, Icarus £15 and Vesta £18. The company adds 20 per cent on to the total cost of each product by way of profit.

    (*i*)   Calculate the prices based upon full cost pricing.

    (*ii*) Advise the company on which products to produce, if competition forces the prices to: Ceres £59, Eros £25, Hermes £80, Icarus £44 and Vesta £92.

    (*iii*) Assuming that output for the month amounts to 100 units of each model; that fixed costs remain the same irrespective of output and that unused capacity cannot be used for other products: calculate the profit or loss if the company continued to produce the whole range at the new prices; AND if the company followed your advice in (*ii*) above.

(London Qualifications Limited: GCE A-level)

12.17 UZ Limited, a local bus operator, is considering adjusting its fare structure. Summer fares are to be increased by 10 per cent. This increase is expected to result in a reduction of no more than 5 per cent in the number of passenger-miles. Winter fares are to be reduced by 20 per cent to increase the number of passenger-miles by at least 10 per cent.

The company's management accounts provide the following information:

UZ Limited
Profit Statement

	Tourist season (seven months)	Winter months (five months)	Annual totals
	£	£	£
Fare income	490,000	200,000	690,000
Operating costs			
Variable	210,000	100,000	310,000
Fixed	70,000	50,000	120,000
Administration	70,000	50,000	120,000
Interest charges	35,000	25,000	60,000
	385,000	225,000	610,000
Profit (loss)	105,000	(25,000)	80,000

Required:

(a) A statement showing the revised profit (loss) if the fare structure is adjusted. *(10 marks)*

(b) Comments on whether or not the changes to fares should be implemented. *(2 marks)*

(c) An explanation of why it is worth while for the company to operate buses during the winter months when it is incurring losses. *(6 marks)*

(Welsh Joint Education Committee: GCE A-level)

12.18X Simons Limited is a small manufacturing company currently making three different types of chair. Each chair is made from the same raw materials by the same labour force.

The managing director presents to you the following details of revenue and cost per unit for the year ended 30 April 20X0:

Type of Chair	Standard	De Luxe	Super
Number of chairs made and sold in the past year	5,000	2,000	3,000

	Per unit £	Per unit £	Per unit £
Selling price	100	120	150
Raw material	16	20	26
Operating labour	16	20	28
Manufacturing overheads:			
Variable	4	7	9
Fixed	8	10	14

Manufacturing fixed overheads are apportioned to the three products in proportion to prime costs (i.e. materials and operating labour). Selling costs are fixed at £160,000. All units produced can be sold as soon as they are made and no stocks are kept.

The directors have been considering their plans for the year ending 30 April 20X1.

The directors intend to introduce a new design of chair to be called the 'Executive'. Raw materials will cost £40 per unit. Operating labour costs £4 per hour throughout the factory and it will take 9 hours to manufacture one 'Executive' chair. Because of labour shortages in the region only 59,300 hours of operating labour will be available to the entire company in the coming year. Variable manufacturing overhead will amount to £9 per unit for the 'Executive' chair.

In the coming year the price of the 'Super' chair will be raised to £170. The price of the 'Standard' and 'De Luxe' chairs will not be increased. It is not thought that the unit sales of each of the three existing chair models can be increased. The fixed selling costs of the company will be increased to £175,000 but other costs will not change.

Required:

(a) Prepare a statement to show the contribution made by each product during the year ended 30 April 20X0 and calculate the company's total profit for the year.

(b) Calculate the selling price of the new 'Executive' chair if the company wishes to make a contribution per 'Executive' chair of £165.

(c) The directors decide to go ahead and introduce the 'Executive' chair. Prepare a budget for the year ended 30 April 20X1 to produce the maximum profit on the basis that market research indicates that 2,500 'Executive' chairs can be made and sold.

(*OCR: from the University of Cambridge Local Examinations Syndicate*)

12.19 Jugs Ltd make five different products – A, B, C, D and E. These have been costed per unit as:
Direct materials and direct labour: A £16; B £19; C £38; D £44; E £23.
Variable overhead: A £11; B £17; C £23; D £14; E £9.
Fixed overhead totalling £3,600 per period is allocated per unit, on a basis of a production of 100 units of each item per period, as A £3; B £4; C £9; D £12; E £8.
When the total cost is found, 10 per cent is added for profit.

You are required to:

(a) Ascertain the selling prices of each item if the full cost pricing system is used.

(b) Owing to competition and the general state of the market, if prices had to be fixed at A £32; B £49; C £56; D £66; E £48, what would be your advice to the directors of Jugs Ltd?

(c) Assuming production of 100 units per item what would be the net profit or loss (*i*) if your advice under (*b*) was adhered to by the company, (*ii*) if the company continued to produce all the items?

(d) Suppose instead that the state of the market was different, and that the prices had to be fixed at A £24; B £38; C £68; D £64; E £29; what would be your advice to the directors?

(e) Assuming production of 100 units per item, what would be the net profit or loss (*i*) if your advice under (*d*) was adhered to by the company, (*ii*) if the company continued to produce all the items?

12.20X Crook plc is a company which produces four different plastic moulded products for the building industry. Central to the production process is a high-pressure moulding machine. The machine is highly capital intensive with a limited capacity and therefore the factory's production capacity cannot increase in the short term.

The machine is operated by a team of four and the direct labour costs of the operation are £20 per hour. The machine's hours of operation are limited to 2,500 per year.

Budgeted details for the year ending 31 August 20X7 are:

	Products			
	Tubing	*Piping*	*Guttering*	*Facing panels*
Annual demand (units)	600	600	600	600
Units details:	£	£	£	£
Selling price	125	116	87	180
Variable costs:				
Material	40	40	30	50
Labour	30	30	20	40
Overheads	25	25	22	56

The budgeted fixed overhead for the period is £30,000.

(*a*) Rank the products in the order in which they should be produced so as to maximise the budgeted profit.

(10 marks)

(*b*) Using the ranking that you have calculated in (*a*), prepare the budgeted profit statement for the year ending 31 August 20X7.

(11 marks)

(*c*) Explain any concerns that you may have about Crook plc using the best product mix calculated in (*a*) above.

(4 marks)

(London Qualifications Limited: GCE A-level)

Standard costing and variance analysis

After you have studied this chapter, you should be able to:

● explain the difference between a standard costing system and an 'actual cost' system;

● explain the advantages of adopting a standard costing system;

● distinguish between ideal standards and attainable standards;

● explain the importance of selecting appropriate standards;

● explain the difference between a favourable and an adverse variance;

● calculate materials usage and price variances;

● calculate labour efficiency and wage rate variances;

● explain the similarity between the calculation of the materials usage variance and the labour efficiency variance;

● explain the similarity between the calculation of the materials price variance and the wage rate variance;

● calculate overhead expenditure variances, volume variances, efficiency variances and capacity variances;

● calculate sales price, volume and mix variances;

● describe the similarities between the variable production overhead efficiency.

Part I STANDARD COSTING AND VARIANCE ANALYSIS

13.1 Comparison with actual costs

A cost accounting system can be said to be either an 'actual cost' system or a 'standard cost' system. The difference is not in the systems themselves but rather in the kind of costs that are used. In the 'actual cost' costing systems already shown, we have seen that they have consisted of the actual costs for direct materials and direct labour, and that overhead has been charged by reference to a predetermined overhead rate.

Standard costing uses instead the costs that *should have been incurred*. **So standard costing has costs that should have been incurred, while 'actual cost' systems use costs that have been incurred.**

In an 'actual cost' accounting system, costs are traced through the records as product costs. On the other hand, **standard costing** uses standards of performance and of prices derived from studying operations and of estimating future prices. Each unit being produced can have a standard material cost, a standard direct labour cost and a standard overhead cost. As with any form of management accounting, this does not in fact have to be carried out fully, for instance some companies will use standard labour and standard overhead costs but may use actual material costs. In the rest of this chapter, we will consider firms that use a standard costing system for all items.

As with all management accounting techniques, the benefits flowing from using standard costing should exceed the costs of operating it, so that there should be advantages accruing from having a standard costing system. These are:

1 Usually it is simpler and needs less work than an 'actual cost' system. This is because once the standards have been set they are adhered to, and the standard costs will remain unchanged for fairly long periods. Other systems need constant recalculations of cost. For instance the average cost method of pricing issues of materials needs a recalculation of the price each time there are further receipts, whereas the standard cost of materials will remain at a constant figure. This can bring about a reduction in the costs of clerical work.

2 The unit costs for each identical product will be the same, whereas this may not be the same with 'actual cost' systems. For instance, in an 'actual cost' system two men making identical units may be paid at different wage rates, the materials issued to one man may have come from a slightly later lot of raw materials received which cost more than the previous lot and therefore the issue price may be higher, and so on. In a standard costing system the same amount would be charged for each of these men, until such time as the standards were altered.

3 A standard cost system provides a better means of checking on the efficiency with which production is carried on, in that the differences between the standard costs and the actual costs, i.e. the **variances**, throw up the changes in efficiency.

4 One important advantage may be that standard costing might make faster reporting available. This is certainly most important, as generally the later information is received the less useful it will be. Standard costing has a great deal of predetermined data when compared with an 'actual cost' system. Therefore, entering up job order sheets, job sheets and many other tasks can be speeded up if the actual costs do not have to be waited for.

The costs that will have been flowing through the standard costing system are those of standard costs and, as actual costs will normally be different, then the difference or variance if adverse (i.e. actual costs have exceeded standard costs) will be debited to the profit and loss account. If the variance is a favourable one (i.e. actual costs have been less than standard costs) then this would be credited to the profit and loss account. This must be done, as all the costs used for the calculation of gross profit, etc. have been standard costs, and if the variances were not put in the profit and loss account then the net profit would not be the net profit actually made.

13.2 Setting standards

Standard costing is a classic case of the use of the principle of 'management by exception'. Put roughly, this means that *when things are going according to plan leave them alone, and concentrate instead on the things that are deviating from planned results.*

With standard costing, the actual results that conform to the standards require little attention. Instead, management's interest is centred on the exceptions to standards. The approach whereby this information is given to management is known as 'exception reporting'.

Getting the 'right' standards is, therefore, of prime importance. If the 'wrong' standards are used, not only will a lot of time and money have been wasted, but it may bring worse results than if no standard had been set at all.

Standards may be unsuitable because they were not set properly, or because conditions have changed greatly since they were set.

Standards of one of two types can be used: ideal standards and maintainable standards. These are as follows:

1 **Ideal standards.** These are set at a maximum level of efficiency, and thus represent conditions that really can very rarely be attained. This approach can be seriously objected to, in that if standards are too high, employees who might otherwise be motivated by standards which are possible to achieve may become discouraged.

2 **Attainable standards.** It is simple for someone to say that individuals will be motivated to attain standards that they are capable of, that they will not exert very much effort to exceed standards, and that standards outside their capabilities will not motivate them. From this follows the also easy conclusion that standards should be neither 'too easy' nor 'too difficult' but should be 'just right'. The difficult part of this is in saying what the 'just right' figures are to set as standards. There is no doubt that the work of behavioural scientists in this area has brought about a far greater insight into such problems. In a very large firm such specialists may be members of the team setting the standards.

The standards for materials and for labour can be divided between (*i*) those which are concerned with prices and (*ii*) those which are concerned with quantities. Standard overhead costs are divided between standard variable overhead costs, and standard fixed overhead costs. The standard fixed overhead costs will be used in absorption costing only, as marginal costing does not bring the fixed costs into its figures.

Finally, in order to obtain maximum benefit from the costing and management accounting systems, it is vitally important that appropriate data and management accounting techniques are used and that they are used in an appropriate and effective manner. Failing to do so is directly wasteful of resources and can also be not just counter-productive but harmful for the organisation.

13.3 Variance analysis

Variance analysis is a means of assessing the difference between budgeted and actual amounts. These can be monetary amounts or physical quantities.

Properly used, variance analysis can improve the operating efficiency of a business by, first of all, setting up the predetermined standard cost structures and, then, measuring actual costs against them in order to measure efficiency.

Variance analysis makes use of the principle of management by exception. When things are going according to plan they can be left alone. Management can then concentrate on the things that deviate from the planned results and, as mentioned above, can adopt exception reporting in order to do so.

13.4 Adverse and favourable variances

The difference between standard cost and actual cost has already been stated to be a variance. Remember these are classified as:

Adverse: actual amount greater than standard amount.
Favourable: actual amount less than standard amount.

The words 'favourable' and 'adverse' should not be confused with their meanings in ordinary language; they are technical terms.

A 'favourable' variance can be 'good', 'bad' or neither. Similarly, an 'adverse' variance can be 'good', 'bad' or neither. It all depends on the circumstances that gave rise to the variance and it is the circumstance you describe when you declare, in your analysis of a variance, that it is 'good' or 'bad' or neither.

Whether a variance is 'good' or 'bad' or neither can only be determined after the cause(s) of the variance have been fully investigated and ascertained.

For example, you may discover an adverse material price variance (i.e. you are paying more per unit of material than you anticipated). This could be because the market price of the materials you buy has risen unexpectedly; or it could be because your purchasing officer is not doing his job properly; or it could be because your production manager has asked your purchasing officer to purchase higher quality materials as the savings in lower production losses will more than offset the rise in the price of the materials.

The first is neither 'good' nor 'bad' – there is nothing you could have done about it. However, having discovered that this has occurred, you now may need to change things so as to ensure you are not simply suffering the increased costs without passing them on to your customers.

The second is 'bad' and needs to be addressed, possibly by replacing the purchasing officer.

The third is 'good'.

What often occurs in this third case is that the purchasing officer is criticised by management as a result of management not properly analysing the variances. The result of this happening is that the purchasing officer refuses to co-operate in future with the production manager and so the business loses in the long run. Proper and thorough analysis of variances is essential. **Partial analysis of variances can do more harm than good.**

13.5 Computation of variances

There is a great deal of difference between the *computation* of the variances and their *analysis*. The computation is simply the mathematical calculation of the variance. The analysis of the variance is a matter requiring a fair amount of judgement, which cannot be performed in a mechanical fashion.

In the rest of this chapter, we'll look at some computations of variances. In fact, there are many variances which can be computed, but we will concentrate on a few of the more important ones. In order that sense can be made of the computations and a reasonable job of analysis done, it will be assumed that the standards set were calculated on a rational basis.

Note: In the computations of variances which follow, there are diagrams to illustrate the variances which have been calculated. The lines drawn on the diagrams will be as follows:

Representing standard costs – – – – –
Representing actual costs - - - - - - - - -
Where actual costs and standard costs are the same —–·—–·

The shaded part(s) of each diagram represent the variance.

13.6 Materials variances

(*a*) Materials price variances

(*i*) Favourable variance:

Material J	
Standard price per metre	£4
Standard usage per unit	5 metres
Actual price per metre	£3
Actual usage per unit	5 metres

Usage is the same as standard, therefore the only variance is that of price calculated:

	£
Actual cost per unit 5 × £3	15
Standard cost per unit 5 × £4	20
Variance (favourable)	5

Exhibit 13.1 shows the variance represented by the shaded area. This is £1 by a quantity of 5, therefore the variance is £5. **The variance extends to the price line and not the quantity line. It is, therefore, a price variance.**

EXHIBIT 13.1 Materials price variance – favourable

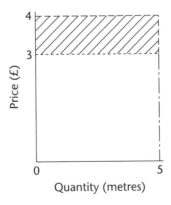

(*ii*) Adverse variance:

Material K

Standard price per metre	£9
Standard usage per unit	8 metres
Actual price per metre	£11
Actual usage per unit	8 metres

EXHIBIT 13.2 Materials price variance – adverse

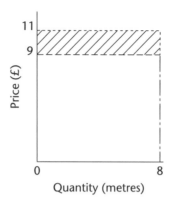

	£
Variance computed:	
Actual cost per unit 8 × £11	88
Standard cost per unit 8 × £9	72
Variance (adverse)	16

The shaded part of Exhibit 13.2 is the variance. This extends £2 times a quantity of 8. Therefore, the variance is £16. Notice that the shaded area is outside the lines marked - - - - - - - - - representing standard costs.

In the diagrams, when the variance is outside the standard cost area as marked by the standard cost lines, it will be an *adverse* variance. When it is inside the standard cost area as marked by the standard cost lines, it will be a *favourable* variance.

(*b*) Materials usage variances

(*i*) Favourable variance:

Material L

Standard price per tonne	£5
Standard usage per unit	100 tonnes
Actual price per tonne	£5
Actual usage per unit	95 tonnes

Cost is the same as standard, therefore the only variance is that of usage calculated:

	£
Actual cost per unit 95 × £5	475
Standard cost per unit 100 × £5	500
Variance (favourable)	25

EXHIBIT 13.3 Materials usage variance – favourable

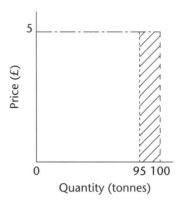

Quantity (tonnes)

(*ii*) Adverse variance:

Material M

Standard price per centimetre	£8
Standard usage per unit	11 cm
Actual price per centimetre	£8
Actual usage per unit	13 cm

EXHIBIT 13.4 Materials usage variance – adverse

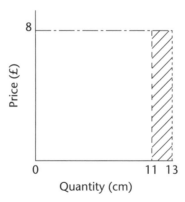

Quantity (cm)

Variance computed:	£
Actual cost per unit $13 \times £8$	104
Standard cost per unit $11 \times £8$	88
Variance (adverse)	16

Here again, the variances for Materials L and M are shown in diagrams by means of shaded areas. **The variances extend to the quantity lines and are, therefore, usage variances.** With Material L, the variance is shown inside the standard cost area, and is, therefore, a favourable variance, whereas Material M shows an adverse variance as it is outside the standard cost area.

(c) Combinations of materials price and usage variances

Most variances are combinations of both material price and usage variances. Sometimes one variance will be favourable whilst the other is adverse, sometimes both will be adverse variances, and at other times both will be favourable variances.

(*i*) Favourable and adverse variances combined:

Material N

Standard price per metre	£6
Standard usage per unit	25 metres
Actual price per metre	£7
Actual usage per metre	24 metres

The net variance is calculated as:

	£
Actual cost per unit 24 × £7	168
Standard cost per unit 25 × £6	150
Variance (adverse)	18

EXHIBIT 13.5 Favourable and adverse variances combined

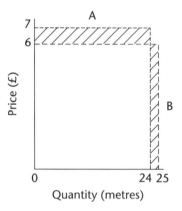

As Exhibit 13.5 shows, this is in fact made up of two variances. The first variance, shown as the shaded portion A, is an adverse price variance (i.e. it is outside the standard cost lines, therefore actual cost has exceeded standard cost). The second variance, shown as the shaded portion B, is a favourable usage variance (i.e. it is inside the standard cost lines, therefore actual usage has been less than standard usage).

The adverse price variance can therefore be seen to be £1 by a quantity of 24 = £24. The favourable usage variance can be seen to be a length of 1 metre by a price of £6 = £6. The net (adverse) variance is therefore made up:

	£
Adverse material price variance	24
Favourable material usage variance	6
Net (adverse) variance	18

(*ii*) Both adverse variances combined:

Material O

Standard price per kilo	£9
Standard usage per unit	13 kilos
Actual price per kilo	£11
Actual usage per unit	15 kilos

The net variance is computed:

	£
Actual cost per unit 15 × £11	165
Standard cost per unit 13 × £9	117
Variance (adverse)	48

EXHIBIT 13.6 Adverse variances combined

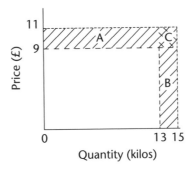

Exhibit 13.6 shows the shaded area A which is definitely a price variance of £2 × 13 = £26 adverse. Shaded area B is definitely a usage variance of 2 × £9 = £18 adverse. This makes up £44 of the variance, but there is the double shaded area, C, of 2 × £2 = £4.

This is really an area which is common to both usage and price. Sometimes, although not very often, this would be treated as a separate variance, but as detail is necessarily limited, in this book we will just add it to the price variance, making it £26 + £4 = £30, the usage variance being left at £18.

(*iii*) Both favourable variances combined:

Material P	
Standard price per tonne	£20
Standard usage per unit	15 tonnes
Actual price per tonne	£19
Actual usage per unit	13 tonnes

The net variance is computed:

	£
Actual cost per unit 13 × £19	247
Standard cost per unit 15 × £20	300
Variance (favourable)	53

EXHIBIT 13.7 Favourable variances combined

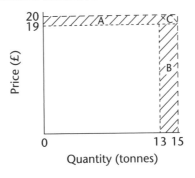

Exhibit 13.7 shows the shaded area A which is definitely a price variance of £1 × 13 = £13 favourable. Shaded area B is a usage variance of 2 × £19 = £38 favourable. The double shaded area C of £1 × 2 = £2, making up the total variance of £53, would normally be added to the usage variance to make it £38 + £2 = £40.

13.7 Materials variances – analysis

(a) Price variances

The price variance is a simple one in that it is obvious that the purchasing department has not been able to buy at the anticipated price. How far this is completely outside the powers of the purchasing department depends entirely on the facts. It may simply be that the rate of inflation is far greater than it had been possible to foresee, or that special forms of extra taxes have been introduced by the government. No one can surely blame the purchasing department for not knowing the secrets of the government's budget each year!

On the other hand, it may have been that poor purchasing control has meant that orders for materials have been placed too late for the firm to manage to get the right price in the market, or that materials which ought to have been bought in bulk have, in fact, been bought in small lots at uneconomic prices. If there are regular suppliers, a short-term gain by buying a cheaper lot from somewhere else could militate against the firm's benefit in the long run if the firm's regular suppliers took umbrage.

Buying the cheapest materials does not always result in the greatest possible profit being attained.

In the end, after all the variance analysis has been undertaken, there must be someone to whom the responsibility for the price variance can be traced and who is then accountable for it. However, care must be taken not to give praise blindly or to criticise unfairly.

(b) Usage variances

There are many reasons for excessive use of material. Inferior materials can bring about a lot of waste, so can workers who are not as skilled as they ought to be. Perhaps the machinery is not suitable for the job, or there might even be deliberate wastage of material, e.g. wood wasted so that it can be taken home by workers as fuel, etc. The theft of material obviously aggravates a usage variance. Here again responsibility must be traced.

When you prepare one of these variance diagrams, there are two simple rules you can use to identify the type (price or usage) and nature (favourable or adverse) of the variance:

Rule 1: if the shaded box is horizontal, it is a price variance; if vertical, it is a usage variance.

Rule 2: if the shaded box lies inside the standard cost line, the variance is favourable; if it lies outside, it is adverse.

13.8 Key questions of variances

Before we look at the computation or analysis of any further variances this is a convenient point to raise some fundamental questions about variances. They are:

1 Why do we wish to calculate this particular variance?
2 When it has been calculated, what action are we going to take about it?
3 If we are not going to make an effective use of the variance, then why bother at all to calculate it?

13.9 Formulas for materials variances

We have deliberately waited until now to give you the formula for calculating each variance. We wanted you to understand what the variances were, rather than simply give you the formula to calculate them. They are as follows:

Materials price variance = (Standard price – Actual price per unit)
× Quantity purchased
= (SP – AP) × QP

Materials usage variance = (Standard quantity required for quantity produced
– Actual quantity used) × Standard price
= (SQ – AQ) × SP

13.10 Inventory records under standard costing

It is worth noting at this point that when a firm adopts a standard costing system it avoids the difficulties involving FIFO, LIFO or average stock methods. In a standard costing system all materials received and issued are valued at the standard cost in the inventory account. There is no recording problem associated with changing prices during the period since they are separately recorded as variances.

Provided that standards are reviewed sufficiently often this system should ensure that the values of inventories are maintained close to their current value.

13.11 Disposition of variances

The question arises as to how the variances are to be brought into the final accounts of the business. There are, in fact, several methods of dealing with them.

They can be treated entirely as costs (if adverse variances) which are period costs and are, therefore, not included in the valuation of closing stocks of finished goods or work in progress. Alternatively they may be brought in as product costs and therefore used in the valuation of closing stocks. Another variation is to treat those variances which are controllable as period costs, but treat the uncontrollable variances as product costs.

All of these methods are acceptable for the financial statements which are used for external reporting.

Before you read further, attempt Review questions 13.3 and 13.4X.

13.12 Costing for labour

Before looking at labour variances, we first need to consider the range of bases upon which labour may be paid. There is no exact definition of 'wages' and 'salaries'. In general, it is accepted that wages are earnings paid on a weekly basis, while salaries are paid monthly.

The methods can vary widely between employers and also as regards different employees in the same organisation. The main methods are:

● Fixed amount salaries or wages – these are an agreed annual amount.
● Piece rate – based on the number of units produced by the employee.
● Commission – a percentage based on the amount of sales made by the employee.
● Basic rate per hour – a fixed rate multiplied by number of hours worked.

Arrangements for rewarding people for working overtime (time exceeding normal hours worked) will vary widely. The rate will usually be in excess of that paid during normal working hours. People being paid salaries will often not be paid for overtime.

In addition, bonuses may be paid on top of the above earnings. Bonus schemes will also vary widely, and may depend on the amount of net profit made by the company, or on the amount of work performed or production achieved, either by the whole company or else by the department in which the employee works.

It is important that the nature of payment to the employees is known before attempting to interpret the results of labour variance calculations. There will be significant differences in the possible explanations when employees are on salaries as opposed to basic rate as opposed to overtime, etc.

13.13 Labour variances

The computation of labour variances is similar to that of materials variances. With labour variances the analysis can be broken down into:

(*a*) Wage rate variances.
(*b*) Labour efficiency variances.

As you read and work through this section, you will notice great similarity between the labour variance formulas and the materials variance formulas. In fact, the only difference is a terminological one. The wage rate formula is identical in method to the materials price formula; and the labour efficiency formula is similarly identical to the materials usage formula. This is something that students frequently fail to grasp. In effect, it means that you need only learn one of the pairs of formulas, along with the terminology for the other pair. You can then complete any variance computation on both pairs of formulas.

Because the computation of labour variances is so similar to that of materials variances only a few examples will be given.

(*a*) Wage rate variance

	Product A
Standard hours to produce	100
Actual hours to produce	100
Standard wage rate per hour	£0.9
Actual wage rate per hour	£1.0

EXHIBIT 13.8 Wage rate variance

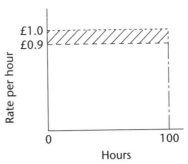

As the actual and standard hours are the same, the only variance will be a wage rate variance, computed as follows:

	£
Actual cost per unit 100 × £1.0	100
Standard cost per unit 100 × £0.9	90
Variance (adverse)	10

Exhibit 13.8 illustrates this in that the variance is represented by the shaded area. This is £0.1 by a quantity of 100, therefore the variance is £10. The variance extends to the wage rate line and it is thus a wage rate variance, and as the shaded area is outside the standard cost lines, indicated by lines marked – – – – – , then it is an adverse variance.

(b) Labour efficiency variance

Product B

Standard hours to produce	400
Actual hours to produce	370
Standard wage rate per hour	£1.0
Actual wage rate per hour	£1.0

EXHIBIT 13.9 Labour efficiency variance

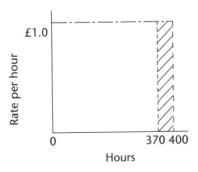

As the actual and standard wage rates are the same, the only variance will be a labour efficiency variance, computed as follows:

		£
Actual cost per unit 370 × £1.0		370
Standard cost per unit 400 × £1.0		400
Variance (favourable)		30

Exhibit 13.9 illustrates this in that the variance is represented by the shaded area. This is a quantity of 30 by a rate of £1.0, therefore the variance is £30. The variance extends to the time line, therefore this is an efficiency variance, as the job has been completed in a different number of hours than standard. As the shaded area is inside the standard cost lines indicated by lines marked – – – – – then it is a favourable variance.

(c) Combined wage rate and efficiency variance

Product C	
Standard hours to produce	500
Actual hours to produce	460
Standard wage rate per hour	£0.9
Actual wage rate per hour	£1.1

EXHIBIT 13.10 Combined wage rate and efficiency variance

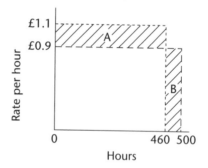

The net variance can be computed as:

		£
Actual cost per unit 460 × £1.1		506
Standard cost per unit 500 × £0.9		450
Variance (adverse)		56

Exhibit 13.10 shows that this is made up of two variances. The first variance, shown as the shaded portion A, is an adverse wage rate variance (it is outside the standard cost lines, therefore it is an adverse variance because actual cost for this has exceeded standard cost). The second variance, shown as the shaded portion B, is a favourable labour efficiency variance (it is inside the standard cost lines, therefore actual hours have been less than standard hours).

The adverse wage rate variance can, therefore, be seen to be £0.2 by a quantity of 460 = £92. The favourable efficiency variance is a quantity of 40 by a price of £0.9 = £36. The net adverse variance is, therefore, made up of:

	£
Adverse wage rate variance	92
Favourable labour efficiency variance	36
	56

13.14 Labour variances – analysis

Labour wage rates will probably be set in conjunction with the trade unions involved, so that this variance may not really be subject to control at any level other than at the bargaining table with the unions involved. Nevertheless such a variance could arise because a higher grade of labour was being used than was necessary, even taking into account trade union needs. It might reflect a job running behind schedule that had to be finished off quickly even though higher grade labour was used. It might have been a rush job that also meant bringing in a higher grade of labour as well. The staffing policy of the firm may have come adrift because the firm had not recruited sufficient numbers of the various grades of labour.

Labour efficiency variances can be caused by a great number of things. Using unsuitable labour, unsuitable machinery, workers trying to slow work up so that more overtime rates of pay are earned, the day after a bank holiday, or the day before it, can affect performance. The morale of workers, the physical state of workers, using poor materials which slows up production, hold-ups because of bottlenecks in production, and so on. The possibilities are almost endless. At the same time, if the variance was worth calculating, some form of action should follow. Otherwise, there is no point at all in calculating such variances.

13.15 Formulas for labour variances

Wage rate variance = (Standard wage rate per hour
– Actual wage rate) × Actual hours worked
= (SR – AR) × AH

Labour efficiency variance = (Standard labour hours for actual production
– Actual labour hours worked) × Standard
wage rate per hour
= (SH – AH) × SR

Don't forget, if you compare these formulas to the materials variance formulas, you will see that they are actually the same, only the terminology is different, i.e. 'wage rate' instead of 'price'; 'efficiency' instead of 'usage'.

Part III OVERHEAD AND SALES VARIANCES

13.16 Management overheads

In your earlier studies of accounting, you may have learnt about the problem of allocating manufacturing overheads to jobs or processes. (If not, you will learn about it when you look at Chapter 18.) In the first instance, the costs are collected in cost centres – normally recognisable departments of the organisation. The total costs of these centres are then applied to products or jobs as they pass through the operations of the cost centre.

Suppose that a firm collects costs into three manufacturing departments, and that the results are as shown in Exhibit 13.11.

EXHIBIT 13.11

Department	A	B	C
	£	£	£
Fixed overhead cost	50,000	40,000	20,000
Variable overhead cost	30,000	35,000	40,000
Total overhead	80,000	75,000	60,000
Direct labour hours	10,000	30,000	15,000
Direct labour cost	£22,000	£59,000	£35,000
Machine hours	20,000	2,000	10,000

A decision has to be taken as to which activity, either labour or machine time, is the dominant factor in the department and will, therefore, provide the most appropriate basis for allocating the overheads.

In the case of Department A, machine hours appear to be the major factor. Overheads will, therefore, be charged on the basis £80,000 ÷ 20,000 hours = £4 per machine hour. The firm will record for each job or process the number of machine hours taken and the overheads will be allocated on this total of hours at £4 per hour.

In Department B, labour appears to be the dominant feature. Overheads will, therefore, be charged on a labour hour rate calculated at £75,000 ÷ 30,000 hours = £2.50 per hour.

Department C does not exhibit any dominant activity and could be expressed in either a machine hour rate or a labour hour rate. Some firms where rates of pay in a department are stable and the mix of labour at different rates of pay stays the same prefer to express the overheads as a percentage of labour cost. In Department C it could be £60,000 ÷ £35,000 = 171 per cent. Thus the labour cost for all work going through Department C would be collected and overheads allocated at 171 per cent of the labour cost figure.

13.17 Predetermined rates

The usual procedure, whether using standard costing or not, is to predetermine the overhead absorption rates using budgeted figures for both the overhead costs and the activity measure, whether machine or labour hours, or cost. This process has a number of advantages. It not only allows appropriate current estimates to be made for things such as price quotations, but also avoids the problem of fluctuating overhead rates at different times of the year due to seasonal variations.

For example, an ice-cream manufacturer is likely to be much more active in the summer months than in the winter. Because activity is low in winter, the rate of absorption is likely to rise steeply in the winter, as costs will not reduce proportionately. It makes more sense to view the overheads in this type of business on an annual cycle and recover the same amount of overhead in both summer and winter.

13.18 Variances in overhead recovery

As in all situations where budgeted figures are used, there are almost certainly going to be variances at the end of a period. Let's take figures from Exhibit 13.11 for Department A as the budget, and compare them with actual performance. This is shown in Exhibit 13.12.

EXHIBIT 13.12

Department A	Budget figures £	Actual figures £
Fixed overhead	50,000	52,000
Variable overhead	30,000	37,000
Total overhead	80,000	89,000
Machine hours	20,000	25,000
Machine hour rate £4		

The actual machine hours worked of 25,000 will have been used to allocate overheads to production at the rate of £4 per hour. As a result, £100,000 will have been allocated. Compared to actual overheads of £89,000 this represents an over-absorption of £11,000. The recovery would only have been exactly equal to actual overhead costs if 22,250 machine hours had been worked – i.e. $22,250 \times £4 = £89,000$.

In a cost accounting system not using standard costing the over- or under-absorption of overheads would be either:

1 transferred wholly to cost of goods sold in the profit and loss account for the period; or
2 allocated between closing inventories and cost of goods sold; or
3 carried forward to the next period.

The first choice would be used if the difference was felt to represent a shortfall in achievement; for example, if the number of hours worked had dropped due to bad management planning. The second would be applied if the differences were felt to be due to poor estimates of the original budgets. **The third would only apply to interim financial statements, not those prepared at a period end, because they are period costs that must be charged to profit and loss during the accounting period.**

Analysing the variances

The £11,000 variance between the amount recovered of £100,000 and the actual overhead cost of £89,000 can be analysed into a number of constituent variances in the normal manner of standard costing. In the above example, the variance can be due to

1 the prices paid for goods and services being different from original estimates or standards – an 'expenditure' variance (sometimes called a 'budget' variance – both terms mean the same thing); or
2 the volume of activity during the period being different from the original estimate – a 'volume' variance (for fixed overheads) or an 'efficiency' variance (for variable overheads).

Expenditure variance

This represents the difference between the actual cost of overhead and the budgeted overhead cost adjusted to the actual level of operational activity. From Exhibit 13.12 the budget figures need to be increased to take account of the fact that activity measured in machine hours has increased from 20,000 to 25,000 hours. This will not, of course, increase the fixed overhead – only the variable overheads which we will assume increase by 25 per cent in line with the hours. (You can see from Exhibit 13.11 that the £4 overhead recovery rate comprised 5/8 i.e. £2.50 for the fixed element and 3/8 i.e. £1.50 for the variable element.) This adjusted budget is shown in Exhibit 13.13.

EXHIBIT 13.13

	A	B	C	B – C
	Original budget	Adjusted budget	Actual	Variance
Fixed overhead	50,000	50,000	52,000	(2,000)
Variable overhead	30,000	37,500	37,000	500
	80,000	87,500	89,000	(1,500)

The actual expenditure exceeds the adjusted budget by £1,500 which represents an adverse fixed overhead expenditure variance of £2,000 and a favourable variable expenditure variance of £500.

Volume variance

Apart from the cost of the overheads, the other factor that was budgeted in developing the predetermined standard was the number of machine hours. In the example, we estimated that 20,000 machine hours would be worked. In fact, 25,000 machine hours were actually worked. This difference would not matter if *all* the overheads were variable, since the rate per hour would be constant at different activities. However, where fixed costs are concerned, increasing the activity will increase the amount recovered above the level required and, if activity is below budget, insufficient fixed overhead will be recovered.

In the example the rate is split:

$$\text{Fixed} \quad \frac{50,000}{20,000} = £2.50$$

$$\text{Variable} \quad \frac{30,000}{20,000} = £1.50$$

$$\underline{4.00}$$

When the machine hours increase from 20,000 to 25,000 we recover $5,000 \times £2.50 = £12,500$ more than required for the fixed overheads.

An alternative way of viewing this is to compare the amount of overheads recovered at 25,000 hours with the flexible budget for this level of activity:

		Total	Fixed	Variable
Recovered 25,000 × £4 =		100,000	62,500	37,500
Budget variable cost 25,000 × £1.50	37,500			(37,500)
Fixed cost	50,000		(50,000)	
		(87,500)		
Volume variance		12,500	12,500	–

This variance shows that by increasing the utilisation of the fixed resources in a business considerable savings are made. The £12,500 is a favourable variance in terms of the original standard.

Summary of variances

The analysis so far shows:

		£	£
Standard overhead recovered at actual level of activity (25,000 × £4)			100,000
Total fixed overhead variance at this level of activity – adverse		2,000	
Total variable overhead variance at this level of activity – favourable		(500)	
			1,500
			101,500
Volume variance – favourable			(12,500)
Actual level of manufacturing overheads			89,000

If this were the limit of the analysis, the variances to be investigated would be the adverse fixed cost variance of £2,000 and the favourable variable cost variance of £500. The remaining £12,500 volume variance is due to the increase in activity and it has been eliminated from further investigation when the budget was adjusted for the change in activity. (This is known as 'flexing' the budget.)

Nevertheless, while it does not require further investigation, it does require to be dealt with. As it stands, £12,500 too much has been recovered. That is, production has been charged with £12,500 too much. If you are not operating a standard costing system, you would need to deal with it using the second of the three approaches described earlier in this section – by allocating it between closing inventories and cost of goods sold.

However, you need to do more than simply find the difference between what it should have cost at the actual level of activity (i.e. the flexed budget) and what it actually cost. You need to look at what was actually produced and use that information to identify precisely what the variances to be investigated are.

13.19 Assessing variances

In an organisation manufacturing products that has adopted a standard costing system, it is common for the cost of the overheads to be related to the product. For example, if a Superwidget is manufactured in Department A and it is estimated that it requires two machine hours per Superwidget, the standard cost of overhead per Superwidget will be $2 \times £4 = £8$.

If in the actual period, a Superwidget takes less than two hours to make there will be a favourable variance which will be costed at £4 per hour. Similarly, if more than two hours are taken, there will be an adverse (i.e. unfavourable) variance costed on the same basis.

Let's use the example from Exhibit 13.11, and assume Department A exclusively manufactures Superwidgets, that the original budget is to make 10,000 Superwidgets and that the actual production of Superwidgets is 12,000. This is shown in Exhibit 13.14.

EXHIBIT 13.14

	Department A	
	Original budget	Actual
	£	£
Total overhead	80,000	89,000
Machine hours	20,000	25,000
Hours per Superwidget	2	
Number of units	10,000	12,000

Note that we are no longer using the machine hours to flex the budget. Instead, we are using the output, the number of Superwidgets produced. Immediately we do this, we identify another variance: to produce 12,000 widgets should take 24,000 hours at the standard rate. Since the actual hours are 25,000 there is an adverse variance of 1,000 hours which costs £4 per hour (note, this is made up of both fixed *and* variable overhead, as it is money wasted through operating at below expected efficiency).

Relating this adverse £4,000 variance to the other overhead variances, we get a standard overhead recovery at the actual level of output of £96,000 (i.e. 12,000 Superwidgets at 2 machine hours each equals 24,000 machine hours at £4 per hour). Actual costs were £89,000. The total variance is, therefore, £7,000. This can be broken down as follows:

	£
Standard cost of overheads for 12,000 actual Superwidgets produced × £8 =	(96,000)
Variable production overhead expenditure variance – favourable (*see* below)	500
Variable production overhead efficiency variance – adverse (*see* below)	(1,500)
Fixed production overhead expenditure variance – adverse (*see* below)	(2,000)
Fixed production overhead volume variance – favourable (*see* below)	10,000
Actual level of manufacturing overhead	(89,000)

13.20 Formulas for overhead variances

The formula for each overhead variance is as follows:

Variable overhead expenditure variance
$$= \text{Actual cost} - (\text{Actual hours worked} \times \text{standard rate})$$
$$= AC - (AH \times SR)$$
$$= £37,000 - (25,000 \times £1.50) = £500 \text{ favourable}$$

Variable overhead efficiency variance
$$= (\text{Actual hours worked} - \text{Actual production in standard hours}) \times \text{standard rate}$$
$$= (AH - APSH) \times SR$$
$$= (25,000 - 24,000) \times £1.50 = £1,500 \text{ adverse}^{Note\ 2}$$

Total variable overhead variance
$$= (APSH \times SR) - AC = (24,000 \times £1.50) - £37,000$$
$$= £1,000 \text{ adverse}$$

Fixed overhead expenditure variance
$$= \text{Budgeted fixed production overheads} - \text{Actual fixed production overheads}$$
$$= BFPO - AFPO$$
$$= £50,000 - £52,000 = £2,000 \text{ adverse}$$

Fixed overhead volume variance[Note 1]
$$= (\text{Actual production in standard hours} \times \text{standard rate}) - \text{Budgeted fixed production overheads}$$
$$= (APSH \times SR) - BFPO$$
$$= (24,000 \times £2.50) - £50,000 = £10,000 \text{ favourable}$$

Total fixed overhead variance
$$= (APSH \times SR) - AFPO = £8,000 \text{ favourable}$$

The fixed overhead volume variance can be further divided into:

Fixed overhead
efficiency variance[Note 1] = (Actual hours worked − Actual production in standard
hours) × standard rate
= (AH − APSH) × SR
= (25,000 − 24,000) × £2.50 = £2,500 adverse

Fixed overhead
capacity variance[Note 1] = (Actual hours worked − Budgeted hours to be worked)
× standard rate
= (AH − BH) × SR
= (25,000 − 20,000) × £2.50 = £12,500 favourable

Note 1: The last three variances (fixed overhead volume variance, efficiency variance and capacity variance) are only calculated when absorption costing is being used. When the basis of the costing system is marginal costing, only the variable overhead expenditure, variable overhead efficiency and fixed overhead expenditure variances are used (because you do not link fixed costs to the level of output). In a marginal costing-based environment, the total standard overhead cost for the 12,000 Superwidgets would be 12,000 at £3.00 variable overhead cost per Superwidget (= £36,000) plus the budgeted fixed cost of £50,000.

Rather than simply calculate the fixed overhead volume variance, you should normally calculate the efficiency and capacity variances. However, you need to be aware that together they represent the fixed overhead volume variance and you should be able to calculate this if required. Replacing the favourable fixed overhead volume variance of £10,000 in the Superwidgets example produces the following breakdown of costs and variances:

	£
Standard cost of overheads for 12,000 actual Superwidgets produced × £8 =	(96,000)
Variable production overhead expenditure variance – favourable	500
Variable production overhead efficiency variance – adverse	(1,500)
Fixed production overhead expenditure variance – adverse	(2,000)
Fixed production overhead efficiency variance – adverse	(2,500)
Fixed production overhead capacity variance – favourable	12,500
Actual level of manufacturing overhead	(89,000)

Obviously, the variable overhead efficiency variance is the same formula as for the fixed overhead efficiency variance, the labour efficiency variance and the materials usage variance.

Note 2: Efficiency variances are adverse when less is recovered than should have been.

13.21 A comprehensive example

The firm in this example operates standard costing based on absorption costing. The data set out below refer to a cost centre for a particular period:

Budget

Variable overheads (extract)

	Output	Cost
In units	*In standard hours*	*£*
9,800	49,000	98,000
9,900	49,500	99,000
10,000	50,000	100,000
10,100	50,500	101,000
10,200	51,000	102,000

Fixed overheads   150,000

Budgeted volume of production 10,000 units

Standard labour hours per unit = 5

Actual

Variable overhead	£104,000	
Fixed overhead	£160,000	
Direct labour hours worked	49,000	hours
Units of production	9,900	units

9,900 units of production is the equivalent of $9,900 \times 5 = 49,500$ standard direct labour hours.

Before making the variance calculations it will be helpful to make some observations on the data given. The flexible budget shows that each unit of production has a standard variable overhead cost of £10. Alternatively, this can be expressed as £10 ÷ 5 = £2 per standard hour of labour. **It should not be assumed that this rate of £2 would also apply to levels of production outside the range shown.** These may well be step costs, such as additional supervision, which would alter the standard variable overhead rate at higher levels of output.

The fixed costs are thought likely to remain fixed provided the range of output does not extend too far above or below the budgeted volume of production. The fixed standard rate is £150,000 ÷ 50,000 = £3 per standard hour of labour, or £150,000 ÷ 10,000 = £15 per unit.

The standard unit cost for overhead is thus £10 + £15 = £25 per unit or £2 + £3 = £5 per labour hour.

This budgeted volume of production is likely to be the level of output thought of as being normal and acceptable in the long run. It is referred to as the normal volume of production or, more commonly, as the 'normal level of activity'.

Calculation of variances

First, it is helpful to calculate the overall overheads variance which is to be analysed. This is developed from the standard cost of the actual units produced:

Actual total overhead costs		£264,000
Standard cost of actual production 9,900 × £25 =		247,500
Total variance	Adverse	(16,500)

This is broken down into the four variances as follows:

Variable overhead expenditure variance

Actual cost			104,000
Actual hours worked at standard rate = 49,000 × £2			98,000
Variable expenditure variance		Adverse	(6,000)

Variable overhead efficiency variance

Actual hours worked	49,000			
Actual production in standard hours	49,500			
Variable efficiency variance	500	× £2	Favourable	1,000

Fixed overhead expenditure variance

Budgeted fixed production overheads			150,000
Actual fixed production overheads			160,000
Fixed expenditure variance		Adverse	(10,000)

Fixed overhead efficiency variance

Actual hours worked	49,000			
Actual production in standard hours	49,500			
Variable efficiency variance	500	× £3	Favourable	1,500

Fixed overhead capacity variance

Actual hours worked	49,000			
Budgeted hours to be worked	50,000			
Fixed volume variance	1,000	× £3	Adverse	(3,000)

Summary of variances

Variable expenditure	Adverse	(6,000)
Variable efficiency	Favourable	1,000
Fixed expenditure	Adverse	(10,000)
Fixed efficiency	Favourable	1,500
Fixed capacity	Adverse	(3,000)
Net Adverse		(16,500)

Reconciliation of standard and actual cost

Standard cost of actual production 9,900 units × £25	(247,500)
Variable expenditure – adverse	(6,000)
Efficiency variance – favourable	1,000
Fixed expenditure – adverse	(10,000)
Fixed efficiency variance – favourable	1,500
Fixed capacity variance – adverse	(3,000)
Actual cost of overheads	(264,000)

13.22 Variances and management action

The calculation of variances and their explanation to managers is of no value unless the information so revealed is put to use in making decisions which change subsequent activities. The question then arises as to whether every variance needs some form of action. It is not possible to be dogmatic here, it really does depend on circumstances. In some cases, a fairly large variance may be fairly insignificant, whereas in others even a small amount may call for urgent action.

There is no doubt that variance calculations of the right type, transmitted to the right people at the right time, and which have an effect upon subsequent operations, can be of immense use. On the other hand, much of the effort put into variance calculation in many firms just goes to waste, as managers do not act on the information. This is very often because a poor 'selling' job has been done by the accounting staff to the managers concerned, in that either they have not been able to convince the managers that variance analysis is worthwhile or, possibly, the information provided is not really what the managers require to enable them to tackle their jobs properly.

13.23 Sales variances

The analysis of the difference between budgeted sales levels and actual levels can have an important bearing on the understanding of results. The main factors which are important in analysing sales are:

(a) selling price variances
(b) volume variances
(c) mix variances

The selling price variance measures the overall profit difference caused by budgeted unit selling price and actual unit selling price being different. If the budget was to sell 100 widgets at £5 each and the actual sales were 100 widgets of £4.50 each, there will be a profit reduction of £50 due to the adverse selling price variance of 50p per unit on the 100 units sold.

The volume variances in sales will be measured in terms of the difference in the total quantity being sold between budget and actual. The impact of changes in volume of sales on profit can only be measured if we know the profitability of the sales. This will be dealt with at gross profit level. Thus if the budget is to sell 100 widgets with a unit gross margin of £2 and the actual sales achieved are only 90 widgets then there is an adverse variance of 10 units at the margin of £2 which represents a loss of profit of £20. If several products are being sold the variance will be worked on total units actually sold in the proportion originally budgeted.

EXHIBIT 13.15

Product	Budget sales units	Budget proportions	Budget gross margin	Total budget margin	Actual sales units	Actual sales in budget proportions
		%	£	£		
X	200	33.3	1.00	200	250	240
Y	200	33.3	1.50	300	190	240
Z	200	33.3	3.50	700	280	240
	600	100.0		1,200	720	720

The volume variance is calculated by comparing actual sales in budget percentage mix with the original budget at budget margins:

Product	Budget sales units	Actual sales in budget proportions units	Variance units	Budget margin	Volume variances
				£	£
X	200	240	40	1.00	40.00
Y	200	240	40	1.50	60.00
Z	200	240	40	3.50	140.00
	600	720	120		240.00

The mix variance arises where more than one product is being sold and the different products have differing profit margins. If the proportions of the actual sales of the products vary from budget then the overall profit will vary as a consequence.

In the example on volume variance the original budget was compared with actual sales split in the budget mix. For the mix variance these figures of actual sales in budget mix are compared with the actual sales and the differences evaluated at the budgeted gross profit margin.

Product	Actual sales in budget proportions units	Actual sales units	Variance units	Budget gross margin	Mix variance
				£	£
X	240	250	10	1.00	10
Y	240	190	(50)	1.50	(75)
Z	240	280	40	3.50	140
	720	720	–		75

The difference in mix between budget and actual has increased profit by £75 due to the influence of more sales of product Z, i.e. there is a favourable mix variance of £75.

EXHIBIT 13.16

			Budget				Actual		
Product	%	Units	Unit selling price	Unit gross profit	Total profit	Units	Unit selling price	Unit gross profit	Total profit
			£	£	£		£	£	£
A	16.7	100	20	5	500	90	21	6	540
B	33.3	200	25	10	2,000	220	24	9	1,980
C	50	300	10	2	600	350	10	2	700
	100	600			3,100	660			3,220

Total variance = Actual profit 3,220
Budget profit 3,100
Favourable variance 120

First, eliminate the price variance using the actual units sold as the basis.

	Actual units sold	Budget price	Actual price	Unit variance	Total price variance
	1	2	3	3 − 2 = 4	1 × 4 = 5
		£	£	£	£
A	90	20	21	1	90
B	220	25	24	(1)	(220)
C	350	10	10	–	
				Adverse price variance	(130)

Secondly, eliminate the volume variance using the unit budgeted gross profit to evaluate the variance.

	Actual units sold	Actual units in budget proportions	Budget units sold	Variance in units	Budget unit gross profit	Total value variance
	1	2	3	2 − 3 = 4	5	4 × 5 = 6
					£	£
A	90	110	100	10	5	50
B	220	220	200	20	10	200
C	350	330	300	30	2	60
	660	660	600	60		
					Favourable volume variance	310

Finally, eliminate the mix variance. This is done by comparing the actual total units sold in the mix as originally budgeted with the actual sales.

	Budget proportions	Actual total sales split in budget proportions	Actual sales units	Difference units	Budget unit gross profit	Mix variance
	1	2	3	3 − 2 = 4	5	4 × 5 = 6
A	16.7	110	90	(20)	5	100
B	33.3	220	220	–	10	–
C	50.0	330	350	20	2	40
		660	660			
					Adverse mix variance	(60)

Summary of variances:

Adverse price variance	(130)
Favourable volume variance	310
Adverse mix variance	(60)
Favourable total sales variance	120

The gross profit margin may change for reasons other than changes in sales – for example, if the cost of materials varies from budgets or wage rates change. This type of variance has, however, already been dealt with under material and labour variances.

Learning outcomes

You should now have learnt:

1 Standard costing is based upon costs that should have been incurred, while other costing systems are based upon actual costs, i.e. costs that have been incurred.

2 The benefits of standard costing.

3 That under a standard costing system, management focuses upon the exceptions to the standards.

4 It is essential that the standards adopted are appropriate and attainable.

5 Variance analysis can improve the operating efficiency of a business by pinpointing items in need of investigation.

6 Adverse variances are not necessarily 'bad'. They result from more having been used or spent than was anticipated. Similarly, favourable variances are not necessarily 'good'. It is the reason for the variance, not the effect, that determines whether it is 'good' or 'bad'.

7 The materials usage variance formula is identical to the labour efficiency variance formula. Only the terminology differs.

8 The materials price variance formula is identical to the wage rate variance formula. Only the terminology differs.

9 How to calculate overhead and sales variances.

10 The similarities between the variable production overhead efficiency variance and both the labour efficiency variance and the materials usage variance.

11 How to identify appropriate reasons why variances found have occurred.

12 That the calculation of variances and explanation of them to managers are of no value unless the information so revealed is put to use in making decisions which change subsequent activities.

REVIEW QUESTIONS

Standard costing and variance analysis

13.1 Rimham plc prepares its budgets annually and as the accountant you are responsible for this task. The following standard data is available:

Material content	Product X	Product Y	Product Z
	kg	kg	kg
Material 1	–	18	24
Material 2	4	14	–
Material 3	12	10	6
Material 4	8	–	18

Material prices	Price per kg
	£
Material 1	0.1
Material 2	0.15
Material 3	0.25
Material 4	0.05

Labour content	Product X hours	Product Y hours	Product Z hours
Department A	2.5	1.5	3
Department B	2.5	1.5	3

Labour rates	Rate per hour £
Department A	1.6
Department B	1.2

Additional budgeted information

Direct labour hours	635,000
Production overheads	£1,143,000

- Production overheads are absorbed on the direct labour hour rate method.
- Administration and selling overheads are absorbed as a percentage of production cost at the rates of 50 per cent and 25 per cent, respectively.
- Profit is estimated at $12\frac{1}{2}$ per cent on budgeted selling price.
- Sales, at standard selling price, for the following year are budgeted as follows:

Product	£
X	800,000
Y	1,280,000
Z	2,400,000

- In order to meet the needs of an expansion programme the company considers it necessary to increase stocks as follows:

Material 1	90,000 kg
Material 2	36,000 kg
Material 3	42,000 kg
Material 4	54,000 kg

Finished goods	
Product X	5,000 units
Product Y	10,000 units
Product Z	10,000 units

You are required to prepare the following:

(a) A schedule giving a detailed standard cost and standard selling price per unit for **each** product,

(b) The sales budget in units,

(c) The production budget in units,

(d) The direct material purchases budget in both units and value.

(AQA (NEAB): GCE A-level)

13.2X Define the terms:

(i)   standard costing
(ii) standard cost
(iii) standard hours
(iv) variance.

(London Qualifications Limited: GCE A-level)

Materials and labour variances

Advice:

Work carefully through Questions 13.3 and 13.4X. If you have any difficulty, repeat them after 24 hours. Once you get into the swing of doing this type of question, it is quite easy to tackle them and get high marks.

13.3 Calculate the materials variances from the following data.

(*i*)	Material Q:	Standard price per tonne	£20
		Standard usage per unit	34 tonnes
		Actual price per tonne	£18
		Actual usage per unit	37 tonnes
(*ii*)	Material R:	Standard price per metre	£17
		Standard usage per unit	50 metres
		Actual price per metre	£19
		Actual usage per unit	46 metres
(*iii*)	Material S:	Standard price per metre	£12
		Standard usage per unit	15 metres
		Actual price per metre	£14
		Actual usage per unit	18 metres
(*iv*)	Material T:	Standard price per roll	£40
		Standard usage per unit	29 rolls
		Actual price per roll	£37
		Actual usage per unit	27 rolls
(*v*)	Material U:	Standard price per kilo	£7
		Standard usage per unit	145 kilos
		Actual price per kilo	£8
		Actual usage per unit	154 kilos
(*vi*)	Material V:	Standard price per litre	£25
		Standard usage per unit	10,000 litres
		Actual price per litre	£22
		Actual usage per unit	9,850 litres

13.4X Calculate the materials variances from the following data.

(*i*)	Material E:	Standard price per metre	£6
		Standard usage per unit	88 metres
		Actual price per metre	£6
		Actual usage per unit	85 metres
(*ii*)	Material F:	Standard price per tonne	£117
		Standard usage per unit	30 tonnes
		Actual price per tonne	£123
		Actual usage per unit	30 tonnes
(*iii*)	Material G:	Standard price per litre	£16
		Standard usage per unit	158 litres
		Actual price per litre	£16
		Actual usage per unit	165 litres
(*iv*)	Material H:	Standard price per foot	£16
		Standard usage per unit	92 feet
		Actual price per foot	£19
		Actual usage per unit	92 feet

    (*v*)   Material I:

Standard price per tonne	£294
Standard usage per unit	50 tonnes
Actual price per tonne	£300
Actual usage per unit	50 tonnes

    (*vi*) Material J:

Standard price per kilo	£27.5
Standard usage per unit	168 kilos
Actual price per kilo	£27.5
Actual usage per unit	156 kilos

13.5 Calculate the labour variances from the following data:

		Standard hours	Actual hours	Standard wage rate	Actual wage rate
(*i*)	Job A	220	218	£2.1	£2.1
(*ii*)	Job B	115	115	£1.7	£1.9
(*iii*)	Job C	200	240	£1.8	£1.8
(*iv*)	Job D	120	104	£2.0	£2.0
(*v*)	Job E	68	68	£1.8	£1.5
(*vi*)	Job F	30	34	£1.7	£1.7
(*vii*)	Job G	70	77	£1.6	£1.6
(*viii*)	Job H	100	100	£1.9	£2.0

13.6X Calculate the labour variances from the following data:

		Standard hours	Actual hours	Standard wage rate	Actual wage rate
(*i*)	Job I	150	142	£2.0	£2.2
(*ii*)	Job J	220	234	£1.9	£1.7
(*iii*)	Job K	50	48	£2.0	£1.9
(*iv*)	Job L	170	176	£2.0	£2.2
(*v*)	Job M	140	149	£2.1	£1.8
(*vi*)	Job N	270	263	£1.6	£2.0

13.7 The company for which you are the accountant manufactures three related, but different, products. These are dishwashers, washing machines and refrigerators. Each product has a standard time per unit of production. These are:

dishwashers	10 hours
washing machines	12 hours
refrigerators	14 hours

In the month of March the actual production was:

dishwashers	150
washing machines	100
refrigerators	90

and the labour details were:

actual hours worked	4,100
standard hourly rate of pay	£4
actual wages incurred	£18,450

You are required to:

(*a*) Explain the term 'standard hour'

(*b*) Calculate the standard hours produced in the month of March

(c) Calculate the following variances, using the above data:
- (i) total direct labour variance
- (ii) direct labour rate variance
- (iii) direct labour efficiency variance

(d) Give **two** possible causes for **each** of the labour rate and efficiency variances in (c).

(AQA (NEAB): GCE A-level)

13.8X Central Grid plc manufactures tungsten parts which pass through two processes, machining and polishing, before being transferred to finished goods. The management of the company have in operation a system of standard costing and budgetary control. The standard cost and budget information for April 20X8 has been established by the management accountant as follows:

Standard cost and budget details for April 20X8

	Machining	Polishing
Standard cost per unit:		
Direct material	£5	–
Direct labour	£12	£4.50
Budgeted output – units	16,000	16,000
(See Note below)		
Budgeted direct labour hours	48,000	24,000

Note: Output passes through both processes and there is no opening or closing work in progress.

Additional information

1 The actual production costs and details for April 20X8 are as follows:
- (i) The output that passed through the two processes was 12,000 units and there was no opening or closing work in progress.
- (ii) Direct material used at standard prices was £64,150.
- (iii) Direct material used at actual prices was £60,390.
- (iv) The direct wages bill and the direct labour hours clocked for the machining department were:

	£	Hours
Machining department	153,000	34,000

2 Variances for the polishing department have been calculated and reveal the following:

Labour efficiency variance	£3,000 Adverse
Labour rate variance	Nil

Required:

(a) Calculate the total direct material variance and its analysis into:
- (i) direct material usage variance
- (ii) direct material price variance.

(b) Calculate the overall direct labour variance for the machining department and analyse this variance into:
- (i) direct labour efficiency variance
- (ii) direct labour rate variance.

(c) Identify the possible reasons for each of the variances calculated for the machining department in (a) and (b) above and also for the variances given for the polishing department.

(d) Discuss possible interrelationships between these variances.

(AQA (AEB): GCE A-level)

13.9 Borrico Ltd manufacture a single product and they had recently introduced a system of budgeting and variance analysis. The following information is available for the month of July 20X1:

1

	Budget £	Actual £
Direct materials	200,000	201,285
Direct labour	313,625	337,500
Variable manufacturing overhead	141,400	143,000
Fixed manufacturing overhead	64,400	69,500
Variable sales overhead	75,000	71,000
Administration costs	150,000	148,650

2 Standard costs were:
Direct labour 48,250 hours at £6.50 per hour.
Direct materials 20,000 kilograms at £10 a kilogram.

3 Actual manufacturing costs were:
Direct labour 50,000 hours at £6.75 per hour.
Direct materials 18,900 kilograms at £10.65 a kilogram.

4 Budgeted sales were 20,000 units at £50 a unit.
Actual sales were:
   15,000 units at £52 a unit
   5,200 units at £56 a unit

5 There was no work in progress or stock of finished goods.

Required:

(*a*) An accounting statement showing the budgeted and actual gross and net profits or losses for July 20X1.
(*b*) The following variances for July 20X1:
   (*i*) Direct material cost variance, direct material price variance and direct material usage variance.
   (*ii*) Direct labour cost variance, direct labour rate variance and direct labour efficiency variance.
(*c*) What use can the management of Borrico Ltd make of the variances calculated in (*b*) above?

(AQA (AEB): GCE A-level)

13.10X (*a*) How does a system of standard costing enable a business to operate on the principle of management by exception?
(*b*) Some of the following materials and labour variances have been wrongly calculated, although the figures used are correct. Recalculate the variances, showing clearly the formulae you have used, and state whether the variances are adverse or favourable.

   (*i*) *Total Materials Variance*
   (Standard price – Actual price)   (Standard quantity – Actual quantity)
   = (£8.42 – £8.24)   (1,940 litres – 2,270 litres)
   = (£0.18)   (−330 litres)
   = £59.40 *adverse*

   (*ii*) *Materials Price Variance*
   (Standard price – Actual price)   Standard quantity
   = (£8.42 – £8.24)   1,940
   = £349.20 *favourable*

(*iii*) *Materials Usage Variance*

(Standard quantity − Actual quantity)   Standard price

= (1,940 − 2,270)   £8.42

= £2,778.6 *adverse*

(*iv*) *Total Labour Variance*

(Actual hours − Standard hours)   (Actual rate − Standard rate)

= (860 − 800)   (£6.14 − £6.53)

= (60 hours)   (− £0.39)

= £23.4 *adverse*

(*v*) *Wage Rate Variance*

(Standard rate − Actual rate)   Actual hours

= (£6.53 − £6.14)   860

= £335.4 *favourable*

(*vi*) *Labour Efficiency Variance*

(Actual hours − Standard hours)   Standard rate

= (860 − 800)   £6.53

= £391.80 *favourable*

(*London Qualifications Limited*: GCE A-level)

13.11X Makers Ltd assembles computer games machines. Standard costs have been prepared as follows:

		Gamesmaster	*Gotchya*
		£	£
Standard cost:			
Direct material:	boards	5	10
	components	20	30
Direct labour:	assembly	5	5
	testing	5	10
Overheads charged at 200%		20	30
		55	85
Profit margin		11	15
Standard selling price		66	100

The standard direct labour rate is £5 per hour.

During May 20X5, 5,000 Gamesmasters were sold at £60 each and 2,000 Gotchyas at £110 each.

Actual costs were incurred as follows:

	£
5,050 Gamesmaster boards	26,000
5,060 sets Gamesmaster components	75,000
2,010 Gotchya boards	28,390
2,025 sets Gotchya components	56,409
10,000 assembly labour hours @ £4.90	49,000
7,000 testing labour hours at £5.10	35,700
Overheads	160,000
	430,499

There are no opening or closing stocks.

Required:

A schedule of direct material and direct labour variances for the month.

(*Welsh Joint Education Committee: GCE A-level*)

13.12X The following diagram reflects costs under a standard costing system. Assume that all the variances are *unfavourable*. State, with reasons, which rectangle(s) represent:

(*i*) the standard cost
(*ii*) the actual cost
(*iii*) the total labour cost variance
(*iv*) the efficiency variance
(*v*) the wage rate variance

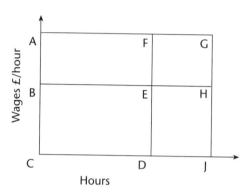

(*London Qualifications Limited*: GCE A-Level)

Overhead and sales variances

Advice: Remember that the overhead variances consist of the difference between the standard costs at the actual level of activity and the actual costs. Remember also that sales variances consist of those for price, volume and mix.

It is important that you answer the parts of the questions that ask you to comment on exactly what might be behind the variances and what action is needed.

13.13 Calculate the overhead variances from the following data. (Hint: if the actual expenditure is given, you should calculate the expenditure variance. If it isn't, you should calculate the volume or efficiency variance.)

(*a*) Budgeted for £6,000 variable overhead and 1,000 machine hours.

Actual overhead	£5,840
Actual machine hours	1,000

(*b*) Budgeted for £20,000 variable overhead and 5,000 machine hours.

Actual overhead	£21,230
Actual machine hours	5,000

(*c*) Budgeted for £12,000 fixed overhead and the actual overhead is found to be £11,770.
(*d*) Budgeted for £40,000 fixed overhead and the actual overhead is found to be £41,390.
(*e*) Budgeted production of 2,000 units in 8,000 hours. Standard variable overhead rate is £3 per hour. In fact 2,000 units are produced in 7,940 hours.
(*f*) Budgeted production of 5,000 units in 15,000 hours. Standard variable overhead rate is £4 per hour. In fact 4,860 units are produced in 15,000 hours.

13.14X Calculate the overhead variances in the following cases. (Hint: if the actual expenditure is given, you should calculate the expenditure variance. If it isn't, you should calculate the volume or efficiency variance.)

(a) Budgeted for £37,000 fixed overhead. The actual fixed overhead turns out to be £36,420.

(b) Budgeted for production of 500 units in 250 hours. The variable overhead rate is £6 per hour. In fact 500 units are produced in 242 hours.

(c) Budgeted for £18,000 variable overhead and 9,000 machine hours. Actual overhead is £18,000 and actual machine hours 8,820.

(d) Budgeted for £9,000 variable overhead and 3,000 machine hours. Actual overhead is £8,790 and actual machine hours 3,000.

(e) Budgeted for £120,000 fixed overhead. The actual fixed overhead turns out to be £129,470.

(f) Budgeted for production of 10,000 units in 30,000 hours. Standard variable overhead rate is £8 an hour. In fact 9,880 units are produced in 30,000 hours.

13.15 You are required to calculate the overhead variances of Joseph Ltd. The budget is prepared as:

(a) Total budgeted variable overhead £400,000.
(b) Total budgeted fixed overhead £160,000.
(c) Budgeted volume of production 80,000 direct labour hours for 40,000 units.

The actual results turn out to be:

(d) Actual variable overhead £403,600.
(e) Actual fixed overhead £157,200.
(f) Actual volume 78,500 direct labour hours which resulted in 42,000 units of production.

13.16X You are required to calculate the overhead variances of Raymond Ltd. The budget is prepared as:

(a) Total budgeted variable overhead £100,000.
(b) Total budgeted fixed overhead £125,000.
(c) Budgeted volume of production 50,000 direct labour hours of 250,000 units.

The actual results turn out to be:

(d) Actual variable overhead £96,500.
(e) Actual fixed overhead £129,400.
(f) Actual volume 52,000 direct labour hours which resulted in 244,000 units.

13.17 The Grange Company had the following results for the year to 31 March 20X1. A single product – a toggle – was made by the company.

	Budget	Actual
Sales in units	125,000	150,000
Sales in £	312,500	356,250

The standard cost of manufacturing each unit was £1.50.

What are the price and volume variances on sales in 20X1?

13.18X Corporec PLC manufactures a detergent in one of its plants. The information for the year to 30 September 20X2 was as follows:

	Budget	Actual
Sales in litres	180,000	170,000
Sales in £	540,000	527,000

The standard cost of manufacturing a litre was £2.

Calculate the price and volume variances for 20X2.

13.19 The following data were collected for Molton Ltd for the year ended 31 March 20X3.

Product	Budget selling price	Budget sales units	Budget sales proportions	Budget gross profit per unit	Budget gross profit total	Actual selling price	Actual sales units	Actual sales proportions	Actual gross profit per unit	Actual gross profit total
	£			£	£	£			£	£
M	5	800	25	1.00	800	5.10	840	30	0.90	756
N	8	1,600	50	1.50	2,400	7.90	1,680	60	1.40	2,352
P	7	800	25	1.20	960	7.30	280	10	1.20	336
		3,200	100		4,160		2,800	100		3,444

Calculate price, volume and mix variances for 20X3.

13.20X The following information relates to Burton Company for the year to 30 June 20X6:

Product	Budget units	Budget sales proportions	Budget selling price per unit	Budget gross profit per unit	Actual units	Actual sales proportions	Actual unit selling price	Actual unit gross profit
			£	£			£	£
A	400	14.3	30	5	500	20.8	29	4
B	600	21.4	25	4	400	16.7	27	5
C	1,800	64.3	40	10	1,500	62.5	39	9
	2,800	100.0			2,400	100.0		

Calculate price, volume and mix variances for 20X6.

13.21 Singleton has been operating for some years as a manufacturer of a single product, and after several years' growth has decided to form a company Singleton Ltd.

His accountant advised him that in an increasingly competitive world he really should achieve greater financial control of his business, and to assist Singleton in this objective the accountant prepared a simple manufacturing budget for the financial year ending 31 August 20X9.

The following schedule provides the detail of the budget and the actual results for the year ended 31 August 20X9. The actual results have been extracted from the ledger as at that date without any adjustments made.

	Budget	Actual
	£	£
Raw materials consumed	80,000	90,000
Factory rent	10,000	12,500
Factory maintenance expenses	6,700	6,100
Heating and lighting	2,900	3,000
Direct labour wages	120,000	110,500
Direct expenses	5,800	6,000
Depreciation of plant and machinery	8,900	10,500
Wages, maintenance labour	18,000	24,000
Other factory overheads	12,700	9,600

Additional information

1 At 31 August 20X9 the following amounts were still owing:

	£
Direct labour wages	5,100
Heating and lighting	900
Other factory overhead	400

2 The factory rent paid covered the period from 1 September 20X8 to 30 November 20X9.
3 During the year the firm sold 90,000 units of its product at £4.50 a unit.
4 There was no work-in-progress. The stocks of finished goods were:

	£
1 September 20X8	28,900
31 August 20X9	35,000

Required:

(a) What is variance analysis and how can it contribute to the operating efficiency of Singleton's business?
(b) For the year ended 31 August 20X9 prepare:
  (i) A manufacturing account and a schedule of the relevant variances;
  (ii) A trading account.
(c) Write a report to advise Singleton whether the principles of budgeting can be applied to:
  (i) Non-manufacturing costs;
  (ii) The control of cash resources.

Your report should indicate in each case the potential benefits that the firm could achieve through extending its use of budgeting.

(AQA (Associated Examining Board): GCE A-level)

13.22X Flint Palatignium Ltd calculates the prices of its output by adding a mark-up of 15 per cent to standard costs. These standard costs are arrived at by reference to budgeted outputs and estimated direct costs as follows:

	£ each	Standard price/rate
Materials	5.00	£1 per unit
Direct labour	2.50	£1.25 per hour
Overheads	7.50	£3.75 per direct labour hour
	15.00	
Mark-up	2.25	
Selling price	17.25	

Management accounts for April 20X8 provide an analysis of operations as follows:

	£
Sales – at standard price	534,750
Standard margin on sales	69,750
Favourable sales price variance	8,691
	78,441
Other favourable variances:	
Material price	4,662
Labour rate	600
Overhead expenditure	147
	83,850
Adverse variances:	
Material usage	(1,743)
Labour efficiency	(292)
Overhead capacity	(9)
Actual operating profit	81,806

Materials in stock are valued at standard cost. At 1 April, 1,000 units of material were held, whereas at 30 April the stock of this material increased to 1,750 units.

Required:

(*i*) A trading account for the month of April 20X8 comparing the budgeted income and expenditure appropriate to actual output, to actual income and expenditure.

(*ii*) An explanation of the value of standard costing and variance analysis to a service business whose custom is to negotiate fixed price contracts.

(*Welsh Joint Education Committee: GCE A-level*)

Materials and labour variances and overhead and sales variances

13.23X HGW Limited produces a product called a Lexton. The standard selling price and the manufacturing costs of this product are as follows:

		£
Standard selling price per unit		86
Standard production costs:		
Direct material	1.5 kilos at £12 per kilo	18
Direct labour	4.4 hours at £7.50 per hour	33
Variable overheads	4.4 hours at £5 per hour	22
		73

The projected production and sales for March 20X4 were 520 units.

On 1 April 20X4 the following actual figures were determined.

Sales	550 units at £85 each
Production	550 units
Direct material	785 kilos at £12.40 per kilo
Direct labour	2,400 hours at £7.80 per hour
Overheads	£12,500 (overall variance £400 adverse)

There was no opening stock of the product Lexton.

Required:

(*a*) Prepare an actual profit and loss statement for HGW Ltd for March 20X4.

(*b*) Calculate the following variances and their respective sub-variances:
   (*i*)   sales – price and volume
   (*ii*) direct material – price and usage
   (*iii*) direct labour – rate and efficiency

(*c*) Prepare a statement reconciling the actual profit calculated in part (*a*) with the budgeted profit on actual sales. (Use the variances calculated in part (*b*) and the given overhead variance.)

(*d*) Write a report to the management outlining the factors that need to be considered when standards are being established.

(*AQA (AEB): GCE A-level*)

13.24 Jasper Ltd is a manufacturer of a single product.

The company has recently introduced a system of standard costing. The material standards are based on average usage in the previous year and suppliers' current trade price lists. Labour standards were set by observing one of the most experienced employees.

The standard production costs per unit are:

Materials	2 kg at £3 per kg
Labour	4.5 hours at £8 per hour
Variable overheads	4.5 hours at £4 per hour

Fixed overheads are estimated at £9,000 per month.

The production and sales budgets for May 20X2 were 1,000 units.

The standard selling price per unit was £80.

Actual results for May 20X2 were as follows:

Production	850 units
Sales	800 units at £78.50 per unit
Materials	£5,670 for 2,100 kg
Labour	£36,900 for 4,500 hours
Variable overheads	£14,880
Fixed overheads	£8,000

Required:

(*a*) Calculate the following variances:

(*i*)	materials – price and usage	(*4 marks*)
(*ii*)	labour – rate and efficiency	(*4 marks*)
(*iii*)	total variable overhead	(*3 marks*)
(*iv*)	total fixed overhead	(*3 marks*)

(*b*) Discuss **three** factors which the management of Jasper Ltd should take into account when setting labour standards. (*9 marks*)

(*Reproduced with the kind permission of OCR: GCE A-level, Paper 2503, Q1, 17/6/2002*)

CHAPTER 14

Capital investment appraisal

Learning objectives

After you have studied this chapter, you should be able to:

- explain why capital investment appraisal is undertaken;
- explain why interest rates are important in financial decision making;
- calculate and compare the net present value (NPV), internal rate of return (IRR) and payback of a series of cash flows;
- choose beween alternative projects on the basis of NPV, IRR and payback.

14.1 Introduction

Let us assume that a man is to start a business making widgets (an imaginary product). If there is only one type of machine that will do the necessary work then that is the machine that he will have to buy. There is no alternative to this if he wants to conduct this type of business. On the other hand, suppose there were two different kinds of machine he could buy, then he would have to buy either machine A or machine B. If both machines were equally efficient, performed the same type of work and would be in use for the same length of time, then the decision would be an easy one. He would simply buy the machine which cost the least amount of money.

Such equality of cost and effective use would be rare. Usually there will be differences in the operation of the machines, what they cost, what they would cost to maintain, exactly what kind of work they could do, and how long they would last in service. Where these differences exist, the proprietor could do with some advice that would help him decide, from a financial point of view, which machine should be chosen.

You should remember that the financial picture is only one aspect of the decision whether to undertake certain kinds of work or to buy a certain fixed asset. Other factors could be:

(*a*) Pollution. One machine may produce obnoxious fumes which might affect workers in the factory or people in the surrounding area. Such pollution might also include noise pollution.

(*b*) One machine might be more dangerous to use.

(*c*) Possibly one machine might be more compatible with other types of machinery which could be needed.

(d) Uncertainty as to whether any necessary repairs to the machinery would be done quickly or not by the supplier, as well as possible problems with spare parts for the machine.

(e) How quickly the machine could be delivered and installed.

(f) Whether or not the workforce would need training to use the machine.

These are only some of the factors which could decide whether or not machine A or machine B is to be bought, and may override the answer which would be given if the decision were based simply on financial considerations. There is a strong link here to what you will read in Chapter 15 on social accounting.

So far we have looked at capital expenditure appraisal in a simple fashion, as though all we had to do was to decide whether to buy one machine or another. In fact the techniques of capital expenditure appraisal extend to issues much wider than that. Instances might be:

(a) Shall we build and operate a factory in Germany or should it be built in Spain?

(b) Shall we buy some expensive footballers for our football club and raise entrance fees to pay for them, or should we use the money to build a better stadium instead?

(c) Should we buy robot machinery to replace our present manually worked machines?

(d) Which site should we choose from the three available for the construction of a new theme park?

Sometimes, therefore, the decision will lie between changing something we are already doing, or deciding which of two or more additional projects should be undertaken without changing our basic existing business.

Remember that in appraising capital expenditure we are dealing with estimates of future costs and future cash inflows. Our assessment of projects will, therefore, only be as good as the accuracy of our estimates of these items.

We will first of all look at how the calculations are made for the various methods in use. Then we will examine the relative strengths and weaknesses of each of the methods used.

14.2 Accounting rate of return

In this method, *profits* are used in the calculations. In the other methods shown in this chapter, it is *cash flows* that are used for the calculations.

The accounting rate of return as a percentage is calculated by using the following formula:

$$\textbf{Accounting rate of return} = \frac{\textbf{Average annual profits}}{\textbf{Average investment}} \times \frac{\textbf{100}}{\textbf{1}}$$

In calculating the average annual profits re the expenditure proposal, only the *additional* revenues and *additional* costs are used. The additional costs (we could call them incremental costs) include the total depreciation charges over the life of the asset.

The average investment figure to be used in the calculation will depend on the method of depreciation which has been used. Where straight line depreciation is used, the figure is found as follows:

$$\frac{\textbf{Amount of initial investment} + \textbf{Scrap value at the end of its life}}{2}$$

At first sight it would be understandable if the reader was to think that the scrap value should be deducted, not added. Rather than elaborate on this point and possibly confuse quite a large number of readers, I would ask the more inquisitive reader to get hold of a more advanced book on the subject to confirm that it is true.

We can now work out the accounting rate of return on two possible projects. In both cases we will assume that there is no scrap value.

	A		B	
	£	£	£	£
Initial cost of investment		6,000		8,000
Additional profits: Year 1	2,000		2,600	
Year 2	3,600		3,000	
Year 3	4,000	9,600	4,000	
Year 4			4,000	13,600

Average profits: A (9,600 – 6,000) ÷ 3 = £1,200
B (13,600 – 8,000) ÷ 4 = £1,400

Average investment: A £6,000 ÷ 2 = £3,000
B £8,000 ÷ 2 = £4,000

Accounting rate of return: A $\dfrac{1,200}{3,000} \times \dfrac{100}{1} = 40\%$

B $\dfrac{1,400}{4,000} \times \dfrac{100}{1} = 35\%$

Using this form of assessment, project A is preferable to project B, as the rate of return is higher at 40 per cent.

14.3 Payback method

This method is quite a simple one. It is also used by quite a lot of firms, particularly at times when interest rates are high and/or when they are experiencing cash flow problems (i.e. when they are finding it difficult to raise cash to pay bills when due). It measures the length of time it takes to recover the original cash outlay from the stream of net cash proceeds from the investment.

Let us look at three possible projects, D, E and F. The initial costs and the cash inflows are now shown.

	D		E		F	
	£	£	£	£	£	£
Initial cost		50,000		50,000		50,000
Cash inflows: Year 1	20,000		10,000		20,000	
Year 2	30,000		20,000		20,000	
Year 3	20,000		20,000		20,000	
Year 4	10,000		30,000		20,000	
		80,000		80,000		80,000

Each has had the same overall outflows and inflows of cash. However, the payback method will rank as the best choice as it is the one which recovers most quickly the cost of the original investment.

Payback method: D   2 years (£50,000 inflows during the first 2 years)
E   3 years (£50,000 inflows during the first 3 years)
F   2.5 years (£50,000 inflows during the first 2.5 years)

The payback method will therefore select project D.

With D and E, the initial cost is received back in an exact number of years. D took exactly 2 years to get back the cost, whilst E took exactly 3 years. Where the answer is not an exact number of years then in the final year during which costs are recovered it is assumed that the cash inflows are of an equal amount during each month of that final year. With F, £40,000 had been recovered by the end of Year 2. In Year 3, £10,000 still had to be recovered, and £20,000 was the total of cash inflows for Year 3, therefore it is assumed that it took a 10,000/20,000 part of Year 3, i.e. 0.5 year, to recover the final £10,000. If the final amount to be received during Year 3 had been £15,000 then it would be taken as a 15,000/20,000 part of the year, i.e. 0.75 year.

It is quite possible that use of only the payback method can mean the selection of the (eventually) least profitable project. For instance:

		G		H		I	
		£	£	£	£	£	£
Initial cost			40,000		40,000		40,000
Cash inflows:	Year 1	20,000		10,000		10,000	
	Year 2	20,000		25,000		10,000	
	Year 3	10,000		15,000		10,000	
	Year 4	–		5,000		30,000	
			50,000		55,000		60,000

Payback method: G   2.00 years
H   2.33 years
I   3.33 years

If the payback method of selection was used, project G would be taken, although the overall profit during each project's life would be

G Revenue £50,000 – cost £40,000 = profit £10,000
H Revenue £55,000 – cost £40,000 = profit £15,000
I Revenue £60,000 – cost £40,000 = profit £20,000

14.4   The time value of money

The methods we have looked at so far have both contained defects. The accounting rate of return method ignored the 'time value' of money. The payback method ignored both the 'time value' of money and the cash flows which occurred after the investment costs had been recovered. The net present value method which we will look at in Section 14.7 does not have these defects.

To explain the 'time value' of money: if you were offered the choice of £1 now or £1 in a year's time, then obviously you would prefer to have £1 now. If you wanted to (assuming that you could invest such a small sum of money) you could invest the £1 now at (say) 10 per cent interest, and get back £1 + 10 per cent = £1.10 in one year's time. Therefore £1 now is better than £1 in a year's time.

Businesses adopt this same outlook when they are comparing the benefits to be gained from differing capital expenditures. Rather than simply compare the actual amounts to be received and paid, they take into account the *time* value of the projected future inflows and outflows of cash. We can now start to look at how they arrive at an adjusted set of figures for comparison.

14.5 Cost of capital

Before we can use the net present value method we will need to know the *cost of capital* for the firm. By this we mean the interest factor representing the cost of the funds needed to finance the projects.

This is based on the idea of *opportunity cost* which some readers will have studied in economics. Suppose you have the choice of investing in securities available on the stock markets, such as ordinary shares or government securities, or alternatively you can invest the funds in one of your own projects. Let us also imagine that the risks involved in the stock market shares or securities are exactly the same as those for your possible project. In that case you would not put your funds into your own project if the stock market investment would give you a higher return.

If you could get a 15 per cent return on your money from a stock market investment, you simply would not put your money into another project, with the same risk, which gave less than 15 per cent return. It would not make sense.

The rate of return we could get from an alternative investment, with the same degree of risk, is known as the cost of capital. In most examples in this chapter, we are going to assume, from now on, that the cost of capital will be 10 per cent. It will make calculations easier to do and to understand. Following the same principle of trying to make things easier to understand for the reader, we are not going to use mathematical formulae but rely, instead, on basic arithmetical skills.

14.6 Present values

The next step is to put calculations on to a common basis to make comparisons possible, as we can only compare like with like.

To do this we use a technique called 'discounted cash flow' abbreviated as DCF. To try to understand this, let us look at what would happen if we invested £10,000 in a security which was free from risk, and which yields a return of 10 per cent per annum. Exhibit 14.1 shows the increase in the value of the investment if it is allowed to accumulate at 10 per cent per annum.

Note that 'Year 0' represents the start of the project – that is, the start of Year 1. We use 'Year 0' because you have to invest cash in the project at the start. All income and all other expenditure is assumed to be incurred and to be received at the end of each year.

EXHIBIT 14.1

Year end	Interest	Total value of investment
		£
0		10,000
	10% × £10,000	1,000
1		11,000
	10% × £11,000	1,100
2		12,100
	10% × £12,100	1,210
3		13,310

Now if we try to compare these figures we can say that, with 10 per cent interest, £13,310 at the end of Year 3 is equivalent to £10,000 at the start of Year 1. Similarly £12,100 at the end of Year 2 is equivalent to £10,000 at the start of Year 1, as also is £11,000 at the end of Year 1.

Now different investments result in cash flows at different points in time. If we want to compare such cash flows we need somehow to be able to get a common measure.

We can do this by discounting the cash flows (DCF) of the future back to what the values of such cash flows were at the start of the investment, given the cost of capital, e.g. in Exhibit 14.1 £13,310 at the end of Year 3 is equivalent, given the cost of capital, to £10,000 at the start of Year 1. This means that if we are comparing different projects, one which has cash flows for three years, another for four years, and the final one for five years, then the thing which is common to them all is the present value at the start of Year 1 for each investment.

What we need to help us is a set of tables which shows us, given the cost of capital, what the present value of £1 received *x* years hence is at the start of Year 1. A table covering ten years is now shown as Exhibit 14.2.

EXHIBIT 14.2 Present value of £1

Year	1%	2%	3%	4%	5%	6%	7%	8%	9%	10%	12%	14%	15%
1	0.990	0.980	0.971	0.961	0.952	0.943	0.935	0.926	0.917	0.909	0.893	0.877	0.870
2	0.980	0.961	0.943	0.925	0.907	0.890	0.873	0.857	0.842	0.826	0.797	0.769	0.756
3	0.971	0.942	0.915	0.889	0.864	0.840	0.816	0.794	0.772	0.751	0.712	0.675	0.658
4	0.961	0.924	0.889	0.855	0.823	0.792	0.763	0.735	0.708	0.683	0.636	0.592	0.572
5	0.951	0.906	0.863	0.822	0.784	0.747	0.713	0.681	0.650	0.621	0.567	0.519	0.497
6	0.942	0.888	0.838	0.790	0.746	0.705	0.666	0.630	0.596	0.564	0.507	0.456	0.432
7	0.933	0.871	0.813	0.760	0.711	0.665	0.623	0.583	0.547	0.513	0.452	0.400	0.376
8	0.923	0.853	0.789	0.731	0.677	0.627	0.582	0.540	0.502	0.467	0.404	0.351	0.327
9	0.914	0.837	0.766	0.703	0.645	0.592	0.544	0.500	0.460	0.424	0.361	0.308	0.284
10	0.905	0.820	0.744	0.676	0.614	0.558	0.508	0.463	0.422	0.386	0.322	0.270	0.247

Year	16%	18%	20%	24%	28%	32%	36%	40%	50%	60%	70%	80%	90%
1	0.862	0.847	0.833	0.806	0.781	0.758	0.735	0.714	0.667	0.625	0.588	0.556	0.526
2	0.743	0.718	0.694	0.650	0.610	0.574	0.541	0.510	0.444	0.391	0.346	0.309	0.277
3	0.641	0.609	0.579	0.524	0.477	0.435	0.398	0.364	0.296	0.244	0.204	0.171	0.146
4	0.552	0.516	0.482	0.423	0.373	0.329	0.292	0.260	0.198	0.153	0.120	0.095	0.077
5	0.476	0.437	0.402	0.341	0.291	0.250	0.215	0.186	0.132	0.095	0.070	0.053	0.040
6	0.410	0.370	0.335	0.275	0.227	0.189	0.158	0.133	0.088	0.060	0.041	0.029	0.021
7	0.354	0.314	0.279	0.222	0.178	0.143	0.116	0.095	0.059	0.037	0.024	0.016	0.011
8	0.305	0.266	0.233	0.179	0.139	0.108	0.085	0.068	0.039	0.023	0.014	0.009	0.006
9	0.263	0.226	0.194	0.144	0.108	0.082	0.063	0.048	0.026	0.015	0.008	0.005	0.003
10	0.227	0.191	0.162	0.116	0.085	0.062	0.046	0.035	0.017	0.009	0.005	0.003	0.002

Exhibit 14.2 is an extract from a full table which is shown as Exhibit 14.6 at the end of the chapter.

On looking at Exhibit 14.2 you can see that the present value of £1 received in five years' time, given a cost of capital of 10 per cent, is £0.621, i.e. line 5 under the column headed 10%. The tables show everything in terms of £1. If therefore £10,000 was received at the end of five years then the answer would be 10,000 × £0.621 = £6,210, or for £6,000 received at the end of five years it would be 6,000 × £0.621 = £3,726.

On the other hand if, given a cost of capital of 5 per cent, and if the cash flows from the investment would be £2,000 in two years' time, followed by £3,000 in three years' time, and a final £5,000 at the end of five years, the total present value of future cash inflows would be as follows:

		£
2,000 × £0.907	=	1,814
3,000 × £0.864	=	2,592
5,000 × £0.784	=	3,920
Total present value		8,326

In case you have had any problems in understanding that, you need to look at the columns under the heading 5%. The second line, which represents the present value based on receipt of £1 in two years' time, is £0.907. As there was £2,000 received rather than £1 it has been multiplied by 2,000 to give £1,814. For Year 3 you look at the same column, line 3, £0.864 and then multiply by 3,000 as there was £3,000 received, to give £2,592. Then, under the same column, line 5 representing the end of Year 5 the figure of £0.784 is taken and multiplied by 5,000, because the final sum received was £5,000, to give £3,920. Adding the figures together gives a present value for all the cash flows of £8,326.

14.7 Net present value

The difference between the amount invested and the present value of future cash flows is called the *net present value*. This can be either a positive net present value or a negative net present value. This can now be illustrated in Exhibit 14.3.

EXHIBIT 14.3

George is considering whether or not to invest in one of two alternative projects. Details are as follows:

		Project K £	Project L £
Investment needed at start		10,000	10,000
Estimated future cash inflows:	Year 1	4,000	1,000
	Year 2	4,000	2,000
	Year 3	4,000	2,000
	Year 4	1,000	5,000
	Year 5	–	4,000
		13,000	14,000

Cost of capital is 10 per cent.

You then perform the following calculations:

Year	Project K			Project L		
	Amount	Present value factors	Present value	Amount	Present value factors	Present value
	£		£	£		£
1	4,000	0.909	3,636	1,000	0.909	909
2	4,000	0.826	3,304	2,000	0.826	1,652
3	4,000	0.751	3,004	2,000	0.751	1,502
4	1,000	0.683	683	5,000	0.683	3,415
5	–		–	4,000	0.621	2,484
		Total present value	10,627			9,962
		Less initial outlay	(10,000)			(10,000)
		Net present value	627			(38)

Project K has a positive net value of £627 as its total of present values exceeds the outlay by £627. Project L has a negative present value of £38, shown as being negative by being enclosed in brackets. Of the two projects Project K would be chosen for financial reasons, as it shows the larger net present value.

Even if Project L was the only project under consideration other than investing on the stock markets with a similar risk, it would still not be chosen because it shows a negative net present value, which means that it would bring back a lower return than from a stock market investment, so there would be no point in taking up project L.

14.8 Internal rate of return (IRR)

This is an alternative technique which also takes into account the time value of money. It uses as a measure the 'true' rate of interest which, when applied to the cash flows and discounted back to the initial outlay, will give a present value calculation of zero.

To find this 'true' rate involves trial and error methods. We proceed as follows:

1 Choose two rates for discounting back future receipts, one of the rates to give a positive net present value, and the other to give a negative net present value.
2 Calculate the net present values using the rates as per 1.
3 Then apply a formula which can be stated as:

$$\text{IRR} = \text{lower rate} + \left(\% \text{ difference between rates} \times \frac{\text{NPV using lower } \% \text{ rate}}{\text{Total difference between the two NPVs}} \right)$$

EXHIBIT 14.4

A project involves an initial outlay of £10,000. It results in cash inflows at the end of Year 1 of £5,000, Year 2 of £4,000, Year 3 of £3,000.

Using discount rates of 10 and 12 per cent, obtaining the necessary figures from the tables in Exhibit 14.2, the NPVs are:

Discount rates	10%		12%	
		£		£
Cash inflows £5,000 × 0.909 =		4,545	£5,000 × 0.893 =	4,465
£4,000 × 0.826 =		3,304	£4,000 × 0.797 =	3,188
£3,000 × 0.751 =		2,253	£3,000 × 0.712 =	2,136
		10,102		9,789
Less Investment		(10,000)		(10,000)
Net present value		102		(211)

The internal rate of return (IRR) is therefore:

$$10\% + \left(2\% \times \frac{102}{102 + 211} \right) = 10.65\%$$

The formula is an approximate one, it is not absolutely correct, but it gives an answer which is satisfactory for all normal practical purposes.

If we were now to repeat the calculation, taking the discount factor as 10.65 per cent, we would see that it would produce a net present value of zero.

Once calculated, the IRR is compared with the cost of capital. If the cost of capital is higher than the IRR then the project should not be taken up. If you are comparing two alternative projects the one with the higher IRR would be selected for investment, assuming that it was above the cost of capital.

14.9 Relevant and irrelevant costs

When decision making, some costs and revenues are relevant to a decision that is to be taken, whilst other costs and revenues are not, i.e. they are irrelevant. The *relevant costs and revenues* are those costs and revenues of the future that will be affected by the decision, whereas irrelevant costs and revenues will not be so affected.

Take as an example a decision as to whether or not we should telephone a lot of our customers in a sales campaign. The cost of the phone rental is irrelevant in the decision whether or not to conduct the campaign, as we will still have to pay exactly the same rental whether or not we engage in the campaign. On the other hand, the cost of making the extra phone calls will be a relevant cost as they would not have been incurred if the campaign had not gone ahead.

With revenues, take the case of buying a new car for a salesman. If the revenues he would help create by sales would remain unchanged no matter which car he were to have, then the revenues would be completely irrelevant in taking the decision as to the type of car to be bought.

However, take the case of a salesman who sells some of his products to farmers. With a four-wheel drive car he could get to farms which would otherwise be inaccessible to an ordinary two-wheel drive car. In this case the revenues would be relevant to the decision as to the type of car to be bought, as they would be affected by the decision.

14.10 Sunk costs

This is a term which can be confusing, since it really means an irrelevant cost which has already occurred. It is a past cost, not a future cost.

Let us take the case of a machine which was bought several years ago, and now has a written down value of £10,000. The scrap value is nil. We can either use the machine on a project we are considering or else we can scrap it. Let us suppose that the revenue from the project will be £25,000 and the future relevant costs will be £18,000. If we added the written down value of the machine to the £18,000 costs then we would make a loss of £3,000 (£25,000 − £28,000). Looking at it that way, we would not tackle the project.

However, the cost of the machine was a past cost. If we do not use the machine on this project the only alternative is to scrap it. Such a past cost is said to be a *sunk cost* and is irrelevant to the decision to be taken. We therefore take on the project (assuming there is no better alternative project) and are better off by £7,000 (£25,000 − £18,000).

14.11 A comparison of the methods

We will now look at a case where each of the methods already described will be used to try to select the best investment. You will see that the different methods can give different answers as to which project should be chosen.

EXHIBIT 14.5

ABC Ltd is wondering whether or not to invest in one of three possible projects. The initial investment will be £10,000, and the cost of capital is 10 per cent. There is no scrap value for fixed assets used. Details of the net cash inflows are as follows:

	M £	N £	P £
Year 1	3,000	5,000	4,000
Year 2	6,000	5,000	5,000
Year 3	4,000	2,000	3,000
Year 4	–	1,600	1,000
Year 5	–	–	1,400
	13,000	13,600	14,400

1 Accounting rate of return:

$$\frac{\text{Average yearly profit}}{\text{Average investment}} \times \frac{100}{1} \qquad \frac{1,000}{5,000} = 20\% \qquad \frac{900}{5,000} = 18\% \qquad \frac{880}{5,000} = 17.6\%$$

2 Payback: 2.25 years 2 years 2.33 years

3 Net present value (cost of capital 10%)

Discount factors per tables				Present values in £s			
			M	N		P	
£0.909	× 3,000 =	2,727	× 5,000 =	4,545	× 4,000 =	3,636
£0.826	× 6,000 =	4,956	× 5,000 =	4,130	× 5,000 =	4,130
£0.751	× 4,000 =	3,004	× 2,000 =	1,502	× 3,000 =	2,253
£0.683			× 1,600 =	1,092	× 1,000 =	683
£0.621					× 1,400 =	869
Total value of present value		10,687		11,269		11,571
Less Investment		(10,000)		(10,000)		(10,000)
Net present values		687		1,269		1,571

4 Internal rate of return

Stage 1: Use a rate of return which will give negative net present values. In this instance it is taken to be 18%.

Discount factors per tables at 18%		*M*		*N*		*P*
£0.847	× 3,000 =	2,541	× 5,000 =	£4,235	× 4,000 =	3,388
£0.718	× 6,000 =	4,308	× 5,000 =	3,590	× 5,000 =	3,590
£0.609	× 4,000 =	2,436	× 2,000 =	1,218	× 3,000 =	1,827
£0.516			× 1,600 =	825	× 1,000 =	516
£0.437					× 1,400 =	611
Total of present value		9,285		9,868		9,932
Less Investment		(10,000)		(10,000)		(10,000)
Net present values		(715)		(132)		(68)

(*Present values in £s*)

Stage 2: Calculate the internal rate of return (IRR), using figures for positive present value figures already calculated in **3** above.

M $10\% + \left(8\% \times \frac{687}{687 + 715}\right) = 13.92\%$

N $10\% + \left(8\% \times \frac{1{,}269}{1{,}269 + 131}\right) = 17.25\%$

P $10\% + \left(8\% \times \frac{1{,}571}{1{,}571 + 68}\right) = 17.67\%$

If used on its own, without reference to the other methods:

1 Accounting rate of return would choose project M, as it gives highest rate of 20 per cent.
2 Payback would choose project N, as it pays back in the shortest time of two years.
3 Net present value would choose project P, as it gives the highest net present value of £1,571.
4 Internal rate of return would choose project P, as it shows highest return of 17.67 per cent, which is itself higher than the cost of capital.

14.12 Merits and demerits of the techniques

Accounting rate of return

Although it is generally easy to calculate, ARR produces a percentage figure that is of little practical use. It cannot, for example, be compared to an organisation's cost of capital in order to assess whether a project would achieve a greater return than the cost of the capital that financed it. It also ignores the timing of cash flows – a project whose profits all arose at the start would be rejected in favour of one with a higher ARR whose profits all came at the end, even if inflation meant that those later period profits were worth significantly less in present value terms than the earlier profits of the rejected project.

Payback

This method is easy to calculate, and is also easy for anyone to understand. As it concentrates on cash flows in the near future many people will tend to accept it, as they are more wary when the cash flows several years hence are used in the other methods. This is because the further away the estimates of cash flows are the less accurate they will tend to be.

However, the method completely ignores the time value of money. It also ignores the cash flows received after the payback period has been reached.

There is no doubt that where there are severe cash flow problems the payback method will be more appealing than the more theoretically correct present value techniques.

Net present value

Theoretically this is the best method. It takes into account all the cash flows, the time value of money and the amounts involved.

Normally the IRR and the net present value method will rank the projects in the same order. For some rather complicated reasons which it is preferred not to consider here, the IRR does, in certain cases, give the wrong ranking compared with the net present value method.

Internal rate of return

This takes into account the time value of money and it is also easy for people to understand, as it is expressed as a percentage.

However, giving a return simply as a percentage can be misleading. Comparing a 50 per cent return which amounts to £100 with a 40 per cent return of £1,000 when just looking at the percentage figures alone, would not be very sensible.

14.13   Surveys of practice

The various surveys as to which techniques are used do vary somewhat, but there is a general picture available, although this varies between the UK and the USA.

1 Most firms use more than one method to evaluate an investment.
2 The payback method is that most frequently used, although it is less used in the USA than in the UK. The IRR method is the second most widely used method.
3 The use of both net present value method and IRR is growing, although the IRR is preferred by more firms than the superior NPV method. This seems to be because managers can understand the IRR method more easily than the NPV method.

It would appear that the popularity of the payback method is due to the fact that most firms place undue emphasis on the short term, such an outlook not being too conducive to DCF methods.

Before we look at any of the methods in use we should bear in mind that estimates concerning cash flows in the very near future are normally more accurate than those for several years ahead. We do know what is going on at the present time, probably there will not be too much change very quickly, but we cannot pretend that we can be so certain about cash flows in five or six years' time.

There are mathematical methods dealing with probability that can help with this sort of problem. They are, however, outside the scope of the A-level syllabuses and will not be included in this book.

EXHIBIT 14.6 Present value of £1

Year	1%	2%	3%	4%	5%	6%	7%	8%	9%	10%	12%	14%	15%
1	0.990	0.980	0.971	0.961	0.952	0.943	0.935	0.926	0.917	0.909	0.893	0.877	0.870
2	0.980	0.961	0.943	0.925	0.907	0.890	0.873	0.857	0.842	0.826	0.797	0.769	0.756
3	0.971	0.942	0.915	0.889	0.864	0.840	0.816	0.794	0.772	0.751	0.712	0.675	0.658
4	0.961	0.924	0.889	0.855	0.823	0.792	0.763	0.735	0.708	0.683	0.636	0.592	0.572
5	0.951	0.906	0.863	0.822	0.784	0.747	0.713	0.681	0.650	0.621	0.567	0.519	0.497
6	0.942	0.888	0.838	0.790	0.746	0.705	0.666	0.630	0.596	0.564	0.507	0.456	0.432
7	0.933	0.871	0.813	0.760	0.711	0.665	0.623	0.583	0.547	0.513	0.452	0.400	0.376
8	0.923	0.853	0.789	0.731	0.677	0.627	0.582	0.540	0.502	0.467	0.404	0.351	0.327
9	0.914	0.837	0.766	0.703	0.645	0.592	0.544	0.500	0.460	0.424	0.361	0.308	0.284
10	0.905	0.820	0.744	0.676	0.614	0.558	0.508	0.463	0.422	0.386	0.322	0.270	0.247
11	0.896	0.804	0.722	0.650	0.585	0.527	0.475	0.429	0.388	0.350	0.287	0.237	0.215
12	0.887	0.788	0.701	0.625	0.557	0.497	0.444	0.397	0.356	0.319	0.257	0.208	0.187
13	0.879	0.773	0.681	0.601	0.530	0.469	0.415	0.368	0.326	0.290	0.229	0.182	0.163
14	0.870	0.758	0.661	0.577	0.505	0.442	0.388	0.340	0.299	0.263	0.205	0.160	0.141
15	0.861	0.743	0.642	0.555	0.481	0.417	0.362	0.315	0.275	0.239	0.183	0.140	0.123
16	0.853	0.728	0.623	0.534	0.458	0.394	0.339	0.292	0.252	0.218	0.163	0.123	0.107
17	0.844	0.714	0.605	0.513	0.436	0.371	0.317	0.270	0.231	0.198	0.146	0.108	0.093
18	0.836	0.700	0.587	0.494	0.416	0.350	0.296	0.250	0.212	0.180	0.130	0.095	0.081
19	0.828	0.686	0.570	0.475	0.396	0.331	0.276	0.232	0.194	0.164	0.116	0.083	0.070
20	0.820	0.673	0.554	0.456	0.377	0.319	0.258	0.215	0.178	0.149	0.104	0.073	0.061
25	0.780	0.610	0.478	0.375	0.295	0.233	0.184	0.146	0.116	0.092	0.059	0.038	0.030
30	0.742	0.552	0.412	0.308	0.231	0.174	0.131	0.099	0.075	0.057	0.033	0.020	0.015

Year	16%	18%	20%	24%	28%	32%	36%	40%	50%	60%	70%	80%	90%
1	0.862	0.847	0.833	0.806	0.781	0.758	0.735	0.714	0.667	0.625	0.588	0.556	0.526
2	0.743	0.718	0.694	0.650	0.610	0.574	0.541	0.510	0.444	0.391	0.346	0.309	0.277
3	0.641	0.609	0.579	0.524	0.477	0.435	0.398	0.364	0.296	0.244	0.204	0.171	0.146
4	0.552	0.516	0.482	0.423	0.373	0.329	0.292	0.260	0.198	0.153	0.120	0.095	0.077
5	0.476	0.437	0.402	0.341	0.291	0.250	0.215	0.186	0.132	0.095	0.070	0.053	0.040
6	0.410	0.370	0.335	0.275	0.227	0.189	0.158	0.133	0.088	0.060	0.041	0.029	0.021
7	0.354	0.314	0.279	0.222	0.178	0.143	0.116	0.095	0.059	0.037	0.024	0.016	0.011
8	0.305	0.266	0.233	0.179	0.139	0.108	0.085	0.068	0.039	0.023	0.014	0.009	0.006
9	0.263	0.226	0.194	0.144	0.108	0.082	0.063	0.048	0.026	0.015	0.008	0.005	0.003
10	0.227	0.191	0.162	0.116	0.085	0.062	0.046	0.035	0.017	0.009	0.005	0.003	0.002
11	0.195	0.162	0.135	0.094	0.066	0.047	0.034	0.025	0.012	0.006	0.003	0.002	0.001
12	0.168	0.137	0.112	0.076	0.052	0.036	0.025	0.018	0.008	0.004	0.002	0.001	0.001
13	0.145	0.116	0.093	0.061	0.040	0.027	0.018	0.013	0.005	0.002	0.001	0.001	0.000
14	0.125	0.099	0.078	0.049	0.032	0.021	0.014	0.009	0.003	0.001	0.001	0.000	0.000
15	0.108	0.084	0.065	0.040	0.025	0.016	0.010	0.006	0.002	0.001	0.000	0.000	0.000
16	0.093	0.071	0.054	0.032	0.019	0.012	0.007	0.005	0.002	0.001	0.000	0.000	
17	0.080	0.060	0.045	0.026	0.015	0.009	0.005	0.003	0.001	0.000	0.000		
18	0.069	0.051	0.038	0.021	0.012	0.007	0.004	0.002	0.001	0.000	0.000		
19	0.060	0.043	0.031	0.017	0.009	0.005	0.003	0.002	0.000	0.000			
20	0.051	0.037	0.026	0.014	0.007	0.004	0.002	0.001	0.000	0.000			
25	0.024	0.016	0.010	0.005	0.002	0.001	0.000	0.000					
30	0.012	0.007	0.004	0.002	0.001	0.000	0.000						

Learning outcomes

You should now have learnt:

1 That as time passes, money loses value and this loss of value must be allowed for when considering long-term investments.

2 Net present value (NPV) and internal rate of return (IRR) usually lead to the same selection being made between mutually exclusive projects. When they differ, it is the NPV selection that should be followed.

3 Accounting rate of return (ARR) is still used, but the rate it produces cannot be compared to the cost of capital and the technique is not recommended.

4 How to calculate NPV, IRR, Payback and ARR.

5 The relative merits of the four methods.

6 What is meant by relevant and irrelevant costs.

7 What is meant by sunk cost.

8 How to select the 'best' project for an organisation to pursue at a given time from a range of possible alternative projects.

9 How to explain why, from a financial perspective, the selected project is the 'best' one for the organisation to pursue.

REVIEW QUESTIONS

Advice: The chances of your examinations containing a question on the appraisal of capital expenditure are quite high.

There will be occasions when you can bring in the factors other than financial ones which should be taken into account. This will gain you important marks, as examiners like to see answers which are not limited simply to computations. This is probably more true of A-level examinations than in some other accounting examinations. Study the points raised in Section 14.1. Also think about it and bring in some points of your own.

Make certain that you can manage the computations required in Questions 14.1 and 14.2X.

Make certain that you know Section 14.11, as the merits and demerits of the techniques used will often be asked.

When you see a set of net present value tables such as those in Exhibit 14.6, you will need to perform calculations such as those shown in Section 14.7.

The payback method, the net present value method and the internal rate of return are all concerned with cash inflows and outflows. Remember that depreciation is neither of these; it should be adjusted to remove it from the calculations. On the other hand, the accounting rate of return includes depreciation as an expense.

In an examination you may well be given the task of comparing two projects, one costing less than the other. Frequently the more expensive project will give a slightly greater net cash flow. The examiner may well expect you to point out that if the project costing less had been taken up, it could be possible that the return from that project plus income earned by investing the difference in initial costs could result in a greater return than that from the more costly project.

14.1 RST Ltd has to decide which one of three projects should be taken up. The following information is available:

● The initial investment would be £20,000, and the cost of capital is 8 per cent. There is no scrap value for the fixed assets used.

● The net cash inflows from the three projects are estimated as:

	F £	G £	H £
Year 1	10,000	6,000	8,000
Year 2	8,000	5,000	9,000
Year 3	7,000	5,000	5,000
Year 4		5,000	4,000
Year 5		6,000	
	25,000	27,000	26,000

In respect of each project you are required to calculate the following:
(*i*)   Accounting rate of return
(*ii*) Payback
(*iii*) Net present values
(*iv*) Internal rate of return.

14.2X   Doldrums Ltd is trying to decide which project should be taken up, out of three possible investments.

● The initial investment would amount to £30,000. Scrap value at end of use would be nil. Cost of capital is 9 per cent.
● The net cash inflows from the three projects under consideration are:

	N £	V £	Q £
Year 1	7,000	12,000	10,000
Year 2	6,000	12,000	10,000
Year 3	8,000	15,000	10,000
Year 4	10,000		11,000
Year 5	12,000		
	43,000	39,000	41,000

For each possible project you are required to calculate:

(*i*)   Accounting rate of return
(*ii*) Payback
(*iii*) Net present value
(*iv*) Internal rate of return.

14.3   Two years ago Sandstone Ltd conducted market research at a cost of £16,000 to investigate the potential market for new products. They are now considering two new product developments, only one of which will be undertaken. The anticipated profitabilities of these two separate projects A and B are given below.

	Project A £	Project A £	Project B £	Project B £
Annual sales		80,000		100,000
Cost of sales	40,000		50,000	
Administration costs	15,000		10,000	
Depreciation	5,000		10,000	
		60,000		70,000
Net profit		20,000		30,000

It is expected that the above will continue for each year of each project's forecast life. The capital cost for Project A is £45,000 and for Project B £53,000.

The expected economic lives are

Project A   8 years
Project B   5 years

Depreciation has been calculated on a straight-line basis, and assumes estimated scrap values of £5,000 for Project A at the end of Year 8, and £3,000 for Project B at the end of Year 5. All costs and revenue take place at the end of each year. The cost of capital is 12 per cent.

Extract from Present Value Table of £1 @ 12 per cent:

Year 1	0.893	Year 5	0.567
Year 2	0.797	Year 6	0.507
Year 3	0.712	Year 7	0.452
Year 4	0.636	Year 8	0.404

Required:

A Calculate the payback period and net present value of each project.   *(14 marks)*

B State, with reasoning, which of the two projects you would recommend.   *(3 marks)*

C Briefly explain why net present value is considered a more meaningful technique compared to payback when making capital expenditure decisions.   *(4 marks)*

D Explain how you have treated the original market research costs in relation to the evaluation of the projects.   *(2 marks)*

    (Total marks 23)

(OCR – University of Oxford Delegacy of Local Examinations: GCE A-level)

14.4X   Eastinteg plc, a major chemical company, had been invited to set up a plant in Eastern Europe in order to provide work in a region of high unemployment. The regional government also hoped that plant modernisation may be possible as well.

Eastinteg have the choice of two alternative plants:

(i) *Plant A.* A modern complex from Japan; highly efficient but expensive. Its capital cost is £85m.

Its expected annual output is:

20X3	20X4	20X5	20X6
Tonnes	Tonnes	Tonnes	Tonnes
30,000	36,000	41,500	80,000

This plant produces a high quality output and fetches the following prices on the open market.

	20X3	20X4	20X5	20X6
	£	£	£	£
Price per tonne	1,000	1,100	950	1,150

(ii) *Plant B.* This plant is manufactured locally in Eastern Europe and is relatively unsophisticated and inefficient. Many experts have reported that it pollutes the environment.

The plant will cost £45m, but since many regional government officials were keen to have locally provided plant, there would be a government grant for the initial capital cost of £20m.

In addition an annual subsidy would also be paid for the first four years of £5m per year. This is to offset some of the plant's running costs.

The expected annual output is:

	20X3 Tonnes	20X4 Tonnes	20X5 Tonnes	20X6 Tonnes
	26,000	28,000	27,000	60,000

The output quality of Plant B is relatively inferior to Plant A and is expected to fetch the following lower prices.

	20X3 £	20X4 £	20X5 £	20X6 £
Price per tonne	600	650	570	750

Additional information

(1) The forecast operating payments for the plants are as follows:

	Payments per tonne of output			
	20X3 £	20X4 £	20X5 £	20X6 £
Plant A	400	450	460	500
Plant B	450	500	500	550

(2) Both plants have an expected life of ten years, but it is known that Plant B becomes even less operationally efficient after six years.

(3) Whilst the East European regional government is aware of the pollutive effect of Plant B, it feels that pollution is so common in the region that the additional amount caused by this plant can be ignored.

(4) The company's cost of capital is 12 per cent per annum.

(5) It should be assumed that all costs are paid and all revenues received at the end of each year.

(6) The following is an extract from the present value table for £1:

	11%	12%	13%	14%
Year 1	£0.901	£0.893	£0.885	£0.877
Year 2	£0.812	£0.797	£0.783	£0.769
Year 3	£0.731	£0.712	£0.693	£0.675
Year 4	£0.659	£0.636	£0.613	£0.592

Required:

(*a*) The forecast revenue statements for each of the years 20X3–20X6 and for each of the plants being considered. Show the expected yearly net cash flows. *(8 marks)*

(*b*) Appropriate computations using the net present value method for each of the Plants A and B, for the first four years. *(6 marks)*

(*c*) A report providing a recommendation to the management of Eastinteg plc as to which plant should be purchased. Your report should include:
(*i*) a critical evaluation of the method used to assess the capital project;
(*ii*) a social accounting assessment of the effects of chemical pollution. *(11 marks)*

(AQA (AEB): GCE A-level)

14.5 Barchester United (a football club) is negotiating with an Italian club for the transfer of the noted player Luciano Gudshotti to the Barchester United team. It is now the start of the new season and you have been asked to advise on the financial aspects of the transfer negotiations.

The average home gate for Barchester is 30,000 people, 30 times a season and the spectator entrance fee is currently £2.50. The present team of 15 players earn on average a total of £6,000 per week (assume a 50-week year) and the existing team has cost £3,200,000 in transfer fees. At present and after all expenses, the Barchester United Football Club makes an annual profit of £150,000.

The directors consider that if an additional £240,000 is spent each year on new promotional activities and with Gudshotti in the team, it will be possible to increase the number of spectators to 33,000 per game and to raise the entrance fee to £3 per person. A new sponsorship deal to be agreed with a local company if Gudshotti joins the club would bring in an additional £50,000 a year in income.

The Italian club requires a transfer fee of £900,000 of which one half would have to be paid at once, and the balance payable equally in three annual instalments beginning at the end of year 1. Gudshotti requires a four-year contract paying him £50,000 a year plus a signing-on fee (payable at once on signing the contract) of £200,000. Additionally the rest of the team would expect a 20 per cent pay rise because more will be expected from the whole team in terms of performance.

The cost of capital to Barchester United is estimated to be 14 per cent and the club also expects a payback of not more than three years. You may assume that unless otherwise indicated all costs are to be paid and all revenues received at the end of each year and you are not required to consider the position beyond four years.

Required:

(a) Calculate the payback period over which the proposed expenditure will be recovered.

(5 marks)

(b) Calculate the net present value of the proposal using the discounted cash flow method.

(11 marks)

(c) Calculate the approximate internal rate of return of the proposal. *(6 marks)*

(d) Advise the directors as to whether or not they should sign Gudshotti and list two other factors which could have an effect on the decision. *(3 marks)*

Note: Table of present value factors:

Tn	$i = 14\%$	18%	22%	26%	30%
t0	1.000	1.000	1.000	1.000	1.000
t1	0.877	0.847	0.820	0.794	0.769
t2	0.769	0.718	0.672	0.630	0.592
t3	0.675	0.609	0.551	0.500	0.455
t4	0.592	0.516	0.451	0.397	0.350

The above table shows the present value of £1 when received at time tn, where n is the number of years before payment is received and i is the rate of interest used in discounting.

(OCR: from the University of Cambridge Local Examinations Syndicate)

14.6X Richards Chemicals Ltd currently disposes of its waste material by using waste skips (large refuse containers) located around its site. The company has ten skips on site, with each skip being able to hold 16m^3 of waste.

Each skip is only emptied when full, and there are an average of 12 collections in total for the company, each week throughout the year. The company pays a rental charge of £3 per day for each skip, and the collection charge for emptying is £10 per skip.

As part of its four-year plan from 1 January 20X3, the company is reviewing its waste disposal method, and wishes to evaluate alternatives. The amount of waste is expected to remain at current levels each year throughout the four-year period.

Option 1 - Current method

The current prices would remain fixed for the first two years (20X3 and 20X4), they would then be increased by 10 per cent and remain fixed for a further two years. All charges would be payable in arrears at the end of each year.

Option 2 - Waste Compactor

This would replace all skips on site, and waste would be put directly into a compactor (for compressing), and when full a collection would be made.

The price quoted from the supplier for a suitable compactor is £31,000, this including a delivery charge of £1,000. The full amount would be payable on 1 January 20X3.

The capacity of the compactor is the equivalent of $64m^3$ of waste, and the collection charge for emptying would be £17.50 per collection. This price would be fixed for the first two years, and would then be increased by 10 per cent and remain fixed for a further two years. These charges would be payable in arrears at the end of each year.

A maintenance contract would also be required, the charge is £500 p.a., payable in advance, and in addition to regular maintenance it includes all running costs throughout the year. The maintenance contract would be fixed in price for the first two years, but would increase by 10 per cent in year 3, with the new rate fixed until the end of the four-year period.

The compactor is expected to last four years, and would have a residual value of £400.

Option 3 - Gas Incinerator

This would again replace all skips on site, and would have the capacity to burn all the waste. The company had investigated this method in 20X0, and special gas pipes had been installed at a cost of £1,200. The project had been planned for the north end of the works overlooking a residential area. It did not continue at that time due to the possibility of toxic fumes and the concern of local residents. The new project would be located at the west end of the works overlooking open land and sports playing fields.

The price quoted from the supplier is £32,000, this includes a delivery charge of £1,000. The full amount would be payable on 1 January 20X3.

Installation of additional special gas pipes would cost £2,000. This would be payable on 1 January 20X3.

A maintenance contract would also be required, the charge is £500 p.a., payable in advance, and in addition to regular maintenance it includes the provision of smoke filters which would help reduce the smoke emissions given from the plant. The maintenance contract would be fixed in price for the first two years, but would increase by 10 per cent in year 3, with the new rate then fixed until the end of the four-year period.

The gas supply running costs would be £1,500 p.a., payable in arrears at the end of each year. These costs would be fixed for the first three years, but would then increase by 8 per cent in year 4.

The incinerator is expected to last four years and would not have any residual value at the end of the period.

One of the directors has already added up the various costs as listed, and states option 3 is the best.

The cost of capital for the company is 12 per cent.

Extract from Present Value Table of £1 @ 12%.

Year 1	0.893
Year 2	0.797
Year 3	0.712
Year 4	0.636
Year 5	0.567

Required:

A A net present value evaluation of each of the three options (all calculations are to be rounded to the nearest £). *(23 marks)*

B State with reasoning whether you agree with the comments of the director. What is your recommendation, giving brief reasons for your choice? *(3 marks)*

C (*i*) Outline the non-accounting factors which the company should consider when making its decision.

(*ii*) What measures could a government take to deal with any environmental concerns?
(5 marks)

(Total marks 31)

(OCR – University of Oxford Delegacy of Local Examinations: GCE A-level)

14.7 (*a*)

| | Capital structure | |
| | (£000) | |
	Ajax	Borg
Ordinary shares (16%)	700	300
Preference shares (14%)	200	200
Debentures (12%)	100	500

(*i*) Calculate the weighted average cost of capital for each of the companies above, on the assumption that debenture interest is an allowable expense against corporation tax, which stands at 40 per cent.

(*ii*) Explain fully the reasons for any differences in the weighted average cost of capital for the two companies. *(9 marks)*

(*b*) Ajax and Borg both have an opportunity to invest in project Cymberline which requires an initial investment of £300,000, and which is thought will generate the following net cash flows:

| | Cymberline |
	(£)
Year 1	55,000
Year 2	60,000
Year 3	145,000
Year 4	170,000

(*i*) What is the maximum cost of financing that can be considered when investing in this project?

(*ii*) From the information given, state with reasons whether you would advise either of the two companies to invest in Cymberline.

Note: Assume that the cash inflow arises at the end of each year. *(10 marks)*

| Present Value of 1 | | | | | |
	12%	13%	14%	15%	16%
Period 1	0.893	0.885	0.877	0.870	0.862
2	0.797	0.783	0.769	0.756	0.743
3	0.712	0.693	0.675	0.658	0.641
4	0.636	0.613	0.592	0.572	0.552

(London Qualifications Limited: GCE A-level)

14.8 The Grubby Brushes Co. Limited has the following capital structure:

	£000
Ordinary shares (fully paid)	1,000
Preference shares (11%)	400
Debentures (10%)	600

The holders of the ordinary shares expect a dividend of 14 per cent per annum. Debenture interest is an allowable charge against corporation tax which stands at 30 per cent.

The directors are considering the re-equipment of the production departments to enable the company to compete more effectively in overseas markets. Two schemes have been proposed, details of which are as follows:

	Scheme 1 £	Scheme 2 £
Initial capital cost	50,000	70,000
Estimated net cash flows:		
Year 1	14,000	14,000
Year 2	10,000	18,000
Year 3	19,000	27,000
Year 4	24,000	31,000

(a) Calculate the company's weighted average cost of capital (to nearest whole per cent).

(6 marks)

(b) Using your answer to (a) calculate the NPV (Net Present Value) of the two projects.

(8 marks)

(c) Using your answer to (b) state which project you would recommend and why. *(5 marks)*

(d) Would your answer to (c) be different if you knew that the estimated net cash flows for the two projects in year 5 were (Scheme 1) £23,000 and (Scheme 2) £32,000? Give your reasons.
(6 marks)

Discount Factors

	9%	10%	11%	12%	13%	14%	15%
Year 1	0.917	0.909	0.901	0.893	0.885	0.877	0.870
2	0.842	0.826	0.812	0.797	0.783	0.769	0.756
3	0.772	0.751	0.731	0.712	0.693	0.675	0.658
4	0.708	0.683	0.659	0.636	0.613	0.592	0.572
5	0.650	0.621	0.594	0.567	0.543	0.519	0.497

(London Qualifications Limited: GCE A-level)

14.9X Following a particularly stormy board meeting several of the directors are having a private conversation, on the following lines:

(i) The sales director says, 'I think someone has been stealing cash. We have been making reasonable profits but we now have a bank overdraft. Surely that's impossible.'

(ii) The production director says, 'I don't think we should charge anything for depreciation this year. The machinery is in perfect condition because we have spent a lot of money on maintenance.'

(iii) 'I am stuck with a lot of outdated and unusable computer equipment,' says the director of administration. 'However, the accountant won't let me scrap it as it still has a lot of book value.'

(iv) 'We badly need a new warehouse,' says the merchandising director. 'We have got over £2 million in our general reserve. We should take the cash out of that to buy a new warehouse.'

Comment on each of these statements.

14.10X A recent survey showed that in investment appraisal, the popularity of *payback* as an evaluation method continues to grow in spite of its known drawbacks. Of some 92 per cent of firms which use the method, approximately one half require its calculation for all projects.

(*a*) What are the main drawbacks to payback in investment appraisal? Briefly examine two other methods that overcome these disadvantages. *(8 marks)*

(*b*) Why do you think payback is so popular as a method as compared to the other methods you have examined in (*a*)? *(12 marks)*

(London Qualifications Limited: GCE A-level)

14.11X André Lefevre runs a car valeting business and now wishes to expand his operations into car hire. He is considering purchasing a small fleet of five identical cars. His accountant has provided him with the following information on each of the three models under consideration.

Model	Country of manufacture	Cost per car (£)
Armada	UK	7,000
Biarritz	Spain	12,000
Carioka	Japan	16,000

Additional information

(1) Dealers are prepared to allow the following discounts on the purchase of a fleet of five cars:

	%
Armada	5
Biarritz	10
Carioka	15

(2) Market research has indicated that likely demand for the hire of each fleet will yield the following total incomes per year:

	£
Armada	30,000
Biarritz	35,000
Carioka	44,000

(3) It is intended to sell the cars immediately at the end of three years. Estimated selling prices for each car then being:

	£
Armada	2,500
Biarritz	5,000
Carioka	7,000

(4) Insurance premiums are to be paid at the start of each year and are expected to rise over the next three years. Insurance for each fleet is expected to cost:

	Year 1 £	Year 2 £	Year 3 £
Armada	7,000	8,050	9,257
Biarritz	9,000	10,350	11,902
Carioka	10,500	12,075	13,886

(5) Servicing and fuel charges are also expected to rise over the next three years. Servicing and fuel charges for each fleet are expected to cost:

	Year 1	Year 2	Year 3
	£	£	£
Armada	4,050	4,155	4,270
Biarritz	5,400	5,520	5,652
Carioka	6,700	6,870	7,057

(6) All cash flows except insurance arise at the end of the relevant year.

(7) The rate of interest applicable is 12% per annum.

(8) The following extract is from the present value table for £1:

Year	12%
1	0.893
2	0.797
3	0.712

Required:

(*a*) A financial statement using the net present value method for **each** fleet of cars being considered. (Workings to the nearest pound.) *(35 marks)*

(*b*) A report for André Lefevre advising him which fleet of cars should be purchased. Indicate any reservations you may have regarding the net present value method of evaluating a project. *(7 marks)*

(*c*) A discussion of any other factors which may influence André in his decision. *(8 marks)*

(AQA (AEB): GCE A-level)

14.12X Study the passage below and then answer the questions which follow.

'. . . The Government should make auditors produce a standardised set of accounts on a single piece of paper aimed at shareholders – not finance directors. This would force all companies to report their profits on a common definition with suitable comparisons for previous years accompanied by a series of performance indicators like return on capital employed, profit margins, money spent on capital investment, research and development and so on.' (from an editorial in *The Guardian* newspaper)

(*a*) The author of this article appears to have made a fundamental error regarding the role of an *auditor* in relation to company accounting. What is the error? *(4 marks)*

(*b*) Explain how each of the four '*performance indicators*' mentioned in the article would assist shareholders in interpreting their company's financial results. *(12 marks)*

(*c*) Explain the significance of *Companies Act Formats* in helping to standardise company accounting. (You are *not* required to reproduce the formats as part of your answer.) *(4 marks)*

(London Qualifications Limited (University of London): GCE A-level)

CHAPTER 15

Other factors affecting decision making – social accounting

15.1 Introduction

Over time, the objective of financial statements has changed. In addition to reporting to shareholders of the company, directors are aware of a wide range of other user groups who are interested in accounting information. These user groups include employees of the company and, more controversially, the public at large. The controversy arises when considering whether or not organisations are responsible for 'social actions', that is, actions which do not have purely financial implications.

15.2 Costs and measurement

One of the problems associated with actions of this type is the difficulty of identifying costs and measuring the effects of (often intangible) factors that contribute to the 'value' of an organisation. It is obvious that employee loyalty and commitment to quality performance increase this value, but how are such intangibles to be measured using objective and verifiable techniques?

Some of the input costs of 'social' activities can be evaluated reasonably accurately. Providing 'social' information required under the 1985 Companies Act is not particularly difficult – it requires information regarding employees to be presented in the accounts, including numbers of employees, wages and salaries data, and details regarding the company's policy on disabled persons. Also, even where 'social' actions are required by legislation, they can often be costed reasonably accurately. For example, there are a large number of European Community directives which have been implemented in the UK relating to social and environmental policies, including the monitoring and control of air and water pollution.

The costs of complying with these disclosure requirements and operational control measures can be high and, as the numbers of regulations increase, these costs will become a basic and essential part of financial statements. It will become increasingly important that not only the costs are reported, but also the benefits, and this is where the difficulties arise – how can the benefits of controlling pollution from a factory be evaluated? Indeed, should an attempt be made to evaluate them at all? Would they be better reported in qualitative or non-financial quantitative terms?

As soon as a company seeks to incorporate social criteria alongside other more traditional performance measures, problems of objectivity, comparability and usefulness arise. For example, social criteria for a paper manufacturer may include environmental issues concerning reforestation. An oil extraction company would include the environmentally safe disposal of oil rigs at the end of their useful economic lives among its social criteria.

However, issues of this type become problematic when viewed using conventional capital appraisal techniques. Not only may the measurable financial payback be so long as to be immaterial – as in the case of an environmental project such as reforestation – it may be virtually non-existent, as in the case of the disposal of obsolete oil rigs. Assessment of issues of this type require different techniques from those traditionally used, and organisations' accounting information systems will need to take this into account, not just in terms of using more qualitative value criteria, but also in selecting the information which is sought in order to assist in the decision-making process.

15.3 The pressure for social actions and social accounting

Despite the existence of many environmental laws, much of the pressure for social actions comes from pressure groups like Greenpeace. These groups can have an enormous impact upon an organisation's profitability, in ways that governments have singularly failed to do. For example, an air pollution law may concentrate on monitoring the quality of air around a factory, rather than on measuring emissions from the factory, making it far more difficult to enforce action against the factory as it can always argue that another factory is the cause of any pollution found. Also, powerful cartels can influence legislation to create enormous delays in introducing socially responsible legislative controls. A pressure group, on the other hand, can stop demand for a company's products, or make it difficult for it to send its products to its customers, and may give it so much negative publicity that it can find its public image materially and irreversibly altered in a very short time.

While pressure groups are not a new phenomenon, their power is now far greater than it has ever been. Organisations need to be aware of the social, particularly environmental, issues inherent in and/or related to their activities, and must be in a position to assess how best to approach these issues. They can only do so if they identify all the variables, both quantitative and qualitative, and both the inputs (costs) and the outputs (effects) of these variables, and determine methods with which to determine what actions to take. Social accounting is concerned with how to report upon the application of the social policies adopted by an organisation, and upon how they have impacted upon the organisation and its environment. An organisation that does so effectively will not only be providing user groups with rich information from which to form a view concerning its social ethos, but also be enhancing its ability to take decisions appropriate for its own longer-term survival and prosperity.

15.4 Corporate social reporting

The reporting of the social effects of a company's activities became an issue in the UK in the 1970s. The reporting of non-financial information usually takes the form of narrative disclosure, sometimes supported by a statistical summary. As much social reporting is non-mandatory, comparison with other companies is difficult, if not virtually pointless and misleading. This is partially due to a positive bias in what is reported – most companies tend to report only 'good news' in their social reports. It is also due to the lack of standards governing what to include and how to present social reports.

Environmental issues have been firmly on the political agenda since the early 1980s and large corporations have responded to public demands for more information about 'green issues'. Oil companies, in particular, produce a notable amount of additional information in their annual reports. This environmental information usually includes details about the company's waste disposal practices, attitudes towards pollution and natural resource depletion, as well as the overall corporate environmental policy. However, many continue to avoid any non-mandatory social reporting, and many instances have been reported of organisations claiming to be socially responsible, when they were, in fact, anything but.

15.5 Types of social accounting

Social accounting can be divided into five general areas:

- national social income accounting;
- social auditing;
- financial social accounting in profit-oriented organisations;
- managerial social accounting in profit-oriented organisations;
- financial and/or managerial social accounting for non-profit organisations.

15.6 National social income accounting

Such accounts have now been in existence for many years. The measure of the nation's productivity recorded in the accounts – basically in sales terms – gives a figure called the Gross National Product, usually referred to as GNP.

To an outsider an increase in GNP would seem to indicate a betterment or progress in the state of affairs existing in the country. This is not necessarily true. The following example illustrates this point.

A new chemical factory is built in a town. Fumes are emitted during production which cause houses in the surrounding areas to suffer destruction of paintwork and rotting woodwork, and it also causes extensive corrosion of bodywork on motor vehicles in the neighbourhood. In addition it also affects the health of the people living nearby. An increase in GNP results because the profit elements in the above add to GNP. These profit elements include:

- to construction companies and suppliers of building materials: profit made on construction of plant;
- to house paint dealers and paint manufacturers, painters and decorators, joiners and carpenters: profit made on all work needed for extra painting, woodwork, etc.;

- to garages and car paint manufacturers: profit made on all extra work needed on motor vehicles;
- to chemists and medical requirement manufacturers: profit made on dealing with effects on residents' health, because of extra medical purchases, etc.

However, in real terms one can hardly say that there has been 'progress'. Obviously the quality of life has been seriously undermined for many people.

As national income accounts do not record the 'social' well-being of a country, other national measures have been proposed. The one most often mentioned is a system of 'social indicators'. These measure social progress in such ways as:

- national life expectancies;
- living conditions;
- levels of disease;
- nutritional levels;
- amount of crime;
- road deaths.

Thus if national life expectancies rose, or road deaths per 100,000 people decreased, etc. there could be said to be social progress, while the converse would apply were the opposite signals found to be occurring.

The main difficulty with this approach is that (given present knowledge and techniques) it cannot be measured in monetary terms. Because of this, the national social income accounts cannot be adjusted to take account of social indicators. On the level of an individual organisation, however, social indicators similar to the above are used in planning, programming, budgeting systems (PPBS). This will be discussed later.

15.7 Social auditing

While national social accounting would measure national social progress, many individual people or organisations are interested in their own social progress. This form of social progress is usually called 'social responsibility'.

To discover which of their activities have to be measured a 'social audit' is required. This is an investigation into:

(a) which of their activities contribute to, or detract from, being socially responsible;
(b) measurement of those activities;
(c) a report on the results disclosed by the investigation.

An example of this might be to discover how the organisation had performed in respect of such matters as:

- employment of women;
- employment of disabled people;
- occupational safety;
- occupational health;
- benefits at pensionable age;
- air pollution;
- water pollution;
- charitable activities;
- help to third world countries.

Social audits may be carried out by an organisation's own staff or by external auditors. The reports may be for internal use only or for general publication.

15.8 Financial social accounting in profit-oriented organisations

This is an extension to normal financial accounting. The objective may either be to show how the social actions have affected financial performance, or otherwise to put a social value on the financial statements of the organisations. The two main types of financial social accounting envisaged to date are those of human resource accounting and how the organisation has responded to governmental or professional bodies' regulations concerning environmental matters.

Human resource accounting

One of the main limitations of normal financial accounting is the lack of any inclusion of the 'value' of the workforce to an organisation. The value may be determined by:

- capitalising recruitment and training costs of employees and apportioning value over employees' period of employment; or
- calculating the 'replacement cost' of the workforce and taking this as the value of human resources; or
- extending either of the above to include the organisation's suppliers and customers.

It is contended that such measurements have the benefits that (a) financial statements are more complete, and (b) managerial decisions can be made with a fuller understanding of their implications.

For instance, suppose that a short-term drop in demand for a firm's goods led to a manufacturer laying off part of the workforce. This might mean higher profits in the short term because of wages and salaries saved. In the long term it could do irreparable damage, because recruitment could then be made difficult in future, or because of the effect on the morale of the rest of the workforce, or changes in attitudes of suppliers and customers.

Compliance costs of statutory/professional requirements

As the effects of organisations upon societies are more widely recognised there will be more and more regulations with which to comply. The costs of compliance will obviously then become a basic and essential part of financial statements.

15.9 Managerial social accounting in profit-oriented organisations

All that has been described above has an effect upon the accounting information systems of an organisation. They will have to be established on an ongoing basis, rather than be based purely on adjustments to the financial accounts at the year end.

The information will affect the day-to-day decisions needed to run the organisation.

15.10 Financial and/or managerial social accounting for non-profit organisations

As profit is not a measure in these organisations it can be difficult to measure how well they are performing. Two approaches to measurement have been used, **planning, programming, budgeting systems (PPBS)**, and **social programme measurement**.

Both of these approaches can be said to be part of what politicians in recent years have called 'value for money'. The general attitude is that while there may be a need for all sorts of social programmes, including health, there is a great need for ensuring that money is not wasted in providing them. The demand is that we should ensure that we get 'value for money' in that the outputs from such schemes should be worth the amount of money expended in carrying them out.

Planning, programming, budgeting systems (PPBS)

It has been said that in the past there was a great deal of confusion between planning and budgeting. Annual budgeting takes a short-term financial view. Planning on the other hand should be long term and also be concerned with strategic thinking.

PPBS gives management of non-profit organisations a better-informed basis on which to make decisions about the allocation of resources to achieve their overall objectives. PPBS works in four stages:

1 Review organisational objectives.
2 Identify programmes to achieve objectives.
3 Identify and evaluate alternative ways of achieving each specific programme.
4 On the basis of cost-benefit principles, select appropriate programme.

PPBS necessitates the drawing up of a long-term corporate plan. This shows the objectives which the organisation is aiming to achieve. Such objectives may not be in accord with the existing organisational structure.

For instance, suppose that the objective of a local government authority, such as a city, is the care of the elderly. This could include providing:

● services to help them keep fit;
● medical services when they are ill;
● old people's housing;
● 'sheltered' accommodation;
● recreational facilities;
● educational facilities.

These services will usually be provided by separate departments, e.g. housing, welfare, education. PPBS relates the total costs to the care of the elderly, rather than to individual departmental budgets.

Management is therefore forced by PPBS to identify exactly which services or activities should be provided, otherwise the worthiness of the programme could not be evaluated. PPBS also provides information which enables management to assess the effectiveness of their plans, such as giving them a base to decide whether for every thousand pounds they are giving as good a service as possible.

As the structure of the programme will not match up with the structure of the organisation, e.g. the services provided will cut across departmental borders, one particular individual must be made responsible for controlling and supervising the programme.

Social programme measurement

The idea that governmental social programmes should be measured effectively is, as yet, in its infancy.

A government auditor would determine whether the agency had complied with the relevant laws, and had exercised adequate cost controls. The auditor would determine whether or not the results expected were being achieved and whether there were alternatives to the programmes at a lower cost.

There should be cost–benefit analyses to show that the benefits are worth the costs they incur. However, the benefit side of the analysis is often very difficult to measure. How, for instance, do you measure the benefits of not dumping a particular substance or an obsolete oil rig into the sea?

As a consequence, so far most social programmes do not yet measure results (benefits). Instead they measure 'outputs', e.g. how many prosecutions for dumping waste. Therefore, a high number of prosecutions is 'good', a low number 'bad'. This is hardly a rational way of assessing results, and quite a lot of research is going into better methods of audit.

15.11 Conflict between shareholders' interests and social considerations

Obviously, an organisation has to come to a compromise about how far it should look after the interests of its shareholders and how far it should bother about social considerations. For instance, a company could treat its employees so well in terms of pay, pensions and welfare that the extra costs would mean very low profits or even losses.

On the other hand there must be instances when, no matter what the effects on profits, the expenses just have to be incurred. If the company has a chemical plant which could easily explode, causing widespread destruction and danger to people, then there cannot be any justification for not spending the money either to keep the plant safe or to demolish it. The full severity of the law must bear down on transgressors of the law in such cases of wilful neglect.

All the facts of the particular case must be brought into account. Let us look at a typical case where the answer may seem obvious, but perhaps there may be other factors which may make the answer not so obvious. Workers in underdeveloped countries are usually paid far lower wages than those in the developed countries. What happens if a large multinational company pays its workers in a given country three or four times as much as home-based companies? Immediately everyone wants to work for the multinational company, which can afford high wages, and leave the home-based companies which cannot. Is that sensible? What chance is there for the development of the country's own home-based industries if the outside companies constantly take all the best brains and most able people?

In such a case it would probably make more sense for the multinational company to pay wages more in keeping with the particular economy, and to help that country in other ways such as by improving the health care generally for all, better education for all, and so on. Obviously a topic such as this will engender discussions and arguments for some considerable time.

15.12 Reports from companies

Companies, mainly those in the USA at first, have begun to declare their philosophy towards such matters as the environment. Such statements are usually included in the annual reports which accompany the accounts.

For example, a company may have decided to have the following ten principles of environmental policy:

1 To comply with both governmental and community standards of environmental excellence.
2 To use only materials and packaging selected to be good for the health of consumers, and for the safety and quality of the environment.
3 To keep energy use per unit of output down to a low level.
4 To minimise waste.
5 To get the discharge of pollutants to as low a level as possible.
6 To use other firms in business which have shown commitment to environmental excellence.
7 To research fully the ecological effect of the company's products and packaging.
8 To carry on business operations in an open, honest and co-operative manner.
9 To make certain that on the board of directors there would be scientifically knowledgeable directors, and ensure that they were provided with environmental reports regularly.
10 To ensure that all the above principles are fully observed and that challenges posed by the environment are vigorously and effectively pursued.

Learning outcomes

You should now have learnt:

- What is 'social accounting'.
- About the implications of social accounting for the accounting function.
- Five general areas of social accounting.
- Some of the difficulties in the measurement of qualitiative factors.
- About the conflict between the shareholders' interests and social considerations.
- About the extent to which social accounting is becoming part of company reporting.

REVIEW QUESTIONS

Advice: Social accounting is as yet in its infancy. There is obviously a great difficulty in trying to put money values on the various aspects of being 'better off' or 'worse off'. There are also problems connected with exactly what 'better off' and 'worse off' means. One person's 'worsening' in some way may be someone else's 'betterment'.

15.1 Describe how an increase in Gross National Product may not have a positive effect on the well-being of the country.

15.2 What types of measures could be used to measure social well-being? What difficulties would be discovered in trying to use accounting in measuring these?

15.3 What aspects of an organisation's activities could be measured in a 'social audit'?

15.4 Describe how there could be conflicts between short-term and long-term benefits.

15.5 Describe how PPBS may conflict with departmental budgets.

15.6X The Board of Directors of a multinational chemical producing company are considering the final accounts for the year and are discussing the emphasis to be made in the Annual Report.

- The Financial Director claims that the main features should be the 20% increase in both the profit after tax and earnings per share plus the record dividend payout.
- The Production Director wants to highlight the massive amounts of capital expenditure this year on safety improvements at one of the chemical plants in Scotland. The plant had previously come under severe public pressure due to the potential health hazards to the local population.
- The Human Resources Director is concerned about the alarming increase in the rate of labour turnover. The trade unions claim that 20% of their workforce earn well below the European average.
- The Managing Director reminds the Board of the significant donations the company has made this year to overseas aid in the countries where they had previously been criticised for the exploitation of cheap labour.

(*a*) Suggest the ways in which companies are likely to experience conflicts between managing shareholders' interests and companies' social responsibilities. *(10 marks)*

(*b*) What might be the consequences for this company if it fails to address these issues?
(10 marks)
(Total 20 marks)

(AQA (NEAB): GCE A-level)

Part 4

MANAGEMENT ACCOUNTING PRINCIPLES AND BUDGETING

16 Elements of costing

17 Contract accounts

18 Job, batch and process costing

19 Budgeting and budgetary control

20 Cash budgets

21 Co-ordination of budgets

Elements of costing

16.1 Costs for different purposes

Cost accounting is needed so that there can be an effective management accounting system. Without a study of costs, such a system could not exist. Before entering into any detailed description of costs it is better if we ask ourselves first what use we are going to make of information about costs in the business.

This can best be done by referring to something which is not accounting, and then relating it to accounting. Suppose that your employer asked you to measure the distance between Manchester and London, but walked away from you without giving any further information. As you thought about this request the following thoughts might go through your head:

1 *HOW* is the distance to be measured? Some possibilities are:
   - from the southern outskirts of Manchester to the northern outskirts of London
   - from the accepted geographical centre of London to the accepted geographical centre of Manchester
   - to the centres of the two cities calculated as mathematically precise points
   - by road; this could be just major roads, just minor roads, or either major or minor roads with the main requirement being the quickest route by road
   - by canal

- by air; allowance may or may not be made for the distance covered by the aircraft which would include climbing to an altitude of 5,000 feet or perhaps 40,000 feet, or might ignore the distance travelled in achieving an altitude.

2 The *COST* of obtaining the information. Measuring distances (or measuring costs) is not costless itself. Using very sophisticated instruments to get accurate measurement can be very expensive indeed. On the other hand it might just be a matter of measuring the distance on a map with a rule and converting it into miles – this would cost hardly anything at all.

3 What is the *PURPOSE* for which the measurement will be used? This has been deliberately left as the last point but, in fact, it should have been the first question that came into your mind. Illustrations of the use could have been as follows:
- he is going to drive from Manchester to London by car and wants a rough idea of the mileage so that he can gauge what time to set off if he is to arrive before it goes dark in London
- he might conceivably want to walk it
- perhaps he wants to send goods by canal
- he might be an amateur pilot who wants to fly from Manchester Airport to London Airport
- he might be submitting a tender for the building of a motorway by the shortest possible route, cutting tunnels through ranges of hills.

The lesson to be learnt from this is that measurement depends entirely on the use that is to be made of the data. Far too often firms make measurements of financial and other data without looking first at the use that is going to be made of the data. In fact it could be said that 'information' is useful data that are provided for someone.

Data given to someone which are not relevant to the purpose required are just not information. Data which are provided for a particular purpose, and which are completely wrong for the purpose, are worse than having no data at all. At least when there are no data managers know that they are making a guess. When useless data are collected they first of all cost money to collect, in itself a waste of money; secondly they often are taken to be useful data and mislead managers into taking steps which are completely wrong and would not have happened if they had relied instead on their own hunches; thirdly, such data clog up the communication system within a firm, so that other data are not acted on properly because of the general confusion that has been caused.

How is all this reflected in a study of costs?

1 What are the data on costs wanted for? They might be needed for the financial accounts, for management control or for decision making. Different sets of data on costs are wanted for different purposes.

2 How are the costs to be measured? Only when the purpose for which the costs are to be used has been decided can the measurement process be decided. Financial accounting, for instance, needs a certain precision in calculating costs which is often not needed in management accounting, where sometimes the nearest thousand pounds will be good enough for the purpose.

3 The cost of obtaining costing data should not exceed the benefits to be gained from having such data. This does not refer to some cost data which are needed to comply with various provisions of the law. We can, however, look at several cases to illustrate the cost–benefit factor:

- Spending £100 to obtain costs which will be used as a basis for pricing many of the products of the firm. If the costs had been 'guessed' an error could have meant large losses for the firm.
- Spending £10,000 to find data on sales which the sales manager will toss into the wastebasket, because they are not the sorts of data he wants, is obviously money wasted.
- Spending a lot of time and money to find out that the stock values on a particular day were £2,532,198, when such precision was not needed. Perhaps the chairman was having a general chat with the bank manager, and all he needed to know was an approximate figure for stock of £2,500,000. The approximate figure could have been found easily and at little cost, so here costs have exceeded benefits.

When it is known what the costs are for, and how much is to be spent on studying them, the appropriate method for measuring them can be decided.

16.2 Past costs in trading companies

Past costs – more commonly called 'historic costs' – are part of the ordinary financial accounting done in firms. Exhibit 16.1 shows costs flowing through financial accounts.

EXHIBIT 16.1 Costs flowing through financial accounts

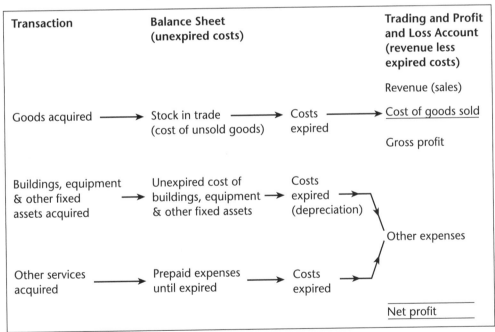

16.3 Past costs in manufacturing companies

You have probably already covered the topic of manufacturing accounts earlier in your studies. In this chapter we will examine some of the detailed aspects of them a little further, as this is essential for a study of costing.

Exhibit 16.2 shows costs flowing through a manufacturing company.

EXHIBIT 16.2 Costs flowing through a manufacturing company

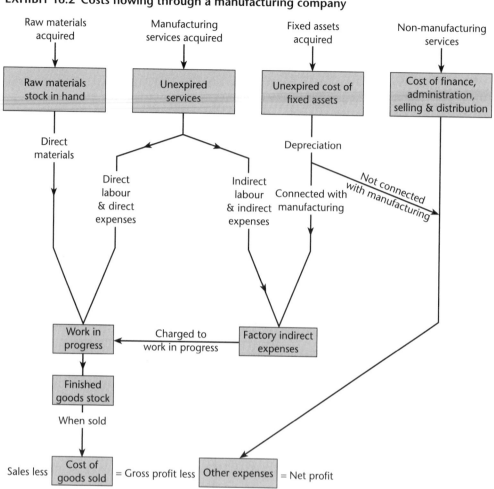

The following is a more detailed description of costs than you will have encountered previously.

● *Direct materials* are those materials which become part of the finished goods, subject to the proviso that the expense involved in tracing the cost is worthwhile. Some items, usually of insignificant amounts, are treated as indirect materials even though they are part of the finished product because the cost cannot be ascertained easily.

● *Direct labour* means those labour costs which are applied to convert the direct materials into the finished goods, also subject to the proviso that the expense involved in tracing this cost is worthwhile.

● *Direct expenses* are those expenses which can be traced directly to the product being manufactured. These are fairly rare, but an instance would be a royalty where the production of each item resulted in, say, £1 being due to the owner of a patent.

● *Prime cost*: The total of Direct materials + Direct labour + Direct expenses is called prime cost.

Naturally there will be disagreement between accountants as to whether certain costs are worth tracing. As some costs are of a direct type, it will often be a matter of judgement which defies any easy proof whether or not the expense of tracing the cost exceeds the benefit from so doing. You should by now be used to the idea in accounting that disagreement often occurs, which can only be settled by a compromise or appeal to someone in higher authority to settle the argument. This obviously relates to many things in accounting besides the decision as to whether an item is of a direct type or not.

● *Factory indirect expenses or manufacturing overheads* are all those other expenses concerned with the manufacturing process which have not been treated as of the direct type. Because there is no easily traceable direct connection with the goods being manufactured these costs must be apportioned between the goods being manufactured in a logical fashion.

● *Production cost*: The total of Prime cost + Factory indirect expenses is called production cost.

● *Administration, selling and distribution and finance expenses* are common to both trading and manufacturing firms.

● *Total cost*: If we add together production cost and administration, selling and distribution, and finance expenses, the resultant figure is known as total cost. To summarise:

	Direct materials
ADD	Direct labour
ADD	Direct expenses
Gives:	PRIME COST
ADD	Factory indirect expenses
Gives:	PRODUCTION COST
ADD	Administration expenses
ADD	Selling and distribution expenses
ADD	Finance expenses
Gives:	TOTAL COST.

Exhibit 16.3 is a list of typical types of expenses found in a manufacturing firm. These can be classified as direct materials, direct labour, direct expenses, factory indirect expenses, administration expenses, selling and distribution expenses, or finance expenses. See how well you can do yourself by covering up the right-hand column with a piece of paper, then sliding your paper down to reveal one answer at a time after you have mentally analysed it yourself.

EXHIBIT 16.3

	Cost	Cost analysis
1	Raw materials for goods – identifiable with product made	Direct materials
2	Rent of factory buildings	Factory indirect expenses
3	Sales staff salaries	Selling and distribution
4	Wages of machine operators in factory	Direct labour
5	Wages of workers in office	Administration expenses
6	Depreciation of lathes in factory	Factory indirect expenses

Continued

7	Depreciation of computers in office	Administration expenses
8	Depreciation of fixtures in sales showrooms	Selling and distribution expenses
9	Supervisors' wages in factory	Factory indirect expenses
10	Royalty paid for each item manufactured	Direct expenses
11	Works manager's salary: he reckons that he spends $3/4$ of his time in the factory and $1/4$ in general administration of the firm	$3/4$ Factory indirect expenses $1/4$ Administration expenses
12	Raw materials incorporated in goods sold, but too difficult to trace to the goods being made	Indirect expenses
13	Depreciation of motor vehicles used for delivery of finished goods to customers	Selling and distribution expenses
14	Interest on bank overdraft	Finance expenses
15	Wages of crane drivers in factory	Factory indirect expenses
16	Discounts allowed	Finance expenses
17	Company secretary's salary	Administration expenses
18	Advertising	Selling and distribution expenses
19	Wages of staff of canteen used by factory staff only	Factory indirect expenses
20	Cost of hiring special machinery for use in manufacturing one special item	Direct expenses

16.4 Product costs and period costs

Product costs are those costs which are allocated to the units of goods manufactured. In fact product costs make up production cost. Such costs are charged up to the cost of goods manufactured in the trading account, and would normally be part of the valuation of unsold goods if the goods to which they refer had not been sold by the end of the period. Product costs are therefore matched up against revenue as and when the goods are sold and not before.

Period costs are those of a non-manufacturing nature and represent the selling and distribution, administration and financial expenses. They are treated as expenses of the period in which they were incurred irrespective of the volume of goods sold.

16.5 Advantages of a costing system

You have now looked at the various elements of cost as far as the whole of the firm is concerned. Such a classification of costs is necessary so that the overall production cost can be ascertained in the case of a manufacturing company with its effect on the valuation of the closing stock of finished goods and of work in progress. What most businesses want to know is how much each item has cost to make. This means that the total costs for the whole firm are not sufficient, and so these costs must be analysed further.

Any costing system must bring about the better control of the firm in guiding it towards its objectives, and the benefits to be derived from the costing system must be greater than the expense of operating the costing system. We must, therefore, look at the possible advantages to be gained in carrying on further analyses of cost:

(*a*) Because expenditure is traced down to each item produced, or each batch of items, it becomes possible to ascertain the contribution of each item to the profitability of the business. The desirability of stopping unprofitable activities can then be assessed.

(b) Once the profitability of each item is known, the reasons for increases or decreases in profits can be seen more clearly.

(c) It becomes easier to forecast future results if we know more about the operations of all the various parts of the business. When forecasted results are not achieved it becomes possible to highlight the reasons for the failure to achieve the forecasted results.

(d) Estimates and tenders can be prepared in future with far greater confidence – previously such calculations as were done must have been largely guesswork. Fewer errors should be made because of the greater knowledge gained via the costing system.

(e) Improvements in various activities of the firm may come about because of the more relevant information that can be supplied. Thus a machine which had always been thought to be quite cheap to use may turn out to be very expensive to use. This may bring about an investigation which would not otherwise have happened, and it may consequently be found that a simple attachment to the machine costing £10 brings about a saving of £100 a year.

(f) As we will see, a very important advantage is the control of expenditure, and it can be achieved because an individual can be made responsible for the expenditure under his/her control.

The possible advantages which can be gained from having a costing system can be seen to be quite considerable. It is, however, now a convenient point to remind you that accounting techniques themselves do not solve problems. Instead it is people within the organisation who, when armed with the information that accounting techniques can provide, are far more able to make sensible decisions about what should be done to aid the progress of the firm towards its objectives.

Imagine trying to decide which item to stop producing out of 12 items made by a firm if you have little information as to the contribution of each item towards the profitability of the firm. Very often the solution will be a new layout in the factory, special training given to certain employees, changes made in the system of remunerating employees, and so on. The information provided by accounting is, therefore, only one part of the whole story for any problem. It is important to remember that often it will be the least important information available to the decision taker.

16.6 The control of costs

One of the most important features of cost accounting is its use for control purposes, meaning in this context the control of expenditure. But control of expenditure is possible only if you can trace the costs down to employees who are responsible for such costs. A convenient area for collecting costs is called a 'cost centre'. In a manufacturing firm all direct materials, direct labour and direct expenses are traced to cost centres; in this case they would be known as 'product centres'. A product centre may be, for example, a single machine used for jobbing work, i.e. where quite a lot of separate jobs are performed specially to conform with the customer's specifications. It could, alternatively, be a group of similar machines or a production department.

By comparison factory indirect expenses by definition, i.e. because they are 'indirect' expenses, cannot be traced (or it is not worthwhile tracing them) to product centres.

These are traced to cost centres which give service rather than being concerned with work directly on the products, and such cost centres are, therefore, known as 'service centres'. Examples of service centres would be the factory canteen or the maintenance department. The costs from these service centres will then need allocating to the product centres in a logical fashion.

In practice there are a number of possible ways of allocating costs to cost centres. What must not be lost sight of is the endeavour to trace costs to a person responsible for the expenditure so that the costs can be controlled.

16.7 Costing: manufacturing firms compared with retailing or wholesale firms

It is quite wrong to think that costing is concerned only with manufacturing firms. Both textbooks and examination papers often give the impression that only in manufacturing is costing needed or found. This is quite incorrect, as costing is just as relevant to retailing and wholesaling firms, service industries and not-for-profit organisations as it is to those in manufacturing. It is simply that manufacturing, which usually has more complex sorts of activities because of the manufacturing element, has attracted greater attention than other types of firms. There are, in addition, many other forms of organisations such as farming, shipping, banking and even charitable organisations where costing can aid management control. It would indeed be difficult to find any organisation which could not use some form of costing system profitably.

Learning outcomes

You should now have learnt:

1 Cost accounting is needed for there to be an effective management accounting system.

2 The benefits of operating a costing system should always outweigh the costs of operating it.

3 To be useful, information must be fit for the purpose for which it is to be used.

4 When it is known what costs are for, and how much is to be spent on studying them, the appropriate method for measuring them can be decided.

5 In the case of a manufacturing company, classifying costs appropriately is necessary so that the overall production cost can be ascertained and so enable appropriate valuation of the closing stock of finished goods and of work in progress.

6 Accounting techniques themselves do not solve problems; it is people within the organisation who, when armed with the information that accounting techniques can provide, are far more able to make sensible decisions about what should be done to aid the progress of the organisation towards its objectives.

7 Appropriate cost allocation is very important for control.

8 When costs are assigned to an individual cost centre, they are 'allocated'; when they are assigned to two or more cost centres, they are 'apportioned'.

REVIEW QUESTIONS

Advice: This chapter is basically for background information. There have not been any recent A-level questions concerned simplyn with the contents of this chapter.

16.1 Analyse the following costs between:
(i) Direct materials
(ii) Direct labour
(iii) Factory indirect expenses
(iv) Administration expenses
(v) Selling and distribution expenses
(vi) Finance expenses.

(*a*) Wages for staff maintaining machines in factory
(*b*) Wages for staff maintaining accounting machinery
(*c*) Expenses of canteen run exclusively for factory workers
(*d*) Expenses of canteen run exclusively for administrative workers
(*e*) Grease used for factory machinery
(*f*) Cost of raw materials
(*g*) Carriage inwards on fuel used in factory boiler-house
(*h*) Carriage inwards on raw material
(*i*) Wages of managing director's chauffeur
(*j*) Wages of cleaners in factory
(*k*) Discounts allowed
(*l*) Rent of salesrooms
(*m*) Wages of lathe operators in factory
(*n*) Wages of security guards; the area of the factory buildings is four times as great as the other buildings
(*o*) Debenture interest
(*p*) Rent of annexe used by accounting staff
(*q*) Managing director's remuneration
(*r*) Sales staff salaries
(*s*) Running costs of sales staff cars
(*t*) Repairs to factory buildings
(*u*) Audit fees
(*v*) Power for machines in factory
(*w*) Rates: $^3/_4$ for factory buildings and $^1/_4$ for other buildings
(*x*) Rent of internal telephone system in factory
(*y*) Bank charges
(*z*) Costs of advertising products on television.

16.2X Analyse the following costs between:
(i) Direct materials
(ii) Direct labour
(iii) Factory indirect expenses
(iv) Administration expenses
(v) Selling and distribution expenses
(vi) Finance expenses.

(*a*) Interest on bank overdraft
(*b*) Factory storekeepers' wages
(*c*) Hire of Rolls-Royce for managing director's use

(*d*) Repairs to factory roof

(*e*) Hotel bills incurred by sales staff

(*f*) Motor tax for vans used for delivering goods to customers

(*g*) Chief accountant's salary

(*h*) Lubricants for factory machinery

(*i*) Cost of disks for firm's computer

(*j*) Helicopter hire charges re special demonstration of company's products

(*k*) Debt collection costs

(*l*) Costs of painting advertising signs on London buses

(*m*) Cost of aeroplane tickets for sales staff

(*n*) Wages of painters engaged in production

(*o*) Wages of timekeepers in factory

(*p*) Postal charges for letters

(*q*) Wages of office boy in general office

(*r*) Postal charges – parcels sent to customers

(*s*) Repairs to vans used for taking goods to customers

(*t*) Cost of raw materials included in product

(*u*) Wages for cleaners engaged in administration block

(*v*) Carriage inwards on raw materials

(*w*) Repairs to neon sign in Piccadilly Circus

(*x*) Advertising agency fees

(*y*) Wages of crane drivers in factory

(*z*) Power costs of accounting machinery.

16.3 From the following information work out:

(*a*) Prime cost

(*b*) Production cost

(*c*) Total cost

	£	£
Wages and salaries of employees:		
In factory (70 per cent is directly concerned with units being manufactured)		220,000
Salaries sales staff		8,000
Commission on sales paid to sales staff		1,400
Salaries of administrative staff		72,000
Travelling expenses:		
Sales staff	2,900	
Factory workers not directly concerned with production	100	
Administrative staff	200	
		3,200
Haulage costs on raw material bought		4,000
Carriage costs on goods sold		7,800
Depreciation:		
Factory machinery	38,000	
Accounting and office machinery	2,000	
Motor vehicles:		
Sales staff	3,800	
Administrative staff	1,600	
Sales display equipment	300	
		45,700
Royalties (total amount payable based on units produced)		1,600

	£	£
Canteen costs used by all the workers, $^2/_3$ work in the factory, $^1/_3$ in other parts of the firm		6,000
Raw materials:		
Stock at start of period		120,000
Stock at close of period		160,000
Bought in the period		400,000
Interest on loans and overdrafts		3,800
Other factory indirect expenses		58,000
Other administrative expenses		42,000
Other selling expenses		65,000

16.4X From the following information work out:

(*a*) Prime cost

(*b*) Production cost

(*c*) Total cost

	£	£
Wages and salaries of employees:		
In factory (60 per cent is directly concerned with units being manufactured)		150,000
In sales force		15,000
In administration		26,000
Carriage costs:		
On raw materials brought into the firm		1,800
On finished goods delivered to customers		1,100
Rent and rates:		
Of factory block	4,900	
Of sales department and showrooms	1,000	
Of administrative block	1,100	
		7,000
Travelling expenses:		
Sales staff	3,400	
Administrative staff	300	
Factory workers not connected directly with production	200	
		3,900
Raw materials:		
Stock at start of period		11,400
Bought in the period		209,000
Stock at close of the period		15,600
Royalties: payable per unit of production		400
Depreciation:		
Sales staff cars	500	
Vehicles used for deliveries to customers	300	
Cars of administrative staff	400	
Machinery in factory	1,800	
Office machinery	200	
		3,200
Interest costs on borrowed money		800
Other factory indirect expenses		6,000
Other administrative expenses		4,000
Other selling expenses		1,000

16.5X (a) The terms *cost behaviour* and *analysis of total cost* are regularly used in cost accounting to classify costs. Distinguish between the two terms. *(12 marks)*

(b) Explain how the following costs will:
(*i*) behave;
(*ii*) be analysed.
- Factory power and lighting
- Production line workers' wages
- Sales manager's salary
- Office rent

(8 marks)

(*London Qualifications Limited: GCE A-level*)

CHAPTER 17

Contract accounts

Learning objectives

By the end of this chapter, you should be able to:

- explain why long-term contracts are treated differently from normal production or service work;
- explain how an appropriate amount of profit may be recognised on a long-term contract before it is completed;
- describe, in brief, how the accounting standard, SSAP 9, prescribes that long-term contracts be dealt with in the financial statements.

17.1 Accounts and the business cycle

The span of production differs between businesses, and some fit into the normal pattern of annual accounts more easily than others. Farmers' accounts are usually admirably suited to the yearly pattern, as the goods they produce are in accordance with the seasons and therefore repeat themselves annually. With a firm whose production span is a day or two, the annual accounts are also suitable.

On the other hand, there are businesses whose work does not conform to a financial year's calculation of profits. Assume that a firm of contractors has only one contract being handled, and that is the construction of a very large oil refinery complex. This might take five years to complete. Until it is completed, the actual profit or loss on the contract cannot be correctly calculated. However, if the company was formed especially with this contract in mind, the shareholders would not want to wait for five years before the profit could be calculated and dividends paid. Therefore an attempt is made to calculate profits yearly. Obviously, most firms will have more than one contract under way at a time, and also it would be rare for a contract to take such a long time to complete.

17.2 Opening contract accounts

For each contract, an account is opened. It is, in fact, a form of trading account. Therefore, if the firm has a contract to build a new technical college it may be numbered Contract 71, and a *Contract 71 Account* would be opened. All expenditure traceable to the contract will be charged to the contract account. This is far easier than ascertaining direct expenses in a factory, as any expenditure on the site will be treated as direct, e.g. wages for the manual workers on the site, telephone rental for telephones on the site, hire of machinery for the contract, wages for the timekeepers, clerks, etc., on the site.

17.3 Certification of work done

With contracts of this type, the contractor is paid by agreement on the strength of architects' certificates, in the case of buildings, or engineers' certificates, for an engineering contract. The architect, or engineer, will visit the site at regular intervals and will issue a certificate giving an estimate of the value of the work done. Thus the certificate may state that work completed has a value of £10,000. A few months later, another certificate will be issued stating that the value of work certified (i.e. the work completed to date) is now £15,000.

Normally, the terms governing the contract will contain a clause concerning retention money. This is the amount, usually stated as a percentage, which will be retained, i.e. held back, in case the contract is not completed by a stated date, or against claims for faulty work, etc. A 10 per cent retention when the value of work certified is £10,000 would lead to £9,000 being payable by the person for whom the contract was being performed at the date when the certificate was issued.

17.4 Allocation of overheads

The administration overhead expenses not traceable directly to the sites are sometimes split on an arbitrary basis and charged to each contract. Of course, if there were only one contract then all the overhead expenses would quite rightly be chargeable against it. On the other hand, if there are 20 contracts being carried on, any apportionment must be arbitrary. No one can really apportion on a 'scientific' basis the administration overhead expenses of the managing director's salary, the cost of advertising to give the firm the right 'image' or the costs of running computers for the records of the whole firm, and these are only a few of such expenses. Any attempt at apportionment is likely to give misleading results, and it is therefore far better for the administrative overhead expenses which are obviously not chargeable to a contract to be omitted from the contract accounts. The surplus left on each contract account is thus the 'contribution' of each contract to administrative overhead expenses and to profit.

17.5 Example

EXHIBIT 17.1

Contract 44 is for a school being built for the Blankshire County Council. By the end of the year the following items have been charged to the contract account:

Contract 44

	£
Wages – Labour on site	5,000
Wages – Foreman and clerks on the site	600
Materials	4,000
Subcontractors on the site	900
Other site expenses	300
Hire of special machinery	400
Plant bought for the contract	2,000

The entries concerning expenditure traceable directly to the contract are relatively simple. These are charged to the contract account. These can be seen in the contract account below.

Architects' certificates have been received during the year amounting to £14,000. It has been assumed for this example that the certificates relate to all work done up to the year end. (It is not always the case that engineers or architects will certify the work done up to the financial year end. They may call several days earlier than the year end. The cost of work done, but not certified at the year end, will therefore need to be carried down as a balance to the next period when another certification will take place.)

A retention of 10 per cent is to be made, and the Blankshire County Council has paid £12,600. The £14,000 has been credited to a holding account called an Architects' Certificates Account and debited to the Blankshire County Council Account. The total of the Architects' Certificates Account now needs to be transferred to the Contract 44 Account. It is, after all, the 'sale' price of the work done so far, and the contract account is a type of trading account. The £12,600 received has been debited to the cash book and credited to Blankshire County Council Account, which now shows a balance of £1,400. Not surprisingly, this is equal to 10 per cent of the value of the work certified and is, of course, the amount of the retention.

As you would expect, the cost of the unused stock of materials on the site is not included in the value of the architects' certificates and is, therefore, carried forward to the next year at cost price. The value of the plant at the end of the year is also carried forward. In this case the value of the cost of the plant not yet used is £1,400 (a). This means that £2,000 (b) has been debited for the plant and £1,400 credited, thus effectively charging £600 for depreciation. Assume that the stock of unused materials cost £800 (c).

The Contract 44 Account will now appear:

Contract 44

	£		£
Wages – Labour on site	5,000	Architects' certificates	14,000
Wages – Foreman and clerks on the site	600	Stock of unused materials c/d	800(c)
Materials	4,000	Value of plant c/d	1,400(a)
Subcontractors on the site	900		
Other site expenses	300		
Hire of special machinery	400		
Plant bought for the contract	2,000(b)		

17.6   Profit estimation

The difference between totals of the two sides (Credit side £16,200; Debit side £13,200) can be seen to be £3,000. It would be a brave person indeed who would assert that the profit made to date was £3,000. The contract is only part completed, and costly snags may crop up which would dissipate any potential profit earned, or snags may have developed already, such as subsidence which has remained unnoticed as yet. The concept of prudence now takes over. For many years, the normal custom, barring any evidence to the contrary, was for the apparent profit (in this case £3,000) to have the following formula applied to it:

$$\text{Apparent profit} \times \frac{2}{3} \times \frac{\text{Cash received}}{\text{Work certified}}$$

$$= \text{Amount which can be utilised for dividends, etc.}$$

In this case this turns out as $£3,000 \times \dfrac{2}{3} \times \dfrac{12,600}{14,000} = £1,800.$

The Contract 44 Account can now be completed.

Profit and Loss Account

	£
Profits from contracts (see Section 17.8 below)	
Contract 43	
Contract 44	1,800
Contract 45	

Contract 44

	£		£
Wages – Labour on site	5,000	Architects' certificates	14,000
Wages – Foreman and clerks		Stock of unused materials c/d	800
on the site	500	Value of plant c/d	1,400
Materials	4,000		
Subcontractors on the site	1,000		
Other site expenses	300		
Hire of special machinery	400		
Plant bought for the contract	2,000		
Profit to the profit and loss account	1,800		
Reserve (the part of the apparent profit			
not yet recognised as earned) c/d	1,200		
	16,200		16,200
Stock of unused materials b/d	800	Reserve b/d	1,200
Value of plant b/d	1,400		

17.7   Anticipated losses

In the case shown there has been an apparent profit of £3,000 but the action would have been different if, instead of revealing such a profit, the contract account had in fact shown a loss of £3,000. In such a case it would not be two-thirds of the loss to be taken into account but the whole of it. Thus £3,000 loss would have been transferred to the profit and loss account. This is in accordance with the concept of prudence which states that profits may be underestimated but never losses.

17.8 SSAP 9

When a revised version of the Statement of Standard Accounting Practice 9 (SSAP 9), *Stocks and long-term contracts*, was issued in 1988, this custom-based *rule of thumb* was replaced with a far more complex calculation that focuses on turnover and the work certified valued in relation to the overall contract amount.

SSAP 9 requires that long-term contracts should be assessed on a contract-by-contract basis. They should be reflected in the profit and loss account by recording turnover and related costs as contract activity progresses. Turnover should be ascertained in a manner appropriate to the stage of completion of the contract, the business and the industry in which it operates. Where the outcome of the contract can be assessed with reasonable accuracy, profit should be recognised (so far as prudence permits) as the difference between recognised turnover and related costs. As previously, any foreseeable losses identified should be immediately recognised and charged as an expense to profit and loss.

The amount of long-term contracts, at costs incurred, net of amounts transferred to cost of sales, after deducting foreseeable losses and payments on account not matched with turnover, should be classified as 'long-term contract balances' and separately disclosed within the balance sheet heading of 'stocks'. The balance sheet note should disclose separately the balances of 'net cost less foreseeable losses' and 'applicable payments on account'.

However, this topic is really beyond the scope of most A-level syllabuses, and therefore of this book. Instead, this chapter is intended to provide an introduction to the subject of accounting for long-term contracts. Students who require a sound understanding of the SSAP 9 rules concerning long-term contracts should refer to the standard, where the appendix covers the topic in detail, or to a specialised text on the subject.

Learning outcomes

You should now have learnt:

1 That a separate contract account should be opened in respect of every contract.

2 That profits or losses on each uncompleted contract must be estimated at the end of each accounting period.

3 That losses should be written off immediately they are identified.

4 That an appropriate amount of any profit should be included in the financial statements.

5 Some of the definitions and requirements of SSAP 9 relating to long-term contracts.

6 That the rule of thumb profit/loss ascertainment approach adopted in this chapter is necessarily simplified in order to ensure the topic is well understood; SSAP 9 should be consulted for the definitive approach to adopt when preparing financial statements.

REVIEW QUESTIONS

Advice: As you can see, each contract account is a type of profit and loss account for each contract. The profit to date on a contract which can be taken to the main profit and loss account is calculated per Section 17.6, unless the examiner gives you another method of calculating it.

17.1 Barley Construction plc are the contractors for the building of a replacement high technology factory for a multinational company. The total value of the contract is £8,500,000 over a three-year period. The contract commenced on 1 March 20X0, and the following details are available as at 28 February 20X1.

	£
Materials purchased	765,000
Material transfers in from another site	23,000
Material transfers out to another site	8,000
Materials on site, not yet used	38,000
Direct labour	448,000
Direct labour accrued	19,500
Indirect labour	63,000
Indirect labour accrued	2,400
Plant delivered to site	120,000
Hire of equipment	57,000
Hire charges owing	3,200
Head office charges	48,000
Cost of work not yet certified	86,000

Barley Construction plc have received payment of £1,555,500 which represents work certified as completed by the architects as at 28 February 20X1, less a 15 per cent retention. The company takes credit for two-thirds of the profit on work certified (less retention).

The plant is estimated to last the life of the contract, and no residual value is expected.

Required:

A The contract account for the year ended 28 February 20X1, together with a calculation of the value of work in progress as at that date.   *(15 marks)*

B Briefly explain the accounting concept involved in the calculation of profit to be credited to the accounts for the year ended 28 February 20X1.

   In the event of a loss being made, how would this be dealt with?   *(3 marks)*

C It is intended that the new factory be fully automated with the consequence of a number of redundancies amongst existing employees. From the social responsibility viewpoint, what factors should the company consider, and what assistance could it give to employees who will eventually be made redundant at the site (the majority of whom it is anticipated will be taking early retirement)?   *(5 marks)*

(Total marks 23)

(OCR: GCE A-level)

17.2X The final accounts of Diggers Ltd are made up to 31 December in each year. Work on a certain contract was commenced on 1 April 20X5 and was completed on 31 October 20X6. The total contract price was £174,000, but a penalty of £700 was suffered for failure to complete by 30 September 20X6.

The following is a summary of receipts and payments relating to the contract:

	During 20X5	During 20X6
Payments:	£	£
Materials	25,490	33,226
Wages	28,384	45,432
Direct expenses	2,126	2,902
Purchases of plant on 1 April 20X5	16,250	–
Receipts		
Contract price (*less* penalty)	52,200	121,100
Sale, on 31 October 20X6, of all plant purchased on 1 April 20X5	–	4,100

The amount received from the customer in 20X5 represented the contract price of all work certified in that year less 10 per cent retention money.

When the annual accounts for 20X5 were prepared it was estimated that the contract would be completed on 30 September 20X6, and that the market value of the plant would be £4,250 on that date. It was estimated that further expenditure on the contract during 20X6 would be £81,400.

For the purposes of the annual accounts, depreciation of plant is calculated, in the case of uncompleted contracts, by reference to the expected market value of the plant on the date when the contract is expected to be completed, and is allocated between accounting periods by the straight line method.

Credit is taken, in the annual accounts, for such a part of the estimated total profit, on each uncompleted contract, as corresponds to the proportion between the contract price of the work certified and the total contract price.

Required:

Prepare a summary of the account for this contract, showing the amounts transferred to profit and loss account at 31 December 20X5 and 31 December 20X6.

17.3 Skimpy plc is a construction company currently undertaking three large construction contracts in its South West Division. Information relating to these three contracts for the year ended 31 October 20X9 is as follows:

	Plymouth contract £000	Torquay contract £000	Truro contract £000
Fixed contract price	600	800	1,200
Balances brought forward at 1 November 20X8			
Cost of work completed	240	80	–
Materials on site	18	6	–
Plant at written down value	90	25	–
Transactions during year			
Materials delivered to site	60	130	80
Wages	75	105	30
Payments to subcontractors	10	46	–
Salaries and other direct costs	18	32	8
Plant at written down value			
– issued to sites	6	115	77
– transferred to other sites	13	–	–

	Plymouth contract £000	Torquay contract £000	Truro contract £000
Balances carried forward at 31 October 20X9			
Materials on site	12	28	35
Plant at written down value	55	80	52
Value of work certified at end of year	500	450	125

Skimpy operates a local head office in the South West Division, the costs of which totalled £70,000 in the year ended 31 October 20X9. These costs are to be apportioned over the three construction contracts in the region in proportion to the wages paid.

The Plymouth contract is nearing completion and the site architect estimates that the additional costs to complete the contract will total £60,000. This sum includes an allowance for all anticipated costs including overheads and contingencies.

Required:

(*a*) Prepare a cost account for each of the three contracts for the year ended 31 October 20X9 and show the cost of the work completed at the end of the year.   *(16 marks)*

(*b*) For each contract recommend, giving reasons, how much profit or loss should be taken for the year ended 31 October 20X9.   *(9 marks)*

(*OCR: GCE A-level*)

17.4X (*a*) How and why do companies account for profits on uncompleted contracts?   *(8 marks)*

(*b*) From the following information prepare a contract account for the year ending 31 December 20X0. Show clearly the amount of profit that may prudently be taken.

Paddy Quick Construction Co
Contract No. 1234 (Start date 1 January 20X0)

	£
Contract price	850,000
Materials issued to site during 20X0	120,480
Materials returned to stores	1,460
Materials on site, 31 December 20X0	15,340
Direct wages	134,200
Wages owing at 31 December 20X0	5,220
Plant issued to contract (at cost)	82,600
Plant value at 31 December 20X0	63,200
Subcontractors' charges	27,560
Head office expenses charged to contract	71,430
Direct expenses (site expenses)	42,570
Direct expenses owing at 31 December 20X0	2,840
Work certified by architect	500,000
Cost of work not yet certified	27,350

The money received from the client (£425,000) was equivalent to the value of work certified less the agreed 15 per cent retention. Paddy Quick uses the fraction $^2/_3$ in calculating the profits on uncompleted contracts.   *(17 marks)*

(*London Qualifications Limited: GCE A-level*)

17.5X (*a*) Define the term *contract costing* and explain what differences exist between contract and job costing.   *(8 marks)*

(b) If a lengthy contract is being undertaken, profit must be accounted for in different accounting periods. A common formula for that allocation is:

$$\frac{2}{3} \times \frac{\text{notional profit}}{1} \times \frac{\text{cash received}}{\text{work certified}}$$

(i) Clearly explain the terms *notional profit* and *work certified*. (4 marks)

(ii) As prudence is a fundamental accounting concept, how can it allow profit to be taken during the contract period rather than on its completion? (8 marks)

(London Qualifications Limited: GCE A-level)

17.6 Loyal Construction plc commenced a new long-term contract on 1 April 20X1. At the financial year end, 31 March 20X2, the following details are available.

	£
Plant purchased and delivered to site on 1 April 20X1	94,000
Materials purchased to site	968,000
Materials returned to suppliers	7,500
Materials on site as at 31 March 20X2 not yet used	15,300
Direct labour paid	471,000
Plant hire paid	52,600
Paid to subcontractors	102,300
Architect's fees paid	31,700
Cost of work not yet certified	136,000
Payment received from customer	1,800,000

Additional information available:
(i) Direct labour accrued as at 31 March 20X2 amounted to £19,200.
(ii) The plant purchased on 1 April 20X1 is estimated to last three years from the date of purchase, with a residual value of £4,000. The company uses the straight line method of depreciation.
(iii) The payment received from the customer represents payment for all work certified by the architect, less a 10% retention.
(iv) The company policy is to charge head office expenses to the Contract Account each year at a rate of 8% of the value of work certified by the architect for the year.
(v) The attributable profit formula used by the company is:

$$\text{apparent (notional) profit } \frac{2}{3} \times \frac{\text{cash received}}{\text{work certified}}$$

Required:
(a) The Contract Account for the year ended 31 March 20X2, showing all appropriate balances brought down as at 1 April 20X2. (21 marks)
(b) The value of the work in progress as at 31 March 20X2. (2 marks)
(c) Briefly explain the purpose of the 10% retention in note (iii). (3 marks)
(d) (i) State and briefly explain the accounting concept involved in the calculation of profit to be credited to the accounts for the year ended 31 March 20X2. (3 marks)
(ii) In the event of a loss being made, how would this be dealt with in the accounts? (3 marks)

(OCR: GCE A-level, Paper 2504, Q1, 17/6/2002)

Job, batch and process costing

Learning objectives

By the end of this chapter, you should be able to:

- explain the difference between job, batch and process costing;
- explain how service costs can be apportioned across a range of production departments;
- explain the difference between the accounting treatment of normal and abnormal losses;
- discuss some of the issues relating to cost allocation between joint products.

18.1 Introduction

The earlier chapters on costing have been concerned mainly with the firm as a whole. You have seen the effects of marginal and absorption costing if applied to the firm, and you have seen the flow of costs through manufacturing and retail businesses. Now we have to consider the use of these concepts in the application of costing in firms. So far there has been a certain amount of simplification so that the concepts could be seen without too much detail obscuring your view. For instance, it has been assumed in most of the Exhibits that the firms have been making only one kind of product, and that there has really been only one cost centre. Without stretching your imagination greatly you will realise that firms manufacture many different types of goods, and that there are many cost centres in most firms.

When looking at the costing systems in use it can be seen that they can usually be divided into two main types, (*a*) job costing, and (*b*) process costing. These two main types have either an absorption or marginal costing approach, they use FIFO or LIFO or AVCO methods of pricing stock issues, etc. It is important to realise that marginal costing is not a costing system, it is instead an approach to costing which is used when job or processing costing systems are used. The same applies to absorption costing.

18.2 The choice of job costing or process costing

Process costing is relevant where production is regarded as a continuous flow, and would be applicable to industries where production is repetitive and continuous. One example would be an oil refinery where crude oil is processed continually, emerging as different grades of petrol, paraffin, motor oil, etc. Another instance would be a salt works where brine (salt water) is pumped into the works, and the product is slabs or packets of salt. Salt works and oil refineries will have a repetitive and continuous flow of production and would, therefore, use process costing.

Contrasted with this would be production which consisted of separate jobs for special orders which could be just one item or of a batch of items. For instance where bodies of Rolls-Royce cars are made to each customer's specifications, each car can be regarded as a separate job. Compared with this would be a printer's business where books are printed, so that the printing of say 5,000 copies of a book can also be regarded as a job. The 'job' can thus be one item or a batch of similar items.

Two terms are used to describe this 'specific order' form of costing – 'job costing', when costs are to be attributed to an individual job (a customer order or task of relatively short duration); and 'batch costing', when costs are to be attributed to a specific batch of a product (a group of similar items which is treated as a separate cost unit – a unit of product or service in relation to which costs are ascertained). In effect, the accounting treatment is the same. For our purposes, we shall focus in this chapter upon job costing. If you are asked to perform batch costing, remember that the process is the same. (You will find that Question 18.9 at the end of this chapter is on batch costing.)

We can compare the process costing and job costing approaches in the diagrams shown as Exhibit 18.1.

EXHIBIT 18.1 Process costing and job costing

Process costing

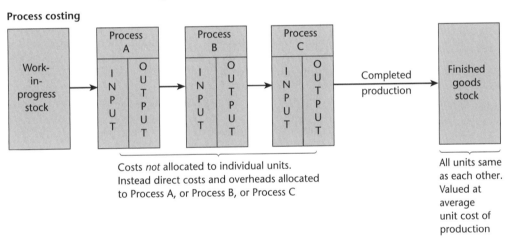

Job costing

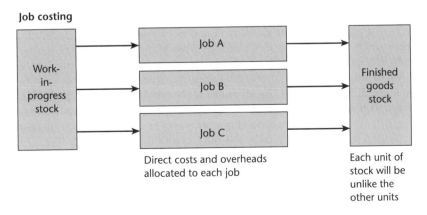

18.3 Job costing

Each job will be given a separate job number, and direct materials and direct labour used on the job will be charged to the job. The accumulation of the costs will be done on a 'job cost sheet'. The materials will have been charged to the job on the FIFO, LIFO or AVCO basis. The direct labour costs will be found by recording the number of direct labour hours of each type of direct worker, and multiplying by the labour cost per hour for each type.

The job is thus the cost centre, and direct labour and direct materials can be charged direct to the cost centre. The indirect expenses cannot be charged direct to the job; such costs are charged instead to a service cost centre and the cost of the service centre is then apportioned between the various jobs to give the cost of each job including indirect expenses.

It is only after the accounting period is over that the exact costs of each service centre are known, but you will want to know how much each job costs as it is finished. You will not want to wait months to find out the cost of each job. This is solved by estimating the indirect expenses, and then fixing the method of apportioning these estimated expenses.

For example, suppose there are three jobs being performed and these are in separate production departments, Departments A, B and C. There are also two service centres, Departments G and H. Some of the indirect labour expenses and other indirect expenses can be allocated direct to the production departments – for instance the wages of the foremen of each of Departments A, B and C, or items such as lubricating materials if each department used quite different lubricants. Other indirect labour can be traced to the two centres G and H as well as expenses. The problem then is that of apportioning the costs of G and H between Departments A, B and C. We can now look at Exhibit 18.2, and see what answer this firm came up with.

EXHIBIT 18.2

Indirect labour costs and other indirect expenses have been allocated to Production Departments A, B and C and Service Departments G and H as follows:

	Production Departments			Service Departments	
	A	B	C	G	H
Indirect labour	2,000	3,000	4,000	500	1,000
Other expenses	1,000	2,000	3,000	1,500	2,000
	£3,000	£5,000	£7,000	£2,000	£3,000

The problem is to apportion the costs of G and H to the production departments. G was a department which maintained factory buildings while H maintained factory machinery. A study of the costs of G produced a very easy answer. There was no doubt that the costs were in direct relationship to the floor space occupied by each department. But it must not be overlooked that Department H also needed the attention of G's workforce so that part of the costs of G would have to be apportioned to H. These costs would then increase the total of costs of Department H which would then need apportioning to the production departments. Floor space in square metres was A 2,000, B 4,000, C 3,000 and H 1,000. The £2,000 costs of Department G were therefore apportioned:

$$\text{Each department: } \frac{\text{Its floor space}}{\text{Total floor space}} \times £2,000$$

Therefore:

$$A \quad \frac{2,000}{10,000} \times £2,000 = £400 \qquad B \quad \frac{4,000}{10,000} \times £2,000 = £800$$

$$C \quad \frac{3,000}{10,000} \times £2,000 = £600 \qquad H \quad \frac{1,000}{10,000} \times £2,000 = £200$$

(Department H's costs have now increased by £200 and become £3,200)

Department H's costs presented a far more difficult problem. Consideration was given to apportionment based on numbers of machines, volumes of production and types of machinery. It was, however, felt that there was a high relationship in this case (although this would certainly not always be true in other firms) between the values of machinery in use and the costs of maintaining them. The more costly equipment was very complicated and needed a lot of attention. Consequently it was decided to apportion H's costs between A, B and C on the basis of the value of machinery in each department. This was found to be A £3,000; B £6,000; C £7,000. The costs were therefore apportioned:

$$\frac{\text{Value of machinery in department}}{\text{Total value of machinery in all 3 departments}} \times £3,200$$

Therefore

$$A \quad \frac{3,000}{16,000} \times £3,200 = £600 \qquad B \quad \frac{6,000}{16,000} \times £3,200 = £1,200$$

$$C \quad \frac{7,000}{16,000} \times £3,200 = £1,400$$

The costs and their apportionment can, therefore, be shown:

| | Production Departments | | | Service Departments | |
	A	B	C	G	H
Indirect labour	2,000	3,000	4,000	500	1,000
Other expenses	1,000	2,000	3,000	1,500	2,000
	3,000	5,000	7,000	2,000	3,000
Department G's costs apportioned	400	800	600	(2,000)	200
					3,200
Department H's costs apportioned	600	1,200	1,400		(3,200)
	£4,000	£7,000	£9,000	–	–

This method of apportioning service department overheads is sometimes called the repeated distribution (or continuous apportionment) method. (*See* Question 18.7 for a discussion of this and another method.)

Now we have the estimated overhead for each department for the ensuing accounting period. We now have another problem as to how the overhead is going to be taken into the calculation of the cost of each job in these departments. After investigation the conclusion is that in Departments A and B there is a direct relationship between direct labour hours and overhead, but in Department C the guiding fact is machine hours. If the total overheads of Departments A and B are therefore divided by the estimated number of direct labour hours this will give the overhead rate per direct labour hour, while in

Department C the total overhead will be divided by the estimated machine hours. The calculation of the overhead rates is therefore as follows:

	Production Departments		
	A	B	C
Direct labour hours	5,000	4,000	
Machine hours			6,000
Overhead rate per			
direct labour hour	£4,000	£7,000	
	5,000	4,000	
	= £0.8	= £1.75	
Overhead rate per			£9,000
machine hour			6,000
			= £1.5

We can now calculate the costs of four jobs performed in this factory:

Job A/70/144

Department A
Started 1.7.20X2. Completed 13.7.20X2
Cost of direct materials £130
Number of direct labour hours 100
Cost rate of direct labour per hour £0.9

Job B/96/121

Department B
Started 4.7.20X2. Completed 9.7.20X2
Cost of direct materials £89
Number of direct labour hours 40
Cost rate of direct labour per hour £1.1

Job C/67/198

Department C
Started 8.7.20X2. Completed 16.7.20X2
Cost of direct materials £58
Number of direct labour hours 50
Cost rate of direct labour per hour £1.0
Number of machine hours 40

Job AC/45/34

Departments A and C
Started in A 3.7.20X2. Passed on to C 11.7.20X2. Completed in C 16.7.20X2
Cost of materials £115
Number of direct labour hours (in Dept A) 80
                                   (in Dept C) 90
Cost rate per direct labour hour (in Dept A) £0.9
                                   (in Dept C) £1.0
Number of machine hours (in Dept C) 70

The job cost sheets for these four jobs are shown below. At no point in this Exhibit has it been stated whether a marginal costing or an absorption costing approach has been adopted. If an absorption costing approach had been used, overhead would include both fixed and variable overheads. If a marginal costing approach had been used, the overhead brought into the calculations of job costs would exclude fixed overhead, so that the overhead rate would be a variable overhead rate.

Job Cost Sheet. Job No. A/70/144			
Started 1.7.20X2		Completed 13.7.20X2	
			£
Materials			130
	Hours	Rates £	
Direct labour	100	0.9	90
Factory overhead	100	0.8	80
Total job cost			300

Job Cost Sheet. Job No. B/96/121			
Started 4.7.20X2		Completed 9.7.20X2	
			£
Materials			89
	Hours	Rates £	
Direct labour	40	1.1	44
Factory overhead	40	1.75	70
Total job cost			203

Job Cost Sheet. Job No. C/67/198			
Started 8.7.20X2		Completed 16.7.20X2	
			£
Materials			58
	Hours	Rates £	
Direct labour	50	1.0	50
Factory overhead	40	1.5	60
Total job cost			168

Job Cost Sheet. Job No. AC/45/34			
Started 3.7.20X2		Completed 16.7.20X2	
			£
Materials			115
	Hours	Rates £	
Direct labour (Dept A)	80	0.9	72
Direct labour (Dept C)	90	1.0	90
Factory overhead (Dept A)	80	0.8	64
Factory overhead (Dept C)	70	1.5	105
Total job cost			446

18.4 Cost centres – job costing and responsibility

It must be pointed out that a cost centre for job costing is not necessarily the same as tracing the costs down to the individual who is responsible for controlling them. There are two questions here: (*a*) finding the cost of a job to check on its profitability and (*b*) controlling the costs by making someone responsible for them so that he/she will have to answer for any variations from planned results. Many firms therefore keep separate records of costs to fulfil each of these functions.

18.5 Process costing

Job costing treats production as a number of separate jobs being performed, whereas process costing sees production as a continuous flow. In process costing there is correspondingly no attempt to allocate costs to specific units being produced.

There is, however, usually more than one process in the manufacture of goods. We can take for an example a bakery producing cakes. There are three processes: (*a*) the mixing of the cake ingredients, (*b*) the baking of the cakes, (*c*) the packaging of the cakes. Each process is treated as a cost centre, and therefore costs for (*a*), (*b*) and (*c*) are collected separately. Overhead rates are then calculated for each cost centre in a similar fashion to that in job costing.

In the case of the bakery, each accounting period would probably start and finish without any half-mixed or half-baked cakes, but some types of firms which use process costing have processes which take rather longer to complete than baking cakes. A typical case would be the brewing of beer. At the beginning and end of each period there would be partly processed units. It is a matter of arithmetic to convert production into 'equivalent units produced' (which is also known as 'equivalent production'). For instance, production during a particular period may be as in Exhibit 18.3.

EXHIBIT 18.3

Started in previous period and ³/₄ completed then, and ¹/₄ completed in	
current period, 400 units, 400 × ¹/₄	100
Started and completed in current period	680
Started in current period and ¹/₈ completed by end of period, 160 units, 160 × ¹/₈	20
Equivalent production	800 units

If the total costs of the cost centre amounted to £4,000 then the unit cost would be

$$\frac{£4,000}{800} = £5.$$

In fact, process costing can become very complicated because some of the part-produced items are complete in terms of say, materials, but incomplete in terms of labour, or else, say, ²/₃ complete for materials and ¹/₄ complete for labour. Although the situation becomes complicated, the principles are no different from those described for calculating equivalent production.

We can now look at an example of process costing in Exhibit 18.4. So that we do not get involved in too many arithmetical complications, we will assume that there are no partly completed goods in each process at the start and end of the period considered.

EXHIBIT 18.4

A bakery making cakes has three processes: (A) the mixing of the cake ingredients, (B) the baking of the cakes, (C) the packaging of the cakes.
January activity was as follows:

	£
Materials used:	
Process (A)	4,000
Process (B)	–
Process (C)	1,000
Direct labour:	
Process (A)	1,500
Process (B)	500
Process (C)	800

Factory overhead:
  Variable:
  Process (A)   400
  Process (B)   1,300
  Process (C)   700
  Fixed (allocated to processes):
  Process (A)   600
  Process (B)   500
  Process (C)   400

During January, 100,000 cakes were made.
The process cost accounts will appear as:

Process (A)

	£		£
Materials	4,000	Transferred to Process (B)	
Direct labour	1,500	100,000 units at £0.065	6,500
Variable overhead	400		
Fixed overhead	600		
	6,500		6,500

Process (B)

	£		£
Transferred from Process (A)		Transferred to Process (C)	
100,000 units at £0.065	6,500	100,000 units at £0.088	8,800
Direct labour	500		
Variable overhead	1,300		
Fixed overhead	500		
	8,800		8,800

Process (C)

	£		£
Transferred from Process (B)		Transferred to finished goods stock	
100,000 units at £0.088	8,800	100,000 units at £0.117	11,700
Materials	1,000		
Direct labour	800		
Variable overhead	700		
Fixed overhead	400		
	11,700		11,700

18.6 Normal and abnormal losses

There are some losses that are basically part of the production process and cannot be eliminated. For instance, when printing books, losses occur in the cutting of paper, when brewing beer there will be losses due to evaporation, when cutting steel there will be losses. These losses are inevitable, even in the most efficient firms, and as such they are called normal or uncontrollable losses.

On the other hand, there are losses which should be avoided if there are efficient operating conditions. Such things as the incorrect cutting of cloth so that it is wasted unnecessarily, not mixing ingredients properly so that some of the product is unusable, and the use of inferior materials so that much of the product cannot pass production tests and is wasted, are abnormal or controllable losses.

The accounting treatment varies between these two sorts of losses.

- *Normal losses*: These are not transferred from the process account but are treated as part of the process costs.

- *Abnormal losses*: These are transferred from the process account to an abnormal loss account. The double entry is:

Dr   Abnormal loss account
    Cr   Process account

The abnormal loss is then treated as a period cost. Accordingly it is written off as an expense to the debit of the profit and loss account at the end of the period.

18.7 Under/overabsorption of overheads

When an overhead rate is based on estimated annual overhead expenditure and estimated activity, it would be very rare for it to be exactly the same as the actual overhead incurred. Either the costs themselves will have changed, or the activity, or both.

If £300,000 has been allocated to the year's production, but actual costs were £298,000 then too much has been allocated; in other words, it is a case of overabsorption of overheads amounting to £2,000.

If, on the other hand, £305,000 had been allocated, but the actual costs were £311,000 then too little has been allocated, and this is an underabsorption of overheads amounting to £6,000.

At the closing balance sheet date, the stock in trade has been valued and this will include something for overheads. In the case of an underabsorption the question arises as to whether the closing stock valuation should be amended to include something for the underabsorbed overheads. The accounting answer is that no adjustment should be made to the stock valuation. Similarly the stock valuation should not be reduced to take account of overabsorption of overheads.

Exhibit 18.5 shows how the costs should be treated for underabsorption of overheads.

EXHIBIT 18.5 Costs treatment for underabsorption of overheads

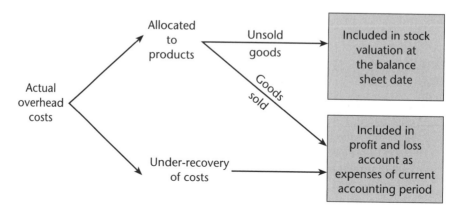

18.8 Other kinds of firms

Process costing is found most often in industries such as oil, canning, paint manufacture, steel, textiles and food processing.

18.9 The problem of joint costs

A manufacturing operation often results in one simple product being produced. Any excess output other than the product is regarded as scrap, and the small cost that could be traced to it is ignored. For example, in the manufacture of a suit, when the cost is traced to the suit, the small unusable bits of cloth that are left over are ignored.

This is not always the case, and where a group of separate products is produced simultaneously, each of the products having relatively substantial sales values, then the products are called 'joint products'. Thus crude oil taken into an oil refinery is processed and the output is in terms of different grades of petrol, paraffin, motor oil, etc. This means that in costing terms the costs of the materials, processes, etc. have to be split between the joint products.

Many problems exist in this area. Perhaps you will see why when the problem of allocating costs between joint products is concerned with the cutting up of a cow for beef. From a cow there is rump steak, the fillet steaks, the T-bone steaks, sirloin, silverside, brisket, etc. If the cow costs the butcher £300, then how would you allocate the cost between all of these various joint products? This gives you some idea of the problem which exists; in many industries this becomes involved with complex technological problems.

In effect, you can allocate the joint costs on the basis of the sale price of each of the joint products, or on the basis of the relative weight or volume of the joint products. In fact, you could allocate the costs on any basis and none would be indisputably 'correct'. With joint products, there is no rational reason or basis for splitting their costs that cannot be argued against.

Sometimes, a minor (i.e. much lower-value) but nevertheless distinguishable product is produced at the same time as the main product. One example is the sawdust that is created when wood is being converted into furniture. Such a product is known as a 'by-product'. One way of dealing with the costs involved is to ignore them and simply credit any income derived from sale of the by-product against the cost of producing the main product.

Learning outcomes

You should now have learnt:

1 That neither marginal costing nor absorption costing is a costing 'system'; rather, they are approaches to costing which are used when job or processing costing systems are used.

2 The differences between job (and batch) costing and process costing.

3 That direct costs can be allocated directly to the relevant cost centre. However, indirect costs have to be approtioned among cost centres on an appropriate basis, as there is no way of knowing precisely how much indirect cost was incurred on each item produced.

4 How indirect costs can be apportioned across cost centres.

5 How to deal with normal and abnormal losses.

6 About the problems relating to cost allocation between joint products.

REVIEW QUESTIONS

Advice: Questions on job and process costing are usually fairly easy to answer and it is also relatively simple to gain quite high marks by tackling them.

18.1 In a firm there are four types of jobs performed in separate production departments A, B, C and D. In addition there are three service departments, K, L and M. Costs have been allocated to the departments as follows:

	Production Departments				Service Departments		
	A	B	C	D	K	L	M
	£	£	£	£	£	£	£
Indirect labour	4,000	6,000	8,000	2,000	1,500	3,000	4,100
Other expenses	2,700	3,100	3,600	1,500	4,500	2,000	2,000

The expenses of the service departments are to be allocated between other departments as follows:

Dept K to Depts A 25 per cent, B 30 per cent, C 20 per cent, D 10 per cent, M 15 per cent.
Dept L to Depts A 60 per cent, C 30 per cent, D 10 per cent.
Dept M to Depts B 30 per cent, C 50 per cent, D 20 per cent.

In departments A and C the job costing is to use an overhead rate per direct labour hour, while in B and D a machine hour rate will be used. The number of direct labour hours and machine hours per department is expected to be:

	A	B	C	D
Direct labour hours	2,000	4,000	4,450	2,700
Machine hours	1,900	2,600	2,900	2,400

You are required to calculate:

(*a*) The overhead rates for Departments A and C.
(*b*) The overhead rates for Departments B and D.

(Keep your answer – it will be used as a basis for the next question.)

18.2 In the firm mentioned in Question 18.1 what would be the costs of the following jobs given that the direct labour costs per hour are: Dept A £2.1; B £1.7; C £2.4; D £2.3?

Job 351: Dept A	Direct materials cost	£190
	Number of direct labour hours	56
	Number of machine hours	40
Job 352: Dept B	Direct materials cost	£1,199
	Number of direct labour hours	178
	Number of machine hours	176
Job 353: Dept C	Direct materials cost	£500
	Number of direct labour hours	130
	Number of machine hours	100
Job 354: Dept D	Direct materials cost	£666
	Number of direct labour hours	90
	Number of machine hours	64
Job 355: Dept C	Direct materials cost	£560
	Number of direct labour hours	160
	Number of machine hours	150
	Job passed on to Dept B where additional direct materials cost	£68
	Number of direct labour hours	30
	Number of machine hours	20

18.3X In a firm there are five types of jobs performed in separate production departments P, Q, R, S and T. In addition there are two service departments F and G. Costs have been allocated to the departments as follows:

	Production Departments					Service Departments	
	P	Q	R	S	T	F	G
	£	£	£	£	£	£	£
Indirect labour	5,000	7,000	3,000	6,000	8,000	10,000	9,000
Other expenses	500	1,800	1,000	1,200	1,300	6,000	7,000

The expenses of the service departments are to be allocated between other departments as follows:

Dept F to Depts P 10 per cent, Q 20 per cent, S 30 per cent, T 15 per cent, G 25 per cent.
Dept G to Depts P 12.5 per cent, Q 20 per cent, R 25 per cent, S 30 per cent, T 12.5 per cent.

In departments R and T the job costing is to use an overhead rate per direct labour hour, while in the other production departments a machine hour rate will be used. The number of direct labour hours and machine hours per department are expected to be:

	P	Q	R	S	T
Direct labour hours	4,000	5,000	3,600	10,000	3,550
Machine hours	3,000	4,000	3,000	8,000	2,800

You are required to calculate:

(a) The overhead rates for departments R and T.
(b) The overhead rates for departments P, Q and S.

(Keep your answer – it will be used for Question 18.4X.)

18.4X In the firm mentioned in Question 18.3X what would be the costs of the following jobs, given that the direct labour rate per hour is Dept P £1.9, Q £2.5, R £2.0, S £2.7, T £2.4?

Job 701: Dept R	Direct materials cost	£115
	Number of direct labour hours	35
	Number of machine hours	29
Job 702: Dept T	Direct materials cost	£1,656
	Number of direct labour hours	180
	Number of machine hours	160
Job 703: Dept P	Direct materials cost	£546
	Number of direct labour hours	100
	Number of machine hours	90
Job 704: Dept S	Direct materials cost	£65
	Number of direct labour hours	250
	Number of machine hours	60
Job 705: Dept Q	Direct materials cost	£4,778
	Number of direct labour hours	305
	Number of machine hours	280
Job 706: Dept P	Direct materials cost	£555
	Number of direct labour hours	200
	Number of machine hours	180
	Then passed to Dept T for completion where direct materials cost	£11
	Number of direct labour hours	18
	Number of machine hours	2

18.5 (a) Define the term *equivalent production* and state when the principle is used. *(4 marks)*

(b) During May 20X1, M Wurzel & Co. Limited's output was 4,000 finished items plus 600 partly finished items. There was no work in progress on 1 May 20X1.

	Materials	Labour	Overheads	Total
Total cost (£)	8,172	7,120	5,196	20,488
WIP degree of completion %	90	75	55	–

Calculate for the month of May 20X1:

(i) the total equivalent production for each cost element;
(ii) the cost per complete unit;
(iii) the value of the work in progress. *(11 marks)*

(London Qualifications Limited: GCE A-level)

18.6X (a) What is meant by the term *equivalent production*? *(3 marks)*

(b) At Earith Industries at the beginning of April there were no partially finished goods on hand. During the month, 6,000 completed units were produced, together with 800 units partially completed. Details of the partially finished items were:

	Total cost (£)	Percentage completed
Materials	12,540	75
Labour	8,476	65
Overheads	7,084	55

Calculate:

(i) the total equivalent production,
(ii) the cost per complete unit,
(iii) the total value of work in progress. *(12 marks)*

(London Qualifications Limited: GCE A-level)

18.7 (a) Explain the difference between the terms *overhead allotment*, *overhead apportionment* and *overhead absorption*. *(5 marks)*

(b) Why are *estimated* figures used in calculating overhead absorption rates? *(2 marks)*

(c) The following information relates to the Flyby Knight Plc for the six months ended 31 December 20X1:

	Production Departments			Service Departments	
	A	B	C	X	Y
Overheads (£)	14,000	12,000	8,000	4,000	3,000
Overheads to be apportioned:					
Dept X (%)	35	30	20	–	15
Dept Y (%)	30	40	25	5	–

(i) Use the continuous apportionment (repeated distribution) method to apportion the service departments' overheads between each other.
(ii) Apportion the service departments' overheads calculated in (i) to the production departments.
(iii) Show how the overheads apportioned to the production departments would have differed if the elimination method had been used for the service departments.

(*iv*) State how far it is true to say that the elimination method produces an inaccurate answer, and is therefore not to be recommended. *(18 marks)*

(London Qualifications Limited: GCE A-level)

18.8X Kalmo Ltd offers a subcontracting service in assembly, painting and packing. Components are supplied by customers to the company, the required operations are then carried out, and the completed work returned to the customer. The company is labour intensive, with only a relatively small amount of materials purchased.

Currently, one factory overhead recovery rate is used which is a percentage of total direct labour costs. This is calculated from the following budgeted costs.

Department	Direct labour costs £	Direct labour hours	Machine hours	Factory overheads £
Assembly	450,000	150,000	6,000	180,000
Painting	500,000	140,625	–	225,000
Packing	250,000	100,000	8,000	75,000

The cost sheet for Job 131190 shows the following information:

Department	Direct labour costs £	Direct labour hours	Machine hours	Direct material costs £
Assembly	2,500	1,000	120	100
Painting	2,200	900	–	400
Packing	4,800	960	80	500

General administration expenses of 20 per cent are added to the total factory costs, and then a further 25 per cent of the total cost is added as profit, to arrive at the selling price.

Although the company has been using the blanket factory overhead recovery rate for a number of years, one of the directors has questioned this method, and asks if it would be possible to apply overhead recovery rates for each department.

Required:

A Calculate the current factory overhead recovery rate, and apply this to arrive at the selling price for Job 131190. *(4 marks)*

B In line with the director's comments, calculate overhead recovery rates for each department, using two alternative methods, and apply both to arrive at new selling prices for Job 131190. *(10 marks)*

C Briefly evaluate the methods you have used for the recovery of factory overheads, justifying which one you consider to be most appropriate. *(6 marks)*

D Outline how an unsatisfactory method of overhead absorption can affect the profits of a business. *(3 marks)*

(Total marks 23)

(OCR: GCE A-level)

18.9 (*a*) What is meant by the term, 'specific order costing'? *(3 marks)*

(*b*) In what ways does specific order costing differ from process costing? *(6 marks)*

(*c*) The Acme Shelving Co. Ltd manufactures shelving brackets in batches of 300. During May, Batch No. 23 was machined at a rate of 15 per hour. Sixty of the brackets failed to pass inspection, but of these, 40 were thought to be rectifiable. The remaining 20 were scrapped, and the scrap value was credited to the batch cost account. Rectification work took nine hours.

Batch No. 23

	£
Raw materials per bracket	1.60
Scrap value per bracket	0.86
Machinists' hourly rate	4.20
Machine hour overhead rate	3.60
(running time only)	
Setting up of machine: normal machining	21.00
rectification	18.00

Calculate:

(*i*)   the cost of Batch No. 23 in total and per unit, if all units pass inspection;

(*ii*) the *actual* cost of Batch No. 23, in total and per unit, after crediting the recovery value of the scrapped components, and including the rectification costs;

(*iii*) the loss incurred because of defective work.   *(16 marks)*

(*London Qualifications Limited: GCE A-level*)

18.10X   Horden Products Ltd manufactures goods which could involve any or all of three production departments. These departments are simply entitled **A**, **B** and **C**. A direct wages cost percentage absorption rate for the recovery of production overheads is applied to individual job costs.

Details from the company's budgets for the year ended 31 March 20X5 are as follows:

	Dept A	Dept B	Dept C
Indirect materials	£23,000	£35,000	£57,000
Indirect wages	£21,000	£34,000	£55,000
Direct wages	£140,000	£200,000	£125,000
Direct labour hours	25,000	50,000	60,000
Machine hours	100,000	40,000	10,000

The following information is also available for the production departments:

	Dept A	Dept B	Dept C
Area (square metres)	30,000	20,000	10,000
Cost of machinery	£220,000	£160,000	£20,000
Horse power of machinery	55	30	15

Other budgeted figures are:

	£
Power	120,000
Rent, rates, light, heat	90,000
Insurance (machinery)	20,000
Depreciation	80,000

Machinery is depreciated on the basis of 20% on cost.

Job No. 347 passed through all three departments and incurred the following actual direct costs and times:

	Direct materials	Direct wages	Direct labour hours	Machine hours
	£	£	£	£
Dept A	152	88	35	60
Dept B	85	192	90	30
Dept C	52	105	45	10

A sum amounting to 30% of the production cost is added to every job to enable a selling price to be quoted.

Required:

(*a*) A statement to show the total production overheads per department and calculate the absorption rate which the company has adopted. *(8 marks)*

(*b*) Calculate the selling price to be quoted for Job No. 347. *(8 marks)*

(*c*) Using the available data, calculate absorption rates when based on:
    (*i*) direct labour hour rate *(3 marks)*
    (*ii*) machine hour rate. *(3 marks)*

(*d*) Explain clearly the meaning of the following terms relating to overheads:
    (*i*) allotment *(3 marks)*
    (*ii*) allocation *(3 marks)*
    (*iii*) apportionment. *(2 marks)*

(*AQA (AEB): GCE A-level*)

18.11X (*a*) Explain the following terms as used in process costing:
    (*i*) normal losses
    (*ii*) abnormal losses
    (*iii*) equivalent production
    (*iv*) joint cost
    (*v*) split-off point *(10 marks)*

(*b*) In process costing, it is neither the technology nor the costs incurred, but the market price of the item, which determines whether an item is classed as:
    (*i*) scrap or waste; and
    (*ii*) a joint product or a by-product.

How far do you agree? *(10 marks)*

(*London Qualifications Limited: GCE A-level*)

Budgeting and budgetary control

By the end of this chapter, you should be able to:

- describe the budgetary process;
- explain the importance of budgets for planning and control;
- apply the economic order quantity approach to stock control.

19.1 Financial budgets

Management control is needed to try to ensure that the organisation achieves its objectives. Once the objectives have been agreed, plans should be drawn up so that the progress of the firm can be directed towards the ends specified in the objectives. Now it must not be thought that plans can be expressed only in accounting terms. For example, quality of the product might be best shown in engineering terms, or social objectives shown in a plan concerned with employee welfare. But some of the objectives, such as the attainment of a desired profit, or the attainment of a desired growth in assets, can be expressed in accounting terms. When a plan is expressed quantitatively it is known as a 'budget' and the process of converting plans into budgets is known as 'budgeting'. In this book we are concerned primarily with budgets shown in monetary terms, i.e. financial budgets.

The budgeting process may be quite formal in a large organisation with committees set up to perform the task. On the other hand in a very small firm the owner may jot down a budget on a piece of scrap-paper or even on the back of a used envelope. Some even manage without writing anything down at all; they have done the budgets in their heads and can easily remember them. This book is concerned with budgeting in a formal manner.

19.2 Budgets and people

Probably in no other part of accounting is there a greater need for understanding other people than in the processes of budgeting. Budgets are prepared to try to guide the firm towards its objectives. There is no doubt that some budgets that are drawn up are even more harmful to a firm than if none was drawn up at all.

Budgets are drawn up for control purposes, that is an attempt to control the direction that the firm is taking. Many people, however, look upon them not as a guide, but as a straitjacket. We can look at a few undesirable actions that can result from people regarding budgets as a straitjacket rather than as a guide.

(a) The sales manager refuses to let a salesman go to Sweden in response to an urgent and unexpected request from a Swedish firm. The reason – the overseas sales expenses budget has already been spent. The result – the most profitable order that the firm would have received for many years is taken up instead by another firm.

(b) The works manager turns down requests for overtime work, because the budgeted overtime has already been exceeded. The result – the job is not completed on time, and the firm has to pay a large sum under a penalty clause in the contract for the job which stated that if the job was not finished by a certain date then a penalty of £200,000 would become payable.

(c) Towards the end of the accounting year a manager realises that he has not spent all of his budget for a particular item. He then launches on a spending spree, completely unnecessary items being bought, on the basis that 'If I don't spend this amount this year they will cut down next year when I will really need the money'. The result: a lot of unusable and unnecessary equipment.

(d) The education budget has been spent, therefore the education manager will not let anyone go on courses for the rest of the year. The result: the firm starts to fall behind in an industry which is highly technical, the staff concerned become fed up and the better ones start to look for jobs in other firms which are more responsive to the need to allow personnel to keep in touch with changing technology.

Studies have shown that the more that managers are brought into the budgeting process, the more successful budgetary control is likely to be. A manager on whom a budget is imposed, as opposed to one who had an active part in drafting the budget, is more likely to pay less attention to the budget and use it unwisely in the control process.

Having sounded the warning that needs to be borne in mind constantly when budgeting, we can now look at the positive end of budgeting – to see the advantages of a good budgetary control system.

19.3   Budgets, planning and control

The methodology of budgetary control is probably accountancy's major contribution to management. Before we get down to the mechanics of constructing budgets we should first of all look at the main outlines of drafting budgets.

When the budgets are being drawn up the two main objectives must be uppermost in the mind of top management, that is that the budgets are for:

(a) **Planning**. This means a properly co-ordinated and comprehensive plan for the whole business. Each part must interlock with the other parts.

(b) **Control**. Just because a plan is set down on paper does not mean that the plan will carry itself out. Control is exercised via the budgets, thus the name budgetary control. To do this means that the responsibility of managers and budgets must be so linked that the responsible manager is given a guide to help him/her to produce certain desired results, and the actual achieved results can be compared against the expected, i.e. actual compared with budget.

19.4 Preparation of estimates

The first thing to establish is what the limiting factors are in a firm. It may well be the fact that sales cannot be pushed above a certain amount, because the productive capacity of the firm sets a limit. If this were not the case, the firm could sell as much as it can produce. Whatever the limiting factor is, there is no doubt that this aspect of the firm will need more attention than probably any other. There would not, for instance, be much point in budgeting for the sale of 1,000 units a year if production could not manufacture more than 700, or to manufacture 2,000 a year if only 1,300 of them could be sold.

There is no doubt that usually the most difficult estimate to make is that of sales revenue. This can be done by using one of two methods:

(*i*) Make a statistical forecast on the basis of the economic conditions applying to the goods sold by the company, and what is known about the actions of competitors.
(*ii*) The opposite is to make an internal forecast. This is usually done by asking each member of the sales staff, or group of salespeople, to estimate the sales in their own areas, and then total the estimates. Sometimes the sales staff are not asked at all.

Now we should remember that much of the subject matter that you have read about, or are currently reading in Economics, is very relevant here. A knowledge of elasticity of demand, whether the product is a complementary product, e.g. the price of egg-cups is linked to the demand for eggs, and whether it is a substitute, e.g. a rise in the price of butter may induce people to turn to other commodities instead, is very relevant in this area. Factors such as whether the firm has a monopoly, whether the firm has many small customers, a few large customers or even one large customer, are of crucial importance. Estimating sales revenue is very much a matter of taking all the economic factors into account, along with other factors.

The sales budget is, however, more than just a sales forecast. Budgets should show the actions that management is taking to influence future events. If an increase in sales is desired the sales budget may show extra sales, which may well be an indication of the action that management is going to take by means of extra television advertising, making a better product, or giving retailers better profit margins and pushing up sales in that way.

19.5 The production budget

The production budget stems from the sales budget, but the first question that has to be settled is that of the level of the stock of finished goods which will be held by the firm.

If sales are even over the year, then production can also be in keeping with the sales figure, and the stock figure can remain constant. Suppose that the firm sells 50 units every month, then the firm can produce 50 units per month. In almost every firm, a minimum stock level will have to be maintained. The amount of stock will be dependent on factors such as amount of storage space, the estimated amount needed to cater for breakdowns in production or for delays in receiving raw materials, etc. Nonetheless, if the stock level was to be a minimum of 70 units it would still mean that production was at the rate of 50 units per month.

On the other hand, sales may not be constant. Sales may average 50 units per month, but the figures may well be as follows:

| January | 20 units | February | 30 units | March | 60 units |
| April | 80 units | May | 70 units | June | 40 units |

This would mean that if production levels were kept at 50 units per month, there would be a shortage of 10 units in May – when 70 were demanded but only 60 were available for sale (10 left over from April plus 50 produced in May). An extra 10 units would need to be held to cover this shortfall. If production each month is to be the same, 10 units would need to be held at the beginning of the year.

Any calculation of minimum stock levels must include these 10 units. For example, if minimum stock of 100 is required, stock at the beginning of the year would need to be 110 units.

However, instead of producing the same number of units each month, the monthly production could be set to equal the sales figures. If a minimum stock level of 100 units is required, the number of units held at the beginning of the year would then be 100.

We can now compare the two levels of production in Sections 19.6 and 19.7.

19.6 Even production flow

The problem here is to find the stock level that the firm would need on 1 January if (i) sales are as shown, (ii) the stock must not fall below 100 units, (iii) production is to be 50 units per month. It can be found by trial and error. For instance, if you decided to see what would happen if the firm started off with 100 units in stock at 1 January you would find that, after adding production and deducting sales each month, the stock level would fall to 90 units in May. As 100 units of stock is the minimum needed you would need to start off on 1 January with 110 units. The method is that if you start off your calculation with an estimated figure of stock, which must be at least the minimum figure required, then if you find that the lowest figure of stock shown during the period is 10 units less than the minimum stock required, go back and add 10 units to the stock to be held on 1 January. If the lowest figure is 30 units less than required add 30 units to the 1 January stock, and so on. We can now look at the figures in Exhibit 19.1.

EXHIBIT 19.1

Units	January	February	March	April	May	June
Opening stock	110	140	160	150	120	100
Add Units produced	50	50	50	50	50	50
	160	190	210	200	170	150
Less Sales	(20)	(30)	(60)	(80)	(70)	(40)
Closing stock	140	160	150	120	100	110

Before we look at the implications of maintaining an even production flow we can look at another example. Try and work it out for yourself before looking at the answer in Exhibit 19.2. The sales are expected to be January 70, February 40, March 50, April 120, May 140 and June 70. The stock level must not fall below 120 units and an even production flow of 80 units is required. What would be the stock level on 1 January?

EXHIBIT 19.2

Units	January	February	March	April	May	June
Opening stock	140	150	190	220	180	120
Add Units produced	80	80	80	80	80	80
	220	230	270	300	260	200
Less Sales	(70)	(40)	(50)	(120)	(140)	(70)
Closing stock	150	190	220	180	120	130

It is more important in many firms to ensure a smooth production flow than to bother unduly about stock levels, assuming that the minimum stock level is always maintained. If the work is skilled then that type of labour force may take several years to become trained, and skilled labour in many industries does not take kindly to being sacked and re-employed as the demand for the goods fluctuates. This is not always true with skilled labour; for instance in the building industry such craftsmen as bricklayers may go to a builder until he has completed a contract such as building a college, a hospital or a housing estate, and then leave and go to another employer on the completion of the job.

On the other hand, a skilled engineer, concerned with the manufacture of, say, diesel engines, would not expect to be fired and re-employed continuously. The bricklayer has a skill that is easily transferable to many other building employers in an area, whereas the diesel engineer may have only one firm within fifty miles of his home where he can use his skills properly. A man employed as a labourer might work on a building site in one part of the year and then work as a labourer in an engineering factory in another part of the year.

Whether a firm could carry on production with widely uneven production levels depends very much on the type of firm and the type of labour involved. A firm would only sack skilled labour which it needed again shortly if it could persuade the men or women to come back when required. If the people who had been sacked were likely to find other employment, and not return to the firm when required, then this would mean that the firm would probably keep them on its payroll and production would continue and stocks of finished goods would begin to pile up.

Many firms do in fact realise their social obligations by only laying off workers when no other alternative is at all reasonable. In some organisations there are probably more workers from time to time than the firm actually needs – this is known as 'organisational slack', so that there is a leeway between the increasing of production and having to take on extra workers.

19.7 Uneven production levels

Some firms by their very nature will have uneven production levels, and this will be accepted by their labour force. An ice-cream firm would find sales at the highest levels in summer, tailing off in winter. It is not really possible to build up stock of ice-cream in the winter for summer sales! Even if it could be done technically, the costs of refrigerating large quantities of ice-cream for several months could hardly be economic. The large labour force used in the summer months will probably include students occupying their vacation periods profitably, and not able anyway to work at the job all the year round even if they wanted to. Such a kind of firm will normally have a far greater relationship between current stock levels and current sales than a firm which has even production levels. The calculation of the quantity to be produced is then:

Sales − (Opening stock + Closing stock) = Production

This can also be stated as:

Opening stock + Units produced − Sales = Closing stock

If the opening stock is 80 units, the sales are expected to be 100 units and the desired closing stock is 50 units, it becomes:

	Units
Opening stock	80
Add Production	?
Less Sales	(100)
Closing stock	50

Production will, therefore, be the missing figure, i.e. 70 units (80 + Production 70 = 150 less actually sold 100 = closing stock 50).

Exhibit 19.3 shows the units to be produced if the following information is known – stock required 1 January 40, at end of each month, January 60, February 110, March 170, April 100, May 60, June 20. Sales are expected to be January 100, February 150, March 110, April 190, May 70, June 50.

EXHIBIT 19.3

Units	January	February	March	April	May	June
Opening stock	40	60	110	170	100	60
Production required	120	200	170	120	30	10
	160	260	280	290	130	70
Less Sales	(100)	(150)	(110)	(190)	(70)	(50)
Closing stock	60	110	170	100	60	20

Linked with the production budget will be a materials purchase budget. It may well be that an order will have to be placed in January, received in March and issued to production in April. The purchase of materials will have to be planned as scientifically as possible.

Learning outcomes

You should now have learnt:

1 That budgets are prepared in order to guide the firm towards its objectives.

2 That they should be drawn up within the context of *planning* and *control*.

3 That while budgets are drawn up for control purposes, a budget should not be seen as a straitjacket.

4 That there are a number of methods or techniques available to management wishing to ensure that excessive stocks are not carried by their organisations. These include economic order quantity (EOQ), just-in-time (JIT), and optimised production technology (OPT).

REVIEW QUESTIONS

Advice: It is unlikely that a full question will be devoted to the contents of this chapter. What is far more likely is that this will be part of a larger question.

19.1 For the year ended 31 December 20X6 the sales of units are expected to be:

January	70	May	30	September	60
February	90	June	20	October	70
March	60	July	20	November	90
April	40	August	30	December	50

The opening stock at 1 January 20X6 will be 120 units. The closing stock desired at 31 December 20X6 is 150 units.

(*a*) What will production be per month if an even production flow is required and stock levels during the year could be allowed to fall to zero?

(*b*) Given the same information plus the constraint that stock levels must never fall below 110 units, and that extra production will be undertaken in January 20X6 to ensure this, what will the January production figure be?

19.2 A firm wants to maintain an even production flow for the first six months of 20X4 followed by an even production flow of 20 units more per month for the last six months of 20X4.

Opening stock of units at 1 January 20X4	50
Closing stock of units wanted at 31 December 20X4	120
Sales of units during the year	650

How many units should be manufactured per month (*a*) January to June 20X4, (*b*) July to December 20X4?

19.3X What stock should be held by a firm on 1 July 20X7 if the following data are available?

		Jul	*Aug*	*Sep*	*Oct*	*Nov*	*Dec*
(*i*)	Sales expected to be	100	140	180	270	190	130
(*ii*)	Production expected to be	160	200	220	250	210	180

(*iii*) Desired stock level at 31 December 20X7 is 320 units.

19.4X What would the production levels have to be for each month if the following data were available?

		Jan	*Feb*	*Mar*	*Apr*	*May*	*Jun*
(*i*)	Stock levels wanted at the end of each month	690	780	1,100	1,400	1,160	940
(*ii*)	Expected sales each month	800	920	1,090	1,320	1,480	1,020

(*iii*) The stock level at 1 January 20X5 will be 740 units.

19.5X (*a*) For each of the following, state three reasons why a firm may wish to keep:
   (*i*) a minimum stock level of finished goods, and
   (*ii*) an even level of production in the face of fluctuating demand.

(*b*) The sales forecast for Douglas & Co for July–December 20X7 is:

	J	*A*	*S*	*O*	*N*	*D*
Units	280	200	260	360	400	420

Produce a production budget showing montly opening and closing stock figures if the firm wishes to maintain an even level of producing 300 units each month, and a minimum stock level of 150 units.
   What must the opening stock be at 1 July to achieve this?

(*c*) Under what circumstances, in budgetary control, may a firm's productive capacity prove to be its limiting or key factor?

(AQA (AEB): GCE A-level)

CHAPTER 20

Cash budgets

Learning objectives

By the end of this chapter, you should be able to:

● explain the importance of cash funds to an organisation;

● prepare a cash budget;

● explain the importance of cash budgeting in the control of cash funds;

● explain the difference between profits and cash in the context of organisational survival.

20.1 The need for cash budgets

It is no use budgeting for production and for sales if at some time during the budget period the firm runs out of cash funds. When talking about cash in budgets we are also usually including bank funds. For that reason, we will not be differentiating between cash and cheque payments or between cash and cheques received. As cash is so important, it is budgeted for, so that any shortage of cash can be known in advance and action taken to obtain permission for a loan or a bank overdraft to be available then, rather than wait until the shortage or deficiency occurs. Bank managers, or anyone concerned with the lending of money, strongly resent one of their customers needing a bank overdraft without prior warning when, in fact, the customer could have known well in advance if a cash budget had been prepared.

The finance needed may not just be by way of borrowing from a bank or finance house, it may well be a long-term need that can only be satisfied by an issue of shares or debentures. Such issues need planning well in advance, and a cash budget can reveal (*a*) that they will be needed, (*b*) how much is needed and (*c*) when it will be needed.

We can now look at a very simple case. Without being concerned in this first exhibit with exactly what the receipts and payments are for, just to keep matters simple at this stage, we can see the dangers that are inherent in not budgeting for cash.

EXHIBIT 20.1

Mr Muddlem had a meeting with his accountant on 1 July 20X3. He was feeling very pleased with himself. He had managed to get some very good orders from customers, mainly because he was now allowing them extra time in which to pay their accounts. Sprite, the accountant, said, 'Can you afford to do all that you are hoping to do?'

Muddlem laughed, 'Why, I'll be making so much money I won't know how to spend it.'

'But have you got the cash to finance everything?' asked Sprite.

'If I'm making a good profit then of course I'll have the cash,' said Muddlem. 'I know the bank manager says that any bank overdraft could not be more than £1,000, but I doubt if I need it.'

'Don't let us rely on guesses,' says Sprite. 'Let's work it out.'

After an hour's work the following facts emerge:

(a) Present cash balance (including bank balance) £800.

(b) Receipts from debtors will be: July £2,000, August £2,600, September £5,000, October £7,000, November £8,000, December £15,000.

(c) Payments will be: July £2,500, August £2,700, September £6,900, October £7,800, November £9,900, December £10,300.

This is then summarised:

	Jul £	Aug £	Sep £	Oct £	Nov £	Dec £
Balance at start of the month:	800	300	200			
Deficit at the start of the month:				(1,700)	(2,500)	(4,400)
Receipts	2,000	2,600	5,000	7,000	8,000	15,000
	2,800	2,900	5,200	5,300	5,500	10,600
Payments	(2,500)	(2,700)	(6,900)	(7,800)	(9,900)	(10,300)
Balance at end of the month:	+300	+200				+300
Deficit at the end of the month:			(1,700)	(2,500)	(4,400)	

'I'm in an awkward position now,' says Muddlem. 'I just cannot borrow £4,400 nor can I cut down on my sales, and anyway I don't really want to as these new sales are very profitable indeed. If only I'd known this, I could have borrowed the money from my brother only last week but he's invested it elsewhere now.'

'Come and see me tomorrow,' says Sprite. 'There may well be something we can do.'

Fortunately for Muddlem his luck was in. He arrived to see his accountant the following morning, waving a cheque. 'My wife won £5,000 on a bingo jackpot last night,' he said.

'Thank goodness for that, at least in future you'll learn to budget ahead for cash requirements. You can't be lucky all the time,' says Sprite.

20.2 Timing of cash receipts and payments

In drawing up a cash budget, it must be borne in mind that all the payments for units produced would very rarely be made at the same time as production itself occurred. For instance the raw materials might be bought in March, incorporated in the goods being produced in April and paid for in May. On the other hand, the raw materials may have been in hand for some time, so that the goods are bought in January, paid for in February and used in production the following August. In contrast, the direct labour part of the product is usually paid for almost at the same time as the unit being produced. Even here a unit may be produced in one week and the wages paid one week later, so that a unit might be produced on say 27 June and the wages for the direct labour involved paid for on 3 July.

Similarly, the date of sale and the date of receipt of cash will not usually be the same, except in many supermarkets and retail stores where many of the goods sold are paid for at the time of sale. The goods might be sold in May and the money received in August, or even paid for in advance so that the goods might be paid for in February but the goods not shipped to the buyer until May. This is especially true, at least for part of the goods, when a cash deposit is left for specially-made goods which will take some time to manufacture. A simple example of this would be a made-to-measure suit on which a deposit would be paid at the time of order, the final payment being made when the completed suit is collected by the buyer.

EXHIBIT 20.2

A cash budget for the six months ended 30th June 20X3 is to be drafted from the following information.

(a) Opening cash balance at 1 January 20X3 £3,200.
(b) Sales at £12 per unit; cash received three months after sale.

Units: 20X2			20X3								
Oct	Nov	Dec	Jan	Feb	Mar	Apr	May	Jun	Jul	Aug	Sep
80	90	70	100	60	120	150	140	130	110	100	160

(c) Production in units

20X2			20X3								
Oct	Nov	Dec	Jan	Feb	Mar	Apr	May	Jun	Jul	Aug	Sep
70	80	90	100	110	130	140	150	120	160	170	180

(d) Raw materials used in production cost £4 per unit of production. They are paid for two months before being used in production.
(e) Direct labour: £3 per unit paid for in the same month as the unit is produced.
(f) Other variable expenses: £2 per unit, $^3/_4$ of the cost being paid for in the same month as production, the other $^1/_4$ paid in the month after production.
(g) Fixed expenses of £100 per month are paid monthly.
(h) A motor van is to be bought and paid for in April for £800.

Schedules of payments and receipts are as follows:

Payments (The month shown in brackets is the month in which the units are produced)

	January		£	February		£
Raw materials:	130	(March) × £4	520	140	(April) × £4	560
Direct labour:	100	(January) × £3	300	110	(February) × £3	330
Variable:	100	(January) × $^3/_4$ × £2	150	110	(February) × $^3/_4$ × £2	165
	90	(December) × $^1/_4$ × £2	45	100	(January) × $^1/_4$ × £2	50
Fixed:			100			100
			1,115			1,205

	March		£	April		£
Raw materials:	150	(May) × £4	600	120	(June) × £4	480
Direct labour:	130	(March) × £3	390	140	(April) × £3	420
Variable:	130	(March) × $^3/_4$ × £2	195	140	(April) × $^3/_4$ × £2	210
	110	(February) × $^1/_4$ × £2	55	130	(March) × $^1/_4$ × £2	65
Fixed:			100			100
Motor van:						800
			1,340			2,075

	May		£	June		£
Raw materials:	160	(July) × £4	640	170	(August) × £4	680
Direct labour:	150	(May) × £3	450	120	(June) × £3	360
Variable:	150	(May) × $^3/_4$ × £2	225	120	(June) × $^3/_4$ × £2	180
	140	(April) × $^1/_4$ × £2	70	150	(May) × $^1/_4$ × £2	75
Fixed:			100			100
			1,485			1,395

Receipts (The month shown in brackets is the month in which the sale was made)

			£
January	80 (October)	× £12	960
February	90 (November)	× £12	1,080
March	70 (December)	× £12	840
April	100 (January)	× £12	1,200
May	60 (February)	× £12	720
June	120 (March)	× £12	1,440

Cash Budget

	Jan £	Feb £	Mar £	Apr £	May £	Jun £
Balance from previous month	3,200	3,045	2,920	2,420	1,545	780
Add Receipts (per schedule)	960	1,080	840	1,200	720	1,440
	4,160	4,125	3,760	3,620	2,265	2,220
Less Payments (per schedule)	(1,115)	(1,205)	(1,340)	(2,075)	(1,485)	(1,395)
Balance carried to next month	3,045	2,920	2,420	1,545	780	825

20.3 Advantages of cash budgets

These can be said to be:

1 Having to think ahead and plan for the future, and express the plans in figures, focuses the mind in a way that thinking in a general fashion about the future will not do. A general optimistic feeling that 'all will be well' will often not stand up to scrutiny when the views of the future are expressed in a cash budget.

2 Seeing that money will have to be borrowed at a particular date will mean that you can negotiate for a loan in advance, rather than at the time when you have actually run out of cash. Bankers and other lenders do not like someone attempting to borrow money in a panic, and needing the money to be instantly available.

When borrowing money, you have to give the lender the confidence that the loan will be repaid at the proper time, plus any interest and charges that may accrue. Attempted last-minute borrowing, probably not substantiated by any calmly thought-out plan, will not inspire such confidence, and will often lead to the loan being refused as the lender may think that the risk is too great.

It is not only that you risk the loan being refused. Lenders will often realise that they have you at their mercy, and will charge much higher rates of interest and impose other conditions that otherwise they would not have done.

3 Knowing about the need to borrow in advance also widens the possible pool of lenders. Such people as friends, relations and business people or investors other than bankers rarely have large sums of cash quickly available. They need time to turn their own investments into cash before they can lend to you.

4 Alternatively, you may find that you will have cash funds surplus to requirements. Knowing this in advance will enable you to investigate properly how you can invest this surplus cash until required, thus earning interest or other investment income. Surplus cash lying in bank current accounts very often earns absolutely no interest at all, no matter how large the amount. Banks often have deposit accounts in which surplus current account cash can be invested to earn interest, with the necessary sums being transferred back into the current account when required by the business. There are also other sorts of short-term investments which your bank or accountant can advise you to put your surplus cash into at appropriate times.

20.4 Profits and shortages of cash funds

Just because a firm is making good profits it does not mean that it will not be short of cash funds. Let us look at how some firms may have good profits and yet still be short of cash funds, possibly having bank overdrafts or loans which are getting steadily bigger.

1 *Firm A has increased its sales by 50 per cent, is making the same percentage gross profit and its expenses have hardly increased, yet its overdraft has got bigger. The reason is that it increased its sales by giving all of its customers four months to pay instead of the usual one month. This has attracted a lot of new customers.*

This means that the debtors are increasing by very large amounts, as they can wait another three months in which to pay their bills. Thus the equivalent of three months' cash receipts have not come into the bank. Meanwhile the firm is making extra purchases for goods for the new customers, with a consequent outflow of more cash than usual, especially if it has not got longer credit terms from its suppliers. So hardly any cash is coming in in the short term, while more cash than usual is going out.

The answer to this is: large increase in profits and fewer cash funds probably resulting in higher bank overdrafts or loans.

2 *Firm B has the same sales, purchases and expenses as usual. However, the proprietor, for whatever reason, is now taking much higher drawings than before. In fact his drawings are exceeding the profits he is making.*

Such a situation cannot go on for ever. He will start to find his cash funds in the business are decreasing, possibly meaning higher loans or overdrafts being needed.

3 *Firm C has just spent a lot of money on fixed assets. It will be several years before the firm recoups the money it has paid out. In the meantime only the depreciation provisions are charged against profits. However, the cash funds have seen the disappearance of the whole amount paid for fixed assets. The net result is that profits may be recorded but the firm is hard-up for cash funds.*

4 *Firm D is going through a bad patch in that sales are very difficult to make, but it does not want to get rid of any of its workforce. Production is kept going at normal rates, and the products not sold are simply kept in stock. Thus the stock is increasing at an alarming rate.*

If stock is not being sold then cash obviously is not being received in respect of such production. Meanwhile all the expenses and wages are still being paid for. This can result in a severe shortage of funds if carried on for long if no further finance is received.

5 *A long-term loan has been paid off but no extra finance from anywhere else has been received. This could equally be the situation if a partner retires and the balance due to that partner is paid out of the firm's funds, without a new partner being introduced. Similarly a company buying back its shares without a new issue of shares could face the same situation.*

In the long term there is a connection between profits and cash funds available, even though it may not be very marked. In the short term you can see that there may be no relationship at all. This simple fact is one that surprises most people. It is because the calculation of profits follows one set of concepts, whereas the calculation of cash funds follows a completely different set of rules.

We examined a related aspect of this topic when we looked at 'overtrading' in Chapter 8.

Learning outcomes

You should now have learnt:

1 The difference between profit and cash funds.

2 When undertaking a cash budget, 'cash' includes both money held in cash and amounts held in the bank.

3 The importance of cash funds to an organisation.

4 What is meant by the term 'cash budget'.

5 The importance of preparing and monitoring a cash budget.

6 How to prepare a cash budget.

7 The difference between profits and cash in the context of business survival.

REVIEW QUESTIONS

Advice: Cash budgeting is an extremely important part of accounting. Questions on this topic are relatively easy to do, and high marks can be gained quite easily.

20.1 Ukridge comes to see you in April 20X3. He is full of enthusiasm for a new product that he is about to launch on to the market. Unfortunately his financial recklessness in the past has led him into being bankrupted twice, and he has only just got discharged by the court from his second bankruptcy.

'Look here laddie,' he says, 'with my new idea I'll be a wealthy man before Christmas.'

'Calm down,' you say, 'and tell me all about it.'

Ukridge's plans as far as cash is concerned for the next six months are:

(a) Present cash balance (including bank) £5.

(b) Timely legacy under a will – being received on 1 May 20X3, £5,000. This will be paid into the business bank account by Ukridge.

(c) Receipts from debtors will be: May £400, June £4,000, July £8,000, August £12,000, September £9,000, October £5,000.

(d) Payments will be: May £100, June £5,000, July £11,000, August £20,000, September £12,000, October £7,000.

You are required:

(a) To draw up a cash budget, showing the balances each month, for the six months to 31 October 20X3.

(b) The only person Ukridge could borrow money from would charge interest at the rate of 100 per cent per annum. This is not excessive considering Ukridge's past record. Advise Ukridge.

20.2X Draw up a cash budget for N. Morris showing the balance at the end of each month, from the following information for the six months ended 31 December 20X2:

(a) Opening cash (including bank) balance £1,200.

(b) Production in units:

20X2									20X3	
Apr	May	Jun	Jul	Aug	Sep	Oct	Nov	Dec	Jan	Feb
240	270	300	320	350	370	380	340	310	260	250

(c) Raw materials used in production cost £5 per unit. Of this 80 per cent is paid in the month of production and 20 per cent in the month after production.

(d) Direct labour costs of £8 per unit are payable in the month of production.

(e) Variable expenses are £2 per unit, payable one-half in the same month as production and one-half in the month following production.

(f) Sales at £20 per unit:

20X2

Mar	Apr	May	Jun	Jul	Aug	Sep	Oct	Nov	Dec
260	200	320	290	400	300	350	400	390	400

Debtors to pay their accounts three months after that in which sales are made.

(g) Fixed expenses of £400 per month payable each month.

(h) Machinery costing £2,000 to be paid for in October 20X2.

(i) Will receive a legacy £2,500 in December 20X2.

(j) Drawings to be £300 per month.

20.3 Herbert Limited make a single product, whose unit budget details are as follows:

	£	£
Selling price		30
Less Costs		
Direct material	9	
Direct labour	4	
Direct production expenses	6	
Variable selling expenses	4	23
Contribution		7

Additional information

1 Unit sales are expected to be:

June	July	August	September	October
1,000	800	400	600	900

2 Credit sales will account for 60 per cent of total sales. Debtors are expected to pay in the month following sale for which there will be a cash discount of 2 per cent.

3 Stock levels will be arranged so that the production in one month will meet the next month's sales demand.

4 The purchases of direct materials in one month will just meet the next month's production requirements.

5 Suppliers of direct materials will be paid in the month following purchase.

6 Labour costs will be paid in the month in which they are incurred. All other expenses will be paid in the month following that in which they are incurred.

7 Fixed expenses are £2,000 per month and include £180 for depreciation.

8 The bank balance at 1 July 20X9 is £3,900 favourable to the business.

Required:

(a) A cash budget for Herbert Limited for the three month period ending on 30 September 20X9 showing the balance of cash at the end of each month. *(16 marks)*

(b) List and explain three ways in which the preparation of a cash flow budget could be of advantage to the management of Herbert Limited. *(6 marks)*

(AQA (AEB): GCE A-level)

20.4X Mtoto Ltd operate as wholesale 'cash and carry' stores and in addition to their main store have two other depots.

The company's summarised balance sheet as at 31 August 20X1 was as follows.

	£	£		£	£
Fixed assets			*Authorised and issued capital*		
(at net book value)		549,600	450,000 £1 *Ordinary shares*		
Current assets			Fully paid		450,000
Stock	399,900		Retained earnings at		
Trade debtors	21,000	420,900	1 Sept 20X0	300,000	
			Less Current year ended		
			31 Aug 20X1 loss	130,000	170,000
			Current liabilities		
			Trade (and other)		
			creditors	110,500	
			Bank overdraft	240,000	350,500
		970,500			970,500

- Over the past year the company has experienced increased competition and as a consequence reported a net trading loss for the year ended 31 August 20X1.
- The company has decided that in the new financial year tighter control must be exercised over cash resources.
- The following information is available:

1 All goods are purchased by the main store.

Purchases 20X1

Actual		Forecast			
Jul	Aug	Sep	Oct	Nov	Dec
£	£	£	£	£	£
55,800	61,200	64,300	41,000	46,000	41,800

- Mtoto Ltd pays suppliers two months after the month of purchase.
- Forecast purchases are being reduced since the managing director regarded current stock levels as too high.
- In addition, shop-soiled stock which cost £20,000 is to be sold for cash in October. It is anticipated that this stock will be sold for £17,000. This sale is not included in the sales of note 2 below.

2 All sales are on a cash basis only except for several important customers who trade only with Mtoto's main store.

Sales 20X1

	Actual		Forecast			
	Jul	Aug	Sep	Oct	Nov	Dec
	£	£	£	£	£	£
Main store:						
Cash sales	21,500	21,600	18,000	26,300	19,200	24,700
Credit sales	24,000	21,000	32,500	26,000	25,400	27,800
Depot 1	15,500	17,400	19,700	18,000	17,600	17,900
Depot 2	21,000	24,000	26,300	19,700	21,000	19,100

3 Mtoto Ltd pays £9,500 fixed overhead costs per month.

4 Wages and salaries are paid each month through a centralised payroll system.

Wages and salaries 20X1

Actual	Forecast			
Aug	Sep	Oct	Nov	Dec
£	£	£	£	£
16,000	17,000	19,000	13,000	12,000

In October, 10 staff were made redundant and are to receive their redundancy compensation of £12,000 in December. This amount is not included in the above figures.

5 Other variable overhead charges are paid by Mtoto Ltd in the month following the month they are incurred.

Variable overhead charges 20X1

Aug	Sep	Oct	Nov	Dec
£	£	£	£	£
5,600	6,800	6,100	7,400	6,900

6 Plant surplus to requirement is to be sold in September for £26,500 cash. The plant cost £55,000 and depreciation to date is £20,000.

Required:

(*a*) A detailed cash budget, on a month by month basis, for the first four months of the financial year ending 31 December 20X1 for Mtoto Ltd. *(13 marks)*

(*b*) A report commenting on:
    (*i*) the current and forecast liquidity position. *(7 marks)*
    (*ii*) the action that Mtoto Ltd could take to attempt a return to a profit situation. *(5 marks)*

(AQA (AEB): GCE A-level)

20.5 David Llewelyn has been advised by his bank manager that he ought to provide a forecast of his cash position at the end of each month. This is to ensure that his cash inputs will be sufficient to allow a bank loan to be repaid when due and to check that his outgoings are properly controlled. It is estimated that at 30 June 20X0 his current account will be £5,000 in credit, whereas the amount owing in respect of the bank loan taken out on 1 March 20X0 will be £15,000. Monthly deductions from the current account balance amount to £242 including interest charges on account of this loan. In addition to these outgoings, David has to allow for the following:

(*i*)   The payment of wages of £2,000 per month.
(*ii*)   Personal drawings of £500 per month.
(*iii*) On average David earns a margin of 15 per cent (of sales) and expects to sell stocks purchased in the previous month. Of the sales in any one month, 20 per cent are paid for within that month, 70 per cent the following month and the remainder two months after sale.
       Other receipts from debtors are expected to be £40,000 in July 20X0, £32,000 in August 20X0 and £4,000 in September 20X0.
(*iv*) Purchases of supplies will amount to £38,250 per month from July 20X0 payable one month in arrears. In addition, purchases of £7,500 to increase stocks will be delivered in September 20X0 and must be paid for in October 20X0. Creditors of £34,000 for purchases made in June 20X0 are to be paid in July 20X0.

(*v*)   Monthly payments to the Inland Revenue for the taxation on his employees' earnings will amount to £500 per month.

(*vi*) Rent which has to be paid quarterly in advance amounts to £5,000 per annum. These payments commenced in January 20X0.

(*vii*) Business rates are to be paid in two instalments as due in October 20X0 and in March 20X1. This estimated expenditure will amount to £4,500 per annum.

(*viii*) Payment of Value Added Tax to H.M. Customs and Excise of £5,000 in July 20X0 and every third month thereafter (but see also (ix)).

(*ix*) David intends to purchase a van for £8,150 in August 20X0. He will then be entitled to deduct £1,050 from the VAT payment due to H.M. Customs and Excise in October 20X0.

Required:

A forecast cash flow statement in columnar form showing the estimated current account balance at the close of each of the four months ending 31 October 20X0.   *(28 marks)*

(Welsh Joint Education Committee: GCE A-level)

20.6   The managing director of Pumpkin Ltd was reviewing the results of the company for the financial year ended 31 March 20X2. The following summarised information was available:

<table>
<tr><td colspan="2">*Balances as at 1 April 20X1*</td></tr>
<tr><td>Issued ordinary share capital:</td><td>£</td></tr>
<tr><td>£1 fully paid shares</td><td>150,000</td></tr>
<tr><td>Share premium account</td><td>100,000</td></tr>
<tr><td>Balance of retained earnings</td><td>40,000</td></tr>
<tr><td colspan="2">*Balances as at 31 March 20X2*</td></tr>
<tr><td>Net profit for year 20X1/X2</td><td>70,000</td></tr>
<tr><td>Fixed assets</td><td>300,000</td></tr>
<tr><td>Bank overdraft</td><td>150,000</td></tr>
<tr><td>Other net current assets</td><td>210,000</td></tr>
</table>

Note: There were no other accounts with balances. The balances as at 1 April 20X1 had remained unchanged throughout the year.

The managing director was pleased that the company had made a good profit, but he was rather concerned that a healthy bank balance at the beginning of the year had now become a large bank overdraft.

Consequently he asked the company accountant to prepare forecast information for 20X2/X3 in order that the cash situation could be improved.

The following information was prepared by the accountant:

1 Company sales – March 20X2

<table>
<tr><td></td><td>£</td></tr>
<tr><td>Cash sales</td><td>30,000</td></tr>
<tr><td>Credit sales</td><td>65,000</td></tr>
</table>

In each month April to September (inclusive) the sales per month would be:

<table>
<tr><td></td><td>£</td></tr>
<tr><td>Cash sales</td><td>40,000</td></tr>
<tr><td>Credit sales</td><td>70,000</td></tr>
</table>

All credit sales are settled the month after the sale.

2 All goods purchased are from a single supplier. The goods are purchased on credit and each month's purchases are paid for three months after the month of purchase.

The following purchase schedule had been prepared for the first nine months of 20X2:

	January	February	March
Purchases	£60,000	£58,000	£61,000

Purchases in April, May and June: £55,000 in each month
Purchases in July, August and September: £45,000 in each month

Note: The company had successfully negotiated lower prices from its supplier commencing 1 July 20X2.

3 Dividends would be paid as follows:
  (*i*) Final ordinary dividend of 5p per share payable on 31 May 20X2 in respect of financial year 20X1/X2.
  (*ii*) Interim ordinary dividend of 2p per share payable on 31 July 20X2 in respect of financial year 20X2/X3.

4 Selling and distribution expenses are expected to be 6 per cent of a given month's total sales. They are paid one month in arrears.

5 Administration charges would be incurred as follows:

20X2 February, March, April	£10,000 per month
20X2 May to September (inclusive)	£13,500 per month

Administration charges are settled two months after the month in which they were incurred.

6 The company had decided to make a bonus issue of shares of one share for every three held. The issue would be made on 30 April 20X2. The bonus shares would not qualify for the final dividend of 20X1/X2, but would qualify for the interim dividend to be paid on 31 July 20X2.

Required:

(*a*) Comment on the liquidity of the company as at 31 March 20X2 and explain to the managing director why a company can apparently make a good profit but have no cash in the bank. *(8 marks)*

(*b*) Prepare a cash budget for each of the four months ending 31 July 20X2. *(12 marks)*

(*c*) Comment on the forecast bank balance as shown by your cash budget. Identify ways in which the bank overdraft could be reduced over the last five months of 20X2. *(5 marks)*

(AQA (AEB): GCE A-level)

20.7X Belinda Raglan owns a clothing factory. Trading over the last two years has been very successful and she feels that having achieved good results it is now time to request an increase in the overdraft facility.

● In the past the bank has been willing to offer business overdraft facilities and at present there is an agreed limit of £15,000.
● On 1 May 20X4 the overdraft stands at £5,000.
● In order to support her request for the increased facility, she has produced a forecast profit statement for the four months ended 31 August 20X4 as follows:

	May		June		July		August	
	£000	£000	£000	£000	£000	£000	£000	£000
Sales		74		28		116		168
Cost of sales		51		12		78		101
Gross Profit		23		16		38		67
Less: Rent	4		4		4		4	
Other expenses	8		3		10		14	
Depreciation	5	17	5	12	5	19	5	23
Net profit		6		4		19		44

Although Belinda thought these figures would be sufficient to satisfy the requirements of the bank, the manager has asked for a cash budget for the period concerned to be submitted.

The following additional information concerning the business is available.

1 Rent is paid quarterly in advance on the first day of May, August, November and February.
2 All other expenses are payable in the month in which they are incurred.
3 Purchases for the period are expected to be – May £60,000; June £120,000; July £40,000 and August £43,000. These will be paid for in the month of purchase. Purchases will be unusually high in May and June because they will be subject to a special reduction of 3% of the amounts quoted.
4 80% of the sales are on a credit basis payable two months later. Sales in March and April were £88,000 and £84,000 respectively.
5 A compensation payment of £10,000 to a former employee for an industrial injury, not covered by insurance, is due to be paid in May.

Required:

(a) Prepare a forecast cash budget on a month by month basis for the period May to August 20X4.
(15 marks)

(b) Discuss the advantages and disadvantages of cash budgeting.
(10 marks)

(c) Draft notes, to be used by the bank manager for a letter to Ms Raglan, indicating why the request for an increased overdraft facility may be refused.
(9 marks)

(AQA (AEB): GCE A-level)

20.8X Ian Spiro, formerly a taxi-driver, decided to establish a car-hire business after inheriting £50,000.

His business year would be divided into budget periods each being four weeks.

He commenced business on a Monday the first day of period 1, by paying into a business bank account £34,000 as his initial capital.

All receipts and payments would be passed through his bank account.

The following additional forecast information is available on the first four budget periods of his proposed business venture.

1 At the beginning of period 1 he would purchase 6 saloon cars of a standard type; list price £6,000 each, on which he had negotiated a trade discount of 11 per cent.
2 He estimates that four of the cars will be on the road each Monday to Friday inclusive, and at weekends all six cars will be on the road. Hire charges as follows:

Weekday rate £10 per day per car
Weekend rate £18 per day per car

He estimates that this business trading pattern will commence on the Monday of the second week of period 1, and then continue thereafter.

All hire transactions are to be settled for cash.

Note: a weekend consists of Saturday and Sunday. All remaining days are weekdays.

3 An account was established with a local garage for fuel, and it was agreed to settle the account two periods in arrear. The forecast gallon usage is as follows:

Period 1	Period 2	Period 3	Period 4
200	200	400	500

The fuel costs £1.80 per gallon.

4 Servicing costs for the vehicles would amount to £300 per period, paid during the period following the service. Servicing would commence in period 1.

5 Each of his vehicles would be depreciated at 25 per cent per annum on a reducing balance basis.

6 Fixed costs of £200 per period would be paid each period.

7 He had agreed with a local firm to provide two cars on a regular basis, Monday to Friday inclusive, as chauffeur driven cars. The agreed rate was £60 a day (per car), payment being made in the following period.
    This contract would not commence until the first day of period 2, a Monday.

8 Drawings: Periods 1 and 2: £400 a period.
              Periods 3 and 4: £800 a period.

9 Wages and salaries:
    (a) Initially he would employ 3 staff, each on £320 a budget period. Employment would commence at the beginning of period 1.
    (b) On commencement of the contract the two additional staff employed as chauffeurs would each receive £360 a budget period. Payments are to be made at the end of the relevant period.

10 In anticipation of more business being developed he planned to buy a further three cars for cash in period 4. The cars would cost £6,500 each and it was agreed he would be allowed a trade discount of 10 per cent.

Required:

(a) A detailed cash budget for the first four budget periods.
(b) An explanation as to why it is important that a business should prepare a cash budget.
(c) Identify how a sole proprietor may finance a forecast cash deficit distinguishing between internal and external financial sources.

(AQA (AEB): GCE A-level)

20.9 Melvin Books Ltd manufactures bookmarks, which sell for £1.00 each.
    The bookmarks are made by people working at home, who are paid 20p for every bookmark they produce. The raw materials bought to make one bookmark cost 30p. Salespeople sell the bookmarks and are paid 10p for each bookmark which they sell. The administration costs £42,000 per year. Business rates of £20,400 are also paid annually.

Required:

(a) Classify each cost by completing the following table and total each column: *(7 marks)*

	Total fixed costs £	Variable costs **per unit** in pence
Wages Raw materials Salespeople's wages Administration costs Business rates		
Total		

(b) (i) State the formula used to calculate the contribution per unit. *(1 mark)*

(ii) Calculate the contribution per unit. *(3 marks)*

(iii) Why is the amount of contribution per unit important? *(2 marks)*

(c) Calculate:

(i) the number of bookmarks which must be manufactured and sold per year for the business to break even. State the formula used; *(4 marks)*

(ii) the total revenue at this level of sales; *(2 marks)*

(iii) the profit or loss achieved by Melvin Books Ltd if 150,000 bookmarks are sold.

(2 marks)

(AQA: GCE A-level, Paper ACC4, Q1, 21/1/2002)

Co-ordination of budgets

21.1 Master budgets

The various budgets have to be linked together and a 'master budget', which is really a budgeted set of final accounts, drawn up. We have in fact looked at the sales, production and cash budgets. There are, however, many more budgets for parts of the organisation; for instance there may be:

(*i*)   a selling expense budget,
(*ii*)   an administration expense budget,
(*iii*) a manufacturing overhead budget,
(*iv*)   a direct labour budget,
(*v*)   a purchases budget,

and so on. In this book we do not wish to get entangled in too many details, but in a real firm with a proper set of budgeting techniques there will be a great deal of detailed backing for the figures that are incorporated in the more important budgets.

Now it may be that when all the budgets have been co-ordinated, or slotted together, the master budget shows a smaller profit than the directors are prepared to accept. This will mean recasting budgets to see whether a greater profit can be earned and, if at all possible, the budgets will be altered. Eventually, there will be a master budget that the directors can agree to. This then gives the target for the results that the firm hopes to achieve in financial terms. Remember that there are other targets, such as employee welfare, product quality, etc. that cannot be so expressed.

This section is concerned with the drawing up of budgets for an imaginary firm, Walsh Ltd, culminating in the drawing up of a master budget.

To start with we can look at the last balance sheet of Walsh Ltd as at 31 December 20X4. This will give us our opening figures of stocks of raw materials, stock of finished goods, cash (including bank) balance, creditors, debtors, etc.

Walsh Ltd
Balance Sheet as at 31 December 20X4

Assets employed:

Fixed assets	Cost	Depreciation to date	Net
	£	£	£
Machinery	4,000	1,600	2,400
Motor vehicles	2,000	800	1,200
	6,000	2,400	3,600

Current assets		
Stocks: Finished goods (75 units)	900	
Raw materials	500	
Debtors (20X4 October £540 + November £360 +		
December £450)	1,350	
Cash and bank balances	650	
		3,400
		£7,000

Financed by:		
Share capital, 4,000 shares of £1 each		4,000
Profit and loss account		2,600
		6,600

Current liabilities		
Creditors for raw materials		
(November £120 + December £180)	300	
Creditors for fixed expenses (December)	100	
		400
		£7,000

The plans for the six months ended 30 June 20X5 are as follows:

(*i*) Production will be 60 units per month for the first four months, followed by 70 units per month for May and June.

(*ii*) Production costs will be (per unit):

	£
Direct materials	5
Direct labour	4
Variable overhead	3
	12

(*iii*) Fixed overhead is £100 per month, payable always one month in arrears.

(*iv*) Sales, at a price of £18 per unit, are expected to be:

	January	February	March	April	May	June
No. of units	40	50	60	90	90	70

(*v*) Purchases of direct materials (raw materials) will be:

	January	February	March	April	May	June
	£	£	£	£	£	£
	150	200	250	300	400	320

(*vi*) The creditors for raw materials bought are paid two months after purchase.

(*vii*) Debtors are expected to pay their accounts three months after they have bought the goods.

(*viii*) Direct labour and variable overhead are paid in the same month as the units are produced.

(*ix*) A machine costing £2,000 will be bought and paid for in March.

(*x*) 3,000 shares of £1 each are to be issued at par in May.

(*xi*) Depreciation for the six months: machinery £450, motor vehicles £200.

We must first of all draw up the various budgets and then incorporate them into the master budget. Some of the more detailed budgets which can be dispensed with in this illustration will be omitted.

Materials Budget

	Jan	Feb	Mar	Apr	May	Jun
Opening stock £	500	350	250	200	200	250
Add Purchases £	150	200	250	300	400	320
	650	550	500	500	600	570
Less Used in production:						
Jan–April 60 × £5	(300)	(300)	(300)	(300)		
May and June 70 × £5					(350)	(350)
Closing stock £	350	250	200	200	250	220

Production Budget (in units)

	Jan	Feb	Mar	Apr	May	Jun
Opening stock (units)	75	95	105	105	75	55
Add Produced	60	60	60	60	70	70
	135	155	165	165	145	125
Less Sales	(40)	(50)	(60)	(90)	(90)	(70)
Closing stock	95	105	105	75	55	55

Production Cost Budget (in £s)

	Jan	Feb	Mar	Apr	May	Jun	Total
Materials cost £	300	300	300	300	350	350	1,900
Labour cost £	240	240	240	240	280	280	1,520
Variable overhead £	180	180	180	180	210	210	1,140
	720	720	720	720	840	840	4,560

Creditors Budget

	Jan	Feb	Mar	Apr	May	Jun
Opening balance £	300	330	350	450	550	700
Add Purchases £	150	200	250	300	400	320
	450	530	600	750	950	1,020
Less Payments £	(120)	(180)	(150)	(200)	(250)	(300)
Closing balance £	330	350	450	550	700	720

Debtors Budget

	Jan	Feb	Mar	Apr	May	Jun
Opening balances £	1,350	1,530	2,070	2,700	3,600	4,320
Add Sales £	720	900	1,080	1,620	1,620	1,260
	2,070	2,430	3,150	4,320	5,220	5,580
Less Received £	(540)	(360)	(450)	(720)	(900)	(1,080)
Closing balances £	1,530	2,070	2,700	3,600	4,320	4,500

Cash Budget						
	Jan	Feb	Mar	Apr	May	Jun
Opening balance £	650	550	210			1,050
Opening overdraft £				(2,010)	(2,010)	
Received (see Schedule) £	540	360	450	720	3,900	1,080
	1,190	910	660	1,290	1,890	2,130
Payments (see Schedule) £	(640)	(700)	(2,670)	(720)	(840)	(890)
Closing balance £	550	210			1,050	1,240
Closing overdraft £			(2,010)	(2,010)		

Cash Payments Schedule						
	Jan	Feb	Mar	Apr	May	Jun
Creditors for goods bought two months previously £	120	180	150	200	250	300
Fixed overhead £	100	100	100	100	100	100
Direct labour £	240	240	240	240	280	280
Variable overhead £	180	180	180	180	210	210
Machinery £			2,000			
	640	700	2,670	720	840	890

Cash Receipts Schedule						
	Jan	Feb	Mar	Apr	May	Jun
Debtors for goods sold three months previously £	540	360	450	720	900	1,080
Shares issued £					3,000	
					3,900	

Walsh Ltd: Master Budget
Forecast Operating Statement for the six months ended 30 June 20X5

		£
Sales		7,200
Less Cost of goods sold:		
Opening stock of finished goods	900	
Add Cost of goods completed	4,560	
	5,460	
Less Closing stock of finished goods	(660)	
		(4,800)
Gross profit		2,400
Less:		
Fixed overhead	600	
Depreciation:		
Machinery	450	
Motors	200	
		650
		(1,250)
Net profit		1,150

Walsh Ltd
Forecast Balance Sheet as at 30 June 20X5

Assets employed:

Fixed assets

	Cost	Depreciation to date	Net
	£	£	£
Machinery	6,000	2,050	3,950
Motor vehicles	2,000	1,000	1,000
	8,000	3,050	4,950

Current assets

Stocks:

Finished goods	660	
Raw materials	220	
Debtors	4,500	
Cash and bank balances	1,240	
	6,620	

Creditors

Amounts falling due within one year

Trade creditors	720		
Creditors for overheads	100		
		(820)	
			5,800
			10,750

Financed by:

Capital and Reserves

Called up share capital	7,000
Profit and loss account (2,600 + 1,150)	3,750
	10,750

21.2 Capital budgeting

The plan for the acquisition of fixed assets such as machinery, buildings, etc. is usually known as a capital budget. Management will evaluate the various possibilities open to it, and will compare the alternatives. This is a very important part of budgeting and it is covered in Chapter 14.

21.3 The advantages of budgeting

The process of budgeting, with the necessary participation throughout the organisation finally producing a profit plan, is now a regular feature in all but the smallest firms. Very often, budgeting is the one time when the various parts of management can really get together and work as a team rather than just as separate parts of an organisation. When budgeting is conducted under favourable conditions, there is no doubt that a firm which budgets will tend to perform rather better than a similar firm that does not budget. Budgeting means that managers can no longer give only general answers affecting the running of the firm, they have to put figures to their ideas; and they know that, in the end, their estimated figures are going to be compared with what the actual figures turn out to be.

It has often been said that the act of budgeting is possibly of more benefit than the budgets which are produced. However, the following benefits can be claimed for good budgeting:

(a) The strategic planning carried on by the board of directors or owners can be more easily linked to the decisions by managers as to how the resources of the business will be used to try to achieve the objectives of the business. The strategic plan has to be converted into action, and budgeting provides the ideal place where such planning can be converted into financial terms.

(b) Standards of performance can be agreed to for the various parts of the business. If sales and production targets are set as part of a co-ordinated plan, then the sales department cannot really complain that production is insufficient if they had agreed previously to a production level and this is being achieved, nor can production complain if its production exceeds the amount budgeted for and it remains unsold.

(c) Plans can be expressed in comparable financial terms. Some managers think mainly in terms of, say, units of production, or of tonnes of inputs or outputs, or of lorry mileage, etc. The effect that each of them has upon financial results must be brought home to them. For instance, a transport manager might be unconcerned about the number of miles that his fleet of lorries covers until the cost of doing such a large mileage is brought home to him, often during budgeting. It may be then, and only then, that he starts to search for possible economies. It is possible in many cases to use mathematics to find the best ways of loading vehicles, or to change routes taken by vehicles so that fewer miles are covered and yet the same delivery service is maintained. This is just one instance of many when the expression of the plans of a section of a business in financial terms can spark off a search for economies, when otherwise such a search may never be started at all.

(d) Managers can see how their work slots into the total activities of the firm. It can help to get rid of the feeling of 'I'm only a number not a person', because they can identify their position within the firm and can see that their jobs really are essential to the proper functioning of the firm.

(e) The budgets for a firm cannot be set in isolation. This means that the situation of the business, the nature of its products and its workforce, etc., must be seen against the economic background of the country. For instance, it is no use budgeting for extra labour when labour is in extremely short supply, without realising the implications, such as having to pay higher than normal wage rates. Increasing the sales target during a 'credit squeeze' needs a full investigation of the effect of the shortage of money upon the demand for the firm's goods, and so on.

The charges made against budgeting are mainly that budgets bring about inflexibility, and that managers will not depart from budget even though the departure would bring about a more desirable result. Too many budgets are set at one level of sales or production when, in fact, flexible budgets (discussed later in this chapter) ought to be used. It is very often the case that budgeting is forced upon managers against their will. Instead, the firm should really set out first of all to do a 'selling job' to convince managers that budgets are not the monsters so often thought. A trial run for part of a business is far superior to starting off by having a fully detailed budget set up right away for the whole of the business.

Learning to use budgets is rather like learning to swim. Let children get used to the water first and remove their fear of the water, then they will learn to swim fairly easily. For most children (but not all), if the first visit to the baths meant being pushed into the deep end immediately, then reaction against swimming would probably set in. Let a manager become used to the idea of budgeting, without the fear of being dealt with severely during a trial period, and most managers will then become used to the idea and participate properly.

21.4 The use of computers in budgeting

Years ago budgeting was a task which most accountants hated doing. It was not the concept of budgeting that accountants disliked. Far from it, as it suited their needs perfectly. Instead it was the multitude of numerical manipulations that had to be performed that made the task a formidable one.

Those of you who have done some of the exercises in this book manually know the feeling when after a lot of work your master budget simply will not balance. Searching through to find the error(s) can be a daunting prospect. Imagine how much more complicated it is in a real firm dealing with real figures rather than with the simple sets of data which form your exercises. Also, imagine the feeling when the managing director used to say to the accountant, 'What if we increased our prices by 5 per cent and took an extra month to pay creditors?' The accountant would then have to plough his or her way through a large number of extra calculations.

Most of that is now a thing of the past. Computers are used instead. Either they have a computer program specially written for the task, or else commercial spreadsheets can be used. When the necessary basic figures or 'what if' amendments are keyed in, the computer will automatically produce the budgets or the amended budgets within a very short space of time.

This enables management to see the results that would be expected to be obtained from many separate propositions, thus enhancing the chance of choosing the best solution. Also, as the accounting year unfolds, the changes that have occurred since the year started can be incorporated very easily so as to adjust the budgets as the year progresses.

21.5 Flexible budgets

So far in this book, budgets have been drawn up on the basis of one set of expectations, based on just one level of sales and production. Later, when the actual results are compared with the budgeted results expected in a fixed budget, they may have deviated for either or both of two reasons:

1 While the actual and budgeted volumes of production and sales may be the same there may be a difference in actual and budgeted costs.
2 The volumes of actual and budgeted units of sales and production may vary, so that the costs will be different because of different volumes.

The variations, or 'variances' as they are more commonly known, are usually under the control of different managers in the organisation. Variances coming under 1 will probably be under the control of the individual department. On the other hand variances under 2 are caused because of variations in plans brought about by top management because of changing sales, or at least the expectation of changing sales.

Budgets are used for control purposes, therefore a manager does not take kindly to being held responsible for a variance in his spending if the variance is caused by a type 2 occurrence if he is working on a fixed budget. The answer to this is to construct budgets at several levels of volume, and to show what costs, etc., they should incur at different levels. For instance, if a budget had been fixed at a volume of 500 units and the actual volume was 550, then the manager would undoubtedly feel aggrieved if the costs for producing 550 units are compared with the costs which should have been incurred for 500 units. Budgets which do allow for changing levels are called 'flexible budgets'.

To draft a full set of flexible budgets is outside the scope of this book, but an instance of one department's flexible budget for manufacturing overhead can be shown in Exhibit 21.1. (In reality it would be in greater detail.)

EXHIBIT 21.1

Data Ltd
Budget of Manufacturing Overhead, Department S

Units	400	450	500	550	600
	£	£	£	£	£
Variable overhead	510	550	600	680	770
Fixed overhead	400	400	400	400	400
Total overhead (A)	910	950	1,000	1,080	1,170
Direct labour hours (B)	200	225	250	275	300
Overhead rates (A) divided by (B)	4.55	4.22	4.00	3.93	3.90

Notice that the variable costs in this case do not vary in direct proportion to production. In this case, once 500 units production has been exceeded, they start to climb rapidly. The flexible budget makes far greater sense than a fixed budget. For instance if a fixed budget had been agreed at 400 units, with variable overhead £510, and production rose to 600 units, the manager would think the whole system unfair if he was expected to incur only £510 variable overhead (the figure for 400 units). On the contrary, if the comparison was on a flexible budget then costs at 600 units production would instead be compared with £770 (the figure at 600 units).

Learning outcomes

You should now have learnt:

1 There are a number of budgets that together comprise the master budget and they must all reconcile to each other and to the master budget.

2 That budget preparation is often an iterative process as the master budget is focused more and more tightly to the objectives of the organisation.

3 How to prepare a master budget.

4 That flexible budgeting permits managers to adjust their budgets in the light of variations in plan, often involving items over which they have no control.

REVIEW QUESTIONS

Advice: In many ways drawing up a budgeted set of final accounts is very much like drawing up accounts from single entry records. Accounts from single entry records concern the past; budgeted accounts from estimates concern the future.

21.1 D Smith is to open a retail shop on 1 January 20X4. He will put in £25,000 cash as capital. His plans are as follows:

(i) On 1 January 20X4 to buy and pay for premises £20,000, shop fixtures £3,000, motor van £1,000.

(ii) To employ two assistants, each to get a salary of £130 per month, to be paid at the end of each month. (PAYE tax, National Insurance contributions, etc. are to be ignored.)

(iii) To buy the following goods (shown in units):

	Jan	Feb	Mar	Apr	May	Jun
Units	200	220	280	350	400	330

(iv) To sell the following number of units:

	Jan	Feb	Mar	Apr	May	Jun
Units	120	180	240	300	390	420

(v) Units will be sold for £10 each. One-third of the sales are for cash, the other two-thirds being on credit. These latter customers are expected to pay their accounts in the second month following that in which they received the goods.

(vi) The units will cost £6 each for January to April inclusive, and £7 each thereafter. Creditors will be paid in the month following purchase. (Value stock in trade on the FIFO basis.)

(vii) The other expenses of the shop will be £150 per month payable in the month following that in which they were incurred.

(viii) Part of the premises will be sublet as an office at a rent of £600 per annum. This is paid in equal instalments in March, June, September and December.

(ix) Smith's cash drawings will amount to £250 per month.

(x) Depreciation is to be provided on shop fixtures at 10 per cent per annum and on the motor van at 20 per cent per annum.

You are required to:

(a) Draw up a cash budget for the six months ended 30 June 20X4, showing the balance of cash at the end of each month.

(b) Draw up a forecast trading and profit and loss account for the six months ended 30 June 20X4 and a balance sheet as at that date.

21.2X B Cooper is going to set up a new business on 1 January 20X8. He estimates that his first six months in business will be as follows:

(i) He will put £10,000 into a bank account for the firm on 1 January 20X8.

(ii) On 1 January 20X8 he will buy machinery for £2,000, motor vehicles for £1,600 and premises for £5,000, paying for them immediately out of the business bank account.

(iii) All purchases will be effected on credit. He will buy £2,000 goods on 1 January and he will pay for these in February. Other purchases will be rest of January £3,200, February, March, April, May and June £4,000 each month. Other than the £2,000 worth bought on 1 January all other purchases will be paid for two months after purchase.

(iv) Sales (all on credit) will be £4,000 for January and £5,000 for each month after that. Debtors will pay for the goods in the third month after purchase by them.

(v) Stock in trade on 30 June 20X8 will be £2,000.

(vi) Wages and salaries will be £150 per month and will be paid on the last day of each month.

(vii) General expenses will be £50 per month, payable in the month following that in which they were incurred.

(viii) He will receive a legacy of £5,500 on 21 April 20X8. This will be paid into the business bank account immediately.

(ix) Insurance covering the 12 months of 20X8 will be paid for by cheque on 30 June 20X8, £140.

(x) Rates will be paid as follows: for the three months to 31 March 20X8 by cheque on 28 February 20X8; for the 12 months ended 31 March 20X9 by cheque on 31 July 20X8. Rates are £360 per annum.

(xi) He will make drawings of £80 per month by cheque.

(xii) He has substantial investments in public companies. His bank manager will give him any overdraft that he may require.

(xiii) Depreciate motors 20 per cent per annum, machinery 10 per cent per annum.

You are required to:

(a) Draft a cash budget (includes bank) month by month showing clearly the amount of bank balance or overdraft at the end of each month.

(b) Draft the projected trading and profit and loss account for the first six months' trading, and a balance sheet as at 30 June 20X8.

21.3 Bedford Ltd is a manufacturing business with several production departments. Benjamin Kent, the manager of the machining department, submitted the following figures for the firm's annual budget for his department:

Units produced	64,000
	(Normal
	production
	level)
	£
Raw materials	294,400
Direct labour	236,800
Power	38,400
Repairs and maintenance (25% variable at this level of budgeted cost)	51,200
Insurance	1,300
Heating and lighting	1,250
Indirect wages (15% variable at this level of budgeted cost)	64,000
Total cost	687,350

Total capacity for machining department	80,000 units

Actual production for the period is 68,000 units, and costs are:

Materials	310,750
Direct labour	249,100
Power	39,800
Repairs and maintenance	53,050
Insurance	1,350
Heating and lighting	1,200
Indirect wages	65,250
Total cost	720,500

Benjamin is being criticised for overspending £33,150 compared with his normal budget. It is appreciated that he has made a saving on heating and lighting, but concern is being expressed over the spending on materials and labour. Benjamin feels that he has been able to control the department's costs efficiently.

Required:

A Construct a flexible budget for 60 per cent, 70 per cent, 75 per cent, 85 per cent and 90 per cent of production capacity, calculate any savings or overspending by Benjamin's department and comment on its efficiency.

(17 marks)

B Describe the operation of an efficient system of budgetary control. *(6 marks)*

(Total marks 23)

(OCR: from University of Oxford Delegacy of Local Examinations: GCE A-level)

21.4X (*a*) What is meant by the terms:

  (*i*) Budget

  (*ii*) Operating budget

  (*iii*) Master budget? *(8 marks)*

(*b*) The information below relates to the business of Madingley Ltd:

Balance Sheet as at 30 May 20X0

	Cost	(£000) Aggregate depreciation	Book value
Fixed assets			
Land and buildings	134.00	–	134.00
Plant and machinery	9.40	3.76	5.64
Fixtures and fittings	2.30	1.05	1.25
	145.70	4.81	140.89
Current assets			
Stocks: Raw materials	91.70		
Finished goods	142.40		
Debtors	594.40		
Bank	12.40		
		840.90	
Less: Current liabilities			
Creditors: Raw materials	82.20		
Overheads	127.40		
		209.60	
Working capital			631.30
			772.19
Financed by:			
Share capital		500.00	
Profit and loss account		272.19	
			772.19

The following is a schedule of the budgeted income and expenditure for the six months ended 30 November 20X0 (£000):

	Sales	Materials	Wages	Overheads
June	193.20	41.20	7.60	123.00
July	201.40	42.40	7.90	119.20
August	216.10	49.60	8.80	131.40
September	200.50	31.40	6.10	91.50
October	190.30	21.20	3.70	59.30
November	183.70	19.80	2.60	42.60

Notes:

(*i*) Generally, materials are paid for two months after receipt, and customers pay on average after three months.

(*ii*) Payments outstanding for materials at 1 June 20X0 were: April £38,500; May £43,700.

(*iii*) Debtors were: March £194,300; April £203,600; May £196,500.

(*iv*) Wages are to be paid in the month in which they fall due.

(*v*)   Overheads are to to be paid one month after they are incurred: the figure for May was £127,400.

(*vi*)   Stocks of raw materials are to be kept at £91,700.

(*vii*)   The stocks of finished goods at 30 November 20X0 are to be £136,200.

(*viii*)   There are no stocks of semi-finished items on 31 May 20X0, and none is expected in stock on 30 November.

(*ix*)   Forty per cent of the overheads are to be considered as fixed.

(*x*)   Depreciation on plant and machinery is to be allowed at 10 per cent per annum on cost; the fixtures and fittings are thought to have a value at 30 November of £980.

(*xi*)   There are no sales of finished goods or purchases of raw materials for cash planned during the period.

Prepare:

(*i*) A forecast operating statement for the period June to November 20X0; and

(*ii*) A forecast balance sheet as at 30 November 20X0.   *(17 marks)*

(London Qualifications Limited: GCE A-level)

21.5   The following information has been extracted from the books of Issa Ltd for the financial year ended 31 December 20X0.

Trading and Profit and Loss Account for the year ended 31 December 20X0

	£000s		£000s
Opening stock	90	Sales	750
Purchases	490		
	580		
Less Closing stock	80		
Cost of goods sold	500		
Gross profit	250		
	750		750
Administration expenses	60	Gross profit	250
Selling and distribution expenses	50		
Financial charges	20		
Depreciation of fixed assets	20		
Net profit	100		
	250		250

Balance Sheet as at 31 December 20X0

	£000s	£000s		£000s	£000s
Fixed assets			£1 Ordinary shares:		
At cost		750	Fully paid		200
Less Aggregate depreciation		144	9% £1 Preference shares Fully paid		100
		606			
Current assets			Share premium		150
Stock	80		Retained earnings		350
Trade debtors	75				800
Less Provision for			*Current liabilities*		
doubtful debtors	5	70	Trade creditors	50	
Balance at bank	100	250	Accrued expenses	6	56
		856			856

The company had commenced the preparation of its budget for the year ending 31 December 20X1 and the following information is the basis of its forecast.

1 An intensive advertising campaign will be carried out in the first six months of 20X1 at a cost of £15,000. It is anticipated that as a result of this, sales will increase to £900,000 in 20X1.
2 The gross profit/sales ratio will be increased to 35 per cent.
3 A new stock control system is to be installed in 20X1 and it is expected that the stock level will be reduced by £15,000 as compared to the 20X0 closing stock.
4 Land and buildings which cost £50,000 (nil depreciation to date) will be sold in 20X1 for £200,000 cash. Half of the proceeds will be used to buy ordinary shares in another company, Yates Ltd, at an agreed price of £4 per share. (Ignore share commission, etc.)
5 The company planned to capitalise some of its reserves on 1 April 20X1. New ordinary shares are to be issued on a 1 for 2 basis. Half the funds required will be drawn from the share premium account and the remainder will be taken from retained earnings.
6 Preference share dividends will be paid on 1 May 20X1 and 1 November 20X1. The company planned to pay an interim ordinary share dividend on the increased share capital of 2.5p per share on 1 July 20X1. No final dividend is proposed.
7 Owing to inflation revenue expenses are expected to rise as follows:
Administration expenses will increase by 6 per cent.
Selling and distribution expenses will increase by 8 per cent.
The advertising campaign expenses are in addition to the increase above.
Financial charges will increase by 4 per cent.
These percentage increases are based on the figures for the year ended 31 December 20X0.
8 With the projected sales increases trade debtors are expected to rise to £100,000 by 31 December 20X1. The provision for doubtful debts is to be adjusted to 7½ per cent of forecast trade debtors.
9 Other forecast figures as at 31 December 20X1:

	£000s
Balance at bank	350.1
Trade creditors	56.0
Expense creditors	15.0

10 Depreciation of 10 per cent per annum on cost is to be provided on £600,000 of the company's fixed assets.

Required:

(a) A budgeted trading, profit and loss and appropriation account for the year ending 31 December 20X1. Show the full details of the trading account. *(10 marks)*

(b) A budgeted balance sheet as at 31 December 20X1. *(8 marks)*

(c) What advantages accrue to a business by preparing a budget with respect to:
(i) forecast profitability;
(ii) forecast liquidity? *(7 marks)*

(AQA (AEB): GCE A-level)

21.6X The balance sheet of Gregg Ltd at 30 June 20X6 was expected to be as follows:

Balance Sheet 30 June 20X6 (£s)

	Cost	Depreciation to date	Net
Fixed assets			
Land and buildings	40,000	–	40,000
Plant and machinery	10,000	6,000	4,000
Motor vehicles	6,000	2,800	3,200
Office fixtures	500	220	280
	56,500	9,020	47,480

Current assets		
Stock in trade: Finished goods	1,800	
Raw materials	300	
Debtors (May £990 + June £900)	1,890	
Cash and bank balances	7,100	11,090
		58,570
Financed by		
Share capital		50,000
Profit and loss account		7,820
		57,820
Current liabilities		
Creditors for raw materials		
(April £240 + May £140 + June £160)	540	
Creditors for variable overhead	210	750
		58,570

The plans for the six months to 31 December 20X6 can be summarised as:

(*i*) Production costs per unit will be:

	£
Direct materials	2
Direct labour	5
Variable overhead	3
	10

(*ii*) Sales will be at a price of £18 per unit for the three months to 30 September and at £18.5 subsequently. The number of units sold would be:

Jul	Aug	Sep	Oct	Nov	Dec
60	80	100	100	90	70

All sales will be on credit, and debtors will pay their accounts two months after they have bought the goods.

(*iii*) Production will be even at 90 units per month.

(*iv*) Purchases of direct materials – all on credit – will be:

Jul	Aug	Sep	Oct	Nov	Dec
£	£	£	£	£	£
220	200	160	140	140	180

Creditors for direct materials will be paid three months after purchase.

(*v*) Direct labour is paid in the same month as production occurs.

(*vi*) Variable overhead is paid in the month following that in which the units are produced.

(*vii*) Fixed overhead of £90 per month is paid each month and is never in arrears.

(*viii*) A machine costing £500 will be bought and paid for in July. A motor vehicle costing £2,000 will be bought and paid for in September.

(*ix*) A debenture of £5,000 will be issued and the cash received in November. Interest will not start to run until 20X7.

(*x*) Provide for depreciation for the six months: motor vehicles £600, office fixtures £30, machinery £700.

You are required to draw up as a minimum:

(*a*) Cash budget, showing figures each month.
(*b*) Debtors budget, showing figures each month.
(*c*) Creditors budget, showing figures each month.
(*d*) Raw materials budget, showing figures each month.
(*e*) Forecast operating statement for the six months.
(*f*) Forecast balance sheet as at 31 December 20X6.

In addition you may draw up any further budgets you may wish in order to show the workings behind the above budgets.

21.7 The following information relates to the actual sales of Griffton Ltd during the last four months of its financial year.

	March	*April*	*May*	*June*
Quantity (units)	900	900	900	1,000
Price each	£55	£55	£55	£55

The budgeted information below relates to the next financial year commencing 1 July 20X2:

(*i*) The company forecasts that sales quantity will decrease in July by 10 per cent of the level in June. The reduced quantity will remain for August and September, but will then increase by 10 per cent in October, and remain fixed for the next three months.

The sales price will remain at £55 each until 1 September when it will be increased to £60 per unit; this price will be effective for a minimum of six months.

50 per cent of sales are on a cash basis and attract a 2 per cent cash discount; the remaining 50 per cent of sales are paid two months in arrears.

The company arranges its purchases of raw materials such that the closing stock at the end of each month exactly meets the requirement for the following month's sales. Each unit sold requires 2 kg of material at £15 per kg; this price is fixed until December 20X3.

(*ii*) As a separate exercise, the managing director asks for stock levels to be reviewed, and asks you about the use of Economic Order Quantities at some time in 20X3. The following budgeted data would apply to this exercise:

Material	2,000 kg per month
Price	£15 per kg
Stockholding costs	20% p.a. on average stock value
Ordering costs	£10 per order

Required:

Draw up monthly budgets for the four-month period commencing 1 July 20X2 for:

(*a*) Debtors in £s.
(*b*) Raw material purchases in kg.

(19 marks)

(OCR: from University of Oxford Delegacy of Local Examinations: GCE A-level)

Part 5

SUPPLEMENTARY TOPICS

22 Break-even analysis

23 The accounting equation and the balance sheet

24 The double entry system

25 Accounting concepts

These topics do not appear in all A2-level syllabuses. In fact, the material in Chapters 23–25 would normally have been covered at the AS-level. It is included here so that students can be directed to revise the contents of these chapters, should it be felt necessary for them to do so. Chapter 22 should at least be read, even if it is not in the syllabus being studied. It helps set the context for managerial decision making based on accounting numbers. It should, therefore, aid in the understanding of the relationships between various types of costs, which are dealt with in Chapter 12.

Break-even analysis

By the end of this chapter, you should be able to:

● explain the importance of contribution and fixed costs in identifying the break-even level of sales;

● prepare break-even graphs and contribution graphs;

● use break-even graphs to show the impact of changes in costs, volume and selling price upon profitability;

● describe some of the limitations of break-even charts.

22.1 Introduction

The level of activity achieved by a firm is of paramount importance in determining both whether it makes a profit or loss, and the size of such profits or losses. Let us take an example to which the answer is obvious. If a firm has fixed costs of £10,000 and its total revenue is £8,000 then, no matter how much the variable costs are, the firm is bound to make a loss. A firm has to cover both its fixed costs and its variable costs before it can make a profit. With very low revenue, as in this case, a loss would be bound to be incurred.

There is, therefore, a great deal of interest in exactly how much revenue (i.e. sales) has to be earned before a profit can be made. If revenue is below fixed costs then a loss will be incurred; if revenue is below total costs (i.e. fixed costs + variable costs) a loss will still be incurred. Where revenue is greater than fixed costs plus variable costs then a profit will have been made. The question then arises – at what point does the firm stop incurring a loss and, with the next unit of revenue, make a profit? That is, at what point does the firm break even or make neither a profit nor a loss?

Fixed costs stay unchanged over stated ranges in the volume of production, but variable costs are those that change with volumes in production. As revenue increases so do variable costs, so that the only item that remains unchanged is that of fixed costs. Let us look at an example of a firm showing the changing costs and revenue over differing volumes of production.

Apollo Ltd has fixed costs of £5,000. The variable costs are £2 per unit. The revenue (selling price) is £3 per unit. Looking at production in stages of 1,000 units we can see that the figures emerge as in Exhibit 22.1.

EXHIBIT 22.1

No. of units	Fixed cost	Variable cost	Total cost: Variable + Fixed	Revenue (Sales)	Profit	Loss
	£	£	£	£	£	£
0	5,000	Nil	5,000	Nil		5,000
1,000	5,000	2,000	7,000	3,000		4,000
2,000	5,000	4,000	9,000	6,000		3,000
3,000	5,000	6,000	11,000	9,000		2,000
4,000	5,000	8,000	13,000	12,000		1,000
5,000	5,000	10,000	15,000	15,000	Nil	Nil
6,000	5,000	12,000	17,000	18,000	1,000	
7,000	5,000	14,000	19,000	21,000	2,000	
8,000	5,000	16,000	21,000	24,000	3,000	
9,000	5,000	18,000	23,000	27,000	4,000	

With activity of 5,000 units, the firm will break even, it will make neither a profit nor a loss. Above that the firm moves into profit, below that the firm would never make a profit.

We could have calculated the break-even point without drawing up a schedule of costs, etc. as in Exhibit 22.1. Instead we could have said that for one unit the revenue is £3 and the variable cost is £2, so that the remaining £1 is the amount out of which the fixed costs have to be paid, and that anything left over would be profit.

The £1 is the 'contribution' towards fixed costs and profit. If the contribution was only just enough to cover fixed costs, there would be no profit, but neither would there be any loss. There are £5,000 fixed costs, so that with a contribution of £1 per unit there would have to be 5,000 units to provide a contribution of £5,000 to cover fixed costs. It could be stated as:

$$\text{Break-even point} = \frac{\text{Fixed costs}}{\text{Selling price per unit} - \text{Variable costs per unit}}$$

i.e. in the case of Apollo Ltd:

$$\frac{£5,000}{£3 - £2} = \frac{5,000}{1} = 5,000 \text{ units}$$

22.2 The break-even chart

The information given in Exhibit 22.1 can also be shown in the form of a chart. Many people seem to grasp the idea of break-even analysis rather more easily when they see it in chart form. This is particularly true of people who are not used to dealing with accounting information. We will, therefore, plot the figures from Exhibit 22.1 on a chart which is shown as Exhibit 22.2.

The use of the chart can now be looked at. It would be extremely useful if you could draw the chart as shown in Exhibit 22.2 on a piece of graph paper. The larger the scale you use, the easier it will be to take accurate readings. Plot the lines from the figures as shown in Exhibit 22.1.

EXHIBIT 22.2 Break-even chart for Apollo Ltd

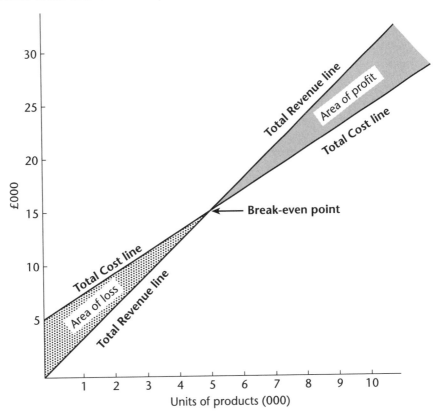

To find the break-even point in terms of units of product, draw a line straight down from the break-even point so that it meets the base line at right angles. This is shown in Exhibit 22.3 as line A which, when read off on the base line, gives units of products and sales as 5,000 units. Now draw a line direct to the vertical line so that it meets that at a right angle. This is line B and shows £15,000. This means that according to the chart the break-even point is shown at 5,000 units where both costs and revenue are equal at £15,000. This is naturally the same answer as was shown in the table of figures in Exhibit 22.1.

As production and sales go above 5,000 units, the firm makes profits. When production and sales are above 5,000 units, the difference represents the 'safety margin', as this is the number of units in excess of the break-even point that it could afford to lose without making a loss.

Look at the chart again and, without looking back at what you have just read, attempt to answer the following by taking readings off your chart:

(*i*) What would the total costs of the firm be at (*a*) 2,000 units, (*b*) 7,000 units, (*c*) 8,500 units?

(Remember: take a line up from the product line for the figure needed, then from where the cost line is bisected draw a line to the £s line to meet it at right angles.)

(*ii*) What is the revenue for (*a*) 3,000 units, (*b*) 6,000 units, (*c*) 7,500 units?

EXHIBIT 22.3 Finding the break-even point

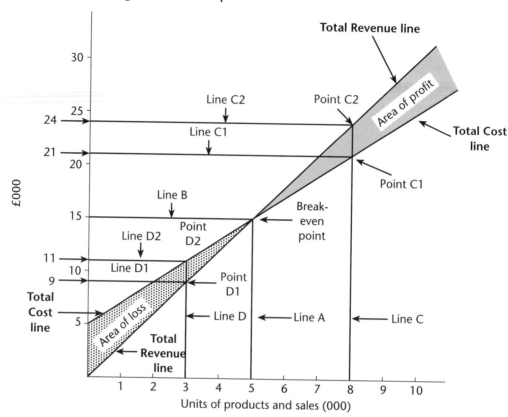

Before proceeding further, look at the answers which are shown at the end of this section.

Now we will try to find the amount of profit or loss at various levels by looking at the chart in Exhibit 22.3. First let us calculate the profit made if 8,000 units are going to be made and sold. Draw a line up from the product line at right angles (shown as line C) until it bisects both the Total Cost line and the Total Revenue line, the points of intersection being shown as C1 for the Total Cost line and C2 for the Total Revenue line. Read off the amounts in £s by taking lines across to the vertical line until they meet it at right angles. These are shown as lines C1 and C2. Line C1 will give a reading of £21,000 and C2 one of £24,000. As the total revenue exceeds the total costs there is a profit, and in this case the profit is £3,000.

If we now try for 3,000 units, the line drawn up from the product line will meet the Total Revenue line at point D1 and the Total Cost line at D2. Reading off to the £s line D1 shows as £9,000 while D2 shows as £11,000. In this case the total cost exceeds the total revenue by £2,000 and there is, therefore, a loss of £2,000.

Before you proceed further, attempt this third question: (iii) from your own chart, find the profit or loss recorded at (*a*) 1,000 units, (*b*) 4,000 units, (*c*) 6,500 units and (*d*) 8,500 units.

The answers to the third question can now be checked.

Answers

(*i*) (*a*) £9,000 (*b*) £19,000 (*c*) £22,000

(*ii*) (*a*) £9,000 (*b*) £18,000 (*c*) £22,500

(*iii*) (*a*) Loss £4,000 (*b*) Loss £1,000 (*c*) Profit £1,500 (*d*) Profit £3,500

22.3 Changes and break-even charts

The effect of changes on profits can easily be shown by drawing fresh lines on the chart to show the changes, or intended changes, in the circumstances of the firm. Let us first of all consider what factors can bring about a change in the profits of a firm. These are:

(*a*) The selling price per unit could be increased (or decreased).
(*b*) A possible decrease (or increase) in fixed costs.
(*c*) A possible decrease (or increase) in variable costs per unit.
(*d*) Increase the volume of production and sales.

We will investigate these by starting with the same basic information for a firm and then seeing what would happen if each of the changes (*a*) to (*d*) were to happen.

The basic information, before suggested changes, is shown in Exhibit 22.4.

EXHIBIT 22.4

No. of units	Fixed cost	Variable cost	Total costs: Variable + Fixed	Revenue (Sales)	Profit	Loss
	£	£	£	£	£	£
100	2,000	400	2,400	900		1,500
200	2,000	800	2,800	1,800		1,000
300	2,000	1,200	3,200	2,700		500
400	2,000	1,600	3,600	3,600	Nil	Nil
500	2,000	2,000	4,000	4,500	500	
600	2,000	2,400	4,400	5,400	1,000	
700	2,000	2,800	4,800	6,300	1,500	
800	2,000	3,200	5,200	7,200	2,000	
900	2,000	3,600	5,600	8,100	2,500	

The table shows that variable costs are £4 per unit and selling price £9 per unit. We can draw a chart to incorporate this information before considering the changes being contemplated. This is shown in Exhibit 22.5.

(a) Increase selling price

Taking a copy of the old chart as a base, we can now draw an extra line on it to represent an increase in selling price. Let us suppose that the selling price could be increased by £2 per unit. This can now be shown on a break-even chart as in Exhibit 22.6. The line shown as 'New Total Revenue' could then be added. This would mean that the break-even point would change as the increased revenue would mean that costs were covered sooner. The dotted area shows the reduction in the loss area that would be incurred at the same volume of sales, whilst the shaded area shows the increase in profit at the various volumes of sales.

EXHIBIT 22.5 Basic break-even chart

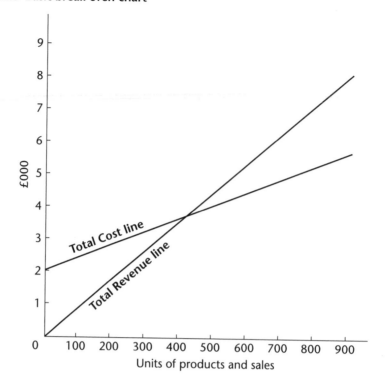

EXHIBIT 22.6 Break-even chart showing increase in selling price

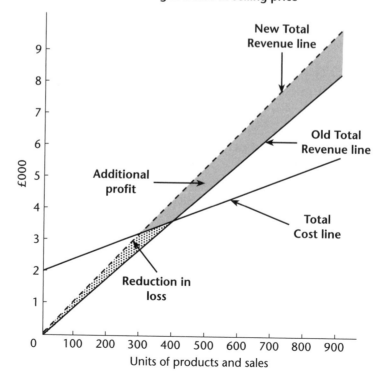

(b) Reduce fixed costs

We can now draw some more lines on the chart shown in Exhibit 22.6, this time to reflect a reduction of £800 in fixed costs. This can be seen in Exhibit 22.7, where a line entitled 'New Total Cost' has been added. The reduction in loss if sales were at a low volume is represented by the dotted area while the shaded area shows the additional profit at various volumes of activity. The change in profit or loss will be constant at £800 over these volumes.

EXHIBIT 22.7 Break-even chart showing reduction in fixed costs

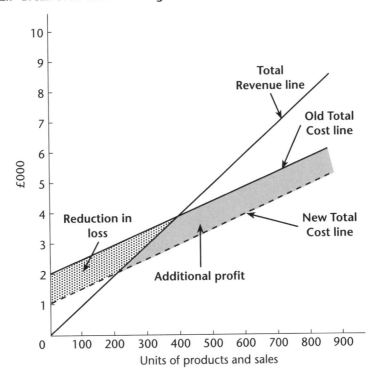

(c) Reduce variable costs

Reverting to the chart shown in Exhibit 22.6, we can see what happens if the variable costs per unit are reduced, in this case by £2 per unit. This is shown in Exhibit 22.8, where the dotted area shows the reduction in loss compared with the position if the costs had not changed, while the shaded area shows the additional profit at different levels of activity.

A reduction in fixed costs in Exhibit 22.7 showed a constant difference of £800 compared with previously over the whole range of activity, whereas a reduction in variable costs as in Exhibit 22.8 brings about different increases of profit, or reductions of loss, over the whole range of activity. The greater the activity the greater the gain with variable cost savings, whereas the gain remains constant with fixed cost savings.

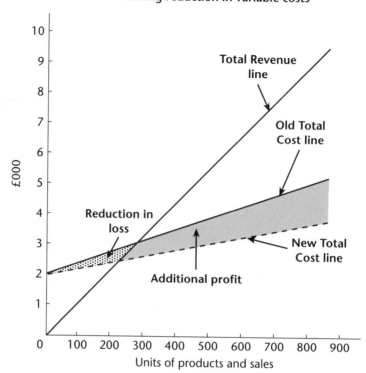

EXHIBIT 22.8 Break-even chart showing reduction in variable costs

(d) Increased production and sales

In this case it is merely a matter of extending the lines for Total Revenue and Total Costs. Exhibit 22.9 shows this for an increase of 300 units. The new profit indicated will be greater than the old profit because all extra units are being sold at a profit.

22.4 The limitations of break-even charts

In each of these cases, it has been assumed that only one of the factors of variable cost, fixed cost, selling price or volume of sales has in fact altered. This is not usually the case. An increase in price may well reduce the number sold. There may well be an increase in fixed cost which has an effect which brings down variable costs. The changes in the various factors should, therefore, be studied simultaneously rather than separately.

In addition, where there is more than one product, the proportions in which the products are sold, i.e. the product mix, can have a very important bearing on costs. Suppose that there are two products, one has a large amount of fixed costs but hardly any variable costs, and the other has a large amount of variable costs but little fixed costs. Therefore if the proportions in which each are sold change very much this could mean that the costs and profit could vary tremendously, even though the total figures of sales stayed constant. An illustration of this can be seen in Exhibit 22.10.

EXHIBIT 22.9 Break-even chart showing increase in production and sales

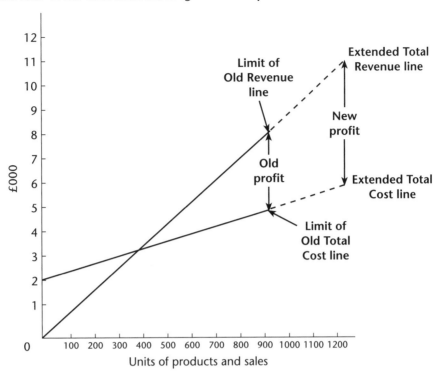

EXHIBIT 22.10

In considering the break-even analysis we may expect that the following will occur:

Fixed costs £1,000, Variable costs: Product A £5 per unit, B £20 per unit.
Selling prices: A £10 per unit, B £30 per unit.
Expected sales: A 150, B 50. Actual sales: A 30, B 90.
The expected sales are A 150 × £10 + B 50 × £30 = £3,000.
The actual sales are A 30 × £10 + B 90 × £30 = £3,000.

The actual and expected sales are the same, but the costs and profit are quite different.

			£
Expected:	Sales		3,000
Less Variable costs:	A 150 × £5 =	750	
	B 50 × £20 =	1,000	
			(1,750)
	Contribution		1,250
Less	Fixed costs		(1,000)
	Net profit		250

			£
Actual:	Sales		3,000
Less Variable costs:	A 30 × £5 =	150	
	B 90 × £20 =	1,800	
			(1,950)
	Contribution		1,050
Less	Fixed costs		(1,000)
	Net profit		50

Variable costs are usually taken to be in direct proportion to volume, so that 1,000 units means (say) £5,000 variable costs and therefore 2,000 units would mean £10,000 variable costs, 3,000 units equal £15,000 variable costs and so on. This is often a reasonable estimation of the situation, but may well hold true only within fairly tight limits. For instance 3,100 units could mean £16,000 costs instead of the £15,500 that it would be if a linear relationship existed. This is also true of sales, because to increase sales beyond certain points some units may be sold cheaply. Thus 1,000 units might be sold for £9,000; 2,000 units sold for £18,000; but to sell 2,200 units the revenue might be only £19,100 instead of the £19,800 (2,200 × £9) that might be expected if a linear relationship existed over all ranges.

It is assumed that everything produced is sold, and that stocks in trade remain constant. It would be difficult to do otherwise as both sales revenue and costs relate to one and the same measure of volume.

22.5 | Contribution graph

Exhibit 22.11 is a redrafting of Exhibit 22.5 that includes the addition of a line representing variable cost. It runs parallel to and below the Total Cost line. This is an alternative method of presentation. It highlights the total contribution. The vertical gap between the Total Cost line and the Variable Cost line at any particular number of units represents the contribution at that number of units.

EXHIBIT 22.11 Contribution graph

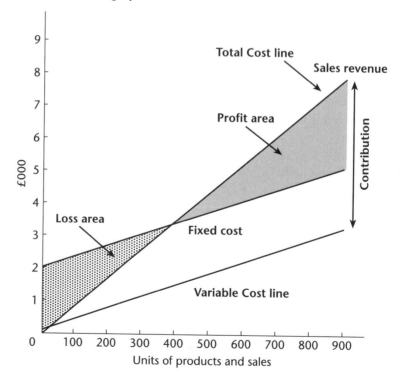

You should now have learnt:

1 How to prepare break-even graphs and contribution graphs.

2 That break-even analysis can be performed using either a formula or a graph.

3 How to use graphs to identify break-even point, the margin of safety and the contribution for any level of activity.

4 How to use a formula in order to calculate the break-even point.

5 That fixed costs are assumed to be fixed for the range of activity being considered, and variable costs per unit and sales revenue per unit are assumed to be constant within that range of activity. It is important to check whether these assumptions are correct when carrying out a break-even analysis. If they are not, the format of the analysis should be adjusted appropriately.

6 How to use break-even graphs to show the impact of changes in costs, volumes and selling price upon profitability.

7 How to explain the relevance of contribution to decision making.

REVIEW QUESTIONS

Advice: Be careful when drawing any charts, as a faulty chart will give you wrong answers for every part of your answer. You cannot expect examiners to assume that your faulty drawing of a graph was a simple error of draughtsmanship instead of being conceptual. They will not give you the marks.

22.1 Hedges Ltd has fixed costs of £8,000. The variable costs are £4 per unit. The revenue (selling price) is £6 per unit.

You are required:

(*i*) to draft a schedule as follows filling in the columns (*a*) to (*f*) for each stage of 1,000 units up to 10,000 units;

No. of units	(*a*) Fixed cost £	(*b*) Variable cost £	(*c*) Total cost £	(*d*) Revenue £	(*e*) Profit £	(*f*) Loss £
0						
1,000						
2,000						
3,000						
4,000						
5,000						
6,000						
7,000						
8,000						
9,000						
10,000						

(ii) also to draw a break-even chart from the data in this schedule. Draw it carefully to scale on a piece of graph paper. Retain your answer: you will need it for some questions which follow later.

22.2 Cover up the schedule you constructed as your answer to 22.1(*i*) and look instead at the break-even chart constructed as the answer to 22.1(*ii*). Answer the following:

(*a*) What are the total costs at production levels of (*i*) 4,000 units, (*ii*) 7,000 units, (*iii*) 9,000 units, (*iv*) 5,500 units?

(*b*) What is the total revenue at (*i*) 3,000 units, (*ii*) 8,000 units, (*iii*) 5,500 units?

22.3X Look at your schedule in answer to 22.1(*i*) and answer the following:

(*a*) What are the total costs at production levels of (*i*) 4,000 units, (*ii*) 7,000 units, (*iii*) 9,000 units, (*iv*) 5,500 units? You will have to deduce this amount as it is not shown as a figure on the schedule.

(*b*) What is the total revenue at (*i*) 3,000 units, (*ii*) 8,000 units, (*iii*) 5,500 units?

22.4 From your break-even chart for 22.1(*ii*) calculate the profit or loss that will be made at levels of (*i*) 3,000 units, (*ii*) 10,000 units, (*iii*) 4,000 units, (*iv*) 7,000 units, (*v*) 8,500 units.

22.5X From the schedule in 22.1(*i*) calculate the profit or loss that would be made at levels of (*i*) 3,000 units, (*ii*) 10,000 units, (*iii*) 4,000 units, (*iv*) 7,000 units, (*v*) 8,500 units (this last figure will have to be deduced as it is not a figure on the schedule).

22.6 Polemic Ltd manufactures and sells a single product. The following information is available for three financial years ending 30 September.

	Price per unit £	Unit volume 000s
Sales		
Actual 20X1	130	50
Forecast 20X2	129	52
Forecast 20X3	128.5	53

Costs per unit produced	Actual 20X1 £	Forecast 20X2 £	Forecast 20X3 £
Direct materials	50	55	55
Direct labour	30	31.5	33
Variable production overhead	10	11	12
Direct expenses	5	5	6
Variable sales overhead	15	16	16

Other costs for the year	£000s	£000s	£000s
Fixed production overhead	50	55	55
Other fixed overhead	200	220	220

Additional information

1 When the management of Polemic prepared its direct labour forecast unit cost for 20X2 and 20X3, direct wages were increased only by the forecast rate of inflation.

2 The trade union representatives of the production workers wished to press for a greater wage increase. They suggested that:

(*i*) Direct wages be increased at twice the rate of inflation. The effect of this would be to increase direct labour costs per unit as follows:

	20X2	20X3
	£	£
Direct labour	33	35

(*ii*) Unit selling prices be increased in order to cover the increased labour costs.

3 It is to be assumed that all expense and revenue relationships will be unchanged except where indicated.

Required:

(*a*) A schedule for 20X1, 20X2 and 20X3 for Polemic Ltd showing:
    (*i*) the break-even points;
    (*ii*) the net profit for each year.
    Base your calculations on the original labour costs.   *(8 marks)*

(*b*) A graph showing a break-even point for 20X2.   *(5 marks)*

(*c*) Advise Polemic Ltd's management as to their response to the trade union's claim for higher wages. Include relevant financial analysis.   *(7 marks)*

(*d*) Explain the limitation of break-even analysis.   *(5 marks)*

(AQA (AEB): GCE A-level)

22.7X The relationship between income/cost/volume suggests that there are four ways by which profit can be increased. These are:

1 Increase unit selling price.
2 Decrease unit variable cost.
3 Decrease fixed costs.
4 Increase volume.

Assume that the current situation for a product is as follows:

Sales volume	1,000 units
Selling price	£2 each
Variable cost	£1 per unit
Fixed costs	£500

You are required to:

(*a*) draw **four** separate break-even charts showing the effect of the following changes on the current situation:
    (*i*)   a 10 per cent increase in volume,
    (*ii*) a 10 per cent increase in unit selling price,
    (*iii*) a 10 per cent decrease in unit variable cost,
    (*iv*) a 10 per cent reduction in fixed costs.   *(16 marks)*

(*b*) Use your charts to state the additional profit resulting from **each** change.   *(4 marks)*
    (Total marks 20)

(AQA (NEAB): GCE A-level)

22.8 At the monthly senior management meeting of Hampshire plc on 1 May 20X0, various suggestions were made to improve the profit to be made by selling the firm's single product in the last quarter of the year ending 30 September 20X0. The product is not subject to seasonal demand fluctuations, but there are several competitors producing similar items. In the first quarter of the year a suggestion was made that profit could be improved if the selling price were reduced by 5 per cent, and this was put into effect at the beginning of the second quarter. As the new price undercut that of the rival firms, demand increased and the firm's break-even point was reduced.

The following suggestions have now been raised:

(*i*) Differentiate the product from its rivals by giving it a more distinctive shape, colour and packaging. This would increase material costs per unit by £0.30, but selling price would not be raised. Demand is then predicted to rise by 10 per cent;

(*ii*) Improve the quality of the product by strengthening it and giving it a one-year guarantee – material costs would then increase by £0.15 per unit and labour costs by £0.30 per unit. Selling price would rise by £0.40 per unit, and demand increase by 7 per cent;

(*iii*) Further reduce the selling price by 10 per cent – demand to rise by 20 per cent;

(*iv*) Pay commission plus salaries instead of fixed salaries only to all sales staff. Variable selling costs would then rise by £0.20 per unit, but fixed costs would fall by £4,100 per quarter;

(*v*) Subcontract the making of some components, and close the department responsible, making six staff redundant at an estimated cost to the firm of £12,000. 30,000 components are currently made per quarter. Each component's variable cost is £0.55. They can be bought from a recently established firm for £0.60 per unit. The department's share of the firm's fixed costs is 20 per cent and £2,500 fixed costs per quarter would cease to arise if the department were to be closed.

Data for:	First quarter	Second quarter
Number of units produced and sold	9,000	10,800
	£	£
Selling price per unit	14.00	13.30
Materials per unit	3.65	3.65
Labour per unit	2.10	2.10
Variable factory overhead per unit	1.40	1.40
Variable selling costs per unit	0.85	0.85
Fixed factory overhead	21,375	21,375
Fixed selling and administration costs	16,125	16,125

Required:

A Calculate the profit made in each of the first and second quarters, showing clearly the contribution per unit in each case.
(*4 marks*)

B Draw one break-even chart showing the total costs and total revenues for the first and second quarters. You should label clearly the two break-even points and margins of safety.
(*7 marks*)

C Taking each suggestion independently, calculate the profit that might be made in the last quarter if each of them were to be implemented.
(*9 marks*)

D Discuss the implications for the firm of undertaking suggestions (i–iv), and for the firm and the local community of undertaking suggestion (v).
(*8 marks*)

E Explain to the senior managers how, while break-even analysis is useful, it has limitations.
(*3 marks*)
(*Total marks 31*)

(*OCR, from University of Oxford Delegacy of Local Examinations: GCE A-level*)

22.9X You are employed by Monarch Ltd which manufactures specialist hydraulic seals for the aircraft industry. The company has developed a new seal with the following budgeted data:

Variable cost per unit	£
Direct materials	8
Direct labour	4
Variable overheads	4
	16

The draft budget for the following year is as follows:

Production and sales	60,000 units
	£
Fixed cost: Production	260,000
Administration	90,000
Selling, marketing and distribution	100,000
Contribution	840,000

Certain departmental managers within the company believe there is room for improvement on the budgeted figures, and the following options have been suggested.

(*i*)   The sales manager has suggested that if the selling price was reduced by 10 per cent, then an extra 30 per cent units could be sold. The purchasing manager has indicated that if material requirements were increased in line, then a material price reduction of 6.25 per cent could be negotiated. With this additional output, fixed production costs would increase by £30,000, administration by £5,000 and selling, marketing and distribution by £10,000. Other costs would remain unchanged.

(*ii*) The export manager has suggested that if the company increased overseas marketing by £15,000 then exports would increase from 15,000 units to 17,000 units. With this suggestion, distribution costs would increase by £12,000, and all other costs would remain unchanged.

(*iii*) The marketing manager has suggested that if an extra £40,000 were spent on advertising, then sales quantity would increase by 25 per cent. The purchasing manager has indicated that in such circumstances, material costs would reduce by £0.30 per unit. With this suggestion fixed production costs would increase by £25,000, administration by £4,000 and other selling, marketing and distribution costs by £7,000. All other costs would remain unchanged.

(*iv*) The managing director believes the company should be aiming for a profit of £486,000. He asks what the selling price would be per unit if marketing were increased by £50,000, this leading to an estimated increase in sales quantity of 30 per cent? Other fixed costs would increase by £67,000, whilst material prices would decrease by 6.25 per cent per unit. All other costs would remain unchanged.

Required:

A Taking each suggestion independently, compile a profit statement for options (*i*) to (*iii*), showing clearly the contribution per unit in each case. For suggestion (*iv*), calculate the selling price per unit as requested by the managing director.   *(13 marks)*

B Calculate the break-even quantity in units if the Managing Director's suggestion were implemented. Draw a contribution/sales graph to illustrate your calculations.
   Read from the graph the profit if 60,000 units were sold.   *(6 marks)*

C Whilst marginal costing has a number of applications, it also has disadvantages. In a report to the managing director, outline the main applications of marginal costing and explain its disadvantages.   *(12 marks)*
          (Total marks 31)

(OCR, from University of Oxford Delegacy of Local Examinations: GCE A-level)

22.10 Magwitch Limited's finance director produced the following forecast break-even chart for the year ending 31 May 20X1:

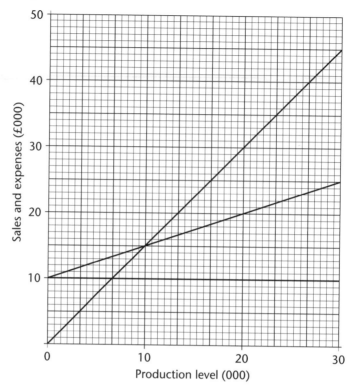

During the year the company produced and sold 20,000 units, and both revenue and expenses were 10 per cent higher than forecast.

Compeyson plc has made an agreed takeover bid for the company at a value of twelve times the net profit for the year ending 31 May 20X1.

Magwitch's assets and liabilities are to be taken over at their balance sheet values, with the exception of fixed assets, which are to be revalued at £40,000.

The summarised balance sheets of Magwitch Limited and Compeyson plc at the takeover date of 31 May 20X1 are as follows:

	Magwitch £000	Compeyson £000
Fixed assets	32	160
Current assets	65	340
Short-term liabilities	(26)	(110)
	71	390
Share capital (£1 shares)	40	200
Reserves	31	190
	71	390

The terms of the takeover are that Compeyson plc will give three of its shares (value £1.80 each) for every two shares in Magwitch Limited, plus a cash payment to make up the total agreed takeover price.

Magwitch Limited will cease to trade on 31 May 20X1, and its assets and liabilities will be assumed by Compeyson plc. Any goodwill arising is to be written off immediately against reserves.

(*a*) Draw up a summarised profit and loss account for Magwitch Limited for the year ended 31 May 20X1. *(5 marks)*

(*b*) Draw up a balance sheet for Compeyson plc after the takeover of Magwitch Limited has taken place. *(15 marks)*

(*c*) Calculate how many shares and how much cash would be received by a holder of 6,000 shares in Magwitch Limited as a result of the takeover. *(5 marks)*

(London Qualifications Limited: GCE A-level)

22.11X (*a*) How far is it true to state that a company's break-even point occurs where the contribution just equals the fixed costs? *(5 marks)*

(*b*) A company's detailed information of costs and sales has been destroyed because of a computer malfunction. The following data has, however, been gleaned from various sources:

Sales volume (units)	10,000	12,000
Costs (£):		
direct materials	30,000	36,000
direct labour	28,000	33,000
overheads	20,500	24,100

Selling price per unit at all volumes of output is £12.30

Calculate:

(*i*) the cost of an additional 2,000 units of output;
(*ii*) the variable costs of 10,000 units of output;
(*iii*) the fixed element – if any – of each component cost;
(*iv*) the break-even point. *(10 marks)*

(London Qualifications Limited: GCE A-level)

The accounting equation and the balance sheet

23.1 What is accounting?

People and businesses

Accounting is something that affects people in their personal lives just as much as it affects very large businesses. We all use accounting ideas when we plan what we are going to do with our money. We have to plan how much of it we will spend and how much we will save. We may write down a plan, known as a **budget**, or we may simply keep it in our minds.

Recording accounting data

However, when people talk about accounting, they are normally referring to accounting as used by businesses and other organisations. The owners of businesses cannot keep all the details in their minds so they have to keep records of it.

Organisations not only record cash received and paid out. They also will record goods bought and sold, items bought to use rather than to sell, and so on. This part of accounting is usually called the *recording of data*.

Classifying and summarising

When the data are being recorded they have to be organised so as to be most useful to the business. This is known as *classifying* and *summarising* data.

Following such classifications and summaries it will be possible to work out how much profit or loss has been made by the business during a particular period. It will also be possible to show what resources are owned by the business, and what is owed by it, on the closing date of the period.

Communicating information

From the data, people skilled in accounting should be able to tell whether or not the business is performing well financially. They should be able to ascertain the strengths and weaknesses of the business.

Finally, they should be able to tell or *communicate* their results to the owners of the business, or to others allowed to receive this information.

Accounting is, therefore, concerned with:

● recording data;
● classifying and summarising data;
● communicating what has been learnt from the data.

23.2   What is bookkeeping?

The part of accounting that is concerned with recording data is often known as **bookkeeping**. Until about one hundred years ago all accounting data were kept by being recorded manually in books, hence the term 'bookkeeping'.

Nowadays, although hand-written books may be used (particularly by smaller organisations), most accounting data are recorded electronically and stored electronically using computers.

Bookkeeping is the process of recording data relating to accounting transactions in the accounting books.

23.3   Accounting is concerned with . . .

Accounting is concerned with the users which accountants might make of the bookkeeping information given to them. This book covers many such uses.

23.4   Users of accounting information

Possible users of accounting information include:

● *Owner(s) of the business*. They want to be able to see whether or not the business is profitable. In addition they want to know what the financial resources of the business are.
● *A prospective buyer*. When the owner wants to sell a business the buyer will want to see such information.

- *The bank*. If the owner wants to borrow money for use in the business, then the bank will need such information.
- *Tax inspectors*. They need it to be able to calculate the taxes payable.
- *A prospective partner*. If the owner wants to share ownership with someone else, then the would-be partner will want such information.
- *Investors*, either existing ones or potential ones. They want to know whether or not to invest their money in the business.

There are many other users of accounting unformation – suppliers and employees, for example. One obvious fact is that without properly recorded accounting data a business would have many difficulties providing the information these various users (often referred to as 'stakeholders') require.

23.5   The accounting equation

By adding up what the accounting records say belongs to a business and deducting what they say the business owes, you can identify what a business is worth according to those accounting records. The whole of financial accounting is based upon this very simple idea. It is known as the *accounting equation*.

It can be explained by saying that if a business is to be set up and start trading, it will need resources. Let's assume first that it is the owner of the business who has supplied all of the resources. This can be shown as:

> **Resources supplied by the owner = Resources in the business**

In accounting, special terms are used to describe many things. The amount of the resources supplied by the owner is called **capital**. The actual resources that are then in the business are called **assets**. This means that when the owner has supplied all of the resources, the accounting equation can be shown as:

> **Capital = Assets**

Usually, however, people other than the owner have supplied some of the assets. **Liabilities** is the name given to the amounts owing to these people for these assets. The accounting equation has now changed to:

> **Capital = Assets − Liabilities**

This is the most common way in which the accounting equation is presented. It can be seen that the two sides of the equation will have the same totals. This is because we are dealing with the same thing from two different points of view – the value of the owners' investment in the business and the value of what is owned by the owners.

Unfortunately, with this form of the accounting equation, we can no longer see at a glance what value is represented by the resources in the business. You can see this more clearly if you switch assets and capital around to produce the alternate form of the accounting equation:

> **Assets = Capital + Liabilities**

This can then be replaced with words describing the resources of the business:

> Resources: what they are = Resources: who supplied them
> (Assets)   (Capital + Liabilities)

It is a fact that no matter how you present the accounting equation, the totals of both sides will *always* equal each other, and that this will *always* be true no matter how many transactions there may be. The actual assets, capital and liabilities may change, but the total of the assets will always equal the total of capital + liabilities. Or, reverting to the more common form of the accounting equation, the capital will always equal the assets of the business minus the liabilities.

Assets consist of property of all kinds, such as buildings, machinery, stocks of goods and motor vehicles. Other assets include debts owed by customers and the amount of money in the organisation's bank account.

Liabilities include amounts owed by the business for goods and services supplied to the business and for expenses incurred by the business that have not yet been paid for. They also include funds borrowed by the business.

Capital is often called the owner's **equity** or net worth. It comprises the funds invested in the business by the owner plus any profits retained for use in the business less any share of profits paid out of the business to the owner.

23.6   The balance sheet and the effects of business transactions

The accounting equation is expressed in a financial position statement called the **balance sheet**.

The balance sheet shows the financial position of an organisation at a point in time. In other words, it presents a snapshot of the organisation at the date for which it was prepared. The balance sheet is not the first accounting record to be made, but it is a convenient place to start.

Let's now look at how a series of transactions affect the balance sheet.

1 The introduction of capital

On 1 May 20X7, B. Blake started in business and deposited £5,000 into a bank account opened specially for the business. The balance sheet would appear:

B. Blake
Balance Sheet as at 1 May 20X7

	£
Assets: Cash at bank	5,000
Capital	5,000

Note how the top part of the balance sheet contains the assets and the bottom part contains the capital. This is always the way the information is presented in a balance sheet.

2 The purchase of an asset by cheque

On 3 May 20X7, Blake buys a building for £3,000 paying by cheque. The effect of this transaction on the balance sheet is that the cash at the bank is decreased and the new asset, the building, is added:

B. Blake
Balance Sheet as at 3 May 20X7

	£
Assets	
Building	3,000
Cash at bank	<u>2,000</u>
	<u>5,000</u>
Capital	
	<u>5,000</u>

Note how the two parts of the balance sheet 'balance'. That is, their totals are the same. This is always the case with balance sheets.

3 The purchase of an asset and the incurring of a liability

On 6 May 20X7, Blake buys some goods for £500 from D. Smith, and agrees to pay for them some time within the next two weeks. The effect of this is that a new asset, **stock of goods**, is acquired, and a liability for the goods is created. A person to whom money is owed for goods is known in accounting language as a **creditor**. The balance sheet becomes:

B. Blake
Balance Sheet as at 6 May 20X7

	£
Assets	
Building	3,000
Stock of goods	500
Cash at bank	<u>2,000</u>
	5,500
Less: Creditor	<u>(500)</u>
	<u>5,000</u>
Capital	
	<u>5,000</u>

Note how the liability (the creditor) is shown as a deduction from the assets. This is exactly the same calculation as is presented in the most common form of the accounting equation.

4 Sale of an asset on credit

On 10 May 20X7, goods which cost £100 were sold to J. Brown for the same amount, the money to be paid later. The effect is a reduction in the stock of goods and the creation of a new asset. A person who owes the firm money is known in accounting language as a **debtor**. The balance sheet is now:

B. Blake
Balance Sheet as at 10 May 20X7

	£
Assets	
Building	3,000
Stock of goods	400
Debtor	100
Cash at bank	2,000
	5,500
Less: Creditor	(500)
	5,000
Capital	5,000

5 Sale of an asset for immediate payment

On 13 May 20X7, goods which cost £50 were sold to D Daley for the same amount. Daley paid for them immediately by cheque. Here one asset, stock of goods, is reduced, while another asset, cash at bank, is increased. The balance sheet becomes:

B. Blake
Balance Sheet as at 13 May 20X7

	£
Assets	
Building	3,000
Stock of goods	350
Debtor	100
Cash at bank	2,050
	5,500
Less: Creditor	(500)
	5,000
Capital	5,000

6 The payment of a liability

On 15 May 20X7, Blake pays a cheque for £200 to D. Smith in part payment of the amount owing. The asset of cash at bank is therefore reduced, and the liability to the creditor is also reduced. The balance sheet is now:

B. Blake
Balance Sheet as at 15 May 20X7

	£
Assets	
Building	3,000
Stock of goods	350
Debtor	100
Cash at bank	1,850
	5,300
Less: Creditor	(300)
	5,000
Capital	5,000

Note how the total of each part of the balance sheet has not changed. The business is still worth £5,000 to the owner.

7 Collection of an asset

J Brown, who owed Blake £100, makes a part payment of £75 by cheque on 31 May 20X7. The effect is to reduce one asset, debtor, and to increase another asset, cash at bank. The balance sheet becomes:

B. Blake
Balance Sheet as at 31 May 20X7

	£
Assets	
Building	3,000
Stock of goods	350
Debtor	25
Cash at bank	1,925
	5,300
Less: Creditor	(300)
	5,000
Capital	5,000

23.7 Equality of the accounting equation

It can be seen that every transaction has affected two items. Sometimes it has changed two assets by reducing one and increasing the other. In other cases, the effect has been different. However, in each case other than the very first (when the business was started by the owner injecting some cash into it), no change was made to the total of either section of the balance sheet and the equality between their two totals has been maintained. The accounting equation has held true throughout the example, and it always will. The effect of each of these seven accounting transctions upon the two sections of the balance sheet is shown below:

Number of transaction as above	Assets	Capital and Liabilities	Effect on balance sheet totals
1	+	+	Each side added to equally
2	+ −		A *plus* and a *minus* both on the assets side *cancelling out* each other
3	+	+	Each side has equal deductions
4	+ −		A *plus* and a *minus* both on the assets side *cancelling out* each other
5	+ −		A *plus* and a *minus* both on the assets side *cancelling out* each other
6	−	−	Each side has equal deductions
7	+ −		A *plus* and a *minus* both on the assets side *cancelling out* each other

These are not the only types of accounting transactions that can take plance. Two other examples arise when the owner withdraws resources from the business for his or her own use; and where the owner pays a business expense personally.

A summary of the effect upon assets, liabilities and capital of each type of transaction you've been introduced to so far is shown below:

Example of transaction	Effect			
1 Owner pays capital into the bank	↑	Increase asset (Bank)	↑	Increase capital
2 Buy goods by cheque	↓	Decrease asset (Bank)	↑	Increase asset (Stock of goods)
3 Buy goods on credit	↑	Increase asset (Stock of goods)	↑	Increase liability (Creditors)
4 Sale of goods on credit	↓	Decrease asset (Stock of goods)	↑	Increase asset (Debtors)
5 Sale of goods for cash (cheque)	↓	Decrease asset (Stock of goods)	↑	Increase asset (Bank)
6 Pay creditor	↓	Decrease asset (Bank)	↓	Decrease liability (Creditor)
7 Debtor pays money owing by cheque	↑	Increase asset (Bank)	↓	Decrease asset (Debtors)

The next two types of transactions do cause the totals of each part of the balance sheet to change (as did the very first, when capital was introduced to the business by the owner). When the capital changes, the totals of the two parts of the balance sheet both change.

Example of transaction	Effect			
8 Owner takes money out of the business bank account for own use	↓	Decrease asset (Bank)	↓	Decrease capital
9 Owner pays creditor from private money outside the firm	↓	Decrease liability (Creditor)	↑	Increase capital

23.8   More detailed presentation of the balance sheet

Let's now look at the balance sheet of B. Blake as at 31 May 20X7, presented in line with how you have learnt to present the information earlier in the book:

B. Blake
Balance Sheet as at 31 May 20X7

	£	£
Fixed assets		
Buildings		3,000
Current assets		
Stock of goods	350	
Debtor	25	
Cash at bank	1,925	
	2,300	
Less Current liabilities		
Creditor	(300)	
		2,000
		5,000
Capital		5,000

You will have noticed in this balance sheet the terms 'fixed assets', 'current assets' and 'current liabilities'. As you recall from earlier chapters, they may be defined as:

- **Fixed assets** are assets which have a long life, and which are bought with the intention to use them in the business and not with the intention to simply resell them, e.g. buildings, machinery, fixtures, motor vehicles.
- **Current assets** are assets consisting of cash, goods for resale or items having a short life. For example, the value of stock in hand goes up and down as it is bought and sold. Similarly, the amount of money owing to us by debtors will change quickly, as we sell more to them on credit and they pay their debts. The amount of money in the bank will also change as we receive and pay out money.
- **Current liabilities** are those liabilities which have to be paid within no more than a year from the date on the balance sheet, e.g. creditors for goods bought.

Learning outcomes

You should now have learnt that:

1 Accounting is concerned with the recording and classifying and summarising of data, and then communicating what has been learnt from it.

2 It may not only be the owner of a business who will need the accounting information; it may need to be shown to others, e.g. the bank or the Inspector of Taxes.

3 Accounting information can help the owner(s) of a business to plan for the future.

4 The accounting equation is: Capital = Assets – Liabilities.

5 The two sides of the accounting equation are represented by the two parts of the balance sheet.

6 The totals of one part of the balance sheet should always be equal to the total of the other part.

7 Every transaction affects two items in the accounting equation. Sometimes that may involve the same item being affected twice, once positively (going up) and once negatively (going down).

8 Every transaction affects two items in the balance sheet.

REVIEW QUESTIONS

23.1 You are to complete the gaps in the following table:

	Assets	Liabilities	Capital
	£	£	£
(a)	12,500	1,800	?
(b)	28,000	4,900	?
(c)	16,800	?	12,500
(d)	19,600	?	16,450
(e)	?	6,300	19,200
(f)	?	11,650	39,750

23.2X You are to complete the gaps in the following table:

	Assets	Liabilities	Capital
	£	£	£
(a)	55,000	16,900	?
(b)	?	17,200	34,400
(c)	36,100	?	28,500
(d)	119,500	15,400	?
(e)	88,000	?	62,000
(f)	?	49,000	110,000

23.3 Distinguish from the following list the items that are liabilities from those that are assets:

(a) Office machinery
(b) Loan from C Shirley
(c) Fixtures and fittings
(d) Motor vehicles
(e) We owe for goods
(f) Bank balance

23.4X Classify the following items into liabilities and assets:

(a) Motor vehicles
(b) Premises
(c) Creditors for goods
(d) Stock of goods
(e) Debtors
(f) Owing to bank
(g) Cash in hand
(h) Loan from D Jones
(i) Machinery

23.5 State which of the following are shown under the wrong classification for J White's business:

Assets	Liabilities
Loan from C Smith	Stock of goods
Cash in hand	Debtors
Machinery	Money owing to bank
Creditors	
Premises	
Motor vehicles	

23.6X Which of the following are shown under the wrong headings?

Assets	Liabilities
Cash at bank	Loan from J Graham
Fixtures	Machinery
Creditors	Motor vehicles
Building	
Stock of goods	
Debtors	
Capital	

23.7 A Smart sets up a new business. Before he actually sells anything, he has bought motor vehicle £2,000, premises £5,000, stock of goods £1,000. He did not pay in full for his stock of goods and still owes £400 in respect of them. He had borrowed £3,000 from D Bevan. After the events just described, and before trading starts, he has £100 cash in hand and £700 cash at bank. You are required to calculate the amount of his capital.

23.8X T Charles starts a business. Before he actually starts to sell anything, he has bought fixtures £2,000, motor vehicle £5,000 and a stock of goods £3,500. Although he has paid in full for the fixtures and the motor vehicle, he still owes £1,400 for some of the goods. J Preston had lent him £3,000. Charles, after the above, has £2,800 in the business bank account and £100 cash in hand. You are required to calculate his capital.

23.9 Draw up A Foster's balance sheet from the following as at 31 December 20X8:

	£
Capital	23,750
Debtors	4,950
Motor vehicles	5,700
Creditors	2,450
Fixtures	5,500
Stock of goods	8,800
Cash at bank	1,250

23.10X Draw up M Kelly's balance sheet as at 30 June 20X6 from the following items:

	£
Capital	15,000
Office machinery	9,000
Creditors	900
Stock of goods	1,550
Debtors	275
Cash at bank	5,075

23.11 Complete the columns to show the effects of the following transactions:

	Effect upon		
	Assets	Liabilities	Capital

(a) We pay a creditor £70 in cash.
(b) Bought fixtures £200 paying by cheque.
(c) Bought goods on credit £275.
(d) The proprietor introduces another £500 cash into the firm.
(e) J Walker lends the firm £200 in cash.

	Effect upon		
	Assets	*Liabilities*	*Capital*

(*f*) A debtor pays us £50 by cheque.

(*g*) We return goods costing £60 to a supplier whose bill
   we had not paid.

(*h*) Bought additional shop premises paying £5,000 by cheque.

23.12X Complete the columns to show the effects of the following transactions:

	Effect upon		
	Assets	*Liabilities*	*Capital*

(*a*) Bought a motor van on credit £500.

(*b*) Repaid by cash a loan owed to P Smith £1,000.

(*c*) Bought goods for £150 paying by cheque.

(*d*) The owner puts a further £5,000 cash into the business.

(*e*) A debtor returns to us £80 goods. We agree to make
   an allowance for them.

(*f*) Bought goods on credit £220.

(*g*) The owner takes out £100 cash for his personal use.

(*h*) We pay a creditor £190 by cheque.

23.13 C Sangster has the following items in his balance sheet as on 30 April 20X8:

Capital £20,900; Creditors £1,600; Fixtures £3,500; Motor vehicle £4,200; Stock of goods £4,950; Debtors £3,280; Cash at bank £6,450; Cash in hand £120.

During the first week of May 20X8:

(*a*) He bought extra stock of goods £770 on credit.

(*b*) One of the debtors paid him £280 in cash.

(*c*) He bought extra fixtures by cheque £1,000.

You are to draw up a balance sheet as on 7 May 20X8 after the above transactions have been completed.

23.14X F Dale has the following assets and liabilities as on 30 November 20X9:

Creditors £3,950; Equipment £11,500; Motor vehicle £6,290; Stock of goods £6,150; Debtors £5,770; Cash at bank £7,280; Cash in hand £40.

The capital at that date is to be deduced by you.

During the first week of December 20X9, Dale:

(*a*) Bought extra equipment on credit for £1,380.

(*b*) Bought extra stock by cheque £570.

(*c*) Paid creditors by cheque £790.

(*d*) Was paid by debtors £840 by cheque and £60 by cash.

(*e*) Put in an extra £250 cash as capital.

You are to draw up a balance sheet as on 7 December 20X9 after the above transactions have been completed.

CHAPTER 24

The double entry system

Learning objectives

By the end of this chapter, you should be able to:

● explain what is meant by the double entry system;

● explain how the double entry system follows the rules of the accounting equation;

● enter transactions using the double entry system.

24.1 Nature of a transaction

In Chapter 23, we saw how various events had changed two items in the balance sheet. Events which result in such changes are known as 'transactions'. This means that if the proprietor asks the price of some goods, but does not buy them, then there is no transaction. If he later asks the price of some other goods, and then buys them, then there would be a transaction, and two balance sheet items would then have to be altered.

24.2 The double entry system

We have seen that every transaction affects two items. If we want to show the effect of every transaction when we are doing our bookkeeping, we will have to show the effect of a transaction on each of the two items. For each transaction this means that a bookkeeping entry will have to be made to show an increase or decrease of that item, and another entry to show the increase or decrease of the other item. From this you will probably be able to see that the term **double entry system** of bookkeeping is a good one, as each entry is made twice (double entry).

It may be thought that drawing up a new balance sheet after each transaction would provide all the information required. However, a balance sheet does not give enough information about the business. It does not, for instance, tell who the debtors are and how much each one of them owes the firm, nor who the creditors are and the details of money owing to each of them.

Instead of constantly drawing up balance sheets after each transaction what we have instead is the 'double entry' system. The basis of this system is that the transactions which occur are entered in a set of **accounts**. An account is a place where all the information referring to a particular asset or liability, or to capital, is entered. Thus there will be an account where all the information concerning office machinery will be entered.

Similarly there will be an account for buildings, where all the information concerned with buildings will be shown. This will be extended so that every asset, every liability and capital will have its own account for transactions in that item.

24.3 The accounts for double entry

Each account should be shown on a separate page. The double entry system divides each page into two halves. The left-hand side of each page is called the **debit** side, while the right-hand side is called the **credit** side. The title of each account is written across the top of the account at the centre.

You must not think that the words 'debit' and 'credit' in bookkeeping mean the same as the words 'debit' or 'credit' in normal language usage. If you do, you will become very confused.

This is a page of an accounts book:

Title of account written here

Left-hand side of the page. This is the 'debit' side.	Right-hand side of the page. This is the 'credit' side.

If you have to make an entry of £10 on the debit side of the account, the instructions could say 'debit the account with £10' or 'the account needs debiting with £10'.

Chapter 23 showed that transactions increase or decrease assets, liabilities or capital. Double entry rules for accounts are:

Accounts	To record	Entry in the account
Assets	an increase a decrease	Debit Credit
Liabilities	an increase a decrease	Credit Debit
Capital	an increase a decrease	Credit Debit

Let us look once again at the accounting equation:

	Assets = Liabilities + Capital		
To increase each item	Debit	Credit	Credit
To decrease each item	Credit	Debit	Debit

The double entry rules for liabilities and capital are the same, but they are the opposite of those for assets. This is because assets are on the opposite side of the equation and, therefore, follow opposite rules. When we look at the accounts the rules will appear as:

Any asset account		*Any liability account*		*Capital account*	
Increases	*Decreases*	*Decreases*	*Increases*	*Decreases*	*Increases*
+	−	−	+	−	+

We have not enough space in this book to put each account on a separate page, so we will have to list the accounts under each other. In a real firm at least one full page would be taken for each account.

24.4 Worked examples

The entry of a few transactions can now be attempted:

1 The proprietor starts the firm with £1,000 in cash on 1 August 20X8. These are entered:

Effect	Action
1 Increases the *asset* of cash 2 Increases the capital	Debit the cash account Credit the capital account

Cash

20X8		£	
Aug 1		1,000	

Capital

			20X8	£
			Aug 1	1,000

The date of the transaction has already been entered. Now there remains the description which is to be entered alongside the amount. This is completed by a cross-reference to the title of the other account in which the double entry is completed. The double entry to the item in the cash account is completed by an entry in the capital account; therefore the word 'Capital' will appear in the cash account. Similarly, the double entry to the item in the capital account is completed by an entry in the cash account; therefore the word 'Cash' will appear in the capital account.

The finally completed accounts are therefore:

Cash

20X8		£	
Aug 1 Capital		1,000	

Capital

		20X8	£
		Aug 1 Cash	1,000

2 A motor van is bought for £275 cash on 2 August 20X8.

Effect	Action
1 Increases the *asset* of motor van 2 Decreases the *asset* of cash	Debit the motor van account Credit the cash account

Motor van

20X8		£		
Aug 2 Cash		275		

Cash

			20X8		£
			Aug 2 Motor van		275

3 Fixtures bought on credit from Shop Fitters for £115 on 3 August 20X8.

Effect	Action
1 Increases the *asset* of fixtures 2 Increases the *liability* to Shop Fitters	Debit the fixtures account Credit the Shop Fitters account

Fixtures

20X8		£		
Aug 3 Shop Fitters		115		

Shop Fitters

			20X8		£
			Aug 3 Fixtures		115

4 Paid the amount owing to Shop Fitters on 17 August 20X8, in cash.

Effect	Action
1 Decreases the *liability* to Shop Fitters 2 Decreases the *asset* of cash	Debit the Shop Fitters account Credit the cash account

Shop Fitters

20X8		£		
Aug 17 Cash		115		

Cash

			20X8		£
			Aug 17 Shop Fitters		115

5 Transactions to date. Taking the transactions numbered **1** to **4** above, the records will now appear:

Cash

20X8		£	20X8		£
Aug 1 Capital		1,000	Aug 2 Motor van		275
			Aug 17 Shop Fitters		115

Capital

		20X8				£
		Aug	1	Cash		1,000

Motor van

20X8			£			
Aug	2	Cash	275			

Shop Fitters

20X8			£	20X8			£
Aug	17	Cash	115	Aug	3	Fixtures	115

Fixtures

20X8			£			
Aug	3	Shop Fitters	115			

Before you read further, work through Review Questions 24.1 and 24.2X.

24.5 A further worked example

Now you have actually made some entries in accounts you are to go carefully through the following example. Make certain you can understand every entry.

Transactions	Effect	Action
20X8 May 1 Started an engineering business putting £1,000 into a business bank account.	↑ Increases *asset* of bank. ↑ Increases *capital* of owner.	Debit bank account. Credit capital account.
May 3 Bought works machinery on credit from Unique Machines £275.	↑ Increases *asset* of machinery. ↑ Increases *liability* to Unique Machines.	Debit machinery account. Credit Unique Machines account.
May 4 Withdrew £200 cash from the bank and placed it in the cash box.	↑ Increases *asset* of cash. ↓ Decreases *asset* of bank.	Debit cash account. Credit bank account.
May 7 Bought a motor van paying in cash £180.	↑ Increases *asset* of motor van. ↓ Decreases *asset* of cash.	Debit motor van account. Credit cash account.

Transactions	Effect	Action
May 10 Sold some of the machinery for £15 on credit to B Barnes.	↑ Increases *asset* of money owing from B Barnes. ↓ Decreases *asset* of machinery.	Debit B Barnes account. Credit machinery account.
May 21 Returned some of the machinery, value £27, to Unique Machines.	↓ Decreases *liability* to Unique Machines. ↓ Decreases *asset* of machinery.	Debit Unique Machines. Credit machinery account.
May 28 B Barnes pays the firm the amount owing, £15, by cheque.	↑ Increases *asset* of bank. ↓ Decreases *asset* of money owing by B Barnes.	Debit bank account. Credit B Barnes account.
May 30 Bought another motor van paying by cheque £420.	↑ Increases *asset* of motor vans. ↓ Decreases *asset* of Bank.	Debit motor van account. Credit bank account.
May 31 Paid the amount of £248 to Unique Machines by cheque.	↓ Decreases *liability* to Unique machines. ↓ Decreases *asset* of bank.	Debit Unique Machines. Credit bank account.

In account form:

Bank

20X8			£	20X8			£
May	1	Capital	1,000	May	4	Cash	200
May	28	B Barnes	15	May	30	Motor van	420
				May	31	Unique Machines	248

Cash

20X8			£	20X8			£
May	4	Bank	200	May	7	Motor van	180

Capital

20X8				20X8			£
				May	1	Bank	1,000

Machinery

20X8			£	20X8			£
May	3	Unique Machines	275	May	10	B Barnes	15
				May	21	Unique Machines	27

Motor Van

20X8			£	
May	7	Cash	180	
May	30	Bank	420	

Unique Machines

20X8			£	20X8			£
May	21	Machinery	27	May	3	Machinery	275
May	31	Bank	248				

B Barnes

20X8			£	20X8			£
May	10	Machinery	15	May	28	Bank	15

24.6 Abbreviation of 'limited'

In this book when we have come across transactions with limited companies the letters 'Ltd' have been used as the abbreviation for 'Limited Company'. Thus, if we see the name of a firm as W Jones Ltd or W Jones plc ('plc' = public limited company) we know that firm is a limited company. The transactions with companies are entered in the same way as for any other customer or supplier.

Learning objectives

You should now have learnt:

1 That double entry follows the rules of the accounting equation.
2 That double entry maintains the principle that every debit has a corresponding credit entry.
3 That double entries are made in accounts in the accounting books.
4 Why each transaction is entered into accounts rather than directly into the balance sheet.
5 How transactions cause increases and decreases in asset, liability and capital accounts.
6 How to record transactions in T-accounts.

REVIEW QUESTIONS

24.1 Complete the following table:

	Account to be debited	Account to be credited
(a) Bought office machinery on credit from D Isaacs Ltd.		
(b) The proprietor paid a creditor, C Jones, from his private monies outside the firm.		

	Account to be debited	Account to be credited

(c) A debtor, N Fox, paid us in cash.

(d) Repaid part of loan from P Exeter by cheque.

(e) Returned some of office machinery to D Isaacs Ltd.

(f) A debtor, N Lyn, pays us by cheque.

(g) Bought motor van by cash.

24.2X Complete the following table showing which accounts are to be debited and which to be credited:

	Account to be debited	Account to be credited

(a) Bought motor lorry for cash.

(b) Paid creditor, T Lake, by cheque.

(c) Repaid P Logan's loan by cash.

(d) Sold motor lorry for cash.

(e) Bought office machinery on credit from Ultra Ltd.

(f) A debtor, A Hill, pays us by cash.

(g) A debtor, J Cross, pays us by cheque.

(h) Proprietor puts a further amount into the business by cheque.

(i) A loan of £200 in cash is received from L Lowe.

(j) Paid a creditor, D Lord, by cash.

24.3 Write up the asset and liability and capital accounts to record the following transactions in the records of G Powell.

20X7

July 1 Started business with £2,500 in the bank.

,, 2 Bought office furniture by cheque £150.

,, 3 Bought machinery £750 on credit from Planers Ltd.

,, 5 Bought a motor van paying by cheque £600.

,, 8 Sold some of the office furniture – not suitable for the firm – for £60 on credit to J Walker & Sons.

,, 15 Paid the amount owing to Planers Ltd £750 by cheque.

,, 23 Received the amount due from J Walker & Sons £60 in cash.

,, 31 Bought more machinery by cheque £280.

24.4 You are required to open the asset and liability and capital accounts and record the following transactions for June 20X8 in the records of C Williams.

20X8

June 1 Started business with £2,000 in cash.

,, 2 Paid £1,800 of the opening cash into a bank account for the business.

,, 5 Bought office furniture on credit from Betta-Built Ltd for £120.

,, 8 Bought a motor van paying by cheque £950.

,, 12 Bought works machinery from Evans & Sons on credit £560.

,, 18 Returned faulty office furniture costing £62 to Betta-Built Ltd.

,, 25 Sold some of the works machinery for £75 cash.

,, 26 Paid amount owing to Betta-Built Ltd £58 by cheque.

,, 28 Took £100 out of the bank and put it in the cash till.

,, 30 J Smith lent us £500 – giving us the money by cheque.

24.5X Write up the asset, capital and liability accounts in the books of C Walsh to record the following transactions:

20X9

June	1	Started business with £5,000 in the bank.
,,	2	Bought motor van paying by cheque £1,200.
,,	5	Bought office fixtures £400 on credit from Young Ltd.
,,	8	Bought motor van on credit from Super Motors £800.
,,	12	Took £100 out of the bank and put it into the cash till.
,,	15	Bought office fixtures paying by cash £60.
,,	19	Paid Super Motors a cheque for £800.
,,	21	A loan of £1,000 cash is received from J Jarvis.
,,	25	Paid £800 of the cash in hand into the bank account.
,,	30	Bought more office fixtures paying by cheque £300.

24.6X Write up the accounts to record the following transactions:

20X7

March	1	Started with £1,000 cash.
,,	2	Received a loan of £5,000 from M Chow by cheque, a bank account being opened and the cheque paid into it.
,,	3	Bought machinery for cash £60.
,,	5	Bought display equipment on credit from Betterview Machines £550.
,,	8	Took £300 out of the bank and put it into the cash till.
,,	15	Repaid part of Chow's loan by cheque £800.
,,	17	Paid amount owing to Betterview Machines £550 by cheque.
,,	24	Repaid part of Chow's loan by cash £100.
,,	31	Bought additional machinery, this time on credit from D Smith for £500.

Accounting concepts

25.1 Introduction

When transactions are recorded in the books, certain assumptions are made. These assumptions are known as the *concepts of accounting*.

The trading and profit and loss accounts and balance sheets are drawn up for the owner(s) of the business. However, the owner of a business may not be the only person to see the final accounts. They may have to be shown to the bank manager if the owner wants to borrow money. The Inspector of Taxes will want to see them for the calculation of taxes. They may also need to be shown to someone if the business is for sale. Similarly, a new partner or investor would want to see them.

25.2 One set of financial statements for all purposes

When financial statements are published, everyone receives the same profit and loss account and balance sheet. For financial statements to be of any use, all the various stakeholders have to believe that the basis and assumptions underlying the financial statements are valid and appropriate. If the stakeholders do not believe this to be the case, they won't trust the financial statements.

Let's consider an example concerning one item in the balance sheet. Assume that you are in a class of students and that you have the problem of valuing your assets, which consist of 10 textbooks. The first value you decide is based upon how much you could sell them for. Your own guess is £30 and that is what you tell everyone that they are worth, but the other members of your class suggest they should be valued at anything from £15 to £50.

Suppose that you now decide to put a value on their use to you. You may well think that the use of these textbooks will enable you to pass your examinations and so you will get a good job. Another person may have the opposite idea concerning the use of the textbooks. The use value placed on the textbooks by others in the class will be quite different. Again, your value may be higher than those of some of your colleagues and lower than those of others.

Finally, you decide to value them by reference to cost. You take out the receipts you received when you purchased the textbooks, which show that you paid a total of £60 for them. If the rest of the class does not think that you have altered the receipts, then they will all agree with you that the value, expressed at original cost, is £60. At last, you have found a way of valuing the textbooks where everyone agrees on the same figure. As this is the only valuation that you can all agree upon, each of you decides to use the idea of valuing the asset of textbooks at their cost price so that you can have a meaningful discussion about what you are worth (in terms of your assets, i.e. your textbooks) compared with everyone else in the class. It probably won't come as a surprise to you to learn that this is precisely the basis upon which the assets of a business are valued. Accountants call it the 'historic cost convention'.

25.3 Objectivity and subjectivity

The use of a method which arrives at a value that everyone can agree on, because it is based upon a factual occurrence – in the above example, the amount you paid for your textbooks – is said to be 'objective'. Valuing assets at their cost to you is, therefore, objective – you are adhering to and accepting the facts. You are not placing your own interpretation on the facts. As a result, everyone else knows where the value came from and can see that there is very good evidence to support its adoption.

If, instead of being objective, you were 'subjective', you would use your own judgement to arrive at a cost. This often results in the value you arrive at being biased towards your own views and preferences – as in the example above when the usefulness of the textbooks to you for examinations was the basis of their valuation. Subjective valuations seem right to the person who makes them, but most other people would probably disagree with the value arrived at, because it won't appear to them to be objectively based.

The desire to provide the same set of accounts for many different parties, and so provide a basis for measurement that is generally acceptable, means that objectivity is sought in financial accounting. If you are able to understand this desire for objectivity, then many of the apparent contradictions in accounting can be understood because objectivity is at the heart of the financial accounting methods in use at the present time.

Financial accounting, therefore, seeks objectivity and it seeks consistency in how information is prepared and presented. To achieve this, there must be a set of rules which lay down the way in which the transactions of the business are recorded. These rules have long been known as 'accounting concepts'. A group of these have become known as 'fundamental accounting concepts' (also referred to as 'accounting principles') and have been enforced through their incorporation in accounting standards issued on behalf of the accountancy bodies and by their inclusion in the relevant legislation governing companies, the Companies Act.

25.4 Accounting standards and financial reporting standards

At one time, there used to be quite wide differences in the ways that accountants calculated profits. In the late 1960s, a number of cases led to a widespread outcry against this lack of uniformity in accounting practice.

In response, the accounting bodies formed the Accounting Standards Committee which issued a series of accounting standards, called *Statements of Standard Accounting Practice* (SSAPs). The ASC was replaced in 1990 by the Accounting Standards Board, which also issued accounting standards, this time called *Financial Reporting Standards* (FRSs). Both forms of accounting standards are compulsory.

25.5 Accounting standards and the legal framework

Accounting standards are drafted so that they comply with the laws of the United Kingdom and the Republic of Ireland. They also comply with European Union Directives. This is all to ensure that there is no conflict between the law and accounting standards. Anyone preparing financial statements which are intended to show a 'true and fair view' (i.e. truly reflect what has occurred and the financial position of the organisation) must observe the rules laid down in the accounting standards.

25.6 Underlying accounting concepts

A number of accounting concepts have been applied ever since financial statements were first produced for external reporting purposes. These have become second nature to accountants and are not generally reinforced, other than through custom and practice.

The historical cost concept

The need for this has already been described in the textbook valuation example. It means that assets are normally shown at cost price, and that this is the basis for valuation of the asset.

The money measurement concept

Accounting information has traditionally been concerned only with those facts covered by (*a*) and (*b*) which follow:

(*a*) it can be measured in monetary units, and
(*b*) most people will agree to the monetary value of the transaction.

This means that accounting can never tell you everything about a business. For example, accounting does not show the following:

(*c*) whether the firm has good or bad managers,
(*d*) whether there are serious problems with the workforce,
(*e*) whether a rival product is about to take away many of the firm's best customers,
(*f*) whether the government is about to pass a law which will cost the firm a lot of extra expense in future.

The reason that (c) to (f) or similar items are not recorded is that it would be impossible to work out a monetary value for them which most people would agree to.

Some people think that accounting and financial statements tell you everything you want to know about a business. The above shows that this is not true.

The business entity concept

This concept implies that the affairs of a business are to be treated as being quite separate from the non-business activities of its owner(s).

The items recorded in the books of the business are therefore restricted to the transactions of the business. No matter what activities the proprietor(s) get up to outside the business, they are completely disregarded in the books kept by the business.

The only time that the personal resources of the proprietor(s) affect the accounting records of a business is when they introduce new capital into the business, or take drawings out of it.

The dual aspect concept

This states that there are two aspects of accounting, one represented by the assets of the business and the other by the claims against them. The concept states that these two aspects are always equal to each other. In other words:

Capital = Assets – Liabilities

As you know, double entry is the name given to the method of recording transactions under the dual aspect concept.

The time interval concept

One of the underlying principles of accounting is that financial statements are prepared at regular intervals of one year. For internal management purposes they may be prepared far more frequently, possibly on a monthly basis or even more frequently.

25.7 Fundamental accounting concepts

These comprise a set of concepts considered so important that they have been enforced through accounting standards and/or through the Companies Act. Five have been enforced through the Companies Act 1985, and a sixth through an accounting standard, FRS 5 (*Reporting the substance of transactions*).

The five enforced through the Companies Act are:

1 Going concern

This fundamental accounting concept implies that the business will continue to operate for the foreseeable future. It means that it is considered sensible to keep to the use of the historic cost concept when arriving at the valuations of assets.

Suppose, however, that a business is drawing up its final accounts at 31 December 20X8. Normally, using the cost concept, the assets would be shown at a total value of £100,000. It is known, however, that the business will be forced to close down in February 20X9, only two months later, and the assets are expected to be sold for only £15,000.

In this case it would not make sense to keep to the going concern concept, and so we can reject the historic cost concept for asset valuation purposes in cases such as this. In the balance sheet at 31 December 20X8 the assets will therefore be shown at the figure of £15,000. Such a case is the exception rather than the rule.

Examples where the going concern assumption should not be made are:

● if the business is going to close down in the near future;
● where shortage of cash makes it almost certain that the business will have to cease trading;
● where a large part of the business will almost certainly have to be closed down because of a shortage of cash.

2 Consistency

Even if we observe every concept already listed in Sections 25.6 and 25.7, there will still be quite a few different ways in which items could be recorded. This is because there can be different interpretations as to the exact meaning of the concept.

Each firm should try to choose the methods which give the most reliable picture of the business.

This cannot be done if one method is used in one year and another method in the next year and so on. Constantly changing the methods would lead to misleading profits being calculated from the accounting records. Therefore the convention of consistency is used. The consistency concept says that when a business has once fixed a method for the accounting treatment of an item, it will enter all similar items that follow in exactly the same way.

However, it does not mean that the business has to follow the method until the business closes down. A business can change the method used, but such a change is not made without a lot of consideration. When such a change occurs and the profits calculated in that year are affected by a material amount (i.e. one that makes a noticeable difference to the figures shown in the financial statements), then either in the profit and loss account itself or in one of the reports that accompany it, the effect of the change should be stated.

3 Prudence

Very often accountants have to use their judgement to decide which figure to take for an item. Suppose a debt has been owing for quite a long time, and no one knows whether it will ever be paid. Should the accountant be an optimist in thinking that it will be paid, or should he or she be more pessimistic?

It is the accountant's duty to see that people get the proper facts about a business. The accountant should make certain that assets are not valued too highly. Similarly, liabilities should not be shown at values too low. Otherwise, people might inadvisedly lend money to a business, which they would not do if they had the proper facts.

The accountant should always exercise caution when dealing with uncertainty while, at the same time, ensuring that the financial statements are neutral – that gains and losses are neither over- nor under-stated – and this is known as prudence.

It is true that in applying the prudence concept, an accountant will normally make sure that all losses are recorded in the books, but that profits and gains will not be anticipated by recording them before they should be. Although it emphasises neutrality, many people feel that the prudence concept means that accountants will normally take the figure relating to unrealised profits and gains which will understate rather than overstate the profit for a period. That is, they believe that accountants tend to choose figures that will cause the capital of the business to be shown at a lower amount rather than at a higher amount.

The recognition of profits at an appropriate time has long been recognised as being in need of guidelines and these have long been enshrined in what is known as the '**realisation concept**'. This is not so much a separate concept. Rather, it is a part of the broader concept of prudence. Its meaning was clarified by FRS 18, which was issued in 2000 and superseded SSAP 2, the accounting standard that first laid down most of the accounting concepts in use today.

The realisation concept holds to the view that profit and gains can only be taken into account when realisation has occurred and that realisation occurs only when the ultimate cash realised is capable of being assessed (i.e. determined) with reasonable certainty. Several criteria have to be observed before realisation can occur:

● goods or services are provided for the buyer;
● the buyer accepts liability to pay for the goods or services;
● the monetary value of the goods or services has been established;
● the buyer will be in a situation to be able to pay for the goods or services.

Notice that it is not the time:

● when the order is received, or
● when the customer pays for the goods.

However, it is only when you can be reasonably certain as to how much will be received that you can recognise profits or gains.

Of course, recognising profits and gains now that will only be 100 per cent known in future periods is unlikely to ever mean that the correct amount has been recognised. Misjudgements can arise when, for example, profit is recognised in one period, only for it to be discovered later that this was incorrect because the goods involved have been returned in a later period because of some deficiency. Also, where services are involved rather than goods, the services can turn out to be subject to an allowance being given in a later period owing to poor performance.

The accountant needs to take every possibility into account yet, at the same time, the prudence concept requires that the financial statements are 'neutral'. That is, that neither gains nor losses should be over- or under-stated.

As you will see if you take your studies to a more advanced stage, there are times other than on completion of a sale when profit may be recognised. These could include profits on long-term contracts spanning several years, such as the building of a hotel or a very large bridge. In this case profit might be calculated for each year of the contract, even though the bridge is not finished at that date.

4 The accruals concept

The accruals concept says that net profit is the difference between revenues and the expenses incurred in generating those revenues, i.e.

$$\textbf{Revenues} - \textbf{Expenses} = \textbf{Net Profit}$$

Determining the expenses used up to obtain the revenues is referred to as *matching* expenses against revenues. The key to the application of the concept is that all income and charges relating to the financial period to which the accounts relate should be taken into account without regard to the date of receipt or payment.

This concept is particularly misunderstood by people who have not studied accounting. To many of them, actual payment of an item in a period is taken as being matched against the revenue of the period when the net profit is calculated. The fact that expenses consist of the assets used up in a particular period in obtaining the revenues of that period, and that cash paid in a period and expenses of a period are usually different, comes as a surprise to a great number of them.

5 Separate determination

In determining the aggregate amount of each asset or liability, the amount of each individual asset or liability should be determined separately from all other assets and liabilities. For example, if you have three machines, the amount at which machinery is shown in the balance sheet should be the sum of the values calculated individually for each of the three machines. Only when individual values have been derived should a total be calculated.

This concept is, perhaps, best described in relation to potential gains and potential losses. If a business is being sued by a customer for £10,000 and there is a high probability that the business will lose the case, the prudence concept requires the £10,000 to be included as a liability in the financial statements. The same business may, itself, be suing a supplier for £6,000 and may have a good probability of winning the case. It might be tempting to offset the two claims, leaving a net liability of £4,000 to appear in the financial statements. Yet, this would be contrary to the realisation concept which would not allow the probable £6,000 gain to be realised until it was viewed with reasonable certainty that it was going to be received. The separate determination concept prohibits the netting-off of potential liabilities and potential gains. As a result, only the probable £10,000 expense would be recognised in the financial statements.

The remaining fundamental accounting concept was established by the issue of FRS 5:

6 Substance over form

It can happen that the legal form of a transaction can differ from its real substance. Where this happens, accounting should show the transaction in accordance with its real substance which is, basically, how the transaction affects the economic situation of the firm. This means that accounting in this instance will not reflect the exact legal position concerning that transaction.

You have not yet come across the best and easiest illustration of this concept. Later in your studies you may have to learn about accounting for fixed assets being bought on hire purchase. We will take a car as an example.

● From a legal point of view the car does not belong to the firm until all the hire purchase instalments have been paid, and an option has been taken up whereby the firm takes over legal possession of the car.
● From an economic point of view the firm has used the car for business purposes, just as any other car owned by the business which was paid for immediately has been used. In this case, the business will show the car being bought on hire purchase in its accounts and balance sheet as though it were legally owned by the business, but also showing separately the amount still owed for it.

In this way, therefore, the substance of the transaction has taken precedence over the legal form of the transaction.

25.8 Materiality

The accounting concepts already discussed have become accepted in the business world, their assimilation having taken place over many years. However, there is one overriding rule applied to anything that appears in a financial accounting statement – it should be 'material'. That is, it should be of interest to the stakeholders, those people who make use of financial accounting statements. It need not be material to every stakeholder, but it must be material to a stakeholder before it merits inclusion.

Accounting does not serve a useful purpose if the effort of recording a transaction in a certain way is not worthwhile. Thus, if a box of paper-clips was bought it would be used up over a period of time, and this cost is used up every time someone uses a paper-clip. It is possible to record this as an expense every time a paper-clip is used but, obviously, the price of a paper-clip is so little that it is not worth recording it in this fashion, nor is the entire box of paper-clips. The paper-clips are not a material item, and therefore the box would be charged as an expense in the period it was bought, irrespective of the fact that it could last for more than one accounting period. In other words, do not waste your time in the elaborate recording of trivial items.

Firms fix all sorts of arbitrary rules to determine what is material and what is not. There is no law that lays down what these should be – the decision as to what is material and what is not is dependent upon judgement. A firm may well decide that all items under £100 should be treated as expenses in the period in which they were bought even though they may well be in use in the firm for the following ten years. Another firm, especially a large one, may fix the limit at £1,000. Different limits may be set for different types of item.

It can be seen that the size and the type of business will affect the decisions as to which items are material. With individuals, an amount of £1,000 may well be more than you, as a student, possess. For a multi-millionaire, what is a material item and what is not will almost certainly not be comparable. Just as individuals vary, then, so do businesses. Some businesses have a great deal of machinery and may well treat all items of machinery costing less than £1,000 as not being material, whereas another business which makes about the same amount of profits, but has very little machinery, may well treat a £600 machine as being a material item as that business has fixed its materiality limit at £250.

25.9 The assumption of the stability of currency

You don't have to be very old to remember that a few years ago many goods could be bought with less money than today. If you listen to any older relative then many stories will be heard of how little this item or the other could be bought for x years ago. The currencies of the countries of the world are not stable in terms of what each unit of currency can buy over the years.

Accounting, however, uses the historic cost concept, this stating that the asset is normally shown at its cost price. This means that accounting statements will be distorted because assets will be bought at different times at the price then ruling, and the figures totalled up to show the value of the assets in cost terms. For instance, suppose that you had bought a building 20 years ago for £20,000. You now decide to buy an identical additional building, but the price has now risen to £40,000. You buy it, and the buildings account now shows buildings at a figure of £60,000. One building is measured cost-wise in terms of the currency of 20 years ago, while the other is taken at today's currency value. The figure of a total of £60,000 is historically correct, but, other than that, the total figure cannot be said to be particularly valid for any other use.

This means that to make a correct assessment of accounting statements one must bear in mind the distorting effects of changing price levels upon the accounting entries as recorded.

25.10 FRS 18, *Accounting policies*

SSAP 2 was the first accounting standard to cover the disclosure of accounting policies which include accounting concepts. It dealt with four of the fundamental accounting concepts, going concern, accruals, consistency and prudence. When FRS 18 was issued in 2000, it superseded SSAP 2. One change it brought in concerned the clarification of what was meant by 'realisation' and so it clarified the position concerning recognition of profits and gains. The other main change it introduced was to amend the SSAP 2 definition of prudence by stating that financial statements must be neutral. A fuller discussion of FRS 18 is presented in Chapter 10 Section 10.6.

Learning outcomes

You should now have learnt:

1 Why one set of financial statements has to serve many purposes.

2 Why the need for general agreement has given rise to the concepts and conventions that govern accounting.

3 What is meant by objectivity and subjectivity.

4 What accounting standards are and why they exist.

5 The assumptions which are made when recording accounting data.

6 The underlying concepts of accounting.

7 How the further overriding concepts of materiality, going concern, consistency, prudence, accruals, separate determination and substance over form affect the recording and adjustment of accounting data and the reporting of accounting information.

8 That an assumption is made that monetary measures remain stable, i.e. that normally accounts are not adjusted for inflation or deflation.

REVIEW QUESTIONS

25.1 'The historical cost convention looks backwards but the going concern convention looks forwards.'

Required:

(*a*) Explain clearly what is meant by:
  (*i*) the historical cost convention;
  (*ii*) the going concern convention.

(*b*) Does traditional financial accounting, using the historical cost convention, make the going concern convention unnecessary? Explain your answer fully.

(*c*) Which do you think a shareholder is likely to find more useful – a report on the past or an estimate of the future? Why?

(Association of Chartered Certified Accountants)

Examination techniques

(If you have not already read the page of advice on exam technique at the end of Chapter 8, you should do so now.)

A large number of students do not think clearly about how they are going to tackle their GCE A-level examinations. They will revise all the necessary stuff, and will then throw away a large number of marks because of poor examination technique. As you have progressed to A-levels you obviously cannot be completely devoid of such technique, but you can certainly improve it by reading and absorbing what is written in this appendix.

Most of the main deficiencies noted by examiners have not changed at all over the past fifty years. We do hope that we can get you to tackle the examinations in the right way.

Commencing the examination

First, take a few long deep breaths to settle your nerves, and then read the examination paper. Pay special attention to how many questions you have to answer from each section, and exactly what each question requires you to do. After this you should then select the questions to be attempted.

Students do not read the questions properly

A large number of students do not answer the questions as set by the examiner, because they have not read the question properly. They answer what they think the examiners want, not what they are asking for.

Let me take a simple example. Suppose the examiner sets the following question: 'Describe the use of accounting ratios in assessing the performance of businesses.'

A lot of students will immediately start to describe how to calculate various accounting ratios. Marks which will be obtained – nil. The question asked for the *use* of accounting ratios, not *how to calculate* them.

Many other students will have concentrated on the word *use*. They will then write their answer based on comparing this year's accounting ratios in a business with those of last year. They may well even mention trend ratios which will earn them some extra marks. If they keep their discussion to comparing ratios in a business in the year with other years, however, they cannot get top marks, no matter how well they have written their answers.

Why not? Well, they picked up the word 'use', but from then on they stopped reading properly. The question does not in any way limit itself to the ratios of one business only. First of all you can compare the performance of a business with its own performance in the past. Secondly, you may be able to compare one business with another business of a similar kind. In addition, if you miss out mentioning inter-firm comparisons you will lose marks.

Therefore, (*a*) *read* the question carefully, (*b*) *underline* the *key* words to get to the meaning of the questions, (*c*) *think carefully* about how widespread your answer should be.

On the other hand, there is no point in widening the question more than is needed. It is for the *use* of *accounting* ratios, *not* the use of *all types* of ratios. Besides accounting ratios there are marketing ratios – e.g. size of share of market, how long it takes to supply orders, ratios of defective goods, etc. The question does not ask for all of these. If you give them, you will not get any extra marks.

Poor time management

Using time well to gain the highest possible marks is essential. Examiners constantly report that examinees are very poor in this aspect of tackling an examination. How, then, can you avoid the usual pitfalls.

First of all read the *rubric* carefully – that is, the instructions at the top of the paper, e.g. 'Attempt four questions only: the three questions in Section A and one from Section B. Begin each answer on a separate page.'

You would be surprised to know that a lot of students would try to answer more than one question from Section B. If you tackle two questions from Section B you will get marks for only one of your answers. No examiner will mark both and then give you marks for your highest marked answer. They will mark the first of the optional questions answered and ignore the next unnecessary answer.

Secondly, don't annoy the examiner by not starting your answer on a separate page. It is your job to make the examiner's work as easy as possible. Examiners are only human, and it would not be surprising if their annoyance did not affect the marking of your paper.

You really must attempt each and every question to fulfil the examination requirements. If you have to answer five questions then you must not tackle only four questions.

Students often feel that they would be better off by handing in the complete answers to only four questions, instead of five incomplete answers. In accounting examinations this is not true. Why is this so?

1 Examiners use positive marking in accounting examinations. If you have done 80 per cent of an answer worth 20 marks in total, and you have got it absolutely correct, then you get 80% × 20 = 16 marks.
2 The first marks in a question are the easiest to obtain. Thus it is easier to get the first 10 marks out of 20 than it is to get the second lot of marks to get full marks. Ensuring that you get the easiest marks on every question therefore makes your task easier.

To ensure that you tackle (not necessarily finish) each question you should mark the number of minutes to be allowed by *yourself* for each question. Thus a 20-mark question in a 100-mark examination should be given 20 per cent of the time, e.g. 3 hours × 20% = 36 minutes. When 36 minutes have gone by, stop *answering the question* unless it is the last question to be attempted, and go on to the next question.

If you don't know the answer, or part of an answer, you should guess. You don't lose marks for guessing, and if you guess correctly you get the marks. Intuition will often give the correct answer. Very often if you don't guess on part of a computational question you will be unable to go on to the remainder of the question which you can answer.

Workings

You may wonder why we have put this under a separate heading. We cannot emphasise enough how important it is that you should:

(*a*) submit all your workings, and
(*b*) ensure that the workings are set out so that the examiner can follow them.

A very high percentage of candidates in an examination are near the pass mark, within either a few percentage points above it or below it. You should know that from your study of natural curves in statistics. If you are one of these candidates, and, as we have said, there are a lot of them, handing in workings which can be understood by the examiner will often ensure you a pass mark. Conversely, no workings, or completely unintelligible workings may well ensure your failing the examination.

Tackle the easiest questions first

Never start off your examination by tackling a difficult question. You have got to be able to settle down properly, and not let your nerves get out of control. Starting off on the easiest question is the best way to enable you to get off to a good start.

State your assumptions

It does happen that sometimes a question can contain ambiguities. Examination bodies try to prevent it happening, but it does occur occasionally. The questions do (unfortunately) sometimes contain errors.

In both of these cases you must point out the ambiguity/error. You should then make an assumption, based on what you thought the examiner meant, and carry on with your answer. You must, however, state what your assumption is. Try to make your assumption as sensible as possible. The examiner will then mark your answer accordingly. If you make a ridiculous assumption, it is unlikely that you will be given any marks for that part of your answer. Don't be sarcastic in your comments or complain about inefficiency, there are other times and places for that.

Computational questions versus essay questions

Provided you know what you are doing, it is easier to gain higher marks on computational questions than on essay questions. Therefore if you have a choice, and you can manage the computational question, then that is the one to tackle.

There are quite a few reasons for this which are all tied up with knowing how examiners set and mark the examination scripts, and using some psychological know-how to work out the best strategy. We do not propose to elaborate on this in greater detail, but can tell you that after over sixty years between us in accountancy education we feel quite happy to give you this advice.

Answering written questions

The problem

Unlike computational-type answers, you will not know whether your written answers are up to the mark until you receive your examination result. Likewise, written questions lack the certainty and precision of accounting problems and it is often difficult to fathom out exactly what the examiners require of you. For this reason sound examination technique is absolutely essential together with precise knowledge of relevant law and regulations.

There are several major aspects to success in written papers. These are:

- *plan* your answer
- answer the question *as set*
- pay attention to good *layout*, and
- explain in clear and simple terms what you are doing.

Remember you can only be marked on what you write down. You have no opportunity to explain some ambiguity or other and if what you write is unclear you will *not* get the benefit of the doubt.

Plan

First read the question and jot down the key *verb*, i.e. your instructions; this may be to discuss, explain, advise, set out, list, draft an audit programme, write a letter, etc.

If the question requires a discussion or an explanation it should be written in proper paragraph form. Each paragraph should be self-contained and explain the point it makes. Sentences should be short and to the point. The ideal length for a paragraph is three sentences with four as a maximum. Over four and you are probably making more than one point and should have gone into two paragraphs.

Plan how many points you are going to make and what the answer is. This is essential as otherwise your answer will 'drift' as you struggle to come to some conclusion. The plan should consist of arrows connecting points to each other so that the answer will flow and be logical. The plan need not be too extensive; it is silly to waste time on a 'mini-answer'. It should consist of the *headings* you are going to use.

Answer the question set

Think while you are writing out your answer to make sure you are answering the question *as set*. Keep on reading the instructions and make sure you are following them. Use the question to help you to get the answer and, while this should be tackled at the planning stage, it is always possible that inspiration will strike while you are writing out your answer. If this happens, jot the point down on your plan, otherwise you might forget it and that can cause frustration. What you say should be relevant but if you are in doubt about the relevance but sure about the accuracy – put it in! You cannot lose and it may be one of the key points the examiner was looking for.

Layout

Whenever examiners meet to discuss results, or write down their commentary on students' performance they all agree on the importance of good layout; yet students generally tend to take no notice. The range of marks between good papers and poor papers tends to be quite small. Anything you can do to put the examiner on your side will pay off in those few extra marks.

The main areas for good layout are:

1 *Tabulate* in numbered points, unless you are writing an essay-type question (as explained above).

2 Leave at least a clear line between each point or paragraph.

3 Use headings whenever possible to indicate what major point or series of points you are about to make. Make it easy for the examiner to read your work and follow what

you are doing. A solid mass of material is difficult to read, provides no respite for the eye and shows a lack of discipline.

4 Take care with your *language*. Be objective and avoid the use of the words 'I' or 'we' at too frequent intervals. Be direct and concise, say what you mean, do not use pompous terminology and use technical words in their correct meaning.

Short sentences are far more effective and punchy than long ones. An accounting programme or evaluation of an internal control system could well start with a series of *verbs*. Good ones are: test, examine, inspect, calculate, reconcile, compare, summarise, enquire, investigate. These key words will help you to make answers to these types of questions much more direct and to the point. If you start with them you are bound to avoid falling into the trap of being long-winded, or of padding out your answer. You only have a limited time and everything you write down must earn you marks.

5 Remember that there may be clues in the exam paper that will help you answer a question – you may, for example, find a balance sheet presented as part of a question, while another question asks that you prepare a balance sheet.

Key points

Do try to find a couple of key points to each question. These are points which you feel are vital to answer the question. You may well be right and, anyway, jotting them down after you have read the question carefully can help to give your answer much needed direction.

Practice

You will need to practise the above routine. Written answers do need more practice than computational ones. Have a go at the question. Write out the answer as you would in the examination. Compare with the suggested answers.

Write out at the foot of your answer *what you left out **and** what you got wrong*.

Learn from the answers, and from the work you do, so that when you see a similar question you will produce a better answer.

Time pressure

You will experience a lot of time pressure as you progress with written questions. Do not worry; this is a good sign.

In the examination, spread your time sensibly. Start with the questions you like the look of most and, if you have to go slightly over time, do so. End with the question you think you cannot answer, but do give yourself time to have a reasonable go at it.

If a written question is included in a computational paper do not go over the time on it but do spend the allocated time. *Examiners pay great attention to the written parts of computational papers*, so do not skimp this part.

All this sounds formidable and, of course, it is. It requires skill and application and, above all, confidence. Practice makes perfect and once the skill is acquired then, like riding a bicycle, it will not be forgotten. Take pride in your work and be critical of your own efforts, but do not imagine your answers will have to be perfect to pass the examination. Suggested answers tend to be too long because tutors are afraid to reveal any signs of weakness or ignorance.

Go for the main points and make them well. That is the secret of success.

Glossary

Abnormal losses	The difference between normal loss and actual loss.
Absorption cost/ full cost	The allocation of all production direct and indirect expenses to products.
Account	Part of double entry records, containing details of transactions for a specific item.
Accounting	The uses to which data recorded by bookkeeping can be put for various purposes.
Accounting equation	A simple representation of the dual nature of accounting transactions: Capital = Assets − Liabilities or alternatively, Assets = Capital + Liabilities Used to introduce the concept of double entry accounting.
Accounting rate of return (ARR)	Average annual profits/Average investment.
Accruals concept	All revenue or other benefit received should be matched to the expenditure incurred in generating that revenue or benefit.
Accumulated fund	A form of capital account for a non-profit-oriented organisation.
Activity-based costing (ABC)	The process of using cost drivers as the basis for overhead absorption whereby costs are attributed to cost units on the basis of benefit received from indirect activities, e.g. ordering, setting up and assuring quality.
Allocation of costs	When costs are assigned to an individual cost centre.
Apportionment of costs	When costs are assigned to two or more cost centres.
Assets	Resources owned by a business.
Attainable standard	What can be achieved under 'normal' conditions.
Authorised share capital	The nominal value of the share capital that the company is allowed to issue under its constitution.
Average cost (of stock) (AVCO)	Total cost of stock divided by units in stock.
Bad debts	Amounts owing to a business that are not expected to be paid.
Balance sheet	A statement showing the assets, capital and liabilities of a business.
Batch costing	When costs are to be attributed to a specific batch of a product (a group of similar items which is treated as a separate cost unit).

Bonus shares (scrip issue)	Shares issued to existing shareholders free of charge.
Bookkeeping	The recording of accounting data.
Break-even	A level of activity at which there is neither a profit nor a loss.
Break-even units formula	Fixed costs/Contribution per unit.
Budget	A plan quantified in monetary terms in advance of a defined time period – usually showing planned income and expenditure and the capital employed to achieve a given objective.
Business entity concept	The affairs of a business are to be treated as being quite separate from the non-business activities of its owner(s).
Called-up share capital	Where only part of the amounts payable on each share has been asked for, the total amount asked for on all the shares is known as the called-up capital.
Calls in arrears	The total amount for which payment has been asked (i.e. called for), but which has not yet been paid by shareholders.
Capital	The total of resources supplied to a business by its owner.
Capital expenditure	Expenditure on fixed assets.
Capital reserve	A reserve which is not available for transfer to the profit and loss appropriation account. Most capital reserves can never be utilised for cash dividend purposes.
Cash flow forecast	A statement produced for management showing cash receipts and payments forecast for future periods.
Cash flow statement	The summarised financial statement that shows the sources and uses of cash of a business over a period of time.
Consistency concept	When a method has been adopted for the accounting treatment of an item, the same method will be adopted for all subsequent occurrences of similar items.
Contribution	Sales – marginal cost *or* Sales – variable cost
Cost centre	A production or service location, function, activity or item of equipment whose costs may be attributed to cost units.
Cost driver	Activities that generate cost.
Cost of capital	The return expected by those who provide capital to an organisation.
Cost pool	A collection of individual costs within a single heading.
Cost unit	A unit of product or service in relation to which costs are ascertained.
Credit	The right-hand side of the accounts in double entry.
Creditor	A person to whom money is owed for goods or services.
Cumulative preference shares	Holders of these shares can receive a dividend up to an agreed percentage each year. Any shortfall of dividend paid in a year can be carried forward. These arrears of preference dividends will have to be paid before the ordinary shareholders receive anything.
Current ratio	Current assets/current liabilities

Debenture	A form of loan to a company, usually in the form of a written acknowledgement of the debt prepared by the company. The acknowledgement includes the rate of interest to be paid and the terms of repayment.
Debit	The left-hand side of the accounts in double entry.
Debtor	A person who owes money to a business for goods or services they have received.
Depreciation	An amount representing the cost to the business of the wearing out or loss in value of a fixed asset over an accounting period.
Deprival value	The value of an asset based on the concept that it is equal to the amount of money the owners would have to receive to compensate them exactly for being deprived of it.
Direct cost	Costs that can easily be identified with units of production, such as the cost of a component.
Direct expenses	Those expenses which can be traced directly to the product being manufactured.
Direct labour	The cost (that can be easily identified) of the labour that was applied to convert the direct materials into the finished goods.
Direct materials	The cost (that can be easily identified) of materials which become part of the finished goods.
Direct method	Cash flow calculated on the basis of all the cash inflows and outflows relating to trading activities.
Directors	Officials appointed by shareholders to manage the company for them.
Discounted cash flow	The discounting of future net cash flows of a capital project to ascertain present value.
Dissolution	When a partnership firm ceases operations and its assets are disposed of.
Dividends	The amount given to shareholders as their share of the profits of the company.
Double entry bookkeeping	A system where each transaction is entered twice, once on the debit side and once on the credit side.
Doubtful debts	Amounts owing to a business that may not be paid.
Dual aspect concept	There are two aspects of accounting, one represented by the assets of the business and the other by the claims against them. The concept states that these two aspects are always equal to each other. This is the basis of double entry.
Economic order quantity (EOQ) formula	A mathematical method of identifying the amount of stock that should be ordered at a time and how frequently to order it, so that the overall total of the costs of holding the stock and the costs of ordering the stock can be minimised. The formula is: $$\sqrt{\frac{(2 \times \text{demand for period} \times \text{order cost})}{\text{unit carrying cost}}}$$
Equity	Another name for the capital of the owner.
Equivalent units	Notional whole units representing uncompleted work. Used to apportion costs between work in progress and completed output.

Exceptional item	An item that is material in amount, falls **within** the ordinary activities of the firm, but is not something that would ordinarily be expected to occur and needs to be shown so that the accounts will give a 'true and fair view'.
Exceptions reporting	Where reporting concentrates upon those items where there is a significant difference between budget and actual.
Extraordinary item	An item that is material in amount, falls **outside** the ordinary activities of the firm, but is not something that would ordinarily be expected to occur and needs to be shown so that the accounts will give a 'true and fair view'.
Factory indirect expenses	All those other expenses concerned with the manufacturing process which have not been treated as of the direct type.
Fair value	The value that assets and liabilities would fetch in a transaction between two strangers.
FIFO	**First In First Out** (stock valuation method).
Financial Reporting Standard (FRS)	Accounting standard issued by the Accounting Standards Board (ASB).
Fixed capital accounts	Capital accounts which consist only of the amounts of capital actually paid into the firm.
Fixed cost	Cost incurred for a period, the total of which, within limits, tends to be unaffected by fluctuations in levels of activity.
Fixed overhead capacity variance	(Actual hours worked − Budgeted hours to be worked) × Standard rate
Fixed overhead efficiency variance	(Actual hours worked − Actual production in standard hours) × Standard rate
Fixed overhead expenditure variance	Budgeted fixed production overheads − Actual fixed production overheads
Fixed overhead volume variance	(Actual production in standard hours × Standard rate) − Budgeted fixed production overheads
Flexible budget	A budget which, by recognising different cost behaviour patterns, is designed to change as volume of output changes.
Fluctuating capital accounts	Capital accounts whose balances change from one period to the next.
FRSSE	Financial Reporting Standard for Smaller Entities.
Fundamental accounting concepts	Accounting concepts considered so important that they have been enforced through accounting standards and/or through the Companies Act.
Fungible assets	Assets that are substantially indistinguishable one from another.
***Garner* v. *Murray* rule**	If one partner is unable to make good a deficit on his/her capital account, the remaining partners will share the loss in proportion to their last agreed capitals, not in the profit/loss sharing ratio.
Gearing	The relationship between shareholders' investment and borrowings.
General reserve	A revenue reserve that was created in order to ensure some accumulated profits were retained in order to meet an unforeseen or non-specific future expense.

Going concern concept	An assumption that the business will continue to operate for the foreseeable future.
Goodwill	The difference between the total fair value of the net assets of a business and its market value.
Historical cost	The value attributed to an item is based on what it originally cost.
Horizontal balance sheet	Where assets are shown on one side of a balance sheet and capital and liabilities on the other side.
Ideal standard	What is possible.
Income and expenditure account	An account for a non-profit-making organisation to find the surplus or loss made during a period.
Incremental cost	The extra cost arising as a result of making a decision *or* the difference in total cost between alternatives.
Indirect cost	Costs that cannot be identified easily with individual units of production, such as the cost per unit produced of oil used to lubricate the machine on which a product is made.
Indirect method	Cash flow calculated by taking accounting profit and adjusting it by all non-cash amounts that were applied in identifying it, such as depreciation. It gives the net cash flow from operating activities.
Information	Data after they have been combined with something else that allows them to be assessed within a relevant context.
Intangible assets	Fixed assets that cannot be touched, such as goodwill.
Interest on capital	An amount at an agreed rate of interest which is credited to a partner based on the amount of capital contributed by him/her.
Interest on drawings	An amount at an agreed rate of interest, based on the drawings taken out, which is debited to partners.
Internal rate of return (IRR)	Indicates the discounted rate of return of a capital project.
International Accounting Standard (IAS)	Accounting standards issued by the International Accounting Standards Committee and the International Accounting Standards Board.
Issued share capital	The nominal value of the share capital that a company has issued to shareholders.
Job costing	The attribution of costs to jobs.
Joint product	Two or more products separated in processing, each having a sufficiently high saleable value to merit recognition as a main product.
Labour efficiency variance	(Standard labour hours for actual production − Actual labour hours worked) × Standard wage rate per hour
Liabilities	Total of money owed for assets supplied to a business.
LIFO	Last In First Out (stock valuation method).
Limited company	An organisation owned by its shareholders, whose liability is limited to their share capital.

Limited partner	A partner whose liability is limited to the capital he or she has put into the firm.
Limiting factor	Anything that limits the activity of an entity.
Margin of safety	The extent by which forecast sales exceeds or falls short of break-even.
Marginal cost	The cost of producing one more unit = Direct materials + Direct labour + Other variable costs
Master budget	A budget summarising the functional budgets.
Materiality	An item is material and should be recognised in the financial statements if its disclosure or non-disclosure would affect the behaviour of users of the accounting statements.
Materials price variance	(Standard price – Actual price per unit) × Quantity purchased
Materials usage variance	(Standard quantity required for quantity produced – Actual quantity) × Standard price (per unit)
Money measurement concept	The concept that accounting is concerned only with facts measurable in money, and for which measurements can obtain general agreement.
Net present value (NPV)	The difference between the amount invested and the present value of future cash flows.
Net realisable value	The estimated amount that would be received from the sale of the asset less the estimated cost of its disposal.
Nominal value	The price put on the description of a share when it is issued. It is used in calculating the value of share capital in the balance sheet.
Non-cumulative preference shares	Holders of these shares can receive a dividend up to an agreed percentage each year. If the amount paid is less than the maximum agreed amount, the shortfall is lost by the shareholder. The shortfall cannot be carried forward and paid in a future year.
Normal level of activity	The level of output thought of as being normal and acceptable in the long run.
Normal losses	The expected proportion of input that is lost during the production process.
Opportunity cost	The value of a benefit sacrificed in favour of an alternative course of action.
Ordinary shares	Shares entitled to dividends after the preference shareholders have been paid their dividends.
Paid-up share capital	The total of the amount of share capital which has been paid for by shareholders.
Partnership	A firm in which two or more people are working together as owners with a view to making profits.
Partnership capital account	The account that records how much has been invested in a partnership by an individual partner. It is usually left unchanged other than by additional investments made by the partner in the business.
Partnership current account	The account that records the share of profit, drawings, etc. relating to a specific partner.

Partnership salaries	Agreed amounts payable to partners in respect of duties undertaken by them.
Payback	The period it takes to recoup the initial investment in a capital project.
Period costs	Costs of a non-manufacturing nature and representing the selling and distribution, administration and financial expenses. They are treated as expenses of the period in which they were incurred irrespective of the volume of goods sold.
Preference shares	Shares that are entitled to an agreed rate of dividend before the ordinary shareholders receive anything.
Preliminary expenses	All the costs that are incurred when a company is formed.
Present value	The value in terms of today's money of future cash flows.
Prime cost	The total of Direct materials + Direct labour + Direct expenses.
Prior period adjustment	A material adjustment applicable to prior periods arising from changes in accounting policies or from the correction of fundamental errors. They do not include normal recurring adjustments or corrections of accounting estimates made in prior periods.
Private company	A limited company that must issue its shares privately.
Process costing	The costing method applicable where goods or services result from a sequence of continuous or repetitive operations or processes.
Product centre	Where all the costs of direct materials, direct labour and direct expenses are collected in a manufacturing firm.
Product cost	Those costs which are allocated to the units of goods manufactured.
Production cost	The total of Prime cost + Factory indirect expenses.
Provision	An amount written off or retained by way of providing for depreciation, renewals or diminution in value of assets; or retained by way of providing for any known liability of which the amount cannot be determined with 'substantial' accuracy.
Prudence concept	Ensuring that profit and asset values are not overstated by recognising all losses (costs) immediately they become known and all gains (revenue) only when they are realised (certain to be received).
Public company	A company that can issue its shares publicly, and for which there is no maximum number of shareholders.
Receipts and payments account	A summary of the cash book of a non-profit-making organisation.
Relevant cost	A cost that will be affected as a result of taking a particular course of action.
Relevant revenue	Revenue that will be affected as a result of taking a particular course of action.
Repeated distribution method	A method of apportioning indirect costs through service centres whereby each service centre in turn has its costs apportioned among the cost centres and the remaining service centres. The process continues until all the service centre costs have been apportioned to cost centres.
Reserve accounts	The transfer of apportioned profits to accounts for use in future years.
Reserves	These are simply a means of communicating with a company's shareholders exactly what has happened to the profits that have not been

	distributed as dividends. Examples of reserves are the Profit and Loss Account Reserve, the General Reserve and the Share Premium Account.
Retained profit	Company profit not paid as a dividend and not set aside for another use, such as future repairs.
Return on capital employed	Operating profit before interest and tax/(total assets – current liabilities)
Revaluation account	An account used to record gains and losses when assets are revalued.
Revenue reserve	An amount that has been voluntarily transferred from the profit and loss appropriation account that may be for some particular purpose, such as a buildings repairs reserve created just in case the organisation should ever need to undertake repairs on its buildings. The amount in a revenue reserve can be transferred back to profit and loss at any time and is available to be used in whatever way the organisation wishes.
Rights issue	The issue of shares to existing shareholders at a price lower than the ruling market price of the shares.
Sale or return	Goods that do not belong to the person holding them and which may be returned to the owner should the holder fail to sell them.
Sales mix variance	(Actual sales units – Actual sales split in budget proportions) × Budget unit gross profit
Sales price variance	(Actual price – Budget price) × Actual sales units
Sales volume variance	(Actual units sold – Budget units sold) × Budget unit gross profit
Scrip issue (bonus shares)	Shares issued to existing shareholders free of charge.
Semi-variable cost	A cost which varies with production but not at a proportionate rate.
Separate determination concept	When calculating the aggregate amount of each asset or liability, the amount of each individual asset or liability should be determined separately from all other assets and liabilities.
Service centre	All factory indirect expenses are collected in cost centres which give service, such as a canteen or a maintenance department.
Share capital	Amounts indicating a class of interest in a company. At the most basic level, share capital is the equivalent of the sole trader's capital introduced. However, companies can have various classes of ownership interest.
Share premium	When companies issue shares they try to obtain as much money as possible from the shareholders. However, they need (for legal reasons) to decide on a value of the shares in advance. This is called the nominal value. The share premium is the difference between the nominal value and the price at which each share is issued.
Share premium account	The share premium account is credited with the amount of money, in excess of the nominal value, that is received when shares are issued.
Shares	The division of the capital of a limited company into parts.
Shares issued at par	Shares issued at their nominal value.
Standard	A predetermined measurable quantity set in defined conditions.
Standard cost	How much something 'should' cost.

Standard costing	A control technique which compares standard costs and revenues with actual results to obtain variances that are used to stimulate improved performance.
Standard hour	The quantity of work achievable at standard performance in an hour.
Statement of affairs	A statement from which the capital of the owner is deducted by estimating assets and liabilities. Then Capital = Assets − Liabilities.
Statements of Standard Accounting Practice (SSAP)	Accounting standards issued by the Accounting Standards Committee.
Step-variable cost	Costs per unit that change in steps, such as where a small rise in the level of production requires that three people work on a job instead of two.
Subjectivity	Using a method that other people may not agree to, derived from one's own personal preferences.
Substance over form concept	Accounting should show each transaction in accordance with its real substance: that is, on the basis of how the transaction affects the economic situation of the firm, even where that does not reflect the exact legal position concerning the transaction.
Sunk cost	Costs already spent.
Super profits	Net profits less allowance for alternative earnings and alternative return on capital invested.
Tangible assets	Physical fixed assets – ones that can be touched.
Time interval concept	Final accounts are prepared at regular intervals.
Uncalled share capital	The total amount which is to be received in future, but which has not yet been asked for.
Variable cost	Cost, the total of which tends to vary with the level of activity *which is the same as*: Marginal cost + Variable non-production overheads
Variable overhead efficiency variance	(Actual hours worked – Actual production in standard hours) × Standard rate
Variable overhead expenditure variance	Actual cost – (Actual hours worked × Standard rate)
Variance	The difference between planned, budgeted, or standard cost/revenue and actual cost/revenue.
Vertical balance sheet	A form of presentation where the balance sheet items are shown listed under each other.
Wage rate variance	(Standard wage rate per hour – Actual wage rate) × Actual hours worked
Working capital	Current assets − Current liabilities

APPENDIX III

Answers to review questions

1.1 B Arkwright

Statement of Affairs as at 31 December 20X5

Fixed assets		
Motor van at cost	2,800	
Less Depreciation	550	2,250
Current assets		
Stock	3,950	
Debtors	4,970	
Prepaid expenses	170	
Bank	2,564	
Cash	55	
	11,709	
Less Current liabilities		
Trade creditors	1,030	
Expenses owing	470	1,500
Working capital		10,209
		12,459
Capital		10,000
Cash introduced		(C)
Add Net profit		(B)
		(C)
Less Drawings		(A)
		5,673

Missing figures (A), (B) and (C) deducted in that order. (A) to balance is 12,459, thus (B) has to be 18,132 and (C) becomes 8,132.

1.3

Workings:

Purchases		
Bank	29,487	
Cash	2,994	
	32,481	
− Creditors 31.12.20X6	5,624	
	26,857	
+ Creditors 31.12.20X7	7,389	
Purchases for 20X7	34,246	

Sales		
Banked	37,936	
Cash	9,630	
	47,566	
− Debtors 31.12.20X6	9,031	
	38,535	
+ Debtors 31.12.20X7	8,624	
Sales for 20X7	47,159	

Opening Capital:		
Bank	405	
Stock	13,862	
Debtors	9,031	
Rates prepaid	210	
Fixtures	2,500	26,008
Less Creditors	5,624	
Rent owing	150	5,774
		20,234

Kelly

Trading and Profit and Loss Account for the year ended 31 December 20X7

Sales		47,159
Less Cost of goods sold:		
Opening stock	13,862	
Add Purchases	34,246	
	48,108	
Less Closing stock	15,144	
		32,964
Gross profit		14,195
Less Expenses:		
Wages	5,472	
Rent (1,650 − 150)	1,500	
Rates (890 + 210 − 225)	875	
Sundry expenses	375	
Depreciation: Fixtures	250	8,472
Net profit		5,723

Balance Sheet as at 31 December 20X7

Fixed assets		
Fixtures at valuation	2,500	
Less Depreciation	250	2,250

545

Current assets

Stock	15,144	
Debtors	8,624	
Prepayments	225	
	23,993	
Less Current liabilities		
Trade creditors	7,389	
Bank overdraft	602	
		7,991
Working capital		16,002
		18,252

Capital

Balance at 1.1.20X7		20,234
Add Net profit		5,723
		25,957
Less Drawings (1,164 + 6,541)		7,705
		18,252

1.5

Jenny Barnes
Trading and Profit and Loss Account for the year ended
30 April 20X9

			Sales* 102,908
Opening stock		9,500	
Add Purchases		78,100	
(70,500 + 7,600)		87,600	
Less Closing stock		13,620	
Cost of goods sold		73,980	
Gross profit c/d		28,928	
		102,908	
			Gross profit b/d 102,908
Sales assistants' wages	5,260		
Vehicle running expenses	1,020		
Bad debts	150		
Miscellaneous expenses**	1,370		
Light and heat	940		
Depreciation: Equipment	720		
Vehicles	1,000		
Net profit	18,468		
	28,928		28,928

* Sales 96,500 + takings in cash later spent 6,408
(drawings 6,000 + expenses 408)
** Bank 962 + cash 408 = 1,370

1.7
(a)

Creditors Control

Bank	101,500	Balances b/d	7,400
Cash	1,800	Drawings: Goods	600
Balances c/d	8,900	Purchases (difference)	104,200
	112,200		112,200

(b)

Janet Lambert
Trading and Profit and Loss Account for the year ended
31 August 20X9

Sales (deduced, as margin is 25% = 4 × gross profit)			128,000
Opening stock		8,600	
Add Purchases		104,200	
		112,800	
Less Closing stock		16,800	
Cost of goods sold			96,000
Gross profit (33⅓% of cost of goods sold)			32,000
Less: Casual labour (1,200 + 6,620)		7,820	
Rent (5,040 + 300 − 420)		4,920	
Delivery costs		3,000	
Electricity (1,390 + 160 − 210)		1,340	
			17,080
Net profit			14,920

Balance Sheet as at 31 August 20X9

Current assets		
Stock	16,800	
Debtors	4,300	
Prepayments	420	
Bank	1,650	
Cash	330	
	23,500	
Less Current liabilities		
Creditors	8,900	
Expenses owing	160	
	9,060	
		14,440
Capital:		
Balance as at 1 September 20X8 (Workings 1)		7,850
Add Net profit		14,920
		22,770
Less Drawings (Workings 2)		8,330
		14,440

Workings:

(1) Capital as on 1.9.20X8. Stock 8,600 + Debtors 3,900 + Prepaid 300 + Bank 2,300 + Cash 360 = 15,460 − Creditors 7,400 − Accruals 210 = 7,850.

(2) Cash drawings. Step (A) find cash received from sales. Debtors b/d 3,900 + Sales 128,000 − Debtors c/d 4,300 = 127,600 cash received.
Step (B) find cash banked. Balance b/d 2,300 + cash received? − payments 117,550 = balance c/d 1,650. Therefore cash banked? = 116,900.
Step (C) draw up cash account:

Balance b/d	360	Labour	1,200
Sales receipts	127,600	Purchases	1,800
		Banked	116,900
		Drawings (difference)	7,730
		Balance c/d	330
	127,960		127,960

(c) Per text.

1.9

David Denton
Profit and Loss Account for the year ended 31 December 20X0

Work done: Credit accounts	29,863	
For cash	3,418	
		33,281
Less Expenses:		
Materials (9,600 – 580)	9,020	
Secretarial salary	3,000	
Rent	225	
Council tax (180 – 45)	135	
Insurance (800 – 200)	600	
Electricity (1,122 + 374 estimated)	1,496	
Motor expenses	912	
General expenses (1,349 + 295)	1,644	
Loan interest (4,000 × 10% × ³⁄₄)	300	
Provision for doubtful debts	425	
Accounting fee	250	
Amortisation of lease (650 × ³⁄₄)	487	
Depreciation: Equipment	960	
Van	900	1,860
		20,354
Net profit		12,927

Balance Sheet as at 31 December 20X0

Fixed assets	Cost	Depreciation	
Lease	6,500	487	6,013
Equipment	4,800	960	3,840
Vehicle	3,600	900	2,700
	14,900	2,347	12,553
Current assets			
Stock		580	
Debtors	4,250		
Less Provision for doubtful debts	425	3,825	
Prepaid expenses (75 + 200)		275	
Bank (see workings)		6,084	
Cash		123	
		10,887	
Less Current liabilities			
Trade creditors	714		
Interest owing	300		
Accountancy fee owing	250		
Rates owing	135		
Electricity owing	374	1,773	
Working capital			9,114
			21,667

Financed by:		
Capital		
Introduced (6,500 + 3,600)	10,100	
Add Net profit	12,927	
	23,027	
Less Drawings (4,680 + 280 + 400)	5,360	
	17,667	
Loan	4,000	
	21,667	

Workings:
Bank 6,500 + 25,613 + 2,600 + 4,000 = 38,713 – 4,680 – 280 – 6,500 – 300 –
3,000 – 8,886 – 4,800 – 1,122 – 912 – 1,349 – 800 = 6,084

1.10

(a)

J Duncan
Capital Account on 1 January 20X8

Bank		8,000
Cash		300
Stock		4,100
Machinery		12,600
Rent prepaid		200
Debtors		6,300
		31,500
Less: Creditors	2,400	
Loan	5,000	7,400
		24,100

(b)

J Duncan
Trading and Profit and Loss Account for the year ended
31 December 20X8

	£	£	£
Sales			40,450
Less: Sales returns			1,200
			39,250
Less: Cost of sales			
Opening stock at 1 January 20X8		4,100	
Add: Purchases		18,950	
		23,050	
Less: Withdrawn by the owner	300		
Less: Closing stock at 31 December 20X8	3,200	3,500	
			19,550
Gross profit			19,700
Add: Discount received			350
			20,050

Less: Expenses

	£	
Rent	1,850	
Bad debts written off	400	
Wages	6,100	
Insurance	1,450	
Loan interest	400	
Depreciation	4,200	
Repairs	300	
Electricity	750	
		15,450
Net profit		4,600

Workings:
Sales 26,000 − 250 + 14,000 + 400 − 6,300 + 5,000 + 1,200 + 400 = 40,450
Purchases 18,500 − 2,400 + 2,500 + 350 = 18,950
Depreciation = balancing figure.

1.11

J Duncan
Balance Sheet as at 31 December 20X8

	£	£	£
Fixed Assets			
Machinery at 1 January 20X8		12,600	
Add: Additions		7,500	
		20,100	
Less: Depreciation		4,200	15,900
Current assets			
Stock		3,200	
Debtors		5,000	
Bank		2,600	
Cash		50	
		10,850	
Current liabilities			
Creditors		2,500	
Accrued charges			
Loan interest	100		
Rent	250	350	
		2,850	
			8,000
			23,900
Capital Account			
Balance at 1 January 20X8			24,100
Add: Net profit			4,600
			28,700
Less: Drawings			9,800
			18,900
Long-term liabilities			
Bank loan 8%			5,000
			23,900

2.1

Uppertown Football Club
Income and Expenditure Account for the year ended
31 December 20X4

	£	
Income		
Collections at matches		1,650
Profit on refreshments		315
		1,965
Less Expenditure		
Rent for pitch (300 − 60)	240	
Printing and stationery (65 + 33)	98	
Secretary's expenses	144	
Repairs to equipment	46	
Groundsman's wages	520	
Miscellaneous expenses	66	
Depreciation of equipment	125	
		1,239
Surplus of income over expenditure		726

Balance Sheet as at 31 December 20X4

	£	
Fixed assets		
Equipment	625	
Less Depreciation	125	500
Current assets		
Prepayment	60	
Cash	879	
	939	
Less Current liabilities		
Expenses owing	33	
Working capital		906
		1,406
Financed by:		
Accumulated fund		
Balance at 1.1.20X4 (500 + 180)		680
Add Surplus of income over expenditure		726
		1,406

2.3
(a)

The Happy Haddock Angling Club
Income and Expenditure Account for the year ended
31 December 20X8

	£	
Income:		
Subscriptions		3,500
Visitors' fees		650
Competition fees		820
Snack bar profit (*see workings*)		1,750
		6,720
Less Expenditure:		
Rent and rates	1,500	
Secretarial expenses	240	
Loan interest	260	
Depreciation on games equipment	400	
		2,400
Surplus of income over expenditure		4,320

Workings: Snack bar profit: 6,000 − (800 + 3,750 − 900) − 600 = 1,750

(c)

Miniville Rotary Club

Income and expenditure account for the year ended 31 July 20X9

Income			
Subscriptions			1,980
Ticket sales		437	
Less Cost of prizes		272	165
Donations received			177
			2,322
Less Expenditure:			
Rent (1,402 – 500)		902	
Visiting speakers' expenses		1,275	
Secretarial expenses		163	
Stationery and printing		179	
Donations to charities		35	
Depreciation		195	2,749
Excess of expenditure over income			427

Balance sheet as at 31 July 20X9

Fixed assets			
Equipment at cost		1,420	
Less Depreciation		640	780
Current assets			
Stocks of prizes		46	
Arrears of subscriptions		85	131
Less Current liabilities			
Creditors for prizes	68		
Advance subscriptions	37		
Bank overdraft	13	118	13
			793
Accumulated fund			
Balance 1.8.20X8		1,220	
Less Excess of expenditure over income		427	
			793

2.7

(a)

Café operations:			
Takings			4,660
Less Cost of supplies:			
Opening stock		800	
Add purchases (1,900 + 80)		1,980	
		2,780	
Less Closing stock		850	1,930
			2,730
Wages			2,000
Profit			730

(b)

Balance Sheet as at 31 December 20X8

Fixed assets			
Club house buildings			20,500
Games equipment		2,000	
Less Depreciation		400	1,600
			22,100
Current assets			
Snack bar stocks		900	
Bank		700	1,600
Less Current liabilities			
Subscriptions received in advance		380	1,220
			23,320
Financed by:			
Accumulated fund			
Balance 1.1.20X8 (*see* workings)		13,500	
Add surplus for year		4,320	17,820
Loan from bank			5,500
			23,320

Workings: 200 + 800 + 12,500 = 13,500

2.5

(a)

Accumulated fund 1 August 20X8

Equipment		975
Stocks of prizes		38
Arrears of subscriptions		65
Cash and bank		210
		1,288
Less Subscriptions in advance	10	
Prizes suppliers	58	68
		1,220

(b)

(i)

Subscriptions			
In arrears b/d	65	In advance b/d	10
In advance c/d	37	Cash	1,987
Income and expenditure	1,980	In arrears c/d	85
	2,082		2,082

(ii)

Competition prizes			
Stocks b/d	38	Creditors b/d	58
Cash	270	Stock c/d	46
Creditors c/d	68	Cost of prizes given	272
	376		376

(b)

Sports equipment:

Sales		900
Less Cost of goods sold:		
Opening stock	1,000	
Add Purchases (1,000 × 50%)	500	
	1,500	
Less Closing stock (see note)	900	600
Profit		300

Note: To find closing stock 900 is sales at 50% on cost profit so cost of sales is 600. By arithmetical deduction closing stock is found to be 900.

Subscriptions

Owing b/d	60	In advance b/d		120
		Cash: 20X7		40
Income and expenditure	1,280	20X8		1,100
		20X9		80
In advance c/d	80	Owing c/d		80
	1,420			1,420

Life Subscriptions

Income and expenditure (11 × 20)	220	Balance b/d	1,400
Balance c/d	1,380	Cash	200
	1,600		1,600

(c)

Happy Tickers Sports & Social Club
Income and Expenditure Account for the year ended 31 December 20X8

Income:		
Subscriptions (1,280 + 220)		1,500
Profit on café operations		730
Profit on sports equipment		300
		2,530
Less Expenditure		
Rent	1,200	
Insurance	600	
Repairs to roller (½ × 450)	225	
Sports equipment depreciation (see note 1)	486	
Depreciation of roller (½ × 200)	100	2,611
Excess of expenditure over income		81

Balance Sheet as at 31 December 20X8

Fixed assets		
Share in motor roller at cost	1,000	
Less Depreciation to date	500	500
Used sports equipment at valuation		700
		1,200

Current assets			
Stock of new sports equipment (see note 2)		900	
Stock of café supplies		850	
Subscriptions owing		80	
Carefree Conveyancers: owing for expenses		225	
Prepaid expenses		350	
Cash and bank (see note 3)		754	
		3,159	
Less Current liabilities			
Café suppliers	80		
Advance subscriptions	80	160	2,999
			4,199

Accumulated fund		
Balance at 1.1.20X8		2,900
Less Excess of expenditure		81
		2,819
Life subscriptions		1,380
		4,199

Notes:

1 | | | | |
|---|---:|---|---:|
| Stock b/d | 700 | Cash | 700 |
| Transferred from purchases | 500 | Income and expenditure a/c | 14 |
| | | Stock c/d | 486 |
| | 1,200 | | 1,200 |

Used Sports Equipment

2 b/d 1,000 + bought (1,000 × ½) 500 = 1,500 – sold 600 = 900

3 b/d 1,210 + receipts 6,994 – paid 7,450 = 754

(d) To most people probably the best description of the item would be as deferred income, i.e. income paid in advance for future benefits.

It could, however, be described as a liability of the club. The club in future will have to provide and finance amenities for life members, but they do not have to pay any more money for it. This is therefore the liability of the future to provide these services without further payment.

3.1

Stephens, Owen and Jones
Appropriation Account for the year ended 31 December 20X6

Net profit b/d			25,200
Less Salaries: Owen		3,000	
Jones		1,000	4,000
Interest on capitals: Stephens		600	
Owen		400	
Jones		200	1,200
			5,200
			20,000
Balance of profits shared: Stephens ²/₅		8,000	
Owen ²/₅		8,000	
Jones ¹/₅		4,000	20,000

3.2
(a)

Roach & Salmon
Profit and Loss Appropriation Account for the year ended 31 December 20X9

Net profit brought down		32,840
Less: Salaries: Roach	9,000	
Salmon	6,000	15,000
Interest on capital:		
Roach	6,000	
Salmon	4,800	10,800
		25,800
		7,040

Balance of profits shared:		
Roach ½	3,520	
Salmon ½	3,520	7,040

Current Accounts (dates omitted)

	Roach	Salmon		Roach	Salmon
Drawings	12,860	13,400	Salaries	9,000	6,000
			Interest on capital	6,000	4,800
Balances c/d	5,660	920	Share of profits	3,520	3,520
	18,520	14,320		18,520	14,320

(b) Partnership Act 1890 (section 24).

3.3
Williams, Powell and Howe
Appropriation Account for the year ended 31 December 20X7

Net profit b/d			30,350
Add Interest on drawings: Williams	240		
Powell	180		
Howe	130		550
			30,900
Less Interest on capitals: Williams	2,000		
Powell	1,500		
Howe	900	4,400	
Salaries: Powell	2,000		
Howe	3,500	5,500	9,900
			21,000
Balance of profits shared: Williams 50%	10,500		
Powell 30%	6,300		
Howe 20%	4,200		21,000

Balance Sheet as at 31 December 20X7 (extracts)

Capitals: Williams	40,000	
Powell	30,000	
Howe	18,000	88,000

Current accounts:

	Williams	Powell	Howe
Balances 1.1.20X7	1,860	946	717
Add Share of profits	10,500	6,300	4,200
Salaries		2,000	3,500
Interest on capital	2,000	1,500	900
	14,360	10,746	9,317
Less Interest on drawings	240	180	130
Drawings	9,200	7,100	6,900
	4,920	3,466	2,287
			10,673

Considerations

3.5

(a) *Legal position re Partnership Act 1890:* Partners can agree to anything. What is most important is mutual agreement. The agreement can be very formal in a partnership deed drawn up by a lawyer, or it can be evidenced in other ways.

The Act lays down the provisions for profit sharing if agreement has not been reached, written or otherwise.

As Bee is not taking active part in the running of the business he could be registered as a limited partner under the 1907 Limited Partnership Act. This has the advantage that his liability is limited to the amount of capital invested by him; he can lose that but his personal possessions cannot be taken to pay any debts of the firm.

(b) As Bee is a 'sleeping partner' you will have to decide whether his reward should be in the form of a fixed amount, or vary according to the profits made. In this context you should also bear in mind whether or not he would suffer a share of losses if they occurred.

If he were to have a fixed amount, irrespective of whether profits had been made or not, then the question arises as to the amount required. This is obviously a more risky investment than, say, government securities. He therefore would naturally expect to get a higher return.

Bee would probably feel aggrieved if the profits rose sharply, but he was still limited to the amounts already described. There could be an arrangement for extra payments if the profits exceeded a given figure.

(c) Cee is the expert conducting the operations of the business. He will consequently expect a major share of the profits.

One possibility would be to give him a salary, similar to his current salary, before dividing whatever profits then remain.

Dee is making himself available, as well as bringing in some capital. Because of this active involvement he will affect the profits made. It would seem appropriate to give him a salary commensurate with such work, plus a share of the profits.

(d) *Interest on capital:* Whatever is decided about profit sharing, it would seem appropriate for each of the partners to be given interest on their capitals before sharing the balance of the profits.

3.6

Mendez & Marshall
Trading and Profit and Loss Account for the year ended 30 June 20X9

Sales		123,650
Less Cost of goods sold:		
Opening stock	41,979	
Add Purchases	85,416	
	127,395	
Less Closing stock	56,340	71,055
Gross profit		52,595
Add Reduction in provision for doubtful debts		80
		52,675
Less Salaries and wages (18,917 + 200)	19,117	
Office expenses (2,416 + 96)	2,512	
Carriage outwards	1,288	
Discounts allowed	115	
Bad debts	503	
Loan interest	4,000	
Depreciation: Fixtures	770	
Buildings	1,000	1,770
		29,305
Net profit		23,370
Add Interest on drawings: Mendez	180	
Marshall	120	300
		23,670
Less Interest on capitals: Mendez	3,500	
Marshall	2,950	6,450
Salary: Mendez		800
		7,250
		16,420
Balance of profits shared: Mendez	8,210	
Marshall	8,210	16,420

Balance Sheet as at 30 June 20X9

Fixed assets	Cost	Depn	
Buildings	75,000	26,000	49,000
Fixtures	11,000	4,070	6,930
	86,000	30,070	55,930
Current assets			
Stock		56,340	
Debtors	16,243		
Less Provision for doubtful debts	320	15,923	
Bank		677	
		72,940	
Less Current liabilities			
Creditors	11,150		
Expenses owing	296	11,446	
Working capital			61,494
			117,424
Financed by			
Capitals: Mendez		35,000	
Marshall		29,500	64,500

Current accounts	Mendez	Marshall
Balance 1.7.20X8	1,306	298
Add Interest on capital	3,500	2,950
Add Salary	800	
Add Balance of profit	8,210	8,210
	13,816	11,458
Less Drawings	6,400	5,650
Less Interest on drawings	180	120
	7,236	5,688
Loan from J King		

3.8
(a)

Brick & Stone
Trading and Profit and Loss Account for the year ended 30 September 20X9

Sales		322,100
Less Returns inwards		2,100
		320,000
Less Cost of goods sold:		
Opening stock		23,000
Purchases (208,200 − 1,000)	207,200	
Carriage inwards	1,700	
	208,900	
Less Returns outwards	6,100	202,800
		225,800
Less Closing stock		32,000
		193,800
Gross profit		126,200
Less Establishment expenses:		
Rent and rates (10,300 − 600)	9,700	
Heat and light	8,700	
Depreciation: Fixtures	2,600	21,000
Administrative expenses:		
Staff salaries	36,100	
Telephone (2,900 + 400)	3,300	
Printing, stationery and postage	3,500	42,900
Sales and distribution expenses:		
Motor expenses	5,620	
Carriage outwards	2,400	
Depreciation: Motors	9,200	17,220
Financial expenses:		
Discounts allowable	950	
Loan interest	250	
	1,200	
Less Discounts receivable	370	830
		81,950
Net profit		44,250
Less Salary: Stone		6,000
Balance of profits shared:		38,250
Brick ³⁄₅		22,950
Stone ²⁄₅		15,300

(b)

Brick & Stone
Balance Sheet as at 30 September 20X9

Fixed assets	Cost	Depn	Net
Fixtures and fittings	26,000	13,800	12,200
Motor vehicles	46,000	34,200	11,800
	72,000	48,000	24,000

Current assets		
Stock		32,000
Debtors (9,300 – 300)		9,000
Prepayments		600
Bank		7,700
		49,300

Less Current liabilities		
Creditors	8,400	
Accrued expenses	400	8,800
		40,500
		64,500
Less: Loan from Brick		10,000
		54,500

Financed by:		
Capitals: Brick (33,000 – 10,000)		23,000
Stone		17,000
		40,000

Current accounts:	Brick	Stone
Balances 1.10.20X8	3,600	2,400
Salary		6,000
Loan interest	250	
Share of profits	22,950	15,300
	26,800	23,700
Less Drawings	24,000	11,000
Goods for own use		1,000
		2,800
	11,700	14,500
		54,500

Balance Sheet as at 1 January 20X8

Net assets		14,000
		14,000

Capitals X (6,000 + 2,400)		8,400
Y (4,800 – 1,500)		3,300
Z (3,200 – 900)		2,300
		14,000

3.12
(a)

Goodwill	Dr	6,000	
Capitals X			3,000
Y			3,000

Cash	Dr	7,000	
Capital Z			7,000

(b)

Balance Sheet

Goodwill		6,000
Fixed and current assets		15,000
Cash		9,000
		30,000

Capitals X	11,000	25,000
Y	7,000	
Z	7,000	
Current liabilities		5,000
		30,000

(c)

Capitals X	Dr	2,400	
Y	Dr	1,800	
Z	Dr	1,800	
Goodwill			6,000

3.14
(a)

Capital Accounts (000s)

	T	U	V	W		T	U	V	W
					Bal b/d	14	18	5	20
					Cash	12	15	3	
					Goodwill			8	20
Bal c/d	26	33	8	20					
	26	33	8	20		26	33	8	20

(b) Goodwill 30,000; Other assets except cash 40,000; cash 26,000; Capitals as in (a); Creditors 9,000.

3.15 The senior partner's objection is a correct response. The money does not belong to the new partner once it has been paid.

This is because a new partner becomes an owner of part of the business, and this includes a part of the goodwill. This payment is specifically for that part of the goodwill. The goodwill was created by previous partners, and this is where the new partner buys his share from them. The £10,000 will be credited to the old partners in their old profit sharing ratio.

3.10
(a)

Balance Sheet as at 1 January 20X8

Goodwill	12,000
Other assets	14,000
	26,000

Capitals X (6,000 + 6,000)	12,000
Y (4,800 + 4,500)	9,300
Z (3,200 + 1,500)	4,700
	26,000

(b) *Goodwill Workings*

		Before		After	Loss or Gain		Action needed	
X	4/8	6,000	3/10	3,600	Loss	2,400	Credit X	2,400
Y	3/8	4,500	5/10	6,000	Gain	1,500	Debit Y	1,500
Z	1/8	1,500	2/10	2,400	Gain	900	Debit Z	900
		12,000		12,000				

If C, the new partner, has paid £10,000 for one-fifth of the goodwill, then total goodwill is £50,000. Should the business be sold at a future date, and the goodwill realises £50,000, then C would receive one-fifth of the proceeds, i.e. £10,000, thus getting his money back. This illustrates the fairness of the accounting treatment of his original payment for goodwill. If anything had been credited to his account from this original payment for goodwill then he would have received that in addition. Obviously this would be unfair.

3.16

(a)

Stone, Pebble & Brick trading as Bigtime Building Supply Company
Profit and Loss Account for the year ended 31 March 20X9

	Apr–Dec	Jan–Mar
Net profit per accounts	27,225	9,075
Less Interest on Stone's loan	–	385
	27,225	8,690
Interest on capitals: Stone		250
Pebble		200
Brick		125
		2,125
Salary: Brick		
Balance of profits shared:		
Stone	1/3 9,075	1/2 2,995
Pebble	1/3 9,075	3/10 1,797
Brick	1/3 9,075	2/10 1,198
	27,225	8,690

(b)

Capitals

	Stone	Pebble	Brick		Stone	Pebble	Brick
Goodwill adjustment		2,000	6,000	Balances b/d	14,000		
Transfer to loan	14,000			Goodwill adjustment			
Balances c/d	20,000	16,000	10,000	(see note)			
	34,000	18,000	16,000		34,000	18,000	16,000

Current Accounts

	Stone	Pebble	Brick		Stone	Pebble	Brick
Drawings	8,200	9,600	7,200	Interest on capital	250	200	125
Balances c/d	4,120	1,472	5,323	Salary			2,125
				Share of profits:			
				Apr–Dec	9,075	9,075	9,075
				Jan–Mar	2,995	1,797	1,198
	12,320	11,072	12,523		12,320	11,072	12,523

Note:

	Value of goodwill taken over	Elimination of goodwill	Net effect
Stone	30,000	22,000	8,000 Cr
Pebble	20,000	22,000	2,000 Dr
Brick	16,000	22,000	6,000 Dr
	66,000	66,000	–

Goodwill:
Stone	30,000
Pebble	20,000
Brick	16,000
	66,000

3.17

(a)

Buildings

Balance b/d	8,000		
Revaluation: Increase	9,500	Balance c/d	17,500
	17,500		17,500
Balance b/d	17,500		

Motor Vehicles

Balance b/d	3,550	Revaluation: Reduction	950
		Balance c/d	2,600
	3,550		3,550

Stock

Balance b/d	2,040	Revaluation: Reduction	150
		Balance c/d	1,890
	2,040		2,040

Office Fittings

Balance b/d	1,310	Revaluation: Reduction	220
		Balance c/d	1,090
	1,310		1,310

Revaluation

Motor vehicles	950	Buildings	9,500
Stock	150		
Office fittings	220		
Profit on revaluation			
Hughes	4,090		
Allen	2,454		
Elliott	1,636	8,180	
	9,500		9,500

Capitals

	Hughes	Allen	Elliott		Hughes	Allen	Elliott
Balances c/d	13,650	8,874	6,476	Balances b/d	9,560	6,420	4,840
				Profit on revaluation	4,090	2,454	1,636
	13,650	8,874	6,476		13,650	8,874	6,476

(b)

Balance Sheet as at 1 January 20X9

Fixed assets		
Buildings at valuation		17,500
Motors at valuation		2,600
Office fittings at valuation		1,090
		21,190
Current assets		
Stock at valuation	1,890	
Debtors	4,550	
Bank	1,390	
		7,810
		29,000

Capitals:
Hughes 13,650
Allen 8,874
Elliott 6,476
29,000 / 29,000

3.19

(a)

Revaluation

Premises	90,000	Premises	120,000
Plant	37,000	Plant	35,000
Stock	62,379	Stock	54,179
Provision doubtful debts	3,000		
Profit on revaluation			
Alan ³/₆	8,400		
Bob ²/₆	5,600		
Charles ¹/₆	2,800	16,800	
	209,179		**209,179**

*Just the net increases/decreases could have been recorded. Either method acceptable.

Goodwill

Goodwill:		Goodwill cancelled	
Capitals: Alan	21,000	Capitals: Alan ³/₇	18,000
Bob	14,000	Bob ²/₇	12,000
Charles	7,000	Don ²/₇	12,000
	42,000		**42,000**

Capitals

	Alan	Bob	Charles	Don		Alan	Bob	Charles	Don
Goodwill	18,000	12,000	–	12,000	Balances b/d	85,000	65,000	35,000	–
Retirement			42,000		Goodwill	21,000	14,000	7,000	–
Cash	21,000				Cash				79,000
Balances b/d	67,000	67,000		67,000					
	106,000	79,000	42,000	79,000		106,000	79,000	42,000	79,000

Current Accounts

	Alan	Bob	Charles	Don		Alan	Bob	Charles	Don
Retirement			7,478		Balance b/d	3,714		4,678	
Cash	9,023	2,509			Profit on revaluation	8,400	5,600	2,800	
Balances c/d	3,091	3,091		3,091	Cash				3,091
	12,114	5,600	7,478	3,091		12,114	5,600	7,478	3,091

Charles: Retirement

Car	3,900	Capital	42,000
Cash	53,578	Current	7,478
Balance c/d	20,000	Loan	28,000
	77,478		**77,478**

Bank

Don: Capital	79,000	Balance b/d	4,200
Don: Current	3,091	Retirement – Charles	53,578
Balance c/d	5,710	Repaid Alan – Capital	21,000
		Current	9,023
	87,801		**87,801**

(b)

Balance Sheet (summarised):
Fixed assets total 168,100 + Current assets 86,919 – Current liabilities 24,746
= 230,273.
Capitals 67,000 each × 3 + Current accounts 3,091 × 3 = Total 230,273.

3.20

S, W and M
Appropriation Account for the year ended 31 December 20X9

Salaries: W	3,000	Net profit b/d	25,200
M	1,000	4,000	
Interest on capital			
S	600		
W	400		
M	200	1,200	
Balance of profits			
S ²/₅	8,000		
W ²/₅	8,000		
M ¹/₅	4,000	20,000	
	25,200		**25,200**

3.22

Realisation

Buildings	800	Cash: Debtors		2,700
Tools and fixtures	850	Buildings		400
Debtors	2,800	Tools etc.		950
Cash: Expenses	100	Discounts		200
		Loss on realisation: Moore		150
		Stephens		150
	4,550			**4,550**

Capital Accounts

	Moore	Stephens		Moore	Stephens
Loss on realisation	150	150	Balance b/d	2,000	1,500
Cash	1,850	1,350			
	2,000	1,500		2,000	1,500

Cash

Balance b/d	1,800	Expenses realisation	100
Debtors	2,700	Creditors	2,550
Buildings	400	Capitals: Moore	1,850
Tools	950	Stephens	1,350
	5,850		**5,850**

3.23

(a)

Realisation

Fixed assets	14,000	Bank: Fixed assets	8,000
Stock	5,000	X: Fixed assets	7,000
Debtors	21,000	Bank: Stock	4,000
Bank: Dissolution costs	800	Bank: Debtors	3,000
		Discounts on creditors	500
		Loss: X 3/6	9,150
		Y 2/6	6,100
		Z 1/6	3,050
			18,300
	40,800		40,800

(b)

Capital Accounts

	X	Y	Z		X	Y	Z
Fixed assets taken over	7,000			Balances b/d	4,000	4,000	2,000
Loss shared	9,150	6,100	525	Deficiency shared: X			525
Deficiency	525	525		Y			525
				Bank to settle	12,675	2,625	
	16,675	6,625	3,050		16,675	6,625	3,050

Bank (as proof only)

Realisation: Fixed assets	8,000	Balance b/d	13,000
Stock	4,000	Creditors	16,500
Debtors	3,000	Realisation: Costs	800
Capital: X	12,675		
Y	2,625		
	30,300		30,300

3.26

(a) (i)

Amis, Lodge & Pym
Trading and Profit and Loss Account for the year ended 31 March 20X8

Sales		404,500
Less Cost of goods sold:		
Opening stock	30,000	
Add Purchases	225,000	
Add Carriage inwards	4,000	
	259,000	
Less Closing stock	35,000	224,000
Gross profit		180,500
Add Bank interest	750	
Discounts received	4,530	5,280
		185,780
Less Office expenses (30,400 + 405)	30,805	
Rent, rates, light and heat (8,800 – 1,500)	7,300	
Carriage outwards	12,000	
Discounts allowed	10,000	
Provision for bad debts	295	
Depreciation: Motor	15,000	
Plant	20,000	95,400

Net profit		90,380
Add Interest on current accounts and drawings:		
Amis	1,000	
Lodge	900	
Pym	720	2,620
		93,000
Less Salary – Pym	13,000	
Interest on capitals: Amis	8,000	
Lodge	1,500	
Pym	500	10,000
		23,000
		70,000
Balance on profit shared:		
Amis 50%		35,000
Lodge 30%		21,000
Pym 20%		14,000
		70,000

(ii)

Current Accounts

	Amis	Lodge	Pym		Amis	Lodge	Pym
Balances b/d	1,000	500	400	Salary			13,000
Drawings	25,000	22,000	15,000	Interest on capital	8,000	1,500	500
Interest on drawings	1,000	900	720	Balance on profits	35,000	21,000	14,000
Transfer to capital	16,000	–	11,380	Transfer to capital		900	
	43,000	23,400	27,500		43,000	23,400	27,500

(b) (i)

Realisation

Motors (80,000 – 35,000)	45,000	Discount on creditors	500
Plant (100,000 – 56,600)	43,400	Amis: Motor	5,000
Debtors (14,300 – 715)	13,585	Bank: Debtors	12,985
Stock	35,000	Fowles Ltd	138,500
		(75,000 + 63,500)	
Profit on realisation			
Amis 50%	10,000		
Lodge 30%	6,000		
Pym 20%	4,000		
	20,000		
	156,985		156,985

(ii)

Bank

Balance b/d	4,900	Office expenses	405
Realisation: Debtors	12,985	Creditors	16,000
Rent rebate	1,500	Capital: Amis	76,000
Fowles Ltd	63,500		
Capitals: Lodge	4,900		
Pym	4,620		
	92,405		92,405

(iii)

Capital Accounts

	Amis	Lodge	Pym		Amis	Lodge	Pym
Current a/c		900		Balances b/d	80,000	15,000	5,000
Fowles Ltd				Current a/c	16,000		11,380
Shares	25,000	25,000	25,000	Profit on			
Realisation:				realisation	10,000	6,000	4,000
Motor	5,000			Bank		4,900	4,620
Bank	76,000	25,900(?)					
	106,000	25,900	25,000		106,000	25,900	25,000

3.28

(a)

Lock, Stock and Barrel

Profit and Loss Account for the six months ended 1 February 20X7

Sales of completed houses		280,000
Less Costs of completing houses		
Houses in course of construction at start	115,000	
Materials used	35,750	
Land used (75,000 × ¹⁄₃)	25,000	
Wages and subcontractors	78,000	253,750
Gross profit		26,250
Less Administration salaries	17,250	
General expenses	12,500	
Depreciation: Freehold land	300	
Plant and equipment ($^6/_{12} × 10\%$)	7,500	
Vehicles ($25\% × ^6/_{12}$)	4,500	42,050
Net loss		15,800
Shared: Lock 40%	6,320	
Stock 30%	4,740	
Barrel 30%	4,740	15,800

Capitals

	Lock	Stock	Barrel		Lock	Stock	Barrel
Drawings	6,000	5,000	4,000	Balances b/d	52,000	26,000	3,500
Loss shared	6,320	4,740	4,740	Balance c/d			5,240
Balances c/d	39,680	16,260					
	52,000	26,000	8,740		52,000	26,000	8,740

Lock, Stock and Barrel

Balance Sheet as at 1 February 20X7

Fixed tangible assets	Cost	Depreciation	
Freehold land and buildings	20,000	3,300	16,700
Plant and equipment	150,000	89,500	60,500
Motor vehicles	36,000	27,500	8,500
	206,000	120,300	85,700
Current assets			
Stock of land for building	50,000		
Stocks of materials	7,500		
Debtors for completed houses	35,000		
	92,500		
Less Current liabilities			
Trade creditors	52,250		
Bank overdraft	75,250	127,500	
Working capital			(35,000)
Net assets			50,700
Financed by:			
Capitals: Lock			39,680
Stock			16,260
Barrel			(5,240)
			50,700

(b) Amounts distributable to partners:

On 28 February there was only (6,200 + 7,000 + 72,500 – 75,250) 10,450 hence there was nowhere near enough to pay off the creditors, and so payment to partners could not be made.

On 30 April we treat it as though no more cash will be received.

(c) *First distribution*

	Lock	Stock	Barrel
Capital balances before dissolution	39,680	16,260	(5,240)
Loss if no further assets realised			
(85,700 + 92,500 – 6,000 – 6,200 – 7,000			
– 72,500 – 35,000 – 50,000) = 1,500			
Loss shared in profit/loss ratios	(600)	(450)	(450)
Cars taken over	(2,000)	(2,000)	(2,000)
	37,080	13,810	(7,690)
Barrel's deficiency shared profit/loss ratio	4,394	3,296	7,690
Paid to partners	32,686	10,514	–

Second and final distribution

	Lock	Stock	Barrel
Capital balances before dissolution	39,680	16,260	(5,240)
Profit finally ascertained			
100,000 – 1,500 = 98,500			
Shared	39,400	29,550	29,550
	79,080	45,810	24,310
Less Distribution and cars	34,686	12,514	2,000
Final distribution (100,000)	44,394	33,296	22,310

3.30

(a)

Dinho and Manueli

Realisation Account

Property	290,000	Creditors	85,800
Equipment	65,000	Bank	56,700
Stock	143,500	Loan	160,000
Debtors	121,000	Bin Ltd	304,000
		Loss: Dinho	6,500
		Manueli	6,500
	619,500		619,500

(b)

Bin Ltd

Goodwill [write downs (30,000 + 5,000) – realisation loss (13,000)]	22,000
Property	260,000
Equipment	65,000
Stocks	143,500
Debtors	116,000
Bank (120,000 – 56,700)	63,300
Creditors	(85,800)
	584,000
Ordinary share capital	300,000
10% preference shares (D = 87,500; M = 16,500; P = 20,000)	124,000
Loan	160,000
	584,000

(c)

(Salary as before, therefore not relevant.) Earnings on savings were 120,000 @ 6% = 7,200; preference dividend will be 20,000 @ 10% = 2,000, therefore 5,200 needed from profit after preference dividend. Profit must be 3 × 5,200 = 15,600 + the total preference dividend of 12,400 = 28,000.

4.1

(i)

(ii) FIFO Closing stock 20 × £40 = £800

LIFO

	Received	Issued	Stock after each transaction		No. of units in stock	Total value of stock
Jan	10 × £30		10 × £30	300	10	£300
Mar	10 × £34		10 × £30 / 10 × £34	300 / 340 = 640	20	£640
Apr		8 × £34	10 × £30 / 2 × £34	300 / 68 = 368	12	£384
Sep	20 × £40		10 × £30 / 2 × £34 / 20 × £40	300 / 68 / 800 = 1,168	32	£1,184
Dec		12 × £40	10 × £30 / 2 × £34 / 8 × £40	300 / 68 / 320 = 688	20	£740

(iii)

AVCO	Received	Issued	Average cost per unit stock held
Jan	10 × £30		£30
Mar	10 × £34		£32
Apr		8	£32
Sep	20 × £40		£37
Dec		12	£37

4.2

Trading Account for the year ended December 31 20X0 (All methods)

		FIFO	LIFO	AVCO
Sales	8 × £46	368	368	368
	12 × £56	672	672	672
		1,040	1,040	1,040
Purchases		1,440	1,440	1,440
Less Closing stock		800	688	740
Cost of goods sold		640	752	700
Gross profit		400	288	340
		1,040	1,040	1,040

4.5

(a) (dates and calculations omitted)

Cash

Loan: School fund	200.00	Purchases	53.50
Sales	53.50		51.36

Purchases

Cash	51.36

Sales

Cash	53.50

(b) Stock valuation:

34	Break × 16p =	Break × 16p	5.44
15	Brunch × 12p =	Brunch × 12p	1.80
			7.24

Stock

Trading account	7.24

(c)

Broadway School
Trading Account for the month of December 20X9

Purchases	51.36	Sales	53.50
Less Closing stock	7.24		
	44.12		
Gross profit	9.38		
	53.50		53.50

(d)

	Break	Brunch
Purchases (units)	240	108
Less Sold	200	90
Stock should have been	40	18
Actual stock	34	15
Missing items	6	3

If there have been no arithmetical errors, one can only assume that someone has stolen 6 Breaks and 3 Brunches.

4.6

(This is a brief answer showing main points to be covered. In the examination the answer should be in report form and elaborated.)

1 For Charles Gray

(i) The concept of prudence says that stock should be valued at lower of cost or net realisable value. As 50% of the retail price £375 is lower than cost £560, then £375 will be taken as net realisable value and used for stock valuation.

(ii) The sale has not taken place by 30 April 20X9. The prudence concept does not anticipate profits and therefore the sale will not be assumed. The gun should therefore be included in stock, at cost price £560.

2 For Jean Kim

It appears that it is doubtful if the business can still be treated as a going concern.

(c) It is inappropriate to include unrealised profit in the balance sheet value of stocks of finished goods. They should be stated at the lower of cost and net realisable value. Assuming cost is the lower of these two amounts, the value she has placed on the stock must be removed through a provision for unrealised profit. This is an application of the prudence concept – see Chapter 25.

3 If the final decision is that the business cannot continue, then the stock valuation should be £510 each, as this is less than cost, with a further overall deduction of auction fees and expenses £300.

For Peter Fox

Stock must be valued at the lower of cost or net realisable value in this case. The cost to be used is the *cost* for Peter Fox. It is quite irrelevant what the cost may be for other distributors.

It would also be against the convention of consistency to adopt a different method. The consistency applies to Peter Fox, it is not a case of consistency with other businesses. Using selling prices as a basis is not acceptable to the vast majority of businesses.

5.1
(a) The amount paid for goodwill.
(b) The excess represents share premium.
(c) Equity shares generally means ordinary shares.
(d) That although issued in 20X6 a dividend *will* not be paid in that year. The first year that dividends *could* be paid is 20X7.

Extract 1

Extract 2
(e) (i) A rate of 8% per annum interest will be paid on them, irrespective of whether profits are made or not.
(ii) These are the years within which the debentures could be redeemed, if the company so wished.
(f) (i) This is the rate per annum at which preference dividends will be paid, subject to there being sufficient distributable profits.
(ii) That the shares could be bought back by the company.
(g) Probably because there was currently a lower interest rate prevailing at the time of redemption and the company took advantage of it.
(h) Large amounts of both fixed interest and fixed dividend funds have resulted in a raising of the gearing.
(j) Debenture interest gets charged before arriving at net profit. Dividends are an appropriation of profits.
(k) Shareholders are owners and help decide appropriations. Debenture holders are external lenders and interest expense has to be paid.

5.2 Points to be made include that there must be an expectation that sufficient profits will be made in future to meet the debenture interest payments when due; also, there may be cheaper sources of finance available; also, if secured debentures are to be issued, there must be sufficient assets available to act as security over the issue. Gearing is also an issue to be considered – see Chapter 8.

4.8
(a) In one respect the consistency convention is not applied, as at one year end the stock may be shown at cost whereas the next year end may see stock valued at net realisable value.

On the other hand, as it is prudent to take the lower of cost or net realisable value, it can be said to be consistently prudent to consistently take the lower figure.

(b) Being prudent can be said to be an advantage. For instance, shareholders can know that stocks are not overvalued so as to give a false picture of their investment.

Someone to whom money is owed, such as a creditor, will know that the stocks in the balance sheet are realisable at least at that figure.

It is this knowledge that profits are not recorded because of excessive values placed on stocks that gives outside parties confidence to rely on reported profits.

4.10 (See text, Section 4.15.)

$$EOQ = \sqrt{\frac{2 \times 12,000 \times £10}{£6}} = 200 \text{ units}$$

(i) Based on estimates which obviously can vary a lot from actual.
(ii) Consumption may be uneven at times, EOQ assumes even usage.
(iii) Such things as strikes, catastrophes, etc. can render it useless.

4.11
(a) The new provision is $\frac{20}{120}$ of £34,200 = £5,700. The adjustment to be shown in the profit and loss account is therefore £5,700 – £5,400 = £300 (increase).

(b)
Nyree Chan
Balance Sheet Extract as at 31 August 20X1

	£	£
Current assets		
Stock of finished goods	34,200	
Less: Provision for unrealised profit	(5,700)	
		28,500

6.1
GWR Ltd
Profit and Loss Appropriation Accounts
(1) For the year ended 31 December 20X6

	£	£
Profit for the year before taxation		42,005
Less Corporation tax		13,480
Profit for the year after taxation		28,525
Less Transfer to general reserve	6,000	
Preference dividend of 10%	5,000	
Ordinary dividend of 12%	12,000	23,000
Retained profits carried forward to next year		5,525

6.2

(2) For the year ended 31 December 20X7

Profit for the tax year before taxation		34,831
Less Corporation tax		11,114
Profit for the year after taxation		23,717
Add Retained profits from last year		5,525
		29,242
Less Transfer to general reserve	4,000	
Preference dividend of 10%	5,000	
Ordinary dividend of 9%	9,000	
		18,000
Retained profits carried forward to next year		11,242

LMS Ltd

Profit and Loss Appropriation Accounts

(1) For the year ended 31 December 20X7

Profit for the year before taxation		27,929
Less Corporation tax		8,331
Profit for the year after taxation		19,598
Less: Transfer to general reserve	3,000	
Preference dividend 8%	3,200	
Ordinary dividend 8%	9,600	
		15,800
Retained profits carried forward to next year		3,798

(2) For the year ended 31 December 20X8

Profit for the year before taxation		32,440
Less Corporation tax		10,446
Profit for the year after taxation		21,994
Add Retained profits from last year		3,798
		25,792
Less: Transfer to general reserve	4,000	
Preference dividend 8%	3,200	
Ordinary dividend 10%	12,000	
		19,200
Retained profits carried forward to next year		6,592

(3) For the year ended 31 December 20X9

Profit for the year before taxation		36,891
Less Corporation tax		12,001
Profit for the year after taxation		24,890
Add Retained profits from last year		6,592
		31,482
Less: Transfer to foreign exchange reserve	2,000	
Preference dividend 8%	3,200	
Ordinary dividend 11%	13,200	
		18,400
Retained profits carried forward to next year		13,082

6.3

Balance Sheet as at 30 June 20X6

Fixed assets	Cost	Depn	
Buildings	105,000	22,000	83,000
Motors	62,500	15,350	47,150
Fixtures	11,500	3,750	7,750
	179,000	41,100	137,900

Current assets			
Stock		16,210	
Debtors		14,175	
Bank (difference)		4,998	
		35,383	
Less Current liabilities			
Creditors	9,120		
Proposed dividend	5,000		
		14,120	
Net current assets			21,263
Total assets less current liabilities			159,163
Debentures: repayable in 20X9			40,000
			119,163

Capital and reserves		
Called-up share capital		100,000
Fixed assets replacement reserve		8,000
General reserve		6,000
Profit and loss account		5,163
		119,163

6.5

Chang Ltd

Trading and Profit and Loss Account for the year ended
31 December 20X8

Sales		316,810
Less Cost of goods sold		
Opening stock	25,689	
Add Purchases	201,698	
	227,387	
Less Closing stock	29,142	
		198,245
Gross profit		118,565
Less expenses		
Wages (54,207 + 581)	54,788	
Rent (4,300 − 300)	4,000	
Lighting	1,549	
Bad debts (748 + 77)	825	
General expenses	32,168	
Depreciation: Machinery	5,500	
		98,830
Net profit		19,735
Add Unappropriated profits from last year		34,280
		54,015
Less Proposed dividend		10,000
Unappropriated profits carried to next year		44,015

Balance Sheet as at 31 December 20X8

Fixed assets		
Premises		65,000
Machinery	55,000	
Less Depreciation	21,300	33,700
		98,700

Current assets
Stock		29,142
Debtors	21,784	
Less Provision	938	20,846
Prepayments		300
Bank		23,101
		73,389

Less Current liabilities
Proposed dividend	10,000	
Creditors	17,493	
Expenses owing	581	28,074
Working capital		45,315
		144,015

Financed by:
Authorised and issued capital		100,000
Revenue reserves		
Profit and loss account		44,015
		144,015

6.7 T Howe Ltd

Trading and Profit and Loss Account for the year ended 31 December 20X8

Sales		135,486
Less Cost of goods sold		
Opening stock	40,360	
Add Purchases	72,360	
Add Carriage inwards	1,570	
	114,290	
Less Closing stock	52,360	61,930
Gross profit		73,556
Less Expenses		
Salaries	18,310	
Rates and occupancy	4,515	
Carriage outwards	1,390	
Office expenses	3,212	
Sundry expenses	1,896	
Depreciation: Buildings	5,000	
Equipment	9,000	
Directors' remuneration	9,500	52,823
Net profit		20,733
Add Unappropriated profits from last year		15,286
		36,019
Less Appropriations		
Proposed dividend	10,000	
General reserve	1,000	
Foreign exchange	800	11,800
Unappropriated profits carried to next year		24,219

Balance Sheet as at 31 December 20X8

	Cost	Depn	Net
Fixed assets			
Buildings	100,000	37,000	63,000
Equipment	45,000	25,000	20,000
	145,000	62,000	83,000
Current assets			
Stock		52,360	
Debtors		18,910	
Bank		6,723	
		77,993	
Less Current liabilities			
Creditors	12,304		
Expenses owing	470		
Proposed dividend	10,000	22,774	
Working capital			55,219
			138,219
Financed by:			
Share capital: authorised and issued			100,000
Reserves			
Foreign exchange		5,000	
General reserve		9,000	
Profit and loss		24,219	38,219
			138,219

6.9

1 Burden plc: Computation of corrected net profit

Recorded net profit		58,070
Add Profit on sale of equipment		500
		58,570
Less Bad debt written off	300	
Stock reduced to net realisable value	700	1,000
Correct figure of net profit		57,570

2 Burden plc
Profit and Loss Appropriation Account for the year ended 31 May 20X9

Net profit for the year brought down		57,570
Add Retained profits from last year		36,200
		93,770
Less Transfer to general reserve	50,000	
Proposed dividend of 10%	20,000	70,000
Retained profits carried forward to next year		23,770

3   **(i)**   *Current assets*

Stock		17,100
Debtors		6,540
Prepayments		760
		24,400
Less Current liabilities		
Trade creditors	8,500	
Accrued expenses	430	
Proposed dividend	20,000	
Bank overdraft	2,400	
		31,330
Working capital deficit		(6,930)

Note: Figures in brackets are negative.

(ii)   *Capital and reserves*

Ordinary share capital: called up	200,000
Share premium	25,000
General reserve	70,000
Profit and loss account	23,770
Shareholders' funds	318,770

4   *Examples:*

Issue of shares: + Bank; + Share capital.

Sales of fixed assets: + Bank; − Fixed assets.

Debentures issued: + Bank; + Debentures.

6.11

(a) This is incorrect. The tax portion has to be counted as part of the total cost, which is made up of debenture interest paid plus tax. Holding back payment will merely see legal action taken by the Inland Revenue to collect the tax.

(b) This cannot be done. The repainting of the exterior does not improve or enhance the original value of the premises. It cannot therefore be treated as capital expenditure.

(c) This is not feasible. Only the profit on the sale of the old machinery, found by deducting net book value from sales proceeds, can be so credited to the profit and loss account. The remainder is a capital receipt and should be treated as such.

(d) This is an incorrect view. Although some of the general reserve could, if circumstances allowed it, be transferred back to the profit and loss account, it could not be shown as affecting the operating profit for 20X9. This is because the reserve was built up over the years before 20X9.

(e) This is not feasible. The share capital has to be maintained at nominal value as per the Companies Act. A share premium cannot be created in this fashion, and even if it could, it would still have to be credited to the *share premium account* and not the profit and loss account.

(f) Incorrect. Although the premises could be revalued the credit for the increase has to be to a capital reserve account. This cannot then be transferred to the credit of the profit and loss account.

6.12

(i)   (for internal use)

Rogers plc

Trading and Profit and Loss Account for the year ended

31 December 20X2

Sales			288,000
Less Returns inwards			11,500
			276,500
Less Cost of sales:			
Stock 1 January 20X2			57,500
Add Purchases	164,000		
Less Returns outwards	2,000		
		162,000	
Carriage inwards		1,300	
		220,800	
Less Stock 31 December 20X2		64,000	
			156,800
Gross profit			119,700
Distribution costs:			
Salaries and wages		2,800	
Rent and rates		3,750	
General distribution expenses		4,860	
Motor expenses		3,600	
Depreciation: Motors		6,500	
Equipment		700	
		22,210	
Administrative expenses:			
Salaries and wages		5,600	
Rent and rates		2,500	
General administrative expenses		3,320	
Motor expenses		3,600	
Auditors' remuneration		500	
Discounts allowed		3,940	
Bad debts		570	
Depreciation: Motors		3,500	
Equipment		1,100	
		24,630	
		46,840	
Other operating income: Royalties receivable			72,860
Income from participating interests			1,800
			74,660
Interest on bank deposit		660	
		770	
		1,430	
			76,090
Interest payable: Debenture interest			2,400
Profit on ordinary activities before taxation			73,690
Tax on profit on ordinary activities			30,700
Profit on ordinary activities after taxation			42,990
Retained profits from last year			15,300
			58,290
Transfer to general reserve		8,000	
Proposed ordinary dividend		30,000	
		38,000	
Retained profits carried forward to next year			20,290

(ii) (published accounts)
Rogers plc
Profit and Loss Account for the year ended 31 December 20X2

	£	£
Turnover		276,500
Cost of sales		156,800
Gross profit		119,700
Distribution costs	22,210	
Administrative expenses	24,630	46,840
		72,860
Other operating income		1,800
		74,660
Income from participating interests		660
Other interest receivable		770
		76,090
Interest payable		2,400
Profit on ordinary activities before taxation		73,690
Tax on profit on ordinary activities		30,700
Profit on ordinary activities after taxation		42,990
Retained profits from last year		15,300
		58,290
Transfer to general reserve	8,000	
Proposed ordinary dividend	30,000	38,000
Retained profits carried forward to next year		20,290

Notes to accounts on debenture interest and auditors' remuneration.

6.13
(i) (for internal use)
Federal plc
Trading and Profit and Loss Account for the year ended 31 December 20X4

	£	£	£
Sales			849,000
Less Returns inwards			5,800
			843,200
Less Cost of sales:			
Stock 1 January 20X4		64,500	
Add Purchases	510,600		
Less Returns outwards	3,300	507,300	
Carriage inwards		4,900	
		576,700	
Less Stock 31 December 20X4		82,800	
Cost of goods sold		493,900	
Wages		11,350	
Depreciation of plant and machinery		1,500	506,750
Gross profit			336,450
Distribution costs:			
Salaries and wages		29,110	
Rent and rates		20,000	
Motor expenses		10,400	
General distribution expenses		8,220	
Haulage costs		2,070	
Depreciation: Motors		15,000	
Plant and machinery		8,000	92,800
Administrative expenses:			
Salaries and wages		20,920	
Rent and rates		5,000	
Motor expenses		5,200	
General administrative expenses		2,190	
Bad debts		840	
Discounts allowed		5,780	
Auditors' remuneration		2,000	
Directors' remuneration		5,000	
Depreciation: Motors		7,000	
Plant and machinery		5,000	
		58,930	
Less Discounts received		6,800	52,130
			144,930
			191,520
Income from participating interests		3,500	
Interest from government securities		1,600	5,100
			196,620
Amount written off investment in related companies		14,000	
Debenture interest		3,800	17,800
Profit on ordinary activities before taxation			178,820
Tax on profit on ordinary activities			74,000
Profit on ordinary activities after taxation			104,820
Retained profits from last year			37,470
			142,290
Transfer to debenture redemption reserve		20,000	
Proposed ordinary dividend		50,000	70,000
Retained profits carried forward to next year			72,290

(ii) (published accounts)
Federal plc
Profit and Loss Account for the year ended 31 December 20X4

	£	£
Turnover		843,200
Cost of sales		506,750
Gross profit		336,450
Distribution costs	92,800	
Administrative expenses	52,130	144,930
		191,520
Income from participating interests	3,500	
Other interest receivable	1,600	5,100
		196,620
Amounts written off investments	14,000	
Interest payable	3,800	17,800
Profit on ordinary activities before taxation		178,820
Tax on profit on ordinary activities		74,000
Profit on ordinary activities after taxation		104,820
Retained profits from last year		37,470
		142,290
Transfer to reserves	20,000	
Proposed ordinary dividend	50,000	70,000
Retained profits carried forward to next year		72,290

6.16
(a)

Wilkinson Ltd
Year ended 31 December 20X0

Gross profit as calculated		97,000
Add 3 reduction in purchases (W1)		3,500
		100,500
Less 4 reduction in sales (W2)		29,525
Gross profit as revised		70,975

(W1)	Returns + VAT =	4,025	
	Less VAT 15/115 × 4,025	525	
	To be deducted from purchases	3,500	

(W2)	Original sales figure	199,525
	Less returns + VAT	4,025
		195,500
	Less VAT 15/115 × 195,500	25,500
	New sales figure	170,000
	i.e. reduction of 199,525 − 170,000 =	29,525

Net profit on ordinary activities as calculated		25,000
Add overprovision tax in previous year (1)		2,000
		27,000
Less:		
Extra depreciation (W3)	500	
Overstatement in gross profit (W4)	26,025	
		26,525
Net profit as revised		475

(W3) Value 100,800 ÷ 48 years = 2,100 per year
2,100 − 1,600 previously = 500

(W4) 97,000 − 70,975 = 26,025

(b)

None of these appears in the suspense account.

6.18

Owen Ltd
Balance Sheet as at 31 December 20X1

			£
Called-up share capital not paid			150
Fixed assets			
Intangible assets			
Development costs	3,070		
Goodwill	21,000		
		24,070	
Tangible assets			
Land and buildings	32,000		
Plant and machinery	7,100		
		39,100	
Investments			
Shares in undertakings in which the company has a participating interest		35,750	
		98,920	
Current assets			
Stock			
Raw materials and consumables	3,470		
Finished goods and goods for resale	18,590		22,060
Debtors			
Trade debtors	17,400		
Amounts owed by undertakings in which the company has a participating interest	3,000		
Prepayments	1,250	21,650	
		43,710	
Creditors: amounts falling due within one year			
Debentures	6,000		
Bank overdrafts	4,370		
Trade creditors	12,410		
Bills of exchange payable	1,600	24,380	
Net current assets			19,330
Total assets less Current liabilities			118,400
Creditors: amounts falling due after one year			
Debentures	4,000		
Bills of exchange payable	2,000		6,000
			112,400
Capital and reserves			
Called-up share capital			75,000
Share premium account			20,000
Other reserves:			
Capital redemption reserve	5,000		
General reserve	4,000		9,000
Profit and loss account			8,400
			112,400

Notes:

(i) Called-up share capital consists of:

	£
50,000 £1 ordinary shares	50,000
50,000 preference shares of 50p each	25,000
	75,000

(ii) Land and buildings:

	£	
Cost		48,000
Depreciation to 31 December 20X0	12,000	
Depreciation for year to 31 December 20X1	4,000	16,000
		32,000

(iii) Plant and machinery:

Cost		12,500
Depreciation to 31 December 20X0	3,600	
Depreciation for year to 31 December 20X1	1,800	5,400
		7,100

6.19

Belle Works plc
Balance Sheet as at 30 September 20X4

Fixed assets			
Intangible assets			
Concessions, patents, licences, trade marks and similar rights and assets	1,500		
Goodwill	17,500	19,000	
Tangible assets			
Land and buildings	72,500		
Plant and machinery	19,400	91,900	
			110,900
Current assets			
Stock			
Raw materials and consumables	14,320		
Work in progress	5,640		
Finished goods and goods for resale	13,290	33,250	
Debtors			
Trade debtors	11,260		
Other debtors	1,050		
Prepayments and accrued income	505	12,815	
		46,065	
Creditors: amounts falling due within one year			
Debenture loans	6,000		
Bank loans and overdrafts	3,893		
Trade creditors	11,340		
Bills of exchange payable	4,000		
Other creditors including taxation and social security	14,675	39,908	
Net current assets			6,157
Total assets less Current liabilities			117,057
Creditors: amounts falling due after more than one year			
Debenture loans	12,000		
Trade creditors	1,260	13,260	
Provisions for liabilities and charges			
Pensions and similar obligations	1,860		
Taxation, including deferred taxation	640	2,500	
			15,760
			101,297
Capital and reserves			
Called-up share capital			70,000
Share premium account			5,000
Revaluation reserve			10,500
Other reserves			
General reserve	6,000		
Foreign exchange reserve	3,500		
Profit and loss account	9,500		
			6,297
			101,297

6.22

(a) Shareholders
• profits before tax have risen by 12%;
• increased profits despite higher costs;
• positive future plans.

(b) Debenture holders
• interest covered over seven times by operating profit;
• increase in profits plus positive future plans suggest no problem in meeting interest payments over the foreseeable future.

(c) Employees
• profits are rising, even though costs have risen. This suggests more might be available for a wage rise;
• positive future plans include growth, which suggests job security and the possibility of greater prospects of promotion within the company.

Notes appended to the accounts on the details of tangible assets and depreciation, also exact details of items lumped under group descriptions.

7.1

Seeds Ltd

Available for dividends		
General reserve	40,000	
Foreign exchange reserve	5,000	
Profit and loss	45,000	
	90,000	
Less retained in profit and loss by company policy	25,000	
	65,000	
Available		65,000
Less 10% preference dividend	5,000	
30% ordinary dividend	60,000	65,000

Answer: 30 per cent ordinary dividend

Plant Ltd

Available for dividends		
General reserve	70,000	
Fixed assets replacement reserve	20,000	
Profit and loss	63,000	
	153,000	
Less Retained in profit and loss by company policy	40,000	
	113,000	
Available		113,000
Less 10% preference dividend	8,000	
35% ordinary dividend	105,000	113,000

Answer: 35 per cent ordinary dividend

7.3

Grimble Ltd

(a) **Profit and Loss Appropriation Account for year to 31 December 20X0**

Net profit for the year (W1)	262,175
Add Retained profits brought forward	188,300
	450,475

Less Taxation on profits ... 60,000 / 390,475

Less Appropriations
9% preference dividends ... 5,040
Ordinary dividend* ... 56,000 / 61,040
Unappropriated profits carried to next year ... 329,435

(W1) Net profit per question ... 265,500
Less $\frac{1}{2}$ year's debenture interest ... 3,325 / 262,175

* Assumed that ordinary shares have nominal value of £1 each

(b) (Revised) Trial Balance as at 31 December 20X0

	Dr	Cr
9% preference share capital		56,000
Ordinary share capital (W2)		420,000
7% debentures		95,000
Capital redemption reserve (W3)		7,000
Profit and loss		329,435
Taxation owing		60,000
Debenture interest	3,325	
Preference dividend (½ year)	2,520	
Ordinary dividend	56,000	

(W2) 280,000 + bonus 140,000 = 420,000
(W3) 147,000 – used for bonus shares 140,000 = 7,000
Note: Fixed assets will have risen by £20,000 (Dr) and the revaluation reserve will have risen by £20,000 (Cr).

7.5
(a)
Expansion plc
Balance Sheet extracts

Paid-up share capital
100,000 preference shares at £1 ... 100,000
1,300,000 ordinary shares at 50p (W1) ... 650,000

Reserves
Share premium (W2) ... 465,000
Capital redemption reserve (75,000 – bonus) ... 25,000
General reserve ... 100,000
Revaluation reserve ... 200,000
Asset replacement reserve ... 50,000
Profit and loss account ... 75,000 / 1,665,000

Also in balance sheet
Allotment monies owing (W3) ... 383,750
(W1) Original 500,000 × 50p ... 250,000
Bonus issue 100,000 × 50p ... 50,000
Rights issue 600,000 × 50p ... 300,000
Additional shares 50,000 + 50,000 = 100,000 × 50p ... 50,000 / 650,000

(W2) Original ... 100,000
Rights issue 600,000 × 40p ... 240,000
Additional issue 100,000 × 1.25 ... 125,000 / 465,000

(W3) Allotment monies owing
On rights issue 600,000 × 40p = ... 240,000
On additional 100,000 × 1.50 = ... 150,000 / 390,000
Less Applications overpaid by public 25,000 × 25p ... 6,250 / 383,750

Note: normally shares would not be allotted until allotment money was received. The examiner indicates otherwise.

(b) Bank
Rights issue: applications (600,000 × 10p) ... 60,000
Applications: additional shares (125,000 × 25p) ... 31,250
Rights issue: allotment (600,000 × 80p) ... 480,000
Additional shares: allotment (100,000 × 1.50) – (25,000 × 25p) ... 143,750

N.B. It is assumed that the bank account should include allotment monies.

(c) A premium is added to the nominal value of the shares so as to raise the issue price to the market value of the shares.

7.6
(a)
T Torrents Ltd
(Corrected) Balance Sheet as at 30 April 20X0

Fixed assets
Freehold land and buildings at valuation ... 70,000
Plant and machinery at cost (W1) ... 35,000
Less Depreciation to date ... 9,600 / 25,400
Motor vehicles at cost ... 16,000
Less Depreciation to date ... 9,600 / 6,400 / 101,800

Current assets
Stock (W4) ... 27,000
Trade debtors and amounts prepaid ... 14,000
Less Provision for bad debts (W3) ... 340 / 13,660
Bank (W2) ... 1,800 / 42,460

Amounts falling due within one year
Trade creditors and accrued charges ... 9,800
Proposed dividend ... 6,500 / 16,300 / 26,160 / 127,960

Amounts falling due after more than one year
8% debentures (40,000 – 6,000) ... 34,000 / 93,960

(b)

Represented by:
Capital and reserves

Ordinary shares (60,000 + 5,000)	65,000
Share premium (W6)	5,800
Asset revaluation reserve	14,000
Retained earnings (W5)	9,160
	93,960

Workings

(W1)

	Cost	Depreciation
Machinery 30 April 20X0	47,000	14,100
Sale (at book values)	12,000	4,500
	35,000	9,600

Sale at net book value 12,000 – 4,500 =	7,500
Sold for	5,000
Loss to profit and loss	2,500

Purchases to be increased by 5,000 (sale price in goods)

(W2)

Bank	7,000
Less debentures bought	5,200
	1,800

Profit on redemption transferred to share premium account

(W3) Debtors 14,000 – prepaid 400 = 13,600
Provision = 13,600 × 2½% = 340

(W4) Stock 29,000 – belonging to customer 2,000 = 27,000

(W5)

Retained earnings		25,500
Less Dividend	6,500	
Less Loss on machine (W1)	2,500	
Less Bad debts provision (W3)	340	
Less Stock (W4)	2,000	
Less Goods for machine (+ purchases)	5,000	16,340
Revised figure		9,160

(W6)

Share premium		10,000
Add Profit on debentures redeemed		800
		10,800
Less Bonus shares		5,000
		5,800

7.7

(a)

Application and Allotment

20X2			20X2		
Jul 10	Bank: Refund of application money (W3)	55,000	Jun 30	Bank: Applications for rights issue (W1)	495,000
Jul 31	Ordinary share capital (rights)	495,000	Jun 30	Bank: Applications for public issue (W2)	165,000
Jul 31	Share premium (on rights issue)	445,500	Jul 31	Bank: Allotment money of rights issue (W4)	445,500
Jul 31	Ordinary share capital (public)	100,000	Jul 31	Bank: Allotment money of public issue (W5)	137,000
Jul 31	Share premium (on rights issue)	150,000	Jul 31	Allotment monies owing (W6) c/d	3,000
		1,245,500			1,245,500
Aug 1	Balance b/d	3,000			

Workings:

(W1) Total shares 240,000 + 90,000 = 330,000
Taken up 90% = 297,000
5 for 3 held = 297,000 × ⁵⁄₃ = 495,000
Application monies 495,000 × £1 = 495,000
Public issue. Applications 90,000 + 60,000 × £1.10 = 165,000

(W2) Refunds 90,000 – 40,000 = 50,000 × £1.10 = 55,000

(W3) 495,000 shares × 90p = 445,500

(W4) 100,000 × £1.40 = 140,000 less unpaid 3,000 = 137,000

(W5) The examiner could have been more specific. It is assumed that the shares have been allotted in full and that the company allows this to be owing. In theory shares would not be allotted until allotment money was paid. However, £3,000 owing divided by £1.40 per share does not work out to be an exact number of shares, i.e. it is 2,142.85

(W6) shares on which allotment is owed.

Ordinary Share Capital

20X2			20X2		
Jul 31	Balance c/d	915,000	Jun 1	Balance b/d	240,000
			Jun 30	Capital redemption reserve	80,000
			Jul 31	Application and allotment	495,000
			Jul 31	Application and allotment	100,000
		915,000			915,000
			Aug 1	Balance b/d	915,000

(b)

Initial number of shares held	900
Add Rights issue 900 × ⁵⁄₃	1,500
Add Bonus issue	300
Add Public issue	500
New shareholding	3,200

(c) Advantages:

(i) Not normally refundable in the short term, e.g. as compared with a bank overdraft.

(ii) Dividends only payable if profits are made.

Disadvantages:
(i) Share issues can be expensive to administer (not rights issues).
(ii) May give control to different parties than at present.

Alternative ways of funding:
(i) Preference shares.
(ii) Debentures.
(iii) Bank loan.

7.9 No. of ordinary shares £2,600,000 ÷ 25p = 10,400,000
Present market capitalisation 10,400,000 × 60p = £6,240,000

1 *Rights issue at par*
This would raise capitalisation (total market value) to
£6,240,000 + £5,000,000 = £11,240,000
Now 10,400,000 + (5,000,000 × 4) = 30,400,000 shares
New market value per share = 37p approx.

Advantages
(i) Gives benefit of obtaining extra shares to existing shareholders.
(ii) As dividends depend on profits, a recession or similar would not have heavy fixed charges such as debenture interest.
(iii) Shareholders can sell 'rights' if they want to.
(iv) It should raise the amount required.

Disadvantages
(i) Rights issues are usually pitched below (new) market price to make them attractive to buy, but this figure is too low.
(ii) Existing shareholders who are short of funds may be annoyed by not getting all the advantages.

2 *Rights issue at premium of 20p per share*
Extra shares £5,000,000 ÷ 45p = 11,111,111
New total shares 10,400,000 + 11,111,111 = 21,511,111
New market value per share = 51.6p approx.

Advantages:
(i) Raises funds needed.
(ii) Pitched slightly below (new) market value which is generally accepted as correct.
(iii) Same as (ii) and (iii) in 1 above.

Disadvantages:
Same as (ii) in 1 above.

3 *Bonus issue of ordinary shares*
Advantages: none
Disadvantages:
Bonus issue does not result in cash received, and is therefore useless.

4 *Issue of 8% preference shares of £1 each at par*
Advantages:
Would raise the amount required if the percentage return was reasonable in current conditions.
Disadvantages:
Means heavy burden of preference dividends before ordinary shareholders get anything.

5 *6% loan stock at par*
Advantages:
Same as in 4.
Disadvantages:
Gearing becomes very high. Heavy burden of fixed charges.

8.1 Liquidity, profitability, efficiency, capital structure and shareholder.

8.3
Liquidity — see text, Section 8.4.
Profitability — see text, Section 8.5.
Efficiency — see text, Section 8.6.
Capital structure — see text, Section 8.7.
Shareholder — see text, Section 8.8.

8.5 (a) Stock turnover.

8.7 (i) (b) and (d).
(ii) (b) and (d).
(iii) (d).
(iv) If current liabilities greater than current assets, (b) and (d); if current assets greater than current liabilities, (a) and (c).
(v) (b) and (d) but only after a customer takes up the offer.

8.9

(a)
(i) Gross profit as % of sales: $\dfrac{20,000}{80,000} \times \dfrac{100}{1} = 25\%$ $\dfrac{24,000}{120,000} \times \dfrac{100}{1} = 20\%$

(ii) Net profit as % of sales: $\dfrac{10,000}{80,000} \times \dfrac{100}{1} = 12.5\%$ $\dfrac{15,000}{120,000} \times \dfrac{100}{1} = 12.5\%$

(iii) Expenses as % of sales: $\dfrac{10,000}{80,000} \times \dfrac{100}{1} = 12.5\%$ $\dfrac{9,000}{120,000} \times \dfrac{100}{1} = 7.5\%$

(iv) Stockturn: $\dfrac{60,000}{(25,000 + 15,000) \div 2} = 3$ times

$\dfrac{96,000}{(22,500 + 17,500) \div 2} = 4.8$ times

8.11

(a) The ratios reveal that L Ltd's relative profitability has fallen between the two years. The gross and net profit margins have both fallen, but this may be due to the new sales manager's price-cutting policy, rather than because of any change in costs.

The fall in return on capital employed is not what was hoped for from the new sales price policy. A drop from 31 per cent to 18 per cent is very significant and suggests that the change in sales policy and the investment in new machinery, although with the related increased borrowings, have led to short-term depressed returns. If the increased market resulting from the new sales policy can be retained, it would be worthwhile considering an increase in sales price to a point where a higher rate of return would be achieved.

The company appears solvent – there is no shortage of liquid assets. However, it has taken on considerably more long-term debt in order to fund the market expansion. This will have to be serviced and the level of profit should be monitored to ensure that margins do not fall further, raising the current level of risk to unacceptable levels. As 38.2 per cent (£192,000) of net current profits before interest (£502,000) are already being used to meet debt interest payments, compared to only 3.8 per cent in 20X2, it would not take very large changes in costs or selling price to cause this to become a major problem. The current level of gearing will also inhibit the company's ability to raise additional loan funding in future.

Profitability	20X2	20X3
Gross profit : sales	$\dfrac{540}{900} \times 100 = 60\%$	$\dfrac{1,120}{2,800} \times 100 = 40\%$
Net profit : sales	$\dfrac{302}{900} \times 100 = 34\%$	$\dfrac{310}{2,800} \times 100 = 11\%$
ROCE	$\dfrac{302+12}{929+100} \times 100 = 31\%$	$\dfrac{310+192}{1,267+1,600} = 18\%$
Liquidity		
Current ratio	$\dfrac{125}{36} = 3.47:1$	$\dfrac{821}{186} = 4.41:1$
Acid test ratio	$\dfrac{125-30}{36} = 2.63:1$	$\dfrac{821-238}{186} = 3.13:1$
Capital structure		
Capital gearing	$\dfrac{100}{100+929} = 10\%$	$\dfrac{1,600}{1,600+1,267} = 56\%$

(v) Rate of return:
$$\frac{10,000}{(38,000+42,000) \div 2} \times \frac{100}{1} = 25\%$$
$$\frac{15,000}{(36,000+44,000) \div 2} \times \frac{100}{1} = 37.5\%$$

(vi) Current ratio: $\dfrac{45,000}{5,000} = 9 \qquad \dfrac{40,000}{10,000} = 4$

(vii) Acid test ratio: $\dfrac{30,000}{5,000} = 6 \qquad \dfrac{22,500}{10,000} = 2.25$

(viii) Debtor : sales ratio: $\dfrac{25,000}{80,000} \times 12 = 3.75$ months
$$\frac{20,000}{120,000} \times 12 = 2 \text{ month}$$

(ix) Creditor : purchases ratio: $\dfrac{5,000}{50,000} \times 12 = 1.2$ months
$$\frac{10,000}{91,000} \times 12 = 1.3 \text{ months}$$

(b) Business B is the more profitable: both in terms of actual net profits £15,000 compared to £10,000, but also in terms of capital employed. B has managed to achieve a return of £37.50 for every £100 invested, i.e. 37.5 per cent. A has managed a lower return of 25 per cent. Reasons – possibly only – as not until you know more about the business could you give a definite answer.

(i) Possibly managed to sell far more merchandise because of lower prices, i.e. took only 20 per cent margin as compared with A's 25 per cent margin.

(ii) Maybe more efficient use of mechanised means in the business. Note that B has more equipment, and perhaps as a consequence kept other expenses down to £6,000 as compared with A's £9,000.

(iii) Did not have as much stock lying idle. Turned over stock 4.8 times in the year as compared with 3 for A.

(iv) A's current ratio of 9 far greater than normally needed. B kept it down to 4. A therefore had too much money lying idle and not doing anything.

(v) Following on from (iv) the acid test ratio for A also higher than necessary.

(vi) Part of the reason for (iv) and (v) is that A waited (on average) 3.75 months to be paid by customers. B managed to collect in 2 months on average. Money represented by debts is money lying idle.

(vii) A also paid creditors more quickly than did B, but not by much.

Put all these factors together, and it is obvious that business B is run far more efficiently, and is more profitable as a consequence.

(b) Current debtor collection period (i.e. debtor days) = $\dfrac{583}{2,800} \times 365 = 76$ days.

If the collection period were 45 days, the new debtors amount would be:

$$\frac{45}{76} \times 583,000 = 345,200$$

The amount released if a 45-day debtors collection period could be imposed would be £237,800.

8.13

(a) Report in outline:

(i) Profitability

This has fallen dramatically over the last five years.

ROCE for 20Y1 is $\dfrac{10}{500 + 100 + 350 + 50 + 20} \times \dfrac{100}{1} = 1\%$ approx.

Return on total assets is $\dfrac{10}{1,000 + 320} \times \dfrac{100}{1} = 0.8\%$ approx.

Return on total assets after revaluation is

$\dfrac{10}{2,800 + 320} \times \dfrac{100}{1} = 0.3\%$ approx.

This shows such a low return that it is probable that the company will have to discontinue trading. The profits are not enough to pay dividends or provide for growth.

(ii) Liquidity

Working capital 320 – stock no value 70 = 250

Working capital ratio $\dfrac{250}{300} = 0.83$ approx.

Acid test 250 – stock 90 = $\dfrac{160}{300} = 0.53$ approx.

Both working capital and liquidity per acid test are inadequate. Would have to investigate whether or not part of land and buildings could be sold to recover liquidity position.

Note: We are not given any indication as to why trading profits have fallen. Needs investigating before one can say much more.

(b) First ask why Positive invested in Minus in the first place:

Was it (i) for ROCE
(ii) for takeover eventually
(iii) for asset stripping purposes?

Why invest more? (i) thought it could be managed more profitably
(ii) sell freehold land and buildings at a profit
(iii) gain access to other markets.

Depending on motive could buy other 75% of capital not yet owned for 1,500,000 × 30p = 450,000 (remember these are 25p shares).
Net assets (at revalued figures) worth 2,000,000 + 800,000 + 320,000 – 70,000 = 3,050,000 *less* current liabilities 300,000 and preference shares 100,000 = 2,650,000.

This gives value per share of $\dfrac{2,650,000}{2,000,000}$ shares = £1.325 per share

Even if only the sale or use of buildings or land is the motive, shares are recommended for purchase.

(c) To buy extra shares
(i) Own cash resources. Cash balances not known.
(ii) Exchanging shares in Positive for those in Minus.
(iii) Combination (i) and (ii).
(iv) Issue of shares or debentures to raise cash.
(v) Bank loans.

(d)

Positive plc
Balance Sheet as at 1 January 20X1

			000s
Fixed assets			2,100
Investment in subsidiary (W1)			396
Current assets (1360 – shares 156)		1,204	
Less Current liabilities		300	904
			3,400
Financed by			
Issued share capital			1,500
Share premium account			750
General reserve			350
Retained earnings			600
			3,200
11% Debentures			200
			3,400

Working
(W1) Shares held 500,000 at cost — 240
Extra shares 520,000 × 30p — 156
396

8.14 Brief points only. The answer should be in report style.

A Advantages
  (i) Interest of £5,000 per year (tax position not known).
  (ii) Financially safe investment.
  (iii) Can realise easily enough.
Disadvantages
  (i) Interest rates may fall.
  (ii) No protection against inflation.

B Advantages
  (i) Chance to improve business and make more profits.
  (ii) Possibly better return than with other forms of investment.
Disadvantages
  (i) Have to cease present occupation with loss of money earned there unless a manager is hired. Should really bring in a deduction of the relevant amount for this to calculate super profits.
  (ii) Takes whole of cash. How about extra cash needed for financing business?
  (iii) Risk element.
  (iv) Unlimited liability.

C Advantages
  (i) Partial security in that limited liability available.
  (ii) Outlay of £50,000 for £53,000 net assets.
  (iii) Chance to improve profitability.
Disadvantages
  (i) Risk element normal in business.
  (ii) Preference dividend £1,000 per year reduces net profit to £6,000.
  (iii) Heavy fixed charges of £1,600 loan stock interest and £1,000 preference dividend have prior claims each year.

D Advantages
  (i) Limited liability
  (ii) No heavy prior charges such as loan interest and preference dividends.
Disadvantages
  (i) Minority shareholders may have difficulty selling their shares and their wishes may be ignored by the majority shareholders.
  (ii) Return only 6.4% even if all profits are paid as dividends.

Further information
  (i) Would like to have seen several years' accounts for each organisation.
  (ii) Would like to know more about future prospects and plans for each organisation.
  (iii) For B, to calculate super profits, would like to know present earnings of Janet James.

8.17

(a)

Trading and Profit and Loss Accounts for the year ended 31 December 20X9

	X		Y	
Sales		480,000		762,500*1
Less Cost of goods sold		400,000 (+10,000)		610,000
Gross profit		80,000		152,500
Less Admin. expenses (−10,000)	40,000		(−2,500) 57,500	
Selling expenses	15,000	55,000	35,000	92,500
Net profit		25,000		60,000

*1 Assumed 25 per cent mark-up despite wrong stock valuation.

(b) Profitability:

	X	Y
Gross profit %	20%	25%

Net profit %   X $\dfrac{25}{480} \times \dfrac{100}{1} = 5.2\%$ Y $\dfrac{60}{762.5} \times \dfrac{100}{1} = 7.87\%$

Stockturn $\dfrac{400,000}{40,000} = 10$ times $\dfrac{610,000}{45,000^{*2}} = 13.6$ times

*2 Adjusted to take into account inaccurate valuation.

Return on capital employed (ROCE) (previous owners)

X $\dfrac{25,000}{200,000} \times \dfrac{100}{1} = 12.5\%$ Y $\dfrac{60,000}{350,000} \times \dfrac{100}{1} = 17.14\%$

Based on purchase price of business the ROCE for Adrian Frampton would be:

X $\dfrac{25,000}{190,000} \times \dfrac{100}{1} = 13.15\%$ Y $\dfrac{60,000}{400,000} \times \dfrac{100}{1} = 15\%$

All ratios are favourable for Y. If gross profit ratios remained the same in future together with other expenses then Y business is best value.

However:
  (i) Can gross profit ratios of X be improved as compared to those of Y?
  (ii) Can stockturn be improved?
If so, then X could be the cheaper business to buy as it gives a better ROCE.

(c)
  (i) Need to know current assets and current liabilities in detail.
  (ii) Are these similar businesses?
  Type of business.
  Areas in which situated.
  Competition.
  Prefer several years' accounts to gauge trends.
  Quality of staff and whether they would continue.

8.19

(a) Ratios:

Working capital 52,000/48,000 = 1.08 : 1

Acid test: 7,000 + 11,000/48,000 = 0.375 : 1

Gearing: $\dfrac{100,000}{100,000 + 400,000} \times \dfrac{100}{1} = 20\%$

The working capital of 52,000 − 48,000 = 4,000 is totally inadequate. As a ratio this is 1.08 : 1.

The acid test ratio reveals that the company is unable to pay its current liabilities on time. This could result in its being forced into liquidation.

The company is low geared. It is highly unlikely that there will be funds available in two years' time to redeem the debentures.

(b) The company has been treading a very dangerous path. Whilst the profits per share have been falling regularly, from 0.9p in 20X7 to 0.6p in 20X0, at the same time the dividends have been rising from 0.2p in 20X7 to 0.5p in 20X0.

It is possible that the directors have authorised the payment of dividends when there have been inadequate cash resources to fund them. This may have been done to keep the share prices up artificially; low dividends would push them down to lower values.

(c) (i) What arrangements are being made to repay the debentures in two years' time?

(ii) Why have higher dividends been paid than justified?

(iii) What is the current value of freehold land and buildings?

9.1

M Daly

Cash Flow Statement for the year ended 31 December 20X4

Net cash flow from operating activities (note 1)		2,850
Returns on investments and servicing of finance		
Payments to acquire tangible fixed assets		(1,000)
Financing		
Loan received	1,000	
Drawings	(1,500)	
		(500)
Increase in cash in the period		1,350

Notes:

1 Reconciliation of net profit to net cash inflow:

Net profit		2,200
Depreciation	460	
Decrease in stock	30	
Decrease in creditors	(360)	
Decrease in debtors	520	
		650
Net cash flow from operating activities		2,850

2 Analysis of changes in cash during the year:

Balance at 1 January 20X4	(640)
Net cash inflow	1,350
Balance at 31 December 20X4	710

9.3

(a)

Malcolm Phillips

Cash Flow Statement for the year ended 30 April 20X9

Net cash flow from operating activities (note 1)		6,600
Returns on investments and servicing of finance		
Payments for fixed assets		(3,000)
Financing		
Capital introduced	2,000	
Drawings	(8,000)	
		(6,000)
Decrease in cash		(2,400)

Notes:

1 Reconciliation of net profit to net cash inflow:

Net profit		8,500
Depreciation	200	
Increase in creditors	200	
Increase in stock	(2,800)	
Decrease in debtors	500	
		(1,900)
		6,600

2 Analysis of changes in cash during the year:

Balance at 1.5.20X8	(900)
Net cash inflow	2,400
Balance at 30.4.20X9	1,500

(b) (i) $\dfrac{7,500}{30,000} \times \dfrac{100}{1} = 25\%$

(ii) $\dfrac{22,500}{(3,100 + 5,900) \div 2} = \dfrac{22,500}{4,500} = 5$

9.4

C Willis

Cash Flow Statement for the year ended 31 December 20X8

Net cash flow from operating activities (note 1)		11,747
Capital expenditure and financial investment		
Receipts from sale of fixed assets		2,300
Financing		
Loan repaid to P Bond	(1,000)	
Drawings	(12,500)	
		(13,500)
Increase in cash		547

Notes:

1 Reconciliation of net profit to net cash inflow:

Net profit		16,122
Depreciation	1,090	
Profit on sale of motor van	(570)	
Increase in bad debt provision	120	
Increase in stock	(6,855)	
Decrease in debtors (5,490 − 3,800)	1,690	
Increase in creditors	150	
		(4,375)
		11,747

2 Analysis of changes in cash during the year:

Balance at 1 January 20X8	1,568
Net cash inflow	547
Balance at 31 December 20X8	2,115

9.6

(a)

Sharma plc

Cash Flow Statement for the year ended 31 December 20X1

	£
Net cash inflow from operating activities	201,000
Taxation	(40,000)
Capital expenditure and financial investment	
Payments to acquire fixed assets	(180,000)
Equity dividends paid	(38,000)
Financing	
Issue of ordinary share capital	50,000
Decrease in cash in the period	(7,000)

(b)

- A cash flow statement presents a summary of the movements of cash during a period and, as a result, it can draw attention to classes of cash flow which are not generating sufficient cash or are channelling too much cash out of the business.
- The cash flow statement highlights how cash is being utilised.
- The cash flow statement enables liquidity to be more effectively assessed than is possible using accrual-based financial statements.

(c)

	20X0	20X1
Current ratio =	$\frac{80,000}{76,000} = 1.05 : 1$	$\frac{69,000}{97,000} = 0.71 : 1$
Acid test ratio =	$\frac{38,000}{76,000} = 0.5 : 1$	$\frac{23,000}{97,000} = 0.24 : 1$

Liquidity is declining. Stock is rising while debtors and cash are falling. This may indicate a growing obsolescence in stock and, if nothing else has changed, falling sales. Dividends payable have risen and there may be problems finding the cash to pay them. While a new share issue raised £50,000, this was more than offset by an investment of £180,000 in fixed assets. Overall, while liquidity is deteriorating and probably needs to return to previous levels, the fall may be due to the investment in fixed assets. If so, stock should be reviewed in case of obsolescence, but otherwise the liquidity position should return to 20X0 levels over the next 12 months.

10.1

(a) While land is not usually depreciated per FRS 15, there are exceptions, and this is one, so depreciation is appropriate.

(b) This is a non-adjusting event per SSAP 17. The previous year's accounts need no adjustment. However, a note to them is appropriate if the amount is material.

(c) Per FRS 12, as a loss of £10 million is almost certain, they should accrue this loss in last year's accounts.

(d) Not allowed per FRS 10. £20 million should instead be treated as negative goodwill and shown in intangible assets in the balance sheet.

(e) Not allowed per SSAP 9. The stock should be at lower of cost or net realisable value.

(f) FRS 14 insists on its disclosure.

(g) It would be possible to publish one of the working capital type, but it would have to be in addition to a cash flow statement, not instead of it. See FRS 3.

10.3

(i) If a reduced level of activity affects the rate of depreciation in this ratio, then the treatment given is permissible.

(ii) Freehold property should be depreciated (see FRS 15). Therefore, unless the valuation is to be altered, depreciation of £8,000 should be charged.

(iii) Capital reserves under company law cannot be used for payment of cash dividends. Therefore transfer to profit and loss is not allowed. Reduce net profit by £18,000.

(iv) Loan stock interest is an expense, not an appropriation. It should therefore be charged in the main profit and loss account, not in the appropriation account.

Adjustments to profit before taxation for year ended 31 May 20X2

Original calculation		40,000
Less Depreciation on freehold property (ii)	8,000	
Less Share premium (iii)	18,000	
Less Loan stock interest (iv)	15,000	41,000
Net loss		(1,000)

10.5

(a) See Chapter 25.

(b)

(i) Consistency concept. One method of depreciation has been used for several years. To change would be inconsistent and make comparisons difficult.

(ii) Accrual concept. This is because expenditure occurs in one period but includes benefit in the following period as well.

(iii) Materiality concept. Bad debts of £3,000 (when compared with £3,000 per year) are significant. They should be brought into account and must be disclosed.

(c)

(i)

Depreciation for 20X1 on straight line basis (15,000 + 11,000)	26,000
Depreciation for 20X1 on reducing balance basis	
(99,000 + 110,000) × 20%	41,800
Reduction in net profit	15,800

(ii) **Revised profit for Paula Rowe Ltd for year ended 31 March 20X1**

Original gross profit	50,000
Less Expenses (40,000 − 7,500 c/d)	32,500
Corrected net profit	17,500

(iii) **Rendell Stott Ltd**

Summarised Profit and Loss Account for year ended 30 April 20X2

Gross profit		80,000
Less: Administrative expenses (W1)	32,350	
Selling and distribution expenses (W2)	12,000	
Financial charges (W3)	4,200	
Bad debts	20,000	68,550
Net profit		11,450

Workings

(W1) $2{,}000 + 1{,}050 + 19{,}000 + 8{,}000 + 1{,}400 + 900$ = 32,350
(W2) $1{,}500 + 4{,}600 + 3{,}400 + 2{,}500$ = 12,000
(W3) $2{,}500 + 1{,}700$ = 4,200

12.1

(a) Answers to be drafted by students in proper memo form.

Introduction:

Marginal cost is:

Direct labour	3.00
Direct materials	3.50
Variable expenses	2.25
	8.75

As selling price £9.00 exceeds marginal cost £8.75 we should accept (but see below).*

Proof:

	Without new order	With new order
Direct labour	6,000	6,300
Direct materials	7,000	7,350
Factory indirect expenses		
Variable	4,500	4,725
Fixed	500	500
Administration expenses	1,200	1,200
Selling and distribution expenses	600	600
Finance expenses	200	200
	20,000	20,875
Sales	22,000	
Sales 22,000 + 900		22,900
Profit	2,000	2,025

* Depends on how other things are affected besides simple accounting calculation.

(b) For extra order:

Marginal costs per unit (see (a))	8.75
Depreciation £300 p.a. ÷ 150	2.00
Running costs £600 p.a. ÷ 150	4.00
Marginal costs per unit	14.75

As £14.75 is greater than selling price £10 do NOT accept.

12.3

Year 1

	(A) Magellan Ltd (Marginal)		(B) Frobisher Ltd (Absorption)	
Sales £29 × 900		26,100		26,100
Less Variable costs				
Direct labour £3 × 1,200	3,600		3,600	
Direct materials £5 × 1,200	6,000		6,000	
Variable overheads £2 × 1,200	2,400		2,400	
Total variable cost	12,000		12,000	
Less in (A) Valuation closing stock 300/1,200 × £12,000	3,000			
		9,000		
Less in (B) Valuation closing stock 300/1,200 × £21,000			5,250	
				6,750
Fixed overhead		9,000		9,000
Total costs		18,000		15,750
Gross profit		8,100		10,350

Year 2

	(A)		(B)	
Sales £29 × 1,200		34,800		34,800
Less Variable costs				
Direct labour £3 × 1,300	3,900		3,900	
Direct materials £5 × 1,300	6,500		6,500	
Variable overheads £2 × 1,300	2,600		2,600	
Total variable cost	13,000		13,000	
Add in (A) Opening stock b/fwd	3,000			
Add in (B) Opening stock b/fwd			5,250	
	16,000		18,250	
Less in (A) Valuation closing stock 400/1,300 × £13,000	4,000			
Less in (B) Valuation closing stock 400/1,300 × £22,000			6,769	
		12,000		11,481
Fixed overhead		9,000		9,000
Total costs		21,000		20,481
Gross profit		13,800		14,319

Year 3

	(A)		(B)	
Sales £29 × 1,100		31,900		31,900
Less Variable costs				
Direct labour £3 × 1,250	3,750		3,750	
Direct materials £5 × 1,250	6,250		6,250	
Variable overheads £2 × 1,250	2,500		2,500	
Total variable cost	12,500		12,500	
Add in (A) Opening stock b/fwd	4,000			
Add in (B) Opening stock b/fwd			6,769	
	16,500		19,269	
Less in (A) Valuation closing stock 550/1,250 × £12,500	5,500			
Less in (B) Valuation closing stock 550/1,250 × £21,500			9,460	
		11,000		9,809
Fixed overhead		9,000		9,000
Total costs		20,000		18,809
Gross profit		11,900		13,091

12.5

(a) Subject to points raised in (c) the extra production should be taken on, as this results in greater profits amounting to £1,562,000. Proof is as follows:

Extra revenue 60,000 × £150		9,000,000
Less Extra costs		
Direct materials (W1)	3,141,600	
Direct labour 60,000 × 18.70 × 120% =	1,346,400	
Variable overhead 60,000 × 7.50	450,000	
Fixed costs	2,500,000	
		7,438,000
Extra profit		1,562,000

(W1) 60,000 × 74.80		4,488,000
Less saving 10% on extra materials	448,800	
saving 10% on materials used on day shift		
10% × 120,000 × 74.80	897,600	
		1,346,400
		3,141,600

(b) Break-even point to justify night shift

Sale price per unit		150.00
Less Costs per unit		
Material	74.80	
Direct labour 18.70 + 20%	22.44	
Variable overhead	7.50	
		104.74
Contribution per unit		45.26

Total fixed costs $= \dfrac{2,500,000}{45.26} =$ Break-even at 55,236 units.

Note: No 10% reduction on materials because demand less than extra 60,000 units.

(c) (i) Would firm be able to maintain selling price of £187 on first 120,000 units per year?
(ii) Would it have been more profitable to subcontract extra units needed?
(iii) Could the firm diversify into a more profitable alternative product?
(iv) Could extra day facilities have been more profitable?

(b) Best product mix for next year:
Crowns manufactured per hour = 20,000/8,000 = 2.5 per hour
Kings manufactured per hour = 10,000/2,000 = 5 per hour
Kings gives best contribution rate, so produce Kings up to maximum requirements.

	Crowns		Kings	
	Units	Hours	Units	Hours
Minimum required	6,000 ÷ 2.5	2,400	6,000 ÷ 5	1,200
Produce up to maximum of 36,000 Kings			30,000 ÷ 5	6,000
		2,400		7,200
Still (10,000 – 7,200 – 2,400) = 400 hours left, so now produce Crowns 1,000 ÷ 25		400		
		2,800		7,200

Best mix is therefore: Crowns (6,000 + 1,000) = 7,000
Kings (6,000 + 30,000) = 36,000

		Crowns		Kings
Sales therefore	7,000 × £3	21,000	36,000 × £2.5 =	90,000
Contributions:	Crowns (33.3%)	7,000		
	Kings (40%)	36,000		43,000
Floor space costs				15,000
Insurances				600
				15,600
Profit				27,400

(c) Product mix with extra machine
As maximum requirements for Kings have already been met in (b), all new output will be of Crowns.

		Crowns	Kings
Sales (as before) in £s		21,000	90,000
Extra (10,000 hours × 2.5) = 25,000 × £3 =		75,000	
		96,000	90,000
Contributions: Crowns (33.3%)		32,000	
Kings (40%)		36,000	
			68,000
Hire of extra machine			20,000
Floorspace costs			15,000
Insurance			600
			35,600
			32,400

(d) Briefly:
(i) Market demand maintained.
(ii) Flexibility of return of extra machine if demand falls.
(iii) To see if wholesaler will guarantee minimum orders.
(iv) Are there outlets possible other than wholesaler?
(v) Selling price to wholesaler?

12.7

(a)

Arncliffe Ltd
Revenue Statement for the year ended . . .

	Crowns		Kings		Total
Sales		60,000		25,000	85,000
Direct costs: Raw materials	8,000		2,000		10,000
Labour	20,000		10,000		30,000
Machine running costs	12,000	40,000	3,000	15,000	15,000
					55,000
Contribution		20,000		10,000	30,000
Rate of contribution to sales		33.3%		40%	35.3%

12.9
(a)

Paul Wagtail
Manufacturing Trading and Profit and Loss Account
for the year ended 30 April 20X9

	Marginal method	Absorption method
Purchases of raw materials (125,000 – 2,100)	122,900	122,900
Carriage of raw materials	1,500	1,500
	124,400	124,400
Less Stock of raw materials	8,900	8,900
Cost of raw materials consumed	115,500	115,500
Production wages	105,270	105,270
Prime cost	220,770	220,770
Factory overhead expenses:		
Factory power	12,430	12,430
Factory supervisors' wages	29,600	29,600
Factory repairs	19,360	19,360
Factory insurance (40%)	1,920	1,920
Factory heating and lighting (40%)	1,440	1,440
Depreciation of plant	17,600	17,600
	82,350	82,350
	303,120	303,120
Less Work in progress (W1)	11,038	15,156
Production cost of goods completed c/d	292,082	287,964
Sales	464,360	464,360
Production cost b/d	292,082	287,964
Less Stock finished goods (W2)	18,447	18,187
	273,635	269,777
Gross profit	190,725	194,583
Less Expenses:		
Administration expenses	46,700	46,700
Distribution expenses	25,400	25,400
Selling expenses	23,800	23,800
Insurance (60%)	2,880	2,880
Heating and lighting (60%)	2,160	2,160
Depreciation: delivery vehicles	35,200	35,200
	136,140	136,140
Net profit	54,585	58,443

Workings:

(W1) 625 × 80% = 500 equivalent making total 9,500 + 500 = 10,000

Valuations: Marginal $\dfrac{500}{10,000} \times 220,770 = 11,038$

Absorption $\dfrac{500}{10,000} \times 303,120 = 15,156$

(W2) Marginal $\dfrac{600}{9,500} \times 292,082 = 18,447$

Absorption $\dfrac{600}{9,500} \times 287,964 = 18,187$

(b) See text.

12.13
(a)

	Q	R	S	T
Direct labour and materials	14	28	60	32
Variable overheads	4	8	13	12
Fixed overhead	2	4	7	6
Total cost per unit	20	40	80	50
Add Profit 10 per cent	2	4	8	5
Selling price	22	44	88	55

(b) Discontinue S. All other items are above marginal cost.

(c)

	(i) Followed our advice	(ii) Produced all items
Sales		
Q 100 × £33	3,300	3,300
R 100 × £39	3,900	3,900
S 100 × £70	–	7,000
T 100 × £49	4,900	4,900
	12,100	19,100
Less Costs		
Direct labour and materials		
(i) (14 + 28 + 32) × 100	7,400	
(ii) (14 + 28 + 60 + 32) × 100		13,400
Variable overhead		
(i) (4 + 8 + 12) × 100	2,400	
(ii) (4 + 8 + 13 + 12) × 100		3,700
Fixed overhead	1,900	1,900
	11,700	19,000
Net profit	400	100

Note: The net profit or loss could have been worked out using contributions per items, e.g. (i) Contributions per unit (i.e. Selling price *less* Marginal cost).

Q 33 – (14 + 4) = 15
R 39 – (28 + 8) = 3
T 49 – (32 + 12) = 5
   Less Fixed costs

Net profit (same as using method shown)

In (ii) the contribution from S would be a negative one.

(d) Discontinue Q and T. All other items are above marginal cost.

(e)

	(i) Followed our advice	(ii) Produced all items
Sales Q 100 × £17	–	1,700
R 100 × £48	4,800	4,800
S 100 × £140	14,000	14,000
T 100 × £39	–	3,900
	18,800	24,400

Less Costs

Direct labour and materials		
(i) (28 + 60) × 100	8,800	
(ii) (14 + 28 + 60 + 32) × 100		13,400
Variable costs		
(i) (8 + 13) × 100	2,100	
(ii) (4 + 8 + 13 + 12) × 100		3,700
Fixed overhead	1,900	1,900
	12,800	19,000
Net profit	6,000	5,400

12.15

(a) (i) Sales revenue: Break-even $= \dfrac{\text{Total fixed costs}}{\text{Selling price per unit} - \text{Variable costs per unit}}$

$$= \frac{200,000 \times (4.50 + 2.00 + 3.50)}{36.00 - 5.00 - 7.00 - 1.00 - 3.00} = \frac{2,000,000}{20}$$

= 100,000 units × 36 = £3,600,000

(ii) Units produced, as (i) 100,000 units

(iii) 100,000/200,000 = 50%

(b)

Profit Statement	(i) 160,000 units £000	(ii) 260,000 units £000
Sales	6,400	7,280
Variable costs (£16 per unit)	2,560	4,160
Fixed costs (£10 × 200,000)	2,000	2,000
	4,560	6,160
Net profit	1,840	1,120

(c) Profitability: 2,000 units

	Ref. 610 £000	Ref. 620 £000
Sales	50	38
Variable costs 610 (16 + 25%)	40	
Variable costs 620 (16 − 25%)		24
Contribution	10	14

The order for Premier Dufton (Ref. No. 620) should be accepted as it gives the greater contribution.

12.17

(a)

	Tourist	Winter	Total
Revised profit/loss Fare income (W1)	512,050	176,000	688,050
Operating costs			
Variable	199,500	110,000	309,500
Fixed	70,000	50,000	120,000
Administration	70,000	50,000	120,000
Interest charges	35,000	25,000	60,000
	374,500	235,000	609,500
Profit/(loss)	137,550	(59,000)	78,550

Workings (W1) (490,000 + 10%) × 95% = 512,050; (200,000 × 80%) + 10% = 176,000.

(b) The proposed changes would result in a net overall drop of £1,450 in profits. This would not be a wise move, unless it was more or less forced by conditions as yet unknown.

If possible, it would have been better to bring in new tourist fares and leave winter fares as they were.

(c) Winter operations, on revised figures as per (*a*) above, offer a positive contribution towards overheads, i.e.

Fare income	176,000
Less Variable costs	110,000
Contribution	66,000

To close in the winter would therefore lose the contribution towards overheads and would lower total annual profits. Therefore do not cease winter operations.

No information is given about whether or not fixed operating costs, administration and interest charges would be affected by closure. This could alter the advice.

12.19

(a)

	A	B	C	D	E
Direct labour and materials	16	19	38	44	23
Variable overhead	11	17	23	14	9
Fixed overhead	3	4	9	12	8
	30	40	70	70	40
Profit 10%	3	4	7	7	4
Selling price	33	44	77	77	44

(b) Discontinue C.

(c)

	(i) Followed our advice	(ii) Produced all items
Sales A 100 × £32	3,200	3,200
B 100 × £49	4,900	4,900
C 100 × £56	–	5,600
D 100 × £66	6,600	6,600
E 100 × £48	4,800	4,800
	19,500	25,100

Less Costs:

Direct labour materials
(i) (16 + 19 + 44 + 23) × 100   10,200
(ii) (16 + 19 + 38 + 44 + 23) × 100   14,000
Variable costs
(i) (11 + 17 + 14 + 9) × 100   5,100
(ii) (11 + 17 + 23 + 14 + 9) × 100
Fixed Costs   3,600
   7,400
   3,600
   18,900   25,000

Net profit   –   –
Net loss   600

(d) Discontinue A and E.

(e)

	(i) Followed our advice	(ii) Produced all items
Sales A 100 × £24	–	2,400
B 100 × £38	3,800	3,800
C 100 × £68	6,800	6,800
D 100 × £64	6,400	6,400
E 100 × £29	–	2,900
	17,000	22,300

Less Costs:

Direct labour and materials
(i) (19 + 38 + 44) × 100   10,100
(ii) (16 + 19 + 38 + 44 + 23) × 100   14,000
Variable costs
(i) (17 + 23 + 14) × 100   5,400
(ii) (11 + 17 + 23 + 14 + 9) × 100   7,400
Fixed costs   3,600   3,600
   19,100   25,000

Net profit   –   –
Net loss   2,100   2,700

It is assumed that the firm is to continue operating though it will make a loss in this period.

Overheads

	X	Y	Z
Production (1.8 per hour)	9.0	5.4	10.8
Administration (50%)	20.0	16.0	24.0
Selling	10.0	8.0	12.0
	5.0	4.0	6.0
Standard cost	35.0	28.0	42.0
Profit (⅛ of standard cost)	5.0	4.0	6.0
Standard selling price	40.0	32.0	48.0

(b) *Sales budget in units*

	X	Y	Z
Budgeted at standard price	800,000	1,280,000	2,400,000
Unit selling price	40.0	32.0	48.0
Sales budget in units	20,000	40,000	50,000

(c) *Production budget in units*

	X	Y	Z
Needed for sales	20,000	40,000	50,000
For stock purposes	5,000	10,000	10,000
To produce	25,000	50,000	60,000

(d) *Direct materials purchases budget*

Materials	1	2	3	4
Product X		100,000	300,000	480,000
Product Y ⎱ kg	900,000	700,000	500,000	1,080,000
Product Z ⎰	–		360,000	
		1,440,000	1,160,000	1,560,000
		2,340,000		
Cost in £		234,000	290,000	78,000

13.3

(i) Net variance:
Actual cost per unit 37 × £18   666
Standard cost per unit 34 × £20   680
Net variance (favourable)   14

Made up of:
Favourable price variance £2 × 34   68
Adverse usage variance 3 × £18   54
Net variance (favourable)   14

(ii) Net variance:
Actual cost per unit 46 × £19   874
Standard cost per unit 50 × £17   850
Net variance (adverse)   24

Made up of:
Favourable usage variance 4 × £17   68
Adverse price variance 46 × £2   92
Net variance (adverse)   24

(iii) Total variance:
Actual cost per unit 18 × £14   252
Standard cost per unit 15 × £12   180
Variance (adverse)   72

Made up of:
Adverse price variance 15 × £2   36
Adverse usage variance 3 × £12   36
Total variance (adverse)   72

13.1

(a) *Standard cost per unit*

	X		Y		Z	
Material 1	0.6		1.8		2.4	
Material 2	3.0		2.1		1.5	
Material 3			2.5		0.9	
Material 4	0.4					
		4.0		6.4		4.8
Labour: Dept A	3.0		1.8		3.6	
Dept B			2.4			
		3.0		4.2		3.6
Production cost		7.0		10.6		8.4
		11.0				13.2

(iv) Total variance:
Actual cost per unit 27 × £37		999
Standard cost per unit 29 × £40		1,160
Total variance (favourable)		161

Made up of:
Favourable price variance 27 × £3		81
Favourable usage variance 2 × £37 (+ £6 common)		80
		161

(v) Total variance:
Actual cost per unit 154 × £8		1,232
Standard cost per unit 145 × £7		1,015
Total variance (adverse)		217

Made up of:
Adverse price variance 145 × £1 (+ £9 common)		154
Adverse usage variance 9 × £7		63
		217

(vi) Total variance:
Actual cost per unit 9,850 × £22		216,700
Standard cost per unit 10,000 × £25		250,000
Total variance (favourable)		33,300

Made up of:
Favourable price variance £3 × 9,850		29,550
Favourable usage variance 150 × £22		3,750
(+ £450 common)		33,300

13.5

(i)
Actual cost per unit	218 × £2.1	457.8
Standard cost per unit	220 × £2.1	462
Favourable labour efficiency variance		4.2

(ii)
Actual cost per unit	115 × £1.9	218.5
Standard cost per unit	115 × £1.7	195.5
Adverse wage rate variance		23.0

(iii)
Actual cost per unit	240 × £1.8	432
Standard cost per unit	200 × £1.8	360
Adverse labour efficiency variance		72

(iv)
Actual cost per unit	104 × £2.0	208
Standard cost per unit	120 × £2.0	240
Favourable labour efficiency variance		32

(v)
Actual cost per unit	68 × £1.5	102
Standard cost per unit	68 × £1.8	122.4
Favourable wage rate variance		20.4

(vi)
Actual cost per unit	34 × £1.7	57.8
Standard cost per unit	30 × £1.7	51
Adverse labour efficiency variance		6.8

(vii)
Actual cost per unit	77 × £1.6	123.2
Standard cost per unit	70 × £1.6	112
Adverse labour efficiency variance		11.2

(viii)
Actual cost per unit	100 × £2.0	200
Standard cost per unit	100 × £1.9	190
Adverse wage rate variance		10

13.7

(a) See text.

(b) Standard hours produced in March
Dishwashers 150 × 10	1,500
Washing machines 100 × 12	1,200
Refrigerators 90 × 14	1,260
Total standard hours	3,960

(c) (i) Standard hours × standard hourly rate
3,960 × £4		15,840
Actual wages		18,450
Total direct labour variance		2,610 (Adverse)

(ii)
Standard pay 4,100 × £4		16,400
Actual pay		18,450
Direct labour rate variance		2,050 (Adverse)

(iii) Direct labour efficiency variance
(Standard hours – actual hours) × standard rate
3,960 – 4,100 × £4 = 560 (Adverse)

(d) Labour rate variance:
1 Higher grade labour used than necessary.
2 Job running behind time so extra people brought in to help.

Direct labour efficiency variance:
1 Using unsuitable machinery.
2 Workers slowing up work so as to get overtime rates paid.

13.9

(a) **Profit Statement for the month of July 20X1**

	Budgeted		Actual	
Sales		1,000,000		1,071,200
Less Manufacturing costs				
Direct materials	200,000		201,285	
Direct labour	313,625		337,500	
Variable overheads	141,400		143,000	
Fixed overheads	75,000		71,000	
		730,025		752,785
Gross profit		269,975		318,415
Less: Variable sales o/h	64,400		69,500	
Administration costs	150,000		148,650	
		214,400		218,150
		55,575		100,265

(b)

(i) Materials price variance =

(Standard price – actual price per unit) × quantity purchased

= 10.00 – 10.65 = 0.65 × 18,900 = 12,285 Adverse

Material usage =

(Standard quantity – actual quantity used) × standard price

= (20,000 – 18,900) × 10 = 11,000 Favourable

Summary: Material price variance	12,285	(A)
Material usage variance	11,000	(F)
Material cost variance	1,285	(A)

(ii) Labour rate variance =

(Standard rate per hour – actual wage rate) × actual hours worked

= (6.50 – 6.75) × 50,000 = 12,500 (A)

Labour efficiency variance =

(Standard labour hours – actual hours) × standard rate per hour

= (48,250 – 50,000) × 6.50 = 11,375 (A)

Summary: Labour rate variance	12,500	(A)
Labour efficiency variance	11,375	(A)
Labour cost variance	23,875	(A)

(c) In each case find out why the variance has occurred. Then it must be established whether the variances were outside the control of anyone in the firm or whether they were caused by the actions, or lack of action, by people within the organisation. Any necessary corrective action can then be taken.

13.13

(a)

Actual overhead	5,840
Overhead applied to production × £6	6,000
Favourable variable overhead expenditure variance	160

(b)

Actual overhead	21,230
Overhead applied to production 5,000 × £4	20,000
Adverse variable overhead expenditure variance	1,230

(c)

Actual fixed overhead	11,770
Budgeted fixed overhead	12,000
Favourable fixed overhead expenditure variance	230

(d)

Actual fixed overhead	41,390
Budgeted fixed overhead	40,000
Adverse fixed overhead expenditure variance	1,390

(e)

Actual hours × standard rate (7,940 × £3)	23,820
Budgeted hours × standard rate (8,000 × £3)	24,000
Favourable variable overhead efficiency variance	180

(f)

Actual hours × standard rate (15,000 × £4)	60,000
Budgeted hours (4,860 × 3) × standard rate (14,580 × £4)	58,320
Adverse variable overhead efficiency variance	1,680

13.15 The standard variable overhead rate is:

$$\frac{400,000}{80,000} = £5 \text{ per direct labour hour and } £10 \text{ per unit}$$

The standard fixed overhead rate is:

$$\frac{160,000}{80,000} = £2 \text{ per direct labour hour and } £4 \text{ per unit}$$

The variances are:

Variable overhead

(i) *Expenditure variance*

Actual overhead	403,600
Overhead applied to production 78,500 × £5	392,500
Adverse expenditure variance	11,100

(ii) *Efficiency variance*

Actual hours × standard rate (78,500 × £5)	392,500
Budgeted hours × standard rate (42,000 units which should be produced in 42,000 × 2 hours = 84,000 hours × £5)	420,000
Favourable efficiency variance	27,500

Fixed overhead

(i) *Expenditure variance*

Budgeted overhead	160,000
Actual overhead	157,200
Favourable fixed overhead expenditure variance	2,800

(ii) *Efficiency variance*

Actual hours × standard rate (78,500 × £2)	157,000
Budgeted hours for actual production × standard rate (42,000 units which should be produced in 42,000 × 2 hours = 84,000 hours × £2)	168,000
Favourable fixed overhead efficiency variance	11,000

(iii) *Capacity variance*

Actual hours × standard rate (78,500 × £2)	157,000
Budgeted hours × standard rate (80,000 × £2)	160,000
Adverse fixed overhead capacity variance	3,000

The variances can be explained further:

Variable overhead

Actual overhead	403,600
Budgeted overhead for actual production (42,000 units × £10)	420,000
Net favourable variance (made up of favourable efficiency variance £27,500 *less* adverse expenditure variance 11,100)	16,400

Fixed overhead

Actual overhead ... 157,200
Overhead based on units of production (42,000 × £4) ... 168,000
Net favourable variance (made up of favourable expenditure variance £2,800 *plus* favourable efficiency variance £11,000 *less* adverse capacity variance £3,000) ... 10,800

13.17

Actual units sold 150,000 × Budget price £2.50 = 375,000
Actual units sold 150,000 × Actual price £2.375 = 356,250
£0.125 18,750

ADVERSE PRICE VARIANCE

Actual units sold 150,000 × Budget gross profit £1.00 = 150,000
Budgets units sold 125,000 × Budget gross profit £1.00 = 125,000

FAVOURABLE VOLUME VARIANCE 25,000

13.19

	Actual units sold	Budget price £	Actual price £	Unit price variance	Total price variance
M	840	5	5.10	+0.10	+84
N	1,680	8	7.90	−0.10	−168
P	280	7	7.30	+0.30	+84
	2,800			Total price variance	0

	Actual units sold	Actual units in budget %	Budget sales units	Variance in units £	Budget gross profit per unit £	Total variance
M	840	700	800	−100	1.00	−100
N	1,680	1,400	1,600	−200	1.50	−300
P	280	700	800	−100	1.20	−120
	2,800	2,800	3,200	−400		−520

adverse volume variance

	Actual units in budget %	Actual units sold	Variance in units £	Budget gross profit per unit £	Total variance £
M	700	840	+140	1.00	+140
N	1,400	1,680	+280	1.50	+420
P	700	280	−420	1.20	−504
	2,800	2,800	—		+56

favourable mix variance

Summary of sales variance
Price variance 0
Volume variance adverse 520
Mix variance favourable 56
Net adverse variance 464

13.21

(a) See text.

(b)

(i) Manufacturing Account for the year ended 31 August 20X9

Singleton Ltd

	Actual £	Budget £	Variance £
Raw material consumed	90,000	80,000	(10,000)
Direct labour wages	115,600	120,000	4,400
Direct expenses	6,000	5,800	(200)
Prime cost	211,600	205,800	(5,800)
Factory overhead expenses:			
Factory rent	10,000	10,000	–
Factory maintenance	6,100	6,700	600
Heating and lighting	3,900	2,900	(1,000)
Depreciation	10,500	8,900	(1,600)
Wages, maintenance labour	24,000	18,000	(6,000)
Other factory overhead	10,000	12,700	2,700
Production cost of goods completed	276,100	265,000	(11,100)

(ii) Trading Account for the year ended 31 August 20X9

	£	£
Sales		405,000
Stock of finished goods 1 Sep X8	28,900	
Production cost	276,100	
	305,000	
Less Stock of finished goods 31 Aug X9	35,000	
Cost of sales		270,000
Gross profit		135,000

(c) See text.

13.24 (See text for formulas to use.)

(a) (i) Materials price variance = (£3 − £2.70) × 2,100 = 630 (F)
Materials usage variance = (1,700 − 2,100) × £3 = 1,200 (A)

(ii) Labour rate variance = (£8 − £8.20) × 4,500 = 900 (A)
Labour efficiency variance = (3,825 − 4,500) × £8 = 5,400 (A)

(iii) Total variable overhead variance = £14,880 − (3,825 × £4) = 420 (F)
Total fixed overhead variance = (3,825 × £2) − £8,000 = 350 (A)

(b) The management of Jasper Ltd should take account of:

- the mix of employee wage rates among those who will be performing the work;
- any need for overtime rates of pay should the level of likely activity require overtime working;
- any increase in wage rates likely in the period.

The rate set should be neither too high (which would be unachievable and demoralising) nor too low (which would be unchallenging) and should represent the average overall wage rate of those working on production of the item.

14.1

(i) Accounting rate of return

$$\frac{\text{Average yearly profit}}{\text{Average investment}} \quad \frac{1,667}{10,000} = 16.67\%$$

(ii) F = 2.29 years; G 3.8 years; H 2.6 years.

(iii)

	F		G		H	
0.926	× 10,000 =	9,260	× 6,000 =	5,556	× 8,000 =	7,408
0.857	× 8,000 =	6,856	× 5,000 =	4,285	× 9,000 =	7,713
0.794	× 7,000 =	5,558	× 5,000 =	3,970	× 5,000 =	3,970
0.735			× 5,000 =	3,675	× 4,000 =	2,940
0.681			× 6,000 =	4,086		
Total PV		21,674		21,572		22,031
Less Investment		20,000		20,000		20,000
NPV		1,674		1,572		2,031

(iv) Internal rate of return

Take 14% to give negative net present value

	F		G		H	
0.877	× 10,000 =	8,770	× 6,000 =	5,262	× 8,000 =	7,016
0.769	× 8,000 =	6,152	× 5,000 =	3,845	× 9,000 =	6,921
0.675	× 7,000 =	4,725	× 5,000 =	3,375	× 5,000 =	3,375
0.592			× 5,000 =	2,960	× 4,000 =	2,368
0.519			× 6,000 =	3,114		
		19,647		18,556		19,680
Less Investment		20,000		20,000		20,000
		(353)		(1,444)		(320)

Also use NPVs given 8% rate shown in (iii)

$$F \quad 8\% + \left(6\% \times \frac{1,674}{1,674 + 353}\right) = 12.96\%$$

$$G \quad 8\% + \left(6\% \times \frac{1,572}{1,572 + 1,444}\right) = 11.13\%$$

$$H \quad 8\% + \left(6\% \times \frac{2,031}{2,031 + 320}\right) = 13.18\%$$

14.3

A Payback period:

		A		B
Capital cost		45,000		53,000
Net cash inflow				
Sales		80,000		100,000
Less Cost of sales	40,000	55,000*	50,000	60,000*
	15,000		10,000	
Admin. exps		25,000		40,000

$$\frac{45,000}{25,000} = 1.8 \text{ years} \qquad \frac{53,000}{40,000} = 1.325 \text{ years}$$

* Note: Depreciation is *not* a cash outflow and should be ignored.

Net Present value:

Year	A		B
1	0.893 × 25,000	22,325	35,720
2	0.797 × 25,000	19,925	31,880
3	0.712 × 25,000	17,800	28,480
4	0.636 × 25,000	15,900	25,440
5	0.567 × 25,000	14,175	20,979
6	0.507 × 25,000	12,675	
7	0.452 × 25,000	11,300	
8	0.404 × 20,000*	8,080	
		122,180	142,499
Less Original investment		45,000	53,000
		77,180	89,499

* Net after receipt of money for scrap.

B Would recommend B. Lower payback period and greater NPV. Also figures too far into the future, as in A, are less reliable.

C See text, Section 14.12.

D Sunk costs, therefore do not concern the future and are not brought into these calculations.

14.5

Workings

Investment in Gudshotti

	Gross		Present value
50% transfer fee now	450,000		450,000
Plus in 1 year's time	150,000	× 0.877	131,550
Plus in 2 years' time	150,000	× 0.769	115,350
Plus in 3 years' time	150,000	× 0.675	101,250
Signing-on fee now	200,000		200,000
Contract: in 1 year	50,000	× 0.877	43,850
in 2 years	50,000	× 0.769	38,450
in 3 years	50,000	× 0.675	33,750
in 4 years	50,000	× 0.592	29,600
	1,300,000		1,143,800

Net cash inflows per year:
If player bought:

Spectators 33,000 × £3 × 30	2,970,000
Sponsorship	50,000
	3,020,000
Less Costs which alter:	
Promotional activities	240,000
Other players' earnings	360,000
(6,000 × 50) + 20%	
Income before fixed expenses	2,420,000

	600,000

Player not bought:

Spectators 30,000 × £2.50 × 30   2,250,000

Less Costs:

Players' earnings

6,000 × 50   300,000

Income before fixed expenses   1,950,000

Therefore extra income per year = 2,420,000 − 1,950,000 = 470,000

(a) Payback period

$$\text{Gross investment} = \frac{1,300,000}{470,000} = 2.77 \text{ years approx.}$$
Extra net inflow

(b) Present value of cash inflows

Year 1	470,000	×0.877	= 412,190
Year 2	470,000	×0.769	= 361,430
Year 3	470,000	×0.675	= 317,250
Year 4	470,000	×0.592	= 278,240
			1,369,110
Less Investment (*see Workings*)			1,143,800
Net present value			225,310

(c) Internal rate of return

Investment

(*See Workings* at start of answer)

Taking interest rate of 30%

Transfer fee   450,000

in 1 year	150,000	×0.769	= 115,350
in 2 years	150,000	×0.592	= 88,800
in 3 years	150,000	×0.455	= 68,250

Signing-on fee   200,000

Contract

in 1 year	50,000	×0.769	= 38,450
in 2 years	50,000	×0.592	= 29,600
in 3 years	50,000	×0.455	= 22,750
in 4 years	50,000	×0.350	= 17,500
			1,030,700

Net income

Year 1	470,000	×0.769	= 361,430
Year 2	470,000	×0.592	= 278,240
Year 3	470,000	×0.455	= 213,850
Year 4	470,000	×0.350	= 164,500
			1,018,020

Net present value is negative

i.e. 1,018,020 − 1,030,700 = 12,680

Internal rate of return (see formula in text, Section 14.8):

$$14\% + \left(16\% \times \frac{225,310}{225,310 + 12,680}\right) = 31.15\% \text{ approx.}$$

(d) Yes, if no better alternative is available. Meets payback criteria and gives positive NPV at cost of capital rate. Although only asked for two other points,

(i) Have we got sufficient liquid funds to pay 450,000 + 200,000 immediately?

(ii) Effect upon morale of other players to see one player rewarded excessively.

(iii) Can we insure Gudshotti against injury?

Note: We have shown the workings in full. You could have taken various short-cuts to the same answer.

14.7

(a) (i)

	Ajax Capital	Net cost	Borg Capital	Net cost
Ordinary 16%	700	112.0	300	48
Preference 14%	200	28.0	200	28
Debentures 12%	100	12.0	500	60
− Tax relief 40%		4.8		24
		7.2		36
	1,000	147.2	1,000	112

Weighted average cost of capital:

$$\text{Ajax} \quad \frac{147.2}{1,000} \times 100 = 14.72\%$$

$$\text{Borg} \quad \frac{112}{1,000} \times 100 = 11.2\%$$

(ii) Ajax has much more ordinary capital at higher percentage dividends. Borg has debentures which are at a lower rate and also has tax relief on them.

(b) (i) First calculate the Internal Rate of Return (IRR) which really represents the cost of investing in this project.

Discount rates		12%		16%	
Year 1	55,000	×0.893 = 49,115		×0.862 = 47,140	
Year 2	60,000	×0.797 = 47,820		×0.743 = 44,580	
Year 3	145,000	×0.712 = 103,240		×0.641 = 92,945	
Year 4	170,000	×0.636 = 108,120		×0.552 = 93,840	
		308,295		278,505	
Less Investment		300,000		300,000	
		8,295		(21,495)	

$$IRR = 12\% + \left(4\% \times \frac{8,295}{8,295 + 21,495}\right) = 13.11\% \text{ approx.}$$

(ii) Borg to invest as the return exceeds the cost of capital at present of 11.2%. Ajax not to invest as the return from investment is lower than the cost of capital.

14.8

(a) Weighted average cost of capital

Ordinary shares	1,000 × 14%	= 140
Preference shares	400 × 11%	= 44
Debentures	600 × 10% = 60	
less tax relief 30%	18	
		42
		226

$$\text{Average cost} = \frac{226}{\text{Total capital}} \times 100 = 11.3\%$$

rounded down to 11%

(b) Using 11% discount

	Scheme 1			Scheme 2		
Year 1	14,000	× 0.901	= 12,614	14,000	× 0.901	= 12,614
Year 2	10,000	× 0.812	= 8,120	18,000	× 0.812	= 14,616
Year 3	19,000	× 0.731	= 13,889	27,000	× 0.731	= 19,737
Year 4	24,000	× 0.659	= 15,816	31,000	× 0.659	= 20,429
			50,439			67,396
Less Investment			50,000			70,000
Net present value			439			(2,604)

(c) Accept Scheme 1. Gives positive NPV.
Reject Scheme 2. Gives negative NPV.

(d)

	Scheme 1			Scheme 2		
PV as (b)			50,439			67,396
Year 5	23,000	× 0.594	13,662	32,000	× 0.594	19,008
			64,101			86,404
Less Investment			50,000			70,000
Net present value			14,101			16,404

Would now choose Scheme 2 as net present value is higher.

15.1 See text, Section 15.6.

15.2 See text, Section 15.6.
Difficulties lie in trying to give these measures a value in money that would get universal acceptance. How can you place a money value on living conditions, for example?

15.3 See text, Section 15.7.

15.4 Basically there are many things which could be done to improve the various parts of 'social well-being':

(i) Benefits cost a lot of money in the short term, and

(ii) Beneficial effects are felt only in the long term.
Examples are better education and housing.

15.5 See text, Section 15.10.

16.1 (i) f, b. (ii) m. (iii) a, c, e, g, j, $^4/_5$ of n, t, v, $^3/_4$ of w, x. (iv) b, d, i, $^1/_5$ of n, p, q, part of $^1/_4$ of u. (v) l, r, s, z, part of $^1/_4$ of w. (vi) k, o, u, y.

16.3

Raw materials consumed (120,000 + 400,000 − 160,000)	360,000
Haulage costs	4,000
Direct labour 70% × 220,000	154,000
Royalties	1,600
Prime cost	519,600

(a)

Factory overhead		
Factory indirect labour	66,000	
Other factory indirect expenses	58,000	
Travelling expenses	100	
Depreciation: Factory machinery	38,000	
Firm's canteen expenses	4,000	
		166,100
Production cost		685,700

(b)

Administration expenses		
Salaries	72,000	
Travelling expenses	200	
Firm's canteen expenses	2,000	
Depreciation: Acctg. & office machinery	2,000	
Cars of admin. staff	1,600	
Other administrative expenses	42,000	
		119,800
Selling and distribution expenses		
Salaries	8,000	
Commission	1,400	
Travelling expenses	2,900	
Depreciation: Equipment	300	
Salesmen's cars	3,800	
Other selling expenses	65,000	
Carriage costs on sales	7,800	
		89,200

(c)

Finance costs	
Interest on loans and overdrafts	3,800
Total cost	898,500

17.1

A

Contract Account

	£		£
Materials purchased	765,000	Materials transfers out	8,000
Materials transfers in	23,000	Architects' certificates	1,830,000
Direct labour	448,000	Stock of materials c/d (W2)	38,000
Direct labour accrued	19,500	Value of plant c/d	80,000
Indirect labour	63,000	Work not certified c/d	86,000
Indirect labour accrued	2,400		
Plant delivered	120,000		
Hire charges	57,000		
Hire charges owing	3,200		
Head office charges	48,000		
	1,549,100		
Profit to profit and loss account (W1)	279,310		
Reserve (part of apparent profit not yet recognised) c/d	213,590		
	2,042,000		2,042,000

Workings:

(W1)

Apparent profit $= 2,042,000 - 1,549,100 = 492,900$

To recognise $= 492,900 \times \frac{2}{3} \times \frac{\text{Cash received}}{\text{Work certified}}$

$= 492,900 \times \frac{2}{3} \times \frac{1,555,500}{1,830,000} = 279,310$

Reserve is $492,900 - 279,310 = 213,590$

(W2)

Architects' certificates $- 1,555,500 \times \frac{100}{85} = 1,830,000$

B

See text.

C

The multinational company should:

(i) As far as possible offer the chance of redundancy for those voluntarily wishing to retire from the company, rather than force it on unwilling employees.

(ii) See if alternative jobs can be offered elsewhere in the multinational.

(iii) Explain to the workforce why the change is necessary.

(iv) Have staff from the job centre explain about any alternative jobs or occupations.

(v) Give the redundant people advice about new skills training.

(vi) Have them given financial advice about investing redundancy monies, etc.

(vii) Advice re possible claims from the DSS.

(viii) Try to ensure fairness and not victimise certain employees.

17.3

(a)

Note that the question asks for *cost* accounts NOT contract accounts.

Cost accounts for year ended 31 October 20X9

Plymouth Contract (£000)

Balance b/f		Plant transferred	13
Work completed	240	Materials on site c/f	12
Materials on site	18	Plant on site c/f	55
Plant at WDV	90	Cost of work completed	462
Materials	60		
Wages	75		
Subcontractors	10		
Salaries	18		
Plant received	6		
Head office charges	25		
	542		542

Torquay Contract (£000)

Balance b/f		Materials on site c/f	28
Work completed	80	Plant on site c/f	80
Materials on site	6	Cost of work completed	466
Plant at WDV	25		
Materials	130		
Wages	105		
Subcontractors	46		
Salaries	32		
Plant received	115		
Head office costs	35		
	574		574

Truro Contract (£000)

Materials	80	Materials on site c/f	35
Wages	30	Plant on site c/f	52
Salaries	8	Cost of work completed	118
Plant at WDV	77		
Head office costs	10		
	205		205

(b)

Plymouth:

	£000
Total contract price	600
Less Costs to date	462
Future costs	60
	522
Total expected profit	78

If the anticipated costs, including contingencies, are adequate the full proportion of profits to date may be taken. Prudence should be the keynote, but this contract is almost complete.

Profit $= \dfrac{\text{Work certified}}{\text{Contract price}} \times \text{Total profit}$

$= \dfrac{500,000}{600,000} \times 78 = 65,000$

(d) (i) This is an example of the prudence concept. Gains should only be recognised when reasonably certain – see Chapter 25.

(ii) The loss should be written off when it is identified. This is another example of the prudence concept being applied.

18.1

	Production Departments				Service Departments		
	A	B	C	D	K	L	M
Indirect labour	4,000	6,000	8,000	2,000	1,500	3,000	4,100
Other expenses	2,700	3,100	3,600	1,500	4,500	2,000	2,000
	6,700	9,100	11,600	3,500	6,000	5,000	6,100

Apportionment of costs:

	A	B	C	D	K	L	M
Dept K	1,500	1,800	1,200	600	(6,000)		900
Dept L	3,000		1,500	500		(5,000)	
							7,000
Dept M		2,100	3,500	1,400			(7,000)
	11,200	13,000	17,800	6,000	–	–	–

(a) Overhead rates per direct labour hour

Department A $\dfrac{£11,200}{2,000} = £5.6$

Department C $\dfrac{£17,800}{4,450} = £4.0$

(b) Overhead rates per machine hour

Department B $\dfrac{£13,000}{2,600} = £5.0$

Department D $\dfrac{£6,000}{2,400} = £2.5$

18.2

Job Cost Sheet Job 351 Dept A

Direct materials	190
Direct labour	56 × £2.1 = 117.6
Factory overhead	56 × £5.6 = 313.6
	621.2

Job Cost Sheet Job 352 Dept B

Direct materials	1,199
Direct labour	178 × £1.7 = 302.6
Factory overhead	176 × £5.0 = 880
	2,381.6

Job Cost Sheet Job 353 Dept C

Direct materials	500
Direct labour	130 × £2.4 = 312
Factory overhead	130 × £4.0 = 520
	1,332

Torquay: As the contract is only about 50 per cent complete, prudence must take over.

Work certified – cost to date = 450 – 466 = loss to date £16,000. Prudence dictates that all the loss, £16,000, should be taken into account.

Truro: As the contract is in its early stages prudence must take over. The formula is:

Apparent profit × ²/₃ = (125,000 – 118,000) × ²/₃ = 4,667

17.6

(a)

Loyal Construction plc
Contract Account for the year ended 31 March 20X2

	£			£
Plant	94,000	Materials returns		7,500
Materials	968,000	Materials c/d		15,300
Direct labour	471,000	Plant c/d (W2)		64,000
Plant hire	52,600	Work certified (W1)		2,000,000
Subcontractors	102,300	Work not yet		
Architects' fees	31,700	certified c/d		136,000
Direct labour accrued c/d	19,200			
Head office (W1)	160,000			
Profit and loss (W3)	194,400			
Reserve (unrecognised profit) (W4)	129,600			
	2,222,800			2,222,800
Materials b/d	15,300	Direct labour accrued b/d		19,200
Plant b/d	64,000	Reserve b/d		129,600
Work not yet certified b/d	136,000			

Workings: W1 £1.8m ÷ (1.0 – 0.1) = £2m; £2m @ 8% = £160,000

W2 £94,000 – £4,000 = £90,000 ÷ 3 = £30,000.
£94,000 – £30,000 = £64,000

W3 £2,222,800 – £1,898,800 × 2/3 × $\dfrac{£1.8m}{£2m}$ = £194,400

W4 (£2,222,800 – £1,898,800) – £194,400 = £129,600

(b) Work in progress as at 31 March 20X2
= (cost to 31 March 20X2 – payments received) + profit recognised at 31 March 20X2
= (£1,812,000 – £1,800,000) + £194,400
= £206,400

(c)
● to encourage completion of the contract;
● to allow for overestimate of value of work certified;
● to act as insurance against faulty or poor quality work;
● to encourage the buyer – buyers want to delay payment as long as possible.

Job Cost Sheet Job 354 Dept D

Direct materials		666
Direct labour	90 × £2.3	207
Factory overhead	64 × £2.5	160
		1,033

Job Cost Sheet Job 355 Depts C and B

Dept C	Direct materials		560
	Direct labour	160 × £2.4	384
	Factory overhead	160 × £4.0	640
Dept B	Direct materials		68
	Direct labour	30 × £1.7	51
	Factory overhead	20 × £5.0	100
			1,803

18.5

(a) See text.

(b) (i)

	Materials	Labour	Overhead
Finished items	4,000	4,000	4,000
Work in progress (600)	540 (90%)	450 (75%)	330 (55%)
Total units	4,540	4,450	4,330

(ii) Cost per complete unit

Material	£8,172 ÷ 4,540	= 1.80	
Labour	£7,120 ÷ 4,450	= 1.60	
Overhead	£5,196 ÷ 4,330	= 1.20	£4.60

(iii) Value of work in progress

Material	540 × 1.80	= 972	
Labour	450 × 1.60	= 720	
Overhead	330 × 1.20	= 396	£2,088

18.7

(a) Allotment: where overheads traced directly to units.
Apportionment: where overheads not directly traceable and have to be apportioned between units.
Absorption rates: the total amount of overheads calculated as being charged to each unit.

(b) Because the figures belong to the future and therefore cannot be known precisely.

(c) (i) and (ii). Note that parts (i) and (ii) illustrate two different methods in use. The method in (iii) is not in the text.
Continuous apportionment (repeated distribution)

	Production departments			Service departments	
Line	A	B	C	X	Y
	14,000	12,000	8,000	4,000	3,000
1 Allocation per analysis					
2 Allocation of X (4,000)	(35%) 1,400	(30%) 1,200	(20%) 800	(4,000)	(15%) 600
3 Allocation of Y (3,600)	(30%) 1,080	(40%) 1,440	(25%) 900	(5%) 180	(3,600)
4 Allocation of X (180)	(35%) 63	(30%) 54	(20%) 36	(180)	(15%) 27
5 Allocation of Y (27)	(30%) 8	(40%) 12*	(25%) 7	(5%) 0	(27)
	16,551	14,706	9,743 (= total 41,000)		

* Rounded off

Explanation:
Steps: (1) Allocate X overheads to others by % shown.
(2) Allocate Y overheads to others by % shown.
Keep repeating (1) and (2) until the figures left under X and Y are insignificant.

(iii) Elimination method.

	Production departments			Service departments	
Line	A	B	C	X	Y
	14,000	12,000	8,000	4,000	3,000
1 Allocation per analysis					
2 Allocate service dept X	(35%) 1,400	(30%) 1,200	(20%) 800	(4,000)	(15%) 600
3 Allocate service dept Y	(30/95) 1,137	(40/95) 1,516	(25/95) 947		(3,600)
	16,537	14,716	9,747 (total 41,000)	–	–

Explanation:
Steps: (1) Allocate overheads of service department which does largest proportion of work for other departments, i.e. department X.
(2) Allocate next service department per (1), in this case there is only Y.
(3) When doing (2) nothing is charged to service departments already allocated, i.e. in this case X.
(4) Note that since (3) happens the ratios in the next allocation change. As X 5% of Y is not returned then A gets 30/95 of Y, not 30% and so on.

(iv) The answer will depend on whichever approach is adopted. No one can categorically state which method is the most accurate; there is no 'ideal' method.

18.9 (a) and (b) – see text.

(c)

(i)

Batch No. 23

Raw materials 300 × 1.60	480
Direct labour 4.20 × 20 hours	84
Setting up of machine	21
Overheads 3.60 × 20 hours	72
Total cost	657

Cost per unit 657 ÷ 300 = £2.19

(ii)

Batch No. 23

Raw materials 300 × 1.60	480.00	
Less Received for scrap 20 × 0.86	17.20	462.80
Direct labour: Normal 20 × 4.20	84.00	
Rectification 9 × 4.20	37.80	121.80
Setting up: Normal	21.00	
Rectification	18.00	39.00
Overheads: Running time 3.60 × 20	72.00	
Rectification 3.60 × 9	32.40	104.40
		728.00

Per usable unit £728 ÷ 280 = 2.60

(iii)

Loss because of extra costs 728 − 657 =	71.00
Loss because of faulty products 657 × 20/300	43.80
	114.80

19.1

(a)

Opening stock	120
Add Production	?
	630
Less Sales	150

By arithmetical deduction the figure of production is 660 units. Divide by 12 to give production figures of 55 per month. This has been tested to ensure that stock never becomes a negative figure.

(b)

Starting with the above figures

	Jan	Feb	Mar	Apr	May	Jun	Jul	Aug	Sep	Oct	Nov	Dec
Opening stock	120	105	70	65	80	105	140	175	200	195	180	145
Add Production	55	55	55	55	55	55	55	55	55	55	55	55
	175	160	125	120	135	160	195	230	255	250	235	200
Less Sales	70	90	60	40	30	20	20	30	60	70	90	150
Closing stock	105	70	65	80	105	140	175	200	195	180	145	50

Lowest figure of closing stock is March 65. If stock is not to fall below 110 units then an extra (110 − 65) 45 units will have to be produced in January, making January's production:

55 + 45 = 100 units

19.2

Opening stock	50
Add Production	?
	650
Less Sales	
Closing stock	120

By deduction the year's production will be 720 units.

Compared with the first half year, the second half will show greater production of 20 × 6 = 120 units. Production first half therefore $\frac{720 - 120}{2} = 300$ units.

(a) Production: January to June   50 units per month = 300

(b) Production: July to December   70 units per month = 420

                                                              720

20.1

(a)

B Ukridge

Cash Budget	May	Jun	Jul	Aug	Sep	Oct
Balance b/fwd	5					
Overdraft b/fwd		5,305	4,305	1,305	6,695	9,695
Receipts from debtors	400	4,000	8,000	12,000	9,000	5,000
Capital	5,000					
	5,405	9,305	12,305	13,305	2,305	(4,695)
Payments	100	5,000	11,000	20,000	12,000	7,000
Balance c/fwd	5,305					
Overdraft c/fwd		4,305	1,305	6,695	9,695	11,695

(b) There are the possibilities of delaying payments to creditors, delaying purchases or somehow getting debtors to pay up more quickly. Apart from these it is possible that a credit factoring firm could help in 'buying' the amounts of debtors from Ukridge.

If none of these is possible, only a really fantastic product could warrant interest at 100 per cent per annum. This could be the case, although there are many people whose optimism about their products exceeds the true profitability.

20.3

(a)

Cash Budget

	Jul	Aug	Sep
Receipts			
Cash sales (W1)	9,600	4,800	7,200
Credit sales (W2)	17,640	14,112	7,056
	27,240	18,912	14,256
Payments			
Purchases	3,600	5,400	8,100
Direct labour	1,600	2,400	3,600
Direct production expenses	4,800	2,400	3,600
Variable selling expenses	4,000	3,200	1,600
Fixed expenses	1,820	1,820	1,820
	15,820	15,220	18,720

(b) Cash Budget

	Apr	May	Jun	Jul
Receipts				
Cash sales	40,000	40,000	40,000	40,000
Credit sales	65,000	70,000	70,000	70,000
	105,000	110,000	110,000	110,000
Payments				
Purchases	60,000	58,000	61,000	55,000
Selling and administration	5,700	6,600	6,600	6,600
Administration charges	10,000	10,000	10,000	13,500
Final dividend 20X1/X2		7,500		
Interim dividend 20X2/X3				4,000
	75,700	82,100	77,600	79,100
Balance overdraft start of month	(150,000)	(120,700)	(92,800)	(60,400)
Balance overdraft end of month	(120,700)	(92,800)	(60,400)	(29,500)

(c) Would seem to be proceeding satisfactorily to eliminate overdraft.
Could be further reduced by:
(i) Issuing new shares
(ii) Getting debtors to pay more quickly
(iii) Delaying payment of creditors
(iv) Selling off fixed assets
(v) Issuing debentures.

20.9

(a)

	Total fixed costs £	Variable cost per unit in pence
Wages		20
Raw materials		30
Salespeople's wages	42,000	
Administration costs	20,400	
Business rates		10
Total	62,400	60

(b)
(i) Contribution per unit = selling price per unit – variable cost per unit.
(ii) Contribution per unit = £1 – 60p = 40p.
(iii) Contribution per unit represents how much of the proceeds of each unit sold is available to pay for fixed costs and provide profit. It is used to calculate break-even point and to indicate the numbers of units that must be sold in order to achieve a particular level of profit.

Balance at start of month +3,900 +15,320 +19,012
Balance at end of month +15,320 +19,012 +14,548

(W1) July   800 × 40% × £30 = 9,600
August 400 × 40% × £30 = 4,800
September 600 × 40% × £30 = 7,200

(W2) July   1000 × 60% × £30 = 18,000 – 2% = 17,640
August 800 × 60% × £30 = 14,400 – 2% = 14,112
September 400 × 60% × £30 = 7,200 – 2% = 7,056

(b)
(i) Can forecast when and if money needs to be borrowed.
(ii) Can forecast when surplus funds are available so that they can be invested elsewhere.
(iii) To use as basis when dealing with supplier as to creditworthiness, or bank for borrowing powers.

20.5

Receipts	Jul	Aug	Sep	Oct
Sales this month 20%	9,000	9,000	9,000	9,000
Sales last month 70%		31,500	31,500	31,500
Sales 2 months ago 10%			4,000	4,500
Other receipts from debtors	40,000	32,000		
	40,000	41,000	44,500	45,000
Payments				
Wages	2,000	2,000	2,000	2,000
Bank loan and interest	242	242	242	242
Drawings	500	500	500	500
Purchases	34,000	38,250	38,250	45,750
PAYE tax	500	500	500	500
Rent	1,250			1,250
Rates				2,250
Value Added Tax	5,000			3,950
Motor van		5,000		
		8,150		
	43,492	49,642	41,492	56,442
Current account balances				
Start of month	5,000	1,508	(7,134)	(4,126)
End of month	1,508	(7,134)	(4,126)	(15,568)

20.6

(a)
In brief:
Current ratio of 210,000 : 150,000 = 1.4 : 1
Acid test ratio not known. Very dangerous situation because if bank manager asks for repayment of overdraft it is unlikely it can be repaid in the short term.
Profits get ploughed back into the company in all sorts of ways, e.g. extra fixed assets, more stock. It has no direct connection with the balance at the bank. (Use cash flow funds statements as an illustration.)

(c)

(i) The formula is $\dfrac{\text{Fixed costs}}{\text{Contribution per unit}}$. Therefore $\dfrac{62,400}{40\text{p}} = 156,000$ bookmarks must be manufactured and sold per year for the business to break even.

(ii) Total revenue at sales of 156,000 bookmarks = £156,000.

(iii) If 150,000 bookmarks are sold, a loss will be made (it is below the break-even level of 156,000 bookmarks). The contribution per unit is 40p, so sales that are 6,000 less than break-even will result in a loss of contribution of £2,400. This is the loss achieved if sales are 150,000 bookmarks. (Alternatively, loss = revenue less all costs. Total variable costs for 150,000 bookmarks = £90,000 so total costs = £152,400. Total revenue at £1 per bookmark = £150,000 so the loss is £2,400.).

21.1 Cash Budget

	Jan	Feb	Mar	Apr	May	Jun
Opening balance	25,000	+890				
Opening overdraft			−370	−600	−740	−600
Received (see schedule)	400	600	1,750	2,200	2,900	3,550
	25,400	1,490	1,380	1,600	2,160	2,950
Payments (see schedule)	24,510	1,860	1,980	2,340	2,760	3,460
Closing balance	+890					
Closing overdraft		−370	−600	−740	−600	−510

Cash Receipts Schedule

	Jan	Feb	Mar	Apr	May	Jun
Cash sales	400	600	800	1,000	1,300	1,400
Credit sales		−	800	1,200	1,600	2,000
Rent received			150			150
	400	600	1,750	2,200	2,900	3,550

Cash Payments Schedule

	Jan	Feb	Mar	Apr	May	June
Drawings	250	250	250	250	250	250
Premises	20,000					
Shop fixtures	3,000					
Motor van	1,000					
Salaries of assistants	260	260	260	260	260	260
Payments to creditors		1,200	1,320	1,680	2,100	2,800
Other expenses		150	150	150	150	150
	24,510	1,860	1,980	2,340	2,760	3,460

D Smith
Forecast Trading and Profit and Loss Accounts
for the 6 months ended 30 June 20X4

Sales		16,500
Less Cost of goods sold		
Purchases	11,410	
Less Closing stock (130 × £7)	910	
		10,500
Gross profit		6,000
Add Rent received		300
		6,300
Less Expenses		
Assistants' salaries	1,560	
Other expenses	900	
Depreciation: Shop fixtures	150	
Motor van	100	
		2,710
Net profit		3,590

Balance Sheet as at 30 June 20X4

	Cost	Depn	Net
Fixed assets			
Premises	20,000	–	20,000
Shop fixtures	3,000	150	2,850
Motor van	1,000	100	900
	24,000	250	23,750
Current assets			
Stock in trade		910	
Debtors		5,400	
		6,310	
Less Current liabilities			
Creditors	2,310		
Other expenses owing	150		
Bank overdraft	510		
		2,970	
Net current assets			3,340
			27,090
Financed by			
Capital			
Cash introduced			25,000
Add Net profit			3,590
			28,590
Less Drawings			1,500
			27,090

21.3
A

Workings:

1 Raw materials 294,400 ÷ 64,000 = 4.6 per unit
2 Direct labour 236,800 ÷ 64,000 = 3.7 per unit
3 Power 38,400 ÷ 64,000 = 0.60 per unit
4 Repairs are 51,200 − 25%(12,800) = 38,400 fixed. Variable 12,800 ÷ 64,000 = 0.20
5 Indirect wages 64,000 − 15%(9,600) = 54,400 fixed. Variable 9,600 ÷ 64,000 = 0.15

B

21.5

(a)

Bedford Ltd
Flexible Budget at varying levels of production

Level of Production	60%	70%	75%	85%	90%	Actual	Variance +(-)
Units	48,000	56,000	60,000	68,000	72,000	68,000	
Variable costs £							
Raw materials	220,800	257,600	276,000	312,800	331,200	310,750	2,050
Direct labour	177,600	207,200	222,000	251,600	266,400	249,100	2,500
Power	28,800	33,600	36,000	40,800	43,200	39,800	1,000
Repairs and maintenance	9,600	11,200	12,000	13,600	14,400	14,650	(1,050)
Indirect wages	7,200	8,400	9,000	10,200	10,800	10,850	(650)
	444,000	518,000	555,000	629,000	666,000	625,150	3,850
Fixed costs							
Repairs and maintenance	38,400	38,400	38,400	38,400	38,400	38,400	–
Insurance	1,300	1,300	1,300	1,300	1,350	1,350	(50)
Heating/lighting	1,250	1,250	1,250	1,250	1,200	1,200	50
Indirect wages	54,400	54,400	54,400	54,400	54,400	54,400	–
	95,350	95,350	95,350	95,350	95,350	95,350	–
Total costs	539,350	613,350	650,350	724,350	761,350	720,500	3,850

Briefly: generally efficient as most variances are favourable. Comment in detail on each variance.

B
See text.

21.6

Issa Ltd
Trading and Profit and Loss Account for the year ended 31 December 20X1

		£000s
Sales		900.0
Less Cost of goods sold		
Opening stock	80.0	
Purchases (difference)	570.0	
	650.0	
Less Closing stock	65.0	585.0
Gross profit		315.0
Less Expenses		
Administration expenses	63.6	
Selling and distribution expenses (54 + 15)	69.0	
Financial charges	20.8	
Provision for doubtful debts	2.5	
Depreciation	60.0	215.9
Net profit		99.1
Profit on sale of land and buildings		150.0
Retained earnings from last year		350.0
		599.1
Less Appropriations		
Bonus share issue	50.0	
Preference share dividends	9.0	
Ordinary dividend	7.5	66.5
Retained earnings carried to next year		532.6

(b)

Balance Sheet as at 31 December 20X1

	£000s	£000s	£000s
Fixed assets at cost (750 – 50)		700.0	496.0
Less Depreciation to date		204.0	
Investment in Yates Ltd at cost			100.0
Current assets			
Stock		65.0	
Trade debtors	100.0		
Less Provision	7.5	92.5	
Bank		350.1	
		507.6	
Less Current liabilities			
Trade creditors	56.0		
Expense creditors	15.0	71.0	436.6
			1,032.6
Financed by			
Ordinary share capital (200 + 100)			300.0
Share premium (150 – 50)			100.0
9% Preference shares			100.0
Retained earnings			532.6
			1,032.6

(c)

Advantages:

(i) Business can establish desired profit in advance. It can then take necessary action to try to achieve it.
Desired ROCE can be set as target.
Also helps in forecasting dividends/planning for taxation purposes/organising necessary finance/for use with financial backers.

(ii) Manage working capital to ensure its sufficiency when needed. Manage cash balances to seek overdrafts/loans from bank when needed. Ensure creditors paid on time to gain discounts. Invest surpluses as and when they may occur.

21.7

(a)

Debtor budget	Jul	Aug	Sep	Oct
Balances from last month	52,250	52,250	49,500	51,750
Add Credit sales	24,750	24,750	27,000	33,000
	77,000	77,000	76,500	84,750
Less Paid by debtors	24,750	27,500	24,750	24,750
Balances at end of month	52,250	49,500	51,750	60,000

Note: Sales are Jul 900, Aug 900, Sep 900, Oct 1,100. October is taken to be June figure + 10%.

(b)

Raw material budget (in kg)	Jul	Aug	Sep	Oct
Stock from last month	1,800	1,800	1,800	2,200
Add purchases	1,800	1,800	2,200	2,200
	3,600	3,600	4,000	4,400
Less Used	1,800	1,800	1,800	2,200
Stock at end of month	1,800	1,800	2,200	2,200

591

Note to exercises on break-even analysis

The general idea of the questions is to get you to draw up the schedules of costs and revenues and then to draw them carefully on graph paper. It will be a waste of time if you do not use graph paper. It illustrates that accounting data can be represented in diagram form for some users in a more effective way than just using figures. It also puts over the idea that businesses exist to make a profit, and that until sufficient volume is achieved then the business will incur losses. The impact of fixed costs on firms can be revealed quite sharply by this sort of analysis.

22.1

(i)

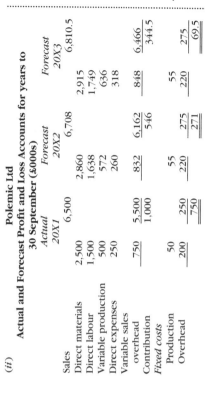

No. of units	Fixed cost	Variable cost	Total cost	Revenue	Profit	Loss
0	8,000	–	8,000	–	–	8,000
1,000	8,000	4,000	12,000	6,000		6,000
2,000	8,000	8,000	16,000	12,000		4,000
3,000	8,000	12,000	20,000	18,000		2,000
4,000	8,000	16,000	24,000	24,000	nil	nil
5,000	8,000	20,000	28,000	30,000	2,000	
6,000	8,000	24,000	32,000	36,000	4,000	
7,000	8,000	28,000	36,000	42,000	6,000	
8,000	8,000	32,000	40,000	48,000	8,000	
9,000	8,000	36,000	44,000	54,000	10,000	
10,000	8,000	40,000	48,000	60,000	12,000	

(ii) The same as Exhibit 22.2 in the textbook. As it really needs graph paper we regret that one cannot be provided in this answer section.

22.2

(a) (i) £24,000 (ii) £36,000 (iii) £44,000 (iv) £30,000
(b) (i) £18,000 (ii) £48,000 (iii) £33,000.

22.4 (i) Loss £2,000 (ii) Profit £12,000 (iii) Nil (iv) Profit £6,000 (v) Profit £9,000.

22.6

(a)

(i)

$$\text{Break-even point} = \frac{\text{Total fixed costs}}{\text{Selling price per unit} - \text{Variable costs per unit}}$$

For 20X1 $= \dfrac{250{,}000}{130 - 110} = 12{,}500$ units

$= $ sales of 12,500 units $\times$ £130 $=$ £1,625,000 sales

For 20X2 $= \dfrac{275{,}000}{129 - 118.5} = $ sales of 26,190 units $\times$ £129 $=$ £3,378,510 sales

For 20X3 $= \dfrac{275{,}000}{128.5 - 122} = $ sales of 42,308 units $\times$ £128.5 $=$ £5,436,578 sales

(ii)

Polemic Ltd
Actual and Forecast Profit and Loss Accounts for years to 30 September (£000s)

	Actual 20X1	Forecast 20X2	Forecast 20X3
Sales	6,500	6,708	6,810.5
Direct materials	2,500	2,860	2,915
Direct labour	1,500	1,638	1,749
Variable production	500	572	636
Direct expenses	250	260	318
Variable sales overhead	750	832	848
	5,500	6,162	6,466
Contribution	1,000	546	344.5
Fixed costs			
Production	50	55	55
Overhead	200	220	220
	250	275	275
	750	271	69.5

(b) Should best be on graph paper. General idea follows:

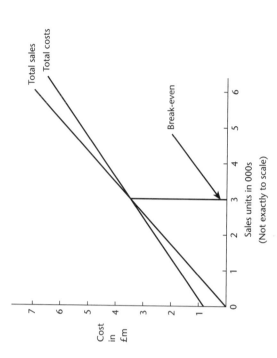

(c) The management of Polemic should be explaining to the union that their demand is unreasonable. As it is, profits have fallen dramatically and the break-even point in 20X3 will be over three times higher than in 20X1.

It is therefore almost impossible for the company to raise prices still further and maintain their level of sales. To try to do so would almost certainly mean a fall in demand and a shedding of a large part of the workforce.

(d) See text, Section 22.4.

22.8

A

Hampshire plc
Profit Statement for first and second quarters

	First quarter		Second quarter	
Sales		126,000		143,640
Materials	32,850		39,420	
Labour	18,900		22,680	
Variable factory overhead	12,600		15,120	
Variable selling costs	7,650		9,180	
		72,000		86,400
Contribution		54,000		57,240
Fixed costs:				
Factory overhead	21,375		21,375	
Selling and administration	16,125		16,125	
		37,500		37,500
Net profit		16,500		19,740

Contribution per unit

$$\text{First quarter} = \frac{54,000}{9,000} = 6.00 \qquad \text{Second quarter} = \frac{57,240}{10,800} = 5.30$$

B Draw on graph paper. Break-even points are at:

$$\text{First quarter} = \frac{37,500}{14.00 - 8.00} = 6,250 \text{ units}$$

$$\text{Second quarter} = \frac{37,500}{13.30 - 8.00} = 7,075 \text{ units}$$

Margins of safety above these points.

C Profit statements incorporating suggestions

	(i)	(ii)	(iii)	(iv)	(v)
No. of units sold	11,880	11,556	12,960	10,800	10,800
Sales (W1)	158,004	158,317	155,131	143,640	143,640
Materials	46,926	43,913	47,304	39,420	
Labour	24,948	27,734	27,216	22,680	
Variable factory o/h	16,632	16,178	18,144	15,120	
Variable selling o/h	10,098	9,823	11,016	11,340	
Total variable costs	98,604	97,648	103,680	88,560	(see W2) 87,900
Contribution	59,400	60,669	51,451	55,080	55,740
Fixed costs					
Factory	21,375	21,375	21,375	21,375	(see W3) 35,000
Selling, etc.	16,125	16,125	16,125	12,025	35,000
	37,500	37,500	37,500	33,400	
Net profit	21,900	23,169	13,951	21,680	20,740
Redundancy					12,000

Workings

(W1) Selling price per unit (i) 13.30 (ii) 13.70 (iii) 11.97 (iv) 13.30 (v) 13.30.

(W2) Per accounts of second quarter in A 86,400 + extra costs 5p per component, 30,000 × 0.5p = 1,500. Total 87,900.

(W3) Fixed costs 37,500 − saving 2,500 = 35,000. Assumed that the 20 per cent of the firm's fixed costs would still continue as they would have to be paid anyway. Question not too clear on this point.

D Briefly:

(i) Would increase profit by 21,900 − 19,740 = 2,160. Seems to be a sensible opportunity which should be considered.

(ii) Apparently increases profit by 23,169 − 19,740 = 3,429. No mention as to what the cost of maintaining the guarantee is likely to be. Until this is known it is impossible to come to a conclusion.

(iii) Fall in profit of 19,740 − 13,951 = 5,789. Should not be considered.

(iv) Increases profit by 21,680 − 19,740 = 1,940. Have to renegotiate terms of employment with sales staff. Worth considering.

(v) Firm

  (a) If we stop making components how can we be certain that suppliers will not later raise prices?

  (b) Would we have to keep larger stocks of components in case of breakdown of supply?

  (c) Possible that newly established firm has got its prices wrong and will be unable to maintain at this price for long.

  (d) Effect on morale of other employees.

  Local community: write generally about effects of unemployment and knock-on effects.

E See text, Section 22.4.

22.10

(a)

Magwitch Ltd
Summarised Profit and Loss Account for the year to 31 May 20X1

Sales volume: units 20,000

	£
Sales £1.50 + 10% = 1.65 per unit	33,000
Variable costs (20 − 10) 0.50 + 10% = 55p per unit	11,000
Contribution	22,000
Fixed costs 0.50 + 10% = 55p per unit	11,000
Profit	11,000

(b)

Compeyson plc
Balance sheet as at 31 May 20X1

Fixed assets (40 + 160)		200
Current assets (65 + 340 − 24) (see W2)	381	
Short-term liabilities (26 + 110)	136	
		245
		445
Share capital (200 + 60) (see W2)		260
Share premium (60 × 0.80)		48
Reserves (190 − 53) (see W1)		137
		445

Workings

(W1) Purchase price 12 × 11 =

Net assets taken over	71
+ revalued property	8
	79
Goodwill written off to reserves	53
	132

(W2) Method of payment of purchase price

Shares 40 × 3/2 = 60 × 1.80	108
Cash (balance)	24
	132

(c) Shares 6,000 × 3/2 = 9,000 shares
Cash 6,000/40,000 × 24,000 = £3,600

23.1 (a) 10,700 (b) 23,100 (c) 4,300 (d) 3,150
(e) 25,500 (f) 51,400

23.3 (a) Asset (b) Liability (c) Asset
(d) Asset (e) Liability (f) Asset

23.5 Wrong: Assets: Loan from C. Smith, Creditors; Liabilities: Stock of goods, Debtors.

23.7 Assets: Motor 2,000; Premises 5,000; Stock 1,000; Bank 700; Cash 100 = total 8,800.
Liabilities: Loan from Bevan 3,000; Creditors 400 = total 3,400. Capital 8,800 – 3,400 = 5,400.

23.9

A Foster
Balance Sheet as at 31 December 20X8

Fixed assets		
Fixtures	5,500	
Motor vehicles	5,700	11,200
Current assets		
Stock of goods	8,800	
Debtors	4,950	
Cash at bank	1,250	
	15,000	
Less Current liabilities		
Creditors	2,450	
		12,550
		23,750
Capital		23,750

23.11

Assets	Liabilities	Capital
(a) – Cash	– Creditors	
(b) – Bank		
+ Fixtures		
(c) + Stock	+ Creditors	
(d) + Cash		
(e) + Cash	+ Loan from J. Walker	+ Capital
(f) + Bank		
– Debtors		
(g) – Stock	– Creditors	
(h) + Premises		
– Bank		

23.13

C Sangster
Balance Sheet as at 7 May 20X8

Fixed assets		
Fixtures	4,500	
Motor vehicle	4,200	8,700
Current assets		
Stock	5,720	
Debtors	3,000	
Bank	5,450	
Cash	400	
	14,570	
Less current liabilities		
Creditors	2,370	
		12,200
		20,900
Capital		20,900

24.1

Debited	*Credited*
(a) Office machinery	D Isaacs Ltd
(c) Cash	N Fox
(e) D Isaacs Ltd	Office machinery
(g) Motor van	Cash

Note: The months are omitted in the ledger accounts which follow. The day of the month is shown in brackets.

24.3

Debited	*Credited*
(b) C Jones	Capital
(d) Loan: P Exeter	Bank
(f) Bank	N Lyn

Bank

(1) Capital	2,500	(2) Office furn.	150
		(5) Motor van	600
		(15) Planers	750
		(31) Machinery	280

Capital

		(1) Bank	2,500

Office furniture

(2) Bank	150	(8) J Walker	60

Machinery

(3) Planers Ltd	750
(31) Bank	280

Cash

		(23) J Walker	60

Planers Ltd

(15) Bank	750	(3) Machinery	750

Motor van

(5) Bank	600

J Walker & Sons

(8) Off. furn.	60	(23) Cash	60

(i) Fixed assets are depreciated over the useful life of the assets. This presupposes that the business will continue to operate during the years of assumed useful life.

(ii) Prepayments also assume that the benefits available in the future will be able to be claimed, because the business is expected to continue.

(iii) Stocks are valued also on the basis that they will be disposed of during the future ordinary running of the business.

(iv) The accruals concept itself assumes that the business is to continue.
All of this shows that the two concepts complement each other.

(c) Shareholders want accounts so that they can decide what to do with their shareholdings, whether they should sell their shares or hold on to them.

To enable them to decide upon their actions, they would really like to know what is going to happen in the future. To help them in this they also would like information which shows them what happened in the past. Ideally therefore they would like both types of report, those on the past and those on the future.

If they had a choice, the logical choice would be to receive a report on the future provided that it could be relied on.

24.4

Cash

(1) Capital	2,000	(2) Bank	1,800
(25) W machinery	75	(30) J Smith	100
(28) Bank	100		

Bank

(2) Cash	1,800	(8) Motor van	950
(26) Betta-Built	500	(26) Betta-Built	58
		(28) Cash	100

Capital

		(1) Cash	2,000

Betta-Built Ltd

(18) Office furn.	62	(5) Office furn.	120
(26) Bank	58		

Office furniture

(5) Betta-Built	120	(18) B Built	62

Evans & Sons

	62	(12) W machinery	560

Motor van

(8) Bank	950		

Works machinery

(12) Evans & Sons	560	(25) Cash	75

J. Smith (Loan)

	75	(30) Bank	500

25.1

(a) See text.

(b) The historical cost convention does not make the going concern convention unnecessary. Several instances illustrate this:

595

Index

Note: entries in the Glossary are indicated by **emboldened page numbers**.

ABC, *see* activity-based costing
abnormal losses, **535**
absorption costing, 303–4, **535**
   allocation of indirect manufacturing costs, 303–4
   compared with activity-based costing, 319–20
   compared with marginal costing, 307–10
   constant sales and uneven production, 310–11
   cost behaviour, 306–7
   effect on future action, 304–6
   fixed costs, 306
   lesson to be learnt, 306
   variable costs, 306
accounting
   classifying and summarising, 501
   communicating information, 501
   functions, 131–3, 500–1, **535**
   purposes, 7, 275
   recording of data, 500
   social, *see*, social accounting
accounting concepts, 521–9
   fundamental, *see* fundamental accounting concepts
   review question on, 529
   underlying, 523–4
accounting equation, 502–3, **535**
   equality, 506–7
Accounting for government grants (SSAP 4), 285
accounting information
   classifying and summarising, 501
   communicating, 501
   recording, 500
   users, 501–2
Accounting for investment properties (SSAP 19), 282
Accounting for leases and hire purchase contracts (SSAP 21), 262
accounting policies
   balance sheet note on, 136
   definition, 278

   examples, 279
   FRS 18 on, 278–9, 529
Accounting for post balance sheet events (SSAP 17), 285–6
accounting rate of return, 373–4, **535**
   compared with other capital investment appraisal methods, 381–2
   merits/demerits, 382
   review questions, 385–94
accounting ratios, *see* ratios
Accounting for research and development (SSAP 13), 277, 283–4
accounting standards, 275–88, 523
   background to, 276, 523
   and GCE A-level syllabuses, 278
   and legal framework, 523
   reason for, 275–6
   review questions, 289–94
   see also Financial Reporting Standards; Statements of Standard Accounting Practice
Accounting Standards Board (ASB), 276–7, 523
accounting statements, 131–73
   limitations, 295–9
   review questions, 235–50
   see also financial statements
accounts, 512–13
   double entry, 513–18
   see also contract accounts; partnership accounts; profit and loss accounts; trading accounts
accruals concept, 27, 161, 223, 526–7, **535**
accumulated fund, non-profit organisation, 28, **535**
acid test ratio, 209–10, 233
acquisitions/disposals, and cash flow statements, 263
activity-based costing (ABC), 319, **535**
   compared with absorption costing, 319–20
   cost drivers, 319
   cost pools, 319
   limitations, 320

actual-cost system, compared with standard accounting, 333–4
adjusting terms (SSAP 16), 285–6
administration expenses, 411, 420
aggregation of financial information, 297–8
allocation of costs, 303–4, 420, **535**
annual general meeting (AGM) of company, 122, 144
annual report, items to be included, 132, 133–6, 143–4, 157–9
answers to review questions, 545–95
anticipated losses, contract accounts, 422–3
apportionment of costs, 430–3, **535**
appropriation accounts, 133–4
   see also profit and loss appropriation accounts
ARR, *see* accounting rate of return
ASB (Accounting Standards Board), 276–7, 523
asset turnover, 217, 233
asset valuation, 93–115
   adjusted historical cost, 107–8
   deprival value, 110–11
   economic value, 109–10
   historical cost, 107
   net realisable value, 109
   present value, 109–10
   replacement cost, 108–9
assets, 502, 503, **535**
   contingent, 287
   current, 508
   disposal of, on dissolution of partnership(s), 61, 68–70
   fixed, *see* fixed assets
   intangible, *see* intangible assets
   purchase of, 504
   replacement of, 108–9
   revaluation of, 58–60, 105–6, 191, 281
   sale of, 504–5
   tangible, *see* tangible assets
   valuation of, 93–115
associated undertakings, reporting requirements, 141
Associates and joint ventures (FRS 9), 262
attainable standards, 335, **535**
audit report, 144
auditors, 122, 144
authorised share capital, 123, **535**
average cost (AVCO) stock valuation method, 95–6, 99, **535**

bad debts, 151, **535**
balance sheet(s), 135–6, 503, **535**
   and bills of exchange, 163
   date of, and stocktaking, 102–3
   detailed presentation, 507–8
   effects of business transactions, 503–6
   and GCE A-level syllabuses, 156–7
   horizontal, **539**
   medium-sized companies, reporting requirements, 161
   notes, 136
   partnerships, 48–9
   post balance sheet events, SSAP on, 285–6
   review questions, 173–88, 509–11
   small companies, reporting requirements, 160
   vertical, **543**
batch costing, 429, **535**
bills of exchange, 162
   and balance sheet, 163
   as contingent liabilities, 162–3
bonus shares, 193–6, **536**
bookkeeping
   double entry system, 512–18
   incomplete records, 7–25
   meaning of term, 501, **536**
   single entry system, 7, 10
borrowing to net worth ratio, 220–1, 234
brackets, use in cash flow statements, 255
break-even analysis, 483–93
   contribution graph, 492
   review questions, 493–9
break-even chart(s), 484–6
   and changes, 487–90
   fixed costs, reduction of, 489
   limitations, 490–2
   production and sales, increase in, 490, *491*
   selling price, increase in, 487–8
   variable costs, reduction of, 489–90
break-even point, 315, 484, 485, **536**
budget variance, 349
budgets/budgeting, 444–9, **536**
   advantages, 469–71
   capital, 469
   cash, *see* cash budgets
   computers used in, 471
   control by, 445
   coordination of, 465–72
   estimates, production of, 446
   financial, 444
   flexible, 471–2, **538**
   master, 465–9
   people and, 444–5
   planning and, 445
   production, 446–7, 467
   review questions, 449–50, 456–64, 472–9
   see also variance analysis
buildings, depreciation of, 106, 281

business cycle, contract accounts and, 419
business entity concept, 524, **536**
business ownership, types, 120
by-products, 437

called-up share capital, 123, **536**
calls in arrears, 123, **536**
capacity variances, 353, 355, **538**
capital, 502, 503, **536**
  cost of, 376
  introduction of, 502
  in partnerships, 42, 46-8
  profit as increase in, 7-10
  return on, 213-16, 229-31, 233
  see also share capital
capital accounts, equivalent for non-profit
    organisations, 28
capital budgeting, 469
capital employed, meaning of term, 213, 215
capital expenditure, 263, **536**
  and cash flow statements, 263
capital gearing ratio, 218-20
Capital instruments (FRS 4), 163-4, 262
capital investment appraisal, 372-85
  review questions, 385-94
capital maintenance, 111-12
  combinations with different valuation
    methods, 112-13
capital redemption reserve, 193
capital reserves, 190-1, **536**
  allowable reductions, 193
  created in accordance with Companies Acts,
    191
  created by case law, 191, 193
capital structure
  balance sheet note on, 136
  ratios, 217-21, 233-4
cash
  and profits, 222-3, 455
  profits available for dividend payments in,
    191-2
  receipts and payments, timing of, 452-4
cash accounts, 11, 27
  see also receipts and payments accounts
cash budgets, 451-6, 468
  advantages, 454
  need for, 451-2
  and profits, 455
  review questions, 456-64
  timing of cash receipts and payments, 452-4
cash flow, 260
  discounted, 376-8
  forecast, 451-6, **536**
  material transactions not resulting in, 264

cash flow statements, 251-69, **536**
  adjustments to net profit, 255-6
  brackets in, 255
  for businesses other than companies, 252
  construction for sole trader, 253-4
  depreciation adjustments, 255-6
  direct method, 259, 261-2, 266-8
  doubtful debts provisions, adjustment for, 256
  examples, 254, 257, 258, 259-60, 264-8
  FRS on, 252, 259-60, 277
  funds movement in, 252-3
  indirect method, 259-64, 265-6
  need for, 251
  and operating activities, 261-4
  and profits and liquidity, 252
  review questions, 270-4
  uses, 268-9
cash sales/purchases, incomplete records, 15
companies, 120, 121-2, **539**
  abbreviation for limited, 518
  auditors, 122
  balance sheets, 135-6
  directors, 122
  finance for, 123-7
  legal status, 122
  limited liability, 121
  private, 121-2
  public, 121, 122
  review questions, 127-8
  trading and profit and loss accounts, 133-5
Companies Acts (1981, 1985, 1989), 121
  and accounting standards, 277
  capital reserves created in accordance with,
    191
  on financial statements, 132, 161
  fundamental accounting concepts enforced
    through, 161, 524-7
  on realised profits and losses, 191
  small/medium-sized companies, definition,
    141, 285
  social information required, 395
comparative figures, in financial statements, 160
computers, use in budgeting, 471
concepts of accounting, 288, 521-9
consistency concept, 99, 161, 525, **536**
contingent asset, definition, 287
contingent liability, definition, 287
continuous apportionment (repeated
    distribution) method, 431
  review question on, 440
contract accounts, 419-23
  allocation of overheads, 420
  anticipated losses, 422-3
  and business cycle, 419

contract accounts (*continued*)
  certification of work done, 420
  example, 420-1
  opening, 419-20
  profit estimation, 422
  review questions, 424-7
  SSAP on, 100-1, 423
contribution, 315, **536**
  graph, 492
  total, maximisation of, 317-18
conventions, 288
conversion costs, 101
coordination of budgets, 465-72
corporate social reporting, 397, 402
corporation tax, 134, 135
cost accounting, 407-14
    control purposes, 413-14
cost-benefit analyses, in social accounting, 401
cost centres, 347, 413, 433, **536**
cost drivers, 319, **536**
cost pools, 319, **536**
cost unit, **536**
cost volume profit analysis, *see* break-even analysis
costing
  absorption, *see* absorption costing
  activity-based, 319-20
  advantages of systems, 412-13
  job, *see* job costing
  manufacturing companies
    compared with retailing or wholesale
      companies, 414
    past costs in, 409-12
  marginal, *see* marginal costing
  process, *see* process costing
  retailing firms, 414
  review questions, 415-18, 438-43
  trading companies, past costs in, 409
  wholesaling firms, 414
costs
  control of, 413-14
  definition, 101
  for different purposes, 407-9
  fixed, 231-3, 306
  full cost pricing, 312-13
  historic, 409
  irrelevant, 380
  opportunity, 376
  past, 409-12
  period, 412, **541**
  product, 412
  relevant, 380
  replacement, 101, 108-9
  sunk, 380-1, **543**
  variable, 231-3, 306

CPP (current purchasing power) accounting,
    108
credit, 513, **536**
credit rating agencies, 138, 208
creditor days ratio, 212, 233
creditors, 504, **536**
  balance sheet note on, 136
  budget, 467
  ratio to purchases, 212, 233
cumulative preference shares, 124, **536**
currency stability assumption, 528-9
current accounts, partnerships, 46-7
current assets, 508
current liabilities, 508
current purchasing power (CPP) accounting, 108
current ratio, 208-9, 233, **536**

DCF (discounted cash flow), 376-8, **537**
death of partners, 57-8
debentures, 125-6, **537**
  distinguished from shares, 125, 220
  interest payable, 125, 133
  naked, 126
  review questions, 127-8
  secured, 126
  simple, 126
debit, 513, **537**
debt ratio, 218, 234
debt to equity ratio, 220, 234
debtor days ratio, 211, 233
debtors, 504, **537**
  balance sheet note on, 136
  and bills of exchange, 162
  budget, 467
  ratio to sales, 211, 233
depreciation, 280, **537**
  accounting for (FRS 15), 105, 106, 280
  and asset revaluation, 105, 106, 107, 299
  and cash flow statements, 255-6
deprival value, 110-11, **537**
*Derivatives and other financial investments:
    disclosures* (FRS 13), 282
direct cost, **537**
direct expenses, 410, **537**
direct labour, 410, **537**
direct materials, 410, **537**
direct method, cash flow statements, 259,
    261-2, 266-8, **537**
directors, 122, **537**
  remuneration/emoluments, 133, 142
  report(s), 143-4
  stewardship responsibilities, 122, 132
discounted cash flow (DCF), 376-8, **537**
discounting, of bills of exchange, 162

discounts, accounting treatment of, 151
disposals/acquisitions, and cash flow
    statements, 263
dissolution of partnership, 60-7, **537**
distribution expenses, 411
dividend(s), **537**
  cover, 222, 234
  effect of inflation, 114
  from joint ventures and associates, 262
  in profit and loss account, 134
  profits available for payment in cash, 191-2
  yield, 221, 234
donations, non-profit organisations, 33
double entry system, 10, 512-18, 524, **537**
  not used for incomplete records, 7
  review questions, 518-20
doubtful debts, **537**
dual aspect concept, 524, **537**

earnings per share (EPS), 221-2, 287
  FRS on, 151, 221, 287
economic order quantity (EOQ), 103-4, **537**
economic value, and asset valuation, 109-10
efficiency ratios, 210-13, 217, 233
efficiency variances, 349, 352, 355, **538**, **543**
employee share ownership plan (ESOP), 282
entrance fees, non-profit organisations, 33
entry value, 108
environmental issues, 396, 397, 402
EOQ (economic order quantity), 103-4, **537**
EPS (earnings per share), 221-2
equity, 503, **537**
equity dividends, and cash flow statements, 263
equivalent units, **537**
ESOP (employee share ownership plan), 282
even production flow, 447-8
examination techniques, 235-6, 530-4
exceptional items in profit and loss accounts,
    153, 159, **538**
  and cash flow statements, 264
exceptions reporting, **538**
exit value, 109
expenditure, capital, *see* capital expenditure
expenditure variances, 349-50, 352, 355, **538**,
    543
expenses, meaning of term in double-entry
    system, 12
extraordinary items, 150, 159, **538**
  and cash flow statements, 264

factory indirect expenses, 411, **538**
fair value, **538**
FIFO (first in, first out) stock valuation method,
    94, 99, **538**

finance, 123-7
  costs/expenses, 411
    and cash flow statements, 262
financial accounting, purposes, 132
financial budgets, 444
financial investment(s)
  and cash flow statements, 263
  FRS on disclosure, 282
  meaning of term, 263
financial planning, effect of price changes, 114
Financial Reporting Standard for Smaller Entities
    (FRSSE), 276-7, 285, **538**
Financial Reporting Standards (FRSs), 276, 523,
    538
  Accounting policies (FRS 18), 278-9, 529
  Associates and joint ventures (FRS 9), 262
  Capital instruments (FRS 4), 163-4, 262
  Cash flow statements (FRS 1), 252, 277
  Derivatives and other financial
    investments: disclosures (FRS 13), 282
  Earnings per share (FRS 14), 151, 221, 287
  Goodwill and intangible assets (FRS 10),
    282
  Impairment of fixed assets and goodwill
    (FRS 11), 282-3
  Provisions, contingent liabilities and
    contingent assets (FRS 12), 286-7
  Reporting financial performance (FRS 3),
    105, 149, 150, 151-3, 157-60, 281, 524,
    527
  Tangible fixed assets (FRS 15), 105, 106,
    279, 280-2
financial social accounting
  in non-profit organisations, 400-1
  in profit-oriented organisations, 399
financial statements, 131-73
  aggregation of information, 297-8
  changes to information sources, 296
  characteristics of useful information, 138-9
  disclosure lacking, 295-6
  examples, 164-72
  externally published, 140-5
  headings for non-profit-oriented
    organisations, 33-4
  historical perspective, 295
  internal compared with published versions,
    132, 147
  limitations, 295-9
  notes to accounts, 140-3, 282
    charges, 142
    directors' emoluments, 142
    staff particulars, 141
    taxation, 143
    turnover particulars, 140-1

financial statements (*continued*)
   objectivity vs. subjectivity, 298
   one set for all purposes, 296-7, 521-2
   problems of information production, 139
   review questions, 173-88
   stages in drawing up, 10
   summary, 161
   timing differences, 299
   'true and fair view' requirement, 140
financing, and cash flow statements, 264
first in, first out (FIFO) stock valuation method,
   94, 99, **538**
fixed assets, 508
   balance sheet note on, 136
   Impairment of fixed assets and goodwill
     (FRS 11), 282-3
   ratios, 218, 234
   revaluation of, 105-6
   Tangible fixed assets (FRS 15), 105, 106,
     279, 280-2
fixed capital accounts, partnerships, 46-7, 48,
   538
fixed costs, 231-3, 306, **538**
   reduction of, and break-even chart, 489
flexible budgets, 471-2, **538**
fluctuating capital accounts, partnerships, 47-8,
   538
freehold land, revaluation of, 105-6, 281
FRSs, *see* Financial Reporting Standards
FRSSEs (Financial Reporting Standards for
   Smaller Entities), 276-7, 285, **538**
full cost pricing, 312-13
   example, 313-14
fundamental accounting concepts/principles,
   161-2, 524-7, **538**
   accruals, 161, 526-7
   consistency, 161, 525
   going concern, 161, 524-5
   prudence, 161, 525-6
   separate determination, 161, 527
   substance over form, 162, 527
fungible assets, **538**

Garner v. *Murray* rule (partnerships), 67-8,
   538
GCE A-level syllabuses
   accounting standards, 278
   balance sheets, 156-7
gearing ratio, 218-20, **538**
   factors affecting, 220
general reserves, 190, **538**
glossary, 535-43
GNP (Gross National Product), 397
going concern concept, 161, 524-5, **539**

goodwill
   amounts written off as, 134
   calculation methods, 50
   existence, 50
   FRSs on, 282-3
   meaning of term, 49, 107, **539**
   partnership, 51-8
   reasons for payment, 49
   review questions, 77-82
   sole trader, 49-50
government aid/grants, 126
   SSAP on, 285
Gross National Product (GNP), 397
gross profit to sales ratio, 213, 233

hire purchase, 126
historical costs, 409, **539**
   asset valuation, 107, 523
   profits and losses, 157-8
horizontal balance sheet format, **539**
human resource accounting, 399

IASB (International Accounting Standards
   Board), 277
IASs (International Accounting Standards),
   277-8, **539**
ideal standards, 335, **539**
Impairment of fixed assets and goodwill (FRS
   11), 282-3
income
   meaning of term, 106, 111
   measurement of, 106-7
income and expenditure accounts, non-profit
   organisations, 27-8, 28-32, **539**
incomplete records, 7-25
   and missing figures, 13-14
   non-profit-oriented organisations, 26
   review questions, 17-25
incremental costs, **539**
indirect manufacturing costs, **539**
   allocation of, 303-4
indirect method, cash flow statements, 259-64,
   265-6, **539**
inflation, effects, 114, 299
input cost, and asset valuation, 109
intangible assets
   FRS on, 282
   meaning of term, 155, 216, **539**
interest, debentures, 125, 133
interest on capital, in partnership accounts, 43,
   539
interest cover, 221, 234
interest on drawings, in partnership accounts,
   43-4, **539**

internal rate of return (IRR), 379–80, **539**
  compared with other capital investment appraisal methods, 381–2
  merits/demerits, 383
  review questions, 385–94
International Accounting Standards Board (IASB), 277
International Accounting Standards (IASs), 277–8, **539**
inventory records
  under standard accounting, 343
  see also stock valuation
investment income, and cash flow statements, 262
investment properties, SSAP on, 282
investment risks, 220
IRR, *see also* internal rate of return
irrelevant costs, 380
issued share capital, 123, **539**

JIT (just-in-time) approach, 104
job costing, 430–3, **539**
  compared with process costing, 428–9
  cost centres, 433
  review questions, 438–43
joint costs, problem of, 437
joint products, 437, **539**
joint ventures, FRS on, 262
just-in-time (JIT) approach, 104

labour, costing for, 343–4
labour efficiency variance, 345–6, 347, **539**
  combined with wage rate variance, 346
labour variances, 344–7
  analysis of, 347
  combined wage rate and efficiency variance, 346
  formulas for, 347
  labour efficiency variance, 345–6, 347
  review questions, 361–6, 370–1
  wage rate variance, 344–5
land, revaluation of, 105–6, 281
last in, first out (LIFO) stock valuation method, 95, 99, 101, **539**
leasing, 126
legal cases, capital reserves created by, 191, 193
legal entity of company, 122
liabilities, 502, 503, **539**
  contingent, 287
  current, 508
  payment of, 505
life membership, non-profit organisations, 33
LIFO (last in, first out) stock valuation method, 95, 99, 101, **539**

limited, abbreviation for, 518
limited liability companies, *see* companies
limited partners, 41, **540**
limiting factor, **540**
liquid resources
  and cash flow statements, 263–4
  definition, 263
liquidity
  and profits, 222–3, 252
  ratios, 208–10, 233
loan capital, 125
loan stock, 125
loans, 126
long-term contracts, *see* contract accounts
long-term finance, 123–6
lost goods, incomplete records, 15–16

maintenance of specific purchasing power of capital, 112
management accounting
  and budgeting, 444–64
  principles, 407–43
  purposes, 132, 297
management accounts, access to, 297
management by exception, 335
management overheads, 347–8
managerial social accounting
  in non-profit organisations, 400–1
  in profit-oriented organisations, 399
manufacturing companies, past costs in, 409–12
manufacturing overheads, 101, 347, 411
margin of safety, **540**
marginal costing
  compared with absorption costing, 307–10
  constant sales and uneven production, 310–11
  review questions, 321–32
marginal costs, 315–17, **540**
market prices, and asset valuation, 109
master budgets, 465–9, **540**
materiality, 528, **540**
materials variances, 337–42
  analysis of, 342
  combinations of price and usage variances, 339–42
  formulas for, 343
  key questions, 342–3
  price variances, 337–8, 342, 343, **540**
  review questions, 361–6, 370–1
  usage variances, 338–9, 342, 343, **540**
maximisation of total contribution, 317–18
medium-sized companies
  definition, 141, 160
  reporting requirements, 161
missing figures, and incomplete records, 13–14

mix variance, 357, **542**
modified financial statements
    medium-sized companies, 161
    small companies, 160
monetary assets, effect of inflation, 114
money, time value of, 375–6
money capital maintenance, 111
    taxation based on, 113
money measurement concept, 523–4, **540**
mortgage loans, 127

naked debentures, 126
national social income accounting, 397–8
net operating profit to operating assets ratio,
        216, 233
net present value (NPV), 378–9, **540**
    compared with other capital investment
        appraisal methods, 381–2
    merits/demerits, 383
    review questions, 385–94
net profit
    adjustments in cash flow statement, 255–6
    meaning of term, 106
    percentage, 213, 227
net profit after tax to total assets ratio, 216, 233
net profit to sales ratio, 213, 233
net realisable value, 96–7, 100–1, 109, **540**
net surplus, 27
net worth, 503
    ratios, 217–18, 233–4
nominal value, **540**
non-adjusting terms (SSAP 16), 286
non-cumulative preference shares, 124, **540**
non-profit-oriented organisations, 26–39
    accumulated fund, 28
    costing in, 414
    donations, 33
    entrance fees, 33
    headings in financial statements, 33–4
    income and expenditure accounts, 27–8, 28–32
    life membership, 33
    profit or loss for special purpose, 28
    receipts and payments accounts, 26–7
    review questions, 34–9
    social accounting in, 400–1
    subscriptions owing, 32
normal level of activity, **540**
normal losses, **540**
notes to accounts, 136, 140–3, 282
NPV, *see* net present value

objectivity, 522
Oil Industry Accounting Committee, Statement
        of Recommended Practice, 283

operating capital maintenance, 113
operating cash flows, 261–2
operating profit to loan interest ratio, 221, 234
opportunity costs, 376, **540**
optimised production technology (OPT), 104
ordinary shares, 124, 220, **540**
overhead variances, 347–56, **538**, **543**
    analysis of, 349
    assessing variances, 351–2
    capacity variances, 353, 355, **538**
    efficiency variances, 349, 352, 355, **538**, **543**
    example of use, 353–5
    expenditure variances, 349–50, 352, 355,
        538, **543**
    formulas for, 352–3
    management overheads, 347–8
    predetermined rates, 348
    recovery of overheads, 348–51
    review questions, 366–70, 370–1
    summary of variances, 350–1
    volume variances, 350, 352, **538**
overheads
    allocation in contract accounts, 420
    manufacturing/production, 101, 347
    under/overabsorption of, 436
overtrading, 222, 223–4
owner's capital, 503, **537**

paid-up share capital, 123, **540**
participating interest, meaning of term, 149
partnership accounts, 40–92
    balance sheets, 48–9
    capital
        accounts, 46–8, **540**
        contributions, 42
        interest on, 43
    current accounts, 46–7, **540**
    fixed capital accounts, 46–7, 48
    fluctuating capital accounts, 47–8
    interest on capital, 43, **539**
    interest on drawings, 43–4, **539**
    profit and loss appropriation account, 45–6
    review questions, 71–92
partnership agreements, 41–4
    contents, 42–4
    lacking, 41–2
partnership(s)
    assets
        disposal on dissolution of, 61, 68–70
        revaluation of, 58–60
    changes in ownership, 49
    characteristics, 41
    death of partners, 57–8
    dissolution of, 60–7

partnership(s) (*continued*)
  drawings, 43–4
  finance, 126–7
  Garner v. *Murray* rule, 67–8, **538**
  goodwill in, 49–58
  limitations, 121
  limited partners, 41
  meaning of term, **540**
  need for, 40–1
  new partners, admission of, 54–7
  performance-related payments to partners, 44
  profit (or loss) sharing, 42–3, 44–5, 51–4
  revaluation of assets, 58–60
  salaries to partners, 44, **541**
  withdrawal of partners, 57–8
past costs
  in manufacturing companies, 409–12
  in trading companies, 409
payback, meaning of term, **541**
payback method, 374–5
  compared with other capital investment appraisal methods, 381–2
  merits/demerits, 382–3
  review questions, 385–94
payments, *see* receipts and payments
performance-related payments, to partners, 44
period costs, 412, **541**
periodic stock valuation, 99
planning, programming, budgeting systems (PPBS), 398, 400
post balance sheet events, SSAP on, 285–6
PPBS (planning, programming, budgeting systems), 398, 400
preference shares, 124, 220, **541**
preliminary expenses, **541**
present value(s), **541**
  and asset valuation, 109–10
  in capital investment appraisal, 376–8
  discount tables, 377, 384
pressure groups, 396
price changes, accounting for, 114
price earnings (P/E) ratio, 222
price variances, 337–8, 342, 343, **542**
pricing policies, 311–12
  full cost pricing, 312–14
  review questions, 321–32
prime cost, 410, **541**
prior period adjustments, 160, **541**
private companies, 121–2, **541**
process costing, 434–5, **541**
  compared with job costing, 428–9
  industries using, 437
  joint costs, problem of, 437

normal and abnormal losses, 435–6
  overheads under/overabsorption, 436
  review questions, 438–43
product centres, 413, **541**
product costs, 412, **541**
production
  budgets, 446–7, 467
  cost(s), 411, **541**
  even production flow, 447–8
  increase in, and break-even chart(s), 490, *491*
  overheads, 101, 347
  uneven, 310–11, 448–9
productivity measure(s), 397
profit and loss accounts, 133–5
  allocation of expenses, 151
  and comparative figures, 160
  in contract accounts, 422
  examples, 12–13, 134–5, 146–7, 150, 152, 165–6, 170
  exceptional items, 153, 159
  extraordinary items, 150, 159
  formats, 145–9, 153–6
  historical cost basis, 157–8
  internal use, 146–7
  layout, 150
  prior period adjustments, 160
  and *Reporting financial performance* (FRS 3), 105, 149, 150, 151–3, 157–60
profit and loss appropriation accounts
  items decreasing balance, 133–4
  items increasing balance, 133
  for partnerships, 45–6
profitability ratios, 213–16, 233
profit(s)
  availability for dividend payments in cash, 191–2
  calculation of, stock valuation and, 96
  and cash, 222–3, 455
  as increase in capital, 7–10
  and liquidity, 222–3, 252
  meaning of term, 107, 111
  non-profit organisations, 28
  sharing in partnership(s), 42–3, 44–5, 51–4
  tax payable on, 134
provision, definition, 286, **541**
Provisions, contingent liabilities and contingent assets (FRS 12), 286–7
prudence concept, 32, 96, 97, 161, 525–6, **541**
public companies, 121, 122, **541**
purchase costs, 101
purchases, meaning of term in double-entry system, 11
pyramid of ratios, 229–30

questions, *see* review questions
'quick' ratio, 209-10

ratios, 205-34
    capital structure ratios, 217-21, 233-4
    comparisons between companies, 225, 228-9
    comparisons over time, 227-8
    efficiency ratios, 210-13, 217, 233
    interpretation of, 224-9
    liquidity/solvency ratios, 208-13, 233
    partnership profit (or loss) sharing, 42-3,
        51-4
    profitability ratios, 213-16, 233
    pyramid of, 229-30
    reason for use, 206-7
    review questions on, 235-50
    sector relevance of comparisons, 225
    shareholder ratios, 221-2, 234
    summary of, 233-4
    trend analysis, 224, 225-7
    users, 207-8
    uses, 207
RC (replacement cost), 101, 108-9
readily disposable investments, meaning of
    term, 263
real capital maintenance, 111
realised profits and losses, 191
receipts and payments accounts, non-profit
    organisations, 26-7, **541**
recoverable amount, definition, 280
relevant costs, 380, **541**
relevant revenue, **541**
repeated distribution (or continuous
    apportionment) method, 431, **541**
    review question on, 440
replacement cost (RC), 101, 108-9
Reporting financial performance (FRS 3), 105,
    149, 150, 151-3, 157-60, 281, 524, 527
research and development, SSAP on, 277,
    283-4
reserve accounts, 190, **541**
reserves
    capital, *see* capital reserves
    general, 190
    nature of, 189, **541-2**
    revenue, 190
    review questions on, 197-204
    transfers to, 133
residual value, definition, 280
retailing firms, costing in, 414
retained profit, **542**
return on capital employed (ROCE), 213-14,
    229-31, 233, **542**
return on owners' equity, 215

return on share capital, 214-16, 233
revaluation, of assets, 58-60, 105-6, 191, 281
revaluation account, **542**
revaluation reserve(s), 193
revenue reserves, 190, **542**
review questions
    absorption costing, 321-32
    accounting concepts, 529
    accounting ratios, 235-50
    accounting standards, 289-94
    analysis of accounting statements, 235-50
    answers to, 545-95
    balance sheets, 173-88, 509-11
    break-even analysis, 493-9
    budgeting and budgetary control, 449-50,
        456-64, 472-9
    capital investment appraisal, 385-94
    cash budgets, 456-64
    cash flow statements, 270-4
    companies, 127-8
    contract accounts, 424-7
    coordination of budgets, 465-72
    costing, 415-18, 438-43
    debentures, 127-8
    double entry system, 518-20
    financial statements, 173-88
    goodwill, 77-82
    incomplete records, 17-25
    interpretation of accounting statements,
        235-50
    labour variances, 361-6, 370-1
    marginal costing, 321-32
    materials variances, 361-6, 370-1
    net present value, 385-94
    non-profit-oriented organisations, 34-9
    overhead variances, 366-70, 370-1
    partnerships, 71-92
    payback method, 385-94
    pricing policies, 321-32
    ratios, 235-50
    sales variances, 366-70, 370-1
    shares, 127-8
    single entry system, 17-25
    social accounting, 402-3
    standard accounting, 359-60
    stock valuation, 115-19
    variance analysis, 359-60
rights issues, 196, **542**
ROCE (return on capital employed), 213-14,
    229-31, 233, **542**

salaries, partners, 44
sale and lease back, 127
sale-or-return goods, 102, **542**

Index

....

sales
    constant, and uneven production, 310–11
    increase in, and break-even chart(s), 490, *491*
    meaning of term in double-entry system, 11
    profit ratios, 213
sales variances, 356–8
    mix variance, 357, **542**
    review questions, 366–70, 370–1
    selling price variance, 356, **542**
    volume variance, 356–7, **542**
Sandilands Committee, definition of profit, 107
scarce resources, 318
scrip issue, 193, **536**
secured debentures, 126
Segmental reporting (SSAP 25), 141, 277
selling expenses, 411
selling price
    increase in, and break-even chart, 487–8
    problems of fixing, 114
    variance, 356
semi-variable cost, **542**
separate determination concept, 161, 527, **542**
service (cost) centres, 414, 430, **542**
share capital, 123–5, **542**
    balance sheet note on, 136
    and cash flow statements, 264
    forms, 124
share premium, **542**
share premium account, 193, **542**
shareholder ratios, 221–2, 234
shareholders' funds, 189
    reconciliation of, 158–9
shareholders' interests, and social
    considerations, 401
shares, 121, **542**
    bonus, 193–6
    compared with debentures, 125
    earnings per share, 221–2
    issued at par, **542**
    ordinary, 124, 220
    preference, 124, 220, **541**
    price earnings ratio, 222
    review questions on, 127–8, 197–204
    rights issues, 196
simple debentures, 126
single entry system, 7, 10
    review questions, 17–25
small companies
    audit exemption, 144
    definition, 141, 160, 285
    Financial Reporting Standards for, 276–7
    reporting requirements, 160, 259, 283
social accounting, 395–402
    compliance costs of statutory/professional
        requirements, 399

corporate social reporting, 397, 402
costs and measurement, 395–6
financial, 399
human resource accounting, 399
national social income accounting, 397–8
pressure for, 396
review questions, 402–3
types, 397–401
social auditing, 398–9
social considerations, and shareholders'
    interests, 401
social programme measurement, 401
sole trader, 120
    cash flow statement, 253–4
    finance, 126–7
    goodwill, 49
solvency ratios, 23, 208–10
specific purchasing power of capital,
    maintenance of, 112
SSAPs, *see* Statements of Standard Accounting
    Practice
standard accounting, 333–7
    comparison with actual-cost system, 333–4
    inventory records under, 343
    review questions, 359–60
    setting standards, 334–5
standard cost, **542**
standard costing, **542**
standard hour, **542**
standards, *see* accounting standards
statements of affairs, 8, 9, 10–11, 27, **543**
Statements of Standard Accounting Practice
    (SSAPs), 276, 523, **543**
    Accounting for government grants (SSAP 4),
        285
    Accounting for investment properties (SSAP
        19), 282
    *Accounting for leases and hire purchase
        contracts* (SSAP 21), 262
    Accounting for post balance sheet events
        (SSAP 17), 285–6
    Accounting for research and development
        (SSAP 13), 277, 283–4
    Segmental reporting (SSAP 25), 141, 277
    Stocks and long-term contracts (SSAP 9),
        100–1, 279, 423
statements of total recognised gains and losses,
    157, 283
step-variable cost, **543**
stock, balance sheet note on, 136
stock levels, methods of controlling, 103–4
stock turnover, 207, 210–11, 233
stock valuation, 93–104
    article method, 98
    AVCO method, 95–6, 99

stock valuation (*continued*)
  category method, 98
  conflict of aims, 101
  different methods, 93-6, 98
  factors affecting decision, 99-100
  FIFO method, 94, 99
  and groups/types of goods, 97-8
  LIFO method, 95, 99, 101
  net realisable value, 96-7
  periodic, 99
  and profit calculation, 96
  review questions, 115-19
Stocks and long-term contracts (SSAP 9),
    100-1, 279, 423
stocks and shares, *see* shares
stocktaking, and balance sheet date, 102-3
stolen goods, incomplete records, 15-16
subjectivity, 522, **543**
subscriptions outstanding, non-profit
    organisations, 32
substance over form concept, 162, 527, **543**
summary financial statements, 161
sunk costs, 380-1, **543**
super profits, 50, **543**

tangible fixed assets, 155, **543**
  FRS on, 105, 106, 279, 280-2
taxation
  basis, 113, 114, 134
  and cash flow statements, 262
  on company profits, 134
  note on accounts, 143
time interval concept, 524, **543**
time value of money, 375-6
total cost, 411
trading accounts, 12, 133
  contract accounts, 419-20
  in non-profit organisations, 28, 30
  in partnerships, 45-6
trading companies, past costs in, 409
transactions, 512
trend analysis, 225-7
'true and fair view', requirement for published
    financial statements, 140
turnover
  definition, 148
  particulars in note to accounts, 140-1

UITF (Urgent Issue Task Force) Abstracts, 277,
  280
uncalled share capital, 123, **543**
uneven production levels, 310-11, 448-9
units of service, and asset valuation, 109
Urgent Issue Task Force (UITF) Abstracts, 277,
  280
usage variances, 338-9, 342, 343
useful economic life, definition, 280

valuation
  of assets, 93-115
  of stock, 93-104
  of work in progress, 101
variable costs, 231-3, 306, **543**
  reduction of, and break-even chart, 489-90
variance analysis, 335-47
  adverse variances, 336, 338, 339, 340, 341,
    346, 358
  computation of variances, 336-7
  disposition of variances, 343
  favourable variances, 336, 337, 338-9, 341,
    357, 358
  formulas for variances, 343, 347, 352-3
  and inventory records under standard
    accounting, 343
  labour, *see* labour variances
  and management action, 356
  materials, *see* materials variances
  overhead, *see* overhead variances
  review questions, 359-60
  sales, *see* sales variances
variances, **538**, **542**
  computation of, 336-7
  disposition of, 343
vertical balance sheet, **543**
volume variances, 350, 352, 356-7, **538**, **542**

wage rate variance, 344-5, **543**
  combined with labour efficiency variance,
    346
weighted average cost stock valuation method,
    99
wholesaling firms, costing in, 414
withdrawal of partners, 57-8
work in progress, valuation of, 101
working capital, **543**